CW01666527

THE HAWKER HURRICANE

THE ROYAL AIR FORCE MUSEUM EDITION

Francis K. Mason

Foreword by Dr. Michael A. Fopp
DIRECTOR, THE ROYAL AIR FORCE MUSEUM

Aston Publications

Published in 1987 by Aston Publications Limited,
Bourne End House, Harvest Hill,
Bourne End, Bucks, SL8 5JJ
Revised Edition published 1990

Copyright Francis K. Mason
1987 and 1990

This book is copyright under the Berne Convention. All rights reserved. Apart from any fair dealing for the purpose of private study, research, criticism or review, as permitted under the Copyright Act, 1956, no part of this publication may be reproduced, stored in a retrieval system, or transmitted in any form or by any means, electronic, electrical, chemical, mechanical, optical, photocopying, recording or otherwise without prior written permission. All enquiries should be addressed to the publisher.

ISBN 0 946627 58 4

Designed by Chris Hand

Printed in England by
The Amadeus Press Limited,
Huddersfield, West Yorkshire

Acknowledgements

Researching historical events, not least those that constituted a World War and especially during the lifetime of its survivors—if the aim is to be objective rather than merely critical, cynical or jingoistic—can be an intensely moving experience, for one may be delving into areas of great emotion and sadness. Many of those with whom I've spoken and corresponded over 20 years recalled with mixed feelings their association with the Hurricane; all those whom I've listed below gave freely of their time to write, talk or look out old mementoes of that association; almost all recalled their affection for the "Hurri". To those of the "other side" every British fighter was a Spitfire, although, on digging further, one arrived at the conclusion that the only RAF fighter they'd ever seen was a Hurricane! Yet they, whatever their association with the aeroplane—having done their utmost to satisfy my enquiries—were invariably anxious to recall the event, their friends and their deeds. The aeroplane, once the ritual of praise was concluded, was brushed aside. It was the people and their circumstance that remained sharpest in memory. And that, as I hope I have reflected in the balance of this book, is as it should be. To them I am most sincerely grateful.

Robert Abbott Esq., Singapore; The Late Gp Capt D. R. S. Bader, ex-No. 242 Squadron, RAF; L. V. Birch Esq., ex-No. 4 FTS, RAF; Jeremy Bird Esq., ex-No. 605 Squadron, RAuxAF; Flt Lt Robin Brown, ex-No. 41 Squadron, RAF; Alvin Bishop Esq., ex-MFSU, Speke; The Late Gp Capt P. W. S. Bulman, Hawker Aircraft Ltd., Mr John W. Caler, California, USA; The late Sir Sydney Camm, Hawker Aircraft Ltd; P. L. Paxton, Esq., ex-RAF Takoradi; R. H. Chaplin, Esq., Hawker Aircraft Ltd.; J. N. Congreve, Esq., ex-RAF Habbaniya; Peter Connon, Esq., Carlisle; John Coombes, Esq., British Aerospace PLC, Kingston-upon-Thames; Mr J. B. Cynk (Polish), London; B. L. Deane, Esq., ex-No. 1 Squadron, RAF; Sqn Ldr P. V. Devitt, ex-No. 615 Squadron, RAuxAF; Sqn Ldr B. H. Drobinski, ex-No. 303 (Polish) Squadron, RAF; F. B. Edge-Hardy, Esq., ex-SAAF; Don Everson, Esq., Oxted; Roger L. Geach, Esq., Truro; Gp Capt T. P. Gleave, ex-No. 253 Squadron, RAF; Herr Gerhard Granz, ex-*Luftwaffe* (Oblt, ZG 2); William Green, Esq., Bromley; Delwyn Griffith, Esq., Birmingham; Herr Fritz Hotzelmann, ex-*Luftwaffe*; Mr Buck Ivers, Iowa, USA; Herr Hans Jenke, *Luftwaffe* next-of-kin, Hamburg; Gp Capt F. W. M. Jenson, ex-No. 601 Squadron, RAuxAF; Sqn Ldr Jozef Koukal, ex-No. 312 (Czech) Squadron, RAF; Sqn Ldr J. H. Lacey, ex-No. 501 Squadron, RAuxAF; Mr Akito Lane, ex-SAAF; L. T. Lee, Esq., Banstead; Mike Llewellyn, Esq., Kent; Philip Lucas, Esq., Hawker Aircraft Ltd.; Mr Leonard Oxenden, ex-RCAF/RCN; Leo Patrick Ricks, Esq., ex-No. 235 Squadron, RAF; R. M. Robinson, Esq., late Royal Fusiliers; Peter Sharpe, Esq., Coventry; R. H. Shaw, Esq., Hawker Aircraft Ltd.; Mr Michael Souprafine, ex-RCAF; Wg Cdr R. R. Stanford-Tuck, ex-No. 257 Squadron, RAF; Sqn Ldr Don Stones, ex-No. 79 Squadron, RAF; Herr Armin Studelmann, ex-*Luftwaffe*; Mrs June Sykes, Peterborough; L. J. Tweed, Esq., ex-No. 111 Squadron, RAF; Robert Unwin, Esq., late of Calcutta; Ivan Venour, Esq., Melbourne, Australia; Flt Lt V. B. S. Verity (New Zealand), ex-No. 73 Squadron *et al.*, RAF; Richard Ward, Esq., Canterbury, Kent; Herr Axel Weese, ex-*Luftwaffe*; Mr Gustav X. Wendell II, California, USA; John Winstanley, Esq., ex-No. 151 Wing, Murmansk, RAF; Gp Capt S. Wroath, ex-A&AEE, RAF; Douglas Young, Esq., ex-RCAF/RAF

I, alas, can write with precious little personal experience of either Hurricane or Spitfire save for a few illicit hours in both aeroplanes in those post-war days when permission from a visiting pilot, endorsed by one's own Wing Commander (Flying), was all that was required to take a "new" aeroplane aloft. Of the Hurricane I could at least make one lasting judgement of my own: It was a "pilot's aeroplane". Those who fly know exactly what I mean. My final acknowledgement must therefore be to those whom I never knew but who gave the nation an aeroplane with which to defend herself.

Foreword by Michael Fopp
Director of the Royal Air Force Museum

It is more than appropriate that Aston Publications have decided to reprint Francis K. Mason's *The Hawker Hurricane* during the year in which we celebrate the 50th Anniversary of the Battle of Britain. In the public's mind the Battle of Britain is synonymous with that elegant thoroughbred the Supermarine Spitfire. But if the Spitfire was, in fact, the thoroughbred then the Hurricane was certainly the workhorse. Three out of five enemy aircraft shot down by all forms of defence during that famous Battle were dispatched by Hurricanes. Although both these famous aircraft were built to the same Government specification Sydney Camm, genius that he was, managed to achieve almost the same performance using a traditional construction whereas Mitchell relied on new methods. This meant that the Hurricane was easier to build, could be produced in greater numbers and this was fundamental to our nation's success in this first decisive victory to be achieved in the air. It is a pity that the Hurricane has become the forgotten aircraft of World War 2 for it was a very noble partner to the Spitfire in the early years of war. Its rate of turn was equal if not better than anything that the Germans could throw against it. Its robust construction and wide track undercarriage made it an ideal mount for the inexperienced fighter pilot. In the hands of the battle-hardened veteran it was a formidable weapon. Sydney Camm's conventional construction meant that, unlike the Spitfire, its eight Browning machine guns were mounted in groups of four centrally in each wing. Apart from the ease of maintaining the guns and re-arming them this meant that the aircraft offered a very stable gun platform in the heat of combat. Famous names such as Bob Stanford-Tuck and Douglas Bader cut their teeth on this machine and in the latter years of their lives would hear not a word said against it.

It is a testimony to its prowess that very few surviving Luftwaffe pilots will admit to having engaged in combat against Hurricanes. When questioned they will invariably insist that they were shot down by a Spitfire! This, of course, could not be the case as the majority of defenders in the Battle of Britain were, in fact, Hurricanes.

Such was the versatility of this machine that it was used for a variety of purposes as the war progressed. It was also flown by the air forces of many foreign lands and formed the basis of a major contribution to the Soviet Union in 1941.

Fifty years on it is pleasing to note that attention is once again being devoted to it and that here and there examples are being restored once again to flying condition. Nevertheless, the Hurricane (particularly when compared to the Spitfire) is now a rarity and this history will enable a much larger group of people to get closer, albeit through text and photographs, to the machine which carried the majority of "The Few" into battle.

DR MICHAEL A. FOPP
Director, Royal Air Force Museum

Contents

Introduction

Picture, if you will, a sunny office of no great size but with large sash windows on two sides, modestly furnished with a big mahogany table and around it set eight chairs, all occupied. Over the mantelpiece hangs a large framed portrait of a young man with high, broad forehead, seemingly uncomfortable in formal suit and severe collar, gazing with lazy eye on the assembled company below. A small brass plate proclaims the subject, HARRY G. HAWKER, 1891–1921.

From the street below come the sounds of a bustling town, the rattle of a lorry as it passes on solid tyres, the occasional trumpeting of an impatient car, the buzzing of a motor-cycle, the chatter of pedestrians.

In the smoky atmosphere of the room the quiet rumble of voices proclaims a discussion rather than a formal meeting. There are few papers in front of the eight men seated round the table. One man holds the rapt attention of the others—none above middle age. He wears the uniform of a very senior officer in the Royal Air Force, the rows of medal ribbons proclaiming long and distinguished service. Occasionally one of his audience interrupts with a question and the conversation becomes momentarily general. One man, smoking heavily, fidgets constantly with a number of blueprint drawings; another appears to be taking notes. The airman talks earnestly and with obvious conviction and authority.

This is a meeting of the Directors of the H. G. Hawker Engineering Company in the boardroom situated on the north side of Canbury Park Road in Kingston-upon-Thames, and the year is 1929. Yet it is *not* a Board Meeting as such but a gathering of key men of the Company, called together to meet the man who would soon be promoted to head the Royal Air Force and whose influence was to set the pattern for the air defence of Britain during the coming decade. The subject of his discussion on that day, by his choice, was the pressing importance to break from the age-old tradition of military aeroplanes, and the responsibility to be borne by industry for meeting the cost to do so. That man was Air Marshal Sir John Salmond.

The history of the Hawker Hurricane was not simply one of a piece of machinery. Its progress from concept and drawing board to the battleskies of the world—more than any other aircraft—embraced the fortunes and destiny of the nation and its aircraft industry, and indeed dictated the course of history of the Royal Air Force for much more than a decade. It was not the product of a flash of inspiration but of years of logical evolution and carefully reasoned development, of a small company staffed by men of loyalty and integrity, led by men of money, yes, but of profound wisdom and considerable professional ability. They gave to the nation the aeroplane it *had* to have, and the Royal Air Force was desperate to get it.

The Hurricane was not a "world beater", yet it matched the best aircraft of Britain's enemies at just the moment of her greatest crisis and was available in adequate quantities. Inevitably you, the reader, will seek comparison with the Spitfire, that beautiful near-contemporary of the Hurricane that was so emotively named, and of course the basis of comparison exists in that both were conceived to perform the same task—to defend Britain against Germany. Yet it was to a far greater degree upon the Hurricane that the responsibility rested to withstand the onslaughts by Germany, Italy and Japan when the world was threatened by those aggressor nations, and to buy time for survival while the arsenals of the West (and the Soviet Union) could forge the weapons of victory. *Indeed the Hawker Hurricane flew and fought in more campaigns, on more fronts and in more theatres and countries than any other aeroplane in the Second World War*—more than the Spitfire, Beaufighter, Mosquito, Lancaster and, of course, the great American aircraft such as the P-40, P-51 and B-17. Only the Bristol Blenheim bomber came near to matching the ubiquity of the Hurricane.

More than 14,000 Hurricanes were produced in the space of seven years and their stories would fill many books—indeed have done so. This book is an attempt to recount the achievements of the "Hurricane men", those who worked to get the aeroplane started, who designed it, who flew it to get it right and, above all, who fought in it. The men—thousands of them—were all individuals, with personal problems and crises of their own; their aeroplane was their common bond. My book can perhaps describe that aeroplane and how it came to fruition; it can outline its great battles and campaigns but, alas, present no more than a whiff of cordite between these covers. It—like the Spitfire, though somewhat sturdier—was a weapon of war, yet one, like so many other great aeroplanes, that evoked a charisma of trust, confidence and character.

Author's Note

It is necessary, for the benefit of aficionados of aviation history and with some deference, to mention that a former book on the Hawker Hurricane, now long since out of print, was produced by this writer some 25 years ago. It has to be said that, having been written so relatively close in time to the events it described, the book could present little more than a rather superficial account of the subject. Many of the personalities involved were constrained by professional limitations at that time from discussing their involvement, while scarcely any of the former enemies' records of the war had been made available for examination. It has to be admitted, therefore, that in some instances events were afforded greater prominence than was their true worth, while others were still cloaked by the various security restrictions. Incredibly, there are even yet some episodes in the Hurricane's story which it is not permitted to disclose. In the course of continuing research down the years I have, however, become aware of the earlier errors of omission and misplaced emphasis. I can only hope that the present work makes amends.

1

LETHARGY

The decade following the "war to end all wars" was for Great Britain a period of political, social, economic and industrial stagnation, a lack of enterprise and direction. Europe's traditional alliances, if not in tatters, were the subject of distrust and suspicion. Britain and France, in winning the war, had been emasculated both in human and material terms, while the former Central Powers lay in ruins, bankrupt and crushed by devastating reparation and ruthless treaty. Well might British politicians seize upon the Ten Year Rule to conceal their reluctance to give thought to military matters. One world war later a British government could at least point to the creation of a Welfare State as demanding prior attention.

After 1918 Britain retained little more than the legend of greatness. She had arrived at the Armistice table armed with the world's most powerful navy and air force yet, within two years, the young Royal Air Force was being chopped up as the admirals and generals fought like alleycats for the pieces. The junior Service was having to fight for its own survival. Moreover the much-popularized "world fit for heroes" remained the pipedream of tired old politicians, unable or unwilling to encourage any alternative to the steadily multiplying soup kitchens. Air travel that should have buoyed up Britain's huge aircraft industry remained the plaything of the rich and all but withered away. There existed no realistic structure in which peacetime aviation, military or commercial, could advance, let alone flourish. The spectre of the chicken farm faced countless skilled airmen peremptorily discharged from a bankrupt Service.

In due course Parliament evolved a formal policy of military stagnation, provided with respectability by the so-called Ten Year Rule. In truth the "rule" was never more than an assumption that a decade's warning was likely to be given of trouble looming on the European horizon. In the event Germany gave just seven years' notice of her ambitions when, in 1932, she walked out of the International Disarmament Conference; and, despite feverish military preparations to meet the Armageddon, no nation in Europe was ready when the blow fell.

Sir Hugh Trenchard, latterly wartime supremo in the new Royal Air Force and always dourly distrustful of the politician, had witnessed the birth-pangs of his Service. The birth had been conceived by the marriage of the army and naval air arms, the shotgun placed in the hands of the government by the British people, outraged by the armed services' inability to protect them from German bombers. The irony was that Trenchard himself was as far removed from understanding the technicalities of an air defence system as Nelson was of a cavalry charge. Sir Hugh was a "bomber man" through and through, his philosophy—seldom coherently expressed—running closely parallel with that of Emilio Douhet, whose precept recognized the aerial bomb as the *raison d'être* of air power. In Trenchard's limited view the need for interceptors was to a large extent superfluous.

While affairs in Europe offered no support for

arguments in favour of his Air Force, those in the Middle East provided better prospects, for here was a region in which post-war "solutions" had simply compounded age-old problems. Britain's mandates in Palestine and Mesopotamia (Iraq), following the crumbling of the Ottoman Empire, placed impossible strains upon the limited Imperial ground forces available to such an extent that Trenchard, seizing on the idea of air policing, was able to demonstrate fairly convincingly that a handful of aeroplanes could accomplish as much as a battalion of infantry—at a fraction of the cost. Such arguments carried weight at the Treasury. The flexibility of deployment of aircraft, compared with that of ground forces, suggested the feasibility of defence of the Suez Canal simultaneously with that of the Mosul oilfields 800 miles distant.

By proving that the rump of the Royal Air Force could establish stability in a traditionally troublesome theatre, Trenchard achieved his aim: survival of the RAF as an independent Service. By contrast most other nations, not forgetting the United States of America, continued to administer their air forces as component parts of their armies. Had such a state of affairs existed in Britain in 1940 the German *Luftwaffe* would have enjoyed a walkover.

Survival of the Service of course resulted in the continuity of staffs and the employment of hand-picked officers and men upon whom the Service would in due course continue to build. Moreover, many of the landing grounds created among the desert wastes of the Middle East as rudimentary bases for wandering Bristol Fighters and DH.9As would one day acquire the dignity of Royal Air Force Stations with hangars, barracks, messes and all the paraphernalia of a regularly established Air Force; many of those Stations will figure prominently later in this story.

Be that as it may, no one could possibly argue that the nature of operations amid the wastes of Mosul in any way demanded the scale of organization, training and equipment relevant to an air force whose responsibilities lay primarily in Europe. And the British Treasury, ever mindful of growing popular pacifism at home, was certainly in no mood to lavish funds on a powerful metropolitan air force.

Thus it was that the elements of the RAF in the Middle East had to make do with barely adequate supplies of war-weary "general purpose" aircraft and a succession of lumbering "bomber transports"—the latter in effect troop-carrying adaptations of wartime bombers—while a relatively small number of wartime scouts (mostly Sopwith Snipes) was saved from the scrapyards and issued to a handful of "fighter" squadrons at home. Lip service was paid to a policy of progressive re-equipment, and a number of aircraft requirements (euphemistically termed Specifications, but in reality seldom displaying more imagination for the next aeroplane than to demand a 20 mph speed increase over the last) was issued by the Air Ministry to the aircraft manufacturers from time to time. Trenchard certainly merited the sobriquet "Father of the Royal Air Force", yet at no time did he espouse a *balanced* air force—such was his preoccupation with the bomber.

Against this background of blurred military planning the survival of the British aircraft industry was nothing short of miraculous. Indeed the fortunes of the H. G. Hawker Engineering Company, which was formed following the voluntary liquidation of the Sopwith Aviation Company, were typical of many of the aircraft manufacturers. A brief excursion into motor-cycles and cars (until Harry Hawker's death while practising for the 1921 Aerial Derby) bought survival, and was followed by repair contracts for Snipes. Even the company's chief aircraft designer was more at home on a horse than in a mechanical vehicle; his first design to achieve material form (a monstrosity which bore the unlikely name of Duiker) proved to be so apallingly inept that it was quietly taken out and buried in a corner of Brooklands—or so the legend goes.

Elsewhere things were little better. However, at least some companies were sharpening their pencils on racing aircraft designs, not least at Supermarine, where a new tradition was being built. Supermarine, Avro, Fairey and Sopwith had all produced racing seaplanes for the ill-fated 1919 Schneider Trophy race, while landplane racers were represented by aircraft from Nieuport and General, Bristol and the Gloucestershire Aircraft Company. None of these designs, however, in any way advanced the development of the aeroplane, merely demanding greater risk for, and courage from, the pilot. At least in the sphere of the bomber there was, perhaps understandably, more activity, albeit little in the way of new development.

Among the leading aircraft designers in the early twenties a number of changes took place that were to have long-lasting results in the industry. At Supermarine a young man called R. J. Mitchell was promoted to succeed F. J. Hargreaves, while at Hawker W. G. Carter stepped up to take over as Chief Designer. Carter remained with the Kingston company until 1925, when, on moving to the Gloucestershire Aircraft Company (to be renamed the Gloster Aircraft Company), his place was taken by Sydney Camm. Camm had spent some seven years with Martin and Handasyde Ltd before joining Carter at Kingston, by which time new fighter designs were beginning to appear in the tiny drawing office.

The first of these designs to materialize was the Woodcock, initiated as a two-bay biplane under the direction of the Duiker's designer, Captain Thomson. Carter quickly realized that in its two-bay configuration the Woodcock, if anything, turned the pages of design back six years, so set about doing what he could to wring some respectability out of the aircraft, fairly quickly producing a single-bay aircraft as the Woodcock Mark II. Camm

*Sydney Camm's first 'solo' design at Kingston in 1925 was the ultra-light Hawker Cygnet. (*Photo: *H. G. Hawker Engineering Co Ltd).*

meanwhile was allowed to cut his teeth on an ultra-light aeroplane, the Hawker Cygnet, a remarkable little biplane by any standards, one of the two examples built surviving to this day.

Compromised from the start, the Woodcock could never be an outstanding aeroplane and returned a performance little better than the wartime Snipe. It was, however, at least rewarded by a small production contract and thereby spelled survival for the Hawker company in Canbury Park Road, Kingston-upon-Thames. Moreover, at the time of Carter's departure for Gloster, the Danes were expressing interest in the Woodcock so that Camm was able to apply himself to a limited re-design and get the feel of producing an aircraft for a military customer.

From the beginning of his appointment as Hawker's Chief Designer, Camm was as much handicapped by his own, almost total lack of experience in working on metal aircraft as by a reluctance of the Air Ministry to demand them. That is not to say that such aircraft had not served in the RAF, yet the woodworking fitter tradesmen in the Service still far outnumbered the "tin bashers". Repairs to and maintenance of metal structures usually required their return to the manufacturer (or a repair depot), while wooden aircraft—fighters, bombers, flying-boats and the rest—could more often than not be repaired on the squadrons. For a Service desperately short of money this was an important consideration.

Nor was the lack of enterprise evident only in airframe design. Aircraft engines underwent little significant development in the early twenties, the aircraft companies having little choice between heavy and bulky derivatives of the Rolls-Royce Eagle, Cub, Condor and Falcon, Siddeley Puma, Napier Lion and Bristol Jupiter. Only Richard Fairey's decision to take the bull by the horns and select the American Curtiss D-12 in-line for his Fox light bomber prompted Rolls-Royce to sit up and take notice. Belatedly the Air Ministry followed suit. The Fox was first flown in 1925 and promptly showed the RAF's latest fighters, the Armstrong Whitworth Siskin and Gloster Grebe, a clean pair of heels.

In long retrospect the Fox proved a heaven-sent blessing for Hawker. The beautiful little aircraft so attracted the bomber barons of the RAF that it came to represent a new yardstick by which future requirements would be measured. Yet, because of antagonism caused within the Air Ministry by Richard Fairey's affrontery in shopping abroad for his engine, the Fox was only rewarded by a very small production order, and only one squadron was so equipped. In other words the Fox had shown the way and created the demand—as well as the vacuum, which Camm now set about filling.

Rolls-Royce, aware that its in-line Falcon represented the most realistic starting point for a new generation of relatively lightweight engines, achieved an important breakthrough when it succeeded in casting single banks of engine cylinders (the former practice being to cast cylinders separately), and the resulting Falcon-development, the F.XI, returned a considerable improvement in power-weight ratio and gave promise of accelerated development. Moreover its compact design and small cross-section suggested the possibility of an exceptionally clean cowling at least as efficient as that of the Fox.

★ ★ ★

It is worth pausing here to look briefly at the situation facing the RAF in its emerging air defence responsibilities towards the end of the 1920s. The annual Hendon air pageant, about the only public manifestation of the RAF's capabilities, had repeatedly focused attention on its supposed ability to destroy canvas replicas of Middle Eastern tribesmen's encampments as stately processions of lumbering bombers slowly moved from one part of the sky to its neighbour and a few brightly painted fighters made apparently fruitless attempts to interfere. For all the public euphoria that this spectacle generated the Air Ministry had unconsciously put its finger on the RAF's impotence as a means of defence over Britain. However, the only foreign air force within attacking range of Britain was that of France, now that Germany was apparently harmless, so that the small number of available RAF fighter squadrons was deployed on a band of airfields in the south and south-east of England—Biggin Hill, Tangmere, Upavon, Hawkinge, Duxford, North Weald, Kenley and Henlow—so sited as to bar the way to London and the industrial Midlands from the south. No warning of approaching bombers would be available, so intercepting fighters would only take off *after* the enemy aircraft (supposedly French) had crossed the English coast. Thereafter, in the absence of overland raid reporting, the fighters would be faced with long stern chases. Aircraft such as the Fox light bomber (top speed 156 mph) and the Gamecock fighter (top speed 155 mph) demonstrated the futility of such tactics. The great expanse of the southern counties, extending from Cornwall to Suffolk, was euphemistically termed the Fighting Area, though it is difficult to imagine what fighting would have taken place—except after the bombers had already attacked their targets.

It fell to that most distinguished airman, Air Marshal Sir John Salmond, appointed Air Officer Commanding-in-Chief, Air Defence of Great Britain (ADGB) in 1925, to emphasize the deficiencies in Britain's air defences, and it was largely thanks to his energies that Service and industry alike set about putting their respective houses in order. Despite continuing limitation of finance for the Services at least Salmond was able to argue the vital importance of increased priority for the interceptor fighter—even at the expense of the heavy bomber, hitherto the Air Staff's sacred cow and powerfully advocated by men like Air Marshal Sir John Steel, Air Officer Commanding the Wessex Bombing Area and former Deputy Chief of the Air Staff. Henceforth, faced with the obvious shortcomings of the fighter defences, not even Trenchard could pursue a "bomber at any cost" policy if his bases were to be fatally vulnerable to enemy attack. For the next ten years it was to be the bomber's turn to enter a decline as the British fighter regained the ascendancy.

First evidence of Salmond's influence was the selection of a "standard" RAF fighter, which emerged as the Bristol Bulldog (top speed 174 mph), an all-metal aeroplane—with fabric covering—which first flew in May 1927 and entered service with No. 3 Squadron at Upavon, replacing Gamecocks. In due course Bulldogs served with ten RAF fighter squadrons and survived in service until 1937.

At Hawker Camm viewed the introduction of the Bulldog with misgivings as he saw the continued acceptance of its bulky Bristol Jupiter radial engine as endangering the development of the much neater in-line. Meanwhile he continued a number of essays to develop airframe design beyond what he saw as no more than a perpetuation of ten-year-old wartime formulae. In this he was ably supported by a triumvirate of highly competent men, each of whom was a master of his profession. Frederick Sigrist had been a long-serving colleague of Sopwith since the pioneering days of aviation and was in effect the Chief Engineer at Canbury Park Road, possessing a priceless instinct in the sphere of aircraft structures; such established influence with Sopwith allowed Camm who, after all, was a relative newcomer to the Company, an almost free rein in the matter of design direction. Camm's right-hand man in the design office was Roy Chaplin, who had come to Hawker in 1926 and was to remain at his side for the next 35 years. The third man was "George" Bulman (so universally known on account of his inability to remember other people's names that everyone else was George to him). Flight Lieutenant P. W. S. Bulman was one of a legendary band of post-war "consultant" test pilots whose services had been widely sought by and freely given to several companies simultaneously in the days when no formal training existed for experimental pilots. Possessed of what were considered to be rare intuitive and analytical flying skills, Bulman joined Hawker in 1925 as Chief (and only) test pilot and was to fly each and every new Hawker aircraft for twenty years.

When Chaplin came to Canbury Park Road Camm's first entirely new fighter, the Hornbill, was undergoing its initial flight tests at Brooklands. This little aircraft employed what was regarded as an immensely powerful Rolls-Royce Condor engine (of 698 hp) and, by attention to detail design, was capable of 187 mph. It was, however, armed with but a single Vickers machine gun and proved more

The standard Fighting Area interceptor between 1930 and 1934, the Bristol Bulldog. It first entered service in 1928 and soldiered on well into the Expansion years. These examples carry the markings of No 3 (Fighter) Squadron at the 1930 Hendon Air Pageant. (Photo: *The Bristol Aeroplane Co Ltd.)*

THE "KINGSTON-HAWKER" TRADITION

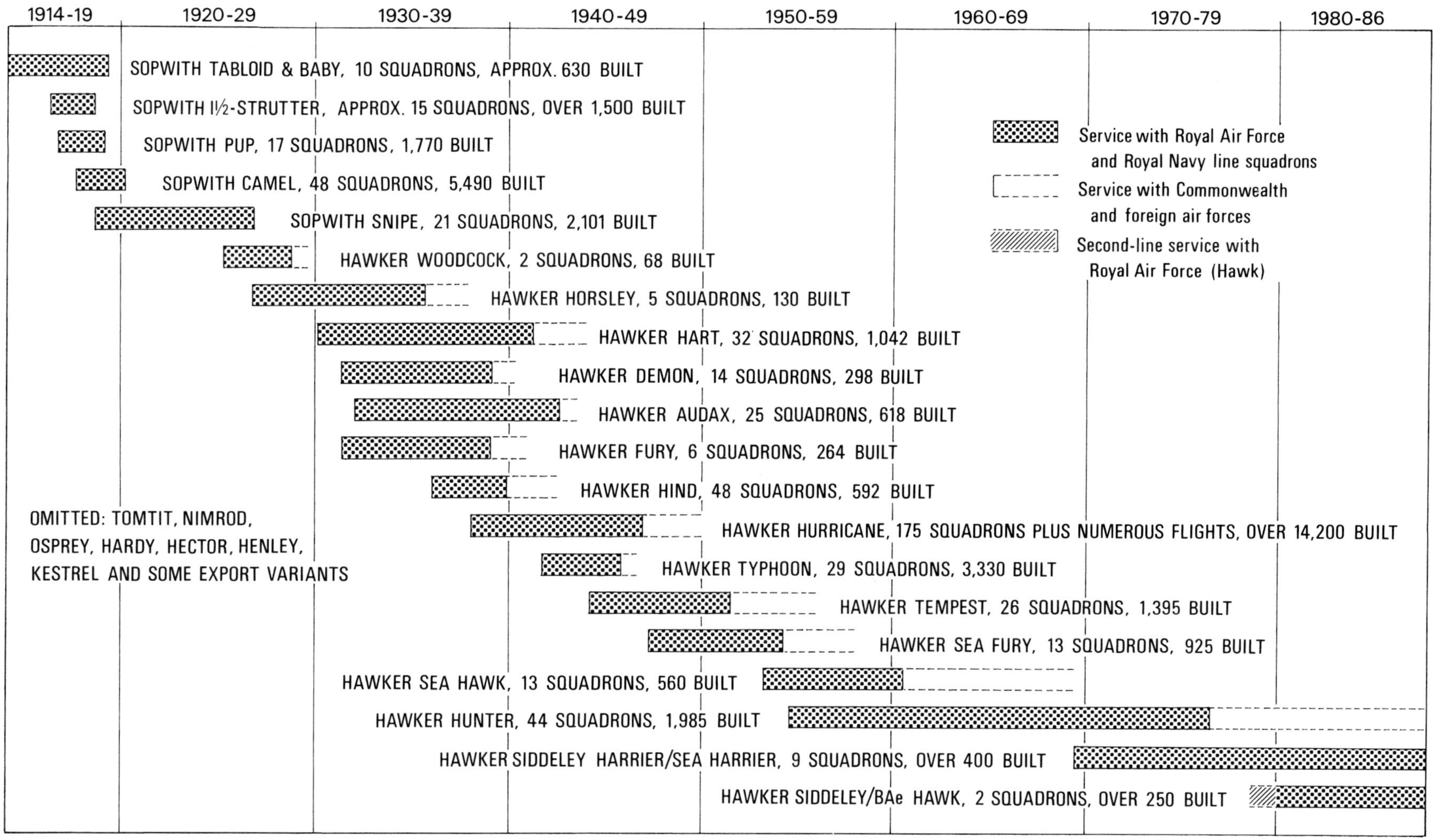

As far as can be established, Kingston-upon-Thames, home of 'Hawker' and its forebear Sopwith Aviation, is unique in having engendered an uninterrupted succession of front-line fighting aeroplanes for Britain's Armed Forces ever since the beginning of the First World War.

than a handful to fly. Moreover, the very efficiency with which Camm managed to enclose the engine resulted in such a narrow fuselage that the cockpit was impossibly cramped—a matter that no doubt Bulman would have been at pains to discuss with Camm.

While the Hornbill was still of predominantly wooden construction, another of Camm's early designs, the private venture Heron—though outwardly of somewhat dated external appearance—employed an all-metal primary structure, originally evolved by Sigrist as early as 1925. This consisted of round steel or duralumin tubes, swaged to rectangular section at their ends; joints were formed by flat plates riveted to the tubes to which other members could be attached. A cupped bolt was passed through the longeron to mount the lugs for cross-bracing wires with turnbuckles for tensioning. Also evolved at this time, and eventually registered for patent by Chaplin, was the famous Hawker dumb-bell spar. This comprised two relatively light-gauge steel strips rolled to polygonal section and connected by a single plate web. These fabricated structures and components were found to be much simpler and rather cheaper to assemble than the alternative welded structure, as well as making for simpler repairs—and no one should have known better than Fred Sigrist, who was himself a master welder; thereafter his oft-quoted words were famous, "Find me a chippy with a spanner and we'll mend the aeroplane."

The Heron, with its untidy Jupiter engine, was never seriously considered as a contender for RAF service, but nevertheless provided Camm with the necessary experience in producing a metal aircraft, so much so that its basic structural philosophy remained essentially unchanged in every one of his aircraft for ten years—up to and including the Hurricane.

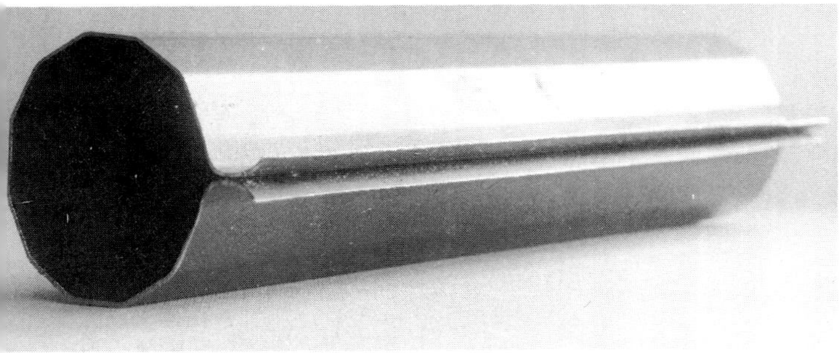

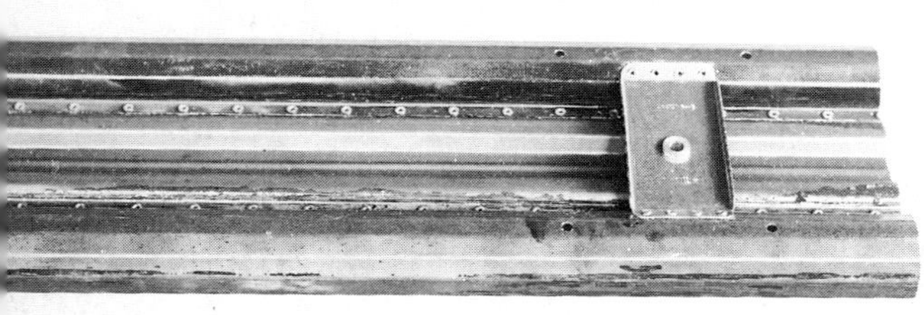

Above: The duodecagonal tubular component of the patent Hawker dumbell wing spar. Below: *The wing spar with corrugated web rivetted to the flanges of the tubular components.* (Photos: *H. G. Hawker Engineering Co Ltd., Neg Nos 47E and 48E dated 1933)*

Thus by 1927 Hawker was safely established with an aircraft, the Horsley bomber, in production for the RAF and several others being examined by the Aeroplane and Armament Experimental Establishment (A&AEE) at Martlesham Heath.

Meanwhile Rolls-Royce had successfully bench-run the F.XI in-line engine, while the Air Ministry had issued a Specification (12/26) for a new light bomber, calling for a top speed of 160 mph. To meet this requirement Camm used as the design basis his Harrier bomber (which, on account of an unsuitable Jupiter engine, had proved desperately underpowered but otherwise had met with Service approval). By substituting the new in-line engine it was possible to clean up the entire fuselage, while the much reduced load demands (1,000 lb bomb load in the Harrier compared with 500 lb in 12/26) enabled Camm to scale down the wings. When ready for flight in June 1928 the new Hawker bomber tipped the scales at an all-up weight of 4,500 lb; more important, it returned a speed of 180 mph and, according to Bulman, proved entirely viceless in the air. The irony of the situation was that it already outpaced the Bulldog fighter, which was still a year away from entry into RAF service.

The new Hawker aircraft embarked on a year-long programme of development trials, during which the Service conducted a series of evaluations in direct competition with the Avro Antelope and Fairey Fox Mark II. The outcome of these was a report by the RAF stating that the Hawker design, now named the Hart, had proved greatly superior in performance, handling and maintenance, leading in turn to the issue of a production Specification (9/29) and a preliminary order for 12 aircraft.

Once more, with the imminent introduction of a light bomber capable of running rings around the best RAF interceptors in service, ADGB faced the same embarrassing problem it had faced in 1926. Moreover, at exactly the moment when ADGB most needed the powerful influence of its Commander-in-Chief, Sir John Salmond became due for promotion away from an operational command. However, in anticipation of this situation, shortly before taking up his appointment as Air Member for Personnel on the Air Staff, Salmond paid a visit to Canbury Park Road in March 1929 for a general discussion with the Hawker Board. It has been suggested that this meeting—which Camm was invited to attend—was one of the most significant of its sort held between a senior Service officer and an industrial Board in the inter-war period. Camm's recollections were that Salmond was shown the completed first prototype of a new Hawker fighter that had been embarked on in considerable secrecy and at private expense and which was about to be loaded on to a lorry and taken to Brooklands for its first flight. No one can have

The Hawker Hornbill interceptor, Sydney Camm's first essay in high-speed fighter design. (Photo: Flight, *Neg No 3880)*

failed to be impressed by the beauty of this fighter—then referred to as the Hornet—while the expectation of a maximum speed of 200 mph must have restored Salmond's confidence in his Command's future defence capabilities after his departure. Salmond urged Hawkers to pursue flight trials with the Hornet with the utmost vigour and promised in return to set in motion the necessary steps to prepare a draft specification to cover official recognition and purchase of the prototype.

Camm, however, recalled Salmond's anxiety that the entire process of "clawing one's way up the speed scale" was fraught with hazard. He felt that the Hornet, for all its elegance, represented merely the ultimate perfection of the old wartime fighter formula—a biplane armed with two guns. Already other manufacturers had been at work on monoplanes; Mitchell's Supermarine S.5 racing seaplane had captured the Schneider Trophy almost two years previously. Admittedly no one had succeeded in producing a realistic monoplane fighter (Camm himself had attempted the design of such an aircraft in February 1925 but, frustrated by his dependence on the Jupiter engine, he had not persevered with it), but it was felt that, in due course, someone, somewhere would acquire sufficient finance for research to develop the means of combining strength and manoeuvrability, demanded by a monoplane interceptor. It seems likely that already forming in Salmond's mind was the belief that, in the unlikely event of increased Treasury finance being available, the burden of responsibility for an initiative would have to be borne by private industry. All that could be expected from the Air Ministry was the formulation of a demand; moreover the demand would have to be phrased in radical terms so as to avoid yet another bomber-versus-fighter stalemate.

After Sir John's departure from ADGB its command passed to Air Marshal Sir Edward Ellington, a man best remembered for his preoccupation with the introduction of new air fighting tactics than for his energy in promoting new fighter aircraft. He had, after all, as one of Trenchard's officers selected for senior command, commanded in turn the Royal Air Force in the Middle East, India and Iraq ever since 1922, theatres in which interceptor fighters had had no place whatsoever, and one has only to refer to the various RAF record books to note that for every visit he paid to a fighter station in ADGB he called on about three bomber stations!

Nevertheless, during his term of command, another famous officer held the key appointment in command of the Fighting Area. Hugh Dowding, then an Air Vice-Marshal, was fully aware of the shortcomings of his fighter force and constantly argued the urgent need to break the bomber-fighter deadlock, and one suspects that he argued his case with such persuasion that he created his own destiny when, in 1930, he found himself promoted after only one year at HQ Fighting Area to the post of Air Member for Research and Development on the Air Council—the very appointment that exercised policy for new aircraft equipment in the RAF.

Thus at this early point was the stage being set on which the story of the Hurricane would unfold. One other significant change in the Royal Air Force occurred at the end of 1929 with the retirement as Chief of the Air Staff of Sir Hugh Trenchard, his

Camm's first fighter of metal construction, the Hawker Heron, at Brooklands; beyond are the original flight sheds of 1910. (Photo: *H. G. Hawker Engineering Co Ltd., Neg No 14N)*

The first Hawker fighter to gain a production contract for the RAF, the Woodcock II, shown here in experimental form with slotted wings, J7974. (Photo: *H. G. Hawker Engineering Co Ltd., Neg No 576W)*

place now to be taken by Sir John Salmond. It would not be too fanciful to suggest that with these changes an era in the history of the Service ended and a new one opened.

★ ★ ★

Before moving on to describe the course of events that led to the conception of the RAF's first monoplane interceptor it may be of interest to take brief note of the current equipment of other major world air forces, for it may be thought from the foregoing that Britain lagged painfully far behind both militarily and technically in aviation affairs at the end of the 1920s.

It is true that at that time France possessed the largest air force in Europe, as well as deploying sizeable forces in North Africa, Syria, the Lebanon and Indo-China. Until December 1928 the *Aviation Militaire* had been administered as the *Cinquième Arme* of the French Army, alongside the Cavalry, Infantry, Artillery and Engineers, but in that month a degree of autonomy was granted with the creation of a separate Air Ministry. Preoccupation with a long and debilitating campaign against the forces of Abd el Krim in Morocco, which lasted from 1925 until 1934 and involved a surprisingly large proportion of the French Air Force, tended to support an aircraft procurement policy of quantity rather than quality while, as in the RAF, bombers enjoyed a higher priority than fighters. Consequently aircraft such as the Nieuport-Delage 62C-1 biplane fighter, which entered service in 1930 with a top speed of 155 mph, were certainly inferior in most aspects of performance to the Bulldog, possessed the same twin-gun armament and employed all-wood structure. More important, perhaps, there existed no independent air command structure through which, as in Britain, any lobby could advocate the development of military aircraft, a state of affairs that was to persist in France for a further seven years—at the end of which time it proved far too late to create an air force capable of matching the might of Germany's *Luftwaffe*.

No nation's air force suffered more at the hands of its own politics in the 1920s than that of the United States, for by 1926, when the Air Service became the US Army Air Corps, there were in first-line service no more than 60 pursuit (or fighter) aircraft—mostly Curtiss PW-8s, P-1s and P-2s—169 observation aircraft and fewer than 100 bombers of many types. The new Air Corps had been authorized to pursue a five-year expansion plan, but financing for this was delayed until mid-1927; two years later the economic depression further restricted aircraft procurement. Fighter equipment still consisted in the main of Curtiss P-1Bs and Cs (top speed around 155 mph), but in 1930 the first Boeing P-12Bs entered service with a speed of 166 mph, a contract for 90 aircraft constituting the largest single Army order for fighters for ten years. The P-12 was a neat, purposeful-looking little biplane employing a large nine-cylinder Pratt & Whitney radial engine; it proved very popular and remained in production until March 1932, by which time a total of 365 had been produced, culminating in the P-12F with a speed of 195 mph. The airframe structure of the early P-12s employed square-section bolted aluminium tubing in the fuselage and fabric-covered wooden spars and ribs in the wings, but the P-12E and F introduced monocoque construction in the fuselage. Armament comprised the familiar twin rifle-calibre machine guns.

2

A STORM BREWS

There can be little questioning that the new broom that swept through the Air Ministry, beginning in 1929 and continuing for three years, resulted in the creation of an initiative to modernize the entire Royal Air Force. Not that symptoms could yet be detected of military danger in Europe, although the more perceptive observers were watching the growth of Mussolini's fascist influence in international circles, particularly as it affected the balance of power in the Mediterranean. This, as well as the emergence of Hitler's NSDAP as the second largest party in the German Reichstag, represented a potentially destabilizing influence in central Europe.

When Sir John Salmond became Chief of the Air Staff on 1 January 1930, he brought with him a first-hand understanding of the problems facing the air defences of Britain. Already there were in existence a number of draft requirements for new interceptor fighters, prepared by the various Directorates, largely as the result of the normal course of discussions with the technical staffs at Farnborough and Martlesham Heath and with leading aircraft designers in industry. The general concensus of opinion had produced a number of conclusions—which generally conformed with opinions expressed during Salmond's visit to Hawker in the previous year.

While there is no doubt that a large degree of agreement existed in the ultimate broad aim of a new interceptor requirement, there were, however, areas of difference, particularly in matters of powerplant configuration, armament and whether night operation should figure in the basic requirement. Fundamental to the requirement was a demand for an increase in maximum speed to 250 mph at 10,000 feet, an arbitrary figure of 75 mph beyond that of the Bulldog, and 50 mph more than the speed of the Hawker Hornet.

The principal bone of contention was less of a technical matter than one of economics. It was pointed out that a standard production-series Jupiter-powered Bulldog cost the taxpayer roughly £4,100, and a Kestrel-powered Hart nearly £4,800; cost of the Hornet in production, just submitted by Hawker, was expected to be about £4,500. To achieve the huge increase in performance would demand costly development of powerplant, particularly if a new radial engine were to be decided upon.

In the matter of powerplant there were still those who remained to be convinced that the in-line necessarily provided the answer to high speed in a military aircraft, pointing to the weight and vulnerability of the cooling system and radiator of the Rolls-Royce F.XI—now named the Kestrel. Nor were they convinced by Rolls-Royce's plans to investigate evaporative cooling—by employing steam condensers along the wing leading edge, the radiator might be discarded altogether.

Arguments about the weight of armament to be specified had been sparked some months earlier at Martlesham Heath, where tests had shown that in a quarter attack by a two-gun fighter possessing a 20 mph speed advantage (that is to say, for example, a

Bulldog attacking a Horsley), the hit expectancy by a line pilot was of the order of 80; if the speed advantage increased to 40 mph the hit expectancy dropped to 20, largely on account of the shorter burst possible. Nor were interceptor squadron pilots particularly impressed by the formation attacks now being introduced throughout the Fighting Area largely at the instigation of Sir Edward Ellington. Moreover, the greater speed advantage did not necessarily permit better results through allowing repeated attacks as it was well known that the old Vickers gun—universally fitted in British interceptors since the war—suffered a far higher incidence of jams during repeated short bursts. One answer lay in mounting the guns outside the propeller arc so as to dispense with the interrupter gear which itself not only reduced the effective rate of fire but also contributed to gun jams. So common was the gun-jam phenomenon that few pilots of those days could countenance a fighter in which its armament was out of physical reach of the cockpit. (One answer, being examined by Gloster, was to mount drum-fed Lewis guns—traditionally reliable weapons—on the aircraft's wings outside the propeller arc, but the 97-round drum severely reduced the length of burst possible.)

The matter of night fighting was not so much concerned with the equipment demanded (such as cockpit lighting, underwing flares and so on) as the ease with which the aircraft could be taken off, flown and landed in the dark. Aircraft with a single radial engine were traditionally difficult to land, while the provision of long flame-damping exhaust pipes on an in-line engine could impose a considerable weight and drag penalty.

Clearly all these esoteric problems were there for the aircraft designers to solve. For the Air Ministry's Directorate of Technical Development (DTD) it was enough to be aware of their existence when formulating the new Specification. Yet one overriding consideration remained: the likely cost of the aircraft. The relatively extensive development of what must surely emerge as a very advanced aircraft would be reflected not only in the unit cost of production aeroplanes but could well demand lengthy testing by the Service as well as more elaborate training both of pilots and maintenance personnel. The answer lay in offering the promise of a large production contract—and this supported the argument that the successful contender should indeed equip both day and night interceptor squadrons.[1] Finally the target date for introduction into service was stated as being "in time for participation in the annual air exercise of 1934".

Not unnaturally the existence of this new Specification, F.7/30, quickly became known throughout the aircraft industry and, in order to counter any suggestion that Hawker was benefiting from preferential knowledge of its terms (for by now the Hornet prototype was undergoing trials at the A&AEE and had been shown to the public at the 1929 Olympia Aero Show), a draft of the Requirement was circulated among most of the major manufacturers in March 1930 by the Air Ministry. At the same time, so as to dissociate the new requirement from the Hornet—now officially renamed the Hawker Fury—a production Specification, 12/30, was issued for that aeroplane and a contract for 21 aircraft raised.

For all the wise counselling that lay behind F.7/30, and there is no doubt that with the promise of large production contracts the industry was spurred to unprecedented excitement and activity, the issue of the requirement was both ill-advised and premature, and led to widespread misinterpretation by the industry at large (a misinterpretation which Hawker avoided, probably as the result of having been privy to Salmond's philosophies from the start). For instance, not all design staffs took adequate note of the overriding demand for greatly increased speed, and some of those that did so lost sight of the fact that the aeroplane was still to be an interceptor fighter in which handling and manoeuvreability were also paramount. Moreover, by the time the Specification was first formally issued towards the end of 1930, the Air Ministry had come down firmly in favour of the steam-cooled Kestrel IV (renamed the Goshawk), which had been test flown by Rolls-Royce in a Hart earlier in the year and had returned promising results. This infatuation with steam cooling was to prove to be the undoing of the whole project and a time-wasting cul-de-sac.

It is not proposed to describe in detail all the attempts made to meet the F.7/30 requirement other than in the manner in which they influenced fighter design in Britain during the early 1930s—beneficially or otherwise. For one thing Hawker now had its hands full with fast-growing orders for the Hart bomber, Fury fighter[2] and Tomtit trainer, while already the Air Ministry was beginning to discuss with Camm a number of variations of the Hart (variations that would in due course emerge as the Demon two-seat fighter, the Audax army co-operation aircraft, the Osprey naval general purpose land- and seaplanes, Hardy, Hartebeeste, Hind and Hector). Camm moreover—perhaps ill-advisedly—decided for the time being to pursue development of his beautiful Fury, which first reached No. 43 (Fighter) Squadron, commanded by Sqn Ldr L. H. Slatter (later Air Marshal Sir Leonard Slatter, KBE, CB, DSC, DFC[3]), at Tangmere in May 1931. With its top speed of 207 mph at 14,000 feet, the Fury represented the pinnacle of every aspiring RAF pilot's ambitions and placed the Service in the forefront of fighter technology. This was a period for Camm in which an extraordinarily close relationship developed with Rolls-Royce—a sort of partnership that was to persist for more than 20 years—and he felt that the promise of increased power from the Kestrel, confidently foreshadowed by its manufacturers, would enable the Fury to meet the demands of F.7/30 without all the expense of a wholly new design (an expense which, the Air Ministry had made all too clear, must be borne by the manufacturer). In this belief he was only partly justified, as will be shown shortly.

Widely regarded as front-runner in the stakes for the new RAF fighter was Reginald Mitchell, by now well known and highly respected for his superb seaplane racers; indeed his S.6 had won the Schneider Trophy in 1929, and the improved S.6B was to take the Trophy outright for Britain in 1931. Yet even Mitchell was to discover the world of difference that existed between the design of a racing seaplane and that of a robust interceptor fighter. The one demanded a capacity for bursts of high speed at sea level and relatively modest stressing, sacrificing such attributes as pilot comfort and field of vision in the interests of low drag; the other would be a fast climbing, highly stressed, armed and radio-equipped fighter in which excellent view from the cockpit and manoeuvreability at high speeds were essential. Nor was a transition from biplane to monoplane a foregone conclusion, for the wings of the racers were far from being cantilever structures but were substantially braced externally. Indeed Mitchell's first essay into an F.7/30 monoplane design reflected all the inherent difficulties: his Supermarine Type 224 (with which he himself expressed disappointment even before it was flown in 1934) proved to be an ungainly monoplane with big inverted-gull wing, large "trousered" landing gear and suspect Goshawk engine. Not surprisingly it failed by a margin of 20 mph to reach the stipulated 250 mph. The large wing was mandatory to keep the wing loading within reasonable bounds, particularly for ease of landing at night.

No better fortune attended Westland's F.7/30 design, which originated as a monoplane on the drawing board but emerged as a hybrid biplane with gull top wing. Continuing development and subsequent re-issue of the Specification had by late 1931 brought forth demands for an armament increased to four machine guns as well as inclusion of full night-flying equipment—indeed the project now became generally known as the "day and night fighter". Westland, in concentrating all four guns around the pilot's cockpit, hit on the idea of mounting the Goshawk engine *behind* the pilot, employing an extension shaft under the cockpit floor to drive the propeller. While this configuration bestowed excellent forward vision for the pilot and eliminated exhaust glare in the cockpit, much of the benefit was lost with the addition of the gull top wing. The end result was a thoroughly ungainly monstrosity whose top speed of 180 mph impressed no one.

If the kindest description of the Westland PV.4 was "ungainly", the Blackburn F.3 was downright grotesque. Also a biplane of singular appearance, the F.3's top wing was attached to the fuselage *below* the cockpit, while the lower wing was attached some three feet below the fuselage by a tunnel fairing which incorporated the Goshawk's steam condenser.

These three prototypes, the Supermarine 224, Westland PV.4 and Blackburn F.3 (given RAF serial numbers *K2890*, *K2891* and *K2892* respectively), were all purchased by the Air Ministry for evaluation in 1934—although the F.3 which suffered continuing engine cooling problems during its taxying trials, never managed to get airborne to corroborate its designers' modest top speed estimate of 190 mph.

Meanwhile Camm, who one feels must have looked askance at the efforts of these manufacturers, had gone ahead with his progressive refinement of the Fury (for which RAF orders totalling 117 had been placed), and, as the original target date of 1934 for service entry by the F.7/30 fighter had long since been abandoned as being quite unattainable, he produced his own contender for the new interceptor requirement. This was the Hawker PV.3, a slightly enlarged derivative of the Fury, powered by a 695 hp Goshawk III engine whose steam condensers occupied almost the entire leading edge of the top wing; to overcome engine overheating on the ground and at low flying speeds he retained a very small retractable radiator whose drag therefore did not compromise the high-speed performance. The PV.3 broke scarcely any new ground: the flame-damping exhausts had been developed on a Demon; installation of the two-decking guns was identical to that of the standard Fury, while the two guns in the sides of the nose were fitted in exactly the same manner as in the Demon; the wheel spats were similar to those flown on a Company-owned Hart; and even the Goshawk engine had been test flown for three months in an otherwise standard Fury. The PV.3, with its top speed of around 220 mph, could be described as "clawing its way up the speed scale".

Alas for all this enterprise (and that of the Bristol company which financed two contenders for F.7/30—the Goshawk-powered Type 123 biplane and the Type 133 monoplane with Bristol Mercury radial) the writing had been on the wall long before the scheduled date of prototype evaluation of F.7/30 competitors (mid-1934). The Goshawk engine, despite its promise of high power, had not lived up to expectations, while the experiences encountered by the Blackburn F.3 were symptomatic of much worse to come; moreover Camm's resort to a "standby" radiator begged the whole question of evaporative cooling's benefit in any case.

F.7/30's failure to bring forth an in-service interceptor by 1934, and the postponement of the final prototype evaluation until 1935, not only focused attention on the glaring absence of a new RAF interceptor, now regarded as essential for 1936, but also permitted an "outsider" to enter the competition. Although Camm's PV.3 underwent further limited improvement and the Bristol Type 133 promised well until it crashed during its final trials before the 1935 evaluation, it was to be another private

The three extraordinary fighter essays originally conceived under the terms of Specification F.7/30. Top: *The Supermarine Type 224,* K2890 (Photo: *Air Ministry Neg No 3400A).* Centre: *The Westland PV.4,* K2891 (Photo: *Air Ministry, Neg No 8161A).* Bottom: *The Blackburn F.3,* K2892 (Photo: *Real Photographs Ltd)*

venture that was to carry off the laurels.

Gloster, whose chief designer W. G. Carter had been quietly pursuing development of a promising biplane fighter, the SS.18, for some years, had succeeded in producing a realistic interceptor, the SS.19B, in 1933. This, the two-bay biplane Gauntlet prototype with Bristol Mercury radial engine, had been rewarded by a contract for 24 production examples. The following year, when Sir Thomas Sopwith purchased the Gloster company—to create the initial basis of the great Hawker Siddeley Group—it was decided to standardize Hawker structural manufacture in the Gauntlet (as the Mark II), effectively extending the development potential of the Gloster fighter. Thus at a very late stage in the F.7/30 saga Carter was able to produce a single-bay derivative, the Gladiator, to conform to the requirement—*including 250 mph speed and four-gun armament*. That the Gladiator was still a biplane, cast in the age-old mould, mattered in 1935 scarcely a jot. What concerned the Air Ministry was that it met the Service demands and could enter service quickly. Thus, as something of an anti-climax, an aeroplane which superficially, at any rate, approximated to those that had entered service half a decade previously, was selected as the winner of Salmond's far-sighted requirement of 1930. Ostensibly the Gladiator was intended as no more than a stopgap fighter, but events were to dictate otherwise. Even stopgap fighters were likely to be needed in large numbers.

★ ★ ★

Germany's walk-out from the international disarmament conference in 1932 and her subsequent withdrawal of membership from the League of Nations on the pretext of humiliation by her neighbours was intended to mask the maturing of long-laid plans for military resurgence under the totalitarian doctrines imposed by the NSDAP. This effectively ended once and for all any possibility of overt examination and control of Germany's military strength by external agencies in 1933.

Be that as it may there was no concealing the activities of such German aircraft manufacturers as Junkers, Heinkel and Dornier, nor of the re-emergence of companies like the Bayerische Flugzeugwerke (later Messerschmitt AG), Fieseler Flugzeugbau and Bücker Flugzeugbau. What was to remain an enigma for those neighbours for several years was the *scale* on which Germany's aircraft industry was engaged in developing modern military aircraft.

Given the totalitarian nature of the Nazi party's grip on the German economy it appeared safe to assume that almost unlimited labour and finance would be available for military procurement—a wise assumption made by British military Intelligence, whose estimates were available to but largely ignored by leading politicians at Westminster, still much preoccupied with the emergence of the nation from the Depression. Not even the warnings of Stanley Baldwin[4] (in 1933 the Lord Privy Seal and Lord President of the Council) impressed upon Parliament the need to take stock of the German danger. Nor perhaps did the appointment of Sir Edward Ellington as Chief of the Air Staff augur well for Britain's fighter defences, although it was quickly seen that this energetic officer had now grasped the vital urgency for immediate and wide-ranging strengthening of those defences—largely one suspects as a result of counselling by Dowding (still Air Member for Research and Development) and by Air Marshal Sir Edgar Ludlow-Hewitt, the newly appointed Director of Operations and Intelligence at the Air Ministry.

At once the fears formerly expressed by Sir John Salmond—that given unlimited financial support and motivation the advance of military technology might suddenly accelerate—seemed likely to be fulfilled. Dowding it was, as well as others at the DTD, who realized that not only were the aspirations of F.7/30 not pitched sufficiently high but that by the time the prototypes were ready for evaluation they would almost certainly be obsolescent. In August 1933 Major John Buchanan of the DTD[5] visited Camm to discuss these problems and to discover whether Hawker was pursuing any substantial advance beyond the PV.3—the only aircraft considered at that time likely to come close to meeting the magic 250 mph target of F.7/30. The most that Camm could demonstrate was a scheme, then only being superficially examined, for a development of the Fury, whose landing gear was intended to be retractable—though not even the manner of its retraction had been decided nor any estimate of speed advantage calculated. Clearly Buchanan had hoped for a more radical departure than this and pressed Camm to concentrate more on the likely benefits of the monoplane.

Although one can speculate that these discussions left Sydney Camm nonplussed—for Hawker could be forgiven for basking in the conviction of Hart Variant and Fury production stretching far into the future (indeed they did not finally run out until 1938)—the challenge was one that the designer could scarcely resist. Indeed, henceforth Camm became engrossed in the evolution of a new monoplane interceptor from that moment on.

It is probably accurate to conjecture that he never seriously considered producing an all-metal stressed-skin monoplane: for such an aircraft to be placed in large-scale production at Kingston (or with Gloster) would have demanded total re-equipment of the factory shops and widespread retraining of the existing workforce—or the recruiting of a new one. Neither course could be countenanced if the new aircraft were to be ordered into production in the next two years. For one thing orders were flowing in almost monthly in 1933 for the Hart and Fury variants; for another, capital investment in extensive plant was still extremely

Landmarks in the Hawker Fury saga. Top: *Fury I*, K1927. Centre: *High-Speed Fury*, K3586, *with Goshawk engine.* Bottom: *Hawker F.7/30 PV.3 four-gun fighter. (*Photos: *Hawker Aircraft Ltd., Neg Nos 67A, 38F and 69F)*

speculative—and would remain so for the foreseeable future. Nevertheless Sopwith's acquisition of the Gloster company was but the first stage in what can now be seen as a farsighted reinforcement of the manufacturing foundations of a very large part of the British aircraft industry, foundations that would embrace such companies as A. V. Roe & Co., Armstrong Siddeley Motors and Sir W. G. Armstrong Whitworth Aircraft in the next few years, and ultimately de Havilland, Blackburn and Folland.

Instead Camm determined initially to wring the last possible potential out of the Fury. A scheme was prepared in which the fuselage of the Fury biplane was retained and a cantilever wing introduced; the undercarriage remained fixed, although it was intended to exploit the cantilever landing gear of the type being proposed for the Gloster design (later to become the Gladiator).[6] As drawn, this scheme for a Fury Monoplane could do no more than perpetuate the latest Kestrel engine (the 745-hp Kestrel XVI, due to be bench run early in 1934) and, with an enclosed cockpit and deepened rear fuselage frames incorporated, performance calculations suggested a top speed in the region of 270 mph. The drawings and calculations were shown to and discussed with Major Buchanan at great length, and there is no doubt that they evoked much more than academic interest. Similar discussions were also being pursued with Mitchell at Supermarines, an intercourse of ideas that now raised the matter of armament once more, and also the practicality of a retractable undercarriage—Major Buchanan himself pointing to the fact that the Americans were already investigating a manually-retractable landing gear in their naval Curtiss XF11C-3 biplane fighter. What little was known of this undercarriage arrangement (the mainwheels being lifted to lie alongside the front fuselage) did not impress Camm—or apparently Mitchell. In the event Camm opted to employ a rectangular wing centre-section of fairly deep section, to which outer wings of two-spar structure would be bolted; the landing gear retracting pivot would be located at the outer edge of the wing centre-section and retract inwards—the wheels almost meeting on the aircraft's centreline. Propeller diameter (and therefore ground clearance of the propeller during take-off) thus dictated the length of landing gear leg, and therefore the spanwise extent of the wing centre-section. Such an arrangement bestowed a wide wheel track—a feature that was to be present in all Camm's fighters for the next 20 years, and one universally applauded by their pilots. The Hurricane's landing gear design was entirely Hawker's, for the retraction necessitated a draw-jack to pull the leg rearwards slightly so as to clear the main spar as the leg was lifted upwards and inwards. Retraction was effected hydraulically by a hand-pump beside the pilot's seat.

It should be mentioned here that—notwithstanding Hawker's performance calculations using the latest Kestrel—the drawings of the Fury Monoplane shown to the DTD in October 1933 were labelled "Goshawk engine", for it must be remembered that this was still very much the favoured powerplant in the Air Ministry. This minor deception was of little consequence because in January 1934 bench figures for a new engine became available from Rolls-Royce—an engine that had been evolved at private expense from the Kestrel and was still known only as the P.V.12. Even before arrangements were made to adapt two Hawker Horsleys, the "High Speed Fury" and a Hart to test fly the new engine, Camm was aware that Rolls-Royce was looking for an installed power output of more than 900 hp for take-off with only relatively small geometric and weight penalties. The P.V.12 was therefore "designed into" the Hawker scheme, now generally referred to as the Interceptor Monoplane.

The much increased structure weight of the cantilever wing, especially in the thick centre-section, as well as the greater weight of engine, combined to limit the performance benefits of retractable undercarriage and increased power. Now the matter of gun armament was raised once more; all the arguments in favour of four guns over two, voiced in 1930, were to be repeated in 1934. In other words, were four guns (so strongly demanded for the F.7/30 prototypes, yet even to be evaluated) still adequate for a fighter expected to possess a top speed well in excess of 275 mph? And if not, where could additional guns be located? If they could not be placed within physical reach of the pilot, was the Vickers gun adequately reliable?

Fortunately the Gunnery Section at the A&AEE had been applying itself to a study of the gun stoppage problem of the Vickers—something that was now realized as being exacerbated by the continued use of wide-tolerance Great War ammunition stocks. In other words, the newly manufactured Vickers Mark III gun demanded better ammunition than was generally available—and so long as stocks of old ammunition remained, funding for new production would not be available. An interesting piece of fortuitous intelligence had, however, reached the Air Ministry from Japan—where until fairly recently retired British naval officers had been seconded in an advisory capacity with the Imperial Navy; a comparative evaluation had been carried out of half a dozen machine guns from various countries in which the Vickers had not only been adjudged the worst of all, but worst by a very long way . . . indeed it was known that the Japanese were trying to negotiate licence agreements to manufacture foreign guns, and, failing that, to place flagrant replicas of them in production.

What was now regarded as something of a crisis in the matter of British aircraft gun armament prompted the creation of an Armament Research Division in the Air Ministry, one of its first tasks being to sponsor a competitive evaluation at the end

The original Hawker Hart test bed for the Rolls-Royce PV.12 engine, K3036. Above: *With midships-mounted radiator and separate oil cooler between the undercarriage legs, and four-blade wooden propeller.* Below: *Later configuration with forward radiator fairing incorporating the oil cooler, and three-blade metal propeller. (*Photos: *Sydney Camm Collection)*

of 1933, in which Colt, Darne, Hispano, Kiraleji, Lewis, Madsen, Spandau and Vickers machine guns were all exhaustively tested in respect of rate of fire, penetration/range and reliability. In every respect one gun surpassed the others, the American Colt, produced by the Colt Automatic Weapon Corporation of Hartford, Connecticut. This gun, however, was designed to fire 0.30-in. rimless ammunition, and was therefore unable to use British ammunition, such as it was. Enquiries were thus made to discover whether the gun could be adapted to cater for wide-tolerance 0.303-in. calibre rounds without compromising the gun's high rate of fire of 1,200 rounds per minute. In January 1934 confirmation that this could be achieved was received from America, and initial negotiations were started to investigate terms available for licence production of the gun in Britain.

Based on the assumption that the Colt gun would be available, the Air Ministry produced a draft Specification written very loosely around the state of design proposals thus far discussed between the DTD and the two aircraft designers, Mitchell and Camm. (Not surprisingly, so great were the commercial stakes, that not even the broad nature of Mitchell's design was divulged to Camm, nor vice versa—although Camm was obviously aware that Mitchell would pursue stressed skin construction throughout his fighter, as he had done in his abortive Type 224.)

This draft Specification, F.5/34, touched only superficially upon the maximum speed of "around 300 mph", but made it clear that the aircraft should be capable of mounting a battery of at least six guns. Architect of this requirement was undoubtedly Sqn Ldr R. S. Sorley (later Air Marshal Sir Ralph Sorley, KCB, OBE, DSC, DFC), then at the Directorate of Operational Requirements, who had followed closely the results in favour of greatly enhanced gun armament; indeed it appears that he it was who first suggested that both Hawker and Supermarine designs be capable of an eight-gun battery.

By March 1934 detail design of a prototype

The Hawker Hind light bomber whose production at Brooklands overlapped that of the Hurricane and represented one of the key stopgap aircraft of the RAF's Expansion period before the War. (Photo: *Hawker Aircraft Ltd.)*

"Interceptor Monoplane to F.5/34" was in the hands of the small experimental design office at Canbury Park Road, although, as no detailed information on the Colt was yet available, it was still only making provision for four fuselage-mounted Vickers guns. The Project Team was, however, investigating how best to accommodate eight guns (using Vickers gun dimensions) in the outer wings, bearing in mind that the primary wing structure was expected to employ a Warren truss between the two wing spars. In June a one-tenth scale model started tests in the compressed-air tunnel at the National Physics Laboratory at nearby Teddington, and two months later these confirmed satisfactory aerodynamic qualities of a full-size aircraft up to a speed of 350 mph. These figures underwent extrapolation assuming a maximum engine power output of 1,000 hp (the latest forecast by Rolls-Royce) and an all-up weight of 4,600 lb, and were submitted to the Air Ministry in August.

Events now moved with considerable urgency, motivated at Hawker—if nowhere else—with the sense that the Company was taking an important step forward into the future; this momentum came to be sustained as realization dawned that Europe could well be plunged into war once more, and in the foreseeable future. A detailed Specification, F.36/34, was prepared and sent to Hawker during the last week in August, virtually written around Camm's submission, and on 4 September the Hawker design was formally tendered to the Air Ministry under the title "*F.36/34 Single-Seat Fighter—High Speed Monoplane*". On 17 November the first manufacturing drawings of the fuselage were issued to the Experimental shops for the purpose of preparing jigs. (Meanwhile similar progress was being made with the Supermarine fighter design, Specification F.37/34 being issued with the requirements of Mitchell's aircraft. Whereas this aeroplane was required to attain a level speed of 330 mph at 15,000 ft—the rated altitude of the P.V.12 engine—Camm's fighter was to be capable of 320 mph at the same height; the difference was based on better drag figures from the Supermarine design. Both aircraft exceeded these speed requirements by four to five per cent when they first entered service).

Two pictures that illustrate the continuity of Hawker structural design. Above: *The primary fuselage structure of a Hart Variant.* Below: *The corresponding structure of a production Hurricane.* (Photos: *Hawker Aircraft Ltd.)*

At the end of November Rolls-Royce notified

Complete rear fuselage structure of the Hurricane prototype, K5083. (Photo: *Hawker Aircraft Ltd., Neg No 30L, dated March 1935)*

Hawker that the engine weight had increased by 80 lb and it was decided, rather than to reposition the powerplant to adjust the aircraft's cg position, to increase the ammunition capacity by 400 rounds (for the four-gun armament, still being considered). Thus the all-up weight increased to 4,800 lb. A wooden mock-up was constructed at Canbury Park Road on which to study such aspects as cockpit layout, pilot's field of view, undercarriage retraction, coolant ducting, radiator location and gun mountings. Further engine details were passed by Rolls-Royce on 18 December which now promised a take-off power rating at 1,025 hp at 2,900 rpm. The "engineers" also undertook not to allow the installed engine weight to exceed 1,200 lb, so that the power/weight ratio at take-off would be 0.85. During the following week a discarded P.V.12 engine (No. 3) was delivered to Kingston for mock-up purposes.

On 10 January 1935, was held the final conference at Canbury Park Road to discuss the results of studies made with the aid of the mock-up. Representing the Royal Air Force were Air Cdre L. A. Pattinson (later Air Marshal Sir Lawrence Pattinson, KBE, CB, DSO, MC, DFC), then Air Officer Commanding Armament Group, Eastchurch, and Wg Cdr Cyril Lowe of HQ, ADGB. Camm explained that he was anxious to go ahead with the wing-gun battery as soon as possible before manufacture of the prototype's wings were too far advanced, explaining that his project designers had already prepared a design to accommodate an eight-gun battery in the outer wings, and that deletion of the four Vickers guns after finalization of the fuselage could well compromise its design by subsequent relocation of equipment and movement of cg. Pattinson, presumably quoting from disappointing results of recent tests with Vickers guns arranged as a wing battery, stated, however, that the eight-gun battery would only be demanded provided that negotiation of a satisfactory licence agreement with Colt could be completed. He also remarked that Wg Cdr Claude Keith of the Air Ministry Ordnance Board and Major H. S. V. Thompson, a Principal Technical Officer of the Directorate-General of Research and Development, had recently returned from America with terms for such a licence to manufacture the Colt and that these terms were then being studied by the Birmingham Small Arms Company.

Contract cover for a prototype of the Hawker fighter (Contract No. 357483/34) was received on 18 February, the aircraft to be given the serial number *K5083*. In the Appendix covering the Standard of Preparation it was stated that no decision had yet been reached regarding the provision of armament, and it was agreed *six weeks later* not to include any armament in the prototype but to ballast it for two fuselage Vickers guns and a Colt in each wing. This prompts the obvious questions: if Colt guns were to be catered for at all, why not the full eight-gun battery? And why the retention of any Vickers guns? This extraordinary lapse of straightforward administrative logic has never been satisfactorily untangled or explained, and was uncharacteristic of the otherwise smooth course of close Ministry–Manufacturer relations that existed in the mid-1930s.[7]

Main landing gear retraction linkage of the Hurricane prototype. (Photo: *Hawker Aircraft Ltd., Neg No 47K)*

The first set of detailed performance estimates was forwarded to the Air Ministry's DTD on 21 February. These now indicated a normal take-off weight of 4,900 lb, and at this figure a wing loading of 19 lb/sq ft (compared incidentally with 14 lb/sq ft of the Fury I biplane). At a flying weight of 4,480 lb the maximum speed was expected to be 330 mph at

15,000 feet, service ceiling 32,500 feet and absolute ceiling 34,800 ft. Landing speed at a weight of 4,200 lb and using full flap was calculated to be about 73 mph TAS. Time to height was expected to be around 12 minutes to 20,000 ft, but no range and endurance figures were yet possible as specific fuel consumption details had not been finalized by Rolls-Royce. All performance figures and weights, however, assumed the inclusion of only four guns. . . .

Final ratification of the gun licence by Colt and BSA was reached in July, and the decision to ballast the prototype for the eight-gun wing communicated to Camm by the Air Ministry on 1 August. Although there was no question in the minds of his design staff that the fabric-covered wings of the new aeroplane—employing an ingenious method of attaching the fabric to the metal structure, developed by Hawker—would not be perfectly capable of withstanding any airspeed likely to be attained by the aircraft, even in a sustained dive, there remained the possibility that, following battle damage, the fabric might balloon and start to disintegrate. By now of course the RAF's great expansion programme was under way, and the Hawker Board saw every reason to plan for improved shop facilities to undertake limited metal stressed-skin production, particularly as the manufacture of metal covered wings—if eventually demanded—required relatively inexpensive plant. Although Camm's staff now embarked on the design of such wings, the first set was not completed until 1938, by which time Hawker was already looking forward two years, when the Company expected to be producing all-over stressed-skin Typhoons and Tornados. (In the event only a small number of Typhoons and a few Tornado prototypes were ever built by Hawker, and production of the Hurricane was concentrated at Kingston, Langley and Brooklands for more than six years—almost the entire wartime production aircraft having "metal wings".)

As construction of the prototype continued apace in the Canbury Park Road Experimental shop (with the design staff able to visit it "from upstairs") a number of relatively minor design matters remained to be settled. Flight tests of the P.V.12 (now named the Merlin, the "C" version being scheduled for installation and flight in Camm's prototype) had disclosed the need for a fairly large radiator, but Hawker was proposing to offset the need for such a high-drag appendage by placing it in a fairing employing a "convergent-divergent" duct to speed up the airflow through the radiator matrix. So as to achieve efficient airflow entry into the duct it was thought necessary to retain an unbroken fuselage undersurface forward of the radiator's face. As the landing gear's mainwheels retracted into cells immediately forward of the radiator fairing it was decided to incorporate D-doors hinged to the leg covers which would fold flush over the wheels when retracted.

Very early photograph of the prototype F.36/34, K5083, *during manufacture, taken at the time when it still featured the Vickers guns on the sides of the fuselage.* (Photo: *Hawker Aircraft Ltd.*, via *Sqn Ldr R. C. B. Ashworth*)

Prototype wing installation of the first eight-gun battery in the Hurricane. Above: *Upper view and* (Below), *viewed from underneath. Staggering the guns alternately allowed the magazines to be mounted in pairs and in tandem. The inscription on the gun bodies reads 'Colt Aircraft Machine Gun, Browning Patent, Cal .303 MG 40. Manufactured by Colt's Patent Fire Arm MFG Co., Hartford, Conn, USA'.* (Photos: *Author's Collection*)

*The Hawker Fury Is of No 43 Squadron ('The Fighting Cocks') at the time of the Munich Crisis in September 1939; the aircraft have been camouflaged and feature the black and white undersurfaces in vogue at the time. (*Photo: Flight, *Neg No 16471S)*

Ballasting for eight guns and deletion of the fuselage Vickers with their mounting structure only shifted the aircraft's cg forward by about half an inch, although the all-up weight now rose to around 5,400 lb.

Work on *K5083* was, as one old Hawker employee recalls, carried out in increasingly cramped conditions as the prototype grew towards completion, for there were after all—apart from the monoplane fighter itself—two wooden mock-ups and three other prototypes under construction (the Hector, the Fury Mark II and the Henley—about which more later), all in a space measuring about 60 by 90 ft. Indeed, considering that production of the Hart Variants was in full swing, all shop space was at a premium at the Hawker factory. Each aircraft was completed in Canbury Park Road—about nine per week in August 1935—before the wings were removed and the whole aeroplane loaded on to a lorry for the journey by road to the final assembly sheds at Brooklands, about eight miles distant, for finishing and preparation for flight.

It is true that the Company owned extensive plant space a mile up the Richmond Road in Kingston, title to it having passed to the H. G. Hawker Engineering Company and thence to Hawker Aircraft Limited when it became a public company in 1933. However, when assembling finance to underwrite work on the Hart and Fury prototypes in 1928, Sopwith had agreed a non-reversionary lease with the Leyland lorry company, and the lease was not due to expire for a further dozen years. There was incidentally a popular belief that no Hawker aeroplane could be put into production with a wing span of more than 40 ft, simply because there was nowhere it could be assembled in the Canbury Park Road shops.[8]

Before returning to the progress of *K5083* towards its first flight it is worth glancing briefly at the men at Hawker who would play key parts in its fortunes during the coming years. On its formation in 1933 Hawker Aircraft Ltd possessed no more than a three-man Board of Directors, T. O. M. Sopwith (Chairman), Frank Spriggs and Fred

*Last of the RAF's biplane fighters: Gloster Gladiators awaiting their turn to practice their flying routine at the 1937 Hendon Air Pageant. (*Photo: Flight, *Neg No T2999)*

Gloster Gauntlet biplane fighters of No 111 Squadron, the famous unit that was to become the first to receive Hurricanes at the end of 1937. (Photo: The Aeroplane)

Sigrist. Spriggs, like Sigrist, had "been with" Sopwith since before the Kaiser's War, but with the outright purchase of Gloster in February 1934 and the formation of Hawker Siddeley in July 1935 he became Gloster's Chairman. As Camm's designs were now to be widely built under licence by many other companies in the industry (at one point 70 per cent of the industry's labour force was engaged in producing Hawker aeroplanes), it was decided that the time had come to substantially strengthen the Board of Hawker at Kingston, and in mid-1935 Sydney Camm (Chief Designer), "George" Bulman (Chief Test Pilot), H. Chandler (Secretary), H. K. Jones and R. W. Sutton were appointed as Directors.

At Brooklands, where all flight testing of Hawker aeroplanes was still carried out (alongside those of Vickers, in the centre of the famous motor racing circuit), George Bulman had long since assumed the formal position of Chief Test Pilot. He had been joined by two other famous test pilots, P. E. G. ("Gerry") Sayer in 1930, and P. G. Lucas in 1931. These three had undertaken the enormous flying programme until John Hindmarsh and Maurice Summers came to Hawker in 1935; Hindmarsh was also well known as a racing driver (winning the Le Mans 24-hour race in a Lagonda), while Summers, younger brother of "Mutt" Summers—who was to take the Spitfire aloft on its maiden flight—stayed only a short time before moving to Vickers, where much of his time was spent production test flying Hawker Harts produced under licence from Hawker. Gerry Sayer also moved to Gloster in 1935, so that by the time Camm's new monoplane was approaching its first flight the Brooklands team still numbered only three pilots, Bulman, Lucas and Hindmarsh.

As tensions increased in Europe the urgency for rearmament by Britain was, by the autumn of 1935, now becoming recognized by all but the dyed-in-the-wool pacifists in the Labour and Liberal parties. Hitler had finally repudiated the military clauses of the Versailles Peace Treaty on 21 May and was demanding massive rearmament by Germany. Ramsay MacDonald resigned as prime minister and was followed by Stanley Baldwin (Conservative), who called a snap election on 14 November; a National Government was returned with a huge majority—the greater number of seats being occupied by Conservatives. On 3 October Italy declared war in Abyssinia. . . .

Seven weeks before Hitler's denunciation of the Peace Treaty his henchman, Hermann Göring, had unveiled the new German air force, which, under General Walther Wever at the *Reichsluftfahrtministerium* (RLM, or air ministry), already possessed more than 20,000 men in uniform; of these, about 3,000 had received some flying training either secretly in the Soviet Union, with the *Lufthansa* airline or with one of the many Government-sponsored civilian flying clubs in Germany. The first military squadrons were flying fighters such as the Heinkel He 51—an aircraft at least capable of matching the RAF's Hawker Fury. Specifications had already been issued to the resurgent aircraft industry for modern aircraft that would emerge as the Messerschmitt Bf 109, Dornier Do 17 and Heinkel He 111. Indeed the prototype Bf 109a made its first flight at Augsburg in September 1935, flown by "Bubi" Knötsch and powered by an imported Rolls-Royce Kentrel V! Moreover this superb fighter was to fire its guns in anger over Spain long before the first Hurricanes and Spitfires even reached the first squadrons of the RAF.

Winston Churchill's warnings in Parliament, so stridently dismissed by the pacifists as so much scaremongering, were if anything understatements of the reality.

3

THUNDER OF THE MERLIN

As the Hawker prototype reached structural completion in August 1935, Rolls-Royce was engaged in certification trials with a Merlin C in a Horsley aircraft so as to be able to obtain a provisional civil 50-hour Certificate of Airworthiness prior to the first flight by *K5083*.

Skinning of the airframe occupied about six weeks and the first flight engine, Merlin C No. 11, was delivered to Canbury Park Road for installation and preliminary systems checks. On 23 October *K5083* was loaded on to the customary lorry and taken—under wraps—to the assembly shed at Brooklands. The fabric-covered wings (complete with gun ballast) were reassembled on to the centre-section and the controls reconnected. Undercarriage (including tailwheel) retraction checks were performed and preliminary engine running started. After weighing the prototype in take-off configuration with full fuel, oil, ballast and pilot, the weight was recorded as 5,416 lb and the cg calculated as being within 0.5 in. of the design location. On 3 November Bulman took the aeroplane out on to the Brooklands grass to start taxying runs to acclimatize himself with the enclosed cockpit and bulky nose—afterwards remarking that without the top wing "there was more daylight in the cockpit" and that the view was "marvellous". Camm also recalled Bulman's wry humour when he reflected on the ease with which one could now vacate the cockpit in a hurry without fear of cracking one's head on the wing! Although the nose contours were slightly wider than those of the Hart and Fury—demanding rather more weaving while taxying so as to see ahead—Bulman foresaw no difficulty when it came to landing.

What seemed at the time to be a major setback occurred on 4 November when Rolls-Royce notified the Hawker Board that the Merlin had failed to pass its 50-hour certification test, although a preliminary inspection had so far failed to disclose the reason for a marked loss of power after completion of more than 40 flying hours. Bulman was consulted and he immediately suggested that the first flight should go ahead without engine certification but that thereafter flights should continue provided only that there was no suggestion of a "mag-drop" and that the engine oil filter should be examined after each flight to ensure freedom from metal particles. Fred Sigrist and the Rolls-Royce engineers agreed and, on 6 November, with about 80 onlookers from the shops, George Bulman taxied out at Brooklands for the first flight.

One of those eyewitnesses of the first flight, Bob Shaw (an old Sopwith "boy"), recalled the sight of the "little silver monoplane with its highly polished cowling panels and huge Watts wooden propeller, seemingly turning very slowly . . ." as it swung into wind prior to take-off. Shaw remembered the "tremendous roar from the Merlin as Bulman thundered across the aerodrome, tail lifting, and off and away, low over the banking of the motor track in no time at all. For more than half an hour we awaited George's return and then, there he was, turning in, sideslipping crabwise over the road, once more that

What would today be termed 'roll-out' pictures, these photographs of K5083 *were taken before Bulman started taxying trials. Note the lower hinged wheel doors, absence of armament and gunsight, short convergent-divergent radiator fairing, absence of radio mast, strut-braced tailplane and very light cockpit canopy structure.* (Photo: *Hawker Aircraft Ltd., Neg Nos 50K, 51K and 52K)*

big propeller turning ever so slowly—as if the engine was no more than ticking over; a burst of throttle as he kicked the aircraft straight, a moment of almost silence as the plane seemed to lose speed quickly, and then the tail dropped to a gentle three-pointer. The men all around started cheering and waving as Tommy and the Old Man (Camm) climbed into the Rolls and set off to welcome George back."

The flight had been kept secret from the daily press and, as far as can be discovered, no photographs were permitted—even by the Company's own photographer—although Cyril Peckham, who was frequently asked to take pictures of the company's new aircraft, was almost certainly present, living as he did not a mile away. The weekly journals *Flight* and *The Aeroplane* had been invited and, though neither was due to visit Brooklands until the middle of the month, must have been aware that the first flight was imminent.

Strange though it may seem, Bulman prepared no formal written Flight Test Report on that momentous first flight (as shown in the extract from the Hawker Register of Test Reports, Appendix I), his impressions being jotted down on "a secretary's threepenny note pad" and passed to Sopwith, Sigrist and Camm orally in the watch office at Brooklands. From Camm's recollections Bulman's report was given quietly and objectively, mentioning that engine temperatures built up very quickly while taxying, but that directional control during take-off was crisp and positive. He also remarked that he didn't like the cockpit canopy and said that it had creaked and flexed continually during the flight; Bulman also stated that the engine temperatures again started to increase quickly after lowering the landing flaps, presumably because they tended to retard the radiator airflow from the rear. It has been said that only after he had given these impressions did Bulman's face break into a broad grin as he playfully punched Camm on the shoulder and exclaimed "Sid, you've most certainly got a winner here!" Such was not Camm's own recollection . . . .

Flight Lieutenant P. W. S. ("George") Bulman, C.B.E., M.C., A.F.C.

Rear view of K5083 *prior to its first flight. Note the massive blade chord of the Watts propeller, the absence of a walk-way on the starboard wing root and the converging canopy rails.* (Photo: *Sydney Camm Collection)*

No attempt had been made to measure performance, Bulman contenting himself with general handling impressions, although he admitted having performed a slow roll and a gentle dive to about 300 mph IAS; he was enthusiastic about the stalling characteristics, stating that with undercarriage down and with little over half the fuel used and flaps up the aeroplane stalled at about 80 mph, and that the stall recovery was immediate and straightforward with only a slight forward pressure required on the stick. But George certainly hated that canopy.

As originally flown, *K5083* displayed a number of features that were progressively altered or removed altogether. For instance, that sliding canopy was a relatively lightweight structure with a single vertical stiffener between front and rear frame. Bulman, who of course fully accepted that enclosed cockpits had come to stay, continued his good-natured grumbling until Camm agreed to sanction the inclusion of two such stiffeners and eventually to a complete redesign of the canopy

Very early flight by Bulman in K5083*; note the retracted tailwheel.* (Photo: *Sydney Camm Collection)*

with heavier framing throughout.

Anticipating the possibility of tail flutter in dives the aircraft retained a single tailplane strut for about six months, but after no such phenomenon had occurred it was removed altogether. And the radiator design, for all its ingenuity, continued to worry the Rolls-Royce engineers on account of engine overheating. As an initial step the central section of the landing flaps was removed, but this gave only a slight improvement, and it was pointed out that during a landing overshoot, when the flaps might remain down for a relatively long time, the engine would almost certainly overheat seriously, and might even fail at full throttle. The entire radiator fairing had therefore to be completely redesigned.

On the other hand the mainwheel D-doors were found to be more trouble than they were worth, stones being thrown up by the wheels during take-off and landing and causing the doors to distort; such damage cancelled any benefit the doors may have had in maintaining a smooth flow to the radiator; these were therefore removed and the "notch" in the leading edge of the undercarriage leg covers filled in to give a smooth line. None of these changes, however, was regarded as vital and, in order to press ahead with the flight test programme, they were incorporated only when the aircraft was already on the ground for a period of scheduled instrumentation or an engine change in the early months of 1936.

Five flights by *K5083* were made during November (all by Bulman) and on 6 December a provisional airworthiness certificate was finally received for the Merlin C. Nevertheless only three further flights were made using engine No. 11, all of them being accompanied by a spate of troubles, including failure of supercharger bearings, collapse of automatic boost control capsules and broken valve springs. When a valve dropped into a cylinder—fortunately while the aircraft was still on the ground—it was decided to change to another engine, Merlin C No. 15.

However, although at least two other Merlin Cs were fitted in *K5083* it had already been decided to continue with this version only for test purposes and to concentrate upon the F version,[9] later to become the Merlin I. Meanwhile the Air Ministry was pressing for *K5083* to make its scheduled visit to Martlesham Heath so that the Service could form its initial impressions of the new fighter and compile a production Specification and, presumably, raise a contract for quantity production. Only two further flights by Bulman sufficed to satisfy him that *K5083* was indeed ready for Martlesham and on 5 March 1936[10]—the same day on which the Spitfire first flew—Bulman delivered the prototype to

First modifications to K5083*, seen here at Brooklands, comprised the revision of the cockpit canopy to include an additional upright stiffening frame and a small fixed rudder tab.* (Photo: *Hawker Aircraft Ltd., Neg No 87K)*

Slight landing gear problems on K5083*: left leg partly retracted with D-door closed.* (Photo: *Sydney Camm Collection)*

the A&AEE. A thorough examination of the aeroplane was made by Service technical officers, whose responsibility it was to prepare reports passing judgement on the ease of servicing, ground handling, equipment and cockpit layout; in this respect one imagines those officers were overawed by the extraordinarily neat and compact layout of Camm's fighter, for their report commended it in glowing terms on its undercarriage configuration, accessibility of refuelling points, gun bays (still only containing ballast) and radio compartment. It was next the turn of the pilots—or rather pilot, for in those days it was customary to detail a single pilot to fly and evaluate new aircraft exclusively, to report his impressions and submit his performance measurements to his commanding officer for consolidation of all the findings of the A&AEE into a single report. The first RAF pilot on whom such responsibility rested was Sgt Samuel Wroath, universally known in the RAF as Sammy.[11]

Reference to Appendix II indicates the nature of flying undertaken by Wroath at Martlesham Heath on *K5083* before its return to Brooklands in mid-April. Problems with the engine continued to dog the aircraft (although engine No. 19 had been fitted in place of Nos. 15 and 17, both of which had failed at Martlesham). The prototype therefore paid a short visit to Rolls-Royce at Hucknall, where it seems that most of the snags were rectified.

Meanwhile the Flight Section at the A&AEE, commanded by Sqn Ldr David Forgham Anderson, DFC, AFC,[12] completed its assessment of *K5083* and submitted its findings to the Air Ministry, including the following details: Maximum speed 315 mph at 16,200 ft and 2,960 rpm at 6 lb boost; climb to 15,000 ft from unstick was achieved in 5.7 minutes, and to 20,000 ft in 8.4 minutes. Extrapolation of heights achieved indicated a service ceiling of 34,500 ft and an absolute ceiling of 35,400 ft (these estimates proved slightly optimistic using the Merlin C). Taking off against a 5 mph headwind at an all-up weight of 5,672 lb, unstick occurred after a ground run of 265 yards and at 81 mph. In a flapless landing the stall occurred at 77 mph, but using the flaps (with their centre section still fitted) reduced this to only 57 mph. The landing ground run without brakes was 525 yards, but use of the brakes produced a run of no more than 205 yards. Apart from an observation that aileron and rudder controls became rather heavy at high speeds (the rudder of *K5083* being mass balanced), consensus was that all departments were well pleased with the aeroplane; not even the cockpit canopy—still without the additional stiffener—was faulted.

It is worth digressing momentarily to mention another, somewhat speculative Air Ministry Specification, F.37/35, which had been issued towards the end of 1935, calling for a fighter with an armament of four 20 mm Oerlikon cannon. Such an armament, envisaged by Ralph Sorley, might be practical in an aircraft of the Bristol Blenheim's size and configuration—proposals for this, the Bristol Type 142M twin-engine light bomber, having been in the Air Ministry's hands since July that year. Camm felt that now that *K5083* had demonstrated its ability to accommodate eight machine guns (as yet

Excellent landing view of K5083 *showing the continuous span-wise landing flaps before removal of the centre section; note that* a third *upright frame has been added to the cockpit canopy, evidence of George Bulman's continuing complaints about the flexing of the canopy panels.* (Photo: *Sydney Camm Collection)*

only on paper), there seemed a realistic chance of interesting the Air Ministry in a four-cannon version of his single-engine fighter. Such a design was submitted on 23 April, 1936, but it failed to impress. It is likely that its current fabric-covered wing was sufficient to discourage support for the idea, and it eventually transpired that the twin-engine Westland Whirlwind succeeded in meeting the requirement. Of course it might be argued that Camm had the last word when in 1941 the first four-cannon Hurricane IICs entered squadron service—roughly 20 times more such aircraft being produced than the Whirlwind. In retrospect, however, it was a blessing that the four-cannon Hurricane idea fell on deaf ears in 1936, for such a distraction would have delayed production of the aircraft so drastically that in all likelihood no Hurricanes at all would have reached the RAF by the outbreak of war.

As various Air Ministry officers visited Canbury Park Road to discuss a likely timetable for the new fighter to achieve production status, rumours abounded that a contract was about to be raised in the near future. It was fairly common knowledge that the Expansion Scheme E, which had called for 800 aircraft (500 fighters and 300 bombers) to be completed by 1937, had been set aside as based on outdated aircraft cost estimates. Already the Hawker Board knew that Ralph Sorley had been pressing since the end of 1935 for a draft production specification for the new Hawker fighter. Thus encouraged, Camm had decided in March to instruct the Production Drawing Office to commence preparing full-series manufacturing drawings, and at the same time the Works planning section applied itself to the matter of exactly how and where a new production line could be accommodated. To begin with negotiations were completed with Westland Aircraft Ltd to take over the entire production of the Hawker Hector army co-operation aircraft, for which a draft contract had just been received by Hawker for 78 aeroplanes, these aircraft following on behind the Hawker Audax at Yeovil. The bulk of the Hawker Fury II production had also reluctantly to be subcontracted to General Aircraft Ltd at Hanworth, that company also undertaking conversion of Harts and Hinds to the training rôle, although the original production of all Hinds (contracts totalling no fewer than 527 aircraft) remained at Kingston and Brooklands. These arrangements were adequate to free a total of 24,000 sq ft of floor space in the Canbury Park Road shops for the new fighter, although much of this would not become available until 1937; a further 14,000 sq ft of space was cleared at Brooklands during that year for final assembly and finishing.

One senses from the tone of surviving internal notes that passed between Camm and other Hawker departments during May 1936 a growing frustration at what seemed to be procrastination at the Air Ministry in raising a production contract, and it was decided therefore to put in hand production arrangements forthwith (recruitment of 280 extra skilled machine operators and fitters, forward purchase of aluminium sheet and steel tubing, and shop clearance) for the production of 1,000 aircraft, without waiting for contract cover. Whether or not a letter from the Hawker Board, notifying the Department for Development and Production of these steps, was instrumental in speeding the contract process will probably never be known. What is now clear is that the administrative process at the Air Ministry *was* moving with unheard-of speed.

Air-to-air study of K5083 *being flown by Bulman early in 1936; the pilot's break-out panel on the starboard side of the cockpit was not fitted until after the prototype had paid its first visit to Martlesham Heath. (*Photo: Flight, *Neg No 12118S)*

Production Scheme E could not be cancelled out of hand by the Air Council as, by implication, it included fairly large numbers of Gladiator fighters, as well as Hind, Wellesley and Whitley bombers, all of which were required by the RAF during 1937, their purchase being allocated in the Air Estimates for 1936–37 and 1937–38. In deciding the composition of a new production scheme, it had to be discovered whether indeed the new Supermarine fighter met the RAF's requirements as well as agreeing the cost of that aircraft in production.

A draft of the new Production Scheme F was

agreed on 1 June, calling for 1,000 fighters—of which all but 100 Hawker fighters were required to be in service by 1 January, 1939. On 3 June a formal contract, No. 527112/36, was received by the Hawker Board for the purchase of 600 "monoplane fighters"; five days later all fuselage manufacturing drawings were issued to the production shops in Canbury Park Road. On 27 June the name Hurricane was formally approved by the Air Ministry. This was a break with tradition which for some years had followed a policy of giving names to fighters implying "aggressiveness", hence names like Gamecock, Bulldog, Fury, Gauntlet, Gladiator and—soon afterwards—Spitfire, a name incidentally of which Reginald Mitchell expressed some dislike. Camm and Sopwith had suggested that the names of violent storms might be no less appropriate for fighters, and subsequent Hawker fighters were to be named Tornado, Typhoon and Tempest, while Westland produced the Whirlwind. Bombers continued, perhaps rather unimaginatively, to be named after towns and cities. On 20 July Hawker received the long-awaited Air Ministry Specification 15/36 setting out the full production standard of the Hurricane.

★ ★ ★

Perhaps surprisingly, there now followed a period of what must have seemed relative inactivity on the Hurricane prototype. However, this was illusory for, while the Martlesham programme had disclosed no significant shortcoming in the airframe (other than the D-doors on the undercarriage), the problems with the Merlin rested entirely with Rolls-Royce for solution before any design alterations to the engine installation could be undertaken by Hawker. Indeed the Merlin certification flight at Hucknall was hard at work carrying out development of the first production engine, the Merlin F, which suggested improved reliability by reducing the rated altitude and shortening the time restriction at full power. This restriction now gave rise to some anxiety owing to the obvious effects on take-off, climb and combat performance of both Hurricane and Spitfire.

Meanwhile, as already mentioned, the centre landing flap section of *K5083* was removed in an effort to alleviate engine overheating by improving the airflow through the radiator, and the aircraft was flown in this configuration on 16 July. (The British public had been given its first glimpse of the Hurricane on 27 June—the day of its official naming—when it was flown before the crowds at the RAF Pageant at Hendon.)

K5083 was now dismantled and returned to Kingston for installation of the fabric-covered eight-gun wings and ring-and-bead gunsight. At the same time the tailplane strut was also removed and a ground-adjustable rudder trim tab fitted. On 17 August the prototype was back at Brooklands to start a further series of flight tests (now fitted with Merlin C No. 17) which lasted for the remainder of the month and included flying without the airscrew nosecone.

It had been intended to deliver *K5083* to Martlesham Heath for its final Service acceptance trials in September 1936 in readiness for entry into RAF service the following spring, but now another setback occurred, resulting from the Air Ministry's refusal to compromise the performance of the Hurricane and Spitfire by adopting the Merlin I. It was becoming clear that the Merlin F was not reaching the required reliability standard demanded by the RAF and it was decided to send *K5083* up to Hucknall for a trial installation of this engine, and for much of September and October the aeroplane flew with this engine in attempts to discover exactly why it was not reaching the necessary standards. These trials, while indicating some shortcomings in the valve and rocker design of the engine itself, showed that much improved cooling was necessary (also clearly confirmed by flight trials on the Spitfire).

Already, however, a new version of the engine, the Merlin G, was being bench run in which the entire camshaft mounting, rocker and valve gear had been redesigned, and improved supercharger bearings, altered airscrew reduction gear ratio and increased carburettor throat area incorporated. These fairly substantial changes gave promise of rather smoother running at full-power settings as well as less critical temperature limitations—although Rolls-Royce engineers continued to press for an improved radiator design. The decision had therefore to be taken to abandon the Merlin F (Merlin I) for the two fighters, the majority of the 180 production examples being set aside for the Fairey Battle light bomber—in which the full-throttle restriction was less critical—and to adopt the G version as the Merlin II in the Hurricane and Spitfire. This change, however, caused all work on Hurricane production at Kingston to be halted in November while preliminary schemes were prepared for new nose contours to be lofted to cater for the engine's new inclined rocker gear covers and a wholly new radiator fairing. It also soon became necessary, owing to the change of nose shape, to relocate the glycol coolant header tank.

Hawker agreed with the Air Ministry that little could be done to improve *K5083* without further delaying the final Service trials, other than to introduce a new radiator fairing. In the meantime a new rudder was introduced incorporating an in-flight adjustable trim tab and limited spinning trials carried out by both Bulman and Lucas during the first week in November. These showed that recovery from spins to the left was less positive than those to the right—though neither was regarded as being below the standard deemed to be the minimum required by the Service. It was moreover, perhaps surprisingly, discovered that recovery was marginally improved in both directions if the tailwheel was fixed in the "down" position, suggesting some ben-

Final standard of preparation reached by K5083 *at the time it took part in the making of the film* Shadow of the Wing *in September 1937; seen here being flown by Philip Lucas the aircraft is fitted with full armament, ring and bead gunsight, radio and aerial mast, landing and navigation lights and production-style radiator; the cockpit canopy has two upright stiffeners and the tailplane strut has been removed.* (Photos: *Sydney Camm Collection*)

eficial airflow instability at the base of the rudder during spin recovery.

At the end of March 1937 Bulman delivered *K5083* to Martlesham Heath once more, the aircraft now fully equipped with guns, ammunition feed, radio, lengthened radiator fairing, fixed tailwheel and a strengthened windscreen and sliding canopy. It had been agreed that performance and handling, using the old Merlin C, should not be allowed to influence the Service's report on the aeroplane. On 3 April Sammy Wroath took the prototype aloft once more to begin the final stage of the RAF's assessment of the Hurricane.

Meanwhile at Kingston two events had occurred, one of which had a direct bearing on the future of the Hurricane and the other, though not in any way influencing it, was wholly associated with it. Now that the RAF Expansion Scheme was at last fully under way it was obvious to the Hawker Board that not only could the other companies of the Hawker Siddeley Group not continue in the long term to produce the Kingston-designed aircraft (their own designs, such as the Avro Anson, Gloster Gladiator and Armstrong Whitworth Whitley, were also already coming into production) but that new contracts for the Hurricane itself could be expected within a couple of years. The latter assumption was made following the creation of RAF Fighter Command in mid-1936—under the command of Air Marshal Sir Hugh Dowding—and the announcement that the Command required a minimum of 52 squadrons with which to defend Britain, each with a unit establishment of 20 fighters. With the inevitable phasing out of Fury IIs, Gladiators and Demons, sufficient Hurricanes and Spitfires simply hadn't yet been ordered to provide any contingency for reserves. The first step to be taken was to announce a considerable increase in the capital of the Hawker Siddeley Group, and against this to secure a substantial loan from the City institutions to enable the building of new factories for aircraft production. Following negotiations with the Buckinghamshire County Council the large expanse of land of Parlaunt Park Farm at Langley was purchased by the Group and plans drawn up to build a large factory, complete with grass airfield adjoining it, it being planned to switch all Hurricane production to this factory early in 1939.

Before Camm's Hurricane design work had finally been transferred from his Experimental Design Office to the Production Office, parallel work was being done to produce schemes for a light bomber originally intended to supersede the Hawker Hart and Hind. The Air Ministry had issued a Specification, P.27/32, for such an aircraft, and the Fairey Aviation Company had tendered a design, the three-seat Fairey Battle, whose prototype made its maiden flight on 10 March, 1936. Employing the same Merlin as the prototype Hurricane, but with an all-up weight almost twice as much, the Battle seemed to Camm as being an extraordinarily unwieldy aircraft and one that would stand little or no chance of survival if confronted by fighters of the calibre of his Hurricane. (The oft-quoted maximum speed of the Battle at 240 mph at 13,000 ft, though confirmed in Service trials, was thoroughly misleading: such a speed could be maintained for no more than a few seconds before the engine began overheating, and when loaded with eight 250 lb bombs the *maximum speed under operational conditions* was 174 mph at 8,000 feet, and the minimum radius of turn almost four times that of the Hurricane.) Whether or not the Air Ministry realized that P.27/32 had been insufficiently reasoned, a new Specification, P.4/34, was issued fairly late in 1934 taking much greater account of fighter performance then being foreshadowed by aircraft like the Hurricane and Spitfire design proposals. The new Specification called for a bomb load of only 1,000 pounds, a top speed of a least 250 mph and a capability of attacking ground targets accurately in a fairly steep dive. Manoeuvreability, particularly the minimum turning radius while carrying its bomb load, was to be considerably better than any aircraft likely to be forthcoming from P.27/32. The Hawker design team therefore set about producing schemes for a two-seat aircraft which employed the Merlin, the outer wings and tail unit of the Hurricane. Because the bomb load was required to be stored internally, a bomb bay was located in a new, deepened fuselage, this bay necessitating the undercarriage to be moved outwards, in turn resulting in an enlarged wing centre-section. The provision of a bomb bay also brought about the transfer of the radiator to the nose, directly below the engine.

Proposals for this aircraft, later to become the Henley, were submitted to the Air Ministry in 1935 and a prototype was ordered. Although P.4/34 called for an armament of only two machine guns—one in the starboard wing and the other in the rear cockpit—it was pointed out in the Hawker proposal that the wings, being produced in the same jigs as those of the Hurricane, could be made to accommodate any number of guns up to eight if necessary.

Preoccupation with the Hurricane during 1936, particularly when the complications of choice of Merlin for that aircraft arose, caused the Henley

The prototype Hawker Henley, K5115, at Brooklands; it is worth noting that the mainwheel D-doors and tailplane strut on this aircraft had already been discarded on the Hurricane prototype. The location of the radiator under the nose was dictated by the provision of a bomb bay in the fuselage. (Photo: *Hawker Aircraft Ltd.*)

The Hawker Hotspur two-seat turret fighter prototype, K8309, *intended to employ many components common to the Hurricane and Henley; it was however too late to compete in trials with the Boulton Paul Defiant in that ill-conceived turret fighter requirement. (*Photo: *Hawker Aircraft Ltd., Neg No HO/64H)*

prototype to suffer reduced priority so that its first flight did not take place until 10 March, 1937. A production order for 350 aircraft was received and immediately subcontracted to Gloster at Hucclecote. However, by early 1938 an extraordinary change in attitudes at the Air Ministry had taken place following the use by the German *Legion Cóndor* of Junkers Ju 87 dive bombers during the Spanish Civil War; widespread public indignation at the use of these "terror" weapons had persuaded members of the Air Council (as well as the British government) that adoption of dive bombing tactics by the RAF would constitute hypocritical endorsement of this form of aerial warfare. Continuation of the Henley as a dive bomber was peremptorily stopped, the production contract reduced to 200 aircraft and the aircraft itself relegated to target towing.

Whether, in the light of the events of May 1940, when Fairey Battle squadrons were massacred by German Messerschmitt Bf 109 fighters, the discontinuation of the Henley as a light bomber was a wise decision has remained a much debated matter. Certainly the running out of the abbreviated Henley production in June 1940 enabled Gloster's production of the much-needed Hurricane to be stepped up just when it was most desperately needed. Moreover no Service trials ever supported a view that the Henley, delivering dive-bombing attacks, would have been any more effective than the Battle; all that can be said is that it *might* have stood a better chance of escaping annihilation.

★ ★ ★

K5083 appears to have performed with flying colours at Martlesham Heath during the spring of 1937 before going its rounds among the various specialist establishments. In particular the Service was delighted with the short gun firing course at Eastchurch, where it flew 18 "fire-outs" on the range at Leysdown on the Isle of Sheppey without a single gun stoppage. The aircraft, however, could now no longer contribute usefully to the Hurricane's development either at Brooklands or at Hucknall and was taken on Royal Air Force charge at Martlesham Heath on 25 May. Four days later it was flown twice by Wroath at the Empire Air Day displays at Martlesham and Felixstowe.

The prototype was now so unrepresentative of the forthcoming production version as to be of little value. Accordingly when the Air Ministry was approached with a request to assist with the making of a film by the agents representing Metro Goldwyn Meyer by providing a modern fighter and a pilot for the flying sequences, someone suggested *K5083* and Sammy Wroath. The proposal was eagerly accepted by MGM, whose cast, including Clarke Gable and Myrna Loy, and camera crews duly arrived at Martlesham Heath during the last week in August. In all, Sammy made 14 flights for the film, some of which purported to show Gable flying the aircraft but which in truth featured the RAF pilot completely obscured by helmet, goggles, oxygen mask and flying suit. In due course the film, which was originally to have been titled *Shadow of the Wing* was issued as *Test Pilot* and became something of a classic of the day.

There is no reference to this episode of *K5083*'s life in any Hawker records and, as far as can be learned, it was to remain unrecorded in any contemporary Press journal as much for commercial purposes as to avoid possible misinterpretation of the old prototype's relegation from the technical and military spotlight. There have been constant claims to have seen the aircraft dismantled in one of Hawker's sheds at Brooklands about two years later, but the aeroplane in question was almost certainly wrongly identified; in any case the prototype ceased to be the property of Hawker Aircraft Ltd on 25 May, 1937.

Meanwhile, however, the Hurricane production lines at Kingston and Brooklands were gathering momentum, and three days before Wroath's last flight in *K5083* a new Hurricane, *L1547*, resplendent in the new camouflage scheme being donned by the RAF's operational aircraft, was wheeled out of the flight shed at Hawker's airfield for its maiden flight.

4

THE STORM GATHERS

It has since been learned from German records that at the time of the first production Hurricane's maiden flight the *Luftwaffe* possessed more than 70 Messerschmitt Bf 109Bs, of which about 55 were in operational service; 24 of these already equipped the *1.* and *2. Staffeln* of *Jagdgruppe J/88* fighting alongside Franco's Nationalist forces in Spain. These fighters, the Bf 109B–1, were handicapped by the low power of their Junkers Jumo 210D engines (only 635 hp) and a relatively light armament of only three rifle-calibre machine guns, but they proved perfectly capable of dealing with the inferior Russian and other aircraft flown by the Republican forces, as well as providing priceless operational experience for Germany's new generation of young fighter pilots. Moreover, just a month after the maiden flight by Hurricane *L1547*, a Bf 109 prototype, powered by a specially boosted Daimler Benz DB601 engine which produced 1,650 hp for short bursts, and flown by Doktor Hermann Wurster, established a new world speed record for landplanes at 378.39 mph.

★ ★ ★

In contrast to the German practice of purchasing a number of initial prototypes—often as many as half a dozen—followed by a dozen or so "pre-production" aircraft with which to conduct the whole range of trials prior to full production for the Service, the procedure adopted for many years by the British Air Ministry involved the acquisition of possibly only one, and seldom more than two prototypes on which all manufacturers' development flying as well as Service evaluation was conducted. Loss of a prototype, even if caused through no fault of the aircraft itself, could and frequently did remove the manufacturer from the running for a big production contract. "Hand-built" prototypes could not be replaced overnight.

Fortunately neither Hurricane nor Spitfire prototypes suffered any serious mishap during their development flying, but both aircraft differed so widely from the finite Service versions that considerable work had still to be carried out by the manufacturers on production aircraft while others were already joining the operational squadrons.

Service plans by the Royal Air Force had included the establishment of four Hurricane squadrons and two of Spitfires during 1937, but these hopes were dashed by the failure of the Merlin I to gain acceptance as a fighter engine.

As it was, the first flight Merlin II (G No. 7) had been delivered to Kingston on 19 April and this engine was initially used to ensure that manufacturing drawings were adequate to enable production to be undertaken of the best possible nose shape and internal layout. Once decided upon, a new model had to be tunnel tested to confirm that there was no significant drag rise or airflow change that might seriously affect the aircraft's performance and handling. It was not until 8 September that *L1547* was completed and moved to Brooklands for final assembly.

Philip Lucas took *L1547* aloft for the first time on

Dick Reynell lost his life on 8th September 1940 in the Battle of Britain during a temporary posting to No. 43 (Fighter) Squadron

The late John Hindmarsh

12 October at an all-up weight of 5,459 lb, fitted with guns and radio but without ammunition or full fuel. During the remainder of the month it was flown six times by Lucas, Bulman and Hindmarsh with the cg at various positions, and on the 23rd with full military load at an all-up weight of 5,993 lb—that is with full fuel and ammunition. By the end of the month deliveries had started of full-standard production Merlin IIs; *L1547* therefore dispensed with G No. 7 and was fitted with engine No. 463 with ejector exhaust manifolds. By the time it was ready for flight once more, on 11 November, three further Hurricanes were flying.

Other than *L1547*, which was to remain at Brooklands for about six months before starting a two-year period with the A&AEE (again flown by Sammy Wroath many times),[13] each production Hurricane had to undergo around six flights before delivery to the Service to check handling and performance both of aircraft and systems, and to adjust the trim controls and throttle settings. Later on, after the establishment of Maintenance Units, a certain amount of Service "bought-out" equipment could be installed after leaving the manufacturer, thereby enabling the production checks to be reduced at Brooklands. As it was, there were few days during 1938 on which each of the Hawker pilots did not make four or five flights (of which about half were still in Hinds). Later that year a new pilot arrived at Brooklands; Richard Carew Reynell, a Flight Lieutenant on the "A" Reserve of Officers, was seconded to Hawker for test-flying duties. Between them the four pilots made just over 3,200 flights at Brooklands during the year, excluding those to deliver aircraft to the Service. It should be remembered that in those years before the establishment of Maintenance Units manufacturers were generally responsible for the delivery of their aircraft direct to the operational squadrons or training units. Only on handing over the aeroplane to the unit commander did ownership pass to the Air Ministry, so that any loss of aircraft prior to that handing over had to be made good at the manufacturer's expense. Indeed it was after John Hindmarsh was killed while testing a production Hurricane (*L1652*) on 6 September that Dick Reynell joined the Company to assist with the tremendous workload.

Occasionally squadron commanders were able to arrange for some of, if not all, their pilots to pay visits to the manufacturer to make a familiarization flight in the new aircraft before delivering it themselves to the squadron; in such cases handover to the Service took place beforehand!

The First Hurricane Squadrons

By mid-December 1937 nine Hurricanes, including *L1547*, had flown, four of which were ready and scheduled for delivery to the Service. No. 111 (Fighter) Squadron, commanded by Sqn Ldr John Woodburn Gillan at Northolt, which had hitherto been flying Gloster Gauntlets, was due to start re-equipping with Hurricanes on 1 January, 1938, but arrangements were made for the four aircraft awaiting delivery at Brooklands to be flown to Northolt without further delay and all (*L1548–L1551*) had arrived by Christmas—although they did not officially appear on RAF charge until their allotted date. Four more aircraft were delivered during January and the initial unit establishment (UE) of 16 Hurricanes had arrived by the end of the follow-

Two views of the first production Hurricane I, L1547. *This aeroplane spent many months at Brooklands and the various test establishments, but was eventually delivered to the RAF during the Battle of Britain; its life ended when it was lost over Merseyside on 10th October 1940 while serving with No 310 (Czech) Squadron.* (Photos: *Hawker Aircraft Ltd., Neg Nos 45/HG2 and 198K, dated October 1937)*

ing month (six aircraft per flight and four in reserve, the latter usually being those undergoing routine maintenance or on-site repair).

Without the benefit of conversion training in a similar high-performance training aircraft (the excellent Miles Master and North American Harvard were still a year away from RAF service), the squadron pilots were faced with the daunting task of advancing from a biplane with a maximum speed of about 230 mph, an open cockpit and fixed landing gear, to a monoplane with a top speed of about 330 mph, enclosed cockpit, landing flaps and retractable undercarriage—the latter innovations having to be operated by hand pump. There was also a psychological handicap of knowing that no "line" pilot had previously flown the Hurricane. Everything depended on the painstaking instruction, advice and encouragement by Gillan and his flight commanders (themselves all "novices" on the new fighter) to bring the squadron up to operationals standards of efficiency, but there was inevitably a number of accidents, including one fatality.

So it was that, in an effort to promote confidence in the aircraft among his pilots, Gillan planned a dramatic high-speed flight from Northolt to Turnhouse in Scotland; it transpired that the spectacular flight was achieved on the return journey. Flying north on the afternoon of 10 February he encountered strong headwinds, so that he did not land at his destination until after four o'clock, but decided to refuel and return south immediately so as to take advantage of those winds. Climbing to 17,000 ft in the gathering dusk, he set course for home, flying above cloud and without oxygen. Only when he spotted the lights of Bedford through a gap in the clouds did he ease the Hurricane into a gentle dive, finally breaking cloud over his home airfield, "startled by the realization that his ground speed was in the region of 450 mph". He landed shortly before six o'clock, having covered the distance of 327 miles from Turnhouse in 48 minutes—an average speed over the ground of 408.75 mph! Moreover the entire flight had been carried out at full throttle (2,950 rpm) and, far from overheating, the Merlin had never missed a beat.

The Press of course had a field day with the news, and of course the Air Ministry did not feel inclined to emphasize the 80 mph tailwind that had contributed to Gillan's spectacular flight. He was nevertheless to be known henceforth in the Service as "Downwind Gillan". There's no doubt that the flight did much to improve the Squadron's confidence in the Hurricane, and overnight the young pilots assumed an élitism within Fighter Command, an image that has remained with "Treble One" ever since. Gillan's careful training of the Squadron and his leadership by example was shortly afterwards recognized by the award of the AFC.

Next to be re-equipped was No. 3 (Fighter) Squadron, commanded by Sqn Ldr Hugh Lewis Pingo Lester, a 40-year-old RFC veteran, at Kenley. For eight years the Squadron had soldiered along on the Bristol Bulldog, but in March 1937 had started to convert to Gloster Gladiators. The first Hurricanes started to arrive in March 1938, but from the outset No. 3 experienced difficulty in operating the new fighters in and out of the relatively small airfield, and a spate of accidents followed, usually involving ground loops or aircraft tipping on to their nose as pilots struggled to avoid ending up in the boundary fence. When two Hurricanes were written off and a pilot was killed in May, however, it was decided to return the Squadron to Gladiators once more, while Kenley airfield was considerably enlarged to cope with modern fighters. Sqn Ldr Hubert Huntlea Chapman took over the Squadron, remaining with it until after the outbreak of war; No. 3 Squadron returned to Hurricanes in July 1939, but by then it had moved to Biggin Hill.

Third Hurricane squadron was No. 56 at North Weald, 20 aircraft being delivered during May and June. (On 1 April Fighter Command decided to increase the UE of Hurricane squadrons to 20 aircraft, nine being allocated to each Flight—three of them being set aside for conversion training.) The CO, Sqn Ldr Charles Leslie Lea-Cox, also an old RFC member, had commanded the Squadron for almost three years, during which time it had flown Bulldogs, Gauntlets and Gladiators. This time the transition to Hurricanes was achieved smoothly and with little difficulty, and by August the Squadron was declared fully operational "by day and night".

Meanwhile development work on the Hurricane had been proceeding apace at Brooklands. Not wholly satisfied with the aircraft's spin recovery characteristics, Bulman had suggested that tunnel tests be carried out to examine the airflow under the tailplane with the aircraft "super-stalled", and in January these had disclosed a complete breakdown of airflow along the lower half of the rear fuselage, confirming a suspicion that the bottom half of the rudder was contributing nothing at all during spin recovery. To overcome this a new ventral spine fairing was incorporated under the rear fuselage (with a cutaway gap to accommodate the tailwheel, now permanently fixed) and extending to the rudder, which itself was extended down by about seven inches. This was first flown on *L1547* on 19 January, 1938, and in a series of exhaustive spinning trials (for which a spin parachute was installed), which took place between then and 9 March, the modification was shown to have transformed the Hurricane's spin recovery, as well as improving lateral control with wheels and flaps down during an approach to landing.

*Close-up view of the starboard side of the Hurricane I's fuselage with access and break-out panels removed. The rubber-handled lever beside the pilot's seat is the manual hydraulic pump for undercarriage retraction, and the large-diameter pipe below is the coolant pipe from engine to radiator. (*Photo: *Sydney Camm Collection)*

By then, however, the 50th Hurricane was approaching completion and it was decided to incorporate the ventral spine in the 61st aircraft, with the result that none of the first three squadrons received modified Hurricanes among their initial deliveries.[14]

In mid-1938 the production rate of Hurricanes reached about five aircraft per week but this dropped temporarily in July and August while a number of modifications were included in the aircraft on the production line; apart from the spin fairing, these included removal of the venturi from the port side of the fuselage, slight relocation of the radio, strengthening of the pilot's oxygen bottle mounting and a small alteration to the nose cowlings to cater for the introduction of ejector exhaust manifolds, soon to become standard in place of the kidney type.

Little has been said thus far on the subject of Hurricane's propeller (or airscrew as it was almost universally known until early in the Second World War, when the word was officially discouraged owing to possible confusion with "aircrew"). The big Watts[15] wooden two-blade fixed-pitch type had been in widespread service for more than a decade, and had sufficed so long as aircraft speeds (particularly in terminal velocity dives) did not exceed about 360 mph. Above that speed the "aircraft drove the propeller" so that not only did tip speeds enter the realm of compressibility—that is, nearing the speed of sound—but the overspeeding of a propeller in relatively coarse pitch could cause fatal damage to the aircraft's engine. The phenomenon was fairly widely understood and as long ago as the late 1920s the Hele-Shaw-Beecham variable-pitch propeller had undergone a number of trials, but the first successful pitch-changing design was produced by Hamilton Standard in the United States, and this had been fairly widely used by military aircraft during the 1930s. Indeed the two-blade Hamilton Standard propeller was fitted on the German Bf

Air-to-air view of L1583, *one of the first Hurricanes to be fitted with the ventral spine fairing; the considerable gap between propeller and fuselage nose, caused by the Watts propeller base-plate, is of interest. The squared-off top of the radio mast was an identifying feature of the early L-series Hurricanes. (*Photo: *Hawker Aircraft Ltd., Neg No HN2)*

109Bs in Spain. By and large, however, it was not regarded with much favour in Britain owing to its high cost, high weight and poor reliability.

The British Air Ministry was moreover unwilling to depend on an overseas source of propellers for its new aircraft, and the de Havilland Airscrew Company was encouraged to negotiate a licence to produce the latest, more reliable version of the three-blade Hamilton Standard for ultimate use on the Hurricane and Spitfire (as well as numerous other new aircraft about to enter production or service). Although representing a marked improvement over the fixed-pitch Watts, whose blade pitch angle was selected as a compromise between take-off (for which a fine blade pitch is most efficient) and combat engine settings (requiring coarse settings), the two-pitch propeller only slightly reduced the danger of engine overspeeding in the dive. A new, highly efficient British airscrew also now became available, the Rotol[16] constant-speed propeller, which, by means of a pitch control lever beside the pilot's throttle, enabled the blade pitch to be infinitely variable according to speed and power requirements and also selected the best possible blade angle, by means of a hydraulic constant speed unit, CSU, to reduce engine overspeeding in high-speed dives. As well as improving the Hurricane's rate of climb, the Rotol propeller enabled the aircraft to fly for endurance more efficiently and was regarded by many as one of the decisive factors contributing to the Hurricane's brilliant combat success during the Battle of Britain.

The first de Havilland Hamilton Standard two-pitch three-blade metal propeller of 11 ft diameter and blade pitches of 30.5 degrees (fine) and 42.5 degrees (coarse) was fitted to Hurricane *L1562* and first flown on 29 August, but was found initially to be extremely sluggish on take-off until the fine-pitch stop was set to give 31.5 degrees.

The American propeller, being bracket-operated, required no hydraulic power lines to the hub through the shaft and could therefore be fitted to the shaft of a standard Merlin II. However, the new Rotol propeller, being hydraulically operated, not only required a different shaft but featured the constant speed unit mounted at the front of the engine itself; Rolls-Royce therefore introduced the Merlin III, which, with a "universal" airscrew shaft, catered for any propeller likely to be fitted in the foreseeable future—DH, Hamilton Standard, Watts, Rotol, Fairey Reed, etc. For the time being, however, the Air Ministry was unwilling to countenance any divergence from the standard of preparation already agreed for the 600 Hurricanes on order, and it was left to the manufacturers to bear the cost of developing any Rotol-equipped Hurricane. Nevertheless Hawker managed to persuade the Air Ministry to release a damaged aircraft to the Company at nominal cost (*L1606*, ex-No. 56 Squadron) for the necessary trials.

This Hurricane was fully repaired and modified with spin fairing, but the radio and guns—being Air Ministry equipment—were removed. In November 1938 Merlin III No. 11111 was delivered together with CSU and Rotol constant-speed propeller (10 ft 6 in. diameter and a pitch range of 23 to 53 degrees) to Kingston. The aeroplane was re-skinned in silver-doped fabric and commercially registered as *G–AFKX*, and in this form was first flown by Philip Lucas on 24 January, 1939. On 7 February Bulman took the aircraft up for performance measurements with full load ballasting at an all-up weight of 6,402 lb, and recorded a maximum level speed of 344 mph at 15,100 ft—the highest level speed yet recorded by a Hurricane. His flight report also reflects the Chief Test Pilot's obvious delight with the excellent handling of the aircraft, its acceleration and exceptional smooth running of the

Groundcrew personnel manhandling a very early Hurricane of No 111 Squadron at Northolt; a stencilled anotation on the wheel chock suggests that this was L1553 *of 'A' Flight. (*Photo: Flight, *Neg No 15542S)*

Merlin throughout its entire speed range. He carried out one dive to an indicated speed of 460 mph from 21,000 feet with the throttle set to give maximum continuous power (2,850 rpm) and recorded no tendency to overspeed.

★ ★ ★

By the time Bulman submitted his report on the Rotol Hurricane to DTD the international situation in Europe had deteriorated sharply to such a level that war with Germany now seemed inevitable. The urgency to introduce the Hurricane and Spitfire into service was paramount.

During September, as the crisis of Munich approached, Fighter Command brought its squadrons to readiness, but far from the 12 or so squadrons of the new fighters originally hoped for by this date only two with Hurricanes were fully operational (Nos. 56 and 111), while no Spitfires were available, only a small handful of very early aircraft having arrived with No. 19 Squadron at Duxford the previous month. However, while deliveries of Spitfires continued desultorily for several more months, those of the Hurricane now accelerated rapidly after the production slowdown, mentioned above. Indeed Hawker was asked to step up production without regard to the cost of "working round the clock", and by October the production rate was sufficient to re-equip a squadron every month, to replace losses *and* to begin to introduce fully modified aircraft (with spin fairings) to the squadrons which still flew the early production Hurricanes. By the end of the year more than 30 aircraft were leaving Brooklands each month.

In July and August two Debden-based Gladiator squadrons began receiving Hurricanes, although the process of re-equipping was complicated by the splitting of No. 87 Squadron, commanded by Sqn Ldr John Rhys-Jones, to provide the nucleus round which No. 85 Squadron was re-formed. The former Squadron had moved north to Debden from Tangmere in June 1937 and had immediately re-equipped with Gladiators, but in June 1938 its "A" Flight, under Flt Lt Donald Eric Turner (RAFO), was ordered to form No. 85 Squadron. For the first two months the Gladiators continued to be used, but as new Hurricanes were delivered to Debden they were distributed fairly evenly between the two units. It was not until November that No. 85 acquired the formal status of an operational squadron with the arrival of that legendary RAF figure, Sqn Ldr David Francis William Atcherley (twin brother of Richard, "Batchy"), as the squadron commander.

In August it was the turn of No. 73 Squadron at Digby in Lincolnshire, under Sqn Ldr Eric Stanley Finch, to re-equip, followed by No. 32 Squadron at Biggin Hill (Sqn Ldr Reginald Pyne, DFC) in September, and then the three Tangmere-based squadrons, No. 1 (Sqn Ldr Ian Anstruther Bertram) in October, No. 43 (Sqn Ldr Richard Erskine Bain) and No. 79 Squadron (Sqn Ldr Geoffrey Donald Emms), both in November. The last squadron to start converting to Hurricanes in 1938 was No. 151 Squadron at North Weald, commanded by Sqn Ldr Edward Mortlock Donaldson.[17]

Thus, although the picture presented by Fighter Command at the time of Munich appeared dismal on paper, with only two Hurricane squadrons operational, the situation was changing rapidly so far as the Hurricane was concerned. Within a couple of months three more squadrons had been declared operational and five others were already flying Hurricanes. By comparison, however, only two Spitfire squadrons (Nos. 19 and 66) had received their new aircraft and neither was yet operational.

The pace of Hurricane deliveries continued without slackening in 1939 with No. 213 Squadron re-equipping at Wittering in January under Sqn Ldr John Humphrey Edwardes-Jones (later Air Chief Marshal Sir Humphrey, KCB, CBE, DFC, AFC), No. 46 in February at Digby (Sqn Ldr Philip

Early Hurricane fuselages under construction at Canbury Park Road in 1938; visible are aircraft L1731–L1740. *In the extreme bottom left of the picture are visible a couple of ventral spine fairings, with one in place on the nearest airframe.* (Photo: *Author's Collection)*

Reginald Barwell), No. 501 at Filton in March (Sqn Ldr Montague Victor Murray Clube, AAF), and No. 504 at Hucknall in April (Sqn Ldr Sir Hugh Michael Seeley, Bt, MP, AAF).

Mention here of the two squadrons of the Auxiliary Air Force, Nos. 501 and 504, being equipped with the latest RAF fighters marked an important change in policy by the Air Ministry. Hitherto the duties of the so-called "weekend Air Force" had until fairly recently been confined to flying light bombers such as the Hart and Hind, or the Hector on army co-operation duties. It had been announced late in 1938 that some of the squadrons would in due course fly interceptor fighters and it was generally assumed that these would be confined to Demons and possibly Gladiators. It came as something of a surprise when the two squadrons mentioned above started receiving new Hurricanes—before many of the Regular fighter squadrons had converted to the monoplanes. The explanation was fairly logical. The two squadrons were part of the old Special Reserve (as distinct from those squadrons which had only ever constituted the Auxiliary Air Force); they possessed a larger complement of pilots, who, generally speaking, were very experienced and, perhaps most important, the Squadrons were based at the airfields of vital aircraft engine factories, Bristol and Rolls-Royce. It was deemed prudent, in the event that war should break out suddenly, to have modern fighters available at short notice capable of defending these vital factories from air attack. Be that as it may, although full complements of Hurricanes were delivered to Filton and Hucknall, the squadrons were able to undertake conversion to the new aircraft only very slowly (although No. 501 Squadron's pilots underwent an advanced training course on Fairey Battles). Events early in the Second World War, when many of the "weekend pilots" were still serving on the Auxiliary squadrons, were to demonstrate that there was little to choose between them and the Regular squadrons when it came to skill and courage in combat.

And so that final year before the war passed all too swiftly; more squadrons were formed, re-formed and re-equipped with Hurricanes and Spitfires. It *was* a race against time, but the Air Ministry's request to Hawker to increase the production rate paid handsome dividends. By April the flow of Hurricanes outstripped the RAF's capacity for the new fighters, and such units as the No. 11 Group Pool (or Advanced Training Pool) at Andover began receiving aircraft to assist squadrons to speed the conversion training of their pilots. Station Flights, which normally existed to provide General Duties officers in administrative posts with aircraft to fly when their other duties permitted now became, in effect, station training flights with Hurricanes.

At the parent company at Kingston the design offices were also now working at full stretch, all experimental design work on the Hurricane having passed to the Production Design Office to speed the preparation of modification drawings. There were, after all, two new Hawker designs now occupying much of Camm's attention—the Tornado and Typhoon fighter—aircraft whose all-metal structure demanded the introduction of new plant in the shops, long foreshadowed for eventual metal-clad wings for the Hurricane. At first the Air Ministry once again urged Hawker not to endanger the flow of Hurricanes by introducing the metal wing, at least for the time being, but Camm was anxious to cut his teeth on these wings and successfully persuaded the DTD to release one of the trials aircraft (*L1877*) for short preliminary assessment of the

Checks being made by AID inspectors on an early Hurricane; at this stage all engine systems, fuel, hydraulics, flaps and undercarriage have been completed and, after priming and painting, the aircraft would be taken to Brooklands for final assembly. (Photo: *Sydney Camm Collection; Hawker Neg No NT5090)*

Assembly of panels prior to finishing of an L-series Hurricane. (Photo: *Author's Collection)*

"prototype" stressed wings, and on 28 April Lucas carried out the first flight. A new set of wings, built in a production-type jig with full provision for eight-gun armament, was then fitted to the Company's own aircraft *G–AFKX*, and flown by K. G. Seth-Smith (a recent arrival at Brooklands) on 4 July. After submission of a preliminary report on the flight trials, continued in *L1856*, the Air Ministry agreed that Hawker should go ahead and produce metal wings at full speed, but use them first to replace damaged wings of aircraft returned to the factory for repair, and later to deliver stocks of the new wings to the Maintenance Units to modify aircraft awaiting delivery to the operational squadrons. Thus arose a seemingly ridiculous situation in which Hawker received a contract for the manufacture of no fewer than 400 sets of metal wings, and yet was continuing to build aircraft for the Service with fabric wings, apparently on the pretext that any negotiation to vary the basic terms of the original 600 aircraft contract might cause interruption to the flow of Hurricanes. This was contradicted by the fact that production of Hurricanes, already subject of new contracts received by Hawker in 1938 (totalling 800 aircraft, as well as one for 1,700 Hurricanes placed with Glosters), had not yet started, and could still be specified as having metal wings without any disruption of the flow of aircraft. As it was, there were still many aircraft with fabric wings in service with operational squadrons in 1940 while large stocks of metal wings (which required no more than three hours' work per aircraft to change) existed at Kingston, Brooklands, Hucclecote and the maintenance units. It is true that as the full situation was reported to Dowding steps were immediately taken to modify the standard of preparation at the manufacturers, though even then the Air Ministry inexplicably insisted that small batches of aircraft still be produced with fabric wings—only to have metal wings fitted as soon as they reached the Maintenance Units. (An interesting sideline on the matter of the interchangeability of fabric and metal wings on the Hurricane is provided by a test flight carried out by Reynell in *L1877*—the DTD aircraft referred to above—on 21 December, 1939; the aircraft was flown with a fabric-covered port wing and a metal-skinned starboard wing!)

All manner of trials were carried out at Brooklands, too numerous to enlarge on, but reference to Appendix I will illustrate their variety. Two other series of tests are, however, of particular interest, as later events will show. As was described in an earlier chapter, the RAF had maintained fairly substantial forces throughout the Middle East, even if their aircraft were, in the main, outdated. In 1935, moreover, the Service had been obliged to send fighter reinforcements to Egypt at the time of Mussolini's Abyssinian adventure, and more recently the overt alignment of the Italian dictator with Hitler threatened danger for the Suez Canal in the event of war with Germany. By 1938 only two fighter squadrons (Nos. 33 and 80 with Gladiators) were deployed in the Eastern Mediterranean, and it was anticipated that Hurricane reinforcements might have to be sent out at short notice should hostilities with Italy occur. The Air Ministry therefore instructed Hawker to undertake preparation of a trials aircraft for evaluation at Khartoum. This involved fitting a dust filter over the carburettor air intake and making provision for a water tank in the fuselage aft of the cockpit. Three DTD aircraft were set aside for trials at Brooklands, *L1669* and *L1893* with Vokes air filters and *L1877* with a filter produced by Rolls-Royce. *L1669* was first flown by Reynell in July 1939 and, after comparison of results with the other aircraft, was selected for despatch to Khart-

The much-used Hurricane I, G-AFKX, *an ex-No 56 Squadron aircraft,* L1606, *retrospectively modified with ventral spine and purchased from the Air Ministry by Hawker; it was employed to flight test various Merlin engines and propellers; the radio mast has been removed. (*Photo: *Hawker Aircraft Ltd.)*

oum for tropical trials, while development went ahead to improve the filters on the other aircraft in this country. In the event *L1669* never returned, as will be related in due course, and the benefits that accrued from the development of tropical air filters were to have a far-reaching influence on the long-term service of the Hurricane with the Royal Air Force.

The other area of research involving the Hurricane concerned the evergreen quest for heavier armament. Both Supermarine and Hawker had been asked in 1938 to investigate the possibility of mounting a pair of 20-mm Oerlikon cannon in or under the wings of their respective fighters. In the case of the Hurricane a design was prepared whereby the cannon were mounted in fairings under the wings (in this instance—at the insistence of the Air Ministry—fabric-covered wings), the gun bodies being mounted within a pair of short banjo frames attached below the main spars, the bodies themselves forming one side of a strong box structure to withstand the shock of the gun recoil springs; belted ammunition feed was from magazines contained within the wings and two chutes in the gun fairing allowed belt links and spent cartridge cases to spill clear of the aircraft. As far as is known this gun installation (in *L1750*) was only required to be checked out briefly for general handling by Hawker (and was flown once by Lucas on 24 May, 1939) before being delivered to Martlesham Heath, where it was flown by Wroath in June before being sent on to Eastchurch for firing trials. Only a brief summary extract from the report on these trials appears to have survived, and this comments that while the gun installation proved satisfactory the pilot found that the sharp nose-down trim change on firing the guns made aiming of a burst of more than 2–3 seconds extremely difficult and, due to the relatively low rate of fire of the Oerlikon, achieving a lethal hit was considered most unlikely. Further reference to *L1750* will occur later.

★ ★ ★

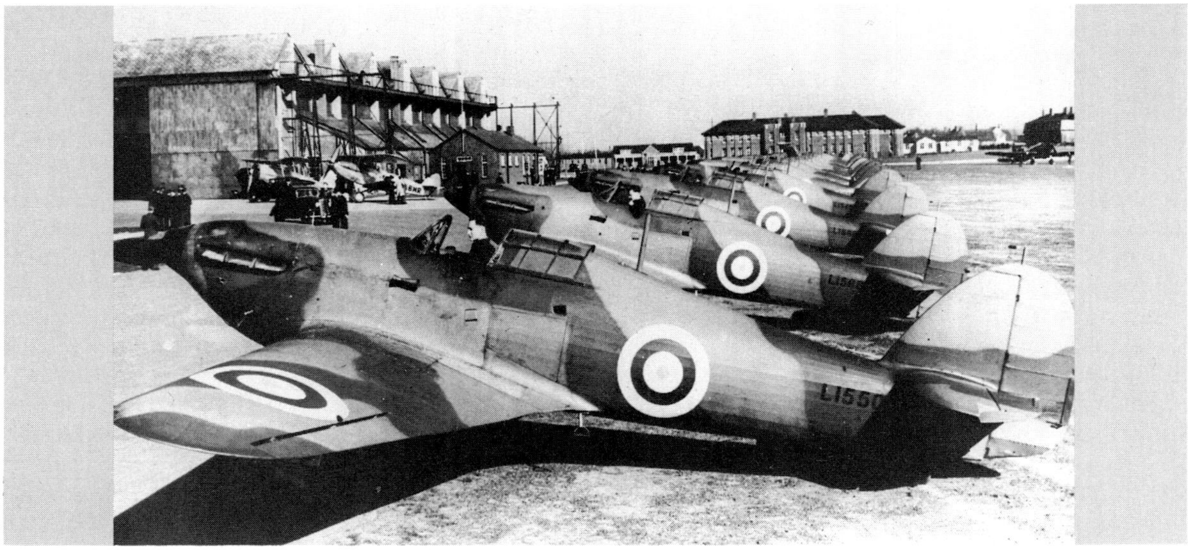

*Early photograph of No 111 Squadron's Hurricanes at Northolt, probably taken in about February 1938. The presence of Hawker's own Hart in the background suggests that Bulman may have been present at Northolt, possibly to give a demonstration to the Press. (*Photo: *US Navy Dept., Neg No 80-CF-4927-1 of the National Archives)*

The Pre-war Hurricane Exports

The absence of any treaty for collective international defence within Europe in the 1930s was caused largely by a widely held belief among the smaller nations that any aggression against them would serve no purpose, and therefore any substantial expenditure upon their armed forces would be profitless. Such a posture was to reckon without the *lebensraum* ambitions of the German dictator. The pacifist parties throughout Europe declined to take seriously the testament of Hitler's *Mein Kampf*, which coherently foreshadowed the creation of a power base in Germany to support totalitarianism. In 1936 he went so far as to publicly claim the right to freedom beyond the recognized German boundaries and set about the remilitarization of the Rhineland while announcing a new four-year German rearmament plan. These events now stirred some of Germany's neighbours to recognize the growing danger, and some of them took such steps as they felt they could afford to bring their armed forces up to date.

Moreover when Albania and Italy completed a series of agreements which served to strengthen the earlier political ties between the two nations, Yugoslavia recognized her growing isolation by the Fascist powers, a feeling of insecurity that was not dispelled even by the Italo-Yugoslav settlement of March 1937. Accordingly, as part of a move to modernize her air force (which already possessed Hawker Furies and had ordered Hind bombers), an application was made to purchase Hurricanes, to which the British government agreed—in line with its policy to support the strengthening of nations friendly towards Britain. As a first step an order for twelve Hurricane Is (with fabric-covered wings) had been placed with Hawker early in 1938, and the first two aircraft—formerly *L1751* and *L1752* of the Air Ministry's first production batch of 600 aircraft—were delivered from Brooklands by air to Belgrade via France and Italy on 15 December, 1938. Soon afterwards a second order, this time for Hurricanes with metal wings, Merlin III engines and DH propellers, was negotiated with the British government, delivery of these starting in February 1940. At the same time a licence agreement for the production of Hurricanes in Yugoslavia by the PSFAZ Rogozarski factory in Belgrade and the *Fabrika Aeroplana I Hidroplana* plant at Zemun was successfully negotiated. The fortunes of Yugoslavia's Hurricanes are recounted on page 137.

The next overseas government to express interest in acquiring Hurricanes was that of South Africa, whose defence minister, Mr Oswald Pirow, had initiated a programme of expansion in the South African Air Force in 1934 with a licence contract to build the Hawker Hartebeeste (a version of the Hardy) at Pretoria. Following representations to the British government in mid-1938 the Air Ministry agreed to release seven Hurricanes from storage and these were crated up at No. 36 Maintenance Unit and shipped out to Cape Town in November; after reassembly they were flown to Pretoria, where they formed part of No. 1 Squadron, SAAF. Not being equipped with tropical air filters, however, these Hurricanes did not survive to participate in operations during the war.

Early production Hurricane Is (LR-O, LR-Q etc) of No 56 Squadron at, above, Ford in 1938 and, below, North Weald (still without ventral spine fairings) early in 1939. (Photo: Courtesy of No 56 Squadron, via R. L. Ward, Farnborough, Neg Ref F27/5/4)

Following the visit to Britain by King Carol of Romania, who watched a display of air drill by RAF squadrons at Odiham in November 1938, a contract came to be negotiated by which 12 Air Ministry Hurricanes would be diverted from the Hurricane production batch and subsequently replaced by new aircraft for the RAF,[18] and delivered to Romania within 12 months.

The British plan to strengthen the Balkan *Entente*'s opposition to German pressure to secure free access to the all-important Romanian oilfields came to nothing, and the Hurricanes—owing to

No 111 Squadron was something of a law unto itself so far as squadron markings were concerned. In this picture, taken at Northolt, the Hurricanes carry the numerals '111', segmented in upper and lower halves in black and white, yellow and white or all-red according to the Flight; the full Squadron Badge was carried on the fin. At one time the Squadron possessed at least one 'training' Hurricane with yellow wing tips and yellow band round the nose. (Photo: *R. L. Ward, Farnborough)*

delays in finalizing the contract—did not start delivery until the eve of the outbreak of the war, and the signature by Romania on 23 November, 1940, of the Axis Tripartite Treaty yielded to that German pressure and thereby avoided any conflict by the *Divisia I-a Aeriana* against the German air force. It is most likely that the Romanian Hurricanes never saw action, and if any survived after the modernization of that air arm by the *Luftwaffe* at the end of 1940 they were probably relegated to second-line duties.

Although senior officers of the Royal Canadian Air Force had first broached the subject of acquiring Hurricanes with the British Air Ministry in 1937 (a suggestion that was dismissed at that time owing to the uncertainty of future deliveries to the RAF), continuing pressure through the Dominion Chiefs of Air Staff Committee at the time of Munich a year later found the British government more amenable to any plan by which fully trained Hurricane squadrons from the British Commonwealth might come to the aid of the RAF in time of war. Arrangements were immediately made to divert 20 Hurricanes from the Kingston production line and ship them to Canada, the first five aircraft leaving Britain in October. Simultaneously agreement was reached for licence production to be undertaken by the Canadian Car and Foundry Company of Montreal, and a pattern aircraft shipped by Hawker on 2 March, 1939. The speed with which Canadian production of Hurricanes got under way was remarkable by any standards and was achieved through extraordinary feats of organization on both sides of the Atlantic—involving, for instance, the committing to microfilm of the drawing of every jig, tool and component at Kingston, and their despatch in duplicate to Canada (a total of 82,000 items). With delivery of the first "Can-Car" Hurricanes starting in 1940, total Canadian production reached 1,451 aircraft. Further references to Canadian-built Hurricanes recur time and again in the remainder of this account.

March 1939 also witnessed the visit by a military mission from Middle Eastern states and resulted in an order by Persia for 18 Hurricanes. Owing, however, to delays in developing a fully tested tropical air filter, already referred to, delivery of these aircraft was also delayed, only one aircraft (*L2079*) being despatched before September and one other in 1940. Neither aircraft was equipped with a tropical filter and, because of the shortage of shipping space and the uncertainties of wartime, the remainder of the contract was held in abeyance until after the war (see page 183).

At roughly the same time that the Persian order was placed the Turkish government sought to purchase 15 Hurricanes as part of a major plan to modernize its air force, an approach that found favour with the British government, anxious to bolster friendly relations with foreign states in the

No photo has been located of the Hurricane I, L1750, *armed with a pair of 20-mm cannon under the wings in April 1939. These two heavily-masked pictures however show the manner in which the guns were mounted (under fabric wings) and the shape of the gun fairings; note the case chute in the rear of the fairings.* (Photo: *Author's Collection, dated April 1939)*

The first tropical trials Hurricane I, L1669, *at Martlesham Heath in 1939 prior to its despatch to Khartoum; as told in Chapter 11 this aeroplane was to enjoy a short but illustrious career in the Western Desert in 1940.* (Photo: *via Sqn Ldr R. C. B. Ashworth*)

eastern Mediterranean. In this instance it was the outbreak of war itself that spurred delivery of the Hurricanes, the entire batch being delivered by sea in September 1939—albeit without tropical air filters.

Much nearer home, the Belgian government in 1939, recalling the events of 1914, woke up at last to the peril of the nation, lying as it did beyond the northern limit of the fortifications of the French Maginot Line. Twenty Kingston-built Hurricanes were ordered in March, the first three being delivered the following month. A manufacturing licence was secured by Avions Fairey (*Société Anonyme Belge*) and an order for a further 80 Hurricanes placed with the Belgian company. By the outbreak of war all the Kingston-built aircraft (with Merlin IIs and Watts propellers) had arrived in Belgium, and the first Belgian-built aircraft was completed before the end of the year at Gosselies. It had been intended to mount an armament of four wing-mounted 12.7-mm heavy machine guns in place of the eight rifle-calibre Brownings, but this scheme suffered delays, so that by the time of the German invasion on 10 May only two such aircraft had been completed. As it was, the Belgian factory had delivered about 20 aircraft, all of which were armed with the standard eight-gun battery. From January 1940, however, all engines delivered from Rolls-Royce to Belgium were Merlin IIIs and the last two aircraft to reach the Belgian air force before disaster struck were fitted with Rotol constant-speed propellers.

Ironically the last nation to place an order for Hurricanes before the war was the one country in direst need of modern fighters—yet on account of a misplaced confidence in her own preparedness delayed taking any realistic steps to modernize her air force. One could also argue that the guarantees given to Poland by Britain and France in March 1939 to support her sovereign rights against any aggression by Germany probably contributed to the Polish government's unwillingness to face realities. In the event a firm order was placed for only one Hurricane for evaluation purposes, with an option to purchase nine more. The first aircraft was indeed shipped from Britain in July and is known to have been unloaded at Stettin on 8 August. Its subsequent fate is unknown, as is that of the nine other aircraft which were hurriedly shipped to Poland early in September; no manifest can be traced to suggest they reached a Polish port and there have been suggestions that they were in fact returned to Britain and taken on charge by the RAF; another report states that they were unloaded into store at Gibraltar to await tropical filters prior to onward shipment to the Middle East at a future opportunity. A consignment of nine filters *did* arrive at Gibraltar in a Lockheed Hudson in June 1940. However to confuse the speculation still further, it is known that in July 1940 a crate, marked with stencils in Polish and containing Hurricane spare parts, turned up at Aden!

★ ★ ★

So it was that on that fateful day, 1 September, 1939, the production and delivery of Hurricane fighters for the Royal Air Force can only have been considered wholly satisfactory by the Air Ministry. Sixteen Hurricane squadrons were fully operational, with one (No. 605 of the Auxiliary Air Force) still working up. Another, No. 610 Squadron, received Hurricanes on the outbreak of war, but did not reach operational status before being reassigned to Spitfires. These squadrons between them had on charge a total of 280 aircraft—the majority, however, still with fabric wings and Merlin II engines—and a further 133 aircraft were either at maintenance units, training units or test establishments. The remaining 169 out of 572 Hurricanes so far completed by Hawker were accounted for by aircraft sold or supplied overseas, those either already written off or being repaired after accidents or awaiting collection from Brooklands. Only 28 of the original order for 600 Hurricanes remained to be completed. Nevertheless with only seven fully operational squadrons of Spitfires, five of Blenheim night fighters, three of Gladiators and one of Gauntlets, the 52-squadron target must still have seemed desperately far away to Hugh Dowding.

5

GERMAN LIGHTNING

Three days after German troops stormed across the Polish border Britain and France declared war. As part of the established agreement with France in such a war with Germany, a British Expeditionary Force (BEF) was assembled and transported across the Channel to take up positions behind the northern sector of the French frontier with Belgium. Two major elements of the Royal Air Force were also ordered to France, the Air Component of the BEF and the Advanced Air Striking Force (AASF); the former, as its title implies, was in effect a force whose purpose was to support and protect the British Army in France, and among the squadrons in the Air Component were two with Hurricanes (Nos. 85 and 87), while the AASF comprised light bomber squadrons with Bristol Blenheims and Fairey Battles for short-range offensive operations, and two further Hurricane squadrons (Nos. 1 and 73) whose main task was the protection of the bombers and their bases, and general air defence of the British-occupied sector of north-eastern France.

While the strength of bombers and army co-operation aircraft contributed by the RAF generally met with French approval, the fighter force (which included no Spitfires) fell far short of French expectations—a tacit admission by that nation that its own fighter force was so archaic as to be quite inadequate to match the strength of the *Luftwaffe*. And it was not long before demands were being made to London for the RAF to send a further six squadrons. Dowding, however, fiercely resisted these demands, but agreed to a small degree of compromise by sending to France two Auxiliary squadrons, Nos. 607 and 615, in November—then still equipped with Gladiators. He did agree to reconsider the situation if a major offensive was launched by the German Army in the west, if the safety of the BEF was seriously threatened and if Fighter Command's strength had moved materially closer to the minimum necessary for the air defence of Britain.

The truth was that Dowding saw no need to waste his valuable fighter units in France so long as air activity over the Western Front posed little threat to the Allies. Activity during that first autumn and winter was confined to occasional local sorties, the *Luftwaffe* content to engage in reconnaissance and isolated bombing raids, seldom by more than two or three aircraft. By far the greater part of the German air force was resting and re-equipping after its *Blitzkrieg* campaign in Poland. For the Hurricane pilots on the airfields at Vassincourt (No. 1 Squadron), Rouvres (No. 79) and Lille/Seclin (Nos. 85 and 87), life consisted of the occasional patrol, a rare scramble and a perpetual battle against the elements, for the French airfields of the north were badly drained and, with the coming of the winter rain and snow, quickly turned to quagmire. Fortunately the Hurricane was better equipped than most fighters to cope with such conditions, with its sturdy wide-track undercarriage, and there were seldom instances when its operations were prevented by the state of the airfields.

The first German aircraft to fall to the Hurricanes

was a Dornier Do 17P reconnaissance aircraft, shot down by Plt Off Peter Mould of No. 1 Squadron (whose motto is *In Omnibus Princeps*—"First in All Things") from 18,000 ft over Toul on 30 October. Mould's aircraft, *L1842*, was to provide excellent testimony of the Hurricane's ability to survive considerable damage in the air, when, on 23 November it was one of a section of three aircraft on patrol, led by Flt Lt George Plinston, that encountered a Heinkel He 111 at 20,000 ft between Verdun and Metz. It required attacks by all three pilots to shoot down the German bomber, and the *coup de grâce* was delivered by Sergeant A. V. ("Taffy") Clowes, flying *L1842*. Just as Clowes broke away six Moranes swept down, their pilots determined to ensure the destruction of the Heinkel, one of them colliding with the Hurricane and carrying away one elevator and half its rudder. Although the Welshman crashed on landing back at Vassincourt his Hurricane was repaired on site, and Clowes escaped with little worse than a few bruises.

No. 73 Squadron had by then also drawn blood. Fg Off Edgar ("Cobber") Kain shot down another Dornier Do 17P from 27,000 ft—quite possibly the greatest height yet for an air combat—on 2 November. No. 85 Squadron's first victim fell on 21 November, when one of its flight commanders, Flt Lt Richard Lee in *L1898*, shot down an He 111 into the sea off Boulogne, and the same month Flt Lt Robert Jeff gained No. 87 Squadron's first victory with the destruction of a reconnaissance He 111 over Hazebrouck.

Meanwhile the last of the L-series Hurricanes (the original batch of 600) had been completed at Brooklands before the end of September and was followed by a new batch of 300 aircraft without interruption of the production line. These aircraft featured Merlin IIIs and either DH or Rotol three-blade propellers, the first 80 being produced with fabric wings. The priority at that time was to replace the aircraft with Merlin IIs and Watts propellers in France, and the majority of the early aircraft were indeed delivered to the Air Component and AASF squadrons.

However, it was in one of the new aircraft that No. 111 Squadron, then flying from Acklington, gained its first victory of the war, when the squadron commander, Sqn Ldr Harry Broadhurst, AFC (later Air Chief Marshal Sir Harry, GCB, KBE, DSO and Bar, DFC and Bar, AFC), flying *N2340* on 29 November, shot down an He 111H into the sea off Newcastle.

This was the period of the "Phoney War", with the Germans flexing their muscles for their next campaign and the Western Allies bracing themselves for the next shock of *Blitzkrieg*. There was, however, nothing phoney about another campaign that now raged in the snows of Finland. Generally referred to as the Winter War (to distinguish it from the later Continuation War), this conflict broke out on 30 November, 1939, following Finland's refusal to accede to Russian demands for military bases on Finnish territory and for a readjustment of the border on the Karelian Isthmus, the latter demand effectively confiscating the Mannerheim Line—Finland's major line of defence against Russia. Equipped with a small but fairly modern air force, the Finns fought with remarkable tenacity, destroying large numbers of the obsolescent Russian aircraft. Though politically sympathetic towards Finland in her fight against the Soviet Union—then allied with Germany—Britain was slow to provide assistance, although plans were afoot to send a squadron of RAF Gladiators. An order to purchase 12 Hurricanes was, however, more swiftly attended to and, taken from stocks held by Nos. 19 and 20 Maintenance Units, these aircraft were shipped in neutral vessels in February 1940. By the time they

L2039, *the CO's aircraft of No 501 Squadron which came to grief at Tangmere late in 1939 during the 'Phoney War' period. Sqn Ldr Montagu Clube's Hurricane displayed the CO's pennant prominently and unusually on the fin. Among the salvaged components in the left foreground can be seen the spinner, indicating that the Hurricane was Merlin III-powered with DH three-blade propeller. The aircraft was subsequently repaired and converted to a Sea Hurricane Mark IA in 1941. (*Photo: *via P. Edmond and R. L. Ward, Neg Ref No F40/3/2A)*

Two Hurricane Is supplied to Finland. Above, HU460, *an ex-L-series aircraft with tail snowskid, pictured shortly after the end of the Winter War.* Below, HU451, *about nine months later with revised markings and conventional tailwheel.* (Photos: *via Sqn Ldr R. C. B. Ashworth)*

had been reassembled in Finland (one aircraft was inexplicably lost *en route*), however, the tide of fortune had turned against the Finns, whose air force and army were slowly being engulfed by the sheer numbers of their enemy. No time remained to bring the Hurricanes into service before hostilities ended on 13 March with the agreement of an armistice.

The 11 Hurricanes, with tail snow skid in place of the customary tailwheel, were eventually introduced into service with the Finnish Air Force and, despite a complete absence of spare parts, most survived to see operational service during the Continuation War against the Soviet Union after the launching of *Barbarossa* by Germany in June 1941. They were employed principally for interception duties owing to their lack of range, but are generally remembered by the Finnish pilots with affection, who judged them to be their best fighters until the arrival of new German aircraft; they gained a number of victories over Soviet aircraft in the early months of that war and none was ever lost in air combat. No record survives to suggest that a Finnish-flown Hurricane ever fought a Russian-flown Hurricane for, as told on page 125, Britain was much more generous with her Hurricanes for the Soviet Union that she had been towards the Finns. . . .

Norwegian Interlude

With the approach of spring in 1940 Hitler now turned his attention to the northern flank, intent on safeguarding the shipping route along the Norwegian coast from the port of Narvik in the far north through which his vital supplies of Swedish iron ore flowed. To do so involved a swift occupation of Denmark, whose bases were necessary for air and sea operations against Norway.

Denmark was swatted like a fly, her air force neglected and starved of modern aircraft for years until it was too late, and was brushed aside in a single day—9 April. German forces made simultaneous attacks in Norway, capturing Narvik, and making landings in force at Oslo, Kristiansand, Arendal, Egersund, Bergen and Trondheim, as the vital airfield at Stavanger-Sola fell to airborne forces—all on that first day.

Britain's reaction to events in Norway was fairly rapid, principally on account of limited preparations she had also been making to attack and secure the port of Narvik when the Germans launched their invasion. However, faced now with a major campaign which demanded support of Norwegian forces in Central Norway, the British forces which now embarked were quite inadequate for the tasks thrust upon them; landing at Harstad, Namsos and Andalsnes between 15 and 18 April, their object was to strike north towards Narvik and then south to link up with the Norwegian Army north of Oslo. However, provided with only one squadron of RAF Gladiators, No. 263 (delivered aboard the carrier HMS *Glorious*), and with only one usable "airfield"—the frozen Lake Lesjaskog—the British forces in central Norway were quickly pinned down and contained by the *Wehrmacht*, while the *Luftwaffe* set about bombing the Gladiators on the lake. Despite tremendous efforts to meet the German bombers in the air, No. 263 was overwhelmed and after a week the pilots and groundcrews were ordered to destroy their surviving aircraft and quit Norway, and by early May all British forces had been evacuated from the country.

The British now reverted to the original plan to gain a foothold in the far north by attacking and capturing Narvik, this time sending No. 263 Squadron—newly re-equipped with fresh Gladiators—and No. 46 Squadron with Hurricanes, commanded by Sqn Ldr Kenneth Brian Boy Cross (later Air Chief Marshal Sir Kenneth, KCB, CBE, DSO, DFC) to support the operation. Eighteen Hurricanes were embarked by lighter in HMS *Glorious* at Greenock on 10 May and, after setting course for Norway, were flown off and landed at Skaanland and Bardufoss on the 26th, this despite the fact that no Hurricane had ever previously flown off a carrier. Of the 18 pilots who accompanied the Squadron, the names of 14 are known for certain: Sqn Ldr K. B. B. Cross (commanding officer), Flt Lts P. G. Jameson and L. R. Stewart (flight commanders), Fg Offs R. M. J. Cowles, P. J. Frost, F. T. Knight, J. W. Lydall and M. C. F. Mee, Plt Offs R. H. Bunker, J. F. Drummond, P. W. Lefevre and P. R. McGregor, F/Sgt Shackley and Sergeant Taylor; their aircraft were *L1793, L1794, L1798, L1804, L1806, L1812, L1814, L1815, L1816, L1853, L1892, L1961, L1980, L1988, N2543, N2633, P2632* and *P2652*. All had been fitted with metal wings and were powered by Merlin IIs with DH propellers. It was decided that the Gladiators should fly from Skaanland (and indeed had already arrived) and the Hurricanes from Bardufoss and on the 25th No. 46 Squadron assembled all its pilots, groundcrews and aircraft at the latter, carrying out a number of "sector reconnaissance" flights to familiarize the pilots with the area around Narvik during the following three days. Being closer to Narvik the Gladiators had already been in action and had destroyed several German aircraft attempting to attack the port. On the 28th, however, it was the turn of the Hurricanes, when Lydall in *L1806* and McGregor in *L1853* caught and destroyed a Junkers Ju 88 over Tjelbotn; that evening the squadron came across a pair of Do 26 flying boats of the *Transozean-Staffel* about to disembark German alpine troops in Rombaksfjord, and shot both down; one managed to make a forced landing near Narvik, where the crew and 10 troops on board were taken prisoner.[19]

As German forces advanced from the south air activity increased steadily and not a day passed during the first week in June on which both RAF squadrons were not in action. From the few surviving records it is estimated that about 20 German aircraft were destroyed for certain (it being customary for the Allied forces to send out search parties to look for survivors stranded in the freezing wastes, so that evidence of German casualties were perhaps more reliable than usual), while *Luftwaffe* records show that at least 28 aircraft were lost around Narvik between 24 May and 7 June—although it is known that some of these were lost as the result of navigational errors. Losses among the Hurricanes were two shot down in combat and two as a result of landing accidents, with one pilot wounded and shipped home.

On 3 June it became clear that the British position at Narvik was untenable, with the *Luftwaffe* now free to use bases in central Norway and becoming stronger every day, and from that date—as another more famous evacuation ended—the Allied forces began embarking for the long and hazardous voyage home. It was thanks to the untiring vigilance of the RAF (and Fleet Air Arm) pilots, who kept up constant patrols, that no serious casualties were suffered from air attack on the sea approaches to Narvik. On the 7th, however, German attacks on the port were stepped up and No. 46 Squadron was in action against He 111s three times. That evening the Squadron personnel were ordered to destroy the surviving Hurricanes and make for a ship in the harbour. Although neither he nor any of his pilots had ever landed on a carrier before, Cross pleaded to be allowed to fly the 10 serviceable Hurricanes on to the *Glorious*, which he knew to be at sea nearby. After being granted permission he called for 10 volunteers. . . .

> "100 per cent volunteered. Tests were carried out with extra weight in the tail of the Hurricanes. At 18.00 hrs Flt Lt Jameson, Fg Off Knight and Sgt Taylor took off for HMS *Glorious* and landed successfully. At 18.10 and 18.15 hrs Fg Off Mee and Plt Off Drummond returned from a patrol over Narvik during which they engaged four Heinkels. Each pilot claimed to have shot down an enemy aircraft, and Plt Off Drummond attacked and damaged the other two.
>
> 8th June 1940. 00.45 hrs. Sqn Ldr Cross, Flt Lt Stewart, Fg Offs Cowles, Frost and Mee, Plt Off Bunker and F/Sgt Shackley took off for HMS *Glorious*."

All ten landed on safely and, after the four unserviceable Hurricanes at Bardufoss had been destroyed, the remaining pilots and the Squadron's ground personnel made their way into Narvik, where they boarded MV *Andora Star* and sailed for home.

All through the morning and early afternoon of 8 June the carrier *Glorious* with her two attendant destroyers, HMS *Acasta* and *Ardent*, steamed westwards to remove themselves from the danger of attack by shore-based bombers—unaware that a much greater hazard lay ahead. At 4 o'clock that afternoon look-outs on the two German battle cruisers *Scharnhorst* and *Gneisenau* sighted the carrier's smoke, and half an hour later the *Scharnhorst* opened fire at a range of 28,000 yards—far beyond the range of the carrier's guns. As the gallant destroyers made straight for the battle cruisers, laying a smokescreen to protect their charge, *Glorious*'s deck crews struggled frantically to make ready to launch a strike by Swordfish (the Hurricanes, whose wings of course did not fold, had probably been stored below), but within minutes hits from plunging fire of the heavy shells set the carrier ablaze, which then took on a heavy list. At 5.20 pm the order was given to abandon ship; 20 minutes later the carrier turned over to starboard and sank. Sixty hours later a small Norwegian fishing vessel came upon rafts supporting three officers and 35 men who, apart from five men who were picked up by a German flying boat and taken prisoner, were the sole survivors from the carrier. Two of the officers rescued were Sqn Ldr Cross and Flt Lt Jameson, who were landed shortly afterwards at the Faeröes. Thus was lost one of Britain's few aircraft carriers, together with 1,515 men of the Royal Navy and Royal Air Force. The loss of ten Hurricanes, whose survival had been so important to Cross only a few hours before, now seemed trivial by comparison.[20]

Blitzkrieg in the West

Almost a month before the end of the Norwegian campaign Germany struck in the West. On 10 May the *Wehrmacht* was launched against Holland, Belgium, Luxembourg and France, its aim (outlined in *Fall Gelb*, Plan Yellow) being to outflank the Maginot Line from the north and to drive an armoured wedge through to the English Channel, thereby isolating the BEF and dividing the French Army before turning south against Paris.

When the blow fell the disposition of the Hurricane squadrons in France had changed somewhat since the winter. No. 1 Squadron was still at Vassincourt, but on that day was re-deployed to Berry-au-Bac; No. 73 was moved to Reims/Champagne; No. 85 was still at Lille/Seclin, but No. 87 had transferred to Senon under French control. The two Gladiator squadrons, Nos. 607 and 615, were in the process of working up on Hurricanes and were not yet fully operational, although each still retained about a dozen Gladiators, No. 607 at Vitry-en-Artois and No. 615 at Abbeville. Between them these six squadrons reported a strength of 96 Hurricanes available on that day.

Since early morning reports had been reaching London of the German attacks and, without hesitation, Dowding ordered three more Hurricane squadrons, Nos. 3, 79 and 504, to France to reinforce the Air Component, and No. 501 Squadron to strengthen the AASF. By that evening No. 3 (Sqn Ldr Patrick Gifford, AFF[21]) had landed at Merville, No. 79 (Sqn Ldr Richard Vernon Alexander) at Mons-en-Chausée and No. 501 (Sqn Ldr M. V. M. Clube) at Betheniville; two days later No. 504 Squadron (Sqn Ldr Rupert Hartley Watson, AAF) arrived at Vitry-en-Artois.[22] One tragedy marred these moves; a transport aircraft bringing the remaining pilots of No. 501 Squadron from Tangmere crashed on landing at Betheniville, killing three and injuring six.

All 10 squadrons of Hurricanes were now to be heavily engaged as the *Luftwaffe*'s aircraft ranged over and ahead of the savage fighting on the ground. In particular No. 501's remaining pilots were stretched to the limit during their first two days in France, claiming the destruction of 15 German bombers and three Bf 110s for the loss of three aircraft and two pilots. On the 12th No. 3 Squadron destroyed eight enemy aircraft without loss.

The Germans certainly suffered their heaviest bomber losses during the first few days of the great offensive as, according to their established rôles, the

A Hawker-built Hurricane I supplied to Belgium ('H-21', an ex-RAF L-series aircraft), pictured in Belgium during the winter of 1939–40. Note the Fairy Fox in the background, an old aircraft in widespread service with the Aéronautque Militaire. *(Photo: R. Ward, Canterbury)*

Believed to be the only Belgian Hurricane to be equipped with a Rotol constant-speed propeller at the time of the German invasion in May 1940. (Photo: *via R. Ward, Canterbury)*

Bf 110s were charged with protecting the bombers while the much more efficient Bf 109Es' responsibilities lay in protecting the *Wehrmacht* from attacks by Allied bombers. The Bf 110s proved unable to give the bombers effective protection and so the Hurricane pilots achieved considerable success in attacks on the Heinkels and Dorniers.

As the situation for the Allied armies quickly deteriorated under the hammer blows of *Blitzkrieg* tactics, much greater demands were made on the Battle and Blenheim light bombers to attack key points in attempts to stem the German advance, and it was in these attacks—and efforts by the Hurricanes to protect the bombers—that the heaviest RAF losses occurred, particularly among the Battles.

Débâcle in Belgium

A contingency plan had been agreed with the Belgians whereby in the event of a German attack on their country the BEF would move forward and take up a defensive line alongside the Belgian Army. This plan took little account of the possibility that the *Wehrmacht* might blast its way deep into Belgium at the outset, so the BEF found itself fighting in the open against an armoured thrust which was already gathering momentum. The Belgian Air Force, with a score of serviceable Hurricanes,[23] 15 Gladiators, about 80 Fairey Fox light bombers, about 20 Fairey Battles, 23 Fiat CR.42s and 20 Renard R–31s, represented on paper a fairly sizeable force, but only the Hurricanes could be regarded as a match for the modern German aircraft. Nevertheless, realizing that despite the age of most of the Belgian aircraft and that in defence of their homeland their crews would inevitably attack the invading *Wehrmacht* with great courage and tenacity if allowed the chance, the *Luftwaffe* had determined on a series of devastating pre-emptive attacks on the Belgian airfields. By the end of the first day 67 Belgian aircraft had been destroyed on the ground, and a further 20 (including half the serviceable Belgian Hurricanes) in the air. The following day an attack by 15 of the Battles on a pontoon bridge at Maastricht was accompanied by the loss of 10 of the bombers. On the 12th a *Staffel* of Bf 109Es ripped through a formation comprising almost all the surviving Belgian Hurricanes over Liège, shooting down three—one of them falling to the guns of JG 27's adjutant—the first victory to be claimed by Hauptmann Adolf Galland.[24]

Failures to prevent key bridges from falling into German hands intact and to destroy them after they had done so were the key to the unchecked advance by the *Wehrmacht* through Belgium. The enormous sacrifices made by the British and French light bombers in their vain attempts to destroy them have passed into military legend.

Owing to the swift advance by the Germans into Holland and Belgium the RAF Hurricanes were not ordered forward from their bases in France; when called on to escort the light bombers on their almost suicidal raids they were thus severely handicapped by fuel shortage owing to the distances they had to fly. Moreover, they flew patrols over the British forces in Belgium as and when they could be spared from their escort duties (for which the Air Component squadrons were not originally intended) and achieved some excellent results, such as when No. 87 Squadron on the 11th twice attacked large formations of Junkers Ju 87 dive bombers near Brussels and Tongres, claiming the destruction of 10, for the loss of two pilots and aircraft.

The decision to hold the Hurricanes on French soil was indeed sensible as later events were to demonstrate. Casualties during those first three days were heavy, but not disastrously so—a total of 12 aircraft lost and seven pilots killed in combat. In anticipation of heavier losses to come, however, Dowding sent over 32 further Hurricanes and pilots on the 13th, as much to bring the two "ex-

The Blackburn Roc floats attached to a Hurricane's wing centresection in the Canbury Park Road experimental shops; the location of the step on the front port strut indicates that the pilot's access to the cockpit would have been over the port wing leading edge. (Photo: *Sydney Camm Collection*)

Gladiator" squadrons up to strength as to replace losses on the others. But from the 14th onwards, as German bombers stepped up their attacks on British-occupied airfields, it became essential to start moving the fighter squadrons from base to base, not only to avoid capture by the advancing Germans but to escape destruction in the raids. This, alas, was what caused the greatest losses of aircraft as the groundcrews with the essential spares and tools could seldom keep pace with the moves by the aircraft, with the result that aircraft that landed with battle damage—which might otherwise be repaired in a matter of a few hours—had to be abandoned. Many such Hurricanes were burned where they stood, while others were left with the object of repairing them as soon as the groundcrews arrived; often they never did. . . .

The movements by No. 1 Squadron, which astonishingly managed to survive intact for five weeks in France after 10 May, served to illustrate the hectic nature of the Battle of France as far as the British fighter squadrons were involved as the German forces swept along the Channel Coast: Berry-au-Bac, 10 May; Condé-Vraux, 17 May; Anglure, 18 May; Chateaudun, 3 June; Boos, 9 June; Angers 13 June; Nantes, 14 June; St Nazaire, 17 June; and finally home to Northolt on 18 June.

The Air Component Hurricane squadrons suffered most; for instance, No. 85 Squadron's pilots shot down 29 German aircraft in the first nine days of the German assault, yet remained at Merville throughout that period. But the loss of six pilots and aircraft—after Dowding's reinforcements had all been swallowed up elsewhere—could not be made good and, although attempts were made to fly the survivors as a combined squadron with No. 87, which had also suffered heavily, both squadrons were ordered back to Britain, No. 85 on 22 May and No. 87 on the 24th.

Dowding was under constant pressure, not only by the French but also by the British Air Staff, to send further Hurricane squadrons to France. Even Churchill waxed eloquent on the need to help the French following demands made to him by the Paris government. Only when Dowding pointed out with some asperity that the French and Norwegian *débâcles* had already drained his home defence resources by one-third of its strength of fighters and some 40 per cent of his Regular pilots did the clamour become muted. To extricate the British Expeditionary Force from the French cauldron was about to cost him more dearly still.

Action in France. Refuelling a Hurricane of No 501 Squadron from an Albion three-point bowser at Betheniville after a combat sortie in May 1940. The wing gun patches have been blown away; the groundcrew all wear steel helmets and two pilots discuss their sortie on the right. Just visible through the bowser's windscreen is the white underside of the aircraft's nose, indicating the black-and-white lower surface colour scheme. (Photo: *Fleet Street News Service*)

The Great Evacuation

When on 21 May the German Panzers reached the Channel coast near Abbeville about half a million British, French and Belgian troops became isolated to the north with their backs to the sea; already pressed on front and flanks, they were now threatened from the rear as Guderian's tank columns turned north towards Boulogne and Calais.

Fortunately for the Allies, at that moment Hitler, influenced by the bragging confidence of his portly air chief, Hermann Göring, and anxious to conserve his strength for the final battles in France, gave orders for the armoured columns to halt. Göring, blinded by the prospect of a shining victory for his *Luftwaffe*, had sought his *Führer*'s sanction to unleash the full might of the air force against the apparently doomed Allied armies in north-eastern France.

Already on the 19th preparations had started to mount an evacuation of the BEF under the code-name Dynamo, and Air Vice-Marshal Charles Hubert Boulby Blount, commanding the Air Component, brought his headquarters back to Hawkinge on the Kent coast, whence he worked in close liaison with Air Vice-Marshal Keith Park, commanding No. 11 Group at Uxbridge, to co-ordinate air fighter cover over the BEF in France; with much greater difficulty he continued to control support operations by the Hurricanes and Lysanders still flying from French soil.

By the time the great evacuation was finally ordered to start on 26 May all RAF squadrons had been recalled from the Pas de Calais, most of the Hurricane squadrons bringing home with them about half their allotted strength of aircraft—all that remained airworthy (on Merville alone about 20 Hurricanes had to be abandoned, some effort having been made to destroy them by setting fire to the rear fuselages). Nos. 607 and 615 Squadrons, most of whose Hurricanes had been transferred to the fully operational squadrons as being of greater combat value in their hands, returned with many of their old Gladiators still intact. All the Lysander squadrons were also back in Britain (other than No. 13, which had lost all its aircraft and whose surviving personnel were to struggle home on the 29th). Two other Hurricane squadrons, No. 213 (Sqn Ldr J. H. Edwardes-Jones) and No. 601 (Sqn Ldr Thomas Loel Evelyn Bulkeley Guinness, MP, AAFRO[25]) had sent detachments to Merville on the 17th for a few days, but both were also back in England.

Henceforth all fighter operations over French soil came under direct control of No. 11 Group, which, despite some risk from German air attacks elsewhere, now brought into action a number of squadrons (Spitfires and Defiants among them) from other Groups in efforts to mount continuous air cover over the evacuation—at least by day. As early as 20 May all available Kent-based Hurricane squadrons had been ordered to attack German motorized columns on the Cambrai-Arras road, and thereafter Hurricanes were sent over to operate from French airfields on a day-to-day basis until all had been overrun. For all the charges levelled at the RAF by soldiers of the BEF for failing to keep the *Luftwaffe* at bay, it must be recorded that at the time Operation Dynamo got under way German army commanders in the Pas de Calais were reporting for the first time since 10 May that the British fighter pilots had achieved air superiority over the ground battle.

On the first full day of the Dunkirk operations Park had at his disposal nine Spitfire squadrons, seven of Hurricanes[26] and No. 264 Squadron of Defiants. Until he could be certain of what the *Luftwaffe*'s tactics would be he preferred to employ no more than one squadron of fighters at a time on patrol over Dunkirk, and by doing so he was able to keep a continuous guard over the evacuation throughout the hours of daylight, with at least one squadron of Spitfires and one of Hurricanes ready at a moment's notice to scramble in case of a large-scale attack. In the event the Germans attacked the embarkation areas in considerable strength, being able to call on more than 220 bombers, about 60 Bf 110s and a single *Gruppe* (I./JG 27) of Bf 109Es; within 48 hours this force was strengthened by some 120 Ju 87 dive bombers and a similar number of Bf 109Es.

Owing to the relatively light fighter escort on the 27th Park's fighters were able to get in among the bombers and shot down about 16 and damaged a dozen others, losing four Hurricanes and four Spitfires. Although the bombers were able to get through and bomb Dunkirk itself, only two ships were sunk. Nevertheless Park realized that, provided no substantial numbers of Bf 109Es were encountered, he could risk doubling the strength of his patrols so as to destroy a larger proportion of the bombers. On the 28th, with most patrols flying at two-squadron strength, his pilots found fewer bombers (most had been prevented from taking off due to bad weather) but many more German fighters. A second *Gruppe* of Bf 109s had arrived on the Channel coast and both Hurricanes and Spitfires were drawn into wasteful and pointless combats; on that day only four bombers were destroyed, but in shooting down 19 German fighters the RAF lost 13 (with five pilots saved).

With the arrival of a fresh Spitfire Squadron and one of Hurricanes (No. 111 Squadron, Sqn Ldr John Marlow Thompson), Park—painfully aware that his fighters had frequently been outnumbered by as many as 10 to one—began operating patrols of four squadrons on the 29th, although they were not flown as wings but operated independently in pairs. On one occasion three Hurricane squadrons and the Defiants of No. 264 Squadron found themselves fighting a skyful of about 80 Bf 109Es attempting to cover a dive bombing attack by Ju 87s. For once the odds were not so heavily stacked against the RAF

The first Canadian-built Hurricane I, P5170, *which made its first flight at the Fort William factory on 9th January 1940 before being shipped to Britain for evaluation by the RAF.* (Photo: *via Sqn Ldr R. C. B. Ashworth)*

fighters and about 22 enemy aircraft were shot down (including 15 claimed by the Defiants); four Hurricanes were lost and many others landed back with battle damage. Moreover, preoccupation with the escorting Messerschmitts had enabled the raid to get through to Dunkirk, where five ships were sunk.

On the 30th bad weather again reduced air activity considerably and by that evening a total of more than 140,000 men had been evacuated since the beginning of Operation Dynamo. By now the *Luftwaffe* was employing its Ju 87s to their best effect on shipping targets; although they remained grounded by continuing bad weather on the 31st they were airborne in strength once more on 1 June and managed to penetrate the RAF's fighter cover by slipping through between patrols—sinking three destroyers (HMS *Basilisk, Keith* and *Skipjack*), laden with troops.

Further air actions were fought during the 2nd and 3rd, but by then the evacuation was being confined largely to the hours of darkness and this certainly kept casualties among men and ships to a minimum. Early on the 2nd a raid by about 120 German aircraft found five RAF fighter squadrons waiting for it over Dunkirk, and the Hurricane and Spitfire pilots kept the enemy bomber crews so busy defending themselves that the attackers failed to do any serious damage among the ships still in the port. This proved to be the last major raid and the *Luftwaffe* contented itself by sending over small numbers of Ju 87s and Ju 88s in bids to sneak through gaps in the fighter cover. Soon after midnight on 3/4 June the evacuation of the Allied troops came to an end; no fewer than 338,226 British and French troops had been brought out of France. Through no fault of the RAF—rather that of disorganization on the ground—about 25,000 French troops had had to be left behind.

The cost of the nine-day operation had been heavy: 135 Spitfires, Hurricanes, Blenheims and Defiants lost, and 84 pilots killed or posted missing. Yet even so, the trauma of the Hurricane squadrons in France was not yet over. Units of the British Army that had not been isolated by the German thrust to the Channel coast were now being forced westwards through northern France, as one by one the ports through which they might have escaped fell to the *Wehrmacht*. All the while the few remaining Hurricanes and Battles of the AASF did what they could to provide air cover. Two squadrons of Hurricanes, Nos. 17 and 242, were sent to France to help, the former occupying the airfield at Le Mans from 8 until 16 June before making hurriedly for the small airstrips on Jersey and Guernsey, and thence to England two days later. No. 242 Squadron, which had been sending detachments to France since late May, was now ordered to move all pilots and aircraft across the Channel, eventually assembling at Ancevis; a move to Nantes was followed by final withdrawal to England on 16 June.

The last of the Hurricane squadrons to leave France were Nos. 1, 73 and 501; No. 1—as already mentioned—was evacuated by sea from St Nazaire, without its aircraft, on the 18th; No. 73, whose surviving aircraft were burned on the airfield at Nantes, escaped through St Malo on the 17th; and No. 501, whose task it was to cover the evacuation of BEF troops from Cherbourg on the 19th while flying from Jersey, brought back to England about eight Hurricanes during that and the following day.

The Battle of France and the Low Countries cost Britain the loss of 949 aircraft, including 477 fighters—of which 386 were Hurricanes from the squadrons which had borne the full brunt of combat. To men of lesser stature than Dowding and Park such sacrifice would have seemed too high for any likelihood of recovery. Worse, of almost 200 pilots killed, severely wounded or posted missing, 29 were squadron and flight commanders and all but about 40 were peacetime Regulars. Their replacement would take months to achieve with men of experience in leadership and skill, as Fighter Command braced itself to meet the full weight of the *Luftwaffe*, already beginning to establish its bases just over the horizon from southern England to the south.

6

FULL FURY OF THE STORM

For twenty-two years, ever since the last German bombers had departed English skies in the Kaiser's War, the problem of Britain's air defence had existed—largely ignored for much of that time, and only relatively recently attended to with urgency by men of ability, farsightedness, technical understanding and, above all, the financial support of a government with fire in its belly. And when the last of the little boats struggled home from Dunkirk with the tattered remnants of the British Expeditionary Force the nightmare reality of RAF Fighter Command's inevitable task loomed stark before its commanders and pilots alike. For in all the calculations on which the RAF's expansion during the past six years had been based, none had countenanced the collapse of France. The 52 fighter squadrons that had been the target strength had never taken account of that collapse, or that many of the fighter squadrons so carefully created and trained on the new fighters would suffer such grievous losses before the Command would be called on to defend British skies. Stanley Baldwin's vision of a war with Germany in which Britain's frontier would lie "on the Rhine"—an excellent cliché to provide awareness of modern warfare in the early 1930s—became suddenly dated as the German *Luftwaffe* occupied its new billets all round the coastline of northern Europe. Göring could actually *see* the RAF's radar station at Dover across the Strait from Calais!

On the credit side, about one-third of Fighter Command—particularly those Hurricane squadrons involved in the Battle of France—had gained priceless combat experience, alas experience that now suggested all too clearly that combat tactics perpetuated among British fighter pilots for almost a decade were not only ineffectual and inflexible but patently dangerous when employed against a German air force whose tactics owed much to the laboratory of Spain and which had been honed to razor sharpness over Poland, Norway, Holland, Belgium and France. In short the old Fighting Area Attacks, which involved set-piece, follow-my-leader formation approach to enemy aircraft, had to be discarded forthwith and replaced by some other, much more flexible style of attack. Unfortunately no time remained in which such tactics could be evolved and taught throughout the Command.

* * *

Fortunately for Dowding there came a month's pause between the end of the Dunkirk evacuation on 3 June and the opening of the *Luftwaffe*'s assault on Britain. Not only did the French continue to resist the German onrush for a further fortnight, thereby delaying the deployment of the German Air Force at its bases on the Channel coast, but a few priceless RAF Hurricane squadrons—with a few of their aircraft intact—were being forced ever westwards through France, unable or unwilling to disengage and return to England while British troops still needed their protection.

When, however, on 1 July, the German Army first set foot on British sovereign territory—the

Channel Islands—all RAF fighter squadrons were safely back home. On that day Fighter Command deployed the forces shown on pages 64 and 65.

From this it may be seen that the Hurricane equipped by far the larger number of Dowding's squadrons (indeed outnumbering all other aircraft combined), and that this numerical superiority existed in the strategically important No. 11 Group, deployed in southern England and commanded by Air Vice-Marshal Keith Park, a New Zealander whose brilliance in handling fighter forces in defensive situations was to stand Britain in good stead throughout the war. What is not evident from the foregoing table is the state of true operational readiness of the various squadrons. For instance, in No. 11 Group's 17 Hurricane squadrons the aircraft serviceability rate stood at about 76 per cent, this despite the fact that well over 100 of the aircraft had experienced prolonged service in France; none of the Spitfires, with a serviceability rate of 72 per cent, had fought in France, although about 35 of them had fought relatively briefly over Dunkirk.

Perhaps reflecting his realization that only the veterans of the French campaign were fully aware of the danger of employing the old FAA tactics Dowding retained these weary, battle-tested pilots in the south. This was particularly true of Nos. 1, 32, 79, 85, 501 and 615 Squadrons, which were carefully distributed among the key Sector airfields of Biggin Hill, North Weald, Kenley and Northolt, where their experienced pilots could "spread the word" among the other squadrons. A good example of this may be seen in the instance of No. 32 Squadron whose CO, John Worrall, had realized the futility of the old formation attacks and, with no time to evolve new tactics, had advocated the head-on charge as an opening attack; on the only occasion that No. 32 had adopted this drastic tactic (near Dunkirk) the German bombers had been forced to scatter, so that any semblance of an accurate bombing run disappeared. Worrall discussed this with John Joslin of No. 79 Squadron, also at Biggin Hill, and the head-on attack came subsequently to be used on a number of occasions, with good results, before Fighter Command started to adopt the paired-aircraft combat unit towards the end of the battle. Coincidentally the same head-on attack had been tried by No. 501 Squadron (an Auxiliary squadron, be it noted)—though with less spectacular results—and it evidently appealed to John Thompson of No. 111 Squadron at Kenley, and again it "caught on". On at least one occasion Nos. 32 and 111 Squadrons went into battle side by side, attacking a formation of Dornier 17s head-on, with fairly dramatic results. It was not, however, a tactic that appealed to the fainthearted (on either side).

One further observation should be made with regard to Dowding's deployment of his fighters; it is also a reflection of the relative combat readiness of the Hurricane compared with that of the Spitfire. Owing to the more modern stressed-skin construction of the Spitfire it was realized by the Air Ministry that—at least in the early months of the war—Spitfires would require special maintenance facilities and servicing personnel; such facilities would first be made available at a few designated "Spitfire bases", of which Hornchurch, Duxford, Biggin Hill and Middle Wallop would be the first, and completed in that order. It may be seen from

Plt Off Albert Gerald Lewis of No 85 Squadron from Kimberley, South Africa, prepares for a sortie in his Hurricane at Croydon during the Battle of Britain. Commissioned in the RAF just before the War, Lewis had shot down nine German aircraft in the Battle of France and destroyed nine more in the Battle of Britain. He later served in Iraq and Ceylon, and finished the War as a squadron leader with 21 victories and two DFCs. (Photo: *via R. L. Ward, Farnborough*)

the quoted Order of Battle that only Hornchurch yet possessed three Spitfire squadrons, and that at Filton, for example, the two Spitfire squadrons suffered a somewhat low serviceability rate—a state of affairs not assisted by "forward" airfields located some distance away.

As powerful justification of Sydney Camm's design philosophy, there were to be countless occasions in the coming months when Hurricane pilots were forced, through battle damage to their aircraft, to land at a forward airfield where only relatively primitive servicing and repair facilities existed, and yet within a few hours were able to take off once more in a fully serviceable aircraft. Unfortunately the same could not be said for the Spitfire—at least during the first half of the battle ahead—which frequently had to be dismantled and transported by road back to its Sector airfield if it had suffered anything but superficial airframe damage.

These remarks are in no way intended to be critical of the Spitfire, but simply to explain the extent to which the Spitfire's combat readiness lagged somewhat behind that of the Hurricane; in many respects the situation improved markedly as the battle proceeded, as servicing and serviceability steadily improved. Yet it has to be said that during the early stages of the battle at least, Dowding and his Group and Sector commanders had still to feel their way when committing many of the Spitfire squadrons to combat; on at least six Spitfire squadrons some aircraft were still subject to combat-at-altitude restrictions as efforts were still being made to overcome gun icing and canopy misting problems. By contrast the Hurricane was by now generally regarded by all as a viceless, "go anywhere, do anything" aeroplane—even if it couldn't quite keep up with its partner in arms.

Thus it was when on 1 July the *Luftwaffe* launched a small number of probing sorties along the east coast of England Dowding possessed a fighter force of 905 aircraft (comprising Hurricanes, Spitfires, Blenheims and Defiants) at first-line strength; in addition 92 Hurricanes, 31 Spitfires, 17 Blenheims and seven Defiants constituted his immediate reserve at maintenance units, plus a total of 38 single-seat fighters (including some Gladiators) which were on strength with Group fighter pools and station flights and could be called on at short notice if desperately required.

The pilot situation was, if anything, less healthy following the *débâcle* in France, the total of 1,103 listed as being on state with the squadrons being somewhat illusory; as far as can be determined only about 820 of these pilots were regarded as fully combat-ready, the remainder not fully "checked out" by their flight commanders and still requiring the final polishing of flying discipline with their squadrons.

Behind the front line the training units were passing out around 20 Hurricane pilots each week as well as about half a dozen pilots trained on Spitfires, but these figures need qualification: almost all newly built aircraft were being delivered to the Maintenance Units for the front line squadrons, while most of the very early production aircraft (such as the original L-batch Hurricanes with wooden propellers, fabric wings and ring-and-bead sights) were being flown by the Operational Training Units. A pilot arriving on his first operational squadron needed a further short spell to acquaint himself with the variable-pitch propeller and reflector gunsight (although many operational pilots still favoured the retention of the bead foresight, even after the reflector gunsight had been fitted). This pattern of competent pilot shortage—and if a squadron remained below its established strength of 18 fully operational pilots there *was* a shortage—compared to aircraft availability was to dog Fighter Command throughout the battle and reached a crisis early in September when pilot losses amounted to the equivalent of two whole squadrons each day. By then training courses at the OTUs had been so shortened that pilots were arriving on the squadrons with fewer than 20 flying hours on Hurricanes and Spitfires, and were obliged to acclimatize themselves with their operational fighters on their first combat sortie!

The July Phase

When German air attacks opened at the beginning of July it was not immediately clear to Dowding or Park what their purpose was, other than that of the reconnaissance aircraft which flew high-level sorties over the industrial Midlands and the sea ports. During the first ten days there was a small number of set-piece raids by Junkers Ju 87 dive bombers, almost certainly of *III.Gruppe, Stukageschwader 51* flying from the Cherbourg area, against British merchant convoys approaching the South Coast, but only when the *Luftwaffe* ventured to attack the ports and naval bases themselves were they intercepted by British fighters; Portland in particular came in for a number of attacks.

However, after a number of attacks, usually by small escorted formations of Dornier Do 17s on coastal convoys in the Channel and off the East Coast, it became clear that their purpose was twofold: to provide experience for German aircrews in over-sea operations (hitherto a type of flying—and navigation—in which the *Luftwaffe* had carried out no training), and to force the British fighters to engage in wasteful and wearing standing patrols over the slow-moving convoys.

The first major convoy attack to confirm the German plan took place on 7 July over a deep-sea convoy which was sailing up the Channel to the Thames Estuary. As the ships approached the Isle of Wight during the morning the standing patrol was assumed by the Hurricanes of No. 145 Squadron, whose CO, Sqn Ldr John Peel, and Plt Off

ROYAL AIR FORCE FIGHTER COMMAND ORDER OF BATTLE, 09.00hrs, 1st July 1940

Sector	*Sqn*	*Aircraft*	*Combat Ready (Unserviceable)*	*Base Airfield*	*Pilots on State*	*Commanding Officer*
No. 11 Group, HQ Uxbridge, Middlesex: Air Vice-Marshal Keith Rodney Park						
Biggin Hill	32 Sqn	Hurricanes	12 (4)	Biggin Hill	16	Sqn Ldr J. Worrall
	79 Sqn (A)	Hurricanes	12 (5)	Biggin Hill	14	Sqn Ldr J. D. Joslin
	245 Sqn (B)	Hurricanes	15 (1)	Hawkinge	16	Sqn Ldr E. W. Whitley
	600 Sqn	Blenheims	8 (6)	Manston	22	Sqn Ldr D. de B. Clarke
	610 Sqn	Spitfires	14 (3)	Gravesend	20	Sqn Ldr A. T. Smith
North Weald	25 Sqn	Blenheims	6 (10)	Martlesham Heath	22	Sqn Ldr K. A. K. McEwan
	56 Sqn	Hurricanes	16 (2)	North Weald	20	Sqn Ldr G. A. L. Manton
	85 Sqn	Hurricanes	15 (3)	Martlesham Heath	21	Sqn Ldr P. W. Townsend
	151 Sqn	Hurricanes	14 (4)	North Weald	20	Sqn Ldr E. M. Donaldson
Kenley	64 Sqn	Spitfires	10 (4)	Kenley	19	Sqn Ldr N. C. Odbert
	111 Sqn	Hurricanes	12 (4)	Croydon	17	Sqn Ldr J. M. Thompson
	501 Sqn	Hurricanes	10 (5)	Croydon	18	Sqn Ldr H. A. V. Hogan
	615 Sqn	Hurricanes	12 (6)	Kenley	21	Sqn Ldr J. R. Kayll
Northolt	1 Sqn	Hurricanes	10 (6)	Northolt	18	Sqn Ldr D. A. Pemberton
	257 Sqn	Hurricanes	13 (5)	Hendon	17	Sqn Ldr D. W. Bayne
	604 Sqn	Blenheims	10 (6)	Northolt	21	Sqn Ldr M. F. Anderson
	609 Sqn	Spitfires	15 (2)	Northolt	18	Sqn Ldr H. S. Darley
Hornchurch	54 Sqn	Spitfires	12 (3)	Rochford	18	Sqn Ldr J. L. Leathart
	65 Sqn	Spitfires	11 (5)	Hornchurch	16	Sqn Ldr D. Cooke
	74 Sqn	Spitfires	10 (7)	Hornchurch	20	Sqn Ldr F. L. White
Tangmere	43 Sqn	Hurricanes	13 (4)	Tangmere	18	Sqn Ldr C. G. Lott
	145 Sqn	Hurricanes	11 (7)	Tangmere	17	Sqn Ldr J. R. A. Peel
	601 Sqn	Hurricanes	15 (2)	Tangmere	19	Sqn Ldr the Hon M. Aitken
	FIU	Blenheims	4 (4)	Tangmere	10	Wing Cdr G. P. Chamberlain
Filton	92 Sqn	Spitfires	11 (6)	Pembrey	19	Sqn Ldr P. J. Sanders
	213 Sqn	Hurricanes	14 (4)	Exeter	20	Sqn Ldr H. D. McGregor
	234 Sqn	Spitfires	9 (6)	St. Eval	21	Sqn Ldr R. E. Barnett
Middle Wallop	236 Sqn	Blenheims	11 (4)	Middle Wallop	19	Sqn Ldr P. E. Drew
	238 Sqn (C)	Hurricanes	10 (2)	Middle Wallop	17	Sqn Ldr H. A. Fenton
Debden	17 Sqn	Hurricanes	14 (4)	Debden	19	Sqn Ldr R. I. G. MacDougall

No. 12 Group, HQ Watnall, Nottingham: Air Vice-Marshal Trafford Leigh Leigh-Mallory						
Duxford	19 Sqn	Spitfires	8 (5)	Fowlmere	24	Sqn Ldr P. C. Pinkham
	264 Sqn	Defiants	11 (7)	Duxford	23	Sqn Ldr P. A. Hunter
Coltishall	66 Sqn	Spitfires	12 (4)	Coltishall	25	Sqn Ldr R. H. A. Leigh
	242 Sqn	Hurricanes	10 (4)	Coltishall	21	Sqn Ldr D. R. S. Bader
Kirton-in-Lindsey	222 Sqn	Spitfires	12 (4)	Kirton-in-Lindsey	21	Sqn Ldr H. W. Mermagen
Digby	29 Sqn	Blenheims	10 (5)	Digby	15	Flt Lt J. S. Adams
	46 Sqn	Hurricanes	15 (3)	Digby	17	Flt Lt A. D. Murray
	611 Sqn	Spitfires	3 (11)	Digby	21	Sqn Ldr J. E. McComb
Wittering	23 Sqn	Blenheims	10 (6)	Colly Weston	20	Sqn Ldr L. C. Bicknell
	229 Sqn	Hurricanes	14 (2)	Wittering	20	Sqn Ldr H. J. Maguire
	266 Sqn	Spitfires	8 (5)	Wittering	21	Sqn Ldr J. W. A. Hunnard
No. 13 Group, HQ Newcastle, Northumberland: Air Vice-Marshal Richard Ernest Saul						
Church Fenton	73 Sqn	Hurricanes	8 (5)	Church Fenton	22	Sqn Ldr J. W. C. More
	87 Sqn	Hurricanes	14 (4)	Church Fenton	23	Sqn Ldr J. S. Dewar
	249 Sqn	Hurricanes	10 (4)	Leconfield	23	Sqn Ldr J. Grandy
	616 Sqn	Spitfires	11 (4)	Church Fenton	19	Sqn Ldr M. Robinson
Catterick	41 Sqn	Spitfires	11 (6)	Catterick	21	Sqn Ldr H. West
	219 Sqn	Blenheims	10 (4)	Catterick	19	Sqn Ldr J. H. Little
Usworth	72 Sqn	Spitfires	12 (4)	Acklington	19	Sqn Ldr R. B. Lees
	152 Sqn	Spitfires	8 (4)	Acklington	25	Sqn Ldr P. K. Devitt
	607 Sqn	Hurricanes	10 (6)	Usworth	17	Sqn Ldr J. A. Vick
Turnhouse	141 Sqn	Defiants	14 (5)	Turnhouse	20	Sqn Ldr W. A. Richardson
	253 Sqn	Hurricanes	13 (5)	Turnhouse	19	Sqn Ldr H. Starr
	602 Sqn	Spitfires	12 (4)	Drem	19	Sqn Ldr G. C. Pinkerton
	603 Sqn (D)	Spitfires	10 (6)	Turnhouse	19	Sqn Ldr E. H. Stevens
	605 Sqn (E)	Hurricanes	8 (6)	Drem	17	Sqn Ldr W. M. Churchill
Dyce	263 Sqn (F)	Hurricanes	3 (2)	Grangemouth	7	Sqn Ldr H. Eeles
Wick	3 Sqn	Hurricanes	12 (2)	Wick	18	Sqn Ldr S. F. Godden
	504 Sqn	Hurricanes	12 (4)	Castletown	15	Sqn Ldr J. Sample

Notes: (A) Squadron moving to Hawkinge. Non-operational during transit.
(B) Squadron ready to move to Turnhouse to rest and re-train.
(C) Squadron non-operational. Still working up after recent formation.
(D) Flights detached at Dyce and Montrose.
(E) Squadron non-operational. Resting and re-training.
(F) One flight only. Still working up after Norwegian campaign; one flight to receive Westland Whirlwinds.

*Aircraft of 'A' Flight, No 56 Squadron, scramble from North Weald during the Battle of Britain, almost certainly towards the end of August 1940. (*Photo: *Star News Service)*

Ernest Wakeham shot down a shadowing Do 17P. Soon afterwards, No. 43 Squadron's Hurricanes took over the escort duties and shot down another Do 17P, which crashed in France. Later still yet another Dornier was shot down by Sqn Ldr the Hon. Max Aitken of No. 601 Squadron. In the late afternoon, as the convoy sailed along the Sussex and Kent coast, the *Luftwaffe* sent over several *Staffeln* of Bf 109E fighters on "free chases" in the hope of catching RAF fighters on their way to and from their standing patrols. Relying on radar to provide warning of attacks on the convoy, Park had no such patrols airborne at that time, and as the low-flying German fighters escaped detection until they reached the Sussex coast the Spitfires of Nos. 64 and 65 Squadrons, scrambled from Kenley and Hornchurch, were too late to meet this wave of Bf 109s. Shortly afterwards, however, a raid by 45 Dorniers *was* detected approaching the convoy, but as the Spitfires were directed to intercept it a free chase by *Jagdgeschwader 27* attacked No. 65 Squadron from above and shot down an entire section of Spitfires.

The air combats on this day had resulted in the destruction of seven German bombers—but no fighters—for the loss of five Spitfires and a Hurricane, with four pilots killed and two slightly wounded. The Hurricane, which crashed near Folkestone (possibly not the result of combat), was flown by Sqn Ldr Joslin of No. 79 Squadron, who tragically lost his life.

Confirmation of the German aims brought no

*Refuelling and re-arming a Hurricane I during the Battle of Britain period. (*Photo: *Fleet Street News Service)*

comfort to Dowding, for at that moment there were seven British coastal convoys at sea and three large deep-sea convoys entering the Western Approaches. Moreover, the launching of free-chase attacks by the Germans over southern England introduced an unexpected and dangerous complication for his fighters as they took off to fly convoy patrols or landed at base short of fuel and ammunition. On the following day the *Luftwaffe* stepped up its attacks on the convoys, dividing its attention between shipping off the Suffolk coast and in the Thames Estuary, English Channel and Bristol Channel. Now determined to avoid exposure of his own fighters to pointless combat with the excellent German Emils, Park was careful not to order the Hurricanes and Spitfires into the air without being certain that no enemy free chases were in progress over the southern counties. Such caution was scarcely practical in the area of Dover, where a free-chasing *Staffel* could appear at no more than two or three minutes' notice. As it was the Spitfire pilots of Nos. 65 and 74 Squadrons had a hectic time in combat with Bf 109Es of Werner Mölders' *Jagdgeschwader 51* near Dover, the former squadron losing its CO, Sqn Ldr Desmond Cooke, on the very day he was due to hand over to Sqn Ldr Henry Sawyer, who himself had narrowly missed being shot down in the morning! Nevertheless, results of this day's fighting were more encouraging, with the Hurricanes shooting down two German bombers off the Sussex and Yorkshire coasts and the Spitfires destroying a reconnaissance Heinkel over the Firth of Forth and four Bf 109Es over Kent. British losses in combat amounted to two Spitfires and two Hurricanes, all of whose pilots were lost—two of them drowned after baling out over the sea.

The first 10 days of July can now be seen as a period of skirmishing by the German Air Force, it being discovered later that the *Luftwaffe* (at the insistence of the *Kriegsmarine*) was under orders to deny British shipping free passage through the English Channel and to discourage the Royal Navy from using its bases at Plymouth, Portland, Portsmouth and Dover. Those 10 days of air combat had cost the *Luftwaffe* the loss of 36 bombers (some of which were shot down by British ground defences), 15 fighters and seven other aircraft. RAF losses amounted to eight Hurricanes, 12 Spitfires and a Blenheim. Spitfires shot down 14 German bombers, six fighters and five other aircraft (reconnaissance aircraft and air-sea rescue seaplanes), and Hurricanes destroyed 13 bombers, seven fighters and a reconnaissance aircraft. Five pilots of Hurricanes and nine of Spitfires had been killed, including the COs of No. 79 (Hurricane) Squadron and No. 65 (Spitfire) Squadron. Sqn Ldr Charles Lott, CO of No. 43 Squadron, had, however, been blinded in one eye when his Hurricane's windscreen was shattered by enemy fire on the 9th and had to hand over command to Sqn Ldr John Badger.

The air fighting of 10 July involved the largest dogfight so far witnessed during the battle when 22 Hurricanes of Nos. 32, 56 and 111 Squadrons and eight Spitfires of No. 74 Squadron fought 26 Dornier Do 17s of *I.Gruppe, Kampfgeschwader 2 "Holzhammer"*, 30 Messerschmitt Bf 110s of *I.Gruppe, Zerstörergeschwader 26 "Horst Wessel"* and 20 Bf 109Es of *I.Gruppe, Jagdgeschwader 3 "Udet"* over convoy "Bread" off the Kentish coast. This was the first occasion on which No. 111 Squadron's Hurricanes entered combat with a line-abreast head-on attack against German bombers, but, in forcing the Dorniers to scatter, it cost the life of Fg Off Tom Higgs. Another 111 pilot, Fg Off Henry Ferris, had his aileron controls shot away, but, instead of putting down at a forward airfield, decided to make for his Sector airfield and, despite being under constant attack by enemy fighters, managed to land safely at Croydon, where he jumped into another Hurricane and immediately took off to rejoin the fight. Ironically Ferris was to lose his life five weeks later—in a head-on attack.

One other event on this day was the withdrawal of No. 79 Squadron from the scene of battle in the south. Its pilots had been in constant action for two months and had suffered heavily, including the loss of the CO and two other pilots during the three previous days. The suggestion that John Joslin may have died in an accident caused by extreme combat fatigue prompted Dowding to order the squadron north to Turnhouse to rest and recover. It was back in the thick of the battle before the end of August.

The *Luftwaffe* continued to press its attacks on the Channel convoys and on the naval bases in the south throughout the remainder of July. On the 11th attacks on a convoy near the Isle of Wight cost the Germans eight bombers and three Bf 110s—all shot down by the Hurricanes of Nos. 145, 238 and 601 Squadrons, which lost two aircraft; both pilots were saved—one of them No. 145's CO, Sqn Ldr John Peel, who was rescued unconscious but unwounded from the sea by the Selsey lifeboat. Off the Norfolk coast near Cromer a weather reconnaissance Dornier 17 was shot down by the famous legless pilot Sqn Ldr Douglas Bader, who commanded No. 242 Squadron at Coltishall.

On the 12th it was the turn of convoy "Booty", off the Suffolk coast, to come under attack by unescorted Dorniers of *Kampfgeschwader 2* and Heinkels of *Kampfgeschwader 53*, whose crews had been ordered to maintain the tightest possible formation even when attacked by British fighters, and their vicious crossfire cost the loss of two Hurricanes of Nos. 85 and 151 Squadrons, both pilots being killed. On this occasion Wg Cdr Victor Beamish (North Weald's station commander) had jumped into a Station Flight Hurricane to fly as No. 2 to Sqn Ldr "Teddy" Donaldson, No. 151's squadron commander; both pilots damaged enemy aircraft but returned to North Weald with plenty of scars on their aircraft. In all, two Do 17s and three Heinkels were destroyed—one of the Dorniers and two He 111s falling to the guns of No. 17 Squadron's Hurricanes.

Further heavy fighting took place over convoy "Bread" in the Channel on the 13th, the Hurricanes of Nos 43, 56 and 238 Squadrons despatching two Dornier 17s, a Junkers 88, a Bf 110 and a Bf 109E for the loss of three aircraft and all their pilots.

The next noteworthy action by Hurricanes was fought on 19 July, although its significance lay not in their pilots' victories but in its circumstance. In a belief that the Defiant two-seat turret fighter might represent a suitable "convoy escort" fighter, Dowding had ordered No. 141 Squadron south from Turnhouse to West Malling in the Biggin Hill Sector to replace No. 79 and to help relieve the single-seaters in some of this wearisome task. During the course of a patrol on this day south of Folkestone by nine Defiants, their pilots were surprised by a devastating attack by 10 Bf 109Es of *II.Gruppe, Jagdgeschwader 2 "Richthofen"*, and in less than a minute five of the British fighters—which possessed no forward-firing wing-guns—were falling in flames; all five gunners were lost, as were four pilots. Only the arrival of John Thompson's Hurricanes of No. 111 Squadron in the nick of time allowed the other four Defiants to disengage and escape. On that day RAF losses exceeded those of the *Luftwaffe*: in addition to the five Defiants (plus another which crashed on landing), four Hurricanes were lost; the four German aircraft shot down comprised a Do 17 and an He 111 claimed by Hurricane pilots, and a Bf 109E and Heinkel He 115 minelayer shot down by Spitfires.

Although the increasing tempo of attacks continued daily for the remainder of the month, only one other day's fighting, that of the 29th, was of particular importance with regard to the Hurricanes' involvement. Early on that day two convoys were at sea off the Kentish coast, and when the CH radars reported a significant build-up of German aircraft over the Pas de Calais, Park naturally anticipated heavy air attacks on the ships. He immediately ordered No. 41 Squadron's Spitfires to stand by for take-off at Manston as well as the Hurricanes of No. 501 at Hawkinge. When it suddenly became evident that the German attack was aimed at neither convoy but at Dover itself the 11 Spitfires and 12 Hurricanes were scrambled to intercept. Their pilots soon spotted a force of 48 Ju 87s, bent on attacking Dover harbour, under a veritable umbrella of about 80 Bf 109Es. In the ensuing fight four of the dive bombers were shot down (two by each squadron)—a score that would probably have been greater had the Dover gun defences not persisted in firing into the dogfight.

The two convoys did not in fact escape the Germans' attention, one being attacked in the Channel by a force of low-flying Ju 88s, which were not spotted by radar and thus escaped interception by No. 610 Squadron's Spitfires (although one of the raiders was brought down—carrying the *Gruppenkommandeur* of *III.Gruppe, Kampfgeschwader 76*, to his death—by a shipborne barrage balloon cable).

The other convoy, northbound from the Thames Estuary, came under attack by 11 bomb-carrying Bf 110Cs of *Erprobungsgruppe 210*, escorted by 30 Bf 110C fighters of *Zerstörergeschwader 26*. From both British and German accounts the air combat that ensued over the ships was brief, vicious and inconclusive; one Spitfire written off and its pilot wounded and two Hurricanes of No. 151 Squadron damaged. At least one of *Erpr.Gr 210*'s aircraft was badly damaged but managed to struggle home.

The significance of this attack lay in the involvement of *Erpr.Gr 210*, an extraordinary unit comprising two *Staffeln* of bomb-carrying Bf 110s and one of bomb-carrying Bf 109Es. It had been formed early in July with the object of introducing fighter-bomber tactics into the *Luftwaffe* under the command of a much-respected junior officer, Hauptmann Walter Rubensdörffer. Fundamental to these tactics were a low fast or diving approach to the target, led by the single-seaters, which made a single pass, each dropping a single bomb before pulling up to act as top cover for the Bf 110s following close behind. The *Gruppe*'s targets at this stage of the Battle of Britain were almost invariably vital and often heavily defended objectives such as fast convoys, dock installations, aircraft factories and radar installations.

However, even as early as June it had been discovered that the much-vaunted Bf 110—despite its high speed (about 350 mph at 22,000 feet) and useful armament of two 20 mm cannon and five or six machine guns—was capable of being matched in combat by the Hurricane. Indeed there had been at least half a dozen instances of hard-pressed Bf 110 formations resorting to their characteristic defensive circle in which the German pilots adopted a circling formation so that each aircraft covered the tail of the aircraft in front, the whole formation gradually moving away from the scene of combat. Hurricane pilots in particular discovered that their own excellent manoeuvrability enabled them to attack these "circles of death" from various angles without exposing themselves to the Bf 110s' front guns and to break away without much loss of height. It was largely *Erpr.Gr 210*'s relatively low altitude of approach that resulted in Hurricane squadrons meeting this formidable unit on numerous occasions during the battle. Indeed the *Gruppe* was to lose three *Kommandeurs* to Hurricanes: Rubensdörffer to No. 111 Squadron on 15 August, von Boltenstern to No. 601 Squadron on 4 September and Werner Weimann to No. 303 (Polish) Squadron on 5 October; seven *Staffelkapitäne* also fell before Hurricane guns.

At the time of the convoy attack on 29 July the RAF was still unaware of *Erpr.Gr 210*'s existence, but as evidence accumulated it was seen to be something of an élite unit and the tenacity with which its attacks were carried out soon became a hallmark of its operations.

And so the skirmishing of July—for such it proved when compared with the very heavy fighting of the next two months—came to an end. During the course of the whole month, during which the *Luftwaffe* had not attempted any major daylight raids beyond the coastal counties, the following casualties were suffered.

GERMAN AIRCRAFT SHOT DOWN, JULY 1940

Shot down by	*Do 17*	*He 111*	*Ju 88*	*Ju 87*	*Bf 109*	*Bf 110*	*Other Aircraft*	*Total*
Hurricanes	15	17	7	10	12	14	12	87
Spitfires	8	12	12	4	26	3	6	71
Blenheims	2	–	1	–	–	–	1	4
Other defences	6	2	5	2	1	3	6	25
Totals	31	31	25	16	39	20	25	187

RAF FIGHTERS SHOT DOWN, JULY 1940

	Hurricanes	*Spitfires*	*Blenheims*	*Defiants*	*Total*
By German fighters	22	33	2	6	63
By German bombers	9	5	–	–	14
By other combat causes	9*	1	5	–	15
Totals	40	39	7	6	92
Pilots/aircrew killed	16	24	5	10	55
Fighters listed as "lost" but salvaged, repaired and returned to Fighter Command	9	2	1	–	12

* Including two shot down by British defences

August and the Defeat of the Dive Bomber

Dowding may have had some cause for qualified satisfaction with the manner in which Fighter Command had withstood the fighting of July. In terms of aircraft destroyed the losses suffered by each side were believed at the time to be roughly three to one in his favour—much later this was found to be no more than about two to one; in terms of losses among pilots and aircrew, at about seven to one in the RAF's favour, the contemporary estimate was much nearer the mark. Losses among his Hurricane pilots had been more than made good, but some of the Spitfire squadrons were still struggling to reach their established strength. The pilot situation had been relieved by the intake of some Fleet Air Arm volunteer pilots as well as the arrival at British ports of a fast-growing number of Czech, Polish and American volunteer pilots, and the first Royal Canadian Air Force squadron, all of whom at this stage were being or had been trained on Hurricanes. The total number of fighter squadrons had been increased slightly, while No. 11 Group, generally felt to be too large for efficient handling from one headquarters, had shed two sectors to form a new Group, No. 10, to cover the West Country and the Bristol Channel.

Yet although the number of squadrons seemed on paper to be approaching the magic figure of 52, the true number of fully operational squadrons still only represented about 75 per cent of the Command's strength. And Dowding realized all to well that the main battle had yet to be fought.

Notwithstanding these problems, the Germans in one respect achieved their initial aim when, at the beginning of August, the British Admiralty decided to discontinue sailing merchant convoys through the English Channel and could therefore move its destroyers and other naval vessels away from the Channel bases. This at least absolved Fighter Command of its responsibility for wasteful standing patrols over slow-moving ships and their understandably trigger-happy gunners.

The first seven days of August witnessed a gradual but temporary reduction in German air activity, partly on account of poor weather and partly of a general redeployment of forces in preparation for the main assault. Sporadic air fighting continued, but Dowding was able to take the opportunity to redeploy some of his squadrons. On the 2nd was formed No. 303 (Polish) Squadron at Northolt, which, like No. 302 (which had been formed on 17 July), was equipped with Hurricanes—but would not figure in Fighter Command's Order of Battle for several more weeks.

On 8 August the battle began in earnest, the *Luftwaffe* now under orders to "wipe out" the RAF fighter defences prior to an air- and seaborne invasion intended to be launched about one month hence. Convinced by his own propaganda reports, Hermann Göring believed that Fighter Command had already been considerably weakened by the fighting of July and now felt that his bombers could attack the RAF's fighter airfields in the southern counties and coastal radar stations without risk of heavy losses. For attacks against pinpoint targets the Junkers Ju 87 dive bomber was regarded as extremely accurate and, given suitable fighter escort, could be expected to devastate Fighter Command's key installations. The fallacy of this lay in the *Luftwaffe*'s inability to provide a *suitable* escort fighter, for the intended aircraft—the Bf 110—was generally unable to hold its own against the Hurricane and Spitfire and, with increasing regularity, had itself to be provided with a covering force of Bf 109Es. Not only were the excellent Emils unable to penetrate far over the English South Coast or linger long when brought to combat, but the preoccupation with the defence of other aircraft markedly reduced the number of "free-chase" sweeps that had been causing such serious problems for Park's squadrons.

Despite the Admiralty's decision to discontinue sailing convoys in the English Channel the recent lull in German air activity encouraged the Royal Navy to shepherd 20 merchantmen in ballast from the Thames Estuary and Medway to the western ports, hoping to pass them undetected through the

ROYAL AIR FORCE FIGHTER COMMAND ORDER OF BATTLE, 09.00hrs, 1st August 1940

Sector	Sqn	Aircraft	Combat Ready (Unserviceable)	Base Airfield	Pilots on State	Commanding Officer
No. 10 Group, HQ Rudloe Manor, Box, Wiltshire: Air Vice-Marshal Sir Christopher Quintin Brand						
Middle Wallop	152 Sqn	Spitfires	10 (5)	Warmwell	20	Sqn Ldr P. K. Devitt
	238 Sqn	Hurricanes	12 (3)	Middle Wallop	18	Sqn Ldr H. A. Fenton
	604 Sqn	Blenheims	10 (5)	Middle Wallop	20	Sqn Ldr M. F. Anderson
	609 Sqn	Spitfires	10 (6)	Middle Wallop	18	Sqn Ldr H. S. Darley
Filton	87 Sqn	Hurricanes	13 (5)	Exeter	20	Sqn Ldr T. G. Lovell-Gregg
	92 Sqn	Spitfires	12 (4)	Pembrey	17	Sqn Ldr P. J. Sanders
	213 Sqn	Hurricanes	12 (5)	Exeter	19	Sqn Ldr H. D. McGregor
	234 Sqn	Spitfires	10 (6)	St Eval	22	Sqn Ldr R. E. Barnett
No. 11 Group, HQ Uxbridge, Middlesex: Air Vice-Marshal Keith Rodney Park						
Biggin Hill	32 Sqn	Hurricanes	11 (4)	Biggin Hill	18	Sqn Ldr J. Worrall
	501 Sqn	Hurricanes	11 (5)	Gravesend	19	Sqn Ldr H. A. V. Hogan
	600 Sqn	Blenheims	9 (6)	Manston	20	Sqn Ldr D. de B. Clarke
	610 Sqn	Spitfires	12 (3)	Biggin Hill	18	Sqn Ldr J. Ellis
North Weald	25 Sqn	Blenheims	7 (7)	Martlesham Heath	22	Sqn Ldr K. A. K. McEwan
	56 Sqn	Hurricanes	15 (2)	North Weald	24	Sqn Ldr G. A. L. Manton
	85 Sqn	Hurricanes	12 (6)	Martlesham Heath	21	Sqn Ldr P. W. Townsend
	151 Sqn	Hurricanes	13 (5)	North Weald	19	Sqn Ldr E. M. Donaldson
Kenley	64 Sqn	Spitfires	12 (4)	Kenley	21	Sqn Ldr A. R. D. MacDonell
	111 Sqn	Hurricanes	10 (2)	Croydon	20	Sqn Ldr J. M. Thompson
	615 Sqn	Hurricanes	14 (2)	Kenley	23	Sqn Ldr J. R. Kayall
Northolt	43 Sqn (1)	Hurricanes	18 (1)	Northolt	18	Sqn Ldr J. V. C. Badger
	257 Sqn	Hurricanes	10 (5)	Northolt	14	Sqn Ldr H. Harkness
Hornchurch	41 Sqn	Spitfires	10 (6)	Hornchurch	19	Sqn Ldr H. West
	65 Sqn	Spitfires	11 (5)	Hornchurch	19	Sqn Ldr H. C. Sawyer
	74 Sqn	Spitfires	12 (3)	Hornchurch	14	Sqn Ldr F. L. White
Tangmere	1 Sqn (2)	Hurricanes	13 (3)	Tangmere	19	Sqn Ldr D. A. Pemberton
	145 Sqn	Hurricanes	10 (7)	Westhampnett	21	Sqn Ldr J. R. A. Peel
	266 Sqn	Spitfires	13 (5)	Tangmere	20	Sqn Ldr R. L. Wilkinson
	601 Sqn	Hurricanes	14 (4)	Tangmere	23	Sqn Ldr W. F. C. Hobson
	FIU	Blenheims	4 (3)	Tangmere	11	Wing Cdr G. P. Chamberlain
Debden	17 Sqn	Hurricanes	14 (5)	Debden	19	Sqn Ldr C. W. Williams

No. 12 Group, HQ Watnall, Nottingham: Air Vice-Marshal Trafford Leigh Leigh-Mallory						
Duxford	19 Sqn	Spitfires	9 (6)	Fowlmere	25	Sqn Ldr P. C. Pinkham
Coltishall	66 Sqn	Spitfires	12 (4)	Coltishall	26	Sqn Ldr R. H. A. Leigh
	242 Sqn	Hurricanes	11 (5)	Coltishall	25	Sqn Ldr D. R. S. Bader
Kirton-in-Lindsey	222 Sqn	Spitfires	14 (3)	Kirton-in-Lindsey	16	Sqn Ldr J. H. Hill
	264 Sqn	Defiants	12 (4)	Kirton-in-Lindsey	21	Sqn Ldr P. A. Hunter
Digby	29 Sqn	Blenheims	8 (4)	Digby	16	Sqn Ldr S. C. Widdows
	46 Sqn	Hurricanes	12 (5)	Digby	23	Flt Lt A. D. Murray
	611 Sqn	Spitfires	6 (7)	Digby and Ternhill	20	Sqn Ldr J. E. McComb
Wittering	23 Sqn	Blenheims	9 (5)	Colly Weston	22	Sqn Ldr L. C. Bicknell
	229 Sqn	Hurricanes	14 (4)	Wittering and Bircham Newton	16	Sqn Ldr H. J. Maguire
No 13 Group, HQ Newcastle, Northumberland: Air Vice-Marshal Richard Ernest Saul						
Church Fenton	73 Sqn	Hurricanes	11 (5)	Church Fenton	20	Sqn Ldr J. W. C. More
	249 Sqn	Hurricanes	11 (5)	Church Fenton	21	Sqn Ldr J. Grandy
	616 Sqn	Spitfires	12 (4)	Leconfield	20	Sqn Ldr M. Robinson
Catterick	54 Sqn	Spitfires	11 (3)	Catterick	15	Sqn Ldr J. L. Leathart
	219 Sqn	Blenheims	10 (5)	Leeming	18	Sqn Ldr J. H. Little
Usworth	72 Sqn	Spitfires	10 (5)	Acklington	19	Sqn Ldr A. R. Collins
	79 Sqn	Hurricanes	10 (2)	Acklington	14	Sqn Ldr J. H. Heyworth
	607 Sqn	Hurricanes	12 (4)	Usworth	15	Sqn Ldr J. A. Vick
Turnhouse	253 Sqn	Hurricanes	12 (4)	Turnhouse	17	Sqn Ldr T. P. Gleave
	602 Sqn	Spitfires	11 (4)	Drem	17	Sqn Ldr A. V. R. Johnstone
	603 Sqn	Spitfires	11 (4)	Turnhouse	20	—
	605 Sqn	Hurricanes	14 (4)	Drem	22	Sqn Ldr W. M. Churchill
Dyce	263 Sqn (3)	Hurricanes	4 (2)	Grangemouth	7	Sqn Ldr H. Eeles
Wick	3 Sqn	Hurricanes	10 (2)	Wick	20	Sqn Ldr S. F. Godden
	232 Sqn	Hurricanes	6 (4)	Sumburgh	9	Flt Lt M. M. Stephens
	504 Sqn	Hurricanes	13 (4)	Castletown	19	Sqn Ldr J. Sample
	804 Sqn, FAA	Gladiators	8 (6)	Wick	13+	Lt Cdr J. C. Cockburn, RN
	808 Sqn, FAA	Fulmars	6 (6)	Castletown	15	—
(Prestwick)	141 Sqn	Defiants	8 (4)	Prestwick	14	Sqn Ldr W. A. Richardson
Aldergrove	245 Sqn	Hurricanes	8 (2)	Aldergrove	15	Sqn Ldr F. W. Whitley

Notes: (1) Squadron moved to Tangmere on this day (1st August). (2) Squadron moved to Northolt on this day (1st August). (3) One flight only (used for local airfield defence).

Dover Strait during the night of 7 August. These hopes were dashed when newly installed *Freya* radar near Calais spotted the ships of convoy Peewit that night; at first light E-boats darted in and sank three merchantmen.

The E-boat attack was then followed by a number of dive bombing raids by the Ju 87s of *Fliegerkorps VIII* during the morning, but it was not until the afternoon, as the convoy passed to the south of the Isle of Wight, that the major attacks developed. Anticipating serious trouble Park, acting on warning from Ventnor CH radar, had put up an escort of 18 Hurricanes of Nos. 145, 238 and 257 Squadrons, with a dozen Spitfires of No. 609 Squadron on their way from Warmwell. The German force comprised 57 Ju 87s covered by 20 Bf 110s and about 30 Bf 109Es of *Jagdgeschwader 27*. Given adequate warning of the raid's approach, the Hurricanes had been able to climb above the German fighters and made their initial attack out of the sun, passing through the escort for a co-ordinated assault on the Ju 87s just as they were starting their diving attacks. No. 145 Squadron managed to shoot down two of the dive bombers before the 30 British fighters were furiously engaged by the German escort. Far below, the approach of the raiders had been a signal for the ships to scatter, but in so doing lost the main benefit of their own protective balloon barrage; this encouraged the Stuka pilots to release their bombs at low level, sinking four merchantmen and damaging seven others with near misses. In the fight overhead the Germans lost another Ju 87, a Bf 110 and three Bf 109Es; two Hurricanes of No. 238 Squadron and one from No. 257 were shot down before the Germans disengaged to protect the dive bombers on their way home. Shortly afterwards Sqn Ldr Fenton, hearing that two of his pilots were down in the sea, took off once more to search for them and came across a Heinkel He 59 seaplane similarly occupied; this he shot down, but in doing so was hit by return fire and had to ditch—being picked up by a British trawler.

Before being shot down the He 59's pilot probably radioed back the information that the survivors of convoy Peewit were trying to reassemble and sail on. A new raid, this time by 82 Ju 87s, covered by 68 Bf 110s and Bf 109Es, set out from France intending to catch the convoy in Weymouth Bay. This time the Hurricanes of Nos. 43 and 145 were waiting and once more attacked out of the sun—not bothering with the Bf 110s, whose pilots seemed engrossed in shooting down the ships' balloons and little else.

The risks taken to sail convoy Peewit had proved expensive, only four of the 20 merchantmen sailing unscathed into Swanage that evening. Its defence had demanded desperate fighting by the Hurricane pilots of Nos. 43, 145, 238 and 257 Squadrons, which lost three, five, three and three aircraft respectively and a total of 12 pilots killed or drowned. The Spitfires of Nos. 64, 65 and 152 Squadrons had been less heavily engaged and lost three aircraft, all of whose pilots were killed. *Luftwaffe* casualties amounted to 10 Ju 87s, 4 Bf 110s, 11 Bf 109Es and the He 59. No. 145 Squadron had been in action three times during the day, shooting down nine Ju 87s, two Bf 110s and four Bf 109Es in spite of its own heavy losses.

It was later realized that the German air force's operations on the 8th had not been part of its premeditated plan and had been launched only when presented with the unexpected convoy target. Two days of little air activity followed, but then on the 11th the whole pattern of German attacks changed. During the course of the day a total of 11 separate raids and sweeps between the Thames Estuary and the Dorset coast was carefully co-ordinated either to catch British fighters in transit to or from patrol, or, through feints, to draw the fighters away from major raids. Park's sector controllers, however, were "acquiring a nose" for the likelihood of such tactics and were attempting to vector fighters in transit through clear skies, or at least tried to cover vulnerable fighter formations with fighters with plenty of fuel and ammunition. These precautions paid off when a free chase on the 11th was frustrated by Spitfires of No. 64 Squadron, whose pilots shot down two Bf 109Es.

It transpired that the Portland naval base was to become this day's major German objective. When the first raid was still forming up over Cherbourg, Park and Brand, acting in unison, between them ordered up more than 70 fighters from eight squadrons, not simply to intercept the threatening raid but to cover the coastal airfields at Tangmere and Warmwell. The raid, consisting of 54 Ju 88s of KG 54, about 20 He 111s of KG 27, 61 Bf 110s of ZG 2 and 30 Bf 109Es of JG 2, was intercepted by 58 Hurricanes of Nos. 1, 87, 145, 213, 238 and 601 Squadrons and 16 Spitfires of Nos. 152 and 609 Squadrons as it approached Weymouth Bay. On this occasion the German fighters were flying well ahead of the bombers and quickly engaged the interceptors before they were able to get through to the bombers; only some of the latecomers—the Hurricanes had had to fly from Exeter—managed to find an opportunity to attack the bombers before being engaged by the German fighters. The *Luftwaffe*'s tactics paid handsome dividends, 16 Hurricanes being shot down (including four further aircraft of No. 145 Squadron) and 13 of their pilots killed; one Spitfire was also lost, together with its pilot. One of the pilots to survive being shot down was No. 145's CO, Sqn Ldr Peel. The German losses totalled 18 aircraft—five Ju 88s, one He 111, six Bf 110s and six Bf 109Es. More important, however, was the loss of three *Gruppenkommandeur* (of II./KG 27, II./KG 54 and I./ZG 2, the first two shot down by Hurricanes). These losses prompted the German bomber crews to question the wisdom of dispensing with close fighter escort, and a growing clamour resulted in the fighter pilots being ordered to stay

One of the most heavily-engaged Hurricane squadrons during the Dunkirk period and early half of the Battle of Britain was John Worrall's No 32 Squadron seen here scrambling from Hawkinge, Biggin Hill's forward airfield. Partway through the Battle all the Squadron's Hurricanes had their DH props changed to Rotols; most other Hurricane squadrons had to await their turn to be re-equipped with new-build Rotol Hurricanes. (Photo: *RAF Museum)*

close to their charges, much to the frustration of the Emil pilots.

Elsewhere on this day *Erpr.Gr. 210* flew two raids, the first on Dover harbour and the second on a convoy off the Suffolk coast, losing two Bf 110s during the latter. The losses sustained by Fighter Command, totalling 25 Hurricanes (with 20 pilots) and six Spitfires (with four pilots), were the heaviest yet suffered in a single day, as were those of the *Luftwaffe*, which lost two Do 17s, one He 111, five Ju 88s, two Ju 87s, eleven Bf 110s, 12 Bf 109s and two He 59s in combat.

The skill with which the British fighters had been positioned to strike the *Luftwaffe*'s raids over England's South Coast on the 11th lent urgency to German plans to attack the RAF radar stations that had obviously provided long-range warning of approaching raids. Now Rubensdörffer's *Erpr.Gr 210* was accordingly selected to "take out" the CH stations at Dover, Rye, Pevensey and Dunkirk (the latter on Kent's north coast covering the Thames Estuary). The audacious attacks early on the 12th, each by four Bf 110s, succeeded in damaging but not destroying three of the installations, but all were operating again the same afternoon. It was while the radars in the south-east were relatively blind that the day's major raid built up over France, comprising 90 Ju 88s of KG 51, 120 Bf 110s of ZG 2 and ZG 76, and 25 Bf 109s of JG 53. As these aircraft were assembling, two raids were slipped in against the airfields at Lympne and Hawkinge, damaging both severely though putting neither out of action.

When the major raid crossed out over the French coast it set course to the north-west and was only spotted fairly late by the Ventnor CH radar as it approached the Isle of Wight, the bombers splitting into two formations at the last moment, one turning towards Portsmouth harbour and the other making straight for the Ventnor radar. At the same time the Bf 110s started to circle just off the Nab, waiting to cover the withdrawal of the bombers.

Once more Brand and Park committed large fighter forces, having ordered up 48 Hurricanes of Nos. 145, 213 and 257 Squadrons and ten Spitfires of No. 266 Squadron. They were, however, careful not to form these into Wings, but instructed the controllers to ensure that they were brought into combat consecutively, thereby avoiding the risk of heavy losses should a free chase interfere. In the event the tactic produced an unexpected result, for the Bf 110 pilots had been ordered not to break out of their circle under any circumstances until the bombers had completed their raids. Thus the British pilots were able to position themselves for a series of attacks on the raiders as they sought to withdraw; in the meantime the Ju 88s were left to the gun defences in Portsmouth. The Bf 109s were also too far away to interfere when two new Spitfire squadrons, Nos. 152 and 609, charged in and shot down two Ju 88s over the Ventnor radar station.

Now the Portsmouth raiders began extricating themselves from the harbour's perimeter balloon barrage, the first one out—carring KG 51's *Geschwaderkommodore*, Oberst Dr Fisser—being pounced on by No. 213 Squadron's Hurricanes and shot down. In all, the British fighters shot down 10 Ju 88s before at last the escort of Messerschmitts could come to their rescue. Moreover, when a free chase was reported approaching from the east with the obvious aim of attacking the RAF fighters as they disengaged over the Solent, Park had the Hurricanes of No. 615 Squadron ideally positioned to bar its way, two Bf 109Es falling to their guns.

The big attack on Ventnor and Portsmouth cost the *Luftwaffe* 11 Ju 88s (five shot down by Hurricanes, five by Spitfires and one by the gun defences), five Bf 110s (three by Hurricanes and two by Spitfires) and two Bf 109s (both by

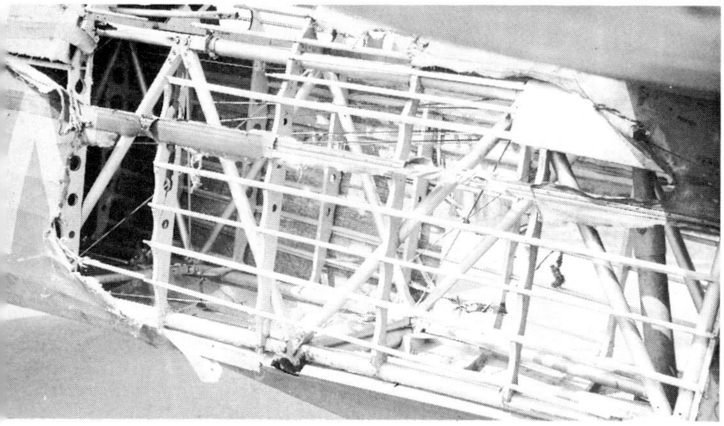

At about 11.30 hrs on 15th August Plt Off A. J. J. Truran of No 615 Squadron was involved in a dogfight with Bf 109Es off Dungeness when his Hurricane KW-W was badly damaged in the rear fuselage by cannon fire; the wings and fuselage were peppered by machine gun bullets and he himself was later wounded. He dropped out of the fight and eventually succeeded in making the 60-mile flight to his home base at Kenley where he made a safe wheels-down landing. (Photos: *Author's Collection)*

Spitfires)—in addition to the two free-chasing victims. Damage had, however, been extremely serious in Portsmouth and its dockyard, while the key Ventnor CH radar was off the air for three days. Moreover, the loss by No. 145 Squadron of three Hurricanes (all of whose pilots were killed) brought the Squadron's casualties up to 13 aircraft and 11 pilots killed since the beginning of the month; Park had no alternative but to pull No. 145 out of the line, John Peel taking his survivors north to Drem on the 14th to rest and train replacements.

After the heavy losses among the Ju 87 dive bombers on the 8th, von Richthofen had withheld their use in any strength until the beginning of the "softening up" phase prior to the launching of the invasion. This phase was now due to start, under the code-name *Adlerangriff*—Attack of the Eagles. However, so complex was the intended co-ordination of raids by all three *Luftflotten*, from bases in Norway to the Brest peninsula (so as to ensure that Fighter Command had no chance to switch its resources from threat to threat) that conditions had to be virtually perfect. Such proved to be far from the case as dawn broke on 13 August.

The events of that day are too complex to be described in detail here. Suffice to state that owing to unfavourable weather forecasts the German OKL decided to postpone the whole operation against England until the afternoon, unaware that some bomber units were already taking off on their first raids; through a series of administrative blunders several of these units had failed to fit the correct radio crystals in their aircraft, so their crews did not receive the recall signal, with the result that they continued on their way without fighter escort. Numerous other units assumed that *only* the planned afternoon operations would be carried out as some fighter *Staffeln* carried out free-chase sorties in the afternoon originally planned for the morning. As a concerted assault on Britain the operations of the 13th proved a fiasco. Nevertheless the *Luftwaffe* succeeded in flying a large number of isolated attacks, including an unescorted raid by 74 Dornier Do 17s of KG 2 over the Isle of Sheppey which severely damaged Eastchurch airfield, destroying a Spitfire and five Blenheims on the ground. Five Dorniers were shot down, all by Hurricanes. One of these was accounted for by Flt Lt Roddick Smith of No. 151 Squadron, who had been given charge of the RAF's single experimental Hurricane *L1750* armed with a pair of 20-mm cannon under the wings.[27] He recounted the action as follows:

> "I ordered the attack, telling my pilots (who I hoped were all there, although one section was not visible in my mirror, and my No. 3 could not keep up) to dive through the enemy formation and on into the clouds, as I assumed the rear formation were Messerschmitt 110s and three-quarters of my pilots were new. I opened fire with my cannon at about 300 yards, firing into the general mass as the enemy were in exceptionally close formation. One immediately burst into flames and another started smoking when my windscreen front panel was completely shattered by enemy fire, and I broke away downwards and returned to North Weald."

If the operations of *Luftflotte 2* got off to a bad start on 13 August, those of *Luftflotte 3* in the afternoon to the west were conducted with careful attention to feints and co-ordinated actions. The major effort involved a large-scale raid by some 120 Ju 88s of LG 1 and KG 54, 79 Ju 87s of St.G 2 and St.G 77, escorted by 30 Bf 110s of V./LG 1 and about 80 Bf 109Es of JG 27 and JG 53. This massive formation advanced across the Channel on a front of about 40 miles towards the English coast west of the Isle of Wight. At the same time three free chases by Bf 109Es of JG 53 were reported over Dorset, their object being to draw any intercepting fighters away to the west. Spitfires were scrambled from Warmwell, but were too late to intercept the 109s which, being short of fuel in any case, ran out across Weymouth Bay and disappeared over the horizon to the south. The effect of these free chases had been to advance the fighter states at Warmwell, Exeter, Middle Wallop and Tangmere so that Brand had plenty of time to scramble more than 90 Hurricanes and Spitfires of seven squadrons from these airfields.

When the German formation reached the coast it split up into three groups, St.G 2 and LG 1 flying up the Solent to attack Southampton, while some Ju 88s attempted a feint raid on Portland, but the Hurricanes of Nos. 213 and 601 Squadrons put the escorting Bf 110s to rout, shooting down three, so the Ju 88s promptly jettisoned their bombs and also hurriedly made off. A third element of the raid, including the 52 Ju 87s of St.G 77 and 80 Ju 88s of LG 1, spread out over Dorset to attack Warmwell and Middle Wallop airfields; unfortunately for them their escorting Bf 109s had to turn for home, already low on fuel, so that the raid on Middle Wallop was broken up by Spitfires of No. 609 Squadron; most of the German crews failed to find their allotted targets and scarcely any damage was caused to Fighter Command installations.

In the late afternoon, however, a devastating raid struck the airfield at Detling in Kent—which was not at that time a component of the fighter defences—thanks to the brilliant timing of a free chase by JG 26's Bf 109s. Forty Ju 87s struck the airfield just as the station's personnel were assembling for their evening meal; three messes were hit and demolished, every hangar was destroyed, the runways and dispersals were heavily cratered, the operations block received a direct hit (killing the station commander), 67 personnel were killed and nearly 300 injured; 22 aircraft were destroyed and about 30 badly damaged. If one of Park's key Sector airfields had suffered such devastation the effect on the air defence of London might have been catastrophic; as it was, the raid went scarcely reported.

Despite the breakdown of German plans on this first day of the *Luftwaffe*'s intended all-out attack on Britain, the casualties on both sides were fairly heavy: six Do 17s were shot down (five by Hurricanes and one by Spitfires), an He 111 was destroyed by Hurricanes, as were eight Ju 88s (six by Hurricanes, two by Spitfires), six Ju 87s (all by Spitfires), 15 Bf 110s (12 by Hurricanes, one by Spitfires and two by airfield guns), and nine Bf 109s (two by Hurricanes and seven by Spitfires); Fighter Command's losses amounted to 12 Hurricanes (with three pilots killed but three others grievously wounded) and one Spitfire (whose pilot was unhurt).

As German air force commanders pondered for much of the 14th on the blunders of the previous day, relatively small *Luftwaffe* formations managed to pierce the fighter defences and reached RAF airfields as far north as Sealand in Cheshire. A Heinkel He 111, which reached Middle Wallop in the evening, was shot down by Spitfires and was found to have carried KG 55's *Geschwaderkommodore*, Oberst Alois Stoeckl, and senior staff officers of *Luftgau VIII* to their deaths. Once more the Hurricanes bore much of the brunt of the day's fighting, four being lost, but shooting down two He 111s, two Ju 87s and four Bf 109s; one Spitfire was lost. Much of Dowding's attention, and that of his Group Commanders, was occupied on this day with rearrangement of their defences. No. 238 (Hurricane) Squadron was moved from Middle Wallop to St Eval in Cornwall to help cover the Western Approaches; "Sailor" Malan and No. 74 (Spitfire) Squadron was withdrawn from Hornchurch north to Wittering and, as already noted, No. 145's battle-weary survivors finally retired to the supposed peace of the north on this day. No. 249 Squadron with Hurricanes, commanded by Sqn Ldr John Grandy, was brought south from Church Fenton to Middle Wallop; in less than 48 hours one of its flight commanders would fight an action that would win him the only Victoria Cross ever awarded to a member of Fighter Command.

★ ★ ★

The battlefield was now clear for action. The *Luftwaffe* could no longer delay the great assault if an invasion was to be launched before the autumn weather set in, and Dowding was as ready as he could possibly be, even if some of his precious squadrons had already been taken out of the line and some of his radar was operating below peak efficiency. Yet there *was* growing unease in the *Luftwaffe*: there was a suspicion that the British fighter

Wg Cdr Victor Beamish, station commander at North Weald during the Battle of Britain (right) with Sqn Ldr 'Teddy' Donaldson, CO of No 151 Squadron. It was not customary for station commanders to fly in combat yet Beamish flew many operational sorties with Nos 17, 46, 56, 151, 249 and 257 Squadrons and shot down two Bf 109Es and two Ju 87Bs, while flying with No 249 Squadron. This indomitable Irishman had been invalided out of the RAF with tuberculosis before the War but had fought his way back to health and rejoined the Service. By the date of his death in action in March 1942 he had destroyed eleven enemy aircraft. (Photo: *RAF Museum)*

pilots could and would tear the heart out of the bomber formations if they penetrated their escort, and the bomber crews were beginning to question whether the Bf 109s possessed sufficient range to be able to protect them *all* the way to their target and all the way back; they were also worried by the escorts' tendency to fly too far ahead to provide adequate cover. The Stuka crews—said to be Göring's "Prussian élite"—had suffered fairly heavily already, having regard to the relatively small force involved. The *Zerstörer* crews, also much favoured by the portly *Reichsmarschall*, were not fulfilling their task of protecting the bombers, and finally the Emil pilots were beginning to fret at their increasing rôle of nursemaid for everyone—instead of being allowed free rein in the English skies.

Thus far the fighting had scarcely involved more than Park's and Brand's Groups, any more than it had involved Kesselring's *Luftflotte 2* and Sperrle's *Luftflotte 3*. Today *Adler Tag*—Eagle Day—Thursday, 15 August, would change all that as Stumpff's Scandinavian-based *Luftflotte 5* joined the battle. The events by nightfall would, however, endorse the day in the *Luftwaffe*'s history as Black Thursday.

The first major attack by nearly 50 Ju 87s under a big umbrella of Bf 109s struck the airfield at Hawkinge shortly before midday and were attacked by 11 Hurricanes of No. 501 Squadron, which shot down two dive bombers but lost two aircraft to the escort. A dozen Spitfires then joined in, destroying three Ju 87s but also losing two aircraft. Meanwhile about half the dive bombers had started an attack on Lympne airfield, where considerable damage was done. At both airfields the Germans used fragmentation bombs to cause the maximum damage among parked aircraft—but there was none at either . . . shortly afterwards a pair of Spitfires was, however, destroyed on the ground at Manston in a snap attack by a dozen low-flying Bf 110s.

As the radar screens cleared after these raids, and Park's fighters returned to refuel and re-arm, it was now the turn of Drone Hill CH radar in the north to report the approach of raids across the North Sea. A total of 63 He 111s of KG 26 with an escort of 21 Bf 110s of ZG 76, flying from Stavanger, were approaching the Firth of Forth as a feint by 17 He 115 seaplanes attempted to draw intercepting fighters further north. When still 50 miles out, the He 111s turned south towards Newcastle and Sunderland, but were successfully attacked by 18 Hurricanes of Nos. 79 and 605 Squadrons and 11 Spitfires of No. 72 Squadron, ordered up from Drem and Acklington. Thirteen Spitfires of No. 41 Squadron were also scrambled from Catterick further south. The resulting running battle cost the *Luftwaffe* eight He 111s (four shot down by Hurricanes, one by Spitfires, one by a Blenheim and two by ground fire) and seven Bf 110s (four by Spitfires and three by Hurricanes); among the latter was the aircraft of I./ZG 76's *Gruppenkommandeur*, Hauptmann Restmeyer.

Almost simultaneously yet another incoming raid was reported to be approaching the Humber at about 13.00 hrs, and 12 Hurricanes of No. 73 Squadron and 12 Spitfires of No. 616 Squadron were ordered off from Leconfield and Church Fenton as 11 Defiants of No. 264 Squadron were directed to cover a nearby coastal convoy. The bombers proved to be about 50 Ju 88s of KG 30, flying unescorted from Aalborg in Denmark, which suddenly swung south to attack the bomber airfield at Driffield, where 10 Whitleys were destroyed. As the low-flying raiders crossed out over the coast near Flamborough Head the British fighters attacked, shooting down seven (five falling to Hurricanes and two to Spitfires). Two other Ju 88s crashed later as the result of battle damage. All these actions were fought without a single loss by the British squadrons, other than a Blenheim which force landed with minor damage at Driffield.

The air battle now returned to the south as Rubensdörffer led his *Erpr.Gr 210* in a superbly executed surprise attack on Martlesham Heath, doing a great deal of damage and putting the airfield out of action for two days. The raid was intercepted by Hurricanes of Nos. 1 and 17 Squadrons, but the Bf 109s of the 3.*Staffel* were ready for them and shot down three; unfortunately 12 Spitfires of No. 19 Squadron, flying from Fowlmere, arrived too late to intercept.

As Rubensdörffer's pilots made good their escape, 88 Do 17s of KG 3, escorted by 130 Bf 109Es of JG 51, JG 52 and JG 54, were approaching Deal and five free chases by 60 Bf 109Es of JG 26 were roaming the skies inland from Dover. Against this threat Park was able to direct 24 Hurricanes and 12 Spitfires already airborne, and scrambled about 40 other Hurricanes from Croydon and Biggin Hill. The escorting Bf 109s remained so close to the bombers as to provide an almost impregnable screen and only two Dorniers were shot down. Over mid-Kent the raid split, one half attacking the Short aircraft factory at Rochester, where much damage was done (including the destruction of seven Stirling bombers), and the other raiding the airfield at Eastchurch.

Meanwhile two heavy raids were in progress over the southern counties, a total of 60 Ju 88s of LG 1, escorted by 40 Bf 110s of ZG 2, attacking Worthy Down and Middle Wallop shortly before 18.00 hrs, and 40 Ju 87s of St.G 1 and St.G 2 with an escort of 20 Bf 110s of LG 2 and 60 Bf 109s of JG 27 and JG 53 carrying out a raid on Portland. These raids were severely mauled by 56 Hurricanes of Nos. 43, 87, 213, 249 and 601 Squadrons and 24 Spitfires of Nos. 234 and 609 Squadrons.

One further noteworthy raid was launched on this memorable day. Flying his third operation of the day, Rubensdörffer led 15 Bf 110s and eight Bf 109s of *Epr.Gr 210* in an audacious attack on Croydon aerodrome at 19.00 hrs. His briefed target was in fact to have been the Kenley Sector airfield, but an escort of JG 52 fighters had failed to make the rendezvous; knowing that his own attack was intended as a diversion to draw RAF fighters away from a raid elsewhere by Dorniers, Rubensdörffer decided to press on with his attack, but instead of breaking cloud over Kenley arrived at Croydon just as the Hurricanes of John Thompson's No. 111 Squadron were taking off. As the German pilots started their bombing runs (which caused widespread damage both on and off the airfield, killed 68 and injured nearly 200 people on the ground), a number of Hurricanes of No. 32 Squadron arrived from nearby Biggin Hill. At once a terrific fight developed, but almost immediately the Bf 109s had to break away owing to fuel shortage, leaving Rubensdörffer's Bf 110s to fend for themselves. Quickly adopting their customary defence circle these pilots struggled to reach cloud cover, but were virtually pinned down by the two Hurricane squadrons. One by one the Germans broke out and attempted to escape to the south. Four Hurricanes of No. 111 Squadron pursued *Erpr.Gr 210*'s Staff Flight, and it happened that Rubensdörffer himself fell to the guns of Thompson—crashing to his death on the outskirts of Rotherfield in Sussex.

So ended a day on which 70 per cent of Fighter Command's pilots had been engaged in battle at least once—some squadrons flew four combat sorties. German losses amounted to four Do 17s, 11 He 111s, 17 Ju 88s, seven Ju 87s, 27 Bf 110s, six Bf 109s, an He 59 and an He 115. Of these 64 German aircraft, Hurricanes accounted for 41 and Spitfires 16, the remainder being destroyed by other defences or by pilots who did not live to establish their claims. RAF losses in air combat totalled 17 Hurricanes (seven pilots killed and two taken prisoner in France) and 11 Spitfires (four pilots killed and three taken prisoner). British aircraft losses on the ground amounted to 10 Whitley bombers, one Battle light bomber, two Spitfires and three Blenheims.

The day's fighting came as a considerable setback to *Luftwaffe* plans. Although serious damage had undeniably been wrought at a number of British airfields and several aircraft factories, Fighter Command appeared to have lost none of its ability to meet almost all the threats posed. Worse, the *Luftwaffe*'s conviction that the entire British fighter strength was concentrated in the south had proved mistaken, as *Luftflotte* 5's losses indicated—12 per cent of the He 111s, 16 per cent of the Ju 88s and 33 per cent of the Bf 110s being shot down. Among the aircrew lost by the *Luftwaffe* on Black Thursday were no fewer than five *Gruppenkommandeur* and eleven *Staffelkapitäne*.

Another bad day for the *Luftwaffe* followed on the 16th with 16 bombers, nine dive bombers, eight Bf 110s and 17 Bf 109s shot down; of these 50 aircraft, 19 fell to Hurricanes, 20 to Spitfires and 11 to other defences. The raids were widespread and caused damage to a number of airfields; the most destructive raid was carried out by Ju 87s of St.G 2 on Tangmere, where five Blenheim night fighters of the Fighter Interception Unit were destroyed; Hurricanes of Nos. 1, 43 and 601 Squadrons and Spitfires of No. 602 Squadron were scrambled and waded into the dive bombers, No. 43 alone accounting for seven.

A particular combat, though probably no more vicious than many another of the Battle of Britain, was to become famous on this day. Three of No. 249 Squadron's Hurricanes were on patrol near Southampton, led by Flt Lt James Nicolson, when their pilots spotted a raid developing over nearby Gosport. As they were manoeuvring to attack, some Bf 109s bounced them from above and behind, setting on fire the Hurricanes of Nicolson and Plt Off M. A. King. The former remained at his controls long enough to complete his attack on a Bf 110 before baling out with extensive burns to his face and hands. King had already baled out and together the two pilots descended by parachute only to come under fire from rifle detachments of the Royal Artillery and Local Defence Volunteers; both airmen were hit, although doubt remains whether King had already succumbed to his wounds. Nicolson survived, and after a long stay in hospital was awarded the Victoria Cross—the only such award ever made to a pilot of Fighter Command. Sad to relate he was to lose his life during the war in the Far East.

On this day British losses in air combat amounted to 11 Hurricanes (four pilots killed) and 10 Spitfires (four pilots killed). One of the Hurricane pilots to lose his life was Plt Off William Fiske of No. 601 Squadron, the first American volunteer pilot to be killed while serving with RAF Fighter Command; he was mortally injured while attempting to land at the height of the raid on Tangmere and died in hospital the next day.

After scarcely any air activity on 17 August, heavy raids were once more launched on the 18th, a day of fighting that was to have a profound effect on German tactics for the remainder of the Battle of Britain. Once more the *Luftwaffe* attempted to synchronize attacks by both *Luftflotten* 2 and 3 to swamp the defences along the English South Coast, and indeed Fighter Command was to suffer heavy casualties—though by no means all of them in air combat. A large number of He 111s, Ju 88s and Do 17s carried out a series of widespread attacks on airfields in the south-east, hitting Biggin Hill and Kenley. At the latter 10 Hurricanes were destroyed on the ground, of which six belonged to No. 615 Squadron; one of the Squadron's flights had managed to get airborne and intercepted the bombers, but had been overwhelmed by free-chasing Bf 109s, whose pilots shot down a further five of the Hurricanes. It immediately became clear to Park's controllers that this was an all-out effort to destroy the southern airfields, and orders were given to keep as many fighters in the air over their bases as possible so long as enemy aircraft were being reported over land. Nevertheless Croydon and West Malling (the latter not yet in full operation) were also hit.

When radar reported another large raid approaching the Isle of Wight it was natural therefore to anticipate a repetition of the devastating raid on Tangmere of two days previously, and Park ordered every available fighter into the air to cover the Sector. However, the targets this time were to be the Poling CH radar station near Littlehampton, the Coastal Command airfield at Thorney Island and the naval airfields at Gosport and Ford. It so happened that the Hurricanes of Nos. 43 and 601 Squadrons were ideally positioned to intercept the raiders making for Poling, and made their initial attacks just as the Ju 87s were starting their dives—while the Spitfires of No. 234 Squadron held the Bf 109 escort at bay. Although Poling radar was very badly damaged (being put out of action for a week) the RAF fighters massacred the dive bombers, No. 43 destroying five, and the Spitfires of Nos. 152 and 602 Squadrons a further 13.

On this day the German air force suffered the combat loss of 66 aircraft—seven He 111s, three Ju 88s, four Do 17s, 18 Ju 87s, 14 Bf 110s and 20 Bf 109s—32 to Hurricanes, 29 to Spitfires, one to a Blenheim and the remainer to the ground defences. Including those destroyed on the ground, Fighter Command lost 36 Hurricanes (with eight pilots killed and several severely wounded) and six Spitfires (one pilot killed).

This was by far the worst day yet for the Hurricane squadrons in terms of aircraft losses; fortunately, however, the pilot losses were less severe, and the aircraft were quickly made good from maintenance unit stocks. Moreover seven of the aircraft struck off charge as "destroyed" were salvaged, repaired and later returned to the Service.

For the *Luftwaffe* two aspects of the day's casualties (apart from the loss of II./KG 53's *Gruppenkommandeur*, Major Tamm, seven *Staffelkapitäne* and more than 100 other officers) were to give rise to considerable concern. The much-vaunted dive-bomber force, which ten days previously numbered 281 aircraft and was regarded as the main assault weapon for the forthcoming invasion, had suffered the loss of 64 aircraft and 136 aircrew—including five *Staffelkapitäne*. It seemed both to Göring and von Richthofen that nothing could prevent the British fighters from penetrating the escort and attacking the dive bombers, and that at the current rate of losses the dive bomber force would effectively cease to exist by mid-September; this prompted Göring to order the withdrawal of the Ju 87 from all operations other than special attacks in which fighter opposition could be avoided with some certainty.

Even higher casualties had been suffered by the *Zerstörerverband*, the period 8 to 18 August having witnessed the loss of 86 Bf 110s and some 180 aircrew, including no fewer than five *Gruppenkommandeur* and seven *Staffelkapitäne*. These formation leaders represented the highly experienced core of the *Luftwaffe*—the men who had led the assaults over half of Europe and would take months to replace with men of similar experience. Accordingly Göring ordered the *Zerstörergeschwader* to shift the emphasis of their rôle from that of escort fighter to autonomous fighter-bomber operations, that is to say operations employing one *Gruppe* as bombers and one or two *Gruppen* as support escort. This would release more Bf 109s for free-chase operations, although many of the single-seaters would still be called on to protect the big bomber formations. These changes of tactics were to herald the onset of an infinitely more hazardous phase of the battle for Fighter Command.[28]

7

THE STORM DEFENCES HOLD

The ferocity of the air battles between 8 and 18 August was bound to cause the *Luftwaffe* to re-examine its tactics for, despite the reports by its air-crews of RAF fighter losses—which were further exaggerated for home consumption in Germany—the OKL itself could as yet detect no significant weakening of the British fighter forces. Dowding on the other hand, despite some heavy losses, knew that so far his fighter factories were steadily building up reserves of replacement aircraft and that new squadrons were becoming operational almost weekly.[29] Moreover a number of volunteer pilots from the Fleet Air Arm were joining the established squadrons, and some ex-Battle pilots were undergoing training on Hurricanes. Provided his losses did not much exceed the average rate of July and August thus far, he probably felt fairly confident of holding the *Luftwaffe* at bay until the onset of the autumn weather.

After the fierce battles of the 18th there followed a relative lull in the air fighting from 19 to 23 August, caused by poor weather. While Dowding took the opportunity to redeploy a few of his squadrons, the German air commanders were planning a phase of new tactics, largely as a result of the clamour by the fighter pilots. Some of the old brigade of fighter commanders—in particular those who had not witnessed modern air combat at first hand—were promoted and posted away from the Channel coast, their place being taken by the "Young Turks". Henceforth increased priority would be given to bombing raids on fighter airfields and factories, but bomber escorts would in future be less generous as the Bf 110s increasingly transferred their activities to the fighter-bombing rôle—at the same time being expected to look after themselves to a much greater extent. The single-seaters were now to concentrate wholly upon offensive sweeps, now employing much greater strength. In other words the *Luftwaffe* was—to the exclusion of all else—to concentrate on the destruction of British fighters, in the air and on the ground. This of course was the move that Dowding and his Group and Sector Commanders most feared.

★ ★ ★

It was the pattern of attack from the start of the new phase, which opened on the 24th. By now Dowding had inexplicably brought his other Defiant squadron, No. 264, south from Kirton to Hornchurch, and it was most unfortunate that this key Spitfire station was to be one of the day's main targets. A belief persists that Dowding felt that the German single-seaters would lack the range to accompany bombers as far as Hornchurch, and that the Defiant—with its complicated tactics expressly developed to attack enemy bombers—would constitute the ideal airfield defence for that airfield. If such was his plan no one told the Hornchurch sector controller, who repeatedly ordered the Defiants to the forward airfield at Manston. They were indeed refuelling at Manston when that airfield was attacked by Ju 88s and hurriedly took off. The commanding officer, Sqn Ldr Philip Hunter, was last seen pursuing a bomber in the direction of France.[30] The Squadron was back at Hornchurch again when He 111s began a series of raids on airfields north of the Thames Estuary with free chases by Bf 109Es in the same area. The Defiants again scrambled—losing two aircraft in a collision on the ground, and three to the roaming German fighters. (Seven more of No. 264 Squadron's Defiants were to be shot down before the unit was finally moved north and out of the daylight battle for good after another disastrous day on the 28th.)

The Heinkels did a lot of damage at Hornchurch, most of the station's Spitfires also being absent on distant patrol or at their forward airfield. At much the same time a raid on North Weald by 46 Do 17s and He 111s was being carried out, covered by the same free chases. This time the Hurricanes of No. 151 Squadron were just able to scramble and claimed four of the Heinkels. It was in fact a fairly good day for the Hurricanes, whose squadrons destroyed a Bf 110 reconnaissance aircraft, two Ju 88s, five He 111s and 10 Bf 110s, losing 10 aircraft but only two pilots; by contrast the Spitfires destroyed four Bf 109Es for the loss of six aircraft but no pilots.

On the 25th the *Luftwaffe* flew a number of free chases just off shore along the South Coast, hoping to attract RAF fighters into the air, but Park and Brand refused to be drawn, preferring to keep their fighters at a high state of readiness on the ground. They were therefore well prepared to meet the day's major attack by Ju 88s and Bf 110s, which fell upon the airfield at Warmwell. They were intercepted by the Hurricanes of No. 17 Squadron and the Spitfires of No. 152. However, while No. 17 lost its CO, Sqn Ldr Cedric Watcyn Williams, shot down by a Bf 110, No. 32 Squadron's loss of a pilot further east reduced its strength to no more than eight and, displaying all the symptoms of advanced combat fatigue, the remnants of the Squadron were ordered north to rest and re-equip; the doughty CO, John Worrall, took over as Sector Controller of the Biggin Hill Sector. During the day Hurricanes destroyed a He 111, two Ju 88s, a Do 17, five Bf 110s and five Bf 109Es, for the loss of eight aircraft and five pilots, while Spitfires shot down a Do 17, four Bf 110s and two Bf 109Es for the loss of eight aircraft and three pilots killed (and one taken prisoner).

The pilot loss rate was now perceptibly creeping up, and with 10 killed, one taken prisoner and nine wounded in hospital, Dowding had lost the equivalent of a squadron in two days. And this rate would continue to rise steadily.

On the following day, when another raid was aimed at fighter airfields north of the Thames, Debden—the main target—escaped serious damage simply because the covering German fighters had to withdraw due to shortage of fuel and constant pressure by the Hurricanes and Spitfires; only a few stout-hearted Dornier crews pushed on to their target, and eventually escaped. However, the free chases over Kent and the Thames Estuary had been committed too soon and were also too short of fuel to attack and prevent the British fighters from intercepting the main bombing effort. Nevertheless Fighter Command suffered heavily once more: 15 Hurricanes, with one pilot killed, and nine Spitfires, with three pilots killed; nine pilots had also been wounded. German losses amounted to 11 Do 17s, four He 111s, five Bf 110s and 14 Bf 109Es. (On this day the Defiants were airborne and attracted the attention of a free chase by Bf 109Es over north Kent, losing three aircraft; they had, however, destroyed three Do 17s and were probably short of fuel and ammunition when attacked themselves—the classic free chase situation.)

There was some respite on the 27th as low cloud with drizzle covered much of southern England. Already there were signs of differences of opinion on defence tactics between Park in No. 11 Group and his northern neighbour, Leigh-Mallory of No. 12 Group. Whatever Park's preferences were in the use of fighter Wings (that is, the assembly of several squadrons into one mass) before committing them to battle—and it is often forgotten that he *did* employ Wings whenever he was able and saw fit to do so—Leigh-Mallory tended to regard the Wing as the be-all and end-all of defensive fighting. Thus on several occasions already, when Park had called for reinforcements to help protect his own northern airfields—Hornchurch, North Weald, Debden and Martlesham which, after all, were scarcely more than five minutes' flying time from Leigh-Mallory's main station at Duxford—the No. 12 Group Wing was still taking off and forming up by the time the German raids were on their way home. Much of the No. 12 Group controllers' difficulty lay in trying to decide, at a moment's notice, which squadrons were immediately available to form a Wing and how to co-ordinate Spitfires and Hurricanes into a single fighting force. This difficulty was frequently compounded by dependence on the most experienced Spitfire Squadron, No. 19, which was not only based on Duxford's satellite at Fowlmere—and not at Duxford itself—and which, because it was attempting to introduce cannon-armed Spitfires into service, was generally regarded as something of a trials squadron.[31]

Park seldom had any alternative but to employ his squadrons individually. His Group's boundary enclosed an enormous front facing the *Luftwaffe* and attacks could be and were launched against his airfields from many directions; for instance, to have committed a Wing of fighters from Biggin Hill southwards to meet a raid approaching over the South Coast would have left his airfields open to attack from the east or from the Thames Estuary.

On the 28th Kesselring's *Luftflotte 2* again aimed its attacks up the Estuary, posing the threat of renewed attacks on the fighter fields north of the Thames. The squadrons at Hornchurch and North

Camouflaged black overall for 'Night Intruder' operations over enemy territory, BE500 was the usual aircraft of Sqn. Ldr. D.C. Smallwood, D.F.C. of No. 87 Squadron. It bore the presentation inscription "United Provinces – Cawnpore 1" painted underneath the cockpit on the side of the aircraft away from the camera. Issued to No. 87 Squadron in November 1941, BE500 served with the squadron for just over a year before going for a short period to No. 533 Squadron, one of the unsuccessful Douglas Havoc "Turbinlite" Squadrons. After a major overhaul BE500 was shipped to the Far East, arriving by November 1943 and it was struck off R.A.F. charge on 31 August, 1944. (Charles E. Brown/Royal Air Force Museum)

Probably a veteran of the Battle of Britain, P3090 served with No. 242 Squadron as LE-S. It was withdrawn for maintenance in mid-September 1940. It was later involved in two separate accidents whilst on ferry flights. P3090 was eventually converted to a 'Sea Hurricane', probably by Gloster, in April 1941, and was delivered to No. 760 Fighter Pool Squadron, Fleet Air Arm at Yeovilton (in whose markings, in a rather shabby state, it is seen here). Its ultimate fate is unknown. (Charles E. Brown/Royal Air Force Museum)

As with most late production Mark Is that were not shipped overseas, Z4791 served at various Training Establishments, one of which was the Empire Central Flying School based at Hullavington. Here Z4791 is seen during 1942 in formation with Spitfires P7926 and P7882 of that unit. Note the school's emblem, "Bird on a Tower", painted on the engine cowling. (Charles E. Brown/Royal Air Force Museum)

Built as a MK IV, KZ193 was one of only three Hurricanes fitted with a Merlin 32 engine which gave greater boost for take-off. The Hurricanes with Merlin 32s were designated the MK V. Trials at Boscombe Down soon revealed that the 32 had an unacceptably short life-span. KZ193 was subsequently returned to Hawker for re-conversion as a MK IV. Whilst at Boscombe Down KZ193 was also used for armament and bomb load trials, and it is seen here fitted with two 40 mm guns. Fitted with these guns it served with No. 164 Squadron, coded FJ-O, on anti-shipping strikes during 1943. (Charles E. Brown/Royal Air Force Museum)

Issued maintenance airframe No. 4150M, subsequently cancelled (presumably because it had been a clerical error), KZ714 went to the Air Fighting Development Unit at Wittering during September 1943. This unit is known to have taken part in operational sorties over enemy territory, but it is not known if KZ714 participated. During March 1944 it moved to 1695 Bomber Defence Training Flight at Dalton, Yorkshire and left there in January 1945. After a major inspection and overhaul at the civil repair organisation, Morrisons at Peterborough, it was shipped to the Far East, arriving at Karachi during August 1945. It was Struck off Charge in December 1946. (Warren M. Bodie)

Here at Wattisham as a member of the Battle of Britain Memorial Flight, PZ865 is seen in the markings of V6962, the aircraft of then Sqdn. Ldr. R.R. Stanford-Tuck, D.S.O., D.F.C.***, Commander of No. 257 squadron during the Battle of Britain.* (Stuart Howe)

PZ865, 'The Last of the Many', was purchased by Hawker from the Air Ministry and used mainly as a 'hack' by Hawker pilots. Issued post-war with the civil registration G-AMAU, it participated in many air races and displays. It remained a member of Hawker's Flying Museum until a major restoration was undertaken during 1960. Later it was used as a 'chase' aircraft during the early trials of the P1127 Vertical Take-Off Prototype. (Charles E. Brown/ Royal Air Force Museum)

Weald were ordered off, but then the German bombers split, one group attacking Rochford and the other Eastchurch. As these raids developed it was presumably assumed that the RAF would order the Kent-based fighters off in an attempt to cut off the retreat of the bombers from the Thames Estuary, and at that moment a series of free chases swept in over the South Coast. Suddenly, instead of intercepting the Dorniers, the British pilots were faced with successive waves of enemy fighters and numerous dogfights broke out all over south-east England. No. 603 Squadron from Hornchurch lost four Spitfires and No. 56 Squadron from North Weald four Hurricanes. Apart from No. 264 Squadron's loss of four Defiants (previously mentioned), the day's fighting cost Fighter Command six Hurricanes with one pilot killed, and seven Spitfires with four pilots killed. Out of 28 German aircraft shot down, no fewer than 15 were Bf 109Es.

Fighting on the 29th was only slightly less furious, but once again the losses on both sides (six Hurricanes, three Spitfires against nine Bf 109Es) indicated the preponderance of fighter-versus-fighter combat. On the 30th, with Park again exhorting his controllers to avoid risking exposure of the fighters to the savage confrontation with free-chasing enemy single-seaters, the Hurricanes of Nos. 1, 56 and 242 Squadrons did succeed in attacking a formation of Heinkels north of London after its fighter escort had turned for home, but one Spitfire squadron, No. 222, which had only recently come down from the North and was still relatively "green", found itself engaged in several combats with Bf 109s and lost eight aircraft. No. 253 Squadron suffered misfortune when a section of four Hurricanes, led by Sqn Ldr Tom Gleave and ordered against what was believed to be a large raid by bombers, broke cloud on the climb and found itself in the middle of a huge formation of about 90 Bf 109s. Acting on the natural impulse of fighter pilots they immediately attacked, Gleave himself shooting down at least three, and probably four aircraft before breaking away and making good his escape. The other three Hurricane pilots were less lucky and all were shot down as the Germans turned against them; Flt Lt George Brown was shot down and wounded near Maidstone, Plt Off C. D. Francis shot down and killed at Redhill and Plt Off D. N. O. Jenkins shot down nearby and killed when his parachute failed to open. Later in the day another No. 253 Squadron pilot, Sergeant J. H. Dickinson, baled out of his Hurricane only to be shot dead by Bf 109s as he descended by parachute over Kent. In all, the operations of the 30th cost the *Luftwaffe* 16 bombers (12 shot down by Hurricanes, two by Spitfires, one by ground fire and one by unknown fighters), six Bf 110s (all by Hurricanes), and 16 Bf 109Es (11 by Hurricanes, four by Spitfires and one by unknown fighters). Fighter Command losses were nine Hurricanes (six pilots killed) and 11 Spitfires (two pilots killed).[32]

31 August was to mark the beginning of the worst week of the whole four-month Battle of Britain for Fighter Command—a week in which combat losses of 107 Hurricanes and 71 Spitfires were accompanied by the loss of 55 pilots killed and 78 seriously wounded. Such losses represented the rate of one squadron each day in pilots and almost two squadrons each day in aircraft. The tempo of fighting forced Dowding to order squadrons out of the battle northwards to rest, often at no more than an hour's notice, to make way on his airfields for replacements already on their way south. Some of the decimated squadrons could muster no more than four or five serviceable fighters for the journey north, and these (mostly Hurricane squadrons) had to be reclassified as training units, so heavy had their losses been among their experienced pilots.

Fortunately Dowding had managed to keep some of his old-established Hurricane squadrons in the North to rest and remuster pilots, and these were now brought south—eager to get back into battle. The worst day for the Hurricane squadrons was undoubtedly the first, 31 August, with 24 aircraft lost, No. 1 (Canadian) Squadron losing three aircraft, No. 56 four, No. 85 three and No. 601 five. Indeed on that day three squadron commanders, Sqn Ldr Peter Townsend of No. 85 Squadron and Sqn Ldr Tom Gleave on No. 253 Squadron were both shot down and wounded,[33] while Gleave's replacement on No. 253, Sqn Ldr Harold Starr, was shot down and killed later the same day.

This phase also included a number of devastating attacks on Park's Sector airfields, Biggin Hill itself being put out of action twice with the operations block receiving a direct hit. Brooklands was also raided three times and although the Hurricane assembly sheds escaped serious damage, the Vickers factory (producing Wellington bombers) was fairly badly damaged and heavy casualties suffered. At Detling—not strictly a fighter airfield—some damage was done, but at Eastchurch on 2 September a bomb dump blew up demolishing almost every building within a quarter of a mile.

The climax of the Battle of Britain, and indeed a critical point in the war, was reached in the late afternoon of Saturday, 7 September, when infuriated at the *Luftwaffe*'s apparent inability to destroy Fighter Command, Hermann Göring took personal charge of the German operations on the Channel coast, and switched his bomber attacks from Fighter Command to the English civilian population with an enormous two-phase raid on London; by so doing he believed he could lure every remaining RAF fighter into the air, where it could be destroyed. In this belief he very nearly proved correct.

The first raid came in along the north Kent coast and shortly afterwards was followed by another huge formation further south. In all, about 1,000 aircraft, comprising five entire Kampfgeschwader (KG 1, 2, 3, 26 and 76), and Bf 110s of ZG 2 and the Bf 109s of JG 2, 3, 51, 52, 54, I./JG 77 and I. and

Formation of No 85 Squadron's Hurricanes towards the end of the Battle of Britain when the squadron was resting and re-equipping at Church Fenton in October 1940. Among the aircraft, which display all manner of marking

The legendary Johnnie Kent (centre) seen as a flight commander of No 303 (Polish) Squadron, soon after its formation in August 1940, with Fg Off Z. Henneburg (left) and Plt Off Miroslav Ferič—both Polish pilots who shot down eight enemy aircraft while flying with the RAF. Kent, a Canadian, had been a pre-War test pilot at Farnborough and had flown the Hurricane prototype; he went on to destroy thirteen German aircraft, and his log book testified to his having flown more than 200 different types of aircraft. (Photo: *Imperial War Museum)*

styles, are N2645, P3409 *(VY-X)*, P3854 *(VY-Q)*, V6611 *(VY-O) and* V7240 *(VY-M)*. *(*Photo: *Sydney Camm Collection)*

*Flt Lt H. P. ('Cowboy') Blatchford, the well-known Canadian pilot and flight commander of No 257 Squadron who led the squadron against the Italian raid of 11th November as the equally well-known CO, Bob Stanford-Tuck, was on leave at the time. On that occasion Blatchford destroyed a Fiat CR.42 by grinding off its wing with his propeller, having run out of ammunition. (*Photo: *RAF Museum)*

ROYAL AIR FORCE FIGHTER COMMAND ORDER OF BATTLE, 09.00hrs, 1st September 1940

Sector	*Sqn*	*Aircraft*	*Combat Ready (Unserviceable)*	*Base Airfield*	*Pilots on State*	*Commanding Officer*
No. 10 Group, HQ Rudloe Manor, Box, Wiltshire: Air Vice-Marshal Sir Christopher Quintin Brand						
Pembrey	92 Sqn	Spitfires	12 (4)	Pembrey	19	Sqn Ldr F. J. Sanders
Filton	87 Sqn	Hurricanes	9 (6)	Exeter	18	Sqn Ldr R. S. Mills
	213 Sqn	Hurricanes	8 (7)	Exeter	19	Sqn Ldr H. D. McGregor
St Eval	236 Sqn	Blenheims	12 (5)	St Eval	22	Sqn Ldr G. W. Montagu
	238 Sqn	Hurricanes	11 (4)	St Eval	20	Sqn Ldr H. A. Fenton (absent wounded)
Middle Wallop	152 Sqn	Spitfires	12 (4)	Warmwell	19	Sqn Ldr P. K. Devitt
	234 Sqn	Spitfires	12 (5)	Middle Wallop	19	Sqn Ldr J. S. O'Brien
	249 Sqn (1)	Hurricanes	15 (1)	Boscombe Down	18	Sqn Ldr J. Grandy
	604 Sqn	Blenheims	11 (3)	Middle Wallop	20	Sqn Ldr M. F. Anderson
	609 Sqn	Spitfires	11 (5)	Middle Wallop	20	Sqn Ldr H. S. Darley
No. 11 Group, HQ Uxbridge, Middlesex: Air Vice-Marshal Keith Rodney Park						
Biggin Hill	79 Sqn	Hurricanes	10 (5)	Biggin Hill	17	Sqn Ldr J. H. Heyworth
	501 Sqn	Hurricanes	12 (5)	Gravesend	22	Sqn Ldr H. A. V. Hogan
North Weald	25 Sqn (2)	Blenheims	14 (2)	Martlesham Heath	24	Sqn Ldr W. W. Loxton (acting)
	56 Sqn (3)	Hurricanes	9 (5)	North Weald	18	(Temporarily unfilled)
	151 Sqn (4)	Hurricanes	9 (4)	Stapleford Tawney	17	(Temporarily unfilled)
Kenley	72 Sqn (5)	Spitfires	15 (3)	Croydon	20	Sqn Ldr A. R. Collins
	85 Sqn	Hurricanes	13 (3)	Croydon	17	Sqn Ldr P. W. Townsend
	253 Sqn	Hurricanes	10 (4)	Kenley	17	(Temporarily unfilled)
	616 Sqn	Spitfires	12 (4)	Kenley	20	Sqn Ldr M. Robinson
Hornchurch	54 Sqn	Spitfires	11 (5)	Hornchurch	14	(Temporarily unfilled)
	222 Sqn	Spitfires	12 (3)	Hornchurch	18	Sqn Ldr J. H. Hill
	600 Sqn	Blenheims	9 (5)	Hornchurch	23	Sqn Ldr D. de B. Clarke
	603 Sqn	Spitfires	13 (3)	Hornchurch	18	(Temporarily unfilled)
Tangmere	17 Sqn	Hurricanes	12 (5)	Tangmere	19	Sqn Ldr A. G. Miller
	43 Sqn	Hurricanes	10 (4)	Tangmere	19	Sqn Ldr C. B. Hull
	602 Sqn	Spitfires	12 (4)	Westhampnett	19	Sqn Ldr A. V. R. Johnstone
Debden	111 Sqn	Hurricanes	11 (5)	Debden	19	Sqn Ldr J. M. Thompson
	257 Sqn	Hurricanes	12 (5)	Debden	20	Sqn Ldr H. Harkness
	601 Sqn	Hurricanes	12 (5)	Debden	22	Sqn Ldr Sir Archibald Hope, Bt.

No. 12 Group, HQ Watnall, Nottingham: Air Vice-Marshal Trafford Leigh Leigh-Mallory						
Duxford	19 Sqn	Spitfires	11 (4)	Fowlmere	22	Sqn Ldr P. C. Pinkham
	310 Sqn	Hurricanes	10 (4)	Duxford	24	Sqn Ldr G. D. M. Blackwood
Coltishall	66 Sqn	Spitfires	10 (6)	Coltishall	19	Sqn Ldr R. H. A. Leigh
	242 Sqn	Hurricanes	11 (4)	Coltishall	21	Sqn Ldr D. R. S. Bader
Kirton-in-Lindsey	264 Sqn	Defiants	8 (7)	Kirton-in-Lindsey	18	Sqn Ldr G. D. Garvin
Digby	29 Sqn (6)	Blenheims	10 (4)	Wellingore	23	Sqn Ldr S. C. Widdows
	46 Sqn (7)	Hurricanes	15 (2)	Digby	20	Flt Lt A. D. Murray
	611 Sqn	Spitfires	12 (6)	Digby	23	Sqn Ldr J. E. McComb
Wittering	23 Sqn	Blenheims	11 (6)	Wittering	26	Sqn Ldr G. F. H. Heycock
	74 Sqn	Spitfires	11 (5)	Wittering	20	Sqn Ldr A. G. Malan
	229 Sqn	Hurricanes	12 (4)	Bircham Newton	18	Sqn Ldr H. J. Maguire
	266 Sqn	Spitfires	8 (4)	Wittering	17	(Temporarily unfilled)
No. 13 Group, HQ Newcastle, Northumberland: Air Vice-Marshal Richard Ernest Saul						
Church Fenton	64 Sqn	Spitfires	12 (6)	Leconfield	22	Sqn Ldr A. R. D. MacDonnell
	73 Sqn	Hurricanes	11 (4)	Church Fenton	19	Sqn Ldr M. W. S. Robinson
	302 Sqn	Hurricanes	12 (4)	Leconfield	26	Sqn Ldr W. A. J. Satchell; Sqn Ldr M. Mumler
Catterick	32 Sqn	Hurricanes	8 (6)	Acklington	15	Sqn Ldr M. N. Crossley
	41 Sqn	Spitfires	14 (3)	Catterick	20	Sqn Ldr H. West
	219 Sqn	Blenheims	8 (5)	Leeming	18	Sqn Ldr J. H. Little
	607 Sqn (8)	Hurricanes	16	Usworth	22	Sqn Ldr J. A. Vick
	610 Sqn	Spitfires	9 (2)	Acklington	18	Sqn Ldr J. Ellis
Turnhouse	141 Sqn	Defiants	9 (7)	Turnhouse	22	Sqn Ldr W. A. Richardson
	605 Sqn	Hurricanes	12 (5)	Drem	19	Sqn Ldr W. M. Churchill
Dyce	145 Sqn	Hurricanes	9 (5)	Montrose; Dyce	18	Sqn Ldr J. R. A. Peel
	263 Sqn (9)	Hurricanes	5 (3)	Grangemouth	10	Flt Lt T. P. Pugh
Wick	3 Sqn (10)	Hurricanes	15 (2)	Wick	22	Sqn Ldr S. F. Godden
	504 Sqn (11)	Hurricanes	14 (2)	Castletown	21	Sqn Ldr J. Sample

Notes: (1) Squadron moved to North Weald later on this day.
(2) Squadron moved to North Weald later on this day.
(3) Squadron moved to Boscombe Down later on this day.
(4) Squadron withdrawn to Digby later on this day.
(5) Squadron had moved from Biggin Hill to Croydon at 07.45 hrs on this day.
(6) Squadron also possessed one Hurricane (*P3201*) on strength.
(7) Squadron moved to Stapleford Tawney later on this day.
(8) Squadron moved to Tangmere later on this day.
(9) One flight only.
(10) Squadron under orders to move to Castletown, Caithness.
(11) Squadron under orders to move to Catterick *en route* for No. 11 Group.

II./LG 2. Within 14 minutes all Fighter Command Hurricane and Spitfire squadrons within 70 miles of London were airborne and flying flat out to intercept—21 squadrons, including the Hurricanes of Nos. 43, 46, 73, 79, 111, 242, 249, 253, 257, 303, 310, 504, 605 and 607, ordered to put up every serviceable fighter.[34]

By the time the picture cleared and showed that the Fighter Command airfields were not the bombers' targets, the first Do 17s were beginning their run in towards London's great sprawling docklands, but because the RAF fighters were all using different radio frequencies it took some minutes before all could be ordered to leave the vicinity of the key airfields which they had been guarding to make for the Thames Estuary. By that time the bombers had turned for home. However, as they passed just to the north of the Isle of Sheppey the second wave of bombers was just to the south, flying towards London. At about that moment, shortly before six o'clock, the full weight of British fighters fell upon the German phalanxes. In one of the war's greatest single air battles—involving more than 1,250 aircraft in an area about 40 by 15 miles—took place, lasting less than half an hour. The Duxford Wing, comprising a Spitfire squadron and three Hurricane squadrons—including No. 310 (Czech) Squadron—had still not properly formed up when it found itself in the battle, an entire *Jagdgeschwader* of Bf 109Es diving through it and shooting down 15 Hurricanes in 19 minutes over a single square mile. No. 249 Squadron lost six aircraft without scoring. No. 43 Squadron lost its popular South African commanding officer, Sqn Ldr Caesar Barrand Hull, as well as the Hawker Test Pilot, Dick Reynell, who was paying the squadron a short visit to obtain first-hand experience in combat operations. As the fire-fighting crews fought a losing battle to control the enormous conflagrations in London's dockland that evening, the wrecks of almost 100 aircraft lay smouldering on the ground in south-east England, a total of 52 German aircraft—including 26 fighters—being destroyed as well as 29 Hurricanes and 14 Spitfires. Seventeen RAF pilots were killed, including two squadron commanders and three flight commanders. By the end of the day No. 41 Squadron with Spitfires, which had lost its CO and both flight commanders in the last few days, was being led by a recently commissioned Pilot Officer, "Ben" Bennions.

Yet this tremendous ordeal by Fighter Command marked the turning point in its fortunes—despite its heavy casualties. Obviously it could not have survived many more days with such crippling losses. Yet, as the *Luftwaffe* switched to attacks on London and other towns and cities, the fighters were no longer forced to defend themselves and their airfields, and there was a considerable falling off of the daylight attacks—at any rate for a week. That respite enabled Dowding to replenish his depleted squadrons, moving rested pilots back to the South to occupy the gaps left by recent casualties.

Be that as it may, Dowding had effectively lost the equivalent of 11 fighter squadrons—far more than the combined strength of all the new squad-

Sqn Ldr Peter Townsend, CO of No 85 Squadron, with some of his sergeant pilots during the Battle of Britain. The picture was probably taken late in September after the Squadron had moved north to rest; Townsend had been wounded in the left foot early in the month, hence the walking stick.

rons formed since the battle started more than two months earlier.

The Final Battles

Time had almost run out for the planned invasion of Britain. However, convinced that the British fighter defences were now all but destroyed, Göring made one final big effort to attack London in daylight with successive waves of bombers on 15 September. This time, however, Fighter Command, much rested and restored to strength, was ready and in a memorable day of fighting over the capital and south-east England the Hurricanes and Spitfires scored a resounding victory—the date ever since commemorated by the nation as "Battle of Britain Day". For the loss of 20 Hurricanes (seven pilots killed and two wounded) and seven Spitfires (three pilots killed, one taken prisoner and two wounded), Fighter Command destroyed 36 bombers and 23 fighters. Perhaps more important in the circumstances, no RAF fighter squadron suffered the loss of more than three aircraft.

Such German losses, involving the death or capture of 163 flying personnel (including the *Gruppenkommandeur* of II./KG 53, Major Max Gruber, and nine *Staffelkapitäne*) finally convinced Hitler of the futility of attempting an invasion while Fighter Command remained so obviously very much in being, and the long-awaited Operation Sealion was finally abandoned—at least until the following spring.

Air attacks by the *Luftwaffe* now lost much of their enthusiasm, and there was a noticeable reduction in the strength of raiding formations for some days. With the night *Blitz* on London now in full swing it was clear to Dowding that not even the *Luftwaffe* possessed the strength to launch sustained attacks on Britain by day *and* night. That is not to suggest that the German air force did not occasionally send over big raids, as witness those on 27 September, when an attack over Surrey and Sussex was intercepted by 120 Hurricanes and Spitfires, and was followed by one of the biggest raids in the west yet seen—led by the Bf 110s of *Erprobungsgruppe 210* as pathfinders—against the Bristol factories at Filton, which was met by five of Brand's fighter squadrons. (On this raid *Erpr.Gr 210* lost its new *Gruppenkommandeur*, Hauptmann Martin Lutz, and a *Staffelkapitän*, the highly experienced veteran Oberleutnant Wilhelm Rössiger. Only after interrogation of a survivor did the RAF now become fully aware of the key rôle played by this extraordinary unit.) On that day the German air force lost 16 bombers, 20 Bf 110s and 18 Bf 109s, compared with 18 Spitfires (ten pilots killed) and 10 Hurricanes (five pilots killed). On the following day, although activity was once again on a smaller scale, RAF losses actually exceeded those of the *Luftwaffe*, resulting from a number of incidents in which Hurricanes were caught by free chases, 11 such aircraft and five Spitfires being shot down. Ten German aircraft were destroyed.

October saw a further reduction of German bomber activity by day over Britain, a change of tactics being made as the *Luftwaffe* embarked on the astonishing use of Bf 109Es as fighter-bombers. These aircraft flew in high over the English South Coast, usually carrying a single 550 lb bomb which was dropped at random over London. There can have been no real intention to bring RAF fighters to combat with these tactics as any study of combat reports by returning German pilots would have shown that very few combats had taken place over 30,000 feet, and most of the *Jagdbomber* sorties were flown at or above that height. Although a fair number of successful interceptions was made, few were accomplished by the Hurricanes.

Only one other incident remains to be mentioned here for, although it occurred shortly after the "official" date of the end of the Battle of Britain, it involved a daylight raid and was of necessity intercepted and dealt with in exactly the same manner by RAF Fighter Command as the attacks of high summer.

Ever since 10 June Mussolini had been at pains to convince his friend the *Reichsführer* that Italy could and would march shoulder to shoulder with the *Wehrmacht, Kriegsmarine* and *Luftwaffe* to final victory for Fascism in Europe. Despite misgivings by Göring, the *Regia Aeronautica* had sent a force of fighters and bombers to bases in Belgium at the end of September. Referred to as the *Corpo Aero Italiano* it comprised the 18° *Gruppo* with 50 Fiat CR.42 *Falco* (Falcon) biplane fighters, the 20° *Gruppo* with 48 Fiat G.50 *Freccia* (Arrow) monoplane fighters, two *Stormi*, the 13° and 43° with 80 Fiat BR.20 *Cicogna* (Stork) bombers and a *Squadriglia* of Cant Z.1007bis bombers. For all the size of this force, the RAF remained unaware of its presence for about a month as almost the entire energies of the Italian airmen were devoted to acclimatizing themselves to the flying conditions of northern Europe.

However, on the very day that Fleet Air Arm Swordfish dealt such a devastating blow against the Italian Navy at Taranto—11 November—the *Corpo Aero Italiano* set out with a force of 10 BR.20s escorted by 40 CR.42s and G.50s (as well as a few German Bf 109Es) to raid the port of Harwich, but were plotted by British radar and intercepted by three squadrons of Hurricanes (Nos. 17, 46 and 257); No. 257 Squadron (now commanded by Sqn Ldr Roland Robert Stanford Tuck, who was absent on leave this day, however) records the fight that followed:

> "Flt Lt Blatchford (Hurricane *V6962*), on running out of ammunition, attacked a CR.42 by ramming it, milling the enemy's top wing with his propeller. The total bag of aircraft destroyed by the Squadron was as follows: Plt Offs North (*V6864*) and Mortimer (*P2835*) shared a BR.20;

Hurricane I EF-R of No 232 Squadron crashed during a transit flight from Manston to Croydon on 10th September 1940 while being flown by Sergeant Alec Butterick. Note that the Browning guns have already been removed by the salvage crew—always one of the first actions taken in such circumstances. The aircraft was later repaired and issued to an Operational Training Unit. (Photo: *via R. L. Ward, Farnborough, Neg Ref F86/1/27A-28A)*

Plt Off North shared a BR.20 with a pilot of No. 46 Squadron; Plt Off Davey (*V7607*) shared a BR.20 with a pilot of No. 46 Squadron; Plt Off Pniak (*V7292*), one BR.20; Sgt Barnes (*V6873*), one CR.42; Sgt Lucas (*R4088*), one CR.42; Plt Off Pniak shared a BR.20 with Plt Off Kay (*V6680*); Plt Off Kay shared a BR.20 with Plt Off Andrews; Plt Off North, one Bf. 109."[35]

Although these victories were by no means outstanding by Battle of Britain standards (there being no losses among the RAF fighters), they were sufficient to discourage further daylight attacks by the Italians and, although there were some light attacks on British coastal targets at night, most of the aircraft and airmen of the *Corpo Aero Italiano* left Belgium in the New Year, and all were gone by April.

★ ★ ★

And so the great daylight Battle of Britain petered out at the end of October 1940. The victory of Fighter Command—for such it was—was not one of destruction of the *Luftwaffe* but one of survival by RAF Fighter Command and frustration of German plans. The *Luftwaffe* was still, after all, a powerful force in being, and one that was now mounting a devastating offensive against Britain by night. The night *Blitz* now found Britain's defences sadly lacking, as the mounting toll of civilian casualties in her cities testified all too clearly.

But the *Luftwaffe*, hitherto invincible throughout Europe, had been checked for the first time and it had suffered very heavy losses among its highly trained flying personnel, men who could not be replaced quickly in wartime. Others, however, hitherto anonymous, now stood head and shoulders above their peers, men such as Werner Mölders, Adolf Galland, Hajo Herrmann, Herbert Ihlefeld, Hans-Joachim Helbig, Dietrich Peltz, Egon Meyer, Paul-Werner Hozzel, Alwin Boerst, Kurt Bühlingen, Gordon Gollob, Walter Oesau, Jochen Muncheberg, Josef Priller, Heinz Bär, Wolf-Dietrich

Reproduction of one of the famous Cuthbert Orde portraits of RAF pilots, here showing Sergeant Jozef František, the Czech pilot who served on No 303 (Polish) Squadron and was the top-scoring RAF pilot in the Battle of Britain. Dated 19th September 1940 the drawing was executed during the short period of this gallant pilot's prolific combat spell; he is pictured wearing the Czech War Cross. (Photo: *Imperial War Museum, Neg No LD421)*

Wilcke, Gerhard Barkhorn, Hans Phillipp and Anton Hackl; all would create a powerful tradition in the *Luftwaffe* that would sustain it for nearly five more years of European war.

The legacy of the battle for the Royal Air Force was perhaps more sombre. The Battle of France and the Battle of Britain destroyed all remnants of the "finest flying club in the world" of pre-war years. Almost half the peacetime Regular pilots in Fighter Command had gone forever. The Command that survived the summer would, however, live to prosper on a newly fostered tradition by the surviving Regulars like Douglas Bader, Bob Stanford Tuck, "Teddy" Donaldson, "Ginger" Lacey, "Sammy" Allard, "Roly" Beamont, Pete Brothers, Mike Crossley, "Butch" Dalton-Morgan, Al Deere, Colin Gray, Johnnie Johnson, Brian Kingcombe, "Sailor" Malan, Des McMullen and "Pancho" Villa, to name but some of the Few; to them were added those who had come to the Colours at the outbreak of war, men like Eric Lock and "Ben" Bennions, and those who fought with the RAF after their own countries had been overrun, Jan Zumbach, Jan Zurakowski and Witold Urbanowicz and the others. The highest-scoring Fighter Command pilot of them all, the Czech Sergeant Jozef František, who flew Hurricanes with No. 303 (Polish) Squadron during September and who shot down 17 German aircraft—all of them in that fateful month—alas had died over Sussex on 8 October.

8

FURTHER STORM PRECAUTIONS

Long before the Battle of Britain was over a new version of the Hurricane was being delivered to Fighter Command, the Mark II with 1,260 hp Rolls-Royce Merlin XX. Indeed the first trial installation had been flown in a Mark I (*P3269*) as early as 11 June, 1940, at Langley by Philip Lucas, and this aeroplane duly became the prototype Mark II Hurricane.[36]

Although the idea of producing a more powerful version of the Hurricane dated back to 1938—a part of the normal development of any fighter—there is no doubt but that the Hawker design staff was more than a trifle disappointed that its fighter was some 25–30 mph slower than the Spitfire; time would show that the decision to opt for a simpler and more easily manufactured airframe was entirely justified, apart from which the Hurricane was to prove superior to the Spitfire in other aspects no less vital than actual combat.

Be that as it may it soon became apparent that the Hurricane would never match the Spitfire in speed performance so long as it retained the relatively thick wing. Nor was the Air Ministry likely under any circumstances to encourage a radical departure from the basic structural configuration simply because—for the time being at any rate—two Hurricanes for every Spitfire was a perfectly satisfactory *status quo*. Camm knew all too well how difficult it had been even to get his metal wing introduced.

Therefore any significant improvement in the Hurricane's performance[37] would have to be achieved using a Merlin of increased power, and one that required little or no alteration to the standard Mark I airframe. Hawker and Rolls-Royce had collaborated "privately" to investigate alternatives to the Merlin II and III, and had flown the RM.3S (a Merlin III with two-stage supercharger, DH propeller and 100-octane fuel, first flown by Reynell on 6 July, 1939), the Merlin XII (flown in *L2026* by Seth-Smith, and later tested with interconnected throttle and pitch controls) and the RM.4S (flown in *G-AFKX* by Reynell on 9 June, 1940, and later to become the Merlin 45 with two-stage supercharger).

The first Merlin XX was delivered to Langley in April 1940, and by June deliveries of 14 such engines had been made to Hawker. Performance measurements returned a maximum true airspeed of 348 mph at 17,500 feet in S-gear, the height at which the two-stage supercharger came into optimum effect. At first the engine produced only 1,180 hp for take-off, but within three months this had been increased to 1,260. In the meantime numerous relatively minor modifications had been introduced which together added some 308 lb to the all-up weight and, according to evaluation figures produced at the time, showed that the newly built Hurricane Mark IIA Series 1 being delivered to RAF Fighter Command in October 1940 possessed a top speed of 342 mph at 17,400 feet in S-gear. Nevertheless the 32 Hurricanes delivered to the squadrons between 4 September and the end of that month were the fastest fully-armed Hurricanes ever flown—but still about 20 mph slower than the Spitfire IIA, then also in service.

In the meantime Hawker had also been able to demonstrate that it was perfectly feasible to install two extra Browning machine guns in each of the Hurricane's wings—believing that this armament, which had been stipulated as one of the alternative armaments for the Typhoon and Tornado, would be eagerly accepted by the Air Ministry. However, for fear that a shortage of Brownings might occur during the Battle of Britain (it never did), the proposal was set aside for a future decision.

An aerial view of 'Claremont', the large mansion near Esher, Surrey, built for Clive of India in 1772 with gardens by Capability Brown, whither Hawker's experimental design staff repaired during the War. Here most of the design work on the Hurricane II and IV, as well as that of the Typhoon, Tempest and Fury monoplane, was carried out in greater safety from bombs than beside the railway line at Kingston. (Photo: *Sydney Camm Collection)*

The Hurricane IIA Series 1 was greeted with enthusiasm by the fighter squadrons and the Air Ministry decided to embark on a programme to convert a number of Hurricane Is that had been returned to maintenance units for fitting of metal wings or in instances where battle damage had been suffered in the nose of the aircraft. In due course 20 such aircraft (in the BV serial range) were modified by MUs, Hawker and Gloster, and 40 (in the DG serial range) by Rolls-Royce. (Later still, because the Russians turned up their noses at Hurricane Is, 40 more Mark Is, in the DR serial range, were converted to Mark IIs, these being shipped to Murmansk late in 1941; see page 115.) By the time these conversions began appearing in 1941 deliveries of Mark IIs from Langley and Hucclecote were in full swing and most "secondhand" Mark IIs were issued to Hurricane training units.

For some months the RAF had been interested in adapting the Hurricane to carry long-range external fuel tanks, the first such trial installation being carried out on the Mark I, *P3462*, and flown by Reynell on 7 May, 1940, at the time of the Norwegian campaign. It was then intended to fly Hurricanes direct to Narvik, and although the highest priority was given to manufacturing these tanks the campaign was called off. However, as is told in Chapter 11, the RAF in the Middle East was calling for urgent reinforcements and the aircraft which had been modified for Norway, as well as the 44-gallon auxiliary fuel tanks, were immediately assembled for a series of flights to Egypt via southern France, Tunisia and Egypt. The tanks were attached by means of twin toggles and a deep fairing (that would today be referred to as a wing pylon) just outboard of the wing centre/outer section joint. These early tanks were non-jettisonable in flight and were not stressed for combat. Starting in September, however, the "Takoradi" reinforcement route across Africa was opened, over which a constant flow of Hurricanes would henceforth pass to the Middle East. Apart from pathfinding Blenheims, Hurricane Is with fixed ferry tanks constituted all the early deliveries—32 in September and 42 in October. As the new-build Hurricane I production would soon run out on all production lines Hawker was asked to incorporate a universal wing centre-section which would be capable of accommodating outer wings with provision for external fuel tanks *and* with either eight or 12 machine guns. This version was termed the Hurricane Mark II Series 2 and, unless fitted with the 12-gun wings, was almost indistinguishable from the Series 1. However, a new production line of Hurricanes was being planned at the Longbridge factory of the Austin Motor Company, with a contract calling for 300 Hurricane IIs; the Standard of Preparation, which was issued by DTD on 18 January, 1941, showed the aircraft to be termed as "tropically-equipped Mark IIA Series 2 aircraft with eight Browning guns and enlarged coolant header tank necessitating the inclusion of additional fuselage nose bay, thus lengthening the aircraft by 6.5 inches". This has always been understood to indicate that *all* Series 2 aircraft possessed a greater overall length, but it is now known that only the first dozen or so aircraft included the enlarged header tank: flight trials of the first Austin aircraft at Langley showed that the aircraft with lengthened nose and Vokes filter suffered from loss of handling crispness and the modification was cancelled. Thereafter the Austin-built Hurricanes reverted to standard (and indeed few of them were completed as "tropicalized" aircraft). Because the relatively small number of photos that were ever published of the Longbridge aeroplanes showed that they included the diaphragm added to the faceplate on the fuselage nose, immediately aft of the propeller, the impression was given of a longer nose.

Although Hurricane IIA Series 2s continued to be produced intermittently from October 1940 until

The Hawker factory at Langley, Bucks, whence Hurricanes flowed for almost five years during the War, with its grass airfield beyond. In post-War years its proximity to London airport led to its disposal and transfer of Hawker's flying operations to Dunsfold in Surrey. (Photo: *Hawker Aircraft Ltd*)

about September 1942, almost all with eight-gun wings, they were generally phased out of front-line service in Britain in mid-1941. The very large production orders for Hurricane IIs placed during the autumn of 1940 seldom differentiated between subvariants and the distribution of these along the production lines was dictated almost invariably by the availability of armament and other equipment.

Authority to go ahead with production of 12-gun wings was received at Canbury Park Road on 2 November, 1940, and by the end of that month seven such sets were already fitted to aircraft being made ready for transporting to Langley. Meanwhile the design offices at Kingston had gone one stage further and produced an adaptation of the light bomb rack which enabled it to be fitted to the ferry tank toggle fasteners under the wings, and a Hurricane I, *P2989*, was accordingly modified for trials at Boscombe Down and flown early in 1941. The aircraft proved to be an ideal choice for low-level bombing and, when the same installation was made in an early, full-power Merlin XX Mark II Hurricane the Air Ministry asked Hawker to modify the armament wiring on all Mark IIs to permit the fitting of bomb racks, and the same modifications were introduced at a convenient stage in the Gloster line.

By the end of 1940 three Fighter Command squadrons were fully equipped with the Hurricane IIA Series 2, No. 46 Squadron (now commanded by Sqn Ldr A. C. Rabagliati, see page 86, note 34) at Digby, No. 303 (Polish) Squadron (Sqn Ldr Ronald Gustav Kellett, AAF) at Leconfield, and No. 605 Squadron at Croydon (Sqn Ldr Gerald Richmond Edge, DFC, AAF). During the next three months Nos. 1, 17, 69, 111, 249, 302 (Polish), 310 (Czech) and 615 Squadrons also took delivery of Mark IIs, and in February 1941 the first Hurricane IIBs (without bombing modifications) were delivered to No. 56 Squadron at Duxford (Sqn Ldr Edgar Norman Ryder, later Gp Capt, CBE, DFC and Bar), No. 242 Squadron now at Martlesham Heath but still commanded by the legless Douglas Bader, and No. 249 Squadron at North Weald (Sqn Ldr Robert Alexander Barton, DFC, later OBE, DFC and Bar). By the summer 24 squadrons in the United Kingdom were flying Hurricane IIAs or IIBs, or a mixed complement of each. The first Mark IIB bombers (or Hurribombers as they were popularly called) reached the squadrons in May, and thereafter working teams from the maintenance units toured the fighter stations to carry out the electrical alterations to enable the earlier Hurricane IIs to carry a pair of 250 lb GP bombs.

From about late May 1941 Hurricane IIBs were beginning to appear at Langley with tropical filters, and in June the first such aircraft reached Malta, where they joined No. 185 Squadron (Sqn Ldr P. W. Mould, DFC, the veteran of No. 1 Squadron in France, see page 53). Although bomb gear also arrived at Hal Far at the same time it was not fitted to the Hurricanes for about a year, the aircraft being initially confined to interception duties.

Four Cannon

To many pilots the Hurricane IIB was the most enjoyable of all versions to fly, retaining all the excellent manoeuvrability of the old Mark I but with a better power/weight ratio and better climb and height performance. It was moreover well able to look after itself in combat with the Messerschmitt Bf 109E. Unfortunately, however, by the time it reached the Service in large numbers in northern Europe, that is the spring of 1941, the German Emil was beginning to be replaced by the 109F and this fighter was in turn superior in most respects to the Hurricane. Most important—and frustrating—was the inability of the British rifle-calibre Browning gun to penetrate German armour, now somewhat increased since the summer of 1940. As one RAF pilot so succinctly put it: "Having 50 per cent more peashooters only means you've got 50 per cent more peas bouncing off Luftwaffe armour." Rifle-calibre guns were still effective when used in the ground attack rôle, but even then only against thin-skinned targets such as truck and troop concentrations.

As has already been shown, the RAF first issued a

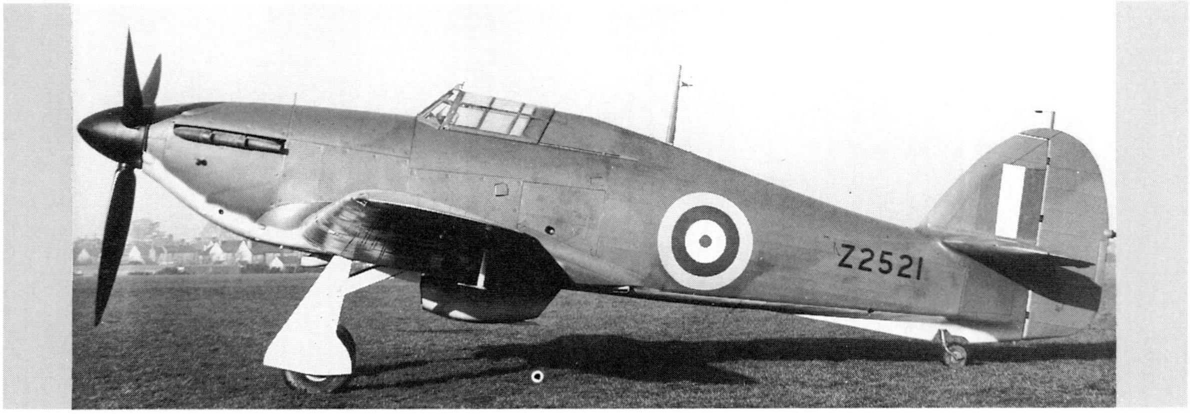

An early Hurricane Mark IIA Series 1, Z2521, with Rotol propeller, Merlin XX and IFF aerials, representative of the version being delivered to Fighter Command before the end of 1940. (Photo: *Hawker Aircraft Ltd., Neg No HG 16)*

A late Hurricane I, V7826, *underwent trials with tropical filter and auxiliary fuel tanks to enable this version to use the tanks in combat in the Middle East in 1941.* (Photo: *Sydney Camm Collection)*

A standard Oerlikon-armed mid-series Hurricane Mark IIC with 44-gallon drop tanks at Brooklands in May 1942. (Photo: *Hawker Aircraft Ltd., Neg No WEY/14/42)*

requirement for an armament of four cannon in a fighter in 1936, to which Hawker had unsuccessfully tendered a scheme for a Hurricane thus armed (see page 35). Sydney Camm, for all his innate conservatism, had remained convinced that the Hurricane could and should be armed with four cannon, but the Air Ministry came as close as it dared to directing Hawker *not* to pursue this line of development. The two-cannon trial installation (in *L1750*), which was a Service experimental requirement, had been a purely academic exercise to discover what effects firing such weapons from high-performance aeroplanes would have in such areas as aircraft trim change, cartridge scatter and discharge under manoeuvring g forces, gun harmonization (that is the range of optimum shot convergence) and icing. After all very little experience existed in Britain of firing guns like the 20-mm Oerlikon or Hispano cannon from aircraft.

Camm, however, got his way in February 1940 (during the period of the so-called Phoney War) and was allowed to undertake a trial installation of four Oerlikon cannon in a pair of damaged metal wings—which the DTD insisted should be purchased by Hawker! The guns acquired were of fairly old naval pattern employing drum feed which demanded winding the drums against strong rotary springs prior to loading, but nevertheless proved capable of being accommodated within the wings, with only small blister fairings on the upper surface. Because the gun barrels projected through the front main spar, access panels had to be provided aft of the rear spar so that the entire gun bodies could be withdrawn rearwards for gun changing.

Fortunately work went ahead very quickly on the trial installation, and using a spare DTD development aircraft, believed to be *P2640*,[38] the first flight was made by Reynell on 27 May. From an exchange of memoranda shortly afterwards it seems that his flight was not sanctioned by DTD and the wings were removed. However, the preliminary handling and performance of this Mark I Hurricane undoubtedly intrigued the Air Ministry (a top speed of only fractionally under 300 mph TAS at 12,800 feet), so much so that, despite an embargo placed on all development work not associated with standard Hurricanes immediately after Dunkirk, the entire installation and wings were repurchased by the Ministry and directed to be fitted on the first available Merlin XX-powered airframe on the production line (*V7360*). The aircraft was completed in great secrecy at Langley and made its first flight on about 10 July; indeed only the one flight was made (by an unknown Hawker pilot) before the aircraft was delivered to Boscombe Down for a total of six trial gun-firing sorties.

Some difficulty was experienced with the drum feed tensioning, which resulted in runaway bursts occurring when firing the guns under g, and on one occasion, when firing the cannon in a simulated quarter attack, two guns ran away on one side while the other two jammed, causing the aircraft to execute the nearest to a true flick roll the Hurricane had ever managed![39] Having adjusted the drum tensioning, *V7360* was delivered to North Weald at the beginning of September for No. 151 Squadron to evaluate it under combat conditions. As already related, this squadron had just been taken out of the battle and the aircraft was passed to Flight Lieutenant Rabagliati of No. 46 Squadron on the 5th (see Ref Note 34).

No record apparently survives of any formal report by Rabagliati (other than his combat reports, Forms 1151), but, bearing in mind the combat damage sustained on the 7th, it is likely that *V7360* was sent to a maintenance unit for repair before being returned either to Boscombe Down or Langley. It next features in Hawker experimental flight test records on 5 December, when Philip Lucas took it aloft for a gun-bay heating test. This is the first reference that can be found to the aeroplane's new designation, the Hurricane Mark IIC, and therefore one assumes that it was regarded as the first prototype.

In the meantime considerable work had been done by the various armament establishments and companies to develop aircraft cannon in Britain, in particular the Oerlikon, whose drum feed, as it stood, was clearly unsuitable. Nevertheless Hawker was now instructed to go ahead with the repair of 30 sets of damaged wings, hand-tooling the modifications necessary to accommodate 12 batteries of drum-fed Oerlikons, 12 of Chatellerault belt-fed Oerlikons and six sets for batteries of Hispano Mark I 20-mm cannon (the last two systems were under development for the four-cannon version of the Typhoon). These wings were fitted to Hurricane IIs on the production lines at Langley and Hucclecote as the guns became available, and by the end of February 11 Hurricane IICs—all regarded as prototypes—were flying, including *V7360, V2461, V2589, Z2885, Z2891, V3521* and *W9314*. Three had already been delivered to Boscombe Down, where performance trials had returned a mean maximum speed recorded as 336 mph TAS at 16,600 feet at an all-up weight of 8,100 lb. Shortly

After the death of the famous pre-War Hurricane squadron commander, Wg Cdr John Gillan of No 111 Squadron, his mother donated to the nation the cost of two Hurricanes one of which, inscribed "OUR JOHN"—a Mark IIC bomber—is seen here at the Hawker factory on the occasion of its dedication by Mrs Gillan. (Photo: *John W. R. Taylor)*

Two views of Z2905 (at Langley, above, and Boscombe Down), the TI Hurricane IIC used to test fly the big 88-gallon ferry tanks that were to play such an important part in enabling the Hurricane to reinforce distant war theatres—though they were less frequently available than the widely-used 44-gallon tanks. (Photos: *Hawker Aircraft Ltd., dated February 1942)*

afterwards two of the aircraft were fitted with Vokes tropical filters and the maximum speed recorded at 320 mph at 16,200 feet at a weight of 8,260 lb.

Initial firing clearance of the Oerlikon guns to Service requirements was obtained at the end of March, by which time about 40 production Hurricane IICs were undergoing final preparation at maintenance units for issue to Fighter Command squadrons. At this stage all aircraft were equipped with drum-fed Oerlikons owing to some work remaining to be done to overcome gun-bay icing affecting the Chatellerault feed.

The first Squadrons to receive the Hurricane IIC, both in April, were No. 3 at Martlesham Heath (Sqn Ldr Russell Faulkner Aitken, later Gp Capt, CBE, AFC) and No. 257 at Coltishall (still commanded by Sqn Ldr Bob Stanford Tuck, DFC). The first Service deliveries of Mark IICs with Chatellerault gun feeds were made to No. 46 Squadron (still led by Rabagliati) at Sherburn-in-Elmet at the end of April, it being intended that this squadron would take them to the Middle East early in May; at the last moment this plan was dropped and, after removal of their tropical filters, the aircraft were handed on to No. 87 Squadron at Charmy Down (Sqn Ldr Ian Richard Gleed, later Wg Cdr, DFC). The first Mark IICs flown in the Middle East were those of No. 229 Squadron (Sqn Ldr Frederick Ernest Rosier, later Air Marshal Sir Frederick, KCB, CBE, DSO[40]) newly arrived in the Western Desert in September.

More Hurricane IICs were produced than any other version—a figure of 4,711 examples being widely quoted as the total—before production finally ended in September 1944. They served initially in the United Kingdom on offensive daylight sweeps, but almost immediately assumed the night fighter rôle as well, both over Britain and as intruders over the Channel and northern France. They were capable of carrying bomb racks from the start, originally for a pair of 250-pounders, but later, in 1942, two 500 lb bombs. They frequently carried 44-gallon drop tanks into combat and, when required to fly the Takoradi reinforcement route from late 1941 across Africa they were invariably fitted with the "big" 88-gallon ferry tanks.

A dedicated night interceptor variant was produced in the late summer of 1941 featuring AI Mark V radar mounted in a special fairing (approximating in shape and size to the 44-gallon drop tank), a fixed 44-gallon fuel tank being carried under the other wing; the associated radar aerials were located on the outer wings. Most Hurricanes used for night operations were fitted with a pair of small horizontal rectangular shields just forward of the windscreen quarterlights to mask the glare from the Merlin's exhaust stubs from the cockpit. (All Hurricane IIs' decking panels were drilled to mount these shields, and it was only the work of a few minutes to attach them prior to a night sortie.)

Numerous trials were carried out on Hurricane IICs during the war. Among the most interesting were those involving the towing of the fighters by Wellington bombers. Originally conceived in 1940 when the lack of long-range fighters posed so many problems for the RAF, the idea of reinforcing Malta by towing Hurricanes from the United Kingdom was examined. The collapse of France put paid to this scheme and, following the loss of HMS *Glorious* and the entry of Italy into the war, it was thought unlikely that an aircraft carrier would be available to carry fighter reinforcements into the Mediterra-

THE TOWED-HURRICANE EXPERIMENTS

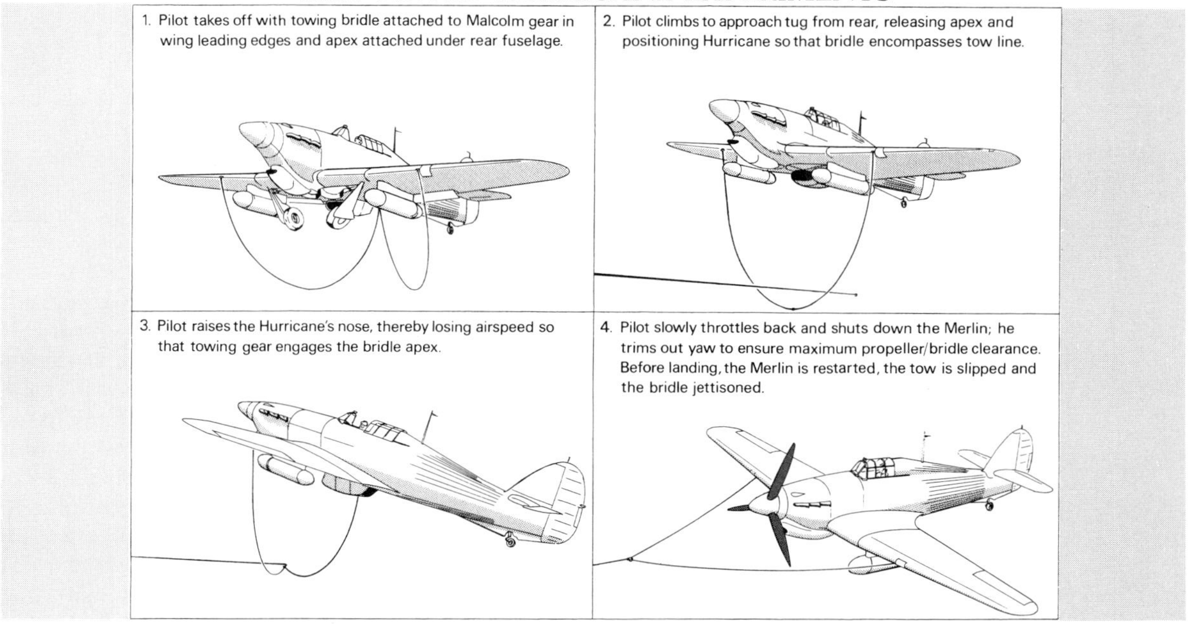

1. Pilot takes off with towing bridle attached to Malcolm gear in wing leading edges and apex attached under rear fuselage.

2. Pilot climbs to approach tug from rear, releasing apex and positioning Hurricane so that bridle encompasses tow line.

3. Pilot raises the Hurricane's nose, thereby losing airspeed so that towing gear engages the bridle apex.

4. Pilot slowly throttles back and shuts down the Merlin; he trims out yaw to ensure maximum propeller/bridle clearance. Before landing, the Merlin is restarted, the tow is slipped and the bridle jettisoned.

nean. Although the Royal Navy quickly came to the rescue with HMS *Argus*, the towing scheme went ahead in 1941 with the idea of using Gibraltar as the point of departure.

Unfortunately, although Wellingtons were already staging through Gibraltar on their own reinforcement flights to the Middle East, the tiny 950-yard airstrip with its swirling crosswinds made it most unlikely that a Wellington with a fighter in tow could have got airborne in the space available. An alternative scheme was therefore evolved in which the tug and fighter took off independently and linked up after take off. Four Gloster-built Hurricane Is were delivered to the airfield at Staverton near Gloucester, where Flight Refuelling Ltd possessed a test facility. The aircraft were fitted with Malcolm hydraulic towing attachments to each outer wing to which were hooked the ends of a steel bridle. Under the direction of Charles Barnard a series of flights was made and the general feasibility of the scheme confirmed. However, apart from some problems (which could have been quite simply overcome) in starting up the Hurricane's engine after being towed for perhaps 700 miles, another factor put paid to the scheme, namely America's entry into the war at the end of 1941 and her offer of a carrier to transport large numbers of fighters into the Mediterranean. Had the towed-fighter scheme been feasible early in 1941 there is little doubt but that it would have been of considerable value in the reinforcement of Malta.

Another scheme involving Hurricanes was their mounting on top of Liberator patrol aircraft of RAF Coastal Command. The purpose of the scheme was to provide the patrol aircraft with its own escort as well as a fighter which might attack enemy patrol aircraft. Responsibility for developing a mounting superstructure on the Liberator was vested in Short Bros Ltd, while Hawker prepared drawings for the modifications necessary in the Hurricane IIC. The ultimate success achieved by Hurricanes catapulted from merchantmen (see Chapter 10)—these fighters also being expendable though with a better chance of rescuing their pilots—the difficulty likely to be encountered in starting the Merlin in mid-Atlantic, and the prolonged discomfort suffered by the Hurricane pilot, caused the project to be discontinued fairly soon, although the scheme *was* briefly studied as an alternative to the towed-fighter idea for theatre reinforcement.

Rockets and Tank-busters

The use of rockets as missiles by British forces dates back to the eighteenth century, and probably reached its zenith in the British Army during the latter half of the last century with the Congreve rocket. Experimental work had continued in fits and starts until shortly before the Second World War, when stocks of cordite-filled three-inch rocket "motors" (in fact no more than three-inch iron pipes with a central ignition core) were created by the Royal Arsenal for possible applications under consideration by the Admiralty and War Office. One of the first major applications was the wide-spread deployment of the so-called UP (unrotated projectile) anti-aircraft rocket barrage batteries introduced for the defence of British cities during the latter half of the winter *Blitz* of 1940–41.

Later in 1941, as part of a programme to investigate arming various RAF aircraft (including Swordfish, Hudsons and Liberators) with the three-inch rocket projectiles for anti-shipping operations, a Hurricane IIA Series 2 (with "universal" wings), *Z2415*, was fitted with three rocket launcher rails under each wing, this aircraft being selected from DTD aircraft at Langley as retaining strengthened wing spars following terminal velocity diving trials in 1941 (such strengthening being thought necessary to withstand high-g manoeuvres rather than any stresses caused by the rockets, which of course impose no firing recoil). This and two further aircraft, similarly modified, were delivered to Boscombe Down later that year.

Work continued on the Rolls-Royce BF 40-mm anti-tank gun long after the Air Ministry selected its rival, the Vickers 'S' gun. This photo, dated 19th November 1942, shows details of the gun body recoil chamber and the method of mounting; the Hurricane wing is shown here inverted on working trestles. (Photo: *Hawker Aircraft Ltd., Neg No 796)*

Never the most accurate weapon against very small targets, the three-inch rockets' optimum firing pattern (using 60 lb explosive warheads) was found to be a ripple salvo firing pairs of missiles at about ten-millisecond intervals by means of a rotary switch, and so, in the instance of the Hurricane—and other RAF fighters—it was decided to increase the normal complement to eight rockets. In the event of attacks on relatively large targets, such as merchant ships and, much later, the flying bomb sites and lock gates, all eight rockets could be fired in a single salvo ... the equivalent of a naval cruiser's main armament broadside.

Although the rocket trials with the Hurricane were concluded quickly and successfully (probably as early as May 1942), no immediate call was made to equip Hurricane squadrons engaged in offensive sweeps with the rockets; indeed the weapon did not come into widespread use until 1943. Two reasons for this delay have been cited in semi-official documents; first, that the Admiralty claimed first priority on rocket stocks for anti-shipping operations, so that Fleet Air Arm and Coastal Command aircraft had first call on the weapons; secondly that Fighter Command wished to gain the maximum benefit of surprise by using the weapons only in the preliminary "softening-up" phase of an invasion of Europe. In the event that the second argument *was* indeed put forward, no more ridiculous policy was ever pursued during the war. The very fact that Coastal Command *did* employ the weapon in 1942 compromised secrecy in any case, whereas the use of rockets by the supporting fighters during the Dieppe raid of August 1942 would have had a shattering effect on the German coastal defences on that occasion, and could well have played an important part in reversing the fortunes of the luckless landing forces.

Two views of the anti-tank TI Hurricane Z2326, a converted Mark IIA. Above, the aircraft at Langley with the Vickers 'S' guns and, below, at Boscombe Down with the Rolls-Royce BF guns. As far as is known no photographs exist of the latter in fairings, but it seems that such fairings would have been extremely bulky compared to those on the production Vickers-armed Hurricane IID. (Photos: *above, Hawker Aircraft Ltd., Neg No HG5/8/20, and below, Author's Collection)*

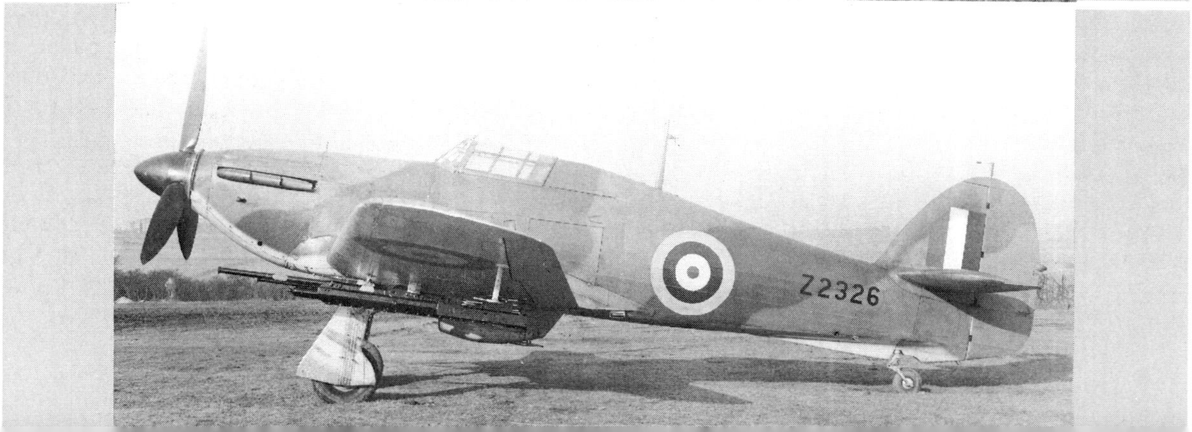

In all likelihood the "delay" in introducing the rocket projectiles into Fighter Command was no more than an excuse voiced later to conceal an attitude of distrust of the weapon that certainly existed among some senior officers and commanders. In some respects the distrust was not misplaced. After all, none of the trials conducted in 1942 demonstrated any great accuracy of the rockets particularly when employed by fighters approaching their targets "at ground level" owing to the big gravity drop, and there was much to be said for the cannon and bomb in such attacks. It was later shown that the rocket was much more accurate when discharged in a fairly steep diving attack. The 20-mm cannon possessed tremendous penetration power against anything but a fairly heavily armoured target. Be that as it may the rocket projectile, once it joined Fighter Command and for all its lack of sophistication and accuracy, survived in RAF service as long as the standard fighter armament of four 20-mm cannon!

★ ★ ★

If the 20-mm cannon was relatively ineffective against heavily armoured ground targets—such as tanks—the other weapon which came to be developed for use by the Hurricane was indeed designed precisely with those targets in mind.

Both Rolls-Royce and Vickers had, since 1939, been working to produce 40-mm guns suitable for mounting in fighter aircraft. To do so, bearing in mind that this was the calibre of the Bofors light anti-aircraft gun, demanded an emphasis on compactness and weight-saving that went far beyond the traditional reputation of gun designers. DTD (Armaments) at the Ministry of Aircraft Production was kept fully informed of the progress of these guns and early in 1941 informed the Air Staff that the basis now existed on which to investigate their installation in a fighter. By then the Hurricane II was demonstrating its ability to accommodate 12 machine guns or four 20-mm cannon, and there seemed no logical reason to suppose the aircraft should not now be able to cope with a pair of 40-mm weapons.

Early in May, therefore, instructions were passed to the Hawker Experimental Design Office (now at Claremont, a requisitioned mansion near Esher, whither the Design Staff had recently moved) to prepare drawings for the necessary modifications to permit two Vickers Type S guns to be mounted under the wings of the Hurricane IIA Series 2. All but two of the Brownings were to be deleted, the remaining two being used to fire alternate ball and tracer ammunition to assist in sighting the big guns. This work started on 30 May and a fortnight later the first pair of guns arrived at Langley for installation in Hurricane II *Z2326*, this aircraft thus becoming the prototype Hurricane IID. Its maiden flight, made by Seth-Smith, was made at an all-up weight (without ammunition and half fuel) of 7,460 lb on 18 September, the guns themselves not being enclosed in fairings. On the following day *Z2326* was delivered to Boscombe Down for preliminary assessment, and after a short visit to the RAE at Farnborough was returned to Langley for installation of the Rolls-Royce BF (belt-fed) 40-mm guns. These cannon were bulkier than the Vickers and carried 12 rounds compared with the Vickers' 15, and after a major failure in one of the BF guns the Rolls-Royce weapon was discontinued and attention was henceforth concentrated on the exceptionally compact and reliable Vickers S.

Much more prolonged firing trials were carried out by the Service, starting in February, using four Hurricane IIDs, a new low-profile fairing now enclosing the gun bodies. The first 92 production aircraft to reach the maintenance units all featured the same armour protection as fitted in the Hurricane IIC, but from July onwards the armour was increased by 368 lb, resulting in a maximum cleared weight for ground attack manoeuvres (3g) of 8,218 lb. By local strengthening of the outer wing attachments this was increased to 8,540 lb—including a tropical filter, at 4g with an ultimate factor of 1.3. Attempts were occasionally made to fly the early Mark IIDs with asymmetric underwing loads on operations, as witness an aircraft of No. 184 Squadron flown in 1943 with a 40-mm gun under one wing and four 60-lb rockets under the other; when the gun was fired the yaw was so sudden and fierce that the rockets and rails broke away from the other side. Soon after, with stronger attachments, such asymmetric loads were commonplace in the Mediterranean and Far East, although aiming only one gun was distinctly difficult.

About 300 Hurricane IID anti-tank fighters were produced, the first production aircraft being despatched by sea to the Middle East in March 1942 and reaching No. 6 Squadron (Sqn Ldr Roger Cave Porteous, DSO) at Shandur in Egypt at the end of the following month. The next two squadrons were both based in the United Kingdom, No. 164 (Sqn Ldr Desmond Papworth McKeown, DFC) and No. 184 (Sqn Ldr Jack Rose, DFC) at Colerne. The great majority of the remainder was shipped to the Middle and Far East; in the latter theatre they equipped Nos. 5 and 20 Squadrons during 1943 and 1944. Following the arrival of the Hurricane Mark IV (see below) in the Middle East, the Mark IID became largely redundant and, when stocks allowed, fairly large numbers joined the flow of aircraft being supplied to the Soviet Union in mid-1943

The "Universal" Hurricane Mark IV

The idea of a "universal" wing, which had been conceived late in 1940, enabled the basic Merlin XX-powered Hurricane IIA to be equipped to mount eight- or 12-gun wings, as well as bombs, drop tanks, ferry tanks and certain other stores,[41]

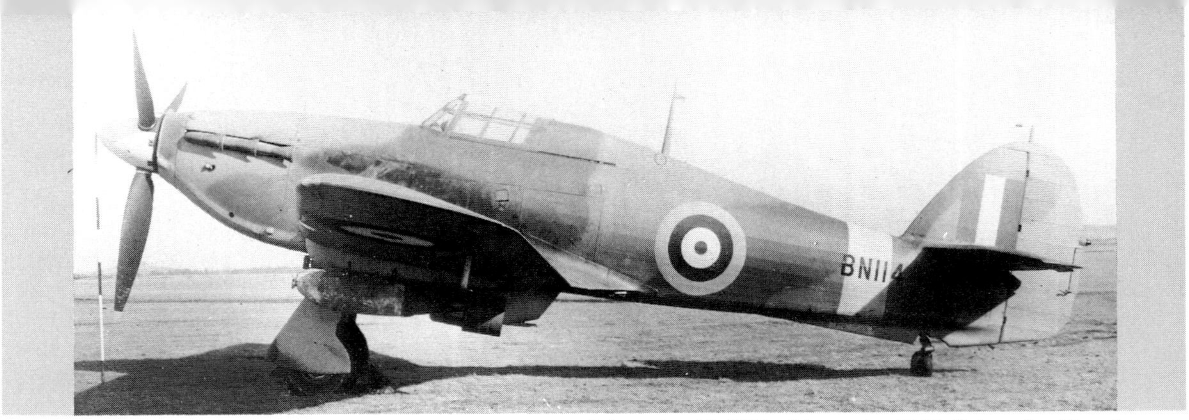

A TI Hurricane Mark IIB, BN114, *undergoing clearance trials at the A&AEE with a pair of 500-lb bombs. Used increasingly against such targets as the flying bomb sites, bridges and lock gates in 1943—when escorts were frequently provided by Typhoons—the Hurricanes suffered heavy losses from* flak *owing to their relatively low speed with these bombs. (*Photo: *Hawker Aircraft Ltd.)*

*Among a host of external stores cleared for use with Hurricanes were such items as Smoke Curtain Installations (SCI) for laying smokescreens during combined operations, and these Small Bomb Carriers (SBC); these were used primarily for carrying six 20-lb practice bombs for training purposes, but on several occasions in 1943 a Hurricane squadron flew with them on operations to drop fragmentation bombs on German airfields in France. (*Photo: *G. W. Wainwright, MLA Ltd.)*

The first installation of rocket projectiles for flight trials by a Hurricane was carried out on a Mark IIA, Z2415, *seen here at Boscombe Down in February 1942. The rather crude arrangement involved only six rocket rails at the outset but was eventually increased to eight on operational aircraft. (*Photos: *Hawker Aircraft Ltd., Neg No 822 and 823 dated 8th February 1942)*

Hurricane Mark IV, LB774, *with Vickers 'S' anti-tank guns pictured at Langley in June 1943.* (Photo: *Sydney Camm Collection)*

One of the 'Towed Hurricane Mark Is', V7480, *at the Flight Refuelling Ltd facility, Staverton, Glos, probably early in 1941. In this instance the fighter took off under its own power with the apex bridle attached under the fuselage aft of the radiator so that the bridle trailed below and behind the undercarriage on each side. When ready to commence towing, the Hurricane pilot released the bridle from the fuselage so that it was suspended from the Malcolm hooks in the wing leading edge on each side. The towing aircraft would then reel out the nylon tow cable and the Hurricane pilot would approach from the rear. When the bridle encompassed the tow cable he would gain height so that the end of the tow cable would engage the apex plate; once engaged, the Hurricane pilot would throttle back slowly until positive tow was accomplished and then shut down his engine.* (Photo: *via R. L. Ward, Farnborough)*

and would today be termed a "force multiplier". The problem, however, became more complicated with the approach to service of rocket projectiles and the anti-tank gun; there was quite simply a limit to the permutations of plumbing and wiring that could be accommodated in a wing joint without the risk of faulty maintenance. For instance an electrical circuit might suffer battle damage while not actually in use, going undetected for days or weeks, and then be required for an operational sortie at short notice having otherwise been declared fully serviceable. This would be particularly dangerous in the case of a drop tank jettison circuit.

Thus in 1941 Hawker put forward the idea for a Hurricane with a universal wing, that is a wing which itself would be capable of mounting different

The development Mark IV, KZ193, *which was later converted to become one of the three Hurricane Mark Vs.* (Photo: *Hawker Aircraft Ltd.)*

*An armoured Hurricane IV equipped with rocket rails. Note the additional armour beside the engine and supercharger. (*Photo: *Hawker Aircraft Ltd., Neg No 843 dated 19th November 1942)*

stores without alteration to the armament circuits and fuel system, and without the necessity to change wing sets. The proposed aircraft—never given a separate designation—was not intended to replace the Mark IIB or IIC, but was not seriously considered by the Air Ministry. Shortly afterwards Rolls-Royce added weight to the proposal by suggesting a new "wide tolerance" long-life Merlin which would be virtually impervious to dust ingestion and therefore could dispense with the bulky air filter on the carburettor air intake; the engine was proposed as being re-rated to produce 1,400 bhp at low level. Even this did not impress the Air Ministry, who considered that the introduction of a radical engine in the Middle East would create servicing problems at the maintenance units; it was also pointed out that an engine specially rated to give maximum power at low level would lose power so rapidly at altitude that the Hurricane would be unable to defend itself in the presence of Axis fighters. The feeling was generally expressed that the existing power ratings represented the best equation of performance at low and medium altitudes.

Although preliminary design work *did* start, under the designation Mark IIE, the new armament configurations—rockets and anti-tank guns—were seen to pre-empt the benefits of the new wing. The new weapons were not simply appendages to be attached to wing pylons. The whole emphasis in the Hurricane was shifting towards operation in the tropics and, when Rolls-Royce offered a new engine, the 1,280-hp Merlin 27 with improved oil system to operate more efficiently in high ambient air temperatures and rated to give optimum power at a slightly lower altitude (S-gear giving best power

Among the more imaginative experiments carried out during the War were the slip-wing trials by F. Hill and Sons Ltd. After preliminary trials with a purpose-built light aircraft, Hills were allocated an old Canadian Hurricane I (originally supplied to Canada in 1938–39 as L1884 *and then shipped back to Britain in 1940 as* 321 *for service with No 1 Squadron RCAF) for modification to accommodate a jettisonable upper wing. The principal purpose of the project was to examine a means of enabling a Hurricane, overloaded with fuel for a very long distance flight, to take off by means of the greatly increased lift. Having reached its cruising altitude the upper wing would then be jettisoned. Like the towed-Hurricane experiments the Hillson F.H.40 slip-wing Hurricane was conceived as a means of flying Hurricanes direct to Malta or the Middle East. The aircraft continued being flown at Boscombe Down until early 1944—long after the need to reinforce Malta had passed. (*Photos: *Hill & Sons Ltd)*

All three Hurricane Mark Vs, KX405 *and* KZ193 *(converted Mark IVs) and the prototype* NL255*; note the fairing on the starboard side of the nose on KX405.* (Photos: *Sydney Camm Collection)*

at 14,800 feet), work on the Mark IIE was stopped. Instead a new prototype was prepared, using an airframe from the Langley Mark II production line, a Merlin 32 (No. 66303) with four-blade Rotol propeller being fitted pending delivery of production Merlin 27s. The aircraft, *KX405*, was fully tropicalized and carried a pair of Vickers S 40-mm guns as being representative of the likely Service configuration, and a new deepened radiator with additional armour protection was included. The first flight by this, then regarded as the prototype, Hurricane Mark IV,[42] was made on 14 March, 1943, flown by Lucas at an all-up weight of 7,215 lb. Its prototype status as a Mark IV, however, survived for only nine days and on the 23rd a new aircraft, *KZ193*, with Merlin 27 and a three-blade Rotol propeller, full ground attack engine and radiator armour, 40-mm guns and ammunition and full fuel, was flown by Lucas at a weight of 8,180 lb. Being wholly representative of the Mark IV, all development trials were to be carried out on *KZ193*, the earlier aircraft now embarking on a completely new series of trials (of which more later).

As further Hurricane IVs began appearing on the production line—approximately 10 Mark IIs continuing to be produced for every one Mark IV—*KZ193* was delivered to Boscombe Down for general assessment and performance measurement with all manner of stores, including asymmetric loading. Full Service clearance was issued on 1 June, permitting the carriage of 250 lb and 500 lb bombs, two, four or eight three-inch rocket projectiles, one or two 40-mm anti-tank guns, one or two 44-gallon drop tanks, or asymmetric combinations of these. The only store that was not permitted to be loaded asymmetrically was the 88-gallon ferry tank.

Despite the earlier emphasis upon operation in the tropics the first Hurricane IVs joined the Mark IIDs with No. 164 Squadron at Colerne in May 1943 and were followed the next month by deliveries to No. 137 Squadron (Sqn Ldr John Basil Wray, later Gp Capt, DFC) at Rochford, having replaced Whirlwinds. Other United Kingdom-based Hurricane IV squadrons were Nos. 63, 184, 186 and 309 (Polish), but the longest serving Squadron was No. 6, which flew the aircraft from July 1943 until January 1947—moving about the Mediterranean, North Africa, Palestine and the Balkans. In Burma the aircraft flew with No. 20 Squadron (Sqn Ldr A. P. Millar, DFC) and No. 42 Squadron (Sqn Ldr G. May, DFC).

A total of 524 Hurricane IVs was built (all at Langley) and apart from their service with 10 operational squadrons they also equipped 11 second-line squadrons (mainly anti-aircraft co-operation units) until shortly after the war's end in Europe.

The Mark IV was not a particularly popular aeroplane among its pilots, the considerable weight of armour and multiplicity of stores depriving it of the crispness of control that had been so evident in the Hurricane IIB; yet it was an extraordinarily tough aeroplane, capable of operating from very primitive airfields that would have denied the use of many a more sophisticated fighter—particularly in the Far East—and of surviving tremendous punishment in combat.

One other version, identified as the Hurricane Mark V, was pursued by Hawker in 1943. Work on the Merlin 32-powered Mark IV "prototype", *KX405*, prompted the manufacturers to persevere with the dedicated "low attack" fighter for the Far East, the engine being capable of being ground-boosted to produce almost 1,700 bhp at low level. When fully equipped in its heaviest configuration (9,300 lb all-up) performance measurements returned a maximum speed of 326 mph at 500 feet

In 1944–45 a large rocket projectile, known as Long Tom, was flight tested on Hurricane IV, KZ706 *(as well as a Mosquito VI,* NT220*). These weapons, of which only one was carried under each wing of the Hurricane, weighed about 500 lb and were powered by five standard three-inch rocket motors. This Hurricane featured the customary late-War ventral blade aerial, but the apparent absence of the carburettor air intake is unexplained. (*Photo: *Author's Collection)*

One of several Canadian-built Hurricanes (shown here is 5624 *with twelve-gun wings) modified with ski undercarriage and snowshoe tail component, intended to enable flying operations to continue unaffected by snow conditions in Canada. Note the fairing over the customary wheel wells. Most Canadian Hurricanes with Hamilton Standard propellers were flown without spinners; later, when a modified diaphragm was developed, the standard Rotol RX5-series spinner was easily adaptable to fit. (*Photo: *Author's Collection)*

when fitted with a Rotol four-blade propeller and tropical filter—roughly the same speed as that of the Hurricane Mark I, despite an increase in weight of more than 57 per cent! From July 1943 *KX405* became known as the Mark V and was followed by a second prototype, *NL255*, towards the end of the year as there were indications that the Air Ministry was considering seeking an "optimized" Hurricane for operations in Burma. However, with large stocks of Hurricanes in India, as well as a number of Hurricane-equipped squadrons of the Indian Air Force—now becoming operational—the decision was reversed and no further work was done on the Hurricane V.

The last Hurricane to emerge from the Langley factory in August 1944 was, appropriately, a Mark IIC, *PZ865*. For almost a year work had been confined to standard Mark IICs and IVs, with scarcely any experimental or development flying undertaken—other than on the abortive Mark V. As a symbolic gesture that final Hurricane, christened "The Last of the Many", was purchased by the manufacturers and survives to this day. Its fortunes in more peaceful skies are recounted in Chapter 14.

The foregoing account of the development of the Hurricane II and IV cannot completely embrace the huge amount of work carried out between 1940 and 1943 on relatively obscure improvements and developments of the Hurricane. However, reference to Appendix I will disclose many areas of this work as it arrived at the flight test stage, and the record of these flights at Brooklands and Langley demonstrated many interesting facets of research undertaken on the Hurricane.

Moreover, a number of other operational versions of the aeroplane were developed by the Royal Air Force and through the Admiralty, often with no more than passing reference to the parent Company. These developments are described in the following chapters as they occurred and in the context of their immediate operational demands in the course of the Hurricane's service following the end of the Battle of Britain.

9

STORM BY NIGHT AND DAY

Throughout the Battle of Britain the *Luftwaffe* flew night sorties over Britain either for training purposes or as nuisance raids intended to unsettle and tire the nation's defences. There were also nightly reconnaissance sorties involving either outward or returning flights during the hours of darkness. Against this constant traffic—amounting to fewer than about 500 sorties during July and August—the British fighter defences were almost impotent. At any one time up to three squadrons of Blenheims (euphemistically classified as night fighters) wandered about the night sky hoping to catch sight of an enemy bomber illuminated by searchlights—and then with the throttles pushed as far from the pilot as possible would attempt to close with a target that was probably capable of a higher speed than the "fighter". No. 25 Squadron and the Fighter Interception Unit were flying Blenheims with rudimentary airborne radar, but even these units achieved precious little success in the way of interceptions and enemy aircraft destroyed; in fairness it should be said, however, that these two units were busy evolving the interception tactics to be employed when Fighter Command eventually received its dedicated night fighter, the Bristol Beaufighter, which was by the standards of the time a formidable aeroplane.

In an effort to discourage such nuisance flights a number of Spitfire and Hurricane squadrons did put up the occasional "cat's-eye" patrols at night, but even these attempts met with little fortune, and the losses among such fighters—due to pilots becoming lost and baling out or crashing on landing—probably exceeded the number of German aircraft actually destroyed.

Relatively early on the Spitfire was withdrawn from cat's-eye sorties as being unsuitable for night fighting, whereas, by contrast, the Hurricane became progressively more widely used as a night fighter. Indeed the squadron commander of No. 29 Squadron, which flew Blenheims, Sqn Ldr Stanley Charles Widdows,[43] was convinced that the use of single-seat fighters by night, and particularly in moonlight, held greater promise of success than twin-engine aircraft without radar and which were generally slower than their targets. He accordingly contrived to acquire his own personal Hurricane (*P3201*) in which he took to roaming the night skies on the look-out for stray bombers. "If persistence had been the yardstick for success, Charles Widdows would have destroyed the entire *Luftwaffe* singlehanded." Alas for a good story, he spotted only two raiders in the course of 40 sorties and failed to score on either occasion.

Towards the end of 1940 German night raids began to increase in size and frequency, although generally the *Luftwaffe* abstained from set-piece raids on British cities until Göring launched his bombers in great strength against London on the evening and night of 7 September. By that date Fighter Command was putting up about 20 Hurricanes on patrol over southern England each night.

Unfortunately London was not the ideal target for defence by single-seaters; for one thing most of the Blenheims were deployed in the south-east and these aircraft, which depended for any hope of success on ground control, tended to clog the available radio frequencies, and the airspace was too confined by gun and balloon barrages to allow freelancing single-seaters any degree of freedom for manoeuvre. Moreover, from mid-September Defiants, which had finally been withdrawn from the daylight battle, began to re-enter the ranks of the night defences as No. 141 Squadron moved down to Gatwick in Sussex.

Among the Hurricane squadrons that were regularly sent up over London during the night *Blitz*—which lasted unabated from 7 September for 55 nights—were the veteran Nos. 73 and 85 Squadrons. The pilots of No. 73, however, flying from Castle Camps during September, found conditions so chaotic over the capital that the squadron suffered heavier losses from the terrific gun barrage (which fired blindly whether or not enemy aircraft were in the vicinity) than it gained victories. No. 85 Squadron, which was later to become a "full-time" night fighter squadron flying Havocs and, much later, Mosquitoes, put in more night flying hours during November 1940 to January 1941 than any other day or night fighter squadron in No. 11 Group, yet failed to destroy a single aircraft until 25 February, when Sqn Ldr Peter Townsend shot down a Dornier Do 17Z. Further to the west No. 32 Squadron, flying from Middle Wallop, sent single aircraft up to patrol the southern approaches to the Midlands, but claimed only a single victim when Flt Lt J. P. Falkowski (Polish) destroyed an He 111 in January.

It is true that the RAF had been desperately trying to introduce the radar-equipped Beaufighter into service since September 1940, but deliveries were initially slow, and the training of radar operators even slower. Moreover, although it was to prove a fairly effective night fighter in due course, the Defiant in those early *Blitz* months proved to be little better than the Hurricane—except that it possessed two pairs of eyes and could shoot sideways if they spotted anything. In an effort to provide some order out of chaos over cities being attacked at night, a system known as Fighter Nights—in fact more a code name than descriptive—was introduced in November. When declared for operation on specific nights and weather conditions allowed Hurricanes to operate, a height band was selected to be free for use by the single-seaters: no guns would be permitted to fire into it and no RAF twin-engine aircraft would fly within it. In theory the system worked very well and certainly reduced casualties among the Hurricane squadrons; in practice, however, less than 10 per cent of enemy raiders chose to fly inside the arbitrary bands (which were changed night by night), so the odds of a Hurricane stumbling on an enemy raider were very slim. Nevertheless, seven German bombers *were* brought down by Hurricanes in the course of Fighter Nights, which continued to be declared until the following summer when the *Blitz* petered out.

Canadian-built Hurricane Is (soon to be re-styled Mark Xs) were coming off the production line at Montreal in fair numbers by the end of 1940, this aircraft, AF964, *being completed early the following year. It is worth remarking that the Canadian aircraft were usually completed with the exhaust-glare shields* in situ, *but that for some unexplained reason these were angled sharply up whereas, when fitted on British-built Hurricanes, they were horizontal. (*Photo: *National Film Board of Canada)*

The slowly mounting tally of night victories by

Fighter Command during that dismal winter have for long been quoted as a measure of the growing efficiency of the Command's radar-equipped Beaufighters, which, by the New Year, flew with three fully operational night fighter squadrons. This is somewhat misleading, as an analysis of the actual number of German aircraft destroyed shows that *all* elements of the night defences were slowly improving—Beaufighters, Defiants, Hurricanes and ground defences—while the guns were taking a declining share of the total numbers of bombers destroyed. Indeed the number of enemy aircraft shot down by Hurricanes increased at a higher rate than those by Defiants and Beaufighters, but this was probably due to the fact that Hurricane squadrons were joining the night defences at a higher rate.

A total of 16 Hurricane squadrons came to be deployed regularly in the night defences during the *Blitz*. No. 87 at Colerne under Sqn Ldr Randolph Stuart Mills (later Gp Capt, DFC) flew patrols over the Bristol Channel and South Wales from November, while a number of recently formed Hurricane day fighter squadrons were hurriedly declared operational by night and others were formed specifically for night fighting. No. 96 Squadron, for instance, was formed in December out of No. 422 (Night Fighter) Flight (which itself had been created to fly Hurricanes at night in defence of London from Shoreham in October) and sent north under Sqn Ldr. R. G. Kellett[44] to cover Liverpool, which had already suffered nine heavy raids, each by more than 50 German bombers. Before starting to re-equip with Defiants at the end of March, No. 96 shot down a Heinkel He 111H to add to two other victories previously scored by No. 422 Flight. No. 151 Squadron, now fully rested from its exertions during the Battle of Britain and equipped with a mixed complement of Hurricanes and Defiants at Wittering and Coltishall to cover the approaches to the Midlands from German bases in Holland, gained its first victory at night on 15 January, when Plt Off R. P. Stevens shot down a Dornier Do 17 while flying Hurricane *V6934*.[45] No. 306 (Polish) Squadron joined the night defences, led by Sqn Ldr Denys Edgar Gillam, AFC (later DSO and two Bars, DFC and Bar, AFC),[46] in February, and was followed in March by No. 308 (Polish) Squadron, which destroyed a Junkers Ju 88 over Coventry during one of its first operational sorties, and No. 310 (Czech) Squadron, which also flew patrols to defend that devastated city.

In Northern Ireland, where the *Luftwaffe* carried out a number of night raids on Belfast, No. 245 Squadron started regular patrols on "Fighter

Hurricane Is of No 306 (Polish) Squadron, the third Polish fighter squadron to be formed during the Battle of Britain; by the time these photos were taken at Ternhill early in 1941 the Squadron, commanded by Sqn Ldr Denys Edgar Gillam AFC, had been declared operational and was engaged in night patrols over the Midlands. (Photos: *J. B. Cynk, via R. Ward, Canterbury)*

Nights" as well as its routine daylight convoy patrols over shipping inbound to the Clyde and Liverpool; its first confirmed night victory was gained by the CO on 13 May, when Sqn Ldr John William Charles Simpson, DFC and Bar, destroyed a Dornier Do 17Z over the Irish Sea. No. 253 Squadron, led by Sqn Ldr Peter Russell Walker (later Air Cdre, CBE, DSO, DFC), moved north to Skaebrae in the Orkneys with Hurricanes in February to cover the naval base at Scapa Flow.

In the case of No. 255 Squadron, based at Kirton-in-Lindsey for the defence of the Midlands and East Coast ports, it was found that on numerous occasions of heavy *Luftwaffe* activity in the area it was unable to react effectively owing to a high accident rate and low serviceability, and so Hurricanes were taken on strength; on 9 May, during a raid on Hull, the squadron claimed the destruction of six enemy raiders—the highest score by any night fighter squadron during the *Blitz*.

As the spring approached, a few Hurricane night fighter squadrons began converting to the American Douglas Havoc twin-engine night fighter. It was during this transition that a legendary Hurricane pilot was to lose his life. The Yorkshireman Geoffrey ("Sammy") Allard, who had flown Hurricanes as a sergeant pilot with No. 85 Squadron in France, shot down 10 German aircraft by the time it returned to England; in the Battle of Britain, during the last nine days of August, he destroyed a further 10, and was commissioned as Pilot Officer. When Peter Townsend was slightly wounded, Allard, as a rapidly promoted Flight Lieutenant at the beginning of September, led his squadron until it was posted north to rest. He was awarded two DFMs and the DFC, but failed to score again during the night fighting of the *Blitz*. His death on 13 March, 1941, was tragic; while collecting a Havoc from Debden a panel came adrift and lodged in the rudder during take-off, causing the aircraft to crash, killing all three occupants.

The night *Blitz* finally came to an end in May, as Göring started to pull most of the *Luftwaffe*'s bombers back from France and the Low Countries to begin redeploying for the great assault on Russia that would open the following month. The night offensive had created enormous damage in London and the other British cities, but had failed to bring the nation to its knees. German records show that 307 bombers had been lost during night operations in seven months, of which the British ground defences had claimed 130 destroyed. Of the remainder it is impossible to be certain exactly what share fell to the guns of Hurricanes as it is obvious that some of the German losses included aircraft which crashed into the sea following combat, unseen by the RAF pilots. The nearest estimate that can be made is between 60 and 80, with the remainder being shared between Defiants, Blenheims and Beaufighters (and various other aircraft pressed into service with the night defences using some distinctly curious tactics).

Use of the Hurricane at night, though by no means entirely unsuccessful, was forced upon Fighter Command through sheer lack of a dedicated night fighter. By the end of the *Blitz* the Beaufighter was well established in service, the ground-controlled interception system had been demonstrated as being highly efficient in most conditions of night activity and the RAF had succeeded in training a fairly large number of aircrew radar operators. While Hurricanes continued to be employed for many months in night defence, some of the squadrons were also now to be switched to other, more profitable duties by night—as will be told shortly.

The Daylight Offensive Fighter Sweeps

Once it was clear to Dowding and his successor at Fighter Command, Air Marshal Sir William Sholto Douglas, KCB, MC, DFC, that the *Luftwaffe* had, at least for the time being, abandoned its daylight offensive against Britain at the end of October 1940, and that there was a practical limit to the number of Hurricane squadrons which could be usefully employed at night, plans were immediately laid to launch British fighters against the Germans based along the coast of France.

The original purpose of these attacks was largely psychological, on the one hand to sustain the morale of the British people now feeling the lash of Göring's bombers with the knowledge that, far from being beaten, Fighter Command was striking back, and on the other to reverse the six-month-old defensive outlook that had permeated the Command itself. Over the coming months the RAF's cross-Channel offensive would assume a number of well-defined forms of attack, some of them closely modelled on the *Luftwaffe*'s *frei Jagd* tactics, and it is convenient to mention briefly here the form these operations took.

*Manned by American volunteer pilots, No 71 Squadron of the RAF was the first of the famous 'Eagle' squadrons, but was formed just too late to fight in the Battle of Britain although several of the pilots did see action while serving with the RAF's regular line squadrons. This picture was probably taken late in 1940. (*Photo: *via R. Ward, Canterbury)*

The smallest attack operation was the *Rhubarb*, usually carried out by up to four fighters (and later fighter-bombers) and authority for which seldom originated above the Wing Leader or Station Commander; targets of opportunity would be sought out and attacked, such as solitary German road vehicles, trains, river craft and such German aircraft as transports, trainers, seaplanes and so on. Next largest form of attack was the *Rodeo*, similar to the Rhubarb but usually carried out at squadron strength; targets of opportunity would still be attacked, but planned targets, such as enemy airfields, came increasingly into the sphere of operations. The largest form of fighter sweep, usually by a Wing of three or four squadrons from a single Sector (such as the Tangmere Wing, Hornchurch Wing, Biggin Hill Wing and the rest), but very occasionally by two or even three Wings together, was the *Ranger*, involving a flight along the enemy coast that was intended to draw German fighters into the air, where they could be overwhelmed by sheer weight of numbers.

There were then the escorted bomber sweeps, which were flown on the principle that bombers (usually Blenheims to begin with) were more likely to attract enemy fighters into the air. The *Circus* was simply a sweep by light bombers—often not even carrying bombs—but with squadrons of fighters providing close escort and top cover. The *Ramrod* was similar except that the bombers were given a specific target, usually an airfield, railway junction, military concentration, headquarters or the like.

Finally anti-shipping attacks, which demanded different attack tactics on account of the presence of flak ships, either against vessels entering or leaving port or sailing along the French coast, came under operations known as *Roadsteads*; later, as shipping attacks assumed greater importance, with German blockade runners attempting to reach northern German ports, Operation *Channel Stop* included all attacks aimed at closing the Strait of Dover to enemy shipping.

* * *

*Dusk take-off by a Hurricane IIB. (*Photo: *Sydney Camm Collection)*

Before describing the cross-Channel operations flown by the Hurricane squadrons, one other limited activity involving Hurricanes by day were the aptly named "Kipper" patrols over the North Sea. Since the beginning of the war fleets of British East Coast drifters had gone about their business of fishing in the North Sea, seldom with any interference from German naval vessels or aircraft; more recently, however, particularly towards the end of the daylight Battle of Britain, a number of spiteful attacks had taken place against these small craft. Fighter Command was accordingly asked by the Admiralty to provide some sort of token protection for the fleets, and from late October Hurricane squadrons based in eastern Britain took turns to put up "Kipper" patrols. Among those involved were No. 257 Squadron flying from Coltishall, No. 258 from Acklington and No. 310 (Czech) from Dyce in Aberdeenshire. Only one German aircraft is believed to have been destroyed during these patrols, but several others were chased away before the winter ended.

*Hurricane IIA of No 247 Squadron at Predannack, Cornwall, in June 1941. At this time the Squadron was engaged in convoy patrols in the Western Approaches, but shortly afterwards with Mark IIBs it went over to intruder operations over North-west France. (*Photo: *via R. Ward, Canterbury)*

*A pair of No 98 Squadron's Hurricanes at Kaldadarnes, Iceland, in June 1941 just prior to the Squadron's redesignation as No 1423 Flight. (*Photo: *via R. Ward, Canterbury)*

Among the first Hurricane squadrons to take the offensive across the English Channel was No. 249 Squadron (commanded by Sqn Ldr Robert Alexander "Butch" Barton, later OBE, DFC and Bar), based at North Weald, two of whose pilots flew a *Rhubarb* in Hurricane Is over Boulogne on 29 December, 1940. In January No. 601 Squadron, recently arrived at Northolt from Exeter with Hurricane Is, joined in with half a dozen *Rhubarbs* and a couple of *Circuses*, but following fairly heavy losses (seven aircraft lost or written off in accidents, and four pilots missing) it was realized that the Hurricane I was no longer suitable for offensive action—particularly in combat at low level at relatively long range—and in March No. 601 began to change to Hurricane IIBs. Two months later, during a typical *Rhubarb* on 22 May, Plt Off A. K. Ogilvie and Plt Off Malczewski were flying from Manston when they met and attacked a Junkers Ju 52/3m transport at 250 feet over France (claiming it probably destroyed), but were themselves almost immediately set on by a pair of Bf 109Es; turning into the attack Ogilvie sent one of the enemy fighters crashing into a wood, whereupon the other made off without pressing the attack.

In February No. 605 Squadron (commanded by

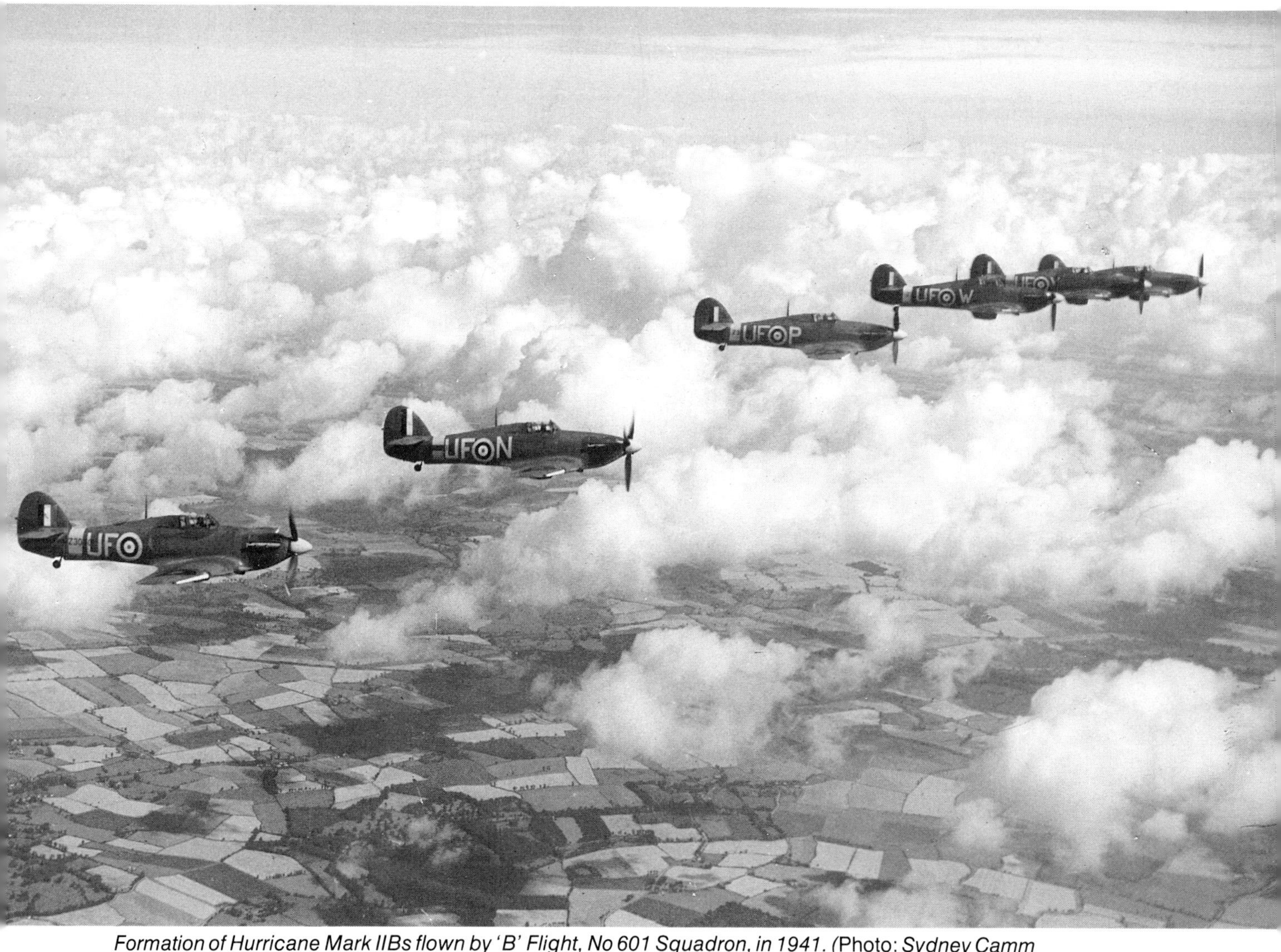

*Formation of Hurricane Mark IIBs flown by 'B' Flight, No 601 Squadron, in 1941. (*Photo: *Sydney Camm Collection)*

Sqn Ldr G. R. Edge, DFC, AAF) arrived at Martlesham Heath with Hurricane IIAs, joining No. 17 Squadron, also with Mark IIAs, and together formed the first Hurricane Wing to participate in *Rangers*. These were, however, shortlived as both squadrons were long overdue for rest (No. 17 having been in the south since before the Battle of Britain), and No. 605 was sent north to Ternhill in March and No. 17 to Castletown, Caithness, in April.

Gradually, however, the number of Hurricane squadrons committed to the daylight offensive increased. Still flying from Coltishall, No. 257 Squadron began flying *Rhubarbs* off the Dutch coast in March, as the recently formed No. 258 Squadron (Sqn Ldr Wilfrid Greville Clouston, DFC) arrived at Kenley with Hurricane IIAs and started *Rhubarbs* over the French coast in May, destroying three Bf 109Es but losing four pilots.

In June, just as the first of the new Messerschmitt Bf 109Fs began arriving in France, the first American "Eagle" Squadron of the RAF, No. 71, moved to North Weald with Hurricane Is; largely composed of volunteer pilots from the United States, but commanded by a British officer (Sqn Ldr Henry de Clifford Anthony Woodhouse, AFC), this squadron continued flying Hurricanes for three months only, but it was a period of hard work and much flying. Before converting to Spitfires No. 71 flew 28 *Rhubarbs*, five *Rodeos*, nine *Circuses* and at least three *Ramrods*, as well as countless convoy patrols in the Thames Estuary; the Squadron's first victory was scored by Plt Off Dunn, who shot down a Bf 109F during a *Circus* over Lille on 21 July. June also saw the arrival of No. 312 (Czech) Squadron at Kenley with Hurricane IIBs and within a month was engaging in *Circuses*; the Squadron claimed the destruction of two Bf 109Es, and two Bf 109Fs, but with three pilots posted missing. No. 312 Squadron then moved to Coltishall to fly convoy patrols off the Norfolk coast under the command of that famous Czech pilot, Sqn Ldr A. Vasatko, DFC.[47]

The Poles of No. 317 Squadron (Sqn Ldr S. Brzezina, DFC, who had flown Spitfires with No. 74 Squadron in the Battle of Britain) arrived at Exeter in July with Hurricane IIAs—having shot down two Bf 109Es with Hurricane Is during a *Circus* on the 10th while based at Fairwood Common.

August 1941 saw No. 247 Squadron flying its first *Rodeo* from Predannack in Cornwall with Hurricane IICs over Morlaix airfield in France, while the first two Canadian Hurricane Squadrons, No. 401 flying from West Malling and No. 402 from Rochford, carried out a number of *Ramrod* escorts; at about this time a number of No 402's pilots were undergoing training with the Air Fighting Development Unit at Duxford in fighter-bombing tactics, and two months later the Squadron's aircraft were modified to carry two 250 lb bombs.

By the late autumn the Hurricane squadrons—of which 16 were regularly flying sweeps along the Dutch, Belgian and French coasts—were suffering their first losses to the pilots of Germany's new fighter, the Focke-Wulf Fw 190A, an aircraft that possessed a speed around 80 mph greater than that of the Hurricane IIB. Even the Spitfire VBs were hard put to it to match this superb fighter. It was therefore decided to discontinue the fighter sweeps, the *Rhubarbs* and *Rodeos*, with Hurricane IIB and IIC aircraft in the purely fighter rôle by day. Instead some of the squadrons with IIBs went over to the fighter-bombing rôle (for which working teams from the maintenance units had been modifying the aircraft during the summer). Occasionally "tip and run" *Rhubarbs* were flown, but these were now regarded as extremely risky; more often, however, the "Hurribombers" would operate as the bombing force in *Circuses* and *Ramrods* with escorts of Spitfire VBs. No. 607 Squadron (Sqn Ldr George Dudley Craig, AAF) carried out the first such attack on 30 October, flying from Manston to drop 250 lb bombs on a transformer station near Tingry. Two days later the Canadians of No. 402 Squadron made a similar attack on Berck-sur-Mer airfield.

The Intruders

Before going on to describe the Hurricane's daylight operations of 1942 and 1943 it is necessary to return to the period of the *Blitz*, when, apart from night defensive operations over Britain, the Hurricane squadrons were beginning to wage their own style of night offensive.

Starting in December 1940, No. 23 Squadron had pioneered the RAF's use of night intruders,[48] flying its Blenheims over German bomber bases to await the return of raiding aircraft from Britain. At much the same time it was suggested at Fighter Command that the Hurricane, already showing promise as a night fighter, might also be ideal as a night intruder—at least against some of the closer German bomber airfields in France. Not surprisingly therefore the first Squadron selected for this work was No. 87 (which had for long been something of a specialist unit in night patrols, having operated a flight exclusively on cat's-eye patrols during the Battle of Britain and gained a rare modicum of success). Late in January 1941 the Squadron sent a flight of Hurricane Is to St Mary's in the Scilly Isles for the dual task of intercepting enemy bombers making for the Bristol Channel, and intruding over German bomber bases in the west of France, particularly the airfield at Vannes in Brittany (suspected—correctly—as being the base of *Kampfgruppe* 100, the *Luftwaffe*'s Heinkel He 111H pathfinder unit). This was a fairly hectic period for No. 87, and in May the intruders' tally of enemy aircraft destroyed began to mount steadily; in June the Squadron started flying Hurricane IICs, in most pilots' opinion the ideal intruder, especially when fitted with a pair of drop tanks.

The tactics employed by the intruder squadrons,

on nights when weather conditions suggested the likelihood of German raids over Britain, often involved a pair of Hurricanes taking off at dusk so as to arrive in the vicinity of enemy bomber bases about one hour after dark to discover whether indeed bombers from those bases were operating that night (by watching for flarepaths being lit). Occasionally the fighters would attack then, although experience showed that the German air gunners were more alert to the danger of intruders at the beginning of a sortie. More often the fighters would return to base with the information of which enemy airfields were operating that night. Shortly afterwards the squadron would put up two or more intruders to lie in wait for the returning bombers at the end of their long and tiring sortie. Stalking the bomber from astern as it started its approach to land, the Hurricane pilot would be well situated to see his quarry dimly silhouetted against the glow of the flarepath. Often no more than a two-second burst from the four 20 mm cannon would suffice to send the bomber crashing onto the runway threshold.

Past masters in the skill of intruding were the pilots of No. 1 Squadron, whose rôle changed from daylight sweeps to training for night intruder work during the period March–July 1941; in the latter month Sqn Ldr James Archibald Findley MacLachlan (later DSO, DFC and Bar) took over command of the Squadron; among his men was a Czech pilot, Karel Kuttelwascher, and together these two perfected their own highly individual form of devastating intruder tactics, which reached a peak of perfection the following spring:

"4 May 1942. One Hurricane IIC with long-range tanks, BE581 JX–E, pilot Flt Lt K. M. Kuttelwascher (Czech), took off from Tangmere at 23.20 hrs to carry out intruder operations at Evreux and St André. Crossed French coast south of Fécamp at 2,000 feet; three searchlights came up from Fécamp, but were doused when our pilot flashed his navigation lights twice... Flew on to St André, which was lit by a double flarepath. Six enemy aircraft, identified as He 111s with white tail lights, were orbiting to land. Circled for two minutes and then came in behind one of them, firing a two-second burst from astern and slightly below; the starboard engine caught fire and the aircraft dived into the ground north-east of the aerodrome. Repeated the same tactics with a second enemy aircraft, which after a one-second burst dived in flames into a wood east of the aerodrome. He then attacked a third aircraft, giving it a two-second burst from dead astern and saw his shells hitting it, the enemy aircraft going down steeply from 1,500 feet. He lost sight of it, but 30 seconds later, as he came round on orbit, there were three separate fires on the ground; all three He 111s are therefore claimed as destroyed...'

These were Kuttelwascher's 10th, 11th and 12th victims and, with a final score of 18, he was awarded a Bar to his DFC. He was then posted away to No. 23 Squadron to fly Mosquitoes, but never achieved the success he had had on the Hurricane—indeed he never again so much as saw an enemy aircraft!

* * *

A much less successful chapter in the Hurricane's night fighting saga was its work with the Turbinlite squadrons. The Turbinlite was the brainchild of Wg Cdr William Helmore, CBE, a technical adviser to the Ministry of Aircraft Production, and comprised a powerful light fitted in the nose of an AI-equipped Havoc night fighter. No fewer than 10 Flights of these Havocs were so equipped and a number of Hurricane night fighter squadrons detailed to work in collaboration. The tactics involved a Hurricane and Havoc flying together as the crew of the latter searched for enemy aircraft using ground control and their own radar. On detecting a target the Havoc would expose its Turbinlite to illuminate the raider so that the Hurricane pilot could close in to attack with his guns.

The general lack of success in combating the German bombers during the *Blitz* of 1940–41 spurred the Air Ministry to order the Havocs' modification during the spring of 1941, and a training unit, No. 1422 (Air Target Illuminating) Flight, was established at Heston to train their crews. The ten Turbinlite Flights were formed during the second half of that year, and at first a line Hurricane squadron was "paired" with each of the Turbinlite Flights, but this proved unsatisfactory as the Hurricanes would not be available for night operations if their pilots had been warned for daylight operations on the following day. In due course each of the Hurricane squadrons gave up one of their flights to the Havoc unit, which then itself assumed the status of

Armourers loading the 20-mm gun magazines of a No 87 Squadron Hurricane Mark IIC night fighter. (Photo: *John W. R. Taylor)*

a squadron. Astonishingly the operations continued throughout 1942, and the following table summarizes the operational fortunes of the dismal project:

Date of Formation	Original Flight No.	Ultimate Turbinlite Sqn No.	Paired Hurricane Sqn	Operating Base(s)	Operational Record
22–5–41	1451	530	No. 3 Squadron	Hunsdon	All patrols uneventful.
7–7–41	1452	531	No. 32 Squadron	West Malling	Trials with Defiants proved unsuccessful. Lost three Havocs in accidents (one colliding with Hurricane). No contacts with enemy aircraft.
10–7–41	1453	532	No. 486 (NZ) Squadron	Wittering and Hibaldstow	Three contacts with enemy aircraft, but Hurricane had become separated (23–7–42). Otherwise uneventful patrols.
4–7–41	1454	533	No. 87 Squadron	Colerne, Exeter and Charmy Down	Four unsuccessful contacts, but otherwise uneventful patrols.
7–7–41	1455	534	Nos. 1 and 3 Squadrons	Tangmere	All patrols uneventful. Attempted trials with Typhoon but fighter found to be too fast.
24–11–41	1456	535	No. 257 Squadron	Honiley and High Ercall	Two unsuccessful contacts, but otherwise patrols uneventful.
15–9–41	1457	536	No. 247 Squadron	Colerne, Exeter, Fairwood Common, Predannack	Contact of Stirling bomber (24–6–42) which was almost shot down; two other contacts on Ju 88s, but both escaped.
6–12–41	1458	537	No. 245 Squadron	Middle Wallop	All patrols uneventful.
20–9–41	1459	538	No. 253 Squadron	Hunsdon and Hibaldstow	On 30–4–42 Flt Lt C. V. Winn illuminated a He 111 which was shot down by Sqn Ldr Derek Sidney Yapp, DFC. Two other inconclusive attacks were made on Do 217s in July 1942.
15–12–41	1460	539	Not known	Acklington	All patrols uneventful.

Of course the entire Turbinlite concept became superfluous once the dedicated AI-equipped night fighters became reliable and effective in service—by the end of the *Blitz* in May 1941—in other words before the first Turbinlite Flight was even formed, and the reason for the persistence with such an obviously wasteful and unwieldy operation for no less than 18 months remains one of the unanswered mysteries of the war.

The Hurricane itself *was* developed to carry airborne interception radar (an adaptation of the pilot-interpreted AI Mark V, see page 94) and these Hurricane IICs were issued to No. 245 Squadron (Sqn Ldr Henry Harold Brownlow Mould) in September 1942; one flight flew patrols from Angle in Pembrokeshire during that winter, but without any known success owing to an absence of enemy air activity.

The Daylight Attacks of 1942–43

Despite the growing menace of the Focke-Wulf Fw 190A to RAF aircraft making daylight sweeps over the French coast during the winter of 1941–42, Hurricane operations had settled into a new pattern, with much greater emphasis on bombing attacks, and by early in the New Year all squadrons flying Mark IIBs and IICs had been modified to carry bombs if the occasion arose. Poor weather curtailed the sweeps for days at a time and it was during one of these spells that the Germans chose to sail the battlecruisers *Scharnhorst* and *Gneisenau*, and the cruiser *Prinz Eugen*, from Brest back to home ports in Germany.

Although the British Admiralty had been expecting a "break-out" for some weeks, the final sortie on 12 February took the Royal Navy and RAF by surprise. Only as the German fleet was approaching the Strait of Dover did Fighter Command, now led by Leigh-Mallory, react. Several Hurricane IIB and IIC bomber squadrons were ordered off, but most were too late to take effective action. Among them were Nos. 3 and 607 Squadrons, which had four-aircraft detachments at Manston:

> "No 607 Squadron. 12 February. Manston, Kent. 12.30 hrs. Four aircraft, flown by Fg Off Lane, Plt Off Cribbs, F/Sgt Walker and Sgt Paul, took off at 12.30 hrs to attack vessels escorting the *Scharnhorst, Gneisenau* and *Prinz Eugen*. The ships were reported to be off Le Touquet, but the aircraft were vectored too far south and only small flak ships were seen. One of these was damaged and set on fire. F/Sgt Walker was seen to secure a direct hit on this ship, but he did not return to base."

Four days later a small convoy of enemy minesweepers was reported off the Brittany coast and No. 402 Squadron, then at Warmwell under the

Ground and flight views of Hurricane IIC BD867QO-Y of No 3 Squadron flying from Hunsdon in September 1941, at about the time the Squadron started night fighting (note the exhaust shields fitted). (Photos: *Sydney Camm Collection*)

command of Sqn Ldr Robert Ellis Evan Morrow, DFC, RCAF, was ordered off with every available aircraft. Morrow took off with eight aircraft to refuel at Perranporth, and having picked up an escort of Spitfires set course south with six Mark IIBs, each with two 250 lb bombs. Flying at no more than 50 feet the Hurricanes came upon the enemy ships, which turned out to be not minesweepers but four destroyers—powerfully armed vessels that had escorted the battlecruisers eastwards on the 12th and which were now returning to their base at Brest. With no time to ponder the wisdom of attack, the six Canadian pilots went straight for the ships, one of which was hit by two bombs and another by one. Both, though fairly badly damaged, reached port safely. All the Hurricanes escaped without damage, although one crashed on landing.

The other major operation which involved bomb-carrying Hurricanes in 1942 was the Allied combined operation at Dieppe on 19 August. For Fighter Command this ill-fated operation imposed the responsibility of giving protection and support for the landing forces and cover for the ships both on their way to and from the beaches, and as they lay offshore. An opportunity was also taken to see how well the Typhoon and Spitfire IX, which had been rushed into service to combat the Fw 190A, behaved in combat, for Leigh-Mallory saw the whole operation as one that would be bound to attract a large proportion of the *Luftwaffe* remaining in France into the air. Accordingly almost every Hurricane and Spitfire squadron participated in some rôle or other. All told, eight Hurricane bomber squadrons were briefed to attack the enemy positions at Dieppe, starting shortly before the first assault troops landed, and continuing until the last ships were finally out of range of the powerful coastal gun batteries.

Typical of the attacks carried out that day was the first sortie by No. 43 Squadron, then commanded

*Loading 250-lb GP bombs on a Hurricane IIB fighter-bomber (*BE417 *AE-K) of No 402 Squadron RCAF at Warmwell during the winter of 1941–42 prior to a cross-Channel sortie. (*Photo: RAF Museum)

by Belgian pilot Sqn Ldr Le Roy Du Vivier, DFC, at Tangmere:

> "No. 43 Squadron. 19 August. Tangmere. The Squadron took an energetic part in the combined operation at Dieppe. We came to readiness at 04.00 hrs and reverted to 30 minutes available at 15.14 hrs—on the top line for 12 hours continuously. During that time we had four complete squadron trips to Dieppe, a total of 48 sorties. This was more than any other squadron in the Tangmere Sector (there were 21 squadrons operating from this Sector). Pilots in the first sortie were Sqn Ldr du Vivier, Flt Lt F. W. Lister, Flt Lt W. Armstrong, Plt Off J. T. Wills, Plt Off Trenghard Smith, Plt Off A. E. Snell, Plt Off J. Daniels, F/Sgt H. Wik (Canadian), F/Sgt J. D. Lewis, Sgt M. Smith, Sgt W. Webster and Sgt G. Ball. No. 43 Squadron was the first to go into the attack against gun positions on the beaches and in the buildings to the west of the harbour. These were the main landing beaches of our troops and were very heavily defended with machine guns, and light and heavy flak. Two attacks were made and all pilots reported hits on gun posts, buildings, wireless masts, etc. However, of the 12 who went out only five came back untouched. F/Sgt Wik is missing from this operation. Plt Off Snell was missing after being heard to say over his R/T that he was baling out, but later he was picked up by air-sea rescue and was unhurt. Flt Lt Lister had the underside of one wing badly shot up by a cannon shell and had to make a wheels-up landing at Tangmere, but was unhurt. The Squadron landed at 06.20 hrs. . . ."

The attacks by the Hurricanes at Dieppe were not afforded close cover, but were flown under an enormous umbrella of Spitfires. Fortunately when the Fw 190As and Bf 109Fs inevitably arrived, they were tackled by the Spitfires; on those occasions when the Fw 190s did get through there were no Hurricanes about!

With passing reference above to the Typhoon it is worth mentioning here that the Dieppe operation was something of a fiasco for the aircraft of which so much was hoped. Two Typhoons were lost—not to the guns of the *Luftwaffe* but when attacked by Canadian-flown Spitfire IXs whose pilots mistook them for Fw 190s! The aircraft were not strictly shot down, but, as they dived away to escape the "friendly guns" their entire tail units broke away following failure of the rear fuselage structure.

Indeed the Typhoon itself proved something of a failure in the dogfighting rôle, being sadly lacking in performance and manoeuvrability at altitude. However, it underwent immediate redevelopment as a ground support fighter with cannon, bombs and rockets, and ultimately re-emerged as one of the finest Allied ground attack aircraft of the European war. And it was to prepare squadrons for its introduction to service in this rôle that Hurricanes came to be more and more employed.

As recounted in the previous chapter, the Hurricane had already undergone development with rocket projectiles and 40-mm anti-tank guns. The first Squadron in Britain to be equipped with the Hurricane IID with the big guns was No. 184 (Sqn Ldr Jack Rose, DFC), specially formed at Colerne on 1 December 1942, to work up and develop anti-tank tactics. Some difficulty was experienced in this as it was soon found that in order to achieve penetration of a tank's armour it was necessary to approach the target horizontally at very low level in order to correct the aim (using the tracer ammunition in the two rifle-calibre machine guns). When these tactics were tried out in Exercise Spartan in March 1943, however, very poor results were obtained—in contrast to the outstanding successes being achieved with the same aircraft by No. 6 Squadron in the Western Desert (see page 157).

As a result of this, use of the 40-mm guns against tanks was largely abandoned, and other types of target were selected. Hurricane IIDs were also delivered to No. 164 Squadron at Middle Wallop in February 1943, and to No. 137 Squadron at Rochford (Southend) in June, both squadrons quickly becoming operational. The first *Rhubarb* with the big guns was flown by No. 137 on 23 July (in Mark IVs with 40-mm Vickers S):

> "No. 137 Sqn. Southend. 23 July. Flt Lt J. M. Bryan, DFC (*KX827*), Fg Off G. S. Chalmers (*KW918*), Fg Off J. T. Davidson (*KZ662*) and Plt Off A. G. Brunet (*KZ661*) flew to Manston to carry out a *Rhubarb* operation. This was the first of this type of operation undertaken by Hurricane IVs with 40-mm cannon and proved highly successful. The four aircraft took off from Manston at 13.10 hrs and landed safely at 15.00 hrs. The Belgian coast was crossed in cloud at 1,500 feet two miles west of Nieuport and a goods train was attacked near Cotemark by all pilots and the engine disintegrated. Two other goods trains were found at Statiestrate; Flt Lt Bryan and Fg Off Chalmers attacked one, seeing strikes and leaving it covered in dirty black smoke. Plt Off Brunet and Fg Off Chalmers dealt with the other, resulting in the engine's disintegration with the boiler knocked off the bogies. Intense light flak was encountered here. Near Lightervelde Plt Off Brunet and Fg Off Chalmers shot up a large army lorry. At Thielt a small train was attacked by all pilots and left emitting smoke. Two barges were cannoned next and badly damaged, and the four aircraft returned to Manston. (Less than a month later Fg Off Davidson was accidentally shot down by a friendly fighter and killed.)"

By now Hurricane IVs were also flying *Roadsteads* using rockets, with Typhoons as close escort:

> "No. 184 Squadron. Manston. 28 June. Four Hurricane IVs were airborne at 04.30 hrs and the Typhoon escort was met at the correct place and time. A convoy of five ships (four of 1,000 tons) was encountered off the Dutch coast. The Typhoons attacked the ships with cannon and drew all the flak from our Hurricanes, which were not fired at until the attack had almost finished. It was a very well co-ordinated attack in which two ships were definitely sunk, one was beached burning furiously and one other was damaged. One Hurricane was lost. (Some of the 3-inch rockets were fitted with 30 lb incendiary heads, the others were 60 lb HE heads.)"

So effective were the 3-inch rocket projectiles proving to be that the 40-mm guns were almost completely discarded for operations in northern Europe by the end of the summer of 1943, and it was now decided to withdraw the Hurricane IV from operational service as being so much inferior in performance to the Typhoon, similarly armed. No. 186 Squadron accordingly began taking delivery of Typhoons in November, followed by Nos. 137 and 164 in January 1944 and No. 184 in March.

Thus ended the operational service of the Hurricane in north-western Europe. Four years had seen the aeroplane fight the greatest defensive air campaign in history and survive to take the offensive—an offensive that progressively eroded the Germans' capacity to counter the invasion of the summer of 1944. One other front in Europe on which the Hurricane fought is less well chronicled and is relatively unknown in the West.

Hurricanes in Russia

Following Hitler's attack on the Soviet Union in June 1941 Winston Churchill had pledged support for Britain's new ally and forthwith plans were laid to ship war materiel to the North Russian ports of Archangel'sk and Murmansk. An account of the Hurricane's defence of the North Cape convoys is given in Chapter 10.

It was, moreover, the Hurricane that also formed a major part of the early cargoes of the North Cape convoys. To begin with, as a means of protecting the disembarkation ports, as well as to assist the Russians in learning to fly and maintain the aircraft, the Royal Air Force despatched two squadrons of Hurricane IIAs and IIBs round the North Cape.

No. 81 Squadron was formed at Debden with Hurricane IIA Series 2s on 29 July, 1941, under Sqn Ldr Anthony Hartwell Rook, AAF, and two days later at Acklington No. 134 Squadron was formed under Sqn Ldr Anthony Garforth Miller. On 12 August, as the groundcrews embarked in ss *Llanstephan Castle* sailing in one of the first PQ convoys, the pilots and aircraft of the two squadrons were taken aboard the carrier HMS *Argus* and on 1 September landed at Vaenga, near Murmansk. As successive convoys arrived hundreds of Hurricanes were disembarked in crates so that the northern ports immediately became strategic targets of the utmost importance for the *Luftwaffe*, against which the RAF squadrons now had to provide adequate air defence, as well as giving training and maintenance instruction to the Russians.

The two squadrons were declared operational at Vaenga on 12 September, although none of their aircraft possessed more than six guns apiece, the other six guns having been removed before flying off HMS *Argus* to reduce weight. Moreover, these guns had been landed at Archangel'sk, and when they eventually arrived at Vaenga it was found that the blast tubes were missing, so the Russian engineers set to to manufacture replacements. Nevertheless No. 81 Squadron was quickly in action on that first day, five aircraft taking off to intercept five Finnish Bf 109Es escorting a German Henschel Hs 126 reconnaissance aircraft. Three of the 109s were claimed shot down and the Hs 126 was damaged; however, Sgt N. H. Smith was shot down and killed. Shortly afterwards Plt Off Bush intercepted and damaged a Bf 110. In the afternoon Plt Off Walker and F/Sgt Haw shot down three more Bf 109s.

Both squadrons were in action several times

OPERATIONAL HURRICANE SQUADRONS BASED IN BRITAIN
(SEE OPPOSITE FOR COMMONWEALTH SQUADRONS)

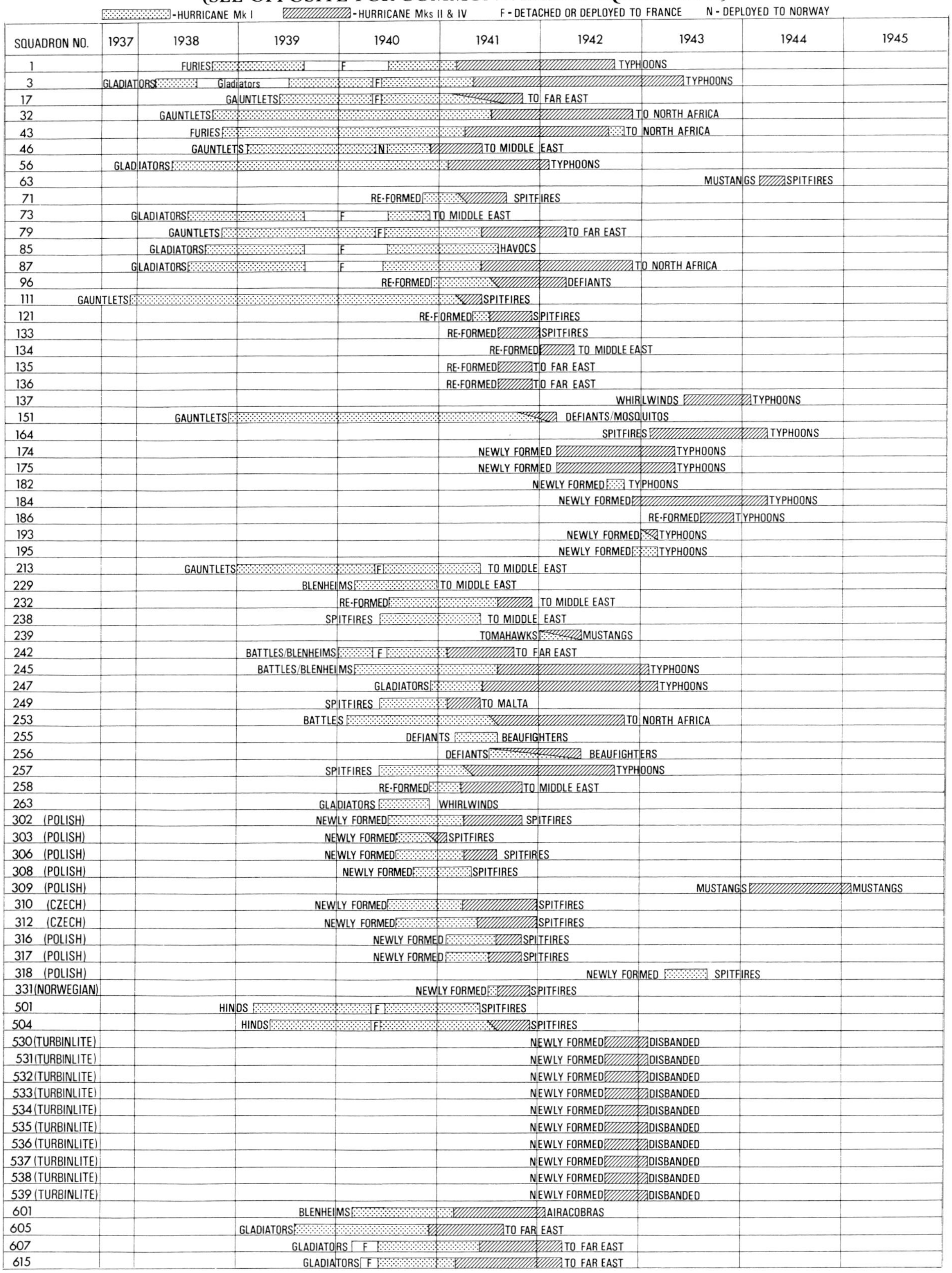

BASES OF OPERATIONAL HURRICANE SQUADRONS IN BRITAIN

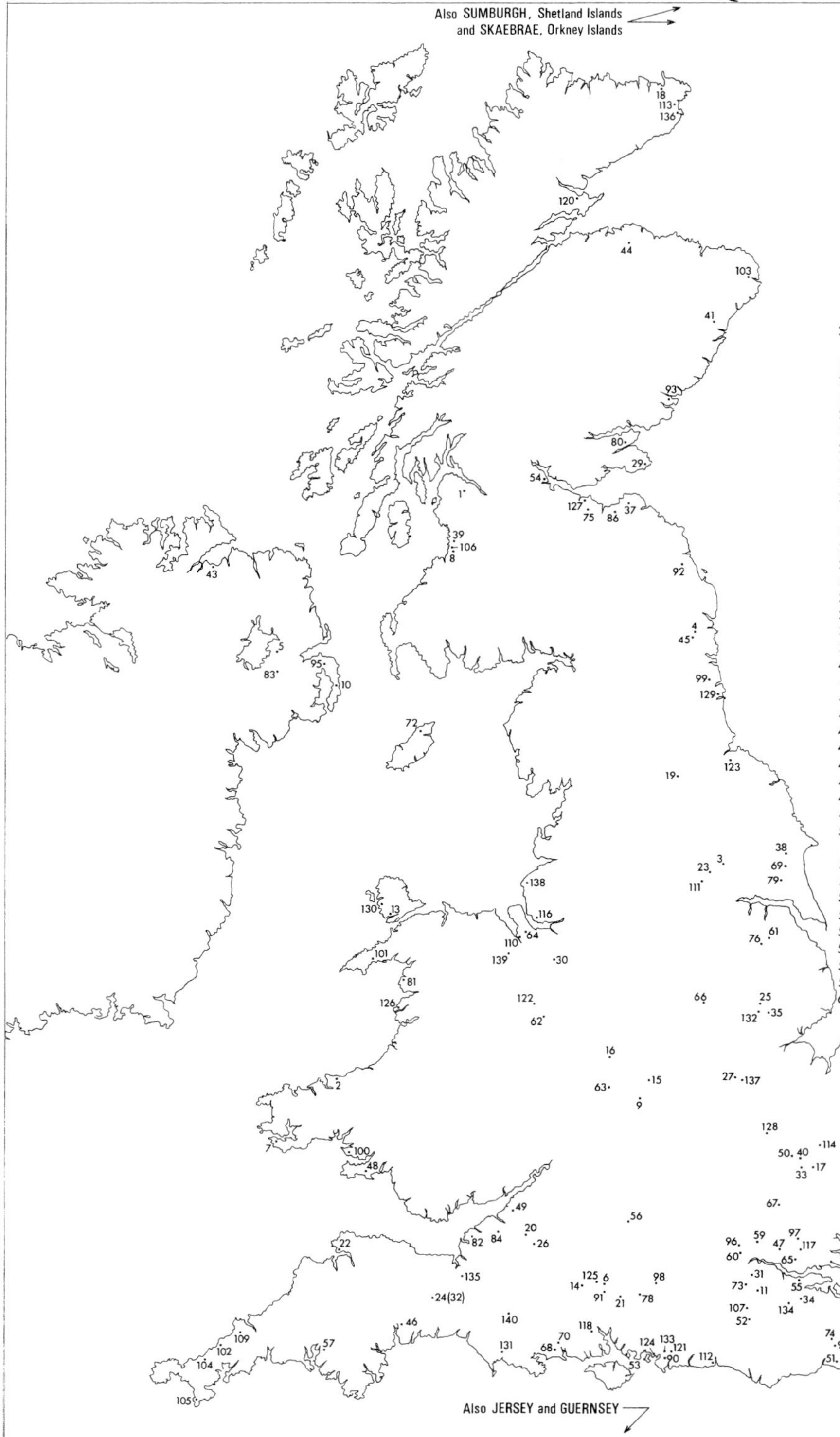

1 ABBOTSINCH
2 ABERPORTH
3 ACASTER MALBIS
4 ACKLINGTON
5 ALDERGROVE
6 ANDOVER
7 ANGLE
8 AYR
9 BAGINTON
10 BALLYHALBERT
11 BIGGIN HILL
12 BIRCHAM NEWTON
13 BODORGAN
14 BOSCOMBE DOWN
15 BRAMCOTE
16 CASTLE BROMWICH
17 CASTLE CAMPS
18 CASTLETOWN
19 CATTERICK
20 CHARMY DOWN
21 CHILBOLTON
22 CHIVENOR
23 CHURCH FENTON
24 CHURCHSTANTON
25 COLEBY GRANGE
26 COLERNE
27 COLLYWESTON
28 COLTISHALL
29 CRAIL
30 CRANAGE
31 CROYDON
32 CULMHEAD
33 DEBDEN
34 DETLING
35 DIGBY
36 DOCKING
37 DREM
38 DRIFFIELD
39 DUNDONALD
40 DUXFORD
41 DYCE
42 EASTCHURCH
43 EGLINTON
44 ELGIN
45 ESHOTT
46 EXETER
47 FAIRLOP
48 FAIRWOOD COMMON
49 FILTON
50 FOWLMERE
51 FRISTON
52 GATWICK
53 GOSPORT
54 GRANGEMOUTH
55 GRAVESEND
56 GROVE
57 HARROWBEER
58 HAWKINGE
59 HENDON
60 HESTON
61 HIBALDSTOW
62 HIGH ERCALL
63 HONILEY
64 HOOTON PARK
65 HORNCHURCH
66 HUCKNALL
67 HUNSDON
68 HURN
69 HUTTON CRANSWICK
70 IBSLEY
71 IPSWICH
72 JURBY
73 KENLEY
74 KINGSNORTH
75 KIRKNEWTON
76 KIRTON-IN-LINDSEY
77 LANGHAM
78 LASHAM
79 LECONFIELD
80 LEUCHARS
81 LLANBEDR
82 LOCKING
83 LONG KESH
84 LULSGATE BOTTOM
85 LYMPNE
86 MACMERRY
87 MANSTON
88 MARTLESHAM HEATH
89 MATLASKE
90 MERSTON
91 MIDDLE WALLOP
92 MILFIELD
93 MONTROSE
94 NEWCHURCH
95 NEWTOWNARDS
96 NORTHOLT
97 NORTH WEALD
98 ODIHAM
99 OUSTON
100 PEMBREY
101 PENRHOS
102 PERRANPORTH
103 PETERHEAD
104 PORTREATH
105 PREDANNACK
106 PRESTWICK
107 REDHILL
108 ROCHFORD
109 ST. EVAL
110 SEALAND
111 SHERBURN-IN-ELMET
112 SHOREHAM
113 SKITTEN
114 SNAILWELL
115 SOUTHEND
116 SPEKE
117 STAPLEFORD TAWNEY
118 STONEY CROSS
119 SWANNINGTON
120 TAIN
121 TANGMERE
122 TERNHILL
123 THORNABY
124 THORNEY ISLAND
125 THRUXTON
126 TOWYN
127 TURNHOUSE
128 TWINWOOD FARM
129 USWORTH
130 VALLEY
131 WARMWELL
132 WELLINGORE
133 WESTHAMPNETT
134 WEST MALLING
135 WESTON ZOYLAND
136 WICK
137 WITTERING
138 WOODVALE
139 WREXHAM
140 ZEALS

Continued from opposite: COMMONWEALTH HURRICANE SQUADRONS IN BRITAIN

401 (No1, RCAF	ARRIVED IN U.K. … SPITFIRES
402 (No2, RCAF	NEWLY FORMED … SPITFIRES
438 RCAF	NEWLY FORMED … TYPHOONS
439 RCAF	NEWLY FORMED … TYPHOONS
440 RCAF	NEWLY FORMED … TYPHOONS
486 RNZAF	NEWLY FORMED … TYPHOONS

RAF and Soviet naval personnel with Hurricane Mark IIBs of Nos 81 and 134 Squadrons, 151 Wing, at Vaenga, North Russia, during the autumn of 1941 before and after the arrival of the snow. The RAF Squadrons used the first letter (F for No 81 and G for No 134) of their normal code plus an individual aircraft identity letter and a pair of Russian-style numerals for Soviet identification purposes. After the Hurricanes were handed over to the Russians the red star replaced the RAF roundels, the RAF code letters were removed, but the Soviet identity numerals and the RAF serials remained. As explained in the text it was some time before the full twelve-gun wing battery was fitted. (Photos: *Sydney Camm Collection)*

during the remainder of September, but it was No. 81 that scored most heavily. In the evening of the 17th the Squadron was covering the withdrawal of Soviet bombers from a raid when it was attacked by eight Bf 109s (this time of the *Luftwaffe*) and Sqn Ldr Rook, Sgt Sims and Sgt Anson each claimed one destroyed—this despite the fact that in the middle of the combat four Russian fighters appeared and promptly attacked the Hurricanes, fortunately without causing any damage. The Squadron was again in action, once more escorting the bombers on the 26th; about nine Finnish Bf 109Fs attempted to attack the bombers, but three were claimed shot down by Plt Off Edmiston (two) and Sgt Reed (one). On the 27th No. 134 Squadron suffered a tragic accident when Flt Lt V. W. Berg in *BG825* took off, unaware that two airmen (Aircraftmen Ridley and Thomas) were still lying on the tail of the aircraft. The Hurricane stalled and crashed from 50 feet; the pilot was uninjured, but the two airmen were killed instantly.[49]

On 6 October No. 134 Squadron intercepted a German raid on Vaenga, shooting down two aircraft and claiming one probably destroyed and damaging two others.

By the end of that month about 60 Hurricane IIs had been assembled from ship cargoes (some of the aircraft still fitted with tropical air filters—evidence of their having been hastily consigned by MUs in Britain to Russia instead of the Middle East) and the pilots of the two RAF squadrons then set about training Soviet pilots in flying the aircraft. On 28 October No. 134 was ordered to hand over its aircraft to the Soviet Air Force and embark in a ship about to sail for Britain. It was followed a month later by No. 81.

It has been said that 2,952 Hurricanes were supplied to the Soviet Union by both Britain and

Canadian Hurricane Mark X AG111 *HK-G of the Fighter Leaders' School in 1942. (*Photo: *Hawker Aircraft Ltd, Neg No MC55/57)*

*Combat operations by Hurricane IID-equipped Squadrons based in the United Kingdom were shortlived before being replaced by Mark IVs; this relatively anonymous aircraft may have served with No 184 Squadron. (*Photo: *Sydney Camm Collection)*

*The sleeve rank badge of the Russian naval Captain suggests that this Hurricane Mark IIB may be one of those that served with the Soviet Baltic Fleet during 1943. (*Photo: *John W. R. Taylor)*

Canada, comprising 210 Mark IIAs, 1,557 Mark IIBs, 1,009 Mark IICs, 60 Mark IIDs and 30 Mark IVs; the remainder were taken from stocks held at RAF maintenance units in the Middle East and sent by rail through Persia; the great majority were, however, shipped from Britain in the North Cape convoys. Little of accuracy is known of their service with the Soviet Air Force, except that the aircraft of Nos. 81 and 134 Squadrons were handed over to the 72nd Regiment of the Red Naval Air Fleet, and that at one stage a number served with a French volunteer Air Regiment in the Soviet Union. As with other aircraft supplied by the Western Allies, wastage was inordinately high simply owing to a general lack of spares and trained groundcrews, and aircraft that would have required no more than a few hours' work to service or repair in the RAF would be consigned to a salvage dump on the Eastern Front or simply abandoned where they stood.

It has also been said that the Russians always suspected that the British supplied old, discarded or "disguised" Hurricane Is—a belief possibly sparked by a very early batch of Mark Is converted to Mark IIs, and by the reduced gun armament in the first Mark IIs at Vaenga. Nevertheless there is little doubt that, witnessing No. 81 Squadron destroy more than a dozen enemy aircraft[50] in the first fortnight of combat at Vaenga must have been of some reassurance especially as the Soviet Air Force itself was suffering such enormous losses elsewhere on the Eastern Front during those early months of *Barbarossa*.

★ ★ ★

A minor operation involving Hurricanes during the sailing of the first North Cape convoys was that by No. 1423 Flight in Iceland. After it had become inevitable that British forces would have to be withdrawn from Norway at the beginning of June 1940 a small contingent was sent to Iceland to frustrate any further moves by the Germans in that direction. These forces remained in Iceland until, on 7 July, 1941, it was announced in Washington that American troops were to take over the garrison duties. Among the RAF forces that had been stationed at the airfield at Kaldadarnes since August 1940 was No. 98 Squadron with Fairey Battles. Now, in July 1941, it fell to No. 98 to provide air cover for the withdrawal of British forces and four Hurricane IIAs (*Z4037*, *Z4045*, *Z4048* and *Z4049*) were despatched in crates from No. 47 Maintenance Unit in Britain. At the end of the month No. 98 Squadron was shipped back to the United Kingdom, leaving one flight behind to fly the Hurricanes, and this was formed into No. 1423 Flight. By now the first North Cape convoy was assembling in Britain and it was decided to strengthen the unit to keep watch for German aircraft that might attempt to interfere with the passage of the convoy, and five more Hurricane IIAs were shipped to Reykjavík (*Z4607*, *Z4617*, *Z4631*, *Z4639* and *Z4702*). In due course the presence of German aircraft was detected flying over Icelandic waters and on 28 August a solitary Heinkel He 111 was spotted and Hurricanes gave chase, but on this and subsequent occasions the German aircraft escaped in cloud. It is now known that KG 26 *was* engaged in reconnaissance patrols, on the look-out for shipping sailing for Russian ports on the North Cape route. In due course No. 1423 Flight was disbanded and its aircraft (less *Z4607*, which had crashed in September) shipped back to the United Kingdom in December 1941.

10

STORM AT SEA

For many years prior to the Second World War the Royal Navy had possessed a succession of carrier-borne fighters, two-gun biplanes whose specifications seemed to compromise rather than enhance their capabilities; yet for all the accoutrements supposedly necessary for aeroplanes which had to fly from the deck of a carrier, operate over the sea and land back on the carrier—catapult spools, flotation gear, dinghy stowage, arrester hook, folding wings and the rest—those aeroplanes, Fairey Flycatchers, Hawker Nimrods and Gloster Sea Gladiators to name but some, managed to retain respectable performance and manoeuvrability. They were in fact not greatly inferior to their landplane contemporaries simply because aircraft designers were *used* to designing fighters to an established formula, the naval requirements scarcely changed from year to year, and most improvements—mainly confined to small increases in engine power—would benefit the naval aircraft equally well.

All that seemed likely to change in the mid-1930s. Not only were modern landplanes making considerable strides in technology, and therefore presumably posing greater threat to their adversaries, but foreign maritime powers, notably Italy and Japan, were beginning to behave in a manner that in the foreseeable future could lead them into conflict with Britain. Their very geographical locations in time of war would seriously threaten the sea routes of the British Empire.

Because the nature of that threat could not accurately be defined in the mid-1930s the Admiralty was content to issue two requirements for naval fighters of no great imagination other than that one should combine the duties of an interceptor with those of a dive bomber and the other, a "pure" fighter, should approximate in most respects to contemporary land-based fighters while carrying an observer/navigator. The first materialized as the Blackburn Skua, which was occasionally to perform creditably (providing the opposition was not too fierce), and the second as the Fairey Fulmar eight-gun fighter, which, although it was to become the Royal Navy's standard fighter for two years and occupied a yawning void in the carriers' inventory, was conspicuously down on performance; it was rather unkindly referred to as a "Fairey Battle weighed down by a Hurricane's armament". Pending the arrival of the Fulmar in service in 1940 the Royal Navy adopted as a stopgap a navalized version of the Gladiator, the Sea Gladiator.

However, it must be emphasized that all the aircraft mentioned above were carrier-borne fighters. At the outbreak of war with Germany the Royal Navy possessed six carriers (HMS *Courageous, Glorious, Furious, Argus, Hermes* and *Ark Royal*), and by the time Italy entered the war on 10 June, 1940, that number had dropped to four, HMS *Courageous* having been sunk early on and *Glorious* sent to the bottom off Norway only two days previously—not what one might regard as a powerful force of carriers having regard to the long merchant sea lanes throughout the world on whose security Britain depended. Certainly the carrier could but only rarely be spared to escort the most important merchant or troop convoy.

★ ★ ★

The first proposal to send the Hurricane to sea had nothing to do with providing a fighter for the Royal Navy as much as to protect British forces in Norway during the campaign of 1940. Following the abortive expedition to central Norway in April that year, when the lack of suitable airfields compromised the efforts by No. 263 Squadron (see page 55) and no fighter existed capable of flying from Britain to provide protection for the ground forces, it was suggested that Hurricanes suitably modified with floats might be capable of operating from the many Norwegian fjords with greater ease and safety. Accordingly Hawker was asked to modify a Hurricane I for evaluation with Blackburn Roc[51] floats so that in the event that a foothold could be gained and held at Narvik a small force of such Hurricanes might be sent out to relieve No. 46 Squadron.

A set of Roc floats was delivered to the experimental department in Canbury Park Road on 23 May and a Hurricane I set aside for modification (the float struts would attach to the wing spars at the mounting points for the outer wings, the wheel undercarriage would be removed and the wheel recesses faired over and the rear spin fairing and rudder increased in depth, see page 195). The necessary drawings were completed by the end of the month but only three days later (3 June, when the evacuation of Narvik was ordered) the Company was told to abandon the project.

In July 1940, when it seemed likely that a shortage of pilots, rather than of aircraft, might occur in Fighter Command, the Royal Navy called for volunteers in the Fleet Air Arm to transfer temporarily to the RAF; about 30 such pilots volunteered and were posted to Gosport for a short conversion course. Eighteen redundant L-series Hurricanes were delivered from RAF maintenance units (several of them being painted in naval colours) and before the end of the month the first half-dozen naval pilots, each with about 18 hours' experience in Hurricanes, reported to various Fighter Command squadrons. These training Hurricanes were no different from standard RAF aircraft, although they have been referred to as the first Sea Hurricanes. By the end of the Battle of Britain about 40 naval pilots had been trained on the Hurricanes, but fewer than half of them had actually transferred to the RAF.

A much greater threat was now becoming apparent as the *Luftwaffe* began to operate a new specialized anti-shipping unit on the Brest peninsula in western France. The German air force had, fairly early in the war, detailed two bomber *Gruppen* to concentrate much of their training on anti-shipping operations, although by and large most of their bombing operations during the daylight Battle of Britain had been little different from those of the other *Kampfgruppen*. (Later on, however, KG 30 and two *Gruppen* of KG 26 would devote all their attention to British convoys sailing to Russia round the North Cape.)

Mixed formation of early Sea Hurricane Mark Is and Hurricane Is transferred to Admiralty charge in about December 1940. The Sea Hurricanes differed only in being equipped with naval radio and painted in two-tone grey camouflage; they were not fitted with catapult spools nor arrester hooks, and were flown as trainers for pilots some of whom would soon be flying the first Sea Hurricane IAs from the catapult-equipped naval auxiliary seaplane tenders Ariguani, Maplin, Patia and Springbank. *(*Photo: *R. Sturtivant via R. Ward, Farnborough)*

Towards the end of the Battle of Britain, however, I./KG 40, flying long-range Focke-Wulf Fw 200 Condor aircraft from Bordeaux-Merignac under the command of Oberstleutnant Edgar Petersen, began patrolling the Western Approaches as well as the sea lanes off the north coast of Ireland, on the look-out for British ships sailing singly and for convoy stragglers. On 26 October a Fw 200, flown by Hauptmann Bernhard Jope, hit and crippled the 42,000-ton *Empress of Britain* (which was torpedoed and sunk soon afterwards). Other ships followed the big liner to the bottom in quick succession.

At a meeting held on 12 November in London, at which Air Chief Marshal Sir Charles Portal, Chief of the Air Staff, and Admiral of the Fleet Sir Dudley Pound, Chief of the Naval Staff and First Sea Lord, were present, the decision was taken to examine the feasibility of carrying "expendable" fighter aircraft in merchant ships and catapulting them on the appearance of a Fw 200 Condor raider. In due course it was decided to adopt the Hurricane I, suitably modified with catapult spools, and an initial order for the conversion of 35 aircraft was placed.[52]

Two types of ship were to be converted. The first, known as Fighter Catapult Ships, of which

Externally indistinguishable from the late series Hurricane Mark I, the Sea Hurricane IA, destined mainly for CAM-ship operations, simply incorporated catapult points and naval radio. Large numbers were converted, and when the CAM-ships were eventually withdrawn from service the Sea Hurricanes were used by the Fleet Air Arm as trainers until the end of the War.

*A pair of Sea Hurricane Mark IAs, bearing Merchant Ship Fighter Unit code letters, being ferried by barge to a CAM-ship anchored in the Mersey. This picture was probably taken early in 1942 when some CAM-ships carried a 'spare' fighter. (*Photo: *Sydney Camm Collection)*

*A Sea Hurricane IA on the fo'c'sle catapult of a CAM-ship; note the flaps pre-selected in the take-off position. The catapult was angled to starboard over the ship's bows as much to prevent the rocket blast from engulfing the bridge as to reduce the risk of the pilot being run down by the ship should he hit the water after launch. (*Photo: *Sydney Camm Collection)*

four were previously banana boats (HMS *Ariguani, Maplin, Patia* and *Springbank*), were already being fitted out as naval auxiliary vessels; they would be crewed exclusively by naval personnel, each carrying two fighters and three pilots of No. 804 Squadron, Fleet Air Arm. These four ships would accompany convoys sailing between Britain and Gibraltar and, not carrying freight, would represent part of the convoys' escorts. The first 35 Sea Hurricane IAs—as they were termed—which became available in January 1941, represented the number anticipated to be required to provide aircraft at sea, replacement stocks in Britain and at Gibraltar and four training aircraft at Sydenham, Belfast, No. 804 Squadron's shore base.

The other type of ship to be converted, the Catapult Aircraft Merchantman, or CAM-ship, was as its name implied a freight-carrying vessel flying the Red Ensign, captained and crewed by merchant seamen, whose Sea Hurricanes would be flown and serviced almost exclusively by RAF volunteers. At first it was suggested that 200 CAM-ships would be converted, but eventually, at Churchill's instigation, the figure was reduced to 35, and in due course 214 further Sea Hurricane IAs were converted, starting in March 1941—some by Hawker and Gloster, but the great majority by General Aircraft Ltd., Hanworth.

The headquarters unit of the CAM-ship Hurricane pilots was the Merchant Ship Fighter Unit (MSFU) at Speke, near Liverpool, under the initial command of Acting Wg Cdr Edward Selwyn Moulton-Barrett and under the jurisdiction of No. 9 Group, Fighter Command. The pilots were drawn from volunteers sought from Fighter Command squadrons during January 1941, and were therefore largely Battle of Britain veterans—though not exclusively so. Initially the catapult training of these pilots was carried out in Fulmars at the RAE, Farnborough, but in July 1941 this work was transferred to Speke under the direction of that most famous and colourful First World War pilot Sqn Ldr Louis Strange, DSO, OBE, MC, DFC and Bar, then aged 51. The rocket catapult at Speke was exactly the same as that to be fitted on the fo'c'sles of the CAM-ships, namely a rocket-propelled structure on a pair of 75-foot rails. No fewer than 13 3-inch solid-fuel rockets, fired electrically, accelerated the Sea Hurricane at full throttle to about 80 mph at some 3.5 g, which, assuming some light headwind and using about half flap, was regarded as a safe flying speed, although most launches were followed by slight "sink" after the aircraft left the catapult rails.

The first launches of "expendable" fighters in defence of convoys, however, involved neither Fighter Catapult Ship, CAM-ship nor Hurricane, but the Royal Navy's seaplane tender, HMS *Pegasus*, and a Fulmar. Sailing with a convoy 250 miles off the Irish coast on 11 January, 1941, Petty Officer F. J. Shaw[53] was catapulted off after a Fw 200, but failed to catch up with the German raider and subsequently managed to reach land, where he put down safely at Aldergrove in Northern Ireland. On 11 May Sub-Lieut F. M. C. Harvey, RNVR, was launched in a Fulmar from HMS *Ariguani*, but after failing to intercept his quarry landed at Kaldadarnes in Iceland. Another of the Fighter Catapult Ships, HMS *Patia*, had already been sunk by a German bomber during her sea trials on 28 April. On 8 June Lieut B. F. Cox was also catapulted in a Fulmar from HMS *Pegasus*, but had no better fortune than Shaw—just reaching Sydenham before his fuel gave out. Two days later Shaw was again launched in a Fulmar, this time from HMS *Springbank*, but again failed to catch a Condor. The lesson was obvious: the Fulmar was simply too slow to catch the Condor, and Sea Hurricanes were to be adopted exclusively in future.

During escort duty with a convoy outward bound not for Gibraltar but for Halifax, Nova Scotia,

The CAM-ship Empire Tide, *one of the most famous of all the catapult merchantment, seen here with a Sea Hurricane IA embarked. (Ministry of Information photo, dated 1943)*

HMS *Maplin* with two Hurricanes embarked (one in reserve) launched a fighter flown by the 40-year-old Australian-born Lieut Robert W. H. Everett against a Fw 200 on 18 July, but just before he could open fire a gun on one of the convoy's ships scored a direct hit, tearing off part of the Condor's wing and causing it to crash. Everett just succeeded in making landfall in Northern Ireland on his remaining fuel. A fortnight later, on 2 August, while sailing with some escort vessels to meet an inbound convoy from Sierra Leone, *Maplin* launched one of her Sea Hurricanes, again flown by Bob Everett, against a Condor. After a long chase and several attempts to dodge the heavy defensive fire from the German bomber, Everett set it on fire and after a few minutes it crashed into the sea from low level. The Hurricane itself had been hit and was losing oil quickly and, after spotting one of the destroyers from his group, the pilot decided to bale out; however, after several attempts to fall out of the cockpit while flying inverted—during which the Hurricane simply pitched down, forcing him back into his seat—he attempted to ditch the fighter. The moment the aircraft touched the water the nose was dragged down by the radiator and the Hurricane disappeared; Everett forced his way to the surface despite not being a strong swimmer, and was rescued none the worst for his experiences. As the first pilot of a catapult Sea Hurricane to destroy a Condor he was to be awarded the DSO.

While HMS *Maplin* continued to sail with convoys to Gibraltar—with an increased complement of three Sea Hurricanes—the other two Fighter Catapult Ships suffered misfortune before the end of the year; HMS *Springbank* was sunk and HMS *Ariguani* badly damaged, both by U-boats—the former having already launched Petty Officer Shaw in a vain effort to destroy a Condor.

Meanwhile the first CAM-ship scheduled to sail with an MSFU pilot had been made ready for catapult trials on the Clyde, and Plt Off H. J. Davidson, RAFVR, made the first launch from SS *Empire Rainbow* on 31 May, steaming downriver at some 10 knots. When two of the rockets on the catapult failed to ignite, and the throttle lever edged back—reducing power—owing to the friction nut not being tightened, the Hurricane only barely escaped striking the water as Davidson struggled to gain airspeed. He eventually climbed away and landed safely at Abbotsinch, having also discovered that he'd forgotten to lower any flap for the launch. He nevertheless accompanied *Empire Rainbow* on her first voyage to Halifax as a CAM-ship, and was followed by Plt Off A. R. McL. Campbell[54] in SS *Empire Moon* within a fortnight. By the end of June six of the 35 CAM-ships had started sailing with the Atlantic convoys.

Unfortunately no CAM-ship Sea Hurricane was successful in bringing down a Condor during 1941, although the presence of fighters in the convoys frequently discouraged the German pilots from attacking and probably prevented them from persistent shadowing, so that the convoys, which might have been attacked by U-boats, escaped unharmed. During the winter of 1941 Moulton-Barrett was posted away from the MSFU, command passing to Acting Wg Cdr George Cannon Pinkerton, AAF (who had been CO of No. 602 Squadron AAF prior to the Battle of Britain).[55]

The winter of 1941–42 saw the sailings of CAM-ships on the North Atlantic crossings suspended, largely because it was thought likely that the weather conditions would prevent the launching of Sea Hurricanes. However, the CAM-ships had previously started sailing on the Gibraltar run, and these continued without interruption. The opportunity was taken therefore to return many of the Sea Hurricanes to the maintenance units for thorough inspection and overhaul, as well as to introduce as many modifications as possible to bring them up to the latest standard without going so far as to rebuild them as Mark IIs.

Sea Hurricanes Round the North Cape

The attack by Germany on Russia in June 1941 had brought forth from Winston Churchill an undertaking to the Soviet dictator that all possible military assistance would be given by Britain to assist in the common struggle to defeat Germany. With British Commonwealth forces stretched to their limit throughout the Middle East, this military aid could only assume material form, other than an invasion of western Europe—the so-called "Second Front"—which was then out of the question, by shipping weapons from Britain to the northern Russian ports of Archangel'sk and Murmansk. Such a voyage would take the convoys far beyond the Arctic Circle and round the North Cape. Because of the ice line to the north these convoys would be obliged to sail well within range of German aircraft known to be based in northern Norway, before turning south into the Kola Inlet.

The first of the convoys (known as PQ convoys for the eastbound voyage and QP for their return) sailed on 12 August, 1941, from Liverpool to Iceland and thence on to Murmansk, and was followed by 10 more at intervals of two of three weeks. At first the Germans underestimated the importance of these convoys and chose not to deploy extra forces to Norway; moreover the first sailings took place during the period of the year when the Arctic enjoys almost continuous darkness, which rendered attacks by aircraft extremely difficult.

By March 1942, however, with daylight hours fast increasing in the far north, the risk of attacks on the convoys was recognized by the British Admiralty, which now allocated a total of six CAM-ships to the North Cape shipping route—that is, one CAM-ship to each convoy; the first of these were *Empire Morn, Empire Lawrence* and *Empire Tide.* (Sailing of CAM-ships were also resumed on the

North Atlantic routes on 3 March, for which 10 ships were allocated, with a further eight—two per convoy—on the Gibraltar run.)

The first North Cape convoy to sail with a CAM-ship was PQ 15, which sailed with *Empire Morn* from Iceland on 26 April. Two Sea Hurricanes were carried, one of them to be disembarked at Murmansk to start creating a pool of aircraft to supply fighters, when needed, for return journeys. The pilots were Fg Off John Kendal and Plt Off D. K. G. Faulks. Constituting the only fighter protection for the convoy, the pilots were told that they would only be launched if there was a reasonable chance of destroying shadowing aircraft, but that in the event of air attacks the Sea Hurricane would not be expended in efforts to shoot down one or two of the attackers and thereby leave the convoy without the means to destroy further shadowers. However, when PQ 15 sighted Fw 200 and Blohm und Voss Bv 138 shadowing aircraft on the 30th, it was decided not to waste the Sea Hurricane so early in the voyage without waiting to see if the Germans intended to attack the convoy at all. It was soon realized that the *Luftwaffe* was bent on keeping a constant watch on the convoy, so it would be pointless to destroy the shadowers when their place could be taken by others immediately. In due course attacks by Ju 88 bombers and He 111 torpedo-bombers developed, sinking three of the 25 merchantmen; three of the raiders fell to the guns of the convoy (including one to the gunners on *Empire Morn*, which herself was narrowly missed by two torpedoes). Yet, having had German aircraft almost continuously in sight for more than half the voyage, the Sea Hurricane pilots' frustration at not being launched can be imagined.

The return of PQ 15 (renumbered QP 12 for the westward journey) was timed to coincide with the sailing of PQ 16, comprising 35 merchantmen from Iceland on 21/22 May. As *Empire Morn* accompanied QP 12, the CAM-ship *Empire Lawrence* sailed with PQ 16, once more with a single Sea Hurricane embarked, its pilots being a South African, Plt Off Alistair Hay, and a Canadian, Fg Off Bruce Macpherson. Both convoys soon came under surveillance and when, on the 25th, some Ju 88s appeared over QP 12 Kendal was launched in an effort to destroy either of the shadowers or a bomber in the hope of breaking the pattern of shadowing. Kendal chose to attack a Ju 88 and succeeded in shooting it down; however, after baling out close to the convoy, his parachute was seen to fail to deploy properly and he died soon after being rescued from the sea. John Kendal was the first MSFU pilot to destroy an enemy aircraft in defence of a convoy . . . and convoy QP 12 reached Iceland without loss.

Distinguishable by its eight-gun wing and A-frame arrester hook, this Sea Hurricane Mark IB is seen at the moment of engaging an arrester cable while landing on a Victorious*-class carrier. (*Photo: *Fleet Air Arm Museum)*

Meanwhile, shortly after Kendal had been in action on the 25th, PQ 16 came under co-ordinated attacks by Ju 88s flying at about 6,000 ft and five He 111 torpedo-bombers at about 100 ft. Al Hay was catapulted from *Empire Lawrence* in an attempt to upset the Heinkels' aim and, although he met with heavy return fire from the German aircraft, he attacked one of the bombers with two three-second bursts and another with a five-second burst, finishing his ammunition on a third; the first was seen to crash by watchers in the convoy, but, more important by far, his spirited attack had completely confused the torpedo bombers, and all their weapons missed. Hay baled out successfully, although he had been wounded in the leg, but on falling into the sea found that his seat-type dinghy had been punctured by the Heinkels' gunfire. He was, however, picked up safely by an escorting destroyer.

Hay's success discouraged further attacks on the convoy that day, and in all probability the German crews, unaware that its sole Hurricane now lay on the sea bed, were briefed to single out *Empire Lawrence* with the prominent catapult on her fo'c'sle for particular attention. The following day the convoy came under renewed assaults and seven merchantmen were sunk—including the CAM-ship (the other Sea Hurricane pilot, Bruce Macpherson,

Standard Sea Hurricane Mark IC with Merlin III and four-canon armament. Though considerably down on performance this version acquitted itself admirably in Fleet Air Arm hands during the Malta convoy battles of 1942. (Photo: *Sydney Camm Collection)*

A late-series Sea Hurricane Mark IIC, pictured at Langley late in 1943; this version remained in operational service with the Fleet Air Arm until the end of the War. (Photo: *Sydney Camm Collection)*

being among the survivors). The remaining 28 ships and their escort sailed into the Kola Inlet on 30 May.

The climax of the battles fought by the North Cape convoys was reached with the sailing of the famous PQ 17 on 27 June, this time with no fewer than 37 merchant ships, including the CAM-ship *Empire Tide*—again with only one Sea Hurricane, with Flt Lt Douglas Richard Turley-George and Plt Off Charles Fenwick as its pilots. However, anticipating a possible attack by heavy enemy surface forces, a covering group including four cruisers had been ordered to sea, as had a much more powerful force from the Home Fleet comprising two battleships, an aircraft carrier (HMS *Victorious*), two cruisers and 14 destroyers.

Although the experiences of QP 12 and PQ 16 had suggested that the Sea Hurricanes had been much better employed in breaking up German bombing and torpedo attacks, and had gained some respite from new attacks—rather than knocking down shadowing aircraft—it seems that the lesson had not been passed to Commander J. E. Broome, who, as commander of PQ 17's close escort, would decide if and when to launch his one and only fighter.

To afford the CAM-ship maximum protection from torpedo attack, Broome stationed her well inside the convoy, but stated that she'd be moved to one wing as the danger of air attacks increased. However, throughout the shadowing phase *Empire Tide* remained in her protected station and was therefore incapable of launching owing to the proximity of other ships in the poor visibility; she was still there when the convoy was attacked by a number of torpedo-carrying Heinkel He 115 seaplanes. Then, as a major attack developed by He 111s, Commander Broome ordered off the fighter; its Merlin was started up and *Empire Tide* prepared to swing out of line to launch, but at that moment every gun in the convoy opened up against the raiders with a positive storm of shell which criss-crossed the sky—including the area in which the Hurricane would have to launch. Reluctantly Turley-George throttled back and switched off. In retrospect it seems that *Empire Tide* should have been moved out to the wing of the convoy so as to be prepared for the inevitable bombing and torpedo attacks. In the event the matter was irrelevant, for about three hours later, in anticipation of an attack by large German warships, the Admiralty signalled to PQ 17 to scatter. The subsequent account of the massacre that befell the convoy, not by the *Tirpitz, Scheer, Lützow* and *Hipper* but by Heinkel He 111s, Junkers Ju 87s and Ju 88s, and U-boats, is now well known. Suffice here to state that only 11 merchantmen straggled into Archangel'sk during the next three weeks, among them *Empire Tide*—her Hurricane still mounted on the catapult.

Obviously shocked by the destruction of PQ 17 the Admiralty sailed the next convoy on 7 September from Iceland with an important addition to the

One of the Canadian Sea Hurricane Mark XIIs (JS310) of No 800 Squadron, Fleet Air Arm, aboard HMS Biter *off Oran on 8th November 1942, during the Torch landings. Shortly after this photo was taken the Squadron was in action against Vichy French fighters.* (Photo: *J. M. Bruen via Sqn Ldr R. C. B. Ashworth)*

escort for its 39 merchantmen, namely one of the first of a new class of escort carriers, HMS *Avenger*. Converted from an American lease-lend merchant ship, the small carrier embarked a complement of 12 Sea Hurricane IBs (see page 130) and three Swordfish. It was also the turn of *Empire Morn* once more to sail to Russia, this time her Sea Hurricane pilots, Fg Off A. H. Burr and a New Zealander, Plt Off John Davies, ordered *not* to launch before *Avenger* turned for home (on meeting up with the returning convoy QP 14) or was sunk.

Four days out from Iceland the convoy came under continuous surveillance by Fw 200s and Bv 138s and the next day, the 13th, the attacks started, *Avenger*'s Sea Hurricanes being ordered off on six occasions in two days, first against Bv 138 flying boats and then against the Ju 88s of KG 30, the He 111s of KG 26 and the He 115s of *Küstenfliegergruppe* 406. Desperate air battles raged over the convoy, the Sea Hurricane pilots seemingly oblivious of the tremendous barrage being put up by the ships' guns. Ten merchant ships were hit and sunk, but this time the *Luftwaffe* suffered the loss of 15 He 111s, 12 Ju 88s and five He 115s; three Sea Hurricanes were shot down—by the guns of the convoy—but their pilots were rescued. On the 16th *Avenger* turned back to join QP 14, leaving *Empire Morn* and her Sea Hurricane to protect PQ 18. After bad weather had frustrated air attacks on the 17th, Burr was catapulted off against 15 He 111 torpedo-bombers attacking the convoy in line abreast. The 23-year-old pilot launched a withering head-on attack, causing one of the Germans to panic and dive into the sea, before exhausting his ammunition in quarter attacks on some of the other attackers. Only one ship was hit. Burr then opted to save his aircraft by going in search of a Soviet airfield and, on his last few drops of fuel, by sheer good fortune stumbled on the small grass airfield of Keg Ostrov—home of the MSFU detachment in Russia.

Flight Decks

After its surprise at finding an aircraft carrier—small though it was—with convoy PQ 18, the *Luftwaffe* showed increasing reluctance to interfere with the North Cape convoys, even though they continued to sail for much of the remainder of the war. From September 1942 it became the exception rather than the rule *not* to include at least one escort carrier in each convoy.

It is now pertinent to recount the manner in which the deck-landing Sea Hurricane came to be introduced—for the CAM-ship aircraft had possessed the means to permit launching by catapult and not for alighting on a flight deck (not withstanding the feat of airmanship that brought the Hurricanes of No. 46 Squadron safely on to the deck of

The two Canadian Sea Hurricanes shot down by French fighters near Oran on 8th November 1942 during the Torch landings, showing the American markings carried by British fighters on that occasion. Left, *a Sea Hurricane Mark X,* AM277, *and,* right, *a Mark XII, JS327, with twelve-gun wings and American personnel in attendance at St Leu*

Sea Hurricane Mark IBs of the Fleet Air Arm aboard an Illustrious*-class fleet carrier, probably in 1942. These fighters were heavily engaged in the Malta convoy battles of 1941–42.* (Photo: *via R. Ward, Canterbury)*

HMS *Glorious* at the conclusion of the Norwegian campaign in June 1940).

Whether or not the success with which Sqn Ldr Kenneth Cross and the pilots of No. 46 Squadron had taken off and landed aboard HMS *Glorious* sowed the seeds of an idea at the Admiralty is not known. Be that as it may, just 48 hours were to elapse before Italy entered the war and the situation in the Mediterranean underwent an immediate change. The swift collapse of France put an end to the tiny trickle of Hurricanes to the Middle East through France, Tunisia and Malta almost before it began.

Indeed the reinforcement of Malta itself quickly became urgent and, on 2 August HMS *Argus* entered the Mediterranean with a dozen Hurricane Is; these were flown off the carrier's deck without difficulty by line pilots of the RAF and landed safely in Malta. No one now doubted the ease with which ordinary Hurricanes could take off from a deck which had been specially cleared for the occasion. Faced with the lack of a fleet fighter with a performance capable of matching most land-based bombers—for the Sea Gladiator was becoming distinctly long in the tooth, the Fulmar already shown to be disturbingly cumbersome and the Skua so puny as to be virtually impotent—it was entirely logical to turn to the Hurricane as the new carrier-borne interceptor.

It had been, however, a relatively simple matter to incorporate spools in an aircraft to transmit the thrust of a powerful catapult to the main structure of the Hurricane, but to restress the fuselage of the aircraft so that an arrester hook did not tear its tail off on engagement with the deck cables on landing involved rather more than local strengthening. Nor was the Air Ministry yet prepared to offset new aircraft, which could result in delays on the RAF Hurricane production line.

Conversion of the Sea Hurricane IA went ahead much faster than that of the deck-landing version, and it was not until March 1941 that a "hooked Hurricane" prototype with an A-frame arrester hook was completed for trials at Farnborough, and later at Boscombe Down, Speke and Lee-on-Solent. The aircraft, an early Canadian-built Mark I (redesignated the Mark X), had already been fitted with catapult spools as a Sea Hurricane IA and now became regarded as the prototype Sea Hurricane IB (*P5187*). Conversion of some low-hour Sea Hurricane IAs and Hurricane Is of all vintages started in May 1941, and by October about 120 Mark IBs had been completed; unfortunately for administrative

The last operational Sea Hurricane in service with the Fleet Air Arm was this Mark IIC, NF700 *of No 835 Squadron, 47th Naval Fighter Wing, aboard HMS* Nairana *in 1945. (*Photo: *K. Armstrong and R. C. Jones)*

tidiness, this designation also covered a small number of early Hurricane IIAs and IIBs as well as some Canadian (Sea) Hurricane Xs, XIs and XIIs with eight- or 12-gun wings. There have been many attempts to exactly define what a Sea Hurricane IB was, and the nearest that can be suggested was "any Hurricane which possessed an arrester hook and whose gun armament did not protrude forward of the wing leading edge", but even this was later complicated by some "hooked Hurricane IIs" (see below).

The armament qualification was necessary when, following a call by the Admiralty for increased armament, about 100 Merlin III-powered Sea Hurricane IBs were rearmed with wings fitted with four 20-mm Oerlikon cannon to become the Mark IC. Although this armament was fairly heavy for the 1,030 hp Merlin III, this naval fighter was still faster than the Fulmar at 296 mph at 15,100 ft, and a good deal more manoeuvrable.

Intended for service aboard the Royal Navy's fleet carriers, which had had to rely almost exclusively on Fulmars until September 1941, the Mark IB was by the end of the year in service with No. 801 Squadron in HMS *Argus* and *Eagle*, No. 806 Squadron in HMS *Formidable*, No. 880 Squadron in HMS *Avenger* (the escort carrier later to join the North Cape convoy PQ 18) and No. 885 Squadron in HMS *Victorious*. The Mark IC joined the Fleet Air Arm in January 1942 and soon afterwards entered service with Nos. 801, 802, 803, 880, 883 and 885 Squadrons. Few Sea Hurricanes were equipped with tropical filters, despite the fact that the majority fought and flew in the Mediterranean and the tropics; a small number of Mark IBs, so equipped, was flown up the Takoradi air bridge to join No. 889 Squadron operating in the Western Desert.

As the sailing of convoys to Malta in 1942 took on new urgency, the Admiralty asked for some Merlin XX-powered Sea Hurricanes to be converted, and in March that year, as an initial step, ordered 70 conversion "kits" to bring Hurricane IICs up to full deck-operating standard; these aircraft, with naval radio, spools and hooks, and a number converted on the production line at Langley, were termed Sea Hurricane IICs, while some training aircraft with Merlin XXs and retaining RAF radio were simply referred to as "hooked Sea Hurricane IIs".

* * *

The biggest naval action involving Sea Hurricanes was that fought in August 1942 by the escort of a convoy (operation Pedestal) that battled its way to Malta from Gibraltar during the build-up of forces in the Mediterranean prior to the great Battle of Alamein. To fight just 14 merchant ships through to the beleaguered island, the escorting naval force comprised four carriers, HMS *Eagle, Furious, Indomitable* and *Victorious* (of which *Furious* was "trucking" Spitfires to Malta and could therefore operate no naval fighters), two battleships, seven cruisers and 24 destroyers. Aboard the carriers were 39 Sea Hurricanes of Nos. 880 Squadron (HMS *Indomitable*), No. 801 (*Eagle*) and No. 885 (*Victorious*), as well as 31 Fulmars and Martlets of Nos. 804, 806, 809 and 884 Squadrons.

The operation got off to a disastrous start on the afternoon of the 11th as the Spitfires started flying off HMS *Furious* while some of the destroyer screen were oiling from tankers; at that moment a German U-boat fired a salvo of torpedoes, four of which struck the *Eagle*, sinking her in eight minutes. Four of her Sea Hurricanes were airborne at the time and these landed on *Indomitable* and *Victorious*; the rest of her air complement was lost.

Available for attacks on the convoy were ranged some 200 German and more than 300 Italian aircraft on bases in Sardinia, Sicily and Italy. That evening the first attacks developed, and although the naval fighters were unable to intercept owing to the failing light, several bombers were destroyed by the gun defences. The following day four attacks were launched, the second of which was intercepted by the Sea Hurricanes and broken up, although one merchant ship was hit and sunk. As *Victorious* began recovering the aircraft of No. 885 Squadron two aircraft suddenly broke from the circling fighters and dived on the carrier, each releasing a 1,100 lb bomb; one exploded on the bows, but the other shattered on the armoured flight deck; neither fortunately affected flight operations or the sailing of the ship (the aircraft were Italian RE.2001 fighter-bombers which were fairly similar in general appearance to the Hurricane).

The third attack of the 12th was made by about 100 aircraft, of which a formation of Ju 87s went straight for the *Indomitable*; she was struck by three 1,100 lb bombs and suffered two near misses, but once more the armoured deck saved the ship, although she could no longer operate her aircraft. Fortunately her Sea Hurricanes were in the air at the time and these were now landed aboard HMS *Victorious*, the only remaining carrier in operation—but with 47 fighters and nine torpedo-bombers crowding her deck and hangar.

As the convoy now entered the Sicilian narrows the naval escort of battleships and carriers turned back to Gibraltar with their destroyer screen as there was inadequate sea room in which to manoeuvre in defence of the convoy. Thus far a carrier, a destroyer and a merchantman had been lost. Now it was the turn of the Axis submarines, torpedo craft, mines and more aircraft to take their toll, yet, despite the further loss of two cruisers and eight merchant ships sunk, the five surviving supply ships (of which three, including the vital tanker *Ohio*, were damaged) proved adequate to sustain the island.[56] Aircraft losses by the carriers amounted to eight in combat and 35 in HMS *Eagle*; German and Italian records show a loss of 31 aircraft in action.[57]

One final major operation in the Mediterranean and North Africa involved Sea Hurricanes. This was the landing by British and American forces in Morocco and Algeria: Operation Torch. The supporting carriers represented the largest force of such ships thus far assembled in the war, comprising four British fleet carriers (HMS *Formidable, Victorious, Furious* and *Argus* with 35 Martlets, 45 Seafires and seven Fulmars), one American fleet carrier (with 54 Wildcats), three British escort carriers (HMS *Biter, Dasher* and *Avenger* with 42 Sea Hurricanes) and four American escort carriers with 57 Wildcats; in addition the carriers had embarked 15 Swordfish, 35 Albacores, 36 Dauntlesses, 27 Avengers and 78 USAAF P-40s.

The main American naval forces were employed to support the landings by US forces on the Atlantic coast far to the west in French Morocco at Casablanca, and it fell to the British Force H and the British Central and Eastern Task Forces to support American and British landings at Oran and Algiers. To avoid confusion among the American ship gunners and pilots—unfamiliar with British and French aircraft—all shipborne fighters involved were painted with the American star insignia, thereby simplifying identification. The principal operations involving the Sea Hurricanes were those in support of the American landings at Oran, which started before dawn on 8 November when *Biter* launched her three Swordfish to drop leaflets on the port urging surrender. *Furious* then launched her eight Albacores to drop bombs on the airfield nearby, but these did no more than encourage French pilots of Dewoitine D.520 fighters to take off in pursuit; all the Albacores were shot down before 12 Sea Hurricanes from *Dasher* and *Biter* could arrive (Canadian-built and converted Mark Xs and XIIAs) and shoot down five of the French fighters, losing two whose pilots were able to force land at St Leu, several miles along the coast from Oran to the east.

This tragic and rather pointless clash of arms was probably as much the result of French impetuosity as the bombing by the Albacores and fortunately was not repeated, although the Sea Hurricanes from *Dasher* and *Biter*, and the Seafires from *Furious*, kept up covering patrols over Oran for the next two days (and carried out a sweep against French artillery on the 9th). The French forces at Oran surrendered on the 10th.

The largest single loss of the entire operation resulted from the torpedoing of the escort carrier *Avenger* by the German submarine *U-155* during the early hours of 15 November; the carrier blew up and sank immediately, taking with her almost the entire crew and all her Sea Hurricanes.

★ ★ ★

The Torch landings marked the beginning of a gradual phasing out of carrier service by Sea Hurricanes, their place being taken by later versions of the Martlet (Wildcat), Seafire, Hellcat and Corsair. Henceforth the carriers would be called on to operate more in confined waters in support of land or landing operations in which their aircraft would be exposed to greater risk of meeting land-based fighters, and the Sea Hurricane—even in its ultimate form, the Mark IIC, with a top speed of no more than 316 mph at 17,000 ft—was clearly no match for German fighters in service by the beginning of 1943.

This Sea Hurricane IIC NF672, *with No 835 Squadron aboard HMS* Nairana, *hit the barrier on 27th June 1945. (*Photo: *K. Amrstrong and R. C. Jones)*

Be that as it may, the CAM-ships and their Hurricanes (now including a few Sea Hurricane ICs) continued to ply the Gibraltar run, with eight ships still allocated to these convoys, occasionally sailing on to Algiers and Casablanca, starting in January 1943. In April that year *Empire Morn* struck a mine off Casablanca but did not sink, her Sea Hurricane being catapulted off and flown to Gibraltar; *Empire Eve* was torpedoed in the Mediterranean in May. By then it was known that the MSFU was due to be closed on 1 July, and the last convoy accompanied by CAM-ships set sail for home from Gibraltar on 23 July. In attendance were *Empire Darwin* and, perhaps appropriately, *Empire Tide*. During that last voyage a total of five Fw 200 Condors appeared, one of which was shot down by a patrolling USAAF B-24 Liberator. Then *Empire Darwin* launched Sub-Lieut John Pickwell in a Sea Hurricane, who shot down a second. Finally *Empire Morn* catapulted her fighter, flown by Plt Off P. J. R. Flynn, who attacked a third, which, according to German records, also fell. Both Hurricane pilots were picked up safely.

And so, after a protracted and frustrating start to their operations, the "expendable" fighters slowly gained the asendancy and finally won the struggle against their traditional enemy, the once-vaunted scourge of the Atlantic convoy, the Condor raider.

11

THE DESERT STORM

Until 10 June, 1940, British shipping had plied the Mediterranean without hostile interference, Germany having neither the ports nor airfields at her disposal from which to operate submarines and aircraft. When, however, on that date Mussolini decided to grab French territory following the *Wehrmacht*'s victorious campaign in the north, and so entered the war, Britain's shipping route (with France's collapse only a week away) faced considerable hazard. Malta, lying roughly half-way between Gibraltar in the west and Alexandria and the Suez Canal in the east, and only some 60 miles from Italian air bases in Sicily, was obviously at greatest risk. Moreover, although scheduled to be provided with four fighter squadrons for the island's defence since the mid-1930s, none had yet been provided.

Indeed when Italy entered the war there was not a single RAF squadron throughout the Mediterranean and Middle East equipped with modern fighters, the best available being the Gladiators of No. 33 Squadron (Mersa Matruh), No. 80 (Amriya) and No. 112 (Helwan) in Egypt, and No. 94 Squadron at Aden. Yet this excellent biplane fighter was considered to be capable of holding its own against the majority of Italian fighters, such as the Fiat G.50 monoplane and the Fiat CR.42 biplane.

Be that as it may, it was essential to send reinforcements to the Mediterranean if the Suez Canal was to be protected from air attack and Malta was to be capable of defending itself from the expected assault by the *Regia Aeronautica*. In the matter of bombers, reinforcement was relatively straightforward, for such aircraft as the Wellington possessed the range to fly from Britain to Gibraltar and thence on to Egypt. For fighters, and that meant Hurricanes (of which there were adequate reserves in Britain, and the aircraft had undergone tropical trials—neither condition applying to the Spitfire), to reach Egypt entailed staging through France, Tunisia and Malta, and there remained little time in which French airfields would be available.

As has already been mentioned (see page 90) Fighter Command had intended flying Hurricanes from Britain to Norway by use of long-range fuel tanks, and these were available at Boscombe Down around 7 June, when the British evacuation of Norway was finally completed. After a short delay in which ferry pilots were assembled, six of the Hurricane Is (minus their guns), led by a Blenheim for navigational purposes, set off for the south of France on 17 June, where arrangements had been made for their refuelling. Owing to some misunderstanding with the French (or possibly as the result of bomb damage on the airfield) the British pilots were refused permission to land; the Blenheim and two of the Hurricanes crashed, but the remaining four Hurricanes landed safely and were refuelled in due course. On the 18th, led by a South African pilot, Flt Lt Barber, these took off and set course for the airfield at Tunis, where further fuel had been promised. This time, however, the pilots failed to find the airfield and, being short of fuel, landed on the coast road further south. All got down safely except Barber himself, who broke his tailwheel; during that night he lashed up a makeshift tail-skid using a quarter-elliptic spring from a derelict truck, while the other pilots set about refuelling from a bowser sent from Tunis. The following day the four pilots took off and landed safely on Malta. Barber was under orders to fly on to Egypt and did so on the 20th.

In the meantime a Hudson had set out from Britain with 48 Browning guns for the original six Hurricanes and, flying via Gibraltar, arrived on Malta on the 21st. However, believing the Hudson to be an excellent aircraft with which to patrol the Central Mediterranean for the benefit of the Royal Navy, Air Commodore Foster Herbert Martin Maynard, AFC, the Air Officer Commanding on Malta, secured permission to retain the aircraft. The Hurricanes, with their guns now stranded on the island, were therefore ordered to be flown back and by the 23rd had been incorporated into Malta's defence. It is believed that Barber and his three other ferry pilots returned to the United Kingdom from Egypt and, because of the loss of French bases, no time remained for further Hurricanes to be sent out by air direct to the Mediterranean.

One other Hurricane *was* in the Middle East in June 1940. It will be recalled that one of the early Mark Is (*L1669*) had been despatched to Khartoum shortly before the outbreak of war with Germany for tropical trials; these trials had long since been completed and after languishing for some months at Khartoum it was taken on strength by No. 80 Squadron at Helwan to provide some flying experience on the type. As the aircraft was now without guns and therefore useless for combat, the Air Officer Commanding No. 202 Group in Egypt, Air Commodore Raymond Collishaw, DSO and Bar, OBE, DSC, DFC,[58] decided to move the Hurricane (dubbed "Collie's Battleship") from airstrip to airstrip in Egypt in an effort to persuade Italian reconnaissance crews that such fighters were present in some numbers in the Middle East. Whether the ruse was successful is not known, but Italian air activity over the Western Desert *was* certainly muted.

Despatch of Hurricanes to Malta was first undertaken by sending HMS *Argus* into the Mediterranean on 2 August, when, in Operation "Hurry", 12 Mark Is were launched and all landed safely at Luqa airfield on Malta. These aircraft comprised No. 418 Flight, which had been formed at Abbotsinch in July and which now combined with Malta's Fighter Flight; the latter unit had been flying the four original Hurricanes, mentioned above, together with a number of Sea Gladiators that had been taken from crates in storage on the island, assembled and flown in combat a number of times by volunteer pilots from Maynard's headquarters. The new unit now formed by these Flights was restyled No. 261 Squadron and commanded by Sqn Ldr Duncan Whiteley Balden.

During those early months of the Mediterranean war Malta suffered relatively few significant attacks by the Italians, who occasionally ventured over the island at fairly high altitude, but turned tail if a Gladiator or Hurricane attacked them. No. 261 Squadron suffered no casualties in combat, but serviceability among the Gladiators inevitably dropped, despite ingenious efforts to cannibalize other aircraft for spares. Moreover, when the Italians started flying German Ju 87B dive bombers over the island, several Hurricanes were badly damaged on the ground at Luqa, but when No. 261 Squadron shot down a couple of the Ju 87s and an escorting G.50 the *Regia Aeronautica* resorted to carrying out desultory night raids which scarcely worried the islanders.

As the island now gave every indication of being capable of defending itself, the Air Ministry decided to start operating bombers and reconnaissance aircraft from Malta. As Wellingtons and three Martin Marylands (of No. 431 Flight) were deployed on the island, 12 more Hurricane Is were sent out aboard HMS *Argus* on 17 November, but on this occasion they were launched at the extreme limit of their range and, their pilots being inexperienced in flying for range, eight Hurricanes and a navigating Skua failed to make landfall and were lost *en route*.

In the meantime a new reinforcement route to the Middle East had opened in September. By employing the former landing grounds established by Imperial Airways in the mid-1930s along an air route from West to East Africa it proved practical—albeit somewhat risky—to fly aircraft from the Gold Coast to Egypt, and since the summer a base had been in the course of preparation at Takoradi. On 24 August a 350-man party plus 25 ferry pilots under the command of Group Captain Henry Karslake Thorold[59] arrived to organize the assembling of aircraft and their despatch across Africa. On 5 September the first consignment of aircraft arrived in crates from Britain (six Hurricane Is and six Blenheim IVs) and the next day HMS *Argus* docked with 30 further Hurricanes. Assembled and test flown, the first group of six Hurricanes and a Blenheim—with a BOAC navigator aboard—took off and started their 3,800-mile flight to the Canal Zone. One week later all but one of the Hurricanes reached Abu Sueir after stops at Kano and Maiduguri in Nigeria, Fort Lami and Ati in the Chad, and El Geneina, El Fasher, El Obeid, Khartoum and Wadi Halfa in the Sudan, and Luxor on the Nile in Egypt. The remaining Hurricane had become unserviceable and was later taken on charge by the South African Air Force at Khartoum.

The early Hurricanes in Africa were a truly veteran bunch of aeroplanes, having been engaged in combat over Dunkirk and in the Battle of Britain; most bore the repaired scars of battle damage, but none had been fitted with tropical air filters. Consequently they had to be stripped down on arrival in Egypt for inspection and in most cases demanded attention to the engines, which were showing signs

Only known photograph of Collie's Battleship, L1669, *taken in the Middle East during 1940 with locally-applied camouflage scheme, probably being flown by No 274 Squadron. Note full-fin flash and 'squared-off' radio mast. The yellow nose-band indicated that no guns were fitted.* (Photo: *Sydney Camm Collection)*

of considerable wear and tear.

A new Squadron, No. 274, had been formed on 19 August at Amriya to fly Gladiators in the Western Desert, and this had been enlarged to absorb a number of Free French pilots who had arrived by a circuitous route from Tunisia, bringing with them a collection of Morane Saulnier 406s and Potez 63s. The French Flight, however, left for Palestine at the end of the month and, under the command of Sqn Ldr Patrick Hunter Dunn,[60] No. 274 Squadron began taking delivery of three of the Hurricanes previously delivered by HMS *Argus* to Malta and flown on to Egypt. The Squadron, which had also been "lent" Collie's Battleship for training purposes, shot down a couple of Savoia Marchetti SM.79 *Sparviero* (Sparrow) bombers over Maaten Bagush on 10 September, and two more five days later. The Gladiators were disposed of in November and the following month No. 274, whose Hurricanes had all now been fitted with tropical air intakes, was heavily engaged in combats with the Italians, shooting down eight aircraft on 9 December and five more on 5 January, 1941.

Another Hurricane squadron was in the process

The only photograph so far traced of Hurricane I (Trop) aircraft of No 418 Flight aboard HMS Argus *en route for Malta. The fighters were flown off on 2nd August 1940 and on the 16th became part of No 261 Squadron at Luqa.* P3733 *seen here features a camouflage scheme of dark earth, mid-stone, duck-egg blue undersides and black spinner.* (Photo: *J. Pickering, via R. L. Ward, Farnborough)*

P3731 *was one of the very early Hurricane Is that equipped No 261 Squadron on Malta, seen here at Ta Kali probably in January 1941; with identical colour scheme and a serial number so close to that of the Hurricane in the previous photograph, it has been conjectured that this had also flown off the* Argus *in August 1940.* (Photo: *via Sqn Ldr R. C. B. Ashworth)*

of redeploying to Egypt at this time, albeit with considerable difficulty. No. 73 Squadron, the veteran of the Battle of France, Battle of Britain and the early weeks of the London *Blitz*, had been ordered to Egypt, its groundcrews being sent aboard a British cruiser through the Mediterranean (being involuntary witnesses to a spirited naval action with the Italian fleet off Cape Spartivento *en route*) and arriving at Alexandria on 11 November. The Squadron's pilots and aircraft sailed for Takoradi, whence they set off for Egypt. On this occasion one of the navigating Blenheims became lost and six of the Squadron's Hurricanes force landed in the desert, killing one pilot and destroying two Hurricanes. The survivors reached Helipolis and, while more Hurricanes were assembled, the pilots were attached to No. 274 Squadron. On 1 January, 1941, No. 73 Squadron was declared operational once more in its own right, and on the 3rd Sergeant Marshall found a small formation of SM.79s while on patrol, shooting down three and damaging another.

The late Squadron Leader M. T. St. J. Pattle, D.F.C., O.C. No. 33 (Fighter) Squadron

The Greek Campaign and the Battle of Crete

Following the Italian attack on Greece from Albania on 28 October, 1940, British air support for the Greeks had been provided largely in the form of bombing raids by Wellingtons based in Egypt and Malta, but on 19 November No. 80 Squadron with Gladiators was ordered to deploy to the Greek airfield at Trikkala. This was followed by No. 112 Squadron, similarly equipped, at Yannina on 24 January. Although these squadrons seemed to be perfectly capable of dealing with the Italians so long as the winter weather kept operations to a low level, pressure began to mount as Mussolini—smarting under rebuke from Hitler for not finishing what he had started—ordered attacks to be stepped up in Greece.

Interesting as a rare photograph of one of the first Takoradi Hurricanes with tropical filter, yet still retaining the early wartime Fighter Command black-and-white undersides (divided on the centreline). An L-series Hurricane believed to have been flown by No 33 Squadron in the Western Desert in about October 1940. (Photo: *via Richard Ward, Canterbury)*

The British Chiefs of Staff in London, acting on intelligence indications that Germany was also preparing to invade the Balkans, ordered Air Chief Marshal Sir Arthur Longmore, GCB, DSO, Commander-in-Chief, RAF Middle East, to send Hurricane squadrons to Greece as well. Determined to hold at least two such squadrons in the Western Desert, Longmore now ordered No. 33 Squadron (which had converted to Hurricanes in September) over to Eleusis under the command of Sqn Ldr Charles Ryley on 19 February.

From the outset the RAF fighter squadrons had had a difficult time coping with poorly drained airfields and, with spare parts in poor supply, serviceability among the aircraft inevitably suffered. In March No. 33 Squadron moved to Larissa, where conditions gradually improved with the approach of spring. The day after No. 33 arrived in Greece No. 80 Squadron received one Flight of six Hurricane Is and this came under the command of a young South African Flight Lieutenant, Marmaduke Thomas St John Pattle, then flying at Paramythia. From now on, with the Gladiators fast succumbing to wear and tear, the Hurricanes' share of operations quickly increased, Pattle himself destroying two CR.42s, three G.50s and two BR.20 bombers in just over three weeks in his new fighter.

The long-anticipated German invasion of the Balkans opened on the morning of 6 April as 27 divisions attacked across the borders of Macedonia in Greece and of Yugoslavia at seven different points, at the same time that the *Luftwaffe* carried out a series of devastating air attacks on the city of Bel-

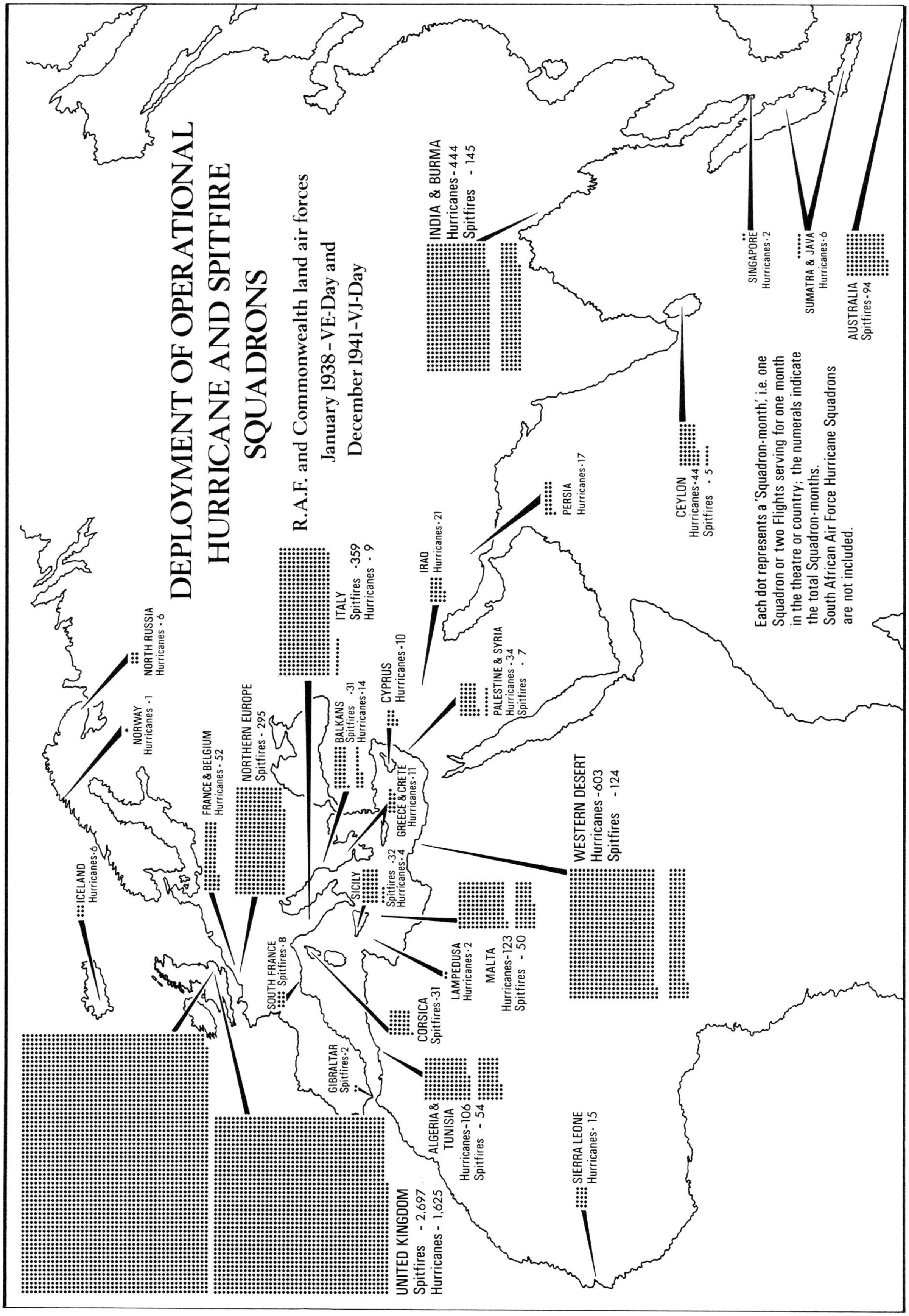
DEPLOYMENT OF OPERATIONAL HURRICANE AND SPITFIRE SQUADRONS
R.A.F. and Commonwealth land air forces
January 1938 – VE-Day and
December 1941 – VJ-Day
UNITED KINGDOM
Spitfires - 2,697
Hurricanes - 1,625
ICELAND
Hurricanes-6
NORWAY
Hurricanes-1
NORTH RUSSIA
Hurricanes-6
FRANCE & BELGIUM
Hurricanes-52
NORTHERN EUROPE
Spitfires-295
SOUTH FRANCE
Spitfires-8
GIBRALTAR
Spitfires-2
CORSICA
Spitfires-31
ALGERIA & TUNISIA
Hurricanes-106
Spitfires - 54
SIERRA LEONE
Hurricanes-15
ITALY
Spitfires -359
Hurricanes - 9
BALKANS
Spitfires -31
Hurricanes-14
SICILY
Spitfires -32
Hurricanes-4
LAMPEDUSA
Hurricanes-2
MALTA
Hurricanes-123
Spitfires - 50
GREECE & CRETE
Hurricanes-11
CYPRUS
Hurricanes-10
WESTERN DESERT
Hurricanes-603
Spitfires -124
PALESTINE & SYRIA
Hurricanes-34
Spitfires - 7
IRAQ
Hurricanes-21
PERSIA
Hurricanes-17
INDIA & BURMA
Hurricanes-444
Spitfires - 145
CEYLON
Hurricanes-44
Spitfires - 5
SINGAPORE
Hurricanes-2
SUMATRA & JAVA
Hurricanes-6
AUSTRALIA
Spitfires-94
Each dot represents a 'Squadron-month', i.e. one Squadron or two Flights serving for one month in the theatre or country; the numerals indicate the total Squadron-months.
South African Air Force Hurricane Squadrons are not included.

Different Hurricanes, same pilot. Left, *Sqdn Ldr Billy Drake as CO of No 128 Squadron at Hastings, Sierra Leone, early in 1942; his aircraft was a Mark IIB with Rotol propeller*

Right, *Sqn Ldr Drake poses with another of No 128 Squadron's Hurricanes, this time a Mark IIA with DH propeller. The Squadron was deployed in West Africa to counter the Vichy French air force threat to British Maritime activities along the African coast*

Squadron Leader Drake was a veteran of the Battle of France (flying Hurricanes) and later commanded a Kittyhawk squadron and a Spitfire Wing in the Mediterranean; he finally led a Typhoon Wing in Britain. His final victory tally was 24+, of which about half were German and Italian fighters

grade. The Yugoslav Air Force at that time possessed a total of 38 Hurricanes, of which about 15 were licence-produced examples; some 30 of them were serviceable at the time of the attack (as were about 70 Messerschmitt Bf 109Es and 30 Hawker Fury biplane fighters). Knowing that this constituted a potentially formidable force of fighters, the *Luftwaffe* made a number of attacks aimed at destroying the Yugoslav Air Force on the ground, but in this was only partially successful. The Yugoslavs deployed 18 Hurricanes with the 51st Fighter Squadron of the 2nd Regiment at Sarajevo and 20 with the 33rd and 34th Fighter Squadrons of the 4th Regiment at Zagreb. Unfortunately the swift advance by the German army prompted the Yugoslav forces to destroy the Zemun factory, thereby depriving the Hurricane units of their source of replacements and spares, although a fighter unit continued to operate from the adjacent airfield for several days. Nevertheless for almost a week the Hurricanes were in constant action both as interceptors over Zagreb and Bosnia and as ground attack fighters against the advancing German infantry. By the 13th, however, their situation had become hopeless as one by one the fighters were shot down or destroyed on the ground while being refuelled and re-armed. One or two Hurricanes managed to escape to Paramythia in Greece, but were almost immediately destroyed by roving *Staffeln* of Bf 109s.

Meanwhile the Greek government, which had declined substantial assistance by British land forces for more than four months (in the belief that to entertain such forces on its soil would be to invite a German invasion), now requested all possible reinforcements; but it was too late. The German army had moved swiftly into Macedonia and was threatening to cut the country in two. Unfortunately the RAF could now spare no more Hurricane squadrons owing to increasing pressure and commitments elsewhere in the Middle East, while No. 112 Squadron, by now operating no more than a handful of Gladiators, was ordered to withdraw its survivors to Crete on 16 April.

One other Squadron had been engaged in moving to Greece with Hurricanes when the German invasion opened, although it was not strictly a fighter squadron. No. 208 Squadron, a tactical reconnaissance (or army co-operation) unit, was equipped with a Flight of Lysanders and a Flight of Hurri-

*A very early tropical Hurricane Tac R Mark I in the Western Desert, almost certainly with No 208 Squadron, showing the 'sand and sphagetti' on spinner, nose and wing leading edge. The groundcrew working under the fuselage are probably either loading or unloading the reconnaissance camera. (*Photo: *via R. Ward, Canterbury)*

*Tropical Hurricane I Z4544 during or shortly after its journey across Africa from Takoradi in June 1941. (*Photo: *Sgt H. Newton, via R. L. Ward, Farnborough)*

*An early tropicalised Hurricane I of No 1 Squadron, South African Air Force, taxying prior to take-off at Agordat, near Kassala in Eritrea during February 1941. The Hurricane flew back to Tessenei each evening at this time to avoid being caught on the ground on the advanced airstrip during daylight. The air-craft shown here was probably a P-series Hurricane, most likely received from the Takoradi run in the previous month. (*Photo: *South African Air Force, via Richard Ward, Canterbury)*

canes; the latter were normally employed as close escort for the Lysanders over the battlefield.

By 19 April the German forces had advanced as far as Larissa, 120 miles to the north-west of Athens; by that date Nos. 33, 80 and 208 Squadrons had all been pulled back to Eleusis for the protection of the Greek capital, Piraeus harbour and the Corinth Canal, and to cover the loading of British troops aboard the evacuation ships. On the previous day five Hurricanes had arrived from Egypt as replacements, bringing the total of serviceable Hurricanes to 22, with seven others being repaired at Eleusis. However, at dawn on the 19th a raid by 15 Ju 88As caught the squadrons unawares and with unerring aim struck the maintenance hangar, destroying it and all seven Hurricanes in a few moments. Three other Hurricanes were lost in combat later that day, although the squadrons destroyed 11 of the enemy.

On the 20th Pattle, who in mid-March had been promoted Squadron Leader to command No. 33 Squadron, now by mutual consent led all the survivors of Nos. 33 and 80 Squadrons as a single unit. That evening, as the pilots were waiting to take off at Eleusis for an offensive sweep, the air raid sirens sounded and reports started coming in that a formation of more than 100 German aircraft was approaching Athens. The remaining Hurricanes—15 in all—took off singly just as a free chase by German fighters swept over the airfield. All the British fighters succeeded in escaping and formed up in a number of small sections, making for Piraeus harbour, where they found a hospital ship being bombed by Ju 88s. Five of these were quickly shot down by Flt Lt Henry John Starrett (South African), Fg Off Peter Reginald Whalley Wickham (British) and Plt Off Newton (Rhodesian), but Starrett's aircraft was damaged and exploded when he attempted to land back at Eleusis (he died shortly after); the other two pilots had time to return, refuel and re-arm and returned to the battle over the Piraeus. Other pilots had between them destroyed two Bf 110s, two Ju 88s and three Bf 109s, but F/Sgt Cottingham and F/Sgt Wintersdorf (French) had been shot down and had baled out. Flt Lt Woods and Sergeant Casbolt had also returned to Eleusis for more ammunition.

Meanwhile Pattle had shot down a Bf 110, but, as he shot down a second in going to the assistance of one of his pilots, he was set on by two other Messerschmitts; his aircraft was set on fire and crashed into Piraeus harbour before he could bale out. So died the highest-scoring RAF pilot of the Second World War.[61]

The 11 Hurricanes were now moved to the airfield at Argos on the 22nd, and on the following day five replacements landed there from Crete. However, later that afternoon, 40 Bf 110s swept down and, having silenced the ground defences, set about the systematic destruction of the fighters—nine of which were reduced to smoking skeletons. At dawn on the 24th the seven surviving Hurricanes took off for Crete, whence they would provide what cover they could for the arrival of the last of the evacuation ships from Greece.

★ ★ ★

Although preparations for the defence of Crete had been proceeding since the previous November following the despatch of the first RAF squadrons to Greece, this work had advanced slowly as it was recognized that little danger of attack would exist so long as Greece resisted the Italians successfully. Now, at the end of April, with German land and air forces occupying the whole of Greece, the situation had become one of the most acute danger. Thousands of Allied troops, who had been evacuated from the north—with precious little of their arms and equipment intact—thronged the island, which itself possessed only two airfields and a landing strip fit for use.

Moreover by mid-May the combined remnants of Nos. 33, 80 and 112 Squadrons amounted to 14 Hurricanes and six Gladiators, to which could be added a handful of Fleet Air Arm Fulmars. Against them were ranged 430 bombers and 180 fighters of *Fliegerkorps VIII* and *XI*, as well as about 600 transport aircraft and troop-carrying gliders.

Enemy air attacks started on the island early in May, concentrating on the ports in the north, but on the 14th the *Luftwaffe* turned its attention to the airfields at Maleme, Heraklion and Retimo. On that first day the Hurricanes accounted for seven Bf 109s, but lost three of their number in combat and one on the ground; two Gladiators had been shot down and all the Fulmars destroyed on the ground. Three replacement Hurricanes arrived from Egypt that evening and three more followed the next day. By the 18th, however, all that remained airworthy were four Hurricanes and three Gladiators; the senior RAF Officer in Greece, Gp Capt George Robert Beamish,[62] sought and gained permission from

Seen en route from Takoradi to Egypt at the end of August 1941, Hurricane IIA Z4769 displays light coloured patches on fuselage and tail whose significance is unknown but may simply be a doping primer applied at Tokoradi. The number '3' is probably the aircraft's batch identification. (Photo: *J. Pickering, via Sqn Ldr R. C. B. Ashworth)*

An early tropical Hurricane I serving on Malta late in 1941, probably with No 261 Squadron. (Photo: *Sgt H. Newton, via R. L. Ward, Farnborough)*

London to evacuate these survivors to Egypt; they left on the 19th.

When, however, the Germans launched their major airborne landings on the 20th the previous decision was reversed and 12 Hurricanes were sent over from Egypt to Heraklion to assist in covering the British evacuation; of these, two were shot down by the guns of the Royal Navy (whose crews had been under heavy enemy air attack on and off for several weeks and were perfectly prepared to fire at anything that flew) and four were damaged when attempting to land on the cratered runway at Heraklion. The remaining fighters gave what cover they could—occasionally supported by sections of about six Hurricanes flying from Egypt with long-range tanks (not quite the first time Hurricanes were in action with auxiliary fuel tanks; see below).

By the end of the month Crete had been lost. Losses, mostly as prisoners, among all three Services had been heavy, some 13,500 Imperial troops and about 280 members of the RAF as well as 38 aircraft. No losses were so grievous as those of the Royal Navy: three cruisers and six destroyers sunk,

Two of the three Hurricanes paid for and presented to the nation by Lady Rachel MacRobert in memory of her three sons who died while flying with the Royal Air Force. All three aircraft served with No 94 Squadron in the Western Desert in 1942—although at least one also flew with No 237 Squadron over the Kirkuk oilfields—the area in which Sir Roderic was shot down and killed the previous year. (Photos: *Sydney Camm Collection)*

and a battleship, an aircraft carrier, six cruisers and eight destroyers damaged—almost all with heavy loss of life.

East Africa and the Middle East

Before describing the fortunes of the Hurricane in the Western Desert it is convenient to mention first a number of "fringe" campaigns which were fought during 1940 and 1941 simply because, like those in Crete and Greece, they caused a drain on the forces available in the Western Desert or released resources after their successful conclusion.

Italy's first significant offensive campaign was launched by her Imperial forces in Abyssinia, Eritrea and Italian Somaliland in August 1940 with some 200,000 troops supported by about 150 aircraft. General Archibald Wavell could muster no more than 19,000 men, including Colonial regiments, and about 180 aircraft, including some Gladiators, Blenheims and Wellesleys, but otherwise obsolete types. The object of the Italian campaign was to overrun French and British Somaliland, and eventually to advance south into Kenya. Although the small Dominion forces fought spirited rearguard actions there was little the ground and air forces could do, especially after the French garrison at Djibouti surrendered and French Somaliland declared for neutrality as a Vichy colony. By the end of the year, despite some extraordinary raids carried out by Wellesleys against such targets as the port of Massawa on the Red Sea, the Italians had succeeded in occupying the whole of British Somaliland and had just penetrated into Kenyan and Sudanese territory. Almost every British soldier was, however, safely evacuated from Berbera under cover of Gladiators based at Aden.

Determined not to allow the Italians any chance to exploit their victory by seriously threatening the British supply route through the Red Sea, Lieut.-Gen. Sir William Platt, commanding British forces in the Sudan, quickly drew up plans for a counter-offensive that comprised a large-scale pincer advance from the Sudan in the north and from Kenya in the south. This time, however, Allied air support would be carefully provided to make the best possible use of the slender resources available.

In one respect Air Commodore Leonard Horatio Slatter, OBE, DSC, DFC, commanding No. 203 Group in the Sudan, was better equipped, as No. 1 Squadron, South African Air Force, was taking delivery of Hurricanes as and when they could be spared from the Takoradi run. Under the command of Brigadier H. Daniel, SAAF, No. 1 Squadron had come north from the Cape fully trained on Hurricanes but without aircraft (those that had been delivered from Britain before the war having long since succumbed to the dust and sand). By the time Platt's offensive opened on 17 January, 1941, the Squadron was established at Khartoum with about six Hurricanes, and increasing in strength by about one aircraft per week. As one of its pilots recalls, the aircraft showed many a scar from their battles in Europe, but, after a thorough overhaul by the Squadron's engineers, were pronounced fit for action. Kassala, in the Sudan near the border with Abyssinia, was retaken on the 19th, after which the South Africans flew a pair of Hurricanes forward at first light each day to mount guard over Platt's ground forces, and continued this routine throughout February and March in support of the advance on Keren, which duly fell on 26 March; thereafter No. 1 Squadron used the airstrips at Kassala and Asmara as its forward landing grounds. Only now did Italian aircraft make any effort to interfere, but were quickly engaged by one or more of the Hurricanes. As far as can be ascertained about eight Fiat CR.32s and CR.42s were shot down, as well as at least one SM.79 and one SM.81, for the cost of one Hurricane slightly damaged. Despite the small number of Hurricanes deployed at any one time (the South Africans were under restraint to safeguard their aircraft from possible attack on the ground owing to the shortage of Hurricanes in the Middle East), their presence was perfectly adequate for the purpose and on no occasion were Platt's forces seriously threatened from the air.

On 8 April Massawa fell to British forces and the defeat of Mussolini's colonial armies was complete, for Addis Ababa had fallen three days earlier. A postscript to this campaign concerned the RAF Gladiator Squadron at Aden, No. 94. Commanded by Sqn Ldr Vernon Crompton Woodward, this Squadron was ordered north to the Canal Zone to convert to Hurricanes and found themselves issued with six very tired Mark Is just disposed of by No. 1 Squadron, South African Air Force!

* * *

About one week before the last shots were being exchanged in Massawa an Iraqi politician, Raschid Ali, with pro-Axis sympathies seized power in Baghdad. The British possessed a number of important treaty rights in Iraq, apart from the considerable oil resources in the areas of Kirkuk and Mosul, whose pipelines ran west to the shores of the Mediterranean. To protect these rights, bases with substantial British garrisons and airfields had been established at Shaibah, near Basra, and at Habbaniya near the banks of the Euphrates, 50 miles to the west of Baghdad. The latter, begun in 1934 and opened three years later, was an extensive base with a seven-mile perimeter enclosing an Aircraft Depot, No. 4 Flying Training School, headquarters of the Royal Air Force in Iraq and, usually, at least one operational squadron of aircraft.

On the night of 28/29 April the Iraqi army arrived at Habbaniya, which it proceeded to invest, bringing with it about 40 pieces of artillery. By that date, however, Air Vice-Marshal Harry George Smart, OBE, DFC, AFC, Air Officer Commanding Iraq at

Habbaniya, had ordered the base to ready itself for such an eventuality, and all manner of training aircraft (mostly Airspeed Oxfords, Fairey Gordons and Hawker Audaxes) had been hastily modified to carry 20 lb or 250 lb bombs, and a small number of Gladiators had been flown in from Egypt. Under orders from London to restore the situation as quickly as possible—for the base possessed food for no more than 12 days—Smart ordered his aircraft into action at first light on 2 May, these thereafter carrying out numerous attacks on the exposed Iraqi positions in the surrounding desert, while Wellingtons from Shaibah joined in. At once the Iraqis started shelling the airfield and by the end of the day losses by No. 4 FTS had reached five aircraft.

This bombardment by the artillery on one side and the aircraft on the other continued for four days, but then it occurred to the Iraqi army that without its own air support (much of the Iraqi Air Force having been destroyed or otherwise prevented from taking off by Wellington raids on Raschid airport) it would achieve little progress at Habbaniya, and during the night of 5/6 May it decamped and withdrew, harried in its retreat by the aircraft and soldiers from Habbaniya. By then a more serious threat had appeared on the horizon when, following information intercepted on the German signalling network, it was learned that two *Luftwaffe* units, II./ZG 76 "*Haifisch Gruppe*" with Messerschmitt Bf 110D-3s and II./KG 4 "*General Wever*" with Heinkel He 111Hs, were under orders to fly to Iraq to support Raschid Ali's revolt. From the 4th onwards a Blenheim took off daily from Habbaniya to search the area around Mosul for signs of German aircraft. On the 10th reports started coming in of German aircraft staging through airfields in Syria—then a self-proclaimed "neutral" under the French Vichy government. On the 13th the Habbaniya Blenheim was attacked by a Bf 110 over Mosul, but escaped to tell the tale. What was not then known was that on the previous day a Heinkel delivering Major Axel von Blomberg to Baghdad was greeted by random rifle shots by exuberant Iraqis as it approached to land at Raschid airport; one of the bullets alas killed the man sent from Germany to co-ordinate the *Luftwaffe*'s collaboration with Raschid Ali.

After an attack on Habbaniya by three He 111s on the 16th, and the destruction of two Bf 110s by Gladiators of No. 94 Squadron over Raschid airport, Sqn Ldr Woodward decided to summon the remainder of No. 94 Squadron from the Canal Zone with their "new" Hurricanes, and on the 20th these fighters gained their first victory by shooting down a Heinkel, which fell in the middle of Habbaniya airfield. On the same day two Hurricane Is equipped with long-range (44-gallon) underwing tanks arrived at the RAF base to carry out "intruder" operations over the Kirkuk-Mosul airfields 160 miles to the north. One of these, flown by Flt Lt Sir Roderick Alan MacRobert, Bt., was refuelled immediately and set off that same afternoon. Alas, neither he nor his aircraft was seen again, although ZG 76's records are said to include mention of a Hurricane being shot down during May.[63] The other long-range aircraft, which was following some distance behind, carried out sweeps over one of the German-occupied airfields, its pilot claiming to have damaged or destroyed several enemy aircraft.

However, as will now be told, the knowledge that the *Luftwaffe* was staging through Syria prompted the RAF to make the first of many attacks on Syrian airfields and these in turn encouraged the *Luftwaffe* to abandon its adventures in Iraq (where Raschid Ali's revolt was finally crushed at the end of May).

The decision to occupy Syria was taken solely to

*Venerable Hurricane I (without tropical filter) of No 213 Squadron at Famagusta, Cyprus, late in 1941. (*Photo: *via R. Ward, Canterbury)*

prevent its airfields being used by the *Luftwaffe*, for Longmore argued that if the Heinkels were able to stage through Damascus on their way to Iraq the same aircraft could use the same airfield as a base from which to attack the Suez Canal. Wavell assembled a force comprising the equivalent of about two divisions of Australian, Free French and Indian troops and a brigade of tanks. Air support at the outset was provided by the Hurricane Is of No. 80 Squadron (now reconstituted and recovered from its mauling in Greece and Crete and commanded by Sqn Ldr Edward Gordon Jones, later Air Vice-Marshal, CB, CBE, DSO, DFC), one Hurricane flight of No. 208 Squadron, as well as No. 3 Squadron, RAAF, with Curtiss Tomahawks, two Blenheim squadrons, a scratch flight ("X" Flight) of Gladiators and two squadrons of Fleet Air Arm Fulmars, the whole force being placed under the command of Air Commodore Leslie Oswald Brown (later Air Vice-Marshal Sir Leslie, KCB, CBE, DSC, AFC).

After No 74 Squadron re-equipped with Spitfire Vs it retained this Hurricane IIC (with guns removed) for general communications duties, seen here late in 1943 at Alexandria. (Photo: *M. Schoeman, via C. F. Shores)*

The advance into Syria began on 8 June (by which date Air Marshal Arthur Tedder, CB, had succeeded Longmore as Commander-in-Chief, RAF Middle East), the Allies pushing ahead simultaneously from Palestine, Trans-Jordan, and from Rutbah and Habbaniya in Iraq. Against Brown's heterogeneous collection of around 60 aircraft were ranged about 100 French aircraft, which included Morane 406s, Dewoitine D.520s and Martin 167 bombers. From the outset it was obvious that the Vichy French pilots were going to resist the Allied advance to the utmost. During the first week, when half the Fulmars were shot down by the superior French fighters, it was decided that the Hurricanes would have to take over the protection of Royal Navy ships operating off the Syrian coast, and in order to relieve the pressure on them another Hurricane squadron, No. 260 (newly arrived from Britain under Sqn Ldr Christopher John Mount, DFC, later Air Cdre, CBE, DSO, DFC) was ordered north to Haifa to join the support forces.

Although the Vichy air force scored a number of notable successes both in combat against the Blenheims and in strikes against the slowly advancing Allied forces on the ground, constant raids on its airfields forced the removal of its aircraft to the north of the country, supposedly out of range of the Blenheims and Hurricanes. When, however, Palmyra fell on 3 July to the forces advancing from Habbaniya up the Euphrates, and the Hurricanes started flying with auxiliary fuel tanks, none of the French airfields was safe from air attack. During the last 10 days of the campaign, during which period the Australians broke through the French defences south of Beirut, the Hurricanes not only kept up constant sweeps over the northern airfields, attacking any French aircraft their pilots found in

As part of the price paid by the Western Allies to encourage Turkey to withstand overtures by the Axis Powers during the mid-War years a quantity of Lend-Lease military equipment was supplied, including Beaufighters, Spitfires, Beauforts, Blenheims, Baltimores and Liberators. The Hurricane IIC, here seen at an RAF airfield in the Middle East, was one of a batch supplied in January 1943 from RAF stocks. With only a pair of sandbags as 'wheel chocks' it is easy to see the danger to which the personnel on the tail were exposed when running up the engine to full power! (Photo: *Author's Collection)*

the open, but also flew defensive patrols off the Syrian coast to guard against any German attempt to fly in reinforcements from the Dodecanese.

In the latter task they were soon to be aided by patrols put up by No. 213 Squadron with Hurricane Is, recently arrived at Nicosia in Cyprus from Britain. The Squadron had flown from HMS *Argus* on 18 May in the western Mediterranean, staged through Malta and eventually arrived at Abu Sueir in Egypt on the 22nd, minus a number of its aircraft and personnel. After a short spell at Haifa, inexplicably flying untropicalized Hurricanes, it arrived at Nicosia on 19 July. It was probably the fact that its aircraft were quickly wearing out that resulted in No. 213 being among the first squadrons in the Mediterranean to receive Hurricane IIAs in August.

Central and West Africa

In the same month that the air force of one Vichy French colony was facing annihilation, 3,300 miles away French aircraft in the West African colonies of Senegal and French Guinea were causing some annoyance to the RAF. In March 1941 the Sunderland flying boats of No. 95 Squadron arrived at Freetown in Sierra Leone to begin anti-submarine patrols over the South Atlantic. All proceeded fairly smoothly for about six weeks, but then it was discovered that Martin 167s of the Vichy French air force were regularly carrying out reconnaissance flights in the area and, for the lack of any more logical explanation, it was reasoned that the purpose of these flights could only be potentially hostile (either by passing information to the Germans about the flying boat patrols or in preparation for some sort of attack—there persisted in the breasts of many a Frenchman much bitterness against the British for their devastation of the French fleet at Oran in 1940).

Accordingly a Fighter Defence Flight (as part of No. 95 Squadron) was created at Hastings, Sierra Leone, with half a dozen Hurricane Is, flown in from Takoradi early in August. Although one of its pilots, Sergeant Todd, quickly opened the Flight's score by destroying a Martin 167 on the 11th, the element of surprise now vanished and the French crews became increasingly circumspect in their activities. In truth the old Hurricane Is proved unable to catch the French aircraft and so, on 7 October, the Flight was expanded to become No. 128 Squadron with 15 Hurricane IIBs under the command of Sqn Ldr Billy Drake (later Wg Cdr, DSO, DFC and Bar). Another Martin 167 was intercepted on the 11th and, although this escaped, the increased performance of the Hurricanes did not go unnoticed, and the French flights quickly tailed off. At the time of the Torch landings in November 1942, with increased maritime patrols necessary over the Atlantic, detachments from No. 128 Squadron were sent to Jeswang in the Gambia to provide protection for the Sunderlands of No. 200 Squadron. However, with the capitulation of the Vichy French forces in Africa following the Allied landings, the danger of French attack on the West African bases disappeared and No. 128 Squadron was disbanded on 8 March, 1943 (and some of its aircraft passed to No. 1432 (Army Co-operation) Flight in Nigeria).

★ ★ ★

Earlier mention of the Heinkel He 111s involved in Iraq brings to mind one other extraordinary mission not irrelevant to the Hurricane saga. With the object of disrupting RAF fighter reinforcements flowing along the Takoradi route, a small German/Italian force, *Sonderkommando Blaich*, was transported early in January 1942 to a remote firm-sand airstrip known as *Campo Uno*, far to the south in the Libyan desert (and which had been surveyed as long ago as 1935). The aircraft flown was a Heinkel He 111H deployed by KG 4 "*General Wever*", flown by Leutnant Bohnsack. Taking off from *Campo Uno* at 08.00 hrs on 21 January with a crew that included the joint commanders of the operation, Hauptmann Theo Blaich (the pre-war explorer) and Major Count Vimercati (the Italian Army's desert expert), the Heinkel arrived at Fort Lamy in the southern Chad at 14.30 hrs and carried out a single bombing run—destroying eight Hurricane IIs and 80,000 gallons of fuel. With little or no interference from the ground, Bohnsack turned the Heinkel north and headed for a forced landing in the desert, with his fuel exhausted after a ten-and-a-half-hour flight. A week later a Junkers Ju 52/3m of the *Wüstennotstaffel* (Desert Rescue Flight) landed close by to refuel the bomber, which was then flown safely to Tripoli. The raid effectively closed the Takoradi route for several weeks while new stocks of fuel were brought overland, causing an accumulation of about 50 Hurricanes to build up at Takoradi and elsewhere.

12

THE STORM PASSES THROUGH THE MEDITERRANEAN

The three-year struggle that eventually ranged along the entire North African coast from the Canal Zone in the east to French Morocco in the west involved Hurricanes in a variety of rôles from beginning to end. For the air forces of both sides it was a struggle fraught with difficulties of supply and reinforcement, which for the Allies were largely concerned with sustaining the island of Malta (which itself lay athwart the Axis supply route to Libya) and with the building of an air force in Africa capable of meeting and beating the combined strengths of the *Luftwaffe* and *Regia Aeronautica*. It was shown in the previous chapter that throughout the first years of operations in the Western Desert the RAF faced constant demands for operational units to be diverted to cope with crises elsewhere.

It was also explained how and why only a tiny trickle of Hurricanes arrived in the Mediterranean by August 1940. During that first summer in the desert General Wavell fought a classic campaign to contain the initial Italian thrust across the Egyptian border from Cyrenaica, allowing it to penetrate as far as Sidi Barrani before it exhausted itself on 16 August. In the air Longmore could call on no more than three Gladiator squadrons, Nos. 33, 80 and 112, to which, with mental apologies to the Italians for the implied insult, he could add a few Gauntlets as temporary reinforcement. The *Regia Aeronautica* was fairly active, but tended not to provide close support for Marshal Graziani's ground forces but rather to carry out set-piece bombing raids using SM.79 bombers with escorts of CR.42 and G.50 fighters.

Although stretched to the full by their own duties of air defence of the Suez Canal as well as protecting Wavell's ground forces, the Gladiator pilots performed magnificently, taking a heavy toll—in relation to the number of Italian aircraft involved—of the enemy. As both sides built up their forces, the one to push on to the Canal and the other to launch a counter-offensive, Longmore was now obliged to send aircraft to Greece. But at least the Takoradi route opened in September and the first Hurricanes started arriving in Egypt. No. 274 Squadron had been formed and was gradually building its strength with Hurricanes which now arrived by sea and from East Africa. No. 73 Squadron also arrived from the United Kingdom, and Hurricanes were also supplied to the two Lysander army co-operation Squadrons, Nos. 208 and No. 3 (RAAF).

On 9 December Wavell's attack was launched as the Hurricanes swept the battle area, on the lookout for Italian troops and soft-skinned vehicles in the open. At first the Hurricanes of No. 208 Squadron were employed as escort or cover for the Lysanders, but, as the Italian air force seldom made any sustained effort to interfere over the battlefield, some of the Hurricanes were themselves given tacti-

*Line-up of Hurricane Is of No 451 Squadron, Royal Australian Air Force, in the Canal Zone, probably late in 1941 after taking over the tactical reconnaissance duties from No 6 Squadron RAF. The nearest aircraft is Z4036, and the third and fifth aircraft in line are not equipped with desert filters. (*Photo: *via D. Howley and R. L. Ward, Neg Ref F.26C/5/3A)*

*Taxying into patches of soft sand frequently caused minor upsets among the desert fighter aircraft. Seen here is a Hurricane IIB EY-Y of No 80 Squadron at Sidi Barrani late in 1941. (*Photo: *J. R. B. Edwards via R. L. Ward, Farnborough)*

cal reconnaissance tasks up to 50 miles behind the front. No. 208, incidentally, was the first of the RAF squadrons to adopt the Italians' "sand-and-spaghetti" style of camouflage, as its pilots themselves could testify to the difficulty of spotting Italian fighters flying low over the desert rocks and scrub; the Hurricanes' new camouflage scheme (usually comprising blotches of dark earth and dark green on a mid-stone background) was normally confined to the nose and wing leading edges, but on some aircraft the "borrowed" scheme was applied over the entire upper surfaces. While on the subject of early desert Hurricane colour schemes, it is worth mentioning that some of the aircraft arriving in Egypt at this time were old Fighter Command aircraft, still displaying the black-and-white undersides. This quickly offended the seasoned desert pilots and, following complaints by the squadrons, aircraft arriving at Abu Sueir and Heliopolis from January 1941 onwards were repainted in the then-customary desert scheme of dark earth and mid-stone on the upper surfaces and "duck-egg" blue undersides. In theory this should have been applied to all aircraft, but during periods of crisis—and there were plenty of them early in 1941—there was no time to correct such matters as paint schemes before the aircraft were rushed to the front line squadrons.

On 10 December Sidi Barrani fell to Wavell's forces, and six days later the last Italian forces were expelled from Egyptian territory as the Hurricanes of No. 33 Squadron carried out highly effective attacks on Italian motor transport beyond the port of Bardia. On 5 January this small town fell to Commonwealth troops, but it was now that Longmore came under pressure from London to send more squadrons to Greece. Although he resisted demands to send his Hurricane squadrons, a compromise was permitted in that no further fighters need be moved until Tobruk had been captured.

Like Dowding some six months earlier, Longmore was now less worried about the supply of Hurricanes (a total of 36 arrived in Egypt by sea and 43 overland from Takoradi between mid-December and mid-January) than about the conversions of Gladiator pilots to Hurricanes. Moreoever, the formation of new squadrons involved much more than the provision of pilots and aircraft. Thus by the date of Tobruk's capture, 22 January, 1941, the muster of Hurricane units in the mediterranean and Middle East was as follows:

No. 33 Squadron	Amriya, Egypt	Warned for move to Greece (effected on 19 February).
No. 73 Squadron	Sidi Haneish, Egypt	Operational in Western Desert.
No. 208 Squadron	Gambut, Libya	Operational with one Flight of Hurricanes and one of Lysanders.
No. 261 Squadron	Hal Far, Malta	Operational with Hurricanes and a few Sea Gladiators.
No. 274 Squadron	Sidi Haneish, Egypt	Operational in Western Desert.
No. 3 Squadron, RAAF	Gambut, Libya	Operational with one Flight of Hurricanes in Western Desert.
No. 1 Squadron, SAAF	Khartoum, Sudan	Equivalent of one Hurricane Flight; pilots converting and operating in Sections in Sudan.

The Luftwaffe Arrives in the Mediterranean

The truly dismal performance by Marshall Graziani's forces in Egypt in December had prompted Hitler to press upon his fellow dictator the services of the *Luftwaffe*, the advanced echelons of whose *Fliegerkorps X* arrived in Sicily during the last fortnight of that month, an event that did not escape the notice of Maynard's reconnaissance Marylands. Painful evidence of the *Luftwaffe*'s presence so close at hand was provided when an eastbound convoy, sailing from Gibraltar to Greece via Malta, came under attack from Heinkel He 111s, Junkers Ju 87s and Ju 88s on 10 January; when the badly damaged carrier HMS *Illustrious* limped into Grand Harbour it was Malta that now felt the weight of German explosive.

Relative failure in November by HMS *Argus*'s Hurricane reinforcements to reach the island left the defences pathetically weak in the face of raids by upwards of 60 aircraft at a time. And even when Wavell's troops continued their advance beyond Tobruk to take Msus on 5 February and Benghazi two days later, Longmore could only spare six Hurricane pilots and their aircraft for Malta; led by Flt Lt Charles Derek Whittingham,[64] on 30 January these aircraft were flown from Gazala on the Libyan coast to Hal Far.

As the advanced Commonwealth forces stumbled to a halt at El Agheila on 8 February, ground and air components began moving across to Greece, so much so that when Axis forces (now including the early elements of the *Afrika Korps* under the command of General Erwin Rommel) attacked just seven weeks later, Wavell simply possessed too few troops, and Longmore too few squadrons of aircraft to withstand the assault, and within a week these had disengaged and were in headlong retreat back across the wastes of Cyrenaica. No. 73 Squadron, which had been flying from Gazala West only since 31 January, now returned to Bu Amud in Egypt; No. 274 Squadron had never even moved base forward from Sidi Haneish. Indeed, to cover the withdrawal by Commonwealth forces under Maj-Gen Philip Neame, VC (amounting to a single division of infantry and an armoured brigade), across 300 miles of desert, Longmore could muster just one Hurricane Squadron, No. 73 (in the process of collecting reinforcements), and the two

Pictures of photographic reconnaissance Hurricanes seem to be extremely rare. This tropical PR Mark IIC (in the DG serial batch) carried the name KATHLEEN on the cockpit sill. Note the prominent camera fairing below the rear fuselage and the absence of radio mast. The colour scheme was a fairly dark blue overall. (Photo: *Howard Levy via Sqn Ldr R. C. B. Ashworth and R. L. Ward, Canterbury*)

Many pictures were published during the War depicting Axis aircraft captured by the Allies; less frequently illustrated were Allied aircraft in German markings. This Hurricane I, V7670, was evidently abandoned on a Cyrenaican airfield during the first Allied retreat in 1941, painted in Luftwaffe *insignia, only to be recaptured during Operation Crusader. Apart from a small tear in the fabric below the radio mast, the aircraft appears to be undamaged.* (Photo: *via Sqn Ldr R. C. B. Ashworth)*

An early Hurricane Tac R Mark I, almost certainly of No 451 Squadron in the Western Desert. Note the 'sand and sphagetti' camouflage and what appears to be an open camera hatch aft of the radiator. (Photo: *via M. Kerr and R. L. Ward)*

Hurricane Flights of Nos. 208 and 3 (RAAF) Squadrons. In an attempt to improve matters Hurricanes were also issued to one Flight of No. 6 Squadron—another short-range tactical reconnaissance unit—an event that was to mark the beginning of a very long association by this squadron with the Hurricane.

Occasionally small formations of Hurricanes engaged German and Italian aircraft and, being so far from their bases and inevitably short of fuel, these were forced to land at forward airstrips only to find that no fuel nor groundcrews remained. During April about 30 Hurricanes were abandoned at Derna, Bomba and Gazala, their pilots seeking lifts in army vehicles as they retreated eastwards.

These were frantic days for No. 73 Squadron. On 5 April its pilots fought a series of running battles with Italian aircraft, destroying 12 for the loss of two Hurricanes. A week later the Squadron was ordered to set up a detached base at Tobruk, together with the Hurricane Flights of Nos. 6 and 3 (RAAF) Squadrons—this despite the fact that the German forces had already pushed on to Bardia and Sollum, thereby isolating the port's garrison. Such was the obvious importance of this port, relatively close to the Egyptian border, that both German and Italian air forces were soon making determined efforts to reduce it. Between them the three squadrons fielded 18 Hurricanes and 31 pilots—including several South Africans who had volunteered to come north from the Sudan. On the 21st, in a typical attack on Tobruk by about 30 Ju 87s with an escort of 18 Bf 109Es, the Hurricanes of No. 73 Squadron shot down two of the dive bombers and a Bf 109E (the latter by one of the South Africans, 2/Lieut Littolff), while No. 3 (RAAF) Squadron claimed two more Ju 87s. On the following day the seven surviving Hurricanes of No. 73 Squadron scrambled to meet a raid by 60 Ju 87s and Bf 109Es, shooing down six for the loss of one Hurricane; the same evening the six survivors took off against a formation of 40, claiming five for the loss of one more Hurricane. In a fortnight the squadron had lost three commanding officers, and was now to be led by Sqn Ldr Peter Guy Wykeham-Barnes (later Air Marshal Sir Peter Wykeham, KCB, DSO and Bar, OBE, DFC and Bar, AFC). On the 25th the survivors flew out of the Tobruk perimeter and landed back at Sidi Haneish in Egypt, leaving just the five Hurricanes of No. 6 Squadron to fight on until 8 May, when the last four pilots also flew back to Egypt.

By May, however, stocks of Hurricanes in the Canal Zone had reached about 110, while Malta had received the first dozen Hurricane IIAs and IIBs to reach the Mediterranean—flown in from HMS *Ark Royal* on 3 April (Operation *Winch*)—with a further 23 arriving by the same method of delivery on the 27th (Operation *Dunlop*). Despite constant visits by German and Italian aircraft the island's defences were now becoming much stronger, particularly in respect of ground radar and anti-aircraft guns. However, No. 261 Squadron, which had constituted the sole fighter defence of the island for more than six months and could now muster fewer than half a dozen experienced pilots, was now disbanded and its survivors incorporated into a new unit, No. 185, which had hitherto existed as No. 1430 Flight. The next batch of Hurricanes, 46 from the carriers *Ark Royal* and *Furious*, which landed at Luqa and Hal Far on 21 May, included 28 Mark IICs and No. 249 Squadron with 18 Mark IIBs led by Sqn Ldr Robert Alexander Barton (later Wg Cdr, OBE, DFC and Bar). At least the fighters on Malta could now match the Bf 109s as well as the latest Italian aircraft, the Macchi C.202 *Folgore* (Lightning)—then about to enter the battle, at heights between about 15,000 and 20,000 feet.[65]

A third Hurricane squadron was created at Ta Kali on 28 June as HMS *Ark Royal* delivered 21 Hurricane IIBs (Operation *Railroad I*), flown by

*Second of the Hurricanes presented by Mrs Gillan in memory of her son John (see page 93) was this early Mark IID tropical anti-tank aircraft pictured in the Middle East. (*Photo: *Imperial War Museum)*

A tropical Hurricane Mark IIB bomber, BP283, *at a Middle East Maintenance Unit, probably early in 1942. (*Photo: *J. Hindley, via R. L. Ward, Farnborough)*

the pilots of No. 46 Squadron, who had embarked in Britain. Originally intended for North Africa, the Squadron had been under orders to fly on to North Africa, but by now the nearest airfield in British hands was too far distant and Air Vice-Marshal Hugh Pugh Lloyd, CBE, MC, DFC (who had succeeded Maynard on 1 June), obtained permission to retain the pilots and aircraft on the island. Thus was formed No. 126 Squadron, commanded by the Battle of Britain veteran, Sqn Ldr A. C. Rabagliati (see footnote 34). Within two days the new Squadron was in action and had opened its score by shooting down two Macchi C.200s. On 4 July it was No. 185 Squadron's turn to destroy a pair of Macchis.

For some weeks it had been noticeable that German aircraft had taken little part in the raids on the island, and it was soon apparent that the *Luftwaffe* had pulled a large proportion of its aircraft strength out of the central Mediterranean for rede-

*The Hurricane IID anti-tank aircraft proved to be something of a 'secret weapon' during the few months prior to the great Battle of Alamein, and No 6 Squadron, whose early examples of the aircraft are seen here, took a respectable toll of Axis tanks and other AFVs both at Bir Hakim and Alamein, although during and after the latter battle it suffered heavy casualties from ground fire. (*Photo: *RAF Museum)*

Hurricane IIs of No 94 Squadron in formation over Egypt in mid-1942; the first, third and fourth aircraft are Tac R Mark IICs (each with two cannon removed), and the other two are normal Mark IICs. The furthest three aircraft are those presented by Lady Rachel MacRobert in memory of her three sons, Sir Alasdair, Sir Roderic and Sir Ian. (Photo: *Sydney Camm) Collection)*

Long-range tropical Hurricane IICs (among them BD872 *and* BN235*) and Shaiba on the Persian Gulf awaiting delivery to the Soviet Union, probably in 1943. These aircraft (all identified by a batch number '7' on rear fuselage) would probably be flown direct to Teheran and thence to Baku in Azerbaijan; other aircraft were dismantled and taken by rail from Teheran to Tbilisi in Georgia.* (Photo: *R. C. Woolven via R. L. Ward, Neg Ref F52B/4/3)*

ployment on the Eastern Front in readiness for the great attack on the Soviet Union. Emboldened by the relative absence of German Messerschmitts, Lloyd now ordered his Hurricane squadrons on to the offensive against Italian air bases in Sicily:

"9 July 1941. Hal Far. Nos. 126 and 185 Squadrons. Four Hurricane IIBs (Sqn Ldr A. C. Rabagliati, No. 126 Sqn., Sqn Ldr P. W. Mould, No. 185 Sqn., Flt Lt Jeffries and Sgt Mackay) took off to strafe the Italian seaplane base at Syracuse. After having destroyed six flying boats and damaged four, and severely shaken everyone in the neighbourhood of Syracuse, Sqn Ldr Mould broke the world's low flying record—four inches above the sea—from Syracuse back to Malta."

On 26 July the Italian Navy attempted an attack on shipping in Grand Harbour, sending six E-boats escorted by some Macchi C.200s. Once again Nos. 126 and 185 Squadrons were ordered off. In the ensuing action the Hurricanes of No. 126 Squadron concentrated on the enemy vessels, destroying four; Flt Lt Peter William Lefevre, DFC, so unnerved the crew of another with his devastating and persistent gun attacks that it ran up the white flag. Plt Off Winton of No. 185 Squadron, which had been engaged in holding off the Macchis, was forced to bale out of his Hurricane and swam to the nearest E-boat only to find the entire crew dead; he accordingly "captured" the vessel, and the Squadron retained its flag as a memento of the action.

Accepting as inevitable that renewed attacks by the Germans would be made sooner or later, particularly as preparations for a new offensive in the Western Desert were now being made, the Air Ministry and Admiralty continued to ship Hurricane IIBs and IICs from Britain to Malta during the second half of 1941. After 34 aircraft arrived from *Ark Royal* on 30 June (Operation *Railroad II*), 14 more from the same carrier were flown off on 9 September (Operation *Status I*), 45 from HMS *Furious* and *Ark Royal* on 13 September (*Status II*), and 34 from HMS *Argus* and *Ark Royal* on 12 November (Operation *Perpetual*). Additional groundcrew personnel were frequently delivered to the island by submarines sailing from Gibraltar.

In July 1941 the 300th Hurricane passed through Takoradi and reinforcements were now reaching the Middle East at a rate which encouraged Tedder to set about increasing the deployment of new Hurricane squadrons, with about half the front-line units now flying Mark IIs.

Operation Crusader

As General Sir Claude Auchinleck succeeded Wavell at the time that British forces in the Western Desert had failed in their bid to relieve Tobruk and recapture airfields in eastern Cyrenaica (Operation *Battleaxe*) during June, both sides now set out to build their strength for new offensives in the late summer. If Auchinleck has since been criticized for excess caution, Tedder was methodical and outspoken in his determination to wrest air supremacy over the Western Desert. Following a visit by the RAF's Inspector General, Air Chief Marshal Sir Edgar Ludlow Hewitt, new OTUs were planned—of which the first, No. 71 (ME) OTU, came into being at Ismailia (formed out of "B" Flight, No. 70 (Middle East) Operational Training Unit) on 1 June. This was primarily a fighter OTU with about 30 Hurricane Is and IIs to begin with, and within three months was turning out about 40 Hurricane pilots every five weeks, some of whom were destined for the "army co-operation" squadrons. In October No. 74 OTU was formed to take over the latter training task at Aqir in Palestine, so that No. 71 OTU could concentrate on air fighting and ground attack training. In the meantime No. 4 FTS at Habbaniya, which had just started a Hurricane training syllabus (following the end of the Iraqi rebellion), was disbanded on 1 July.

Thus by 11 November, the date on which Auchinleck finally launched his offensive across the Egyptian border, Tedder deployed the Hurricane units shown below.

Not only were the squadrons better equipped (more than 90 per cent of the Hurricanes were fitted with tropical filters, while it was a matter of personal choice and specific authority that the remainder were not so encumbered), but the pilots themselves were better trained; many were regarded as "old hands", and others responded very quickly to the improved training and conversion courses. One of the newcomers was an American

Sqn No.	*Hurricane Version*	*Base*	*Remarks*
6	Tac R Mk Is	Kufra, Egypt	Operational with one flight of Hurricanes and one of Lysanders
30	Mk IIAs and IIBs	L. G. 102, Egypt	Operational in Western Desert; Sqn Ldr Frank Albert Marlow
33	Mk Is	Maaten Gerawla, Egypt	Operational in Western Desert; Sqn Ldr James Whittaker Marsden
73	Mk Is and IIAs	Kilo 8, Egypt	Operational in Western Desert; Sqn Ldr Derek Harland Ward
80	Mk IIB bombers	L. G. 111, Egypt	Operational in Western Desert; Sqn Ldr Maurice Michael Stephens
94	Mk Is and IIBs	L. G. 109, Egypt	Operational in Western Desert; Sqn Ldr H. C. Mayers
208	Tac R Mk Is	Maaten Gerawla, Egypt	Operational with one flight of Hurricanes and one of Lysanders
213	Mk IIAs	Idku, Egypt	Operational in Western Desert; Sqn Ldr Lockhart
229	Mk IICs	L. G. 12, Egypt	Operational in Western Desert; Sqn Ldr William Alexander Smith
237	Tac R Mk Is	L. G. 10, Egypt	Operational in Western Desert in Tactical Reconnaissance rôle
260	Mk Is	L. G. 115, Egypt	Operational in Western Desert; Sqn Ldr Derek Ronald Walker
274	Mk IIBs and IICs	Sidi Haneish, Egypt	Operational in Western Desert; Sqn Ldr Dudley Sandry Garton Honor
335 (Greek)	Mk Is	Aqir, Palestine	Not yet operational; Sqn Ldr X. J. Varvaressos (Greek)
1 (SAAF)	Mk IIBs	Not known	Operational in Western Desert; Capt Kenneth Arthur Quirk, SAAF
451 (RAAF)	Tac R Mk Is	Believed L. G. 128, Ft Maddelena, Egypt	Operational in Western Desert in Tactical Reconnaissance rôle
2 PRU	PR Mk Is	Heliopolis, Egypt	Operational. *Ad hoc* detachments throughout Middle East with maximum of five Hurricanes and other aircraft; Sqn Ldr Hugh Charles Macphail, RAFO[66]

An early Hurricane II (identity not known) severely damaged and probably written off after an enemy air raid in mid-1942 on Ta Kali, Malta. The starboard main wingspar appears to have been broken and repair facilities for such damage did not exist. In any case the first Spitfires were probably beginning to arrive at about this time. (Photo: Sgt H. Newton, via R. L. Ward, Farnborough)

from Texas, Plt Off Lance C. Wade, who joined his first operational unit, No. 33 Squadron, in September 1941. By the time Operation *Crusader* started he had destroyed three Italian aircraft, and when he left the squadron a year hence to command No. 145 Squadron flying Spitfires he had shot down a further 12 Axis aircraft. (At that time this was the highest score by an American pilot during the Second World War. He was promoted wing commander in July 1943—the fastest promotion from pilot officer to Wing Leader by a non-Commonwealth pilot in the RAF—and at the time of his death in Italy on 12 January, 1944, his score stood at 25 victories, the highest by an American in the RAF. He had been awarded three DFCs, to which was to be added a rare posthumous Honorary Companionship to the Distinguished Service Order.)

Mention above of the "Tac R" and "PR" Hurricanes requires some qualification, as both these versions came about as the result of local requirements and were not therefore logically described in earlier chapters. The Tac R Mark I was externally scarcely distinguishable from the standard Tropical Mark I, but usually incorporated an additional or alternative radio transmitter for liaison with ground forces; some aircraft had one or two Browning guns removed and a vertical camera installed aft of the cockpit. The Tac R Mark IIC was readily identifiable by the absence of one or two of the cannon to accommodate a camera. As previously mentioned, the Tactical Reconnaissance squadrons often adopted non-standard "desert" camouflage and, following the "sand-and-spaghetti" of No. 208, other squadrons tried all manner of paint schemes from all-over sand finish and all-over mid-stone to grey-and-sand on three aircraft of No. 451 Squadron, RAAF.

The photo-reconnaissance Hurricanes, of which relatively few good pictures have ever been traced, were a rare breed indeed. It is believed that a total of no more than about 12 PR Mark Is was produced by the Service Depot at Heliopolis, all eventually destined for No. 2 Photographic Reconnaissance Unit. The first three (believed to be *P2915*, *W9116* and *W9353*) had been modified at Heliopolis in great secrecy in January 1941 for the Intelligence Photo Flight, set up by Longmore to cover areas of the Middle East not normally accessible to other aircraft. Two of these Hurricanes carried a pair of F24 8-inch cameras, the other one vertical and two oblique F24 14-inch cameras in the rear fuselage aft of the radiator, necessitating a prominent fairing; all had their guns removed and carried extra fuel tanks in the wings. They were followed by five further PR Mark Is in March (among them *V7423* and *V7428*). The colour scheme adopted in the Middle East for these aircraft was a fairly dark blue all over. They were used to considerable effect, particularly during the Iraqi rebellion and Syrian campaign.

In June 1943 No 451 Squadron, Royal Australian Air Force, then flying Hurricanes at Idku in the Western Desert, took a limited part in the tropical trials of the Hawker Typhoon. One of three aircraft, sent out to North Africa, was flown briefly by the Squadron as shown by this very rare photograph. (Photo: via D. Howley and R. L. Ward, Neg Ref F.25A/5/27A)

Two similar PR Mark Is were modified in Malta during April 1941.

In October that year conversion of six Hurricane PR Mark IIs was sanctioned (*Z5132, DG630 et al*), but they were not completed in time to take part in preparations for *Crusader*, the first two being delivered to No. 2 PRU in December; they were said to be capable of a maximum speed of slightly over 350 mph and were able to reach 38,000 feet without trouble. Another batch, believed to number about a dozen aircraft, was converted at the end of 1942 or early 1943, most of these late series Mark IIs being shipped to India for use by No. 3 PRU; however, at least three were flown by a detachment of No. 680 (PR) Squadron from Tocra in Libya as late as July 1944.

★ ★ ★

Operation *Crusader* began well for Auchinleck as the attack caught the Axis forces ill-prepared; Rommel was, on 11 November, himself preparing a final assault on Tobruk. Once again No. 33 Squadron busied itself with ground strafing attacks on Italian motorized transport behind the enemy's lines. However, just as it seemed possible to relieve Tobruk, Rommel suddenly disengaged from the main battle and ordered two Panzer divisions forward to the Egyptian border, at once threatening the rear of the Commonwealth assault forces as well as endangering the RAF's forward landing grounds. At once the Hurricane bombers of No. 80 Squadron were thrown into the attack, destroying large numbers of trucks but doing less damage to the enemy tanks. Now relieved of the weight of German armour, the garrison at Tobruk, assisted by four Hurricane Tac R Mark Is, flown into the perimeter by No. 451 Squadron, RAAF, broke out on 26 November and linked up with New Zealand forces approaching from the south-east. Now himself threatened with encirclement, Rommel abandoned his counter-attack eastwards and a week later the Axis forces started to retire, while the *Luftwaffe*—considerably strengthened once more by reinforcements ordered to the Mediterranean from the Leningrad front—put up strong covering formations of Bf 109s, as well as launching attacks by Junkers Ju 87s on the Eighth Army.

It was at this time that the Hurricane pilots became aware that the Messerschmitt Bf 109F had arrived in North Africa (indeed by the end of the year the whole of JG 27 under Major Bernhard Woldenga was in Cyrenaica and had almost completely re-equipped with the Bf 109F-4/Trop, a fighter capable of about 380 mph at 20,000 feet; it was, however, poorly armed with a single 20 mm cannon and two rifle-calibre machines guns).

No. 208 Squadron saw plenty of action that winter in the desert, flying immediately ahead of the advancing Commonwealth forces and therefore not unnaturally attracting the attention of the enemy fighters:

"29 November. Gerawla. Fg Off P. T. Cotton in *Z4063* (an unarmed Tac R Mark I) was carrying out a reconnaissance of enemy forces in the area of El Adem when he was attacked by two Bf 109Es. Not carrying guns he was unable to join combat and spent almost 30 minutes twisting and turning to avoid the enemy's fire. Eventually the Messerschmitts ran out of ammunition and made off. Cotton's engine just failed to bring him home to base, having been overstrained by the pilot's exertions, and the Hurricane was force landed 15 miles from the airfield."

The pilot was unhurt and was subsequently awarded the DFC; his aircraft was salvaged and repaired. Shortly afterwards No. 208 had its first brush with Bf 109Fs:

"Plt Off C. S. B. Montagu (in *P2646*, an armed Tac R Mark I), while on a tactical reconnaissance over Tmimi, was intercepted by two Bf 109Fs. He successfully evaded four attacks by the enemy and held one of the German fighters in his sights for a long burst, after which it broke away and lost height in the direction of Tmimi. The other pilot also broke off after being fired on by British anti-aircraft guns, which also fired on and hit Montagu's Hurricane; with damaged oil and coolant systems, the engine seized and Montague made a successful wheels-down landing in the desert. Having attracted the attention of an army driver, Montagu attempted to have his aircraft towed the 23 miles to his base, but after covering 12 miles a mainwheel tyre burst and the aircraft had to be abandoned where it stood as no spare was available at the landing ground."

At first Rommel fell back to a prepared defence line based on Gazala, but after a three-day battle which opened on 12 December was able to extricate himself once more. By Christmas the Eighth Army was in Benghazi, with all the Cyrenaican airfields—El Adem, Benina, Berka, Martuba, Gazala, Gambut, Derna and the rest—in Allied hands. Unfortunately, so swift had the advance been that few of the Hurricane squadrons had been able to take full advantage of the captured airfields, with the result that, operating at long range from bases in the rear, they had been unable always to provide adequate support, a lesson of which Tedder was quick to take note. Squadron ground personnel were ordered henceforth always to be ready and able to move into and out of captured enemy airfields at no more than one hour's notice. Furthermore airfield construction units of the RAF were ordered into captured bases more quickly than hitherto to repair runways without waiting for army engineers to do the job.

Once again, on 9 January, 1942, the British advance ran out of momentum at El Agheila and was held. And once more demands from distant theatres threatened a drain on the resources of Com-

HURRICANE BASES: MEDITERRANEAN, AFRICA & MIDDLE EAST

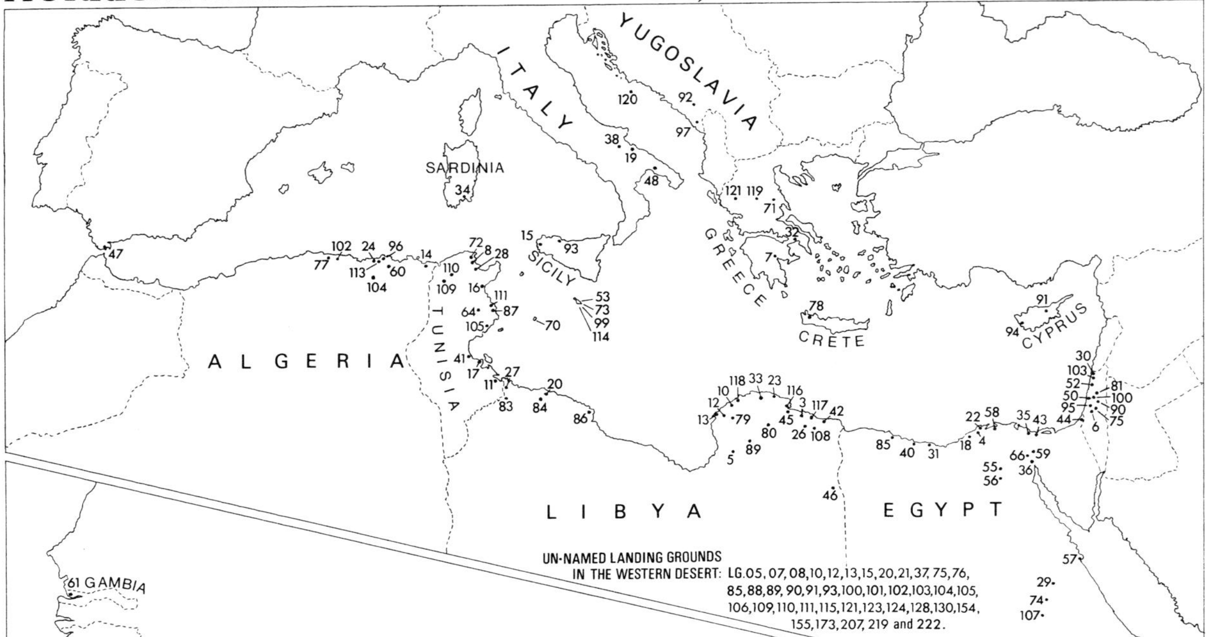

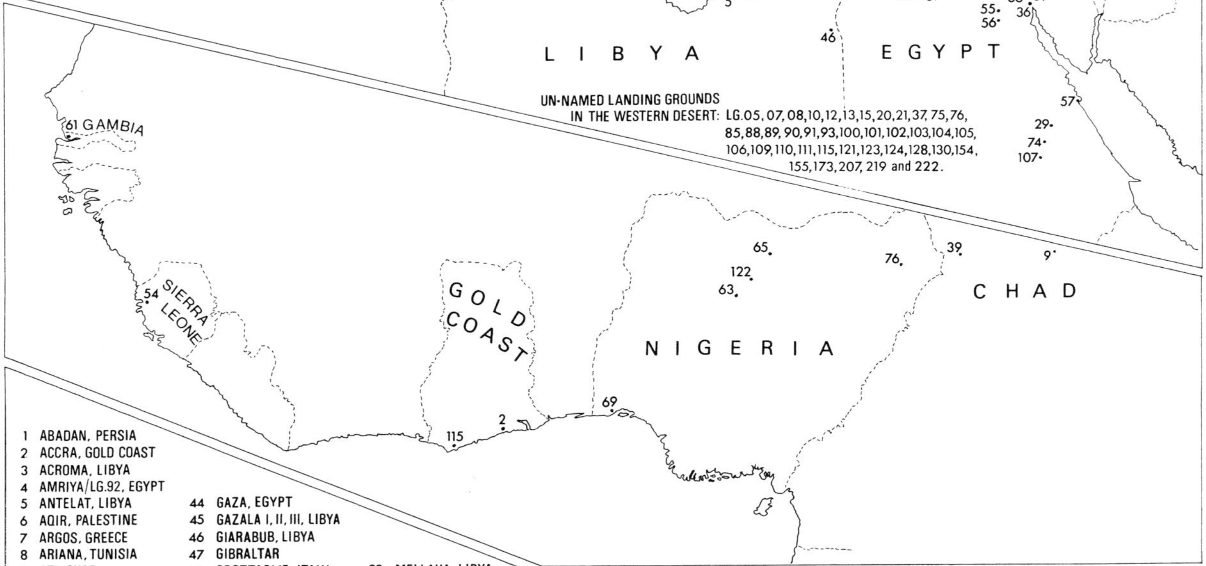

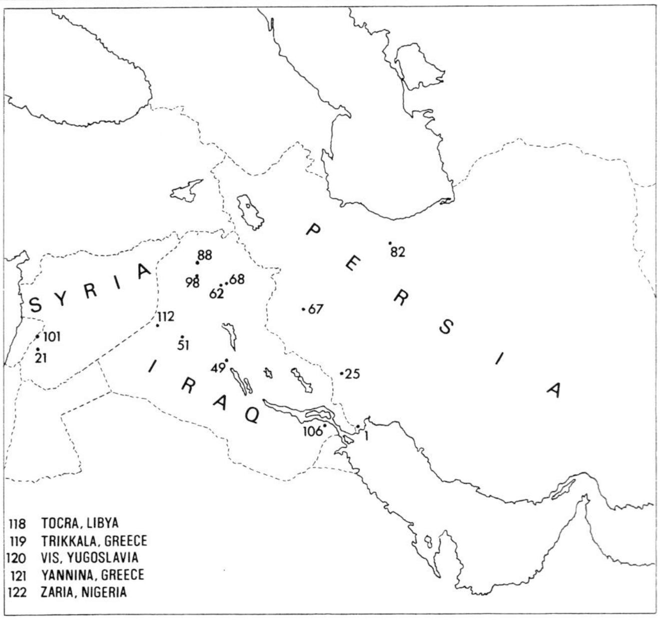

1 ABADAN, PERSIA
2 ACCRA, GOLD COAST
3 ACROMA, LIBYA
4 AMRIYA/LG.92, EGYPT
5 ANTELAT, LIBYA
6 AQIR, PALESTINE
7 ARGOS, GREECE
8 ARIANA, TUNISIA
9 ATI, CHAD
10 BARCE, LIBYA
11 BEN GARDANE, TUNISIA
12 BENINA, LIBYA
13 BERSIS, LIBYA
14 BÔNE/TINGLEY, TUNISIA
15 BO RIZZO, SICILY
16 BOU FICHA, TUNISIA
17 BOU GOURINE, TUNISIA
18 BURG-EL-ARAB, EGYPT
19 CANNE, ITALY
20 CASTEL BENITO, LIBYA
21 DAMASCUS, SYRIA
22 DEKHEILA, EGYPT
23 DERNA, LIBYA
24 DJIDJELLI, ALGERIA
25 DOSHAN TAPPEH, PERSIA
26 EL ADEM/LG.809, LIBYA
27 EL ASSA, LIBYA
28 EL AOUINA, TUNISIA
29 EL BALLAH, EGYPT
30 EL BASSA, PALESTINE
31 EL DABA, EGYPT
32 ELEUSIS, GREECE
33 EL GUBBA, LIBYA
34 ELMAS, SARDINIA
35 EL MATARIYA, EGYPT
36 FAYID, EGYPT
37 FIRDAN, EGYPT
38 FOGGIA, ITALY
39 FORT LAMY, CHAD
40 FUKA, EGYPT
41 GABES, TUNISIA
42 GAMBUT I, II, III, LIBYA
43 GAMIL, EGYPT
44 GAZA, EGYPT
45 GAZALA I, II, III, LIBYA
46 GIARABUB, LIBYA
47 GIBRALTAR
48 GROTTAGLIE, ITALY
49 HABBANIYA, IRAQ
50 HADERA, PALESTINE
51 HADITHA (K.3), IRAQ
52 HAIFA, PALESTINE
53 HAL FAR, MALTA
54 HASTINGS, SIERRA LEONE
55 HELIOPOLIS, EGYPT
56 HELWAN, EGYPT
57 HURGHADA, EGYPT
58 IDKU/LG.229, EGYPT
59 ISMAILIA, EGYPT
60 JEMAPPES, ALGERIA
61 JESWANG, GAMBIA
62 K.1, IRAQ
63 KADUNA, NIGERIA
64 KAIROUAN/ALEM, TUNISIA
65 KANO, NIGERIA
66 KASFAREET, EGYPT
67 KERMANSHAH, PERSIA
68 KIRKUK, IRAQ
69 LAGOS, NIGERIA
70 LAMPEDUSA
71 LARISSA, GREECE
72 LA SEBALA I, II, TUNISIA
73 LUQA, MALTA
74 LUXOR, EGYPT
75 LYDDA, PALESTINE
76 MAIDUGURI, NIGERIA
77 MAISON BLANCHE, ALGERIA
78 MALEME, CRETE
79 MARAUA, LIBYA
80 MECHILI, LIBYA
81 MEGIDDO, PALESTINE
82 MEHRABAD, PERSIA
83 MELLAHA, LIBYA
84 MEROUMA, LIBYA
85 MERSA MATRUH, EGYPT
86 MISURATA I, II, LIBYA
87 MONASTIR, TUNISIA
88 MOSUL, IRAQ
89 MSUS, LIBYA
90 MUQEIBILA, PALESTINE
91 NICOSIA, CYPRUS
92 NIKSIC, YUGOSLAVIA
93 PALERMO, SICILY
94 PAPHOS, CYPRUS
95 PETAH TIQVA, PALESTINE
96 PHILIPPEVILLE, ALGERIA
97 PRKOS, YUGOSLAVIA
98 QAIYARA, IRAQ
99 QRENDI, MALTA
100 RAMAT DAVID, PALESTINE
101 RAYAK, SYRIA
102 REGHAIA, ALGERIA
103 ST JEAN, PALESTINE
104 SETIF, ALGERIA
105 SFAX/EL MAOU, TUNISIA
106 SHAIBAH, IRAQ
107 SHANDUR, EGYPT
108 SIDI REZEGH, LIBYA
109 SOUK-EL-ARBA, TUNISIA
110 SOUK-EL-KHEMIS, TUNISIA
111 SOUSSE, TUNISIA
112 T.1, IRAQ
113 TAHER, ALGERIA
114 TA KALI, MALTA
115 TAKORADI, GOLD COAST
116 TMIMI, LIBYA
117 TOBRUK I, II, LIBYA
118 TOCRA, LIBYA
119 TRIKKALA, GREECE
120 VIS, YUGOSLAVIA
121 YANNINA, GREECE
122 ZARIA, NIGERIA

OPERATIONAL HURRICANE SQUADRONS: MEDITERRANEAN, AFRICA AND THE MIDDLE EAST

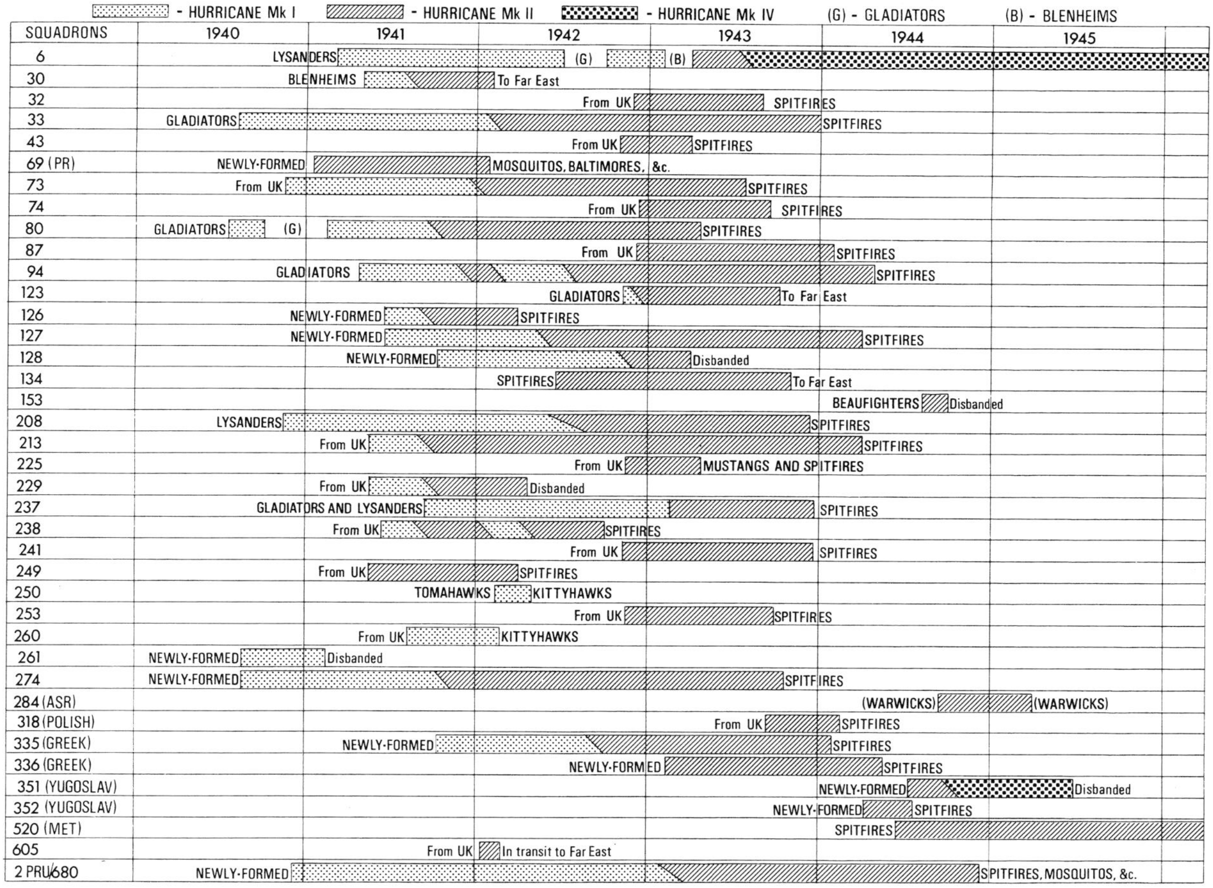

Above: P2638, *an early tropical Hurricane I of No 274 Squadron in the Western Desert displaying unofficial lightning flash markings on the fuselage and, just visible, "sand and spaghetti" streaks on the nose; the aircraft, later converted to PR Mk I with No 208 Squadron at Heliopolis, was shot down by Bf 109Fs in July 1942.* Right: *A Hurricane II of No 71 Operational Training Unit in the Canal Zone.*

monwealth forces in North Africa—this time following the Japanese attacks in South-East Asia. Two Hurricane squadrons, Nos. 17 and 232, both with Hurricane IIBs, had sailed from Britain on 12 November expecting to reach Egypt the following month, but were diverted, the former to Burma and the latter to Singapore. Another squadron, No. 605, became split up as some of its pilots and aircraft were ordered to Malta (arriving in January 1942), while the remainder of the squadron arrived almost simultaneously at Palembang in Sumatra!

Such difficulties were not, however, confined to the Allies in North Africa, for German armies in Russia were being held, and the severe winter conditions on that front demanded that increased use be made of transport aircraft for the movement of supplies, aircraft that would have been of inestimable value for the movement of reinforcements across the Mediterranean to the Axis forces in North Africa.

The island of Malta had indeed been a thorn in the Axis side during the early weeks of *Crusader*, its aircraft and naval units sinking more than 70,000 tons of enemy shipping during November and December. As if to ascribe the loss of Cyrenaica to the toll taken by the Malta forces, Hitler had ordered *Fliegerkorps II* from the Moscow front to Sicily; to Italy came Generalfeldmarschall Albert Kesselring with the headquarters of *Luftflotte 2*. Lloyd at that time could muster some 70 serviceable Hurricanes and about 60 long-range bombers; against him were ranged in Sicily over 400 fighters and bombers. The Germans' aim was clear: to re-establish air superiority in the central Mediterranean by eliminating Malta as a British base.

Before 1941 was out German air attacks on the island were stepped up threefold, their targets almost without exception being the vital airfields. Unfortunately adequate drainage systems on Hal Far and Ta Kali had not been completed and heavy rains now forced all the Hurricanes to be crowded on to Luqa, providing excellent targets for the German bomb aimers. Nevertheless the Hurricane bombers of No. 126 Squadron still managed to carry out occasional attacks on Sicily, while the other Hurricane pilots strove to penetrate the escorts of Bf 109Fs to destroy the Ju 88 bombers. In the three months between December 1941 and February 1942 No. 126 Squadron alone destroyed 34 German and Italian aircraft for the loss of ten Hurricanes and six pilots. The two PR Hurricanes were also kept hard at it, at least one of them being sent out on a sortie every day during December. On 4 January one of their pilots brought back photos of Castelvetrano in the west of Sicily showing the airfield packed with German and Italian transport aircraft; the following day ten Blenheims from Malta paid the base a visit, destroying 11 and damaging 28.

Notwithstanding all these efforts to prevent supplies from being shipped and flown to North Africa, Rommel was not disposed to allow the Eighth Army time to consolidate its position at El Agheila, and launched a powerful frontal attack on 21 January. From the *Luftwaffe*'s viewpoint the timing could not have been better planned. For two days the Ju 87s had pounded the army positions on the ground as the Hurricanes and Tomahawks were kept grounded by torrential rains at their "forward" airfield at Antelat—100 miles to the rear. Conditions at this airfield were chaotic, even though Nos. 238 and 260 Squadrons had managed to extricate themselve to El Gubba and Benina a few days earlier. When, however, the German tanks burst through at El Agheila and covered those 100 miles in little over six hours the squadrons crowded on Antelat (Nos. 33, 94 and 229 with Hurricanes, and No. 112 with Tomahawks) were given no more than 30 minutes' warning to get out. All but four unserviceable Tomahawks and two Hurricanes escaped—as the first German shells were falling—and, thanks to the actions by RAF Armoured Car Companies, the squadrons' ground personnel also escaped. All now made their way to Msus, 100 miles further back to the north-east. Although efforts were made to fly patrols over the ground forces (and indeed the Hurricanes alone destroyed more than 100 Axis vehicles in two days), conditions at Msus were only a little better, but fuel and ammunition stocks soon dwindled. Within four days the fighters were ordered back to Mechili, south of Derna. At this point Air Marshal Sir Arthur Coningham, commanding the Western Desert squadrons, ordered all RAF Maintenance Units to pack up and retire behind the Egyptian border, fearful lest the speed of the Axis advance should threaten the RAF's vital repair organization. Nevetheless it meant that any aircraft suffering anything more than superficial damage had to be abandoned.

Fighting in Cyrenaica during the first week in February became extremely confused, a situation exacerbated by widespread sandstorms, one of which grounded Nos. 33 and 238 Squadrons at Gambut on the 3rd. However, they also prevented German air attacks, particularly by the Ju 87s, on the Eighth Army, now feverishly attempting to establish a line of defence between Gazala and Bir Hakim.

Thus ended Operation *Crusader*, with harsh lessons imposed on the armies and air forces of Axis and Allies alike. All the Hurricane squadrons had been involved in heavy fighting, often with outstanding success; casualties among pilots had not been heavy, but it had become all too clear that not even the Hurricane IIB was a match for the Messerschmitt Bf 109F, and that henceforth its true value lay in the ground attack rôle. On the ground, although heavy fighting continued to flare up in Cyrenaica, the Eighth Army was preoccupied in its efforts to retire intact behind its new defence line. Likewise Rommel, determined to avoid the mistakes and difficulties of the previous Axis offen-

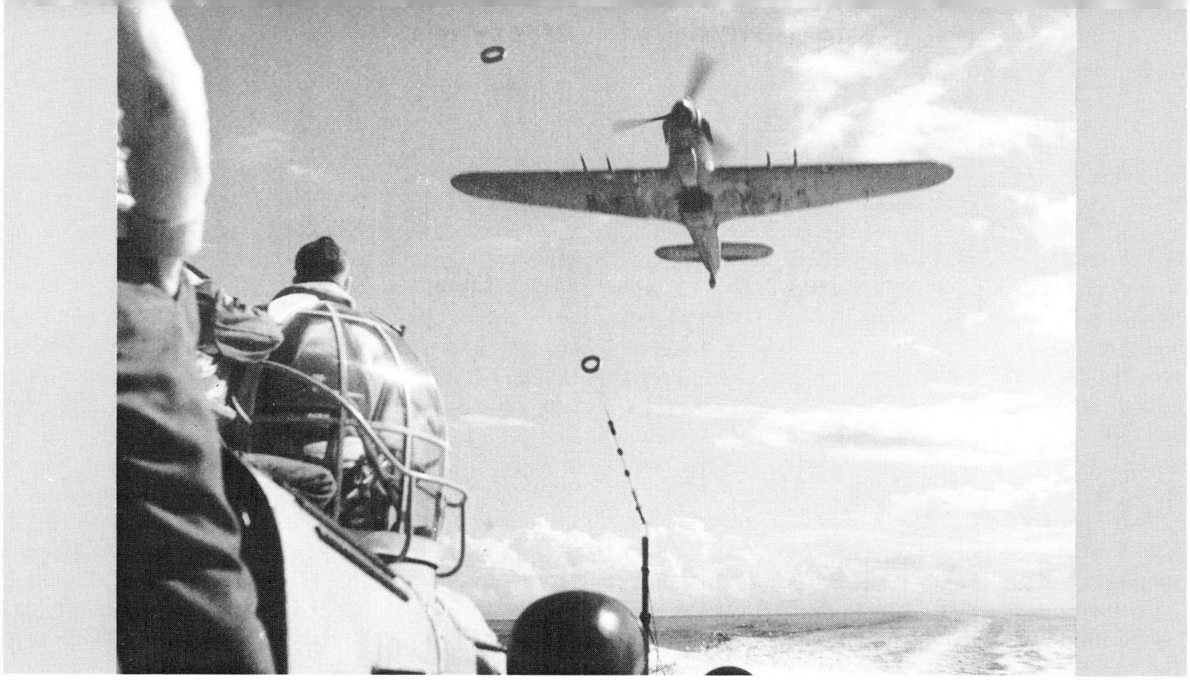

Among the second line duties assumed by Hurricanes in the Mediterranean as they started to be replaced by Spitfires in 1943 was that of air-sea rescue or, to be more precise, of mounting defensive patrols over rescue launches. Seen here is a Hurricane IIC of No 284 Squadron flying from Elmas in Sardinia early in September 1944. (Photo: *Author's Collection*)

sives in the desert, was content to hold his forces against this line; his supply route from Benghazi and Tripoli was shorter by about 100 miles, while that of the Eighth Army was correspondingly longer.

El Alamein

As preparations were made to modify many of the Hurricane IIBs, being held at the maintenance units in the Canal Zone, to carry 250 lb bombs, Malta's ordeal continued. By mid-March 1942 the number of serviceable Hurricanes had fallen to about 30. On only one day of that month were the skies over the island free of the *Luftwaffe* and *Regia Aeronautica*. On 7 March, however, HMS *Eagle* and *Argus* launched 15 Spitfire VCs, and these were followed by 16 more before the end of the month. The first armed Spitfires[67] to be deployed to the Mediterranean theatre, they were taken on charge by Nos. 126 and 249 Squadrons, their few remaining Hurricanes being handed over to No. 185 Squadron, whose pilots continued to fly them until HMS *Eagle* and USS *Wasp* delivered a further 106 Spitfires during April and May. Thereafter, for the next eight months of operations in the central Mediterranean, the air defence of Malta became the responsibility of the Spitfire. In two years of desperate fighting to sustain and defend the vital island a total of 333 Hurricanes had been delivered by Royal Navy carriers; 62 others had been flown in from North Africa when bases in Cyrenaica were available to the RAF, and 19 were delivered as deck cargo in merchant ships.

The difficulty of dealing with Axis tanks now concentrated the minds of the Allied commanders in the Middle East. On the ground the army commanders pressed for immediate delivery of the M.3 Grant and M.4 Sherman tank, while for the RAF representations were made to the Air Ministry to speed the clearance of the Hurricane to carry 500 lb bombs; the latter was not straightforward, and was not cleared on tropical aircraft until rather later owing to the need to concentrate stocks of the "short-finned" bomb in the United Kingdom, but the Air Ministry already had in hand the shipment of an early batch of Hurricane IID anti-tank fighters with 40-mm Vickers "S" guns to the Middle East. No. 6 Squadron was accordingly warned in May 1942 to prepare for a change to the anti-tank role.

On 26 May Rommel launched his attack on the Gazala line, fortunately without catching the Eighth Army unawares; the previous evening the pilot of a Hurricane Tac R Mark II of No. 40 Squadron, South African Air Force, had spotted and reported Italian armour moving forward near the coast. This, however, proved to be a feint as Rommel ordered forward a motorized and two Panzer divisions in an outflanking movement south of Bir Hakim. By the following day these were well round the rear of the Gazala line and were in action near Knightsbridge and El Adem. Nevertheless there could be no immediate danger of complete encirclement so long as Bir Hakim, defended by the 1st Free French Brigade, continued to hold out and in turn threaten the rear of the Panzer divisions. As the Germans now switched their attention to the destruction of this strongpoint by attacking with the 90th Light Division from the east, Coningham switched his fighter squadrons from the Knightsbridge battle to the support of Bir Hakim. On 3 June the anti-tank Hurricane IIDs were sent into action for the first time as Kittyhawk bombers and Tomahawks joined in support operations. Other Hurricanes dropped supply canisters to the defenders.

The battle raged on for nine days, with the RAF

fighters dividing their attention between the Axis air and ground forces. German Ju 87s were much in evidence over Bir Hakim and suffered heavily, and the escorting Bf 109F pilots suddenly found themselves fighting a new adversary when No. 145 Squadron brought Spitfire VCs into combat for their first desert battle. The anti-tank Hurricanes achieved a fair measure of success and claimed the destruction of a score of German tanks, although it was obvious that their pilots needed much more practice to evolve the best tactics for dealing with tanks. By the 10th, however, it was obvious that without considerable Allied artillery support the Free French position was untenable, and the defenders were ordered to retire; about 2,000 men escaped eastwards that night.

The nine days "won" by the defenders of Bir Hakim had been as vital to the Eighth Army as they were disastrous for Rommel, for his entire campaign was based upon his fuel supplies, which would be adequate only if Tobruk was captured by 1 June; as it was the port did not fall until the 21st.

What would have been a rout had the Gazala line crumbled within a week in fact became a costly fighting withdrawal by the Eighth Army, but for the Hurricane pilots it was a period of tremendous battles, often fought to cover the activities of bomb-carrying and anti-tank Hurricanes in action against enemy forces on the ground. No. 73 Squadron, once more in the thick of battle, fought several desperate combats with the Bf 109Fs in June, shooting down two on the 15th, one on the 16th and four on the 17th, for the loss of five pilots (including the CO, Sqn Ldr D. H. Ward, shot down on the 17th in a Mark IIC, *BN277*). The following month, flying from Burg-el-Arab in Egypt, the squadron destroyed 23 more enemy aircraft for the loss of six pilots. It was then pulled out of the battle and transferred to the night defence of the Suez Canal under the command of Sqn Ldr George Robert Arthur McGarel Johnston, RAFVR, on Hurricane NF Mark IICs.

By the beginning of July the British Commonwealth ground and air forces were well back in Egypt behind a line running south from a tiny spot on the map named Alamein, just over 60 miles west of Alexandria. For the next four months Tedder and General Bernard Montgomery (now command-

No 6 Squadron, which was to become the last RAF operational squadron to fly Hurricanes, took its Mark IVs across the Adriatic to Yugoslavia in 1945. Seen here is KZ188 *at Prkos loaded with asymmetric wing stores—a 44-gallon drop tank and four three-inch rockets. (*Photo: *via R. L. Ward, Farnborough)*

*A Hurricane IV of No 6 Squadron, with rockets and drop tank, landing at an airfield in Greece during 1945. (*Photo: *RAF Museum)*

ing the Eighth Army) set about strengthening the desert forces, creating new units, re-equipping and retraining their men. The RAF constructed 33 new desert airstrips on which, together with his established airfields, Tedder deployed a total of 84 squadrons, of which the single-engine fighters comprised 16 squadrons of Hurricanes, seven of Kittyhawks, six of Spitfires, one of Tomahawks and three of USAAF P-40 Warhawks. On the eve of the great battle of Alamein, which opened on 19 October, Tedder fielded the following Hurricane units:

Sqn No.	*Hurricane Version*	*Base*	*Remarks*
6	Mk IID	L. G. 89, Egypt	Operational in Western Desert; anti-tank. Wg Cdr Roger Cave Porteous
33	Mk IIC	L. G. 172, Egypt	Operational in Western Desert; air defence over Eighth Army. Sqn Ldr J. F. F. Finnis
80	Mk IIC	L. G. 37, Egypt	Operational in Western Desert; air defence over Eighth Army. Sqn Ldr Daniel Macfarlane Jack, AAF
94	Mk IIC	El Gamil, Egypt	Operational in Western Desert; air defence of Canal Zone. Sqn Ldr J. H. Cloete (With some Spitfire VCs)
127	Mk IIB	L. G. 37, Egypt	Operational in Western Desert; air defence over Eighth Army. Sqn Ldr Constantine Oliver Joseph Pegge
208	Tac R Mk IIB	L. G. 100, Egypt	Operational in Western Desert; tactical reconnaissance
213	Mk IIC	L. G. 172, Egypt	Operational in Western Desert; offensive sweeps. Sqn Ldr P. Olver
274	Mk IIC bomber	L. G. 37, Egypt	Operational in Western Desert; ground attack. Major J. R. R. Wells, SAAF
335 (Greek)	Mk IIB bomber	L. G. 37, Egypt	Operational in Western Desert; ground attack. Sqn Ldr Hellas (Greek)
417 (RCAF)	Mk IIC	Idku, Egypt	Operational in Canal Zone; defence of Canal Zone. Sqn Ldr P. B. Pitcher, RCAF. (With some Spitfire VCs)
451 (RAAF)	Tac R Mk IIC	L. G. 100, Egypt	Operational in Western Desert; tactical reconnaissance
1 (SAAF)	Mk IIC	Not known	Operational in Western Desert; air defence over Eighth Army
7 (SAAF)	Tac R Mk IIB/C	Not known	Operational in Western Desert; tactical reconnaissance
40 (SAAF)	Tac R Mk IIB/C	Not known	Operational in Western Desert; tactical reconnaissance
2 (PRU)	PR Mk Is and IIs	Heliopolis, Egypt	Operational with detachments throughout Middle East (with several other types of aircraft)
889 (FAA)	Mk IIBs	Not known	Coastal patrols, Mediterranean coast. (With some Sea Hurricane Mk ICs)

On the German side the *Luftwaffe* had brought the new Bf 109G—the Gustav—to North Africa, as well as a fresh *Jagdgruppe*, III./JG 53. The Gustav still suffered a number of structural and engine problems (the top-scoring *Luftwaffe* fighter pilot in North Africa, Hauptmann Hans-Joachim Marseille, had been killed on 30 September baling out from a Bf 109G-2/Trop following engine failure), but when fully serviceable it more than matched the Spitfire VC, let alone the venerable Hurricanes.

After a short period of "softening up" during which the Desert Air Force flew hundreds of sorties, bombing and strafing the *Luftwaffe*'s airfields, Montgomery's artillery opened its famous bombardment of the Axis line on the night of 23/24 October. The preliminary air attacks paid handsome dividends as scarcely any German or Italian aircraft were able to take off to provide cover for the Axis forces. On the afternoon of the 27th, however, 20 Ju 87Ds, with an escort of Bf 109Fs, attempted to support a counterattack by the German 90th Light Division but were intercepted by 24 Hurricanes and 16 USAAF P-40Fs of the 57th Fighter Group. Three Hurricanes were shot down, but JG 27 lost seven Bf 109Fs. The Hurricane IIDs of No. 6 Squadron were in action from the outset, employing new tactics; owing to their vulnerability to *flak* at low level—their maximum speed at sea level was only 210 mph—they attacked the enemy tanks from the rear and broke away by turning rather than climbing. On the 24th, with cover provided by Hurricane IICs of No. 80 Squadron (which drew much of the *flak*), No. 6 destroyed 18 Axis tanks; by the end of the month it had claimed 43 tanks and over 100 other vehicles destroyed, but had lost nine aircraft and six pilots, almost all to *flak*.

On 2 November Montgomery launched his breakthrough thrust, Operation Supercharge. In a dawn combat 24 Hurricanes and Spitfires of Nos. 33 and 238 Squadron engaged about 20 Ju 87s and their escort of Bf 109Fs; later the same day Hurricanes of Nos. 80 and 127 Squadrons intercepted a similar raid. These combats resulted in the shooting down of four of the dive bombers and two Messerschmitts, for the loss of two Spitfires and four Hurricanes. By the 4th Rommel was in headlong retreat. The "fresh" Bf 109 *Gruppe*, III./JG 53, had already succumbed to combat fatigue and had been replaced by Heinz Bär's I./JG 77, but this was now also ordered back to Tripolitania.

Such was the air supremacy now enjoyed by the Desert Air Force that scarcely a single Axis aircraft was seen during Montgomery's advance across Cyrenaica; nor was there any significant check this time at El Agheila. A measure of the initiative that could be maintained by the Allied air force may be judged from an extraordinary move by Coningham, who, during the advance on Benghazi, ordered the Hurricanes of Nos. 213 and 238 Squadrons[68] forward to Martuba, far in the *rear* of the retreating Axis forces; the airfield had been shown by photo reconnaissance to have been abandoned by the enemy. These two squadrons took the retreating convoys completely by surprise and in the course of five days destroyed or disabled about 300 vehicles.

* * *

By now, however, the Axis forces in North Africa faced annihilation from the west as well as the east, for on 8 November British and American forces had landed in Algeria and French Morocco. As was told in Chapter 10, the landings were covered by large forces of carrier-borne fighters—including Sea Hurricanes. Moreover, immediately after the seaborne forces had gone ashore, other RAF and American aircraft were flown in from Gibraltar. The first to arrive was No. 43 Squadron with Hurricane IICs under the command of Sqn Ldr Michael Rook, AAF, whose pilots landed at Maison Blanche, Algiers, on the 8th without being certain whether the airfield had in fact been captured. They were soon in action and the following day shot down a Heinkel He 111 and a Junkers Ju 88. Other Hurricane squadrons which followed No. 43 were No. 225 with Hurricane Tac R Mk IICs and No. 253 with Mk IICs, both of which landed at Maison Blanche on the 13th, and No. 241 Squadron with Tac R Mk IICs on the 19th. No. 32 Squadron with Mk IICs landed at Philippeville on 7 December, followed by No. 87, also with Mk IICs, on the 19th.

Meanwhile in Libya No. 6 Squadron, which had suffered the loss of 14 Hurricane IIDs and seven pilots in the course of more than 300 sorties in October and November, was temporarily withdrawn to fly defensive patrols over Cairo and the Suez Canal in Mark IICs while stocks of the anti-tank aircraft were replenished and modifications made to the aircraft; these included re-rating their Merlin XXs to give more power at sea level (increasing their low-altitude speed by about 40 mph) and providing some armour for the engine and radiator. In February the squadron received these modified Mark IIDs and was back in Libya on 2 March, 1943, now commanded by Sqn Ldr Donald Weston-Burt, DSO.

As the final campaign in Tunisia approached its climax supplies of Spitfires were building up in the

A Hurricane Mark IV, LB886, formerly of No 351 (Yugoslav) Squadron, as it was when handed over to the Yugoslav Partisan Air Force shortly before the War's end. The aircraft is tropicalised although the air intake filter has been removed. (Photo: *Author's Collection)*

HAWKER HURRICANE I

Aircraft representative of the Battle of Britain

Aircraft 'B-Baker', P3144, of No. 32 (F) Squadron, Biggin Hill and Hawkinge, July 1940, as flown variously by Sqn. Ldr. John Worrall and Flt. Lt. Michael Crossley. It destroyed a Messerschmitt Bf 109E before it was itself shot down near Dover on 19th July while being flown by Sgt. G. Turner who was wounded.

STENCILS

A

PATCH TO INSIDE
OF LINE ONLY

Fuselage (port) below radio mast; one-inch characters.

B

OIL
9 GALLS
AIRSPACE
1½ GALLS

Port wing root leading edge, upper surface. 1½-inch characters.

C

FIRST
BREAK HERE
AID

Port side of fuselage above wing trailing edge; one-inch and 1½-inch characters.

D

DO NOT FORGET
TO CHECK
PULL-DOWNSTEP

Port side of fuselage on push-in hand grip. Half-inch characters.

N

NO STEP

Upper trailing edge of wing roots; 2-inch letters

K

GA/LA/41H/
17226D(S)
DTD 512

Starboard fuselage side below hood rail; one-inch numerals.

M

TRESTLE HERE

Beside rear jacking point.

E

COOLANT MIXTURE
GLYCOL WATER
30% 70%

Radiator, both sides.

F

P3144
LFPD/41H/
16120S
DTD 617

Starboard wing tip, lower surface; one-inch characters.

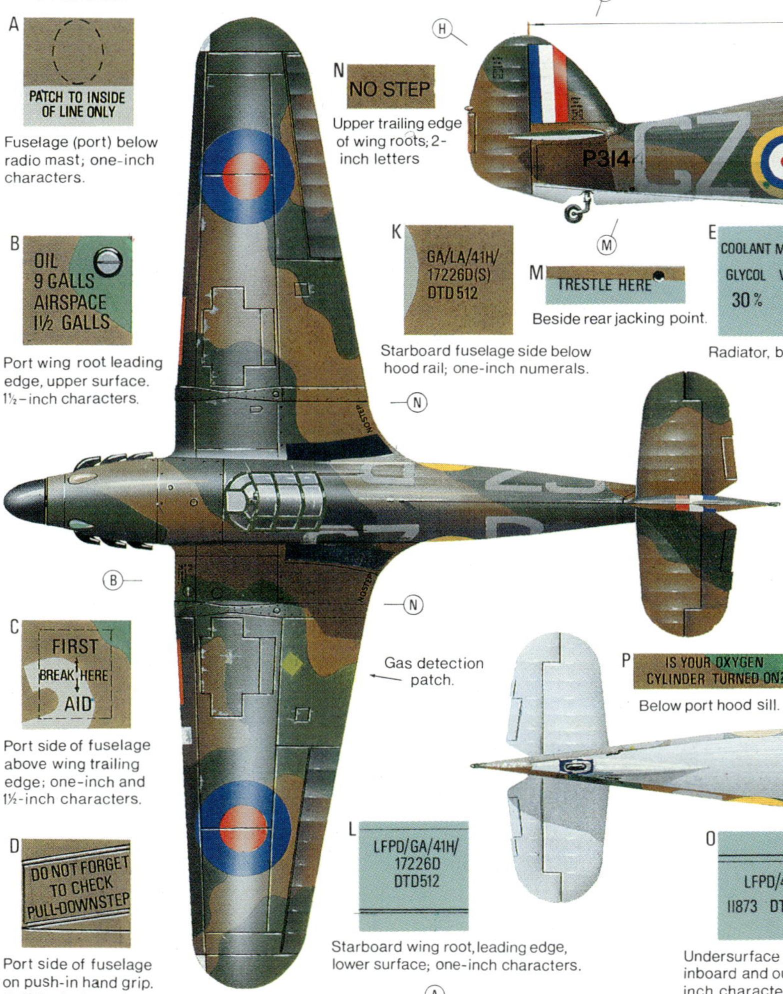

Gas detection patch.

G

LFPD/41H/
1612IP DTD617
W
T

Port wing tip, lower surface; one-inch numerals and 4-inch W/T square.

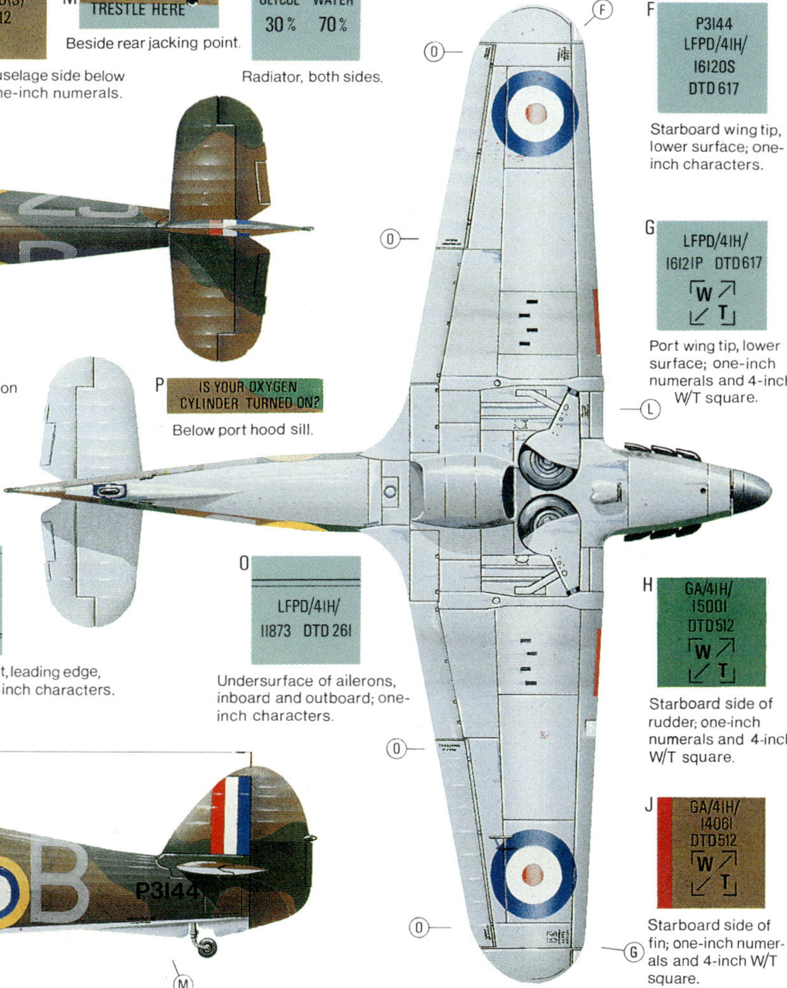

P

IS YOUR OXYGEN
CYLINDER TURNED ON?

Below port hood sill.

L

LFPD/GA/41H/
17226D
DTD512

Starboard wing root, leading edge, lower surface; one-inch characters.

O

LFPD/41H/
11873 DTD 261

Undersurface of ailerons, inboard and outboard; one-inch characters.

H

GA/41H/
15001
DTD512
W
T

Starboard side of rudder; one-inch numerals and 4-inch W/T square.

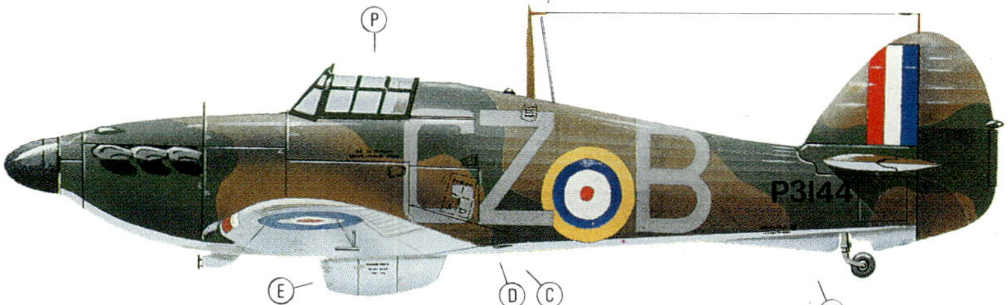

J

GA/41H/
14061
DTD512
W
T

Starboard side of fin; one-inch numerals and 4-inch W/T square.

Gloster-built aircraft with metal wings and Rotol constant-speed propeller. Like many Hurricane squadrons, heavily involved early in the Battle of Britain, No. 32 had little opportunity to apply its code letters according to Fighter Command instructions; as is shown by P3144 the letters were about 25 per cent larger than officially stipulated. Note that although P3144 was fitted with a reflector gunsight the bead foresight had not been discarded.

Until shortly after the Battle of Britain Hurricanes were 'shadow' camouflaged on their upper surfaces; that is to say that aircraft whose serial numbers ended with an even digit were camouflaged as is P3144; those with odd digits displayed a mirrored scheme. There were however many exceptions to the system.

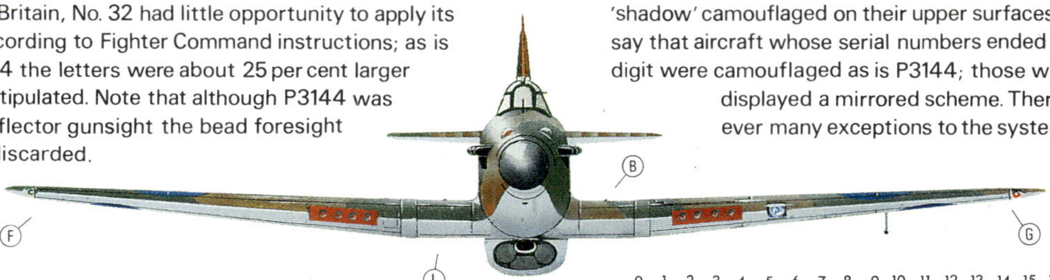

SCALE–FEET 0 1 2 3 4 5 6 7 8 9 10 11 12 13 14 15 16 17 18 19 20

Copyright 1977, 1986 Francis K. Mason FRHistS, AMRAeS

HAWKER HURRICANE IIC

Night fighter/intruder as flown on cross-Channel operations in 1942

Aircraft 'A-Apple', BE500, of No. 87 (F) Squadron, Charmy Down and St Mary's, as flown by the squadron commander, Sqn Ldr D.G.Smallwood, early in 1942. A Hawker (Langley)-built aircraft, BE500 is depicted with a pair of 44-gallon auxiliary fuel tanks and was engaged in night defence and intruder operations over Northern France.

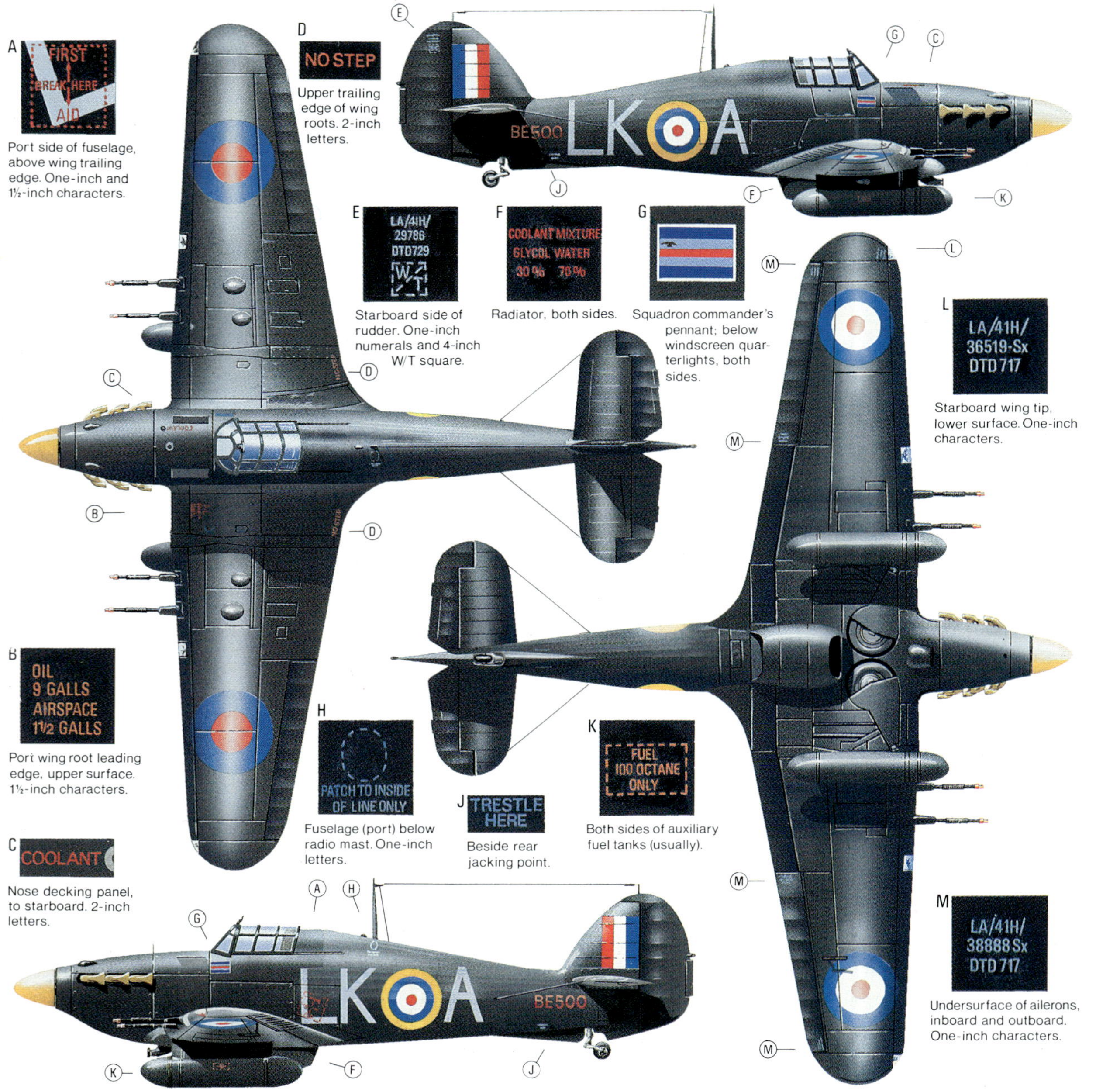

A — Port side of fuselage, above wing trailing edge. One-inch and 1½-inch characters.

D — Upper trailing edge of wing roots. 2-inch letters.

E — Starboard side of rudder. One-inch numerals and 4-inch W/T square.

F — Radiator, both sides.

G — Squadron commander's pennant; below windscreen quarterlights, both sides.

L — Starboard wing tip, lower surface. One-inch characters.

B — Port wing root leading edge, upper surface. 1½-inch characters.

H — Fuselage (port) below radio mast. One-inch letters.

J — Beside rear jacking point.

K — Both sides of auxiliary fuel tanks (usually).

C — Nose decking panel, to starboard. 2-inch letters.

M — Undersurface of ailerons, inboard and outboard. One-inch characters.

BE500 is depicted as it appeared soon after delivery from the Maintenance Unit, with most of the current style of markings and stencils intact. Later in 1942 the underwing roundels were discarded and 'narrow-white' fuselage roundels and fin flashes introduced. BE500 also served as 'B-Baker' with the Squadron for a short time. Its armament was the standard four 20-mm Oerlikon guns.

Sqn Ldr Denis Graham Smallwood (later Air Marshal, CB, CBE, DSO, DFC) enjoyed a distinguished career in the RAF. Having been commissioned shortly before the War, he flew with No 87 Squadron in 1940; in 1941 he was a flight commander on No 247 Squadron (also with Hurricane night fighters) until November that year when he returned to No 87 as its CO, a position he still occupied at the time of the Dieppe landings of August 1942.

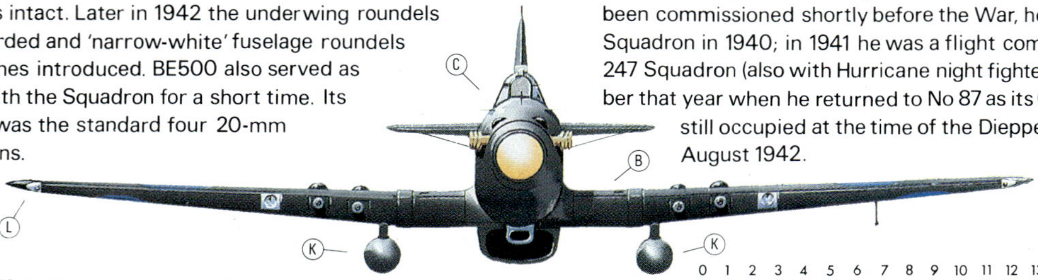

SCALE–FEET 0 1 2 3 4 5 6 7 8 9 10 11 12 13 14 15 16 17 18 19 20

Copyright 1972, 1986 Francis K. Mason FRHistS, AMRAeS

HAWKER HURRICANE IID

Anti-tank aircraft as flown in the Western Desert in mid-1942

Aircraft 'Z-Zebra', BP188 of 'B' Flight, No 6 Squadron, RAF, was a Hawker-built Mark IID which was among the second batch of anti-tank aircraft delivered to the Squadron in July 1942 when at L.G.89.

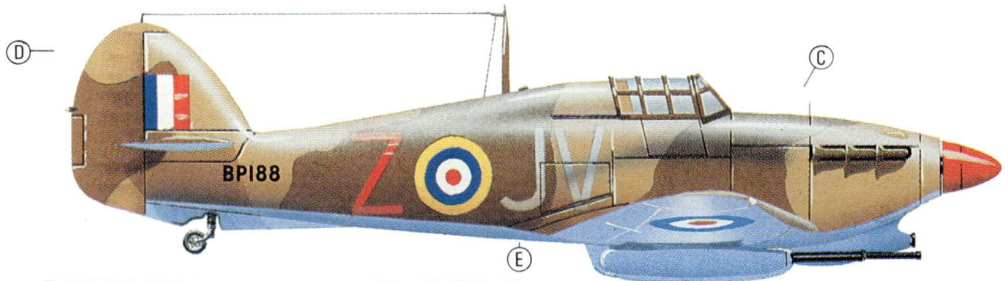

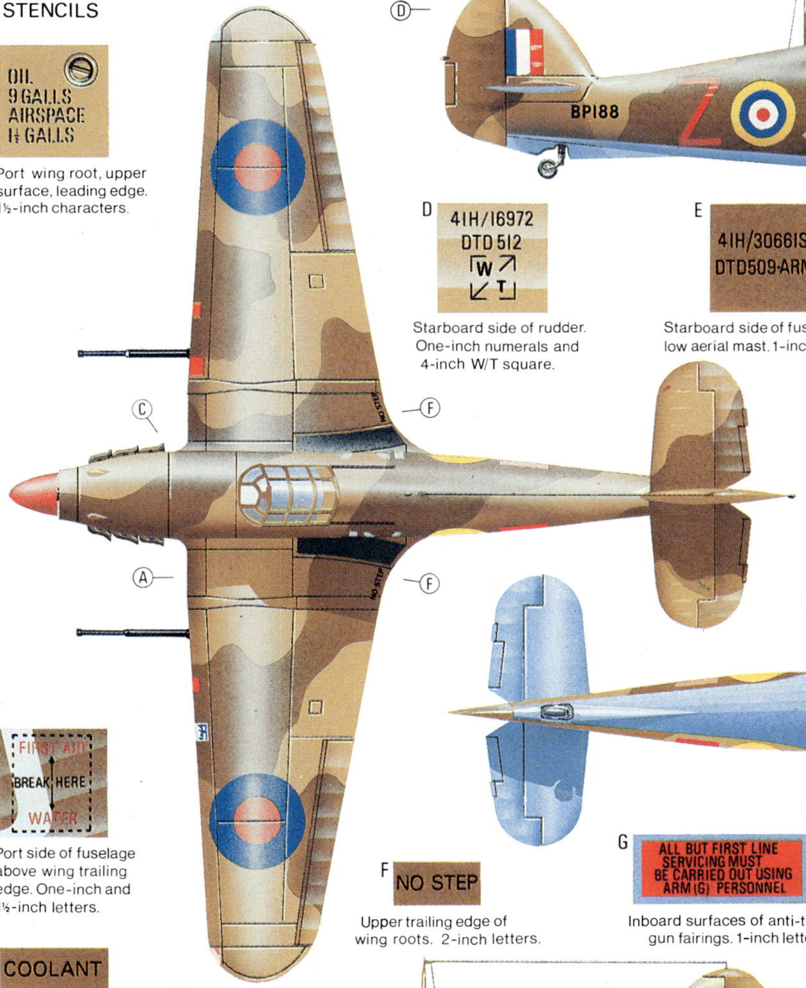

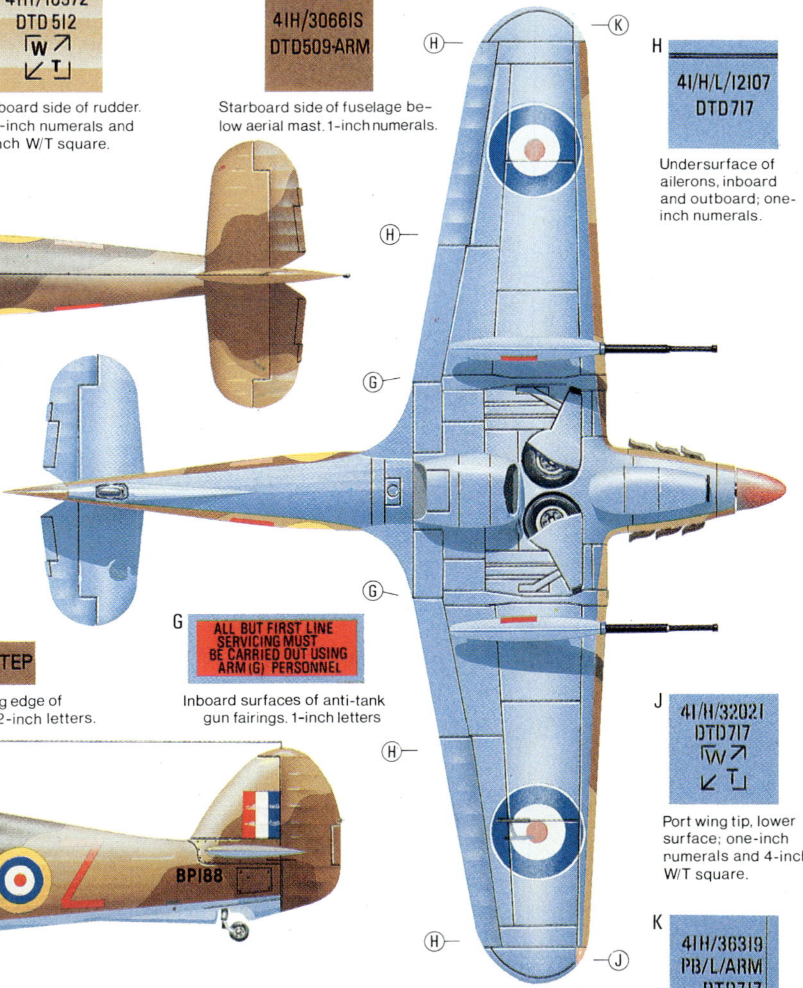

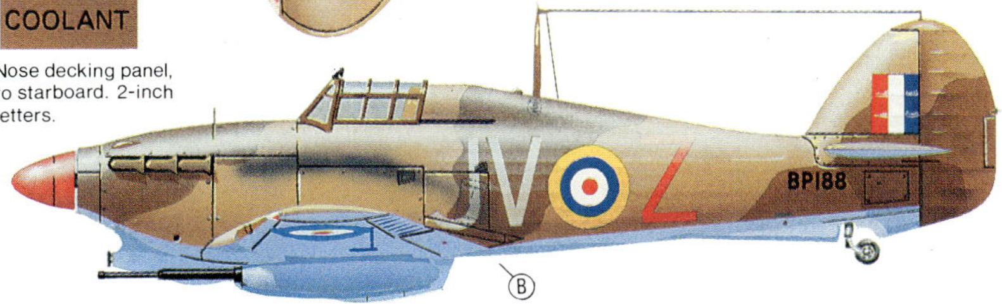

STENCILS

A

OIL
9 GALLS
AIRSPACE
1½ GALLS

Port wing root, upper surface, leading edge. 1½-inch characters.

B

FIRST AID
BREAK HERE
WATER

Port side of fuselage above wing trailing edge. One-inch and 1½-inch letters.

C

COOLANT

Nose decking panel, to starboard. 2-inch letters.

D

41H/16972
DTD 512
W
T

Starboard side of rudder. One-inch numerals and 4-inch W/T square.

E

41H/30661S
DTD509-ARM

Starboard side of fuselage below aerial mast. 1-inch numerals.

F

NO STEP

Upper trailing edge of wing roots. 2-inch letters.

G

ALL BUT FIRST LINE
SERVICING MUST
BE CARRIED OUT USING
ARM (G) PERSONNEL

Inboard surfaces of anti-tank gun fairings. 1-inch letters

H

41/H/L/12107
DTD717

Undersurface of ailerons, inboard and outboard; one-inch numerals.

J

41/H/32021
DTD717
W
T

Port wing tip, lower surface; one-inch numerals and 4-inch W/T square.

K

41H/36319
PB/L/ARM
DTD717

Starboard wing tip, lower surface; one-inch characters.

No 6 Squadron, whose motto is 'The Eyes of the Army' (Oculi Exercitus), was the first to fly this version of the Hurricane. Under the command of Wg. Cdr. Roger Cave Porteous, it was in constant action against Axis armour before, during and after the great Battle of Alamein. Although they destroyed many enemy AFVs the Hurricanes suffered heavy flak casualties.

Colour schemes and markings carried by Allied aircraft in the desert were still, in 1942, of a transient nature. The displaying of squadron code letters was relatively unusual (and was discontinued by No 6 Squadron soon afterwards). Many of the minor stencils were obliterated when 'desert' camouflage was applied.

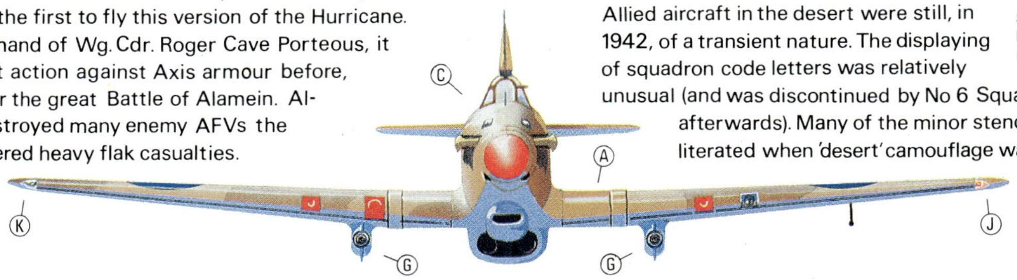

Copyright 1982, 1984, 1986 Francis K Mason FRHistS, AMRAeS

SCALE – FEET 0 1 2 3 4 5 6 7 8 9 10 11 12 13 14 15 16 17 18 19 20

Representative in-service Hurricane colour schemes and markings

Hurricane Mk I, L1584, of No 111 (Fighter) Squadron, Northolt, July 1938. Note the 'kidney' exhaust stubs, Watts wooden propeller, parallel-chord aerial mast and absence of ventral tail fairing. The style of squadron identification was unique.

Hurricane Mk I, N2587 TP-Z of No 73 Squadron, AASF, Norrent Fontes, France, November 1940. The rudder stripes (French style) were applied to assist identification of Allied aircraft; the squadron code letters were removed the following month. Early Rotol propeller.

Sea Hurricane Mk I, P3114 'M', naval operational trainer, Royal Naval Air Station, Gosport, Hants, c. December 1940. No catapult spools nor arrester hook; naval radio fitted and eight-gun armament retained. Rotol RS5/2-derivative propeller.

Hurricane Mk IIB bomber, BD761 SW-F of 'A' Flight, No 253 Squadron, Hibaldstow, Friston, Tangmere and Manston, 1942; cross-Channel 'Rhubarb' and 'Ranger' operations. Rotol RS5/3 propeller.

Hurricane Tac R Mk I, V7818, aircraft 'E' of No 208 Squadron, Tmimi, Libya, January 1941. Single fuselage-mounted oblique F24 camera. Note extemporized 'sand and spaghetti' camouflage. De Havilland variable-pitch propeller.

Hurricane Mk IIC, PG512 DR–L, of the Air Despatch Letter Service, Northolt, July 1944. Underwing tanks used for stowage of despatches, etc.; forward (white) fuselage 'invasion stripe' temporarily omitted. Rotol RS5/13 propeller.

Sea Hurricane Mk IIC, NF672, of No 835 Squadron, Fleet Air Arm, HMS Nairana, Far Eastern waters, June 1945. Note SEAF identification stripes ('extra-dark sea grey'); the underwing tanks were seldom carried. Rotol RS5/11 propeller.

Hurricane PR Mk II, DG613 (ex-P3412), of No 2 Photographic Reconnaissance Unit, Heliopolis, Egypt, 1941-42. Note the ventral fairing for the three cameras, and the absence of an aerial mast. Rotol RS5/3 propeller.

Copyright 1980, 1986 Francis K Mason FRHistS, AMRAeS

Mediterranean and several of the long-serving Hurricane squadrons had either converted to or were in the process of re-equipping with the Spitfire VC. Nevertheless, Tedder, who, on 17 February, 1943, was appointed Air Commander-in-Chief, Mediterranean Air Command, still disposed 23 Hurricane squadrons (compared with 34 of Spitfires, including six of the USAAF):

Although by no means all these squadrons had converted to other aircraft by the date of the invasion of Sicily, 10 July, relatively few Hurricanes took part in the campaign. During the previous night, however, as the transport aircraft and gliders carrying the airborne assault forces neared the Sicilian coast, the Hurricane IICs of No. 253 Squadron, temporarily transferred to night-fighting duties and

Sqn No.	*Hurricane Version*	*Base*	*Remarks*
6	Mk IID	Ben Gardane, Tunisia	Operational in Tunisia; anti-tank operations. Wg Cdr A. E. Morrison-Bell
32	Mk IIC	Tingley, Algeria	Defence of Algerian ports. Sqn Ldr J. T. Shaw. (Also training on Spitfires)
33	Mk IIC	Bersis, Libya	Defence of Benghazi. Sqn Ldr G. May
73	Mk IIC	La Sebala, Tunisia	Operational in Tunisia; night operations. Sqn Ldr R. W. Ellis
74	Mk IIB	Shaiba and Habbaniya, Iraq	Defence on Persian Gulf ports. Sqn Ldr J. C. F. Hayter
87	Mk IIC	Bone and Tingley, Algeria	Defence of Algerian ports. Sqn Ldr William Edward Geoffrey Measures. (Also training on Spitfires)
94	Mk IIC	Savoia, Libya	Defence of Tripoli. Sqn Ldr J. H. Cloete. (Also training on Spitfires)
123	Mk IIB	Bu Amud, Egypt	Convoy protection in eastern Mediterranean. Sqn Ldr K. N. T. Lee
127	Mk IIB	Ramat David, Palestine	Convoy protection in eastern Mediterranean. Sqn Ldr Derek Kane
134	Mk IIB/IIC	Sousse, Tunisia	Air defence of Tunisian ports. Sqn Ldr Percival Stanley Turner
208	Tac R Mk IIB	K. 1, Iraq	Tactical reconnaissance in Iraq
213	Mk IIC	Misurata, Libya	Operational in Libya; defence of Libyan airfields. Sqn Ldr V. C. Woodward
237	Mk IIC	L. G. 106, Egypt	Defence of Canal Zone. Sqn Ldr Eric Thornton Smith, RAFVR
238	Mk IIC	Gamil, Egypt	Defence of Canal Zone. Capt T. W. Phillips
241	Tac R Mk IIC	Arjana, Tunisia	Operational in Tunisia; tactical reconnaissance
253	Mk IIC	Jemappes, Algeria	Defence of Algerian ports. Sqn Ldr L. H. T. Bartlett
274	Mk IIC	Mellaha, Libya	Air defence of Libyan ports. Major J. R. R. Wells, SAAF
335 (Greek)	Mk IIB	Tocra, Libya	Convoy protection off African coast. Sqn Ldr G. Pangalos (Greek)
336 (Greek)	Mk IIB	L. G. 121, Egypt	Convoy protection off African coast. Sqn Ldr S. Diamontopoulos (Greek)
3 (SAAF)	Tac R Mk IIC	Libya (No. 210 Group)	Tactical reconnaissance; detachments to Tunisia
7 (SAAF)	Tac R Mk IIC	Sousse, Tunisia (No. 212 Group)	Operational in Tunisia; tactical reconnaissance
41 (SAAF)	Tac R Mk IIC	Tunisia (No. 212 Group)	Operational in Tunisia, tactical reconnaissance
451 (RAAF)	Mk IIC	Idku, Egypt	Lightened Hurricanes for high-altitude air defence of Canal Zone

based on Lampedusa since the previous month, ranged along the southern coast of Sicily, their pilots ordered to shoot out any searchlight that might expose the invaders. Several of the Hurricane squadrons then based in Cyrenaica, Egypt and Cyprus (notably Nos. 127, 213 and 274) took part in the abortive operations against the Dodecanese islands during September and November 1943, while a number of offensive sweeps were flown over German-occupied airfields in Crete.

Nevertheless Hurricanes did operate from Italy, beginning in February 1944, when No. 6 Squadron, now fully rested from its hard work at Alamein and afterwards[69], and now fully trained and equipped with Hurricane IVs, flew to Grottaglie. Stocks of 3-inch rocket projectiles had built up in the Mediterranean and it was customary to fly with a single 40-mm gun and four rockets; later the gun was discarded altogether owing to the considerable nose-down pitch when firing (with nose armour the Mark IV's cg was very close to the forward limit in any case).

No. 6 Squadron's rôle in Italy was to attack Axis shipping and ports on both coasts of the Adriatic, carrying out its first operation against a German headquarters on the Albanian coast at Durazzo on 29 March. On 4 July it moved north-west to Foggia under Sqn Ldr J. H. Brown so as to be able to cover the entire Yugoslav coastline, usually flying with rockets under one wing and a drop tank under the other. In five months' operations No. 6 took an impressive toll of Axis shipping with its rockets, sinking a 5,000-ton ship, 21 schooners, three ferries and 11 other ships, and severely damaging 27 further vessels.

In August No. 6 Squadron was transferred to the Balkan Air Force, together with two other Hurricane units, Nos. 351 and 352 (Yugoslav) Squadrons, recently formed with Hurricane IICs. While these two Yugoslav-manned squadrons moved to the island of Vis in the Adriatic in October, No. 6 continued to be based in Italy for the time being, sending forward detachments to Niksic deep in Yugoslavia for daily anti-tank patrols. Typical of these was one flown on 3 December and described as follows:

> "3 December, 1944. Niksic. Three Hurricane IVs took off at 12.25 hrs to attack tanks reported on the Klopot–Lijeva–Rijeka road. The pilots found five PzKpfw IIIs and IVs. No. 1 led the section in firing a salvo of four 25 lb armour-piercing RPs, which hit the leading tank, knocking it out. No. 2's salvo of four 60 lb semi-armour-piercing RPs struck a farm building, damaging two tanks parked alongside. No. 3's salvo of 60-pounders struck the same area, further damaging the same two tanks. The pilots made liberal use of their machine guns, but there was no *flak*. All three pilots returned to Niksic at 13.10 hrs."

No. 6 Squadron moved its base to Prkos in Yugoslavia on 9 April, 1945, remaining there until the end of the war in Europe. With just a week to go before Germany's final surrender in May, this longest-serving Hurricane squadron flew a rocket attack on 16 German troopships in the Gulf of Trieste; all hosted white flags in token of their own capitulation![70]

Thus ended the war in Europe and the Mediterranean. The Hurricane had entered the war in the Balkans when German forces invaded Yugoslavia on 6 April, 1941. It was present once more in that country exactly four years later to witness retribution for the devastation of Belgrade and a brutal occupation by German forces. Only its traditional enemy in the air, the Messerschmitt Bf 109, was present to share that sombre anniversary. But the rôles of those classic fighters had been reversed . . .

13

TROPICAL STORMS IN THE FAR EAST

The war in the Far East was but a month old when the first Hurricanes arrived. They were still fighting 44 months later, when the sun finally set on Japan's ambitions in the Pacific and South-East Asia. The first squadrons to arrive at Singapore were equipped with Hurricane Is, IIAs and IIBs and, contrary to reports put about at the time (and to some extent perpetuated ever since), the British aircraft were not generally inferior to the excellent Japanese carrier-borne fighter, the Mitsubishi A6M2 Zero-Sen (ZEKE), possessing similar performance at around 17,000 feet, and a similar wing loading and turning radius. The Hurricane's Merlin produced a better power loading, and even the eight-gun battery discharged a higher weight of fire than the Japanese aircraft. The same assessment could be accorded in a comparison of the Hurricanes in Burma with the Japanese Army's Nakajima Ki-43 Hayabusa (OSCAR). The British pilots were, however, usually overwhelmed by greatly superior numbers and, as was so often the lot of the interceptor, deprived of the initial height advantage in combat owing to inadequate warning of approaching raids. The whole sorry history of Britain's attempts to withstand Japanese aggression in South-East Asia has been succinctly adjudged as "Too little, too late".

* * *

At the moment when Japanese forces first struck at Kota Bharu in northern Malaya in the early hours of 8 December, 1941, there was not one Hurricane within 3,500 miles. The most modern fighters on hand comprised 31 serviceable Brewster Buffalos of No. 243 Squadron, RAF, Nos. 21 and 453 Squadrons, RAAF, and No. 488 Squadron, RNZAF. Despite extraordinary gallantry by the pilots of these obsolescent aircraft (top speed 316 mph at 16,000 feet with an armament, adapted locally, of four 0.303-inch machine guns), they were unable to match the Japanese fighters and came largely to be employed in ground attack operations until the battle moved to Singapore itself.

Ironically the first Hurricane squadron destined for the defence of Singapore had left the United Kingdom three days before the first Japanese attack, with the sailing of No. 242 Squadron from Liverpool on 5 December. Another convoy, which had already sailed for the Middle East with No. 605 Squadron was diverted to Singapore, but this time the aircraft and most of the pilots were well on their way to Malta, and the ground personnel with the remaining pilots continued on their way to Singapore. No. 232 Squadron, *en route* for the Red Sea via the Cape, was diverted to Singapore when it reached Cape Town on 18 December. No. 258 Squadron was also diverted to Singapore.

The first Hurricane aircraft to arrive at Singapore were an assortment of crated Mark Is and IIBs whose ship docked on 3 January together with 24 pilots, including some of the "spare" pilots of No. 605 Squadron, from the Middle East. After being unloaded it was found that all the Hurricanes' Browning guns were choked with thick grease to

The only Hurricane flown by the Royal Australian Air Force in Australia, V7476, *a tropicalised Mark I believed to have been diverted from a shipment to Takoradi.* Top, *as it arrived in Australia in normal RAF colour scheme and markings. (*Photo: *RAAF Official).* Below, V7476 *in 'natural' finish and SEAC markings, looking rather the worse for wear at RAAF Station, Point Cook. The RAAF serial number* A60-1 *was allotted to it, but it is thought that this was never applied. (*Photo: *A. H. Carter,* via *Sqn Ldr R. C. B. Ashworth)*

protect them on the sea voyage; stripping and cleaning them occupied many days, but some of the aircraft had been assembled and pronounced serviceable on the 20th when 27 Japanese bombers, their crews expecting to meet no more than a handful of Buffalos, appeared over Singapore without fighter escort. The RAF fighters disposed of eight of the raiders without loss. The next day the bombers returned, but this time with an escort of A6M2 fighters whose pilots dived on the Hurricanes as they climbed to intercept; this time five Hurricanes were shot down without scoring.

By now all the pilots and groundcrews of Nos. 232, 242, 258 and 605 Squadrons had arrived at Singapore, while HMS *Indomitable* was approaching with 48 further Hurricane IIAs and IIBs, picked up in the Middle East. Because of the vulnerability of concentrating all the squadrons on Singapore island it was decided to retain only Nos. 242 and 258 at Seletar and transfer all members of No. 232 and 605 to Batavia, Java, and Palembang, Sumatra, respectively. On the 26th HMS *Indomitable*

*An extremely rare picture, albeit of poor quality, of a No 135 Squadron Hurricane at Mingaladon, Rangoon, at the time of the Japanese raids on the great port early in 1942. At that time the Squadron was commanded by Frank Carey. (*Photo: *via Sqn Ldr R. C. B. Ashworth)*

launched all her Hurricanes, 15 flying to Seletar and 33 to two airfields, P.I and P.II, near Palembang.

The Japanese air attacks on Singapore continued unabated as the enemy advanced even closer southwards on the Malayan mainland. Radar stations which had provided some early warning of these attacks were overrun or dismantled so that the Hurricanes had frequently to scramble at no more than a few minutes' notice, and were therefore often attacked while still climbing. By the 28th only 21 of the 51 aircraft so recently delivered remained serviceable (plus six Buffalos—all that remained of Nos. 21 and 453 Squadrons, RAAF). Thus it was that on the last day of the month General Sir Archibald Wavell (late of the Middle East, who had been appointed to the Supreme Command of British forces in the Far East on 15 January) ordered all but eight Hurricances and the six Buffalos to withdraw. For ten days these remaining aircraft continued to give what defence they could, with occasional patrols flown up from Sumatra. Not even when Japanese forces landed on Singapore island on 8 February and started shelling the airfields were the pilots discouraged from taking off. On the 9th the Hurricanes destroyed six Japanese bombers and damaged 14 others, for the loss of one pilot. On the 10th, after operating from a makeshift landing strip only 750 yards long, the last Hurricanes were withdrawn to Sumatra. On 15 February the forces in Singapore surrendered.

By then, however, the Japanese had already turned their attention to Sumatra and its two airfields near Palembang. As early as 23 January they had carried out a heavy air raid on P.I and after a paratroop attack on that airfield on 14 February, which caused the loss of several aircraft including Hurricanes, all British and Dutch fighter operations were transferred to P.II. On the following day a Japanese invasion force was successfully attacked off the coast by Hudsons and Blenheims escorted by Hurricanes; that evening the Hurricanes flew a sweep over Banka Island, destroying several ZEKES on the ground. Unfortunately, although the invasion was momentarily forestalled, there were inadequate resources to follow up this minor victory and the Japanese response was as violent as it was immediate. Another airborne attack was made on Palembang, this time threatening the secret airstrip P.II. In some panic and much confusion the airstrip was abandoned and all ground personnel hurriedly embarked at Oesthaven for Java—leaving behind all the spare Merlin engines for the Hurricanes. Such haste was shown to have been unnecessary when, two days later, Gp Capt Gilbert Edward Nicholetts (later Air Marshal Sir Gilbert, KBE, CB, AFC and Bar) returned with 50 volunteers from No. 605 Squadron to recover all available spares and equipment.

By 18 February all remaining Hurricanes, numbering 25, of which 18 were serviceable, were based on Java: No. 232 Squadron (Sqn Ldr Arthur John Alexander Llewellin) at Tjililitan, No. 242 (Sqn Ldr Reginald Edgar Peter Brooker) at Bandoeng, No. 258 (Sqn Ldr Alfred Burke Thompson) at Kemajoran and No. 605 (Sqn Ldr L. E. Andrews) at Andir. The available bomber force comprised 12 Hudsons and six Blenheims, all based at Semplak, but in raids by the Japanese on the 19th and 22nd 15 of the bombers were destroyed. By the 28th Nos. 242 and 258 Squadrons had virtually ceased to exist and their survivors were absorbed into the other two squadrons; the following day, with 12 airworthy Hurricanes remaining, all pilots, groundcrews and aircraft were amalgamated into No. 605 Squadron under Sqn Ldr Brooker. On that day these fighters, in company with ten Dutch P-40s and six Buffalos, made a low-level attack on a Japanese invasion force landing at Eretanwetan, causing some damage and numerous casualties but unable to halt the landings. The following day the surviving pilots were unable to take off from Tjililitan, where they were now concentrated, owing to constant sweeps by the Japanese and damage to the airstrip. On 7 March the last two remaining Hurricanes were destroyed.

The Loss of Burma

With the loss of Java and Sumatra there could be no question of reassembling and re-forming the four Hurricane squadrons. Their survivors, in number fewer than 500 men, took what passage they could. Many died at sea, others were captured by the Japanese, but most reached the shores of Australia.

As much to protect the western flank of the Japanese thrust south in the East Indies as to close the supply route through Rangoon to China, the Japanese attacked Burma from Thailand in mid-January, giving ample warning of their intent by carrying out a ferocious bombing raid on Rangoon on 23 December. At that time the fighter defence of Burma rested on 16 Buffalos of No. 67 Squadron based at Mingaladon on the northern outskirts of Rangoon under the command of Sqn Ldr Robert Alfred Milward (later Wg Cdr., OBE, DFC and Bar). In addition, 650 miles to the north-east at Kunming in China, there was a squadron of the American Volunteer Group with 21 P-40s, whose normal task was to defend the Burma Road, down which the supplies flowed to China from Rangoon.

Unfortunately India itself was no better protected in the air and once more fighter reinforcements had to be assembled from distant sources. No. 17 Squadron, which had sailed from Britain for the Middle East on 12 November with Hurricane IIAs, was diverted *en route* to Rangoon, arriving on 16 January and moving straight to the airfield at Mingaladon under the command of Sqn Ldr Cedric Arthur Cuthbert Stone. No. 135 Squadron had been sailing for India at the same time, but once more the destination was switched; on 28 January it also moved to Mingaladon under the command of

Hurricane IIB, BG872 of No 261 Squadron at Colombo Racecourse, Ceylon, in April 1942 about the time that the Japanese carrier aircraft attacked British naval bases in the island. (Photo: via P. Edmond and R. L. Ward, Farnborough)

Sqn Ldr Frank Reginald Carey.[71] One other Squadron, No. 136, was diverted to Burma while travelling to the Middle East, but did not arrive at Rangoon until 6 February (under Sqn Ldr Thomas Arthur Francis Elsdon), but, being without aircraft, was re-embarked and sent to India to await its Hurricanes.

Thus when, on Christmas Day, the Japanese once more raided Rangoon, this time in considerable force, there were still no Hurricanes on hand. What might have been achieved may be judged by the claims of the P-40 and Buffalo pilots, who stated that they shot down 36 aircraft in the two raids. No. 67 Squadron had, however, been hard pressed to match the Japanese raiders, the pilots' tactics simply being to gain as much height as they could before making a single diving pass through the raiding formation, escaping as best they could at low level; any attempt to climb once more would invite certain destruction by the escorting OSCARS. Many of the Buffalos were destroyed on the ground during the heavy attack of 25 December.

Early in January a consignment of 30 Hurricane Is and IIAs reached Rangoon (it is believed as deck cargo from the Middle East). These were quickly assembled and some flown by pilots of No. 67 Squadron. The arrival of No. 17 Squadron did much to relieve the pressure and Air Vice-Marshal Donald Fasken Stevenson, CB, CBE, DSO, MC, Air Officer Commanding the RAF in Burma, ordered the Hurricanes forward to the airfields in southern Burma—Mergui, Tenasserim, Moulmein and Tavoy—to strike at the Japanese bases in Thailand. They and the Blenheim bombers accounted for the destruction of some 58 aircraft, mostly on the ground at Bangkok during January. During the second half of the month, however, the Japanese opened their invasion, striking from Thailand and overrunning all Stevenson's advanced bases in the south, and all the while air attacks continued on the Rangoon area in attempts to wrest air superiority from the RAF. On the 30th the important airfield at Moulmein, covering Rangoon from the east, fell to the Japanese. Thereafter the only warning of approaching raids was afforded by a constant patrol by a single "Jim Crow" Hurricane over the city.

On 5 February Japanese forces crossed the Salween river 80 miles east of Rangoon and within three weeks were in the outer environs of the great port. Believing that further operations were now impossible at Mingaladon, Stevenson ordered the remaining 24 Hurricanes (and four Buffalos), with the pilots of Nos. 17, 67 and 135 Squadrons, north to a hastily prepared airstrip at Zigon, 100 miles north from Rangoon. On 7 March Rangoon and the airfield at Mingaladon were evacuated under cover of these fighters—now constituting "X" Force under the command of Gp Capt Noel Christie Singer, DSO (later Air Cdre, CBE, DSO, DFC). The efficiency of this support was evident in the fact that throughout the evacuation of Rangoon, which occupied three days, not one Japanese aircraft managed to attack the city or the roads northwards from it.

The Japanese had now developed three parallel northward lines of advance, the most dangerous of which being that towards Mandalay up the Sittang

A Hurricane IIC of No 17 Squadron taking off from Red Road airstrip in Calcutta, probably in the autumn of 1942. (Photo: via Sqn Ldr R. C. B. Ashworth)

*Cox's Bazaar, an important forward airfield on the coast of East Bengal, always presented problems with its poor surface until, relatively late in the War, it was given concrete and tarmac runways and taxyways. Here a Tac R Hurricane IIB (*BG802*) of No 28 Squadron has put a foot wrong in January 1943. (*Photo: *via R. L. Ward, Farnborough)*

River and thus one that threatened to outflank Zigon. By mid-March the dozen remaining Hurricane IIAs of Nos. 17 and 135 Squadrons, a handful of P-40s of the AVG and some Blenheims of No. 45 Squadron had therefore been withdrawn from Zigon to Magwe, and No. 67 Squadron with six surviving Hurricane Is moved to the island of Akyab off the Burma coast. At Magwe, 150 miles to the south-west of Mandalay, the Hurricanes and Blenheims became "Burwing", commanded by Gp Capt Herbert Seton Broughall, MC, DFC, an officer who at once stated his determination "to stop the rot, here and now". On 20 March he ordered Hudsons of No. 139 Squadron at Akyab to cover the airfields in southern Burma to learn the location of the Japanese Army Air Force's main strength. Not surprisingly this was found to be at Mingaladon, where some 50 Mitsubishi Ki-21-II (SALLY) heavy bombers and a similar number of OSCARS were counted. The next day all serviceable aircraft—ten Hurricanes and nine Blenheims—took off from Magwe for Mingaladon. Sixteen of the SALLY heavy bombers were destroyed on the ground and eleven OSCARS in the air (two by Blenheims and the rest by Hurricanes). Two Hurricanes and two Blenheims were lost. Meanwhile ten further Blenheims and 16 Hurricane IIBs had been flown into Magwe from Calcutta, whither they had flown from the Middle East.

Revenge by the Japanese was swift and devastating, as in the next 24 hours Magwe was subjected to a veritable rain of bombs from more than 200 aircraft which virtually destroyed the airfield as well as all but seven Blenheims, a dozen Hurricanes and three P-40s. Broughall now ordered Burwing to disperse, sending the Hurricanes to Akyab, the P-40s to Lashio, 100 miles beyond Mandalay. All but one of the Hurricanes arrived at Akyab on 26 March, only to be ordered into the air the following day to meet successive waves of Japanese bombers. Three Hurricanes were shot down and four others (all Mark Is) were destroyed by bombs. One pilot, baling out over the sea from his Hurricane, and attempting to inflate his Mae West, found that the air he was trying to blow into the life jacket was escaping through a bullet hole in his cheek and jawbone. Nevertheless he succeeded in remaining afloat and after three hours was picked out of the sea by a Burmese fisherman.

*For many years thought to depict a Hurricane IIC trainer with its guns removed, this photo shows one of the early photo reconnaissance aircraft flown to Calcutta from the Middle East in mid-1942. Just visible behind the wing trailing edge is the ventral camera fairing. The outer white rings round the wing roundels were added to avoid confusion with the Japanese red disc markings. As on most PR Hurricanes the radio mast has been deleted. (*Photo: *Flt Lt B. A. Grant, RAAF)*

With the almost total destruction of the RAF at Akyab and Magwe, and the breakdown of organization in the remaining ground forces in central Burma, there remained no course left to Stevenson but to concentrate his forces for the defence of Calcutta and Ceylon. Lashio fell to the Japanese on 29 April, Mandalay on 1 May and Myitkyina on the 8th.

Rebuilding the Air Force in India

Throughout the campaign in Burma Hurricane squadrons had been arriving in a trickle in India and Ceylon. That these had not been thrown into assisting in the defence of Burma was on account of the need to provide some defence for the Royal Navy in Ceylon and the Bay of Bengal, where the Japanese naval forces had already attacked in considerable strength. No. 30 Squadron in Egypt embarked in HMS *Indomitable* and moved to Ratmalana in Ceylon on 6 March under Sqn Ldr George Frederick Chater with Hurricane Mark IIBs; No. 261 Squadron, also brought with Mk IIBs from the Mediterranean in *Indomitable*, arrived at Dum Dum at the end of February, but was then moved to China Bay in Ceylon on 6 March under the command of Sqn Ldr Albert Gerald Lewis. No. 258 Squadron (with no relationship to the Squadron that had disintegrated in Java) was formed under Sqn Ldr Peter Fletcher at Colombo out of a local

A moral for air-to-air photographers. One day in 1944 Ralph Hunter, a pilot of No 28 Squadron, the hard-worked tactical reconnaissance Hurricane squadron, asked a fellow pilot Mike Dewing if he would accompany him aloft for some unofficial air-to-air photography. Together they took off from Dalbhumgahr south of Calcutta, Hunter clutching his box Brownie. Click. *But Hunter was not satisfied. 'Mike, I'm coming a bit closer'.* Click... *'Just a wee bit closer'.* Click. *About two seconds later the Hurricanes collided. Fortunately both pilots managed to make safe landings, little the worse for wear. (*Photos: *Ralph Hunter, via Mike Dewing)*

unit known as "G" Squadron.

This move to strengthen Ceylon was yet another piece of inspired planning by Wavell, who had correctly foreseen that the next Japanese move would be to destroy the Royal Navy's bases and facilities in the island so as to control the eastern half of the Indian Ocean. First reports of Japanese naval forces in the Indian Ocean were received on 4 April, and during the next five days 23 Allied merchant ships were sunk in the Bay of Bengal, 15 of them by carrier-borne aircraft. Early on Easter Sunday, 5 April, 125 Japanese carrier-borne aircraft led by the redoubtable Commander Mitsuo Fuchida—36 ZEKES, 36 VALS (Aichi D3A bombers) and 56 KATES (Nakajima B5N attack aircraft)—assaulted Colombo harbour. In the absence of radar two Catalina flying boats were on patrol and radioed a warning of the approaching raid, and 36 Hurricanes of Nos. 30 and 258 Squadrons and six Fleet Air Arm Fulmars were scrambled to intercept. In the ensuing fight the Japanese ZEKES almost succeeded in preventing the Hurricanes from getting through to the bombers, shooting down 15 Hurricanes and four Fulmars; the British fighters destroyed three ZEKES, two KATES and two VALS, while naval guns shot down two more VALS and a KATE. Although these losses among the Hurricanes were indeed heavy (though eight of the pilots were recovered unhurt), stocks of Hurricane IIBs were adequate for replacements to be issued immediately to the two squadrons.

On the 9th the Japanese returned to Ceylon, this time to attack Trincomalee and the nearby airfield at China Bay with 91 KATES and 38 ZEKES, again led by Commander Fuchida. This raid was intercepted by 17 Hurricanes of No. 261 Squadron and six Fulmars of No. 873 Squadron, Fleet Air Arm. Now the Japanese were able to hold off the interceptors, shooting down eight Hurricanes (of which six pilots were saved) and three Fulmars. The Hurricane pilots shot down twelve ZEKES, the Fulmars three.

The damage done by these two major raids on Colombo and Trincomalee was widespread for, with some warning of Japanese warships in the Bay of Bengal, most of the naval and merchant ships had been able to raise steam and disperse; thus the Japanese crews had concentrated their attacks on the shore installations. Moreover, without adequate naval fighters to protect the ships at sea the Royal Navy suffered heavy losses during this foray by the Japanese into the Indian Ocean; in the first ten days of April the carrier HMS *Hermes*, the cruisers HMS *Cornwall* and *Dorsetshire*, and the destroyers *Hollyhock* and *Vampire* were all sunk by carrier-borne aircraft. The Japanese task force comprised the carriers *Akagi, Hiryu, Shokaku, Soryu* and *Zuikaku*, four battleships, three cruisers and eight destroyers—a force far greater than all the Allied warships in the Indian Ocean, and comprising almost exactly the same ships that had taken such a devastating toll of American warships at Pearl Harbor exactly four months previously.

The Royal Navy now moved its main base facilities further afield, absolving the RAF of further need for reinforcements to be sent to Ceylon for the time being. Instead Hurricane squadrons continued to move to and re-equip in eastern India for the air defence of Calcutta. No. 146 Squadron, which had been flying Buffalos and Mohawks for about three months, re-equipped with Hurricane IIBs at Dum Dum early in May under the command of Sqn Ldr Count Manfred Beckett Czernin,[72] while No. 607 Squadron, which had left Britain in March, arrived at Alipur, near Calcutta, on 25 May commanded by Sqn Ldr Noel Joseph Mowat. This was to become the first squadron in the Far East to be equipped with Hurricane IICs, the initial deliveries being made in June.

The rains of the summer prevented either side from undertaking operations on the Burma front, but it was obvious to Air Chief Marshal Sir Richard Peirse, KCB, DSO, AFC, the Air Officer Commanding-in-Chief, that with British Commonwealth forces not yet strong enough to launch a major offensive in Burma (and with little in the way of reinforcements likely to arrive from the Middle East with the crisis in the Western Desert at its height), the next move would almost certainly be a series of heavy air attacks in the Calcutta areas—possibly as a prelude to a Japanese offensive. The task of the RAF during that autumn of 1942 was therefore straightforward in principle: to build up the air defence of Calcutta so that not only could any significant damage be avoided in the densely packed city of Calcutta but also that the Japanese would quickly recognise that they no longer possessed a semblance of air superiority in the theatre. Apart from this, there was of course still the need to provide Ceylon and its ports with adequate air defence in the event that the Imperial Japanese Navy should pay a return visit to the Indian Ocean. By December that year Peirse deployed the Hurricane squadrons shown below.

Thus, in expectation of the Japanese air attack on Calcutta, there were four Hurricane squadrons operational by day, and one by both day and night. When the attacks were eventually launched they came by night, not by large formations but by about a dozen aircraft. Yet they were enough to send one and a half million people fleeing from the city. Against these tiny raids by scattered aircraft the Hurricanes of No. 146 Squadron were almost powerless to inflict any worthwhile casualties and it fell to a single flight of AI-equipped Beaufighters, hurriedly despatched to Calcutta, to put an end to the attacks in mid-January 1943.

Sqn No.	*Hurricane Version*	*Base*	*Remarks*
17	Mk IICs	Red Road, Calcutta	Air defence of Calcutta. Sqn Ldr M. C. C. Cotton
28	Tac R Mk IIBs	Ranchi, Bihar	Tactical reconnaissance on Burma front; becoming operational
30	Mk IICs	Dambulla, Ceylon	Air defence of ports in Ceylon. Sqn Ldr Alfred William Alexander Bayne
67	Mk IICs	Alipur, Calcutta	Air defence of Calcutta. Sqn Ldr J. H. Buchmann
79	Mk IICs	Kanchrapara, E. Bengal	Air defence of Calcutta. Sqn Ldr C. A. Jones
135	Mk IICs	Dum Dum, Calcutta	Convoy protection and air defence of Calcutta. Sqn Ldr Herbert Selwyn Giddings
136	Mk IIBs/IICs	Chittagong, E. Bengal	Operational patrols over Burma front. Sqn Ldr Arthur Whitaker Ridler
146	Mk IICs	Alipur, Calcutta	Night air defence of Calcutta and railway patrols. Sqn Ldr Geoffrey Reginald Thompson Williams
258	Mk IIBs	Colombo Racecourse, Ceylon	Air defence of Colombo. Sqn Ldr Robert James Walker
261	Mk IIBs	China Bay, Ceylon	Air defence of Trincomalee, Ceylon. Sqn Ldr E. Downey
273	Mk IIBs	Ratmalana, Ceylon	Air defence of ports in Ceylon. Sqn Ldr Alexander Noel Constantine
607	Mk IICs	Jessore, E. Bengal	Air defence of Calcutta, and "Rhubarbs" along Irrawaddy. Sqn Ldr R. H. Holland
615	Mk IICs	Fenny, E. Bengal	Operational patrols and sweeps over Burma front. Sqn Ldr B. L. Buckenfield

HURRICANE SQUADRON BASES: SOUTH-EAST ASIA

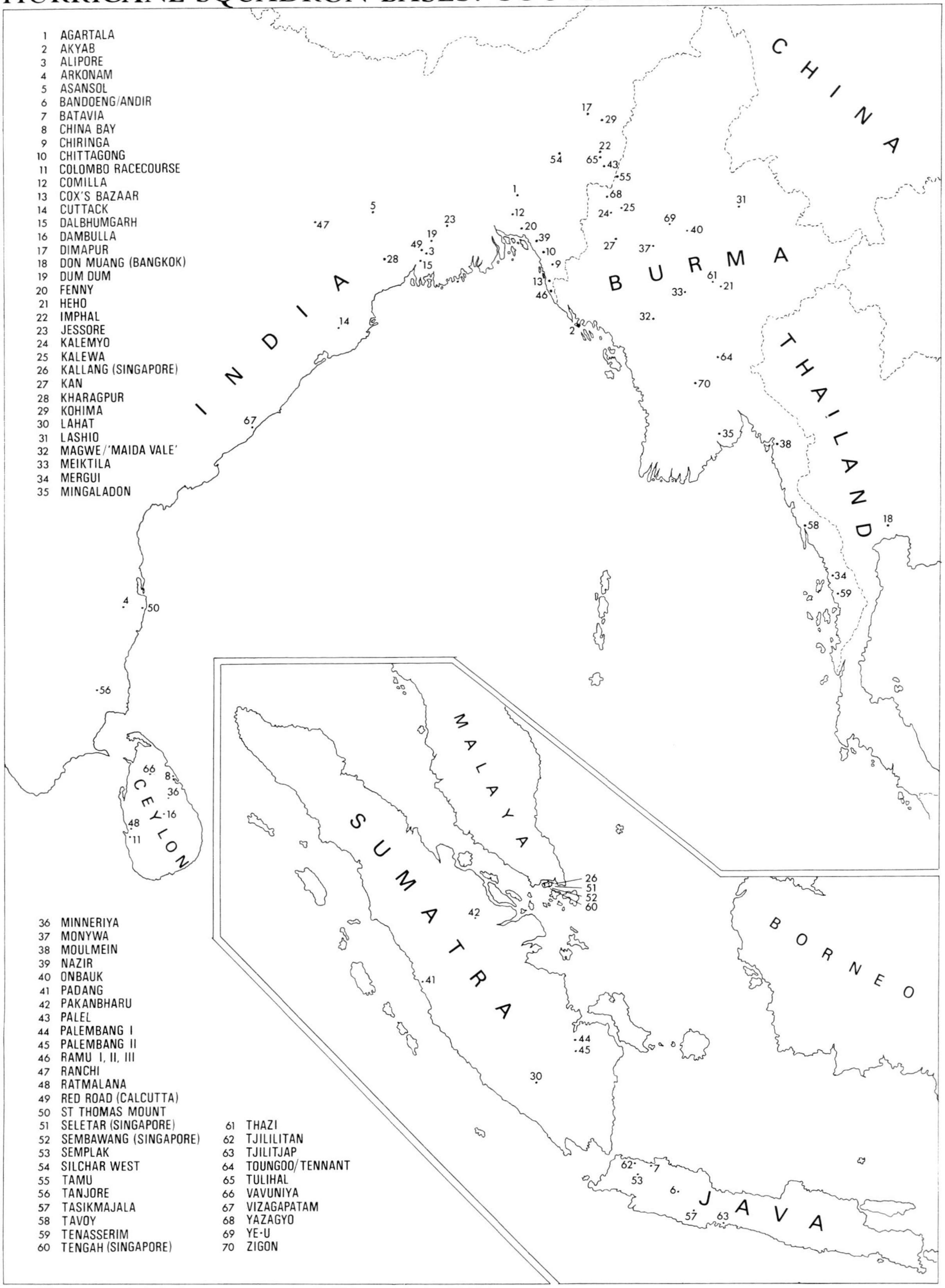

Meanwhile Wavell had decided to mount a limited offensive in the Arakan with the object of establishing an advanced landing ground on Akyab Island. Much depended on the ability of the Japanese to reinforce the Arakan in time, and reconnaissance suggested that the area was only lightly held. Setting out from Cox's Bazaar on 9 December the Eastern Army reached Maungdaw one week later as the tactical reconnaissance Hurricane pilots of No. 28 Squadron flew their first operational sorties, on the look-out for signs of Japanese reinforcements. 30 miles were covered in the next ten days and Indin was occupied on the 27th. However, time now wasted in waiting for supplies to catch up overland allowed the Japanese to strengthen Akyab, and when it was discovered that other enemy forces were preparing to strike towards Maungdaw, thereby threatening to isolate the Commonwealth forces in the south, the Eastern Army was ordered to withdraw once more to Cox's Bazaar in April.

Although this, the first Arakan campaign, failed in its object it afforded extremely valuable experience for the Hurricane pilots of Nos. 28, 67, 136, 607 and 615 Squadrons, which, between them, frequently flew more than 150 sorties a day. The cannon-armed Mark IICs in particular were used to excellent effect against road and river traffic on the Mayu and Kaladan rivers, so that the Japanese were forced eventually to move only at night.

Reference to the reconnaissance over the Arakan prior to and during the first campaign of 1943 prompts a brief account of No. 3 Photographic Reconnaissance Unit, then flying from Dum Dum. During January 1942, while Singapore was fighting to survive Japanese air attacks, Flt Lt Gerald Edwin Frederick Proctor, RAFO, had volunteered with another pilot to ferry two Hurricane PR Mk Is from the Middle East to the colony. Unable to reach Singapore before its surrender, the two pilots set up base at Mingaladon, Rangoon, and subsequently flew about 25 sorties over Thailand and Malaya for Air Vice-Marshal Stevenson before both Hurricanes were eventually written off. The pilots made their way back to Calcutta, where they were joined by three other pilots, two of whom had been posted to India in the belief that Proctor and his companion had been taken prisoner at Singapore. The other pilot, Flt Lt Alexander Cunninghame Pearson,[73] who had been flying with No. 2 PRU in the Middle East, was ordered to Calcutta to establish No. 3 PRU.

In April two Hurricane PR Mk IIBs arrived at

OPERATIONAL HURRICANE SQUADRONS: SOUTH-EAST ASIA

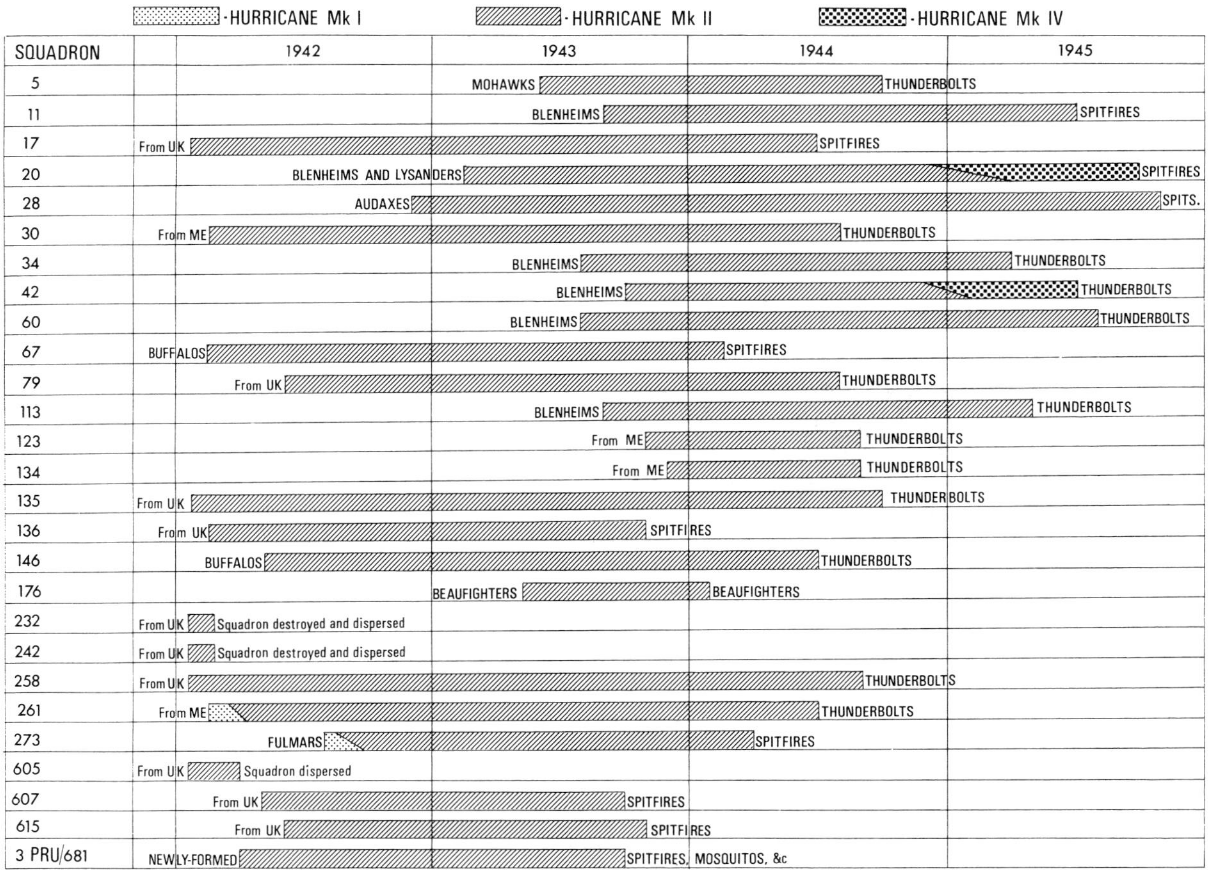

Dum Dum, followed by two more in May and four (including a surplus Mark I) in June. The first successful photographic sorties were flown over northern Burma on 6 June, but until the arrival of adequate stocks of auxiliary tanks the Hurricanes' effective sortie radius was limited to 300 miles. From November 1942 onwards, however, carrying two 44-gallon tanks, Hurricane PR Mk IIs could just cover Mandalay and Rangoon from airfields such as Cox's Bazaar. In January 1943 No. 3 PRU was re-styled No. 681 (Photographic Reconnaissance) Squadron and now came under the command of Wg Cdr Stewart Gordon ("Bill") Wise.[74] The great majority of short-range reconnaissance continued to be undertaken by the half-dozen Hurricane PR Mk IIs remaining until September 1944, when they were retired in favour of Spitfire XIs and Mosquito XVIs.

During the period February–June 1943 Hurricanes were also engaged in operations over the Naga Hills in northern Burma as, led by Brigadier Orde Charles Wingate, specially trained "commando-style" forces were making their way through the jungles to operate behind the Japanese front lines. These Chindit operations were wholly dependent on supplies dropped by RAF Dakotas, which in turn were protected by Hurricanes. Though retained as an obvious protection these escorts encountered scarcely any interference from Japanese aircraft, and long before the campaign ended had petered out altogether. What was not then fully realized by the Allies was that the Japanese, relatively weak in the air over South-East Asia since their initial onrush through Burma a year earlier, were withdrawing their aircraft to fronts in the Pacific, which were now being seriously threatened by the Americans.

Mid-1943 was also a period of change for the Hurricane squadrons. The venerable Blenheim IV light bombers were now finally being retired and the opportunity was taken during the Monsoon season to issue Nos. 11, 34, 42, 60 and 113 Squadrons with Hurricane IIB and IIC bombers, the surplus aircrew members of the Blenheims being withdrawn to India to start conversion to such aircraft as the Beaufort, Mosquito and Liberator. Other squadrons, previously equipped as interceptors, were now given Hurricane bombers. Meanwhile 60 Hurricane IID anti-tank fighters had arrived in India from the Middle East, these aircraft being scheduled for use by Nos. 5 and 20 Squadrons, but owing to a lack of ammunition stocks neither was able to use its 40-mm guns until towards the end of the year. By December a total of 970 Hurricanes were held on charge in India, including about 46 Mark Is, which were in use with No. 151 OTU on the Northwest Frontier—working at full stretch to make ready the stream of pilots arriving in the theatre from all over the Commonwealth for service with new Hurricane squadrons; a further 106 Hurricane IIAs and IIBs had been transferred to the Indian Air Force, whose first Hurricane squadron (No. 1) had just been declared operational. By then moreover the first Spitfire squadrons were becoming operational—in time to inflict heavy losses on the Japanese when raids resumed on Calcutta in December.

By the end of the year South-East Asia Command had been created under Admiral the Lord Louis Mountbatten, with Peirse assuming overall command of the Allied Air Forces in South-East Asia. Mountbatten, like Wavell before him, chose to seize the initiative once the monsoon season was over. This time, however, at the end of 1943, the Allied forces facing Burma were immeasurably stronger and better equipped both on the ground and in the air. Accordingly, just as a year earlier, the first campaign was fought in the Arakan, the object—to capture Akyab—the same but launched sooner so as to forestall a Japanese threat aimed at Chittagong. The main thrust south was made by the 7th Indian Division, which had started out from Cox's Bazaar in November. By 6 February it reached and captured Sinzweya, but was then isolated by a Japanese thrust which cut its overland supply route from the north. Encircled in what became known as the "Admin Box", the 7th Division was sustained wholly by air, large numbers of RAF and USAAF C-47 Dakotas making frequent supply drops under constant cover provided by five Hurricane squadrons and two of Spitfires. On several occasions Japanese aircraft

Hurricane Tac R Mark IIC at Imphal in the Indian state of Manipur. This version was usually identifiable by the removal of the outboard pair of wing cannon, although occasionally only one gun was removed. (Earlier No 28 Squadron had been ordered not to remove any *guns.)* (Photo: *R. L. Ward, Neg Ref No BC1224/28)*

strove to attack, but in every instance were engaged and driven off. The battle raged on around the "Admin Box" for a month, but, after the 5th Indian Division had been landed from the sea, the 7th broke out and at once in turn encircled a large number of Japanese—who fought and died rather than surrender.

Meanwhile on 8 March the Japanese attacked on the central front in Burma with three divisions striking north to cut the main overland supply route for the air bridge which had come into operation (the "Hump" route) following the loss of the Burma Road. These divisions attacked the villages of Imphal and, some 60 miles to the north, Kohima. Imphal was cut off and beseiged, but the Japanese occupied much of Kohima. Once more the forces on the ground were supplied and reinforced entirely by air. The 33rd Indian Corps was flown in to Dinapur under cover of four squadrons of Hurricane IIC bombers (including No. 1 Squadron, Indian Air Force) and closely supported in its advance to relieve the forces fighting at Kohima. In 16 days these four squadrons flew 2,200 sorties, dropping 2,500 250 lb bombs on the Japanese 31st Division, with scarcely ever a sign of Japanese aircraft.

At Imphal the defenders were able to sustain a fairly large perimeter within a horseshoe-shaped valley in which six landing strips were prepared. As the 5th Indian Division was flown in from the Arakan by the C-46s and C-47s, thousands of non-combatant personnel were taken out. Three of the Hurricane squadrons from Kohima were ordered south to join No. 28 Squadron and two of Spitfires at Imphal. In the first fortnight of April the Allied aircraft flew 10,000 sorties in the southern battle, of which about 6,000 were by the Hurricanes.

No. 28 Squadron, which was flying Tac R Mark IICs under the command of Sqn Ldr Henry Larsen (an Englishman born in New York of Danish parents), had brought with it a batch of brand new aircraft from Ranchi; one flight's aircraft were equipped with a single vertical camera in the rear fuselage, those of the other were fitted with an oblique camera. Such was the nature of the surrounding terrain that the ground forces made constant demands for local reconnaissance and there were seldom moments in daylight when at least one of the Squadron's aircraft was not airborne.[75]

On one occasion in the gathering dusk of evening an Indian Hurricane pilot, Sqn Ldr Arjan Singh, spotted a Japanese motorized battalion moving up towards Imphal and radioed his sighting back to his airfield. Soon 33 Hurricane IIC bombers were on their way from Imphal and, with the aid of their landing lights, attacked the column with bombs and cannon. Little could be judged of the effect of the raid, but no attack developed at Imphal; subsequent examination of Japanese documents disclosed that 220 men were killed that evening.

Soon after this event a local Naga succeeded in getting through the Japanese lines to bring details of a Japanese headquarters concealed in the jungle. Having given the exact location to the Hurricane pilots, he then returned to his fellow tribesmen and, at a prearranged time, all in their bright scarlet blankets, stood in a circle around the target. A dozen Hurricanes appeared on the scene, each planting a pair of 250-pounders in the target area. Once again it was only learned later that 100 Japanese had died in the raid.

A Gloster-built Hurricane II, BE193, *flown by Fg Off Buckland at Cox's Bazaar, East Bengal. The steel-mesh airfield surfacing, seen here in 1943, had replaced an earlier kutcha strip which had proved adequate for Hurricane operations but was badly damaged when the first Vultee Vengeance landed on it.* (Photo: *R. Latham, via R. L. Ward, Farnborough)*

Further to the north-east the second Chindit ex-

Not the ideal terrain for a forced landing: a No 28 Squadron Hurricane Tac R Mark IIB flying over the Shan Hills to the north of Imphal in 1943. (Photo: *Mike Dewing)*

A Hurricane IV bomber about to attack a bridge on the Tiddim Road in Burma in 1945. Such targets were constantly bombed by the Hurricanes during the final victorious advance by the Fourteenth Army.

pedition had been under way since December as part of a three-column advance with the Gurkhas, Americans and Chinese, their objective being to cut the main Indaw–Myitkyina railway and to capture Mogaung and Myitkyina itself. Even here two Hurricane squadrons flew in support.

As the monsoon season approached, the Japanese resistance stiffened, and it was not until the beginning of June that the battles at Imphal and Kohima were finally won. At the end of the month the rains broke and only in the nick of time was Mogaung captured on the 20th. Myitkyina did not fall until 3 August. For two months, as 500 inches of rain fell in Assam, operations by the Allied air forces were severely restricted; those by the Japanese came to a complete standstill.

By 1 July Peirse possessed 38 squadrons of fighters, 23 of bombers and 31 other squadrons (transports, flying boats, etc). Of the fighter squadrons 21 flew Hurricanes, eight Spitfires, two Beaufighters, one Thunderbolts and six USAAF squadrons flew P-40s and P-51s. Those with Hurricanes were as listed opposite.

The Final Campaign in Burma

Undertaken in some of the worst fighting terrain in the world, the reconquest of Burma was achieved by the combined advances of IV, XV and XXXIII Corps, the first and third of these constituting the Fourteenth Army commanded by General Sir William Slim; the North Shan States were cleared of the Japanese by the Americans and Chinese.

In the air the Hurricanes were still the most used support aircraft and had long come to be regarded by all and sundry as the most exact air support weapon, even though other recently introduced aircraft possessed higher performance; it was widely felt that this was superfluous in view of the relative absence of Japanese opposition in the air, and the Hurricane remained a firm favourite on account of its ease of maintenance, even under the most primitive conditions—a fact reflected in the extraordinarily high rates of serviceability maintained during this final campaign by a British Commonwealth army during the Second World War.

The first main objective was Mandalay, against which IV and XXXIII Corps moved in outflanking thrusts during January and February following raids by British heavy and medium bombers. During these and subsequent advances the Hurricanes and Thunderbolts operated the "cab rank" tactic, being in radio contact with visual control ve-

In the final stages of the Allied advance south in Burma No 28 Squadron was ordered to keep a constant watch on the numerous river bridges and to report immediately if any were demolished by the retreating Japanese. Shown here is one of the very small number of Tac R Mark IV Hurricanes flown by No 28 Squadron beside the Aya Bridge across the Irrawaddy south of Mandalay in mid-1945. (Photo: *Mike Dewing*)

Sqn No.	*Hurricane Version*	*Base*	*Remarks*
5	Mk IIC/IIDs	Vizagapatam, Madras (Operating from E. Bengal)	Ground attack and bomber escort on Burma front. Sqn Ldr J. M. Cranston
11	Mk IICs	Lanka, India	Day and night "Rhubarbs" on Burma front. Sqn Ldr D. J. T. Sharp. Retained Hurricanes until June 1945
17	Mk IICs	Minneriya, Ceylon	Defence of ports in Ceylon. Sqn Ldr M. C. C. Cotton. Converting to Spitfires
20	Mk IIDs	Chiringa, India	Tactical reconnaissance and anti-tank duties in Burma. Sqn Ldr A. P. Millar. Retained Hurricanes until September 1945
28	Mk IICs	Imphal, India	Tactical reconnaissance on Burma front. Retained Hurricanes until October 1945
30	Mk IIC bombers	Yelahanka, India	Ground attack on Burma front. Sqn Ldr T. A. Stevens
34	Mk IIC bombers	Dergaon, India	Ground attack on Burma front. Sqn Ldr J. A. Bushbridge. Retained Hurricanes until March 1945
42	Mk IIC bombers	Kangla, India	Ground attack on Burma front. Sqn Ldr G. May. Retained Hurricanes until June 1945
60	Mk IIC bombers	Dergaon, India	Ground attack and bomber escort on Burma front. Sqn Ldr R. C. Lindsell. Retained Hurricanes until July 1945
79	Mk IICs	Yelahanka, India	"Rhubarbs" over Burma front. Sqn Ldr D. O. Cunliffe
113	Mk IIC bombers	Palel, India	Ground attack on Burma front. Sqn Ldr Ian Lionel Baber Aitkens. Retained Hurricanes until April 1945
123	Mk IICs	St Thomas Mount, Madras (Operating from E. Bengal)	Bomber and transport escort on Burma front. Sqn Ldr A. J. McGregor
134	Mk IIC bombers	Arkonam, Madras (Operating from E. Bengal)	Patrols on Burma front. Sqn Ldr D. K. McDonald. Converting to Spitfires
135	Mk IICs	Minneriya, Ceylon	Defence of ports in Ceylon. Sqn Ldr L. C. C. Hawkins
146	Mk IIC bombers	Yelahanka, India	Ground attack on Burma front. Sqn Ldr Michael Lawrence O'Leary. Converting to Thunderbolts
258	Mk IICs	Arkonam, India	Bomber and transport escorts on Burma front. Sqn Ldr N. Cameron
261	Mk IIC bombers	Yelahanka, India	Ground attack on Burma front. Sqn Ldr R. E. A. Mason. Converting to Thunderbolts
1 (IAF)	Mk IIBs/IICs	Kangla, India	Ground attack on Burma front, occasional transport escort
4 (IAF)	Tac R Mk IICs	Chiringa, India	Tactical reconnaissance on Burma front
6 (IAF)	Tac R Mk IICs	Chiringa, India	Tactical reconnaissance on Burma front
9 (IAF)	Mk IIC bombers	Palel, India	Ground attack on Burma front, occasional convoy escorts

hicles with the leading troops. Occasionally the Japanese General Kimura would contrive to assemble groups of light tanks with which to counter the advance, but, once detected, they were quickly bombed and cannoned by the ever-present Hurricanes. On 21 March Mandalay fell to XXXIII Corps, IV Corps having swept round from the west to take the important road, rail and river junction of Meiktila 80 miles to the south.

There now followed a pause of about a fortnight while Slim's forces consolidated their gains, winkled out Japanese pockets of resistance in their rear and replenished their supplies of fuel and ammunition. The Hurricane squadrons were still based to the north of Mandalay and most of these were now moved to within 20 miles of the forward Allied positions. By 13 April eight Hurricane squadrons between them fielded 118 Mark IIC bombers and Tac R Mark IICs.

The pause was probably longer than either

A Hurricane Tac R Mark IIC, KZ353 *'G' of No 28 Squadron bearing the light-coloured tail band ordered to be painted on Hurricanes in Burma during the last six months of the War, seen at Meiktila in April 1945.* (Photo: *R. Meadkins, via Sqn Ldr R. C. B. Ashworth)*

Mountbatten or Slim would have wished, for the monsoon would break in six weeks' time and it was essential to have captured Rangoon by then; moreover it was planned to redeploy many elements of the air force in Burma, now commanded by that most experienced New Zealander, Air Chief Marshal Sir Keith Park, in readiness for Operation *Zipper*, the planned invasion of Malaya due to open not later than September. The final advance south, together with a co-ordinated advance down the west coast of Burma by XV Corps, thus became a race against time to Rangoon.

The achievement and spirit of the RAF squadrons during the final weeks of the campaign may be appreciated from No. 20 Squadron's account of its operations in April 1945. This squadron, it will be recalled, was one of the first to be equipped with 40-mm anti-tank guns in Hurricane IIDs late in 1943; since then Mark IVs, similarly armed and with additional armour, had also joined the squadron.

"On 13 April, 1945, the squadron began operations from Thedaw airfield in partnership with No. 28 Tactical Reconnaissance Squadron, also with Hurricanes. For the first few days the taxi strip was used (for take-off) until the engineers, with the aid of 3,000 coolies, completed repairs on the bomb-damaged main runway. The eastern sector, in the Heho area, provided the squadron with a happy hunting ground, the game being mostly motor transport. To the south army air support was given to the 5th Division in its rapid advance on Rangoon via Pyinmana and Toungoo. South of Pyinmana a Japanese convoy of about 40 vehicles was caught trying to make a dash for it. However timely intervention by the squadron accounted for 17 flamers and many damaged; discouraging to say the least for the Japanese troops in the area. To the west, river craft, pontoons, rafts, etc, on the Irrawaddy came in for the Squadron's attention and many successful strikes were made in this area.

"Within two weeks our forward troops in the south had advanced beyond our Hurricanes' range. It was therefore decided to move the squadron to Tennant airstrip at Toungoo, whence Pegu and the Sittang ferry—the main escape route from Burma—would be within our range. The squadron, with the minimum of kit, landed at Tennant on the 28th. In spite of various discomforts experienced at our new location, and what appeared to be colossal administrative disorganization, the Squadron became operational immediately and was rewarded with excellent targets in the Pegu area. It became apparent that the Japanese intended to retreat from Pegu and cross the Sittang by ferry and, as a result, presented the Hurricane IIDs and IVs with ideal targets. The Mark IVs concentrated on the river craft and pontoons on the Sittang while the IIDs dealt with the resulting bottleneck of motor transport on the road leading to the west bank of the ferry. At the end of one day (30 April) the squadron had accounted for 46 flamers and very many vehicles damaged.

A Hurricane IIC, LE787*, used for bomber affiliation in India to assist in training RAF Liberator crews in 1944–45.* (Photo: *via Sqn Ldr R. C. B. Ashworth)*

"On the 30th the squadron received a signal from IV Corps HQ: 'Thank you for your magnificent efforts yesterday on the Mopalin Road. Even more of the little swine will have to walk and its still quite a longish way to Japan.'

"The fall of Rangoon is imminent and it is felt that the squadron's operations in the last four months have, in the air, contributed to this achievement."

On what more apt note could any account of the Hurricane's part in the war against Japan end?

14

PEACEFUL SKIES

From the early months of the Second World War Hurricanes engaged in duties not directly involving combat with the enemy—an anomaly perhaps for an aircraft whose very excellence had so recently been assessed in terms of performance, manoeuvrability and hitting power. Such, however, were the numbers of Hurricanes being produced early in 1940 that it was felt that some could be spared for training young pilots who would soon be needed to man the new fighter squadrons then being formed. The normal procedure hitherto adopted had been for trainee pilots, after completing a short course of flying on two-seat trainers with a fairly respectable performance, such as the excellent Miles Master and North American Harvard, to go straight to their operational squadrons, where not only would they make their first solo on their new fighter but learn the hard way of the finer points of gunnery, combat tactics, scrambles, emergency procedures and so on. Not only did this waste much of the squadrons' time but tended to give the young pilot a very narrow idea of operational flying.

At the beginning of the war Nos. 11 and 12 Groups, Fighter Command, introduced Group Pools at which half-trained pilots assembled and were given a short operational conversion course on the aircraft of the squadrons to which they were likely to be posted. Because these Pools transcended the bounds of responsibility between Fighter and Training Commands, No. 5 Operational Training Unit was established in February 1940 at Aston Down in Gloucestershire, with Hurricanes, Defiants and Blenheims, to take over from No. 11 Group Pool at Andover; then came No. 6 OTU at Sutton Bridge in March (replacing No. 12 Group Pool) with Hurricanes, Masters and Battles, and finally—for the time being—No. 7 OTU at Hawarden with Hurricanes, Spitfires and Masters. These OTUs were later renumbered 55, 56 and 57.

When Hurricanes started being used by these OTUs discarded Mark Is were delivered (with fabric wings and Watts two-blade wooden propellers) as being better than nothing. Pilots were given about 40 hours' flying experience and were instructed—by example rather than lecture room theory—in the rudiments of combat tactics and operational procedures. The new pilots would thus arrive on the operational squadrons with the confidence that they could now put a polish on their *applied* flying in the environment in which they would be fighting. Later, in the most critical stages of the Battle of Britain, such was the shortage of replacement pilots that many a newcomer arrived on his first squadron with no more than twenty hours on Hurricanes at the OTU; a year previously he'd have had none.

Operational training constituted the Hurricane's most widespread rôle among its second line duties throughout the war, continuing in Britain until 1944, when the last Hurricane OTU (No. 55 at Annan, Dumfriesshire) was closed. There were, moreover, two main Hurricane OTUs in the Middle East, No. 71 (ME) OTU for fighter and fighter-bomber training, normally based at Ismailia, and later No. 74 (ME) OTU at Aqir in Palestine for tactical reconnaissance training; and there were at one time three OTUs for training Hurricane pilots in India, the overseas units ultimately receiving late-standard Hurricane IVs. Another important overseas training source of Hurricane pilots was the Rhodesian Air Training Group, which flew Hurricanes from 1942 onwards.

Also in the training rôle, though not for preparing future Hurricane pilots, a new category of unit came into being for training air gunners (and pilots) of RAF heavy bombers in the skills of defending themselves from intercepting fighters. In the early days of the war such training for the bomber crews was provided by operational fighter squadrons, perhaps during a period of "rest"; known as Fighter Affiliation Exercises this work did not particularly appeal to the fighter pilots, who, in spasms of over-indulgence, would carry out most unorthodox manoeuvres, much to the alarm of the bomber crews, who would derive little training benefit in any case. In due course Bomber Defence Flights came into being for such training; the Hurricane pilots usually possessed a fair amount of operational experience and were briefed to carry out standard forms of attack.

The Meteorological Reconnaissance Squadrons and Flights

Since before the war the RAF undertook a small amount of weather reconnaissance, but with the outbreak of hostilities and the need for raid planning the work took on much greater importance. Nowhere was there a greater need than in the Middle East, where tropical storms—often of considerable violence—could develop very quickly.

Unit	*Usual Location*	*Date*	*Hurricane Version(s)*
No. 71 (ME) Operational Training Unit	Ismailia, Egypt	1941–45	Mks Is, PR Is, IIAs, IIBs, IICs, IIDs, IVs and Xs.
No. 73 (ME) Operational Training Unit	Abu Sueir, Egypt	1943–44	Mks I and IICs
No. 74 (ME) Operational Training Unit	Aqir, Palestine	1942–45	Mks I, PR Is, IIBs, IICs and Tac R Mks
No. 75 (ME) Operational Training Unit	Gianaclis, Egypt	1943–44	Mk IICs
No. 79 (ME) Operational Training Unit	Lakatamia, Cyprus	1944–45	Mk IICs
No. 1 Middle East Training School	El Ballah, Egypt	1942–43	Mks Is and IICs
No. 5 Middle East Training School	Shallufa, Egypt	1943–44	Mks IICs and IVs
No. 4 Flying Training School	Habbaniya, Iraq	1941	Mk Is
Advanced Bombing and Gunnery School	El Ballah, Egypt	1943	Mk Is
No. 1 (ME) Check and Conversion Unit	Bilbeis, Egypt	1944	Mks Is and IIBs
No. 2 (ME) Check and Conversion Unit	Palestine	1944	Mk Is
No. 1675 Heavy Conversion Unit	Lydda, Palestine	1944	Mks IIBs and IICs
Air Fighting School	Bilbeis, Egypt	1942	Mk Is
No. 23 Anti-aircraft Co-operation Flight	Foggia and Pomigliano, Italy	1944–45	Mk IVs
No. 26 Anti-aircraft Co-operation Flight	Palestine	1942–45	Mks I, IIB and IIC
Air Defence Co-operation Flight	Bilbeis, Egypt	1942	Mk Is

As RAF Bomber Command heavy bombers began increasingly to be employed in daylight raids over the Continent the need arose to provide crew training in tactics to counter enemy daylight interceptors, and Hurricanes and Spitfires of newly-formed Bomber Defence Training Flights flown by experienced pilots undertook regular bomber affiliation work, a task previously performed on an opportunity basis by operational fighter squadrons whenever they could spare aircraft and pilots. Seen here are, top, a Hurricane IIC of No 1682 Bomber Defence Training Flight at Enstone in mid-1944 and, below, LF537 *of No 1687 Bomber Defence Training Flight.* (Photos: *Upper, Sgt D. Melville; both via Sqn Ldr R. C. B. Ashworth)*

The first Hurricanes to be used solely for weather reconnaissance were those issued to No. 1413 Flight based at Lydda, Palestine, in August 1943—taking over from Gladiators. Operating with detachments at Rayak, Aqir and Damascus, the first Hurricanes were weary Mark Is (including *V4388*, *V6175*, *W9155* and *Z7003*), but the following year, as the weather reporting network expanded, other Flights took on specially prepared Hurricane Met Mark IICs, usually with guns removed and fitted with a psychrometer strut extending from the starboard side of the fuselage below the break-out panel. The other Flights included No. 1412 at Khartoum, No. 1414 at Mogadishu and Eastleigh in East Africa, and No. 1415 at Habbaniya. The normal routine for these Flights was to fly twice-daily "met climbs" to a pre-briefed height, usually about 30,000 feet, but sometimes as high as 35,000 feet—rather a lot to ask of a veteran Hurricane encumbered with a tropical filter.

Hurricanes continued with this work until after the war and in September 1945 Nos. 1413 and 1415 exchanged their Hurricanes for Spitfires, and the other Flights were disbanded. In India and the Far East the Met Flights continued to fly Hurricanes until late in 1946.

In Britain Hurricanes were widely used for weather reconnaissance duties, an example being provided by No. 521 (Weather Calibration) Squadron, based at Langham and elsewhere. New Hurricane Met Mark IICs were received in 1944 and the customary twice-daily met climbs continued until shortly before VE-day.

Ground Defence Equipment Calibration

Since the early days of gun predictors and "sound locators" aircraft had been flown to provide the gun crews with calibration data, and until 1942 this chore had been an extra-mural activity by any conveniently located fighter or bomber unit. Such an expedient had come to be tolerated simply because the equipment was of short range and therefore the aircraft would be absent from operational availability for short periods only—and it *did* permit some officially sanctioned low flying on occasion!

The AMES Type 1 (CH) radar, however, possessed ranges of more than 100 miles and attempts were made to calibrate this equipment using fighter aircraft, and when the PPI displays came into widespread use (with the phenomena known as anomal-

The majority of Hurricanes that carried 'invasion stripes' in June 1944 were second-line aircraft like this unarmed Mark IIC, LF380, *of No 83 Operational Training Unit; it bore the unit codes FI-D.* (Photo: *Sqn Ldr R. C. B. Ashworth)*

A Hurricane Mark IIC, MW339, *of the Air Despatch Letter Service (without 'invasion stripes' and with guns removed). Note the ventral blade aerial, seen increasingly on Hurricanes late in the War.* (Photo: *Sqn Ldr R. C. B. Ashworth)*

ous propagation—the appearance of spurious echoes caused by some atmospheric conditions) demands for calibration became frequent and required long flights involving very accurate navigation. Accordingly several specialist calibration units came into existence.

The first such unit was No. 116 (Calibration) Squadron, which, having formed at Hatfield on 17 February, 1941, moved to Hendon in April and received Hurricane Is in November (among them *V7136*, *V7192* and *AG205*). After a period of work with the Observer Corps and the anti-aircraft gun defences the pilots started work calibrating the early CHL (Chain Home Low) radars on the East Coast and later in 1942 the CHEL (Extra-Low) and Type 7 radars; after the Normandy landings mobile detachments went to the Continent to assist in calibrating the mobile Type 15 radars which accompanied the advancing British and Canadian armies.

Another Hurricane-equipped calibration squadron was No. 527 Squadron, whose Hurricane Is and IIBs, usually equipped with 44-gallon long-range tanks, flew as detachments at Sutton Bridge, Coltishall, Castle Camps, Snailwell and Digby to provide oversea calibration of the CH Type I radars at Stenigot, West Beckham, Stoke Holy Cross, High Street, Bawdsey, Bromley and Canewdon.

Loading despatches and Press material into the underwing auxiliary tanks of an armed ADLS Hurricane IIC on a Continental airfield in 1944 (note the addition of 'invasion stripes' under the wings). (Photo: *via Richard Ward, Canterbury)*

Other Wartime Duties

Among the lesser-known tasks undertaken by Hurricanes towards the end of the war was the simulation of battle conditions during combined operations exercises in preparation for the D-day landings in Normandy. In April 1943 No. 1441 (Combined Operations) Flight, which had been flying Mustangs and Lysanders on "army cooperation" work during battle training in Scotland, was expanded into No. 516 (Combined Operations) Squadron at Dundonald. Hurricane IICs started being delivered to the squadron in November that year and participated in numerous assault exercises at Newton Bay, Oban and Inveraray in the west of Scotland, laying smoke screens and making simulated strafing runs over the landing beaches. By March the following year tactical reconnaissance training sorties were being flown with vertical and oblique cameras; in one of the many rehearsals at Troon for the Normandy landings a low-flying Tac R Hurricane IIC (*LF534*) crashed into a landing craft lying offshore. This training continued after the Normandy landings until December 1944, but with the likelihood of further major seaborne landings in Europe receding the squadron was then disbanded and the Hurricanes disposed of.

While Hurricanes were used in the communications rôle by numerous operational units (such as the photographic reconnaissance units and squadrons which, after the Hurricane had been withdrawn from photographic sorties, still employed them to carry the exposed film and prints to various headquarters), they were also flown in small numbers by established communications flights and squadrons. Nos. 24 and 173 Squadrons at Hendon and Heliopolis respectively maintained a few such elderly Hurricanes simply for use by Staff Officers to visit units within their sphere of command when such visits did not merit the formality of conventional transport.

On the other hand one or two communications units were formed in 1944 exclusively with Hurricanes, among them the Air Despatch Letter Service (ADLS) and the Belgian Communications Flight. The former came into being at Hendon at the time

The only photo so far traced of a Hurricane in the markings of the French Aéronavale. *Believed to be a Canadian Sea Hurricane XIIA (ex-Fleet Air Arm and tropicalised), it was displayed in Paris shortly after the end of the War.* (Photo: *via Sqn Ldr R. C. B. Ashworth)*

*Hurricanes of the Irish Air Corps. The top picture depicts '93' (ex-*P5176*) a very early Canadian-built aircraft which force-landed in Eire during the War. (*Photos: *Irish Air Corps, Ref Nos D77/0 and C39/0 and, bottom, Sqn Ldr R. C. B. Ashworth)*

of the Normandy landings and used about a dozen Hurricane IICs (most of which retained their guns) to carry important despatches between the United Kingdom and airfields in France and Belgium; in due course these aircraft also came to be used to fly up-to-date Press despatches home from the battle fronts, the steadily increasing flow of material being carried in the underwing drop tanks and in a compartment below the radio bay just behind the cockpit. After a couple of the Hurricanes were fired on by American fighters, most of them were painted in the familiar "invasion stripes".

The Belgian Communications Flight also came into being late in 1944 to provide a fast despatch service between London and Brussels once the Belgian capital had been liberated. Two of these aircraft survived the war and one is preserved today in the *Musée de l'Armée et d'Histoire Militaire* at Brussels (*LF345*).

*Hurricane IIC for Portugal. The distortion to the radio mast is caused by the propeller of another Hurricane beyond. Though not fitted here, most aircraft were delivered with tropical filters. (*Photo: *Hawker Aircraft Ltd., Neg No HGP/G/41)*

*One of the Iranian Hurricane IIC single-seat trainers, 2-13, pictured at Langley shortly before delivery. (*Photo: *Hawker Aircraft Ltd, Neg No HPG2)*

The Royal Aircraft Establishment's veteran Hurricane II, Z3687, *fitted with the AWA laminar-flow wing, seen at Farnborough in 1948. (*Photo: *Author's Collection)*

The two Iranian two-seat Hurricane IIC trainers; above, 2-32 *as originally flown with both cockpits open, and below,* 2-31 *in the configuration the aircraft were delivered with an adapted Tempest hood over the rear cockpit. (*Photos: *Hawker Aircraft Ltd)*

A genuine Battle of Britain survivor, L1592, *as it was displayed at Horseguards' Parade shortly after the end of the War. It has since been restored and is today on display at the Science Museum in London. (*Photo: *A. J. Todd)*

Ceremony at Langley on completion of 'The Last of the Many' Hurricane IIC PZ865 *in 1944, seen with the Company's Hart* G-ABMR *which had been used by the Hawker test pilots as an air taxi throughout the War. (*Photo: *Hawker Aircraft Ltd)*

Hurricanes in Foreign Colours

Apart from the Hurricanes sold or supplied before the Second World War, many others came to acquire the markings of other nations by one means or other. As already recounted a large number of Hurricanes had been supplied to the Soviet Union and India during the war, many of these surviving into the post-war years, as did some of those supplied to Egypt, Yugoslavia and Turkey. The French *Aéronavale* acquired about 15 Sea Hurricane IICs and XIIs in 1944 and 1945 (probably in North Africa, as all were fitted with tropical filters) and a few of these remained airworthy until early 1946.

The Irish Air Corps on the other hand obtained at least 19 Hurricane Is and IICs by various means during the war, sufficient to equip its No. 1 Squadron at Baldonnel. At least one Hurricane force landed in Eire during the Battle of Britain and was followed soon after by two others; these became *93* (ex-Canadian Mark I, *P5176*), *94* (ex-*Z2832*) and *95*. Lengthy negotiations with the British Government for the return of the aircraft resulted in *94* and *95* being sent back in exchange for three earlier production Hurricane Is, these becoming *103*, *104* and *105* (ex-V7540). A fourth aircraft, *106* (ex-*Z4037*) was delivered to Baldonnel from RAF Newtownards in 1943, and thereafter seven Mark Is and six Mark IICs followed in 1943 and 1944,[76] some surviving in service until 1947.

With the end of the war Hawker Aircraft Limited returned to its established quest for overseas markets. The first customer, however, who came to purchase Hurricanes after the war did so as the result of wartime Government-to-Government negotiations under which it was agreed that Portugal would acquire aircraft in return for the use of military and naval bases in the Azores (a concession arising out of a 600-year-old pact between Edward III of England and King Ferdinand of Portugal). From the stocks of late-series tropical Hurricane IICs at maintenance units the Air Ministry released 50 aircraft. These were returned to the Hawker factory at Langley, where the engines were exchanged for Merlin 22s, most tropical filters were removed and 40 airworthy aeroplanes prepared for delivery to Portugal, together with a large stock of spares. These were shipped to Portela de Sacavem, Lisbon, and subsequently served at Aerial Base No. 3, Tancos, and with the Lisbon Fighter Defence Flight until about 1951.

Persia, whose purchase of Hurricanes had been interrupted by the war in 1940, resumed its interest after the end of hostilities. To complement ten Hurricanes which had been transferred to the Persian Air Force during the war, 16 Mark IIC single-seaters and two two-seaters were purchased in 1946–47. All were to be used as fighter-trainers by the Advanced Fighter Training Group of the Persian Air Force's Flying Training School at Doshan Teppeh.

Brief moment of reflected glory when the Author was asked to 'start' the Kelmsley Air Trophy Race in 1949. 'Last of the Many' G-AMAU *being flown by Gp Capt Peter Townsend in the blue and gold racing colours of HRH the Princess Margaret in South Wales. (Author's Collection)*

'The Last of the Many' G-AMAU *at another post-War race meeting; colour scheme on this occasion was dark blue and white with gold spinner. (*Photo: *Author's Collection)*

The development of the Hurricane two-seaters was particularly interesting as it stemmed from a project started at Kingston in 1940 intended to evolve a replacement for the Miles Master and North American Harvard (but was terminated during the Battle of Britain)—a scheme in which Persia had also expressed an interest at the time. The design incorporated some of the work carried out during the war in attempts to produce a Hurricane fighter with a single-piece blown cockpit canopy and with cut-down rear fuselage. In the two-seater a second cockpit with dual controls and basic flight instrument panel was inserted behind the existing pilot's cockpit, the radio being excluded. A strengthened pylon and bulkhead were incorporated between the cockpits and it was initially intended to omit canopies from both cockpits, but early flight tests showed that at speeds over 280 mph the occupant of the rear seat suffered such considerable turbulence from the airflow round all the paraphernalia in front of him, and an ingenious adaptation of a Hawker Tempest's sliding canopy was added to the rear cockpit. This was eventually accepted despite results of hood jettison trials, which disclosed the hood's tendency to foul the fin and rudder. The first of the two aircraft was flown by Bill Humble on 27 September, 1946, and both examples were delivered to Doshan Teppeh in

Fine flying view of G-AMAU *rounding a turning point during one of the post-War air races.* (Photo: *Author's Collection)*

1947, possessing a top speed of 320 mph at 21,500 feet and an all-up weight of 8,140 lb (without armament but with tropical filter).

The Surviving Hurricanes

Hurricanes continued to fly in slowly dwindling numbers with the RAF until the end of 1951, although none could be regarded as much more than a "hack". Certainly being the subjects of gratuitous maintenance, they remained serviceable only in the broadest sense! In the words of one user/owner, "I find I have to impose a steadily reducing top speed restriction on the old bird, until I suppose it will coincide with the stalling speed; as the latter seems intent on increasing almost daily, it won't be long before she taxies at high speed off the end of the runway."

One early Hurricane II, *Z3687*, survived at the Royal Aircraft Establishment for a number of years, specially modified with an Armstrong Whitworth laminar flow wing. Painted white overall, filled and polished to high gloss, this aeroplane was used for investigation of airflow behaviour over such wings; even the wing roundels were omitted in the interests of a smooth finish. This old aircraft was presumably scrapped when it ran out of flying hours.

Two examples have, however, remained airworthy since the day they were built. One, *LF363*, has been preserved by the Royal Air Force, having served with No. 309 (Polish) Squadron and an OTU, and flown as part of the Waterbeach Station Flight until 1954, now constitutes part of the RAF Battle of Britain Memorial Flight, its annual allowance of flying hours being carefully allocated to favoured air displays.

More famous by far is *PZ865*, the very last Hurricane completed from new by Hawker Aircraft Limited in 1944. Purchased by the manufacturer from the Air Ministry contract it was christened "*The Last of the Many*". Until the end of the war it was used as a convenient taxi by the Hawker pilots,

'The Last of the Many' G-AMAU *painted in the spurious markings* P2619 *US-B of No 56 Squadron for the filming of ANGELS ONE-FIVE in the 1950s.* (Photo: *Author's Collection)*

After fifteen years of energetic flying the last Hurricane PZ865 *returned to Hawkers for a thorough overhaul amounting to restoration. It is shown here in the maintenance hangar at Dunsfold, Surrey. (*Photo: *Hawker Siddeley Aviation Ltd)*

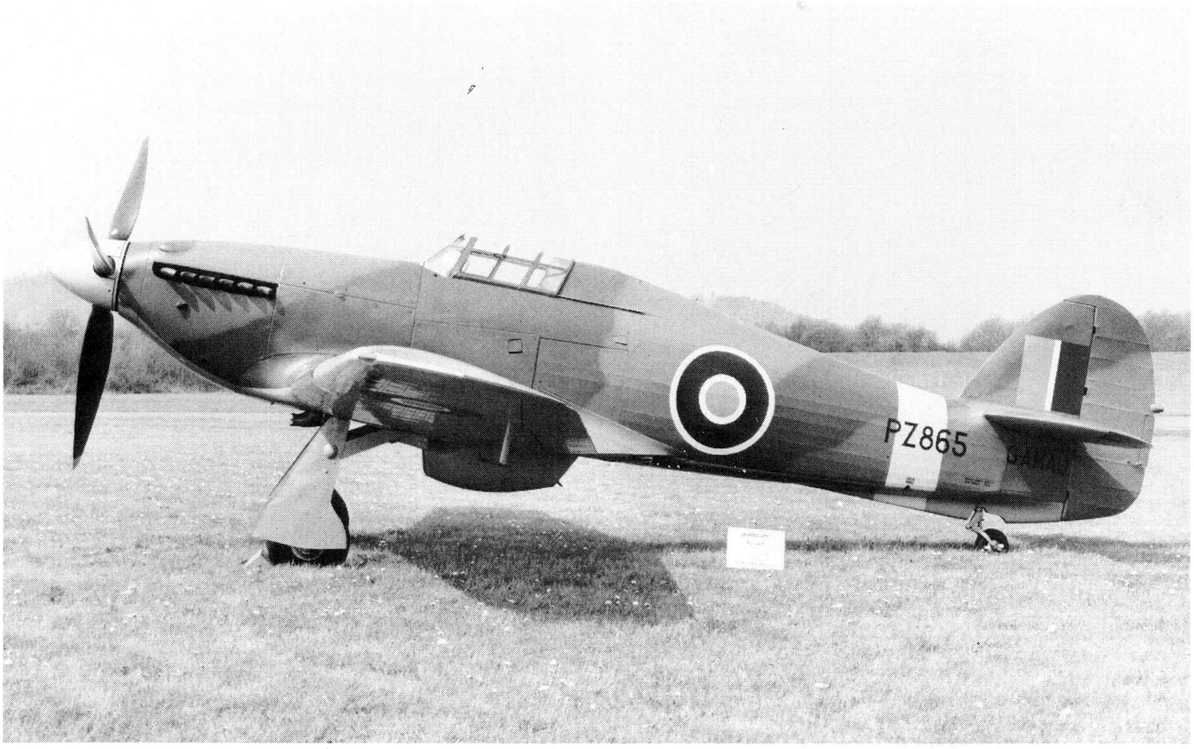

PZ865 *as it emerged in 1961 after its extensive facelift. The military serial had been restored to its conventional prominence while the civil registration letters were relegated to obscurity below the tailplane. Concessions to modernity included a whip radio aerial and individual exhaust stubs. Armament had long since been removed.* (Photo: *Hawker Aircraft Ltd)*

Generally referred to as the 'last Hurricane held on RAF charge', LF363 *was returned to Hawker for general restoration shortly after the War and emerged in all-over silver finish and with guns removed. (*Photo: Hawker Aircraft Ltd*)*

One of the most accurately and beautifully restored of all RAF Hurricanes is the Mark I carrying the markings P2617 *AF-T of No 607 (County of Durham) Squadron, Royal Auxiliary Air Force, seen here at Abingdon on 14th June 1968. (*Photo: *R. L. Ward, Neg Ref Q21/30)*

and was then placed on the civil register as *G-AMAU*. It participated in numerous post-war air displays and was raced on several occasions carrying the racing colours of HRH The Princess Margaret by Group Captain Peter Townsend. It remained a member of Hawker's flying museum (which in time came to include a Cygnet, Tomtit, Hart and Sea Fury) and, repainted from time to time in spurious markings, provided flying sequences in a number of films, including *Hawks in the Sun, Angels One Five* and *The Battle of Britain*; it attended a Vintage Aircraft Rally in 1952, the Royal Aeronautical Society Garden Party in 1953, the National Air Races (flown by Don Lucey) in 1954, and the RAE Jubilee (flown by Bill Bedford) in 1955.

Major overhaul and restoration were completed in 1960 when it was restored to its original paint scheme, and in 1961 it undertook "chase plane" duties during the flight development of the German Sea Fury target tug and, on account of its unusually wide speed range (in those days), was employed as chase plane during the early transition trials of the Hawker P 1127 vertical-take-off prototypes (later to become the Kestrel and Harrier). Today it continues to fly alongside *LF363* as a member of the RAF Battle of Britain Memorial Flight.

Very recently a superbly restored Hurricane has been flown carrying the serial number *P3069* and the squadron code letters of the wartime No. 401 Squadron, RCAF, *YO–A*. Variously described as a Mark I and IIC, the aircraft displays the 12 gun-ports of a Mark IIB or Canadian Hurricane. Owned by the Canadian Warplane Heritage, it is currently the only airworthy Hurricane in North America,

Hurricane Version	*Serial No. Displayed*	*Location and Remarks*
Mark I	*L1592*	London Science Museum; ex-No. 56 and 615 Squadrons; not airworthy.
Mark I	*P2617*	Bicester, Oxon; ex-No. 607 Sqn; not airworthy. Now displayed in R.A.F. Museum, Hendon.
Mark I	*V6846*	Patna, India; ex-Nos. 3, 17, 87, 242 and 312 Squadrons, RAF; not airworthy.
Mark I	*HC452*	Vesivehmaa, Finland; Finnish Hurricane; not airworthy.
Mark I	*Z7015*	Sea Hurricane IA(?); Old Warden (Shuttleworth Collection); not airworthy.
Mark II	*9539*	Belgrade, Yugoslavia; Yugoslav Hurricane; believed possibly airworthy.
Mark II	*P3069*	Canadian Warplane Heritage. Possibly from Canadian-built aircraft; fully airworthy.
Mark IIC	*LF738*	Biggin Hill, Kent; ex-No. 22 OTU; not airworthy.
Mark IIC	*LF686*	Colerne, Wiltshire; not airworthy.
Mark IIC	*LF363*	Coltishall, Norfolk; RAF Battle of Britain Memorial Flight; fully airworthy.
Mark IIC	*PZ865*	RAF Battle of Britain Memorial Flight; "Last of the Many"; fully airworthy.
Mark IIC	*LF751*	Stanmore, Middlesex; ex-No. 24 OTU; not airworthy.
Mark IIC	*LF345*	Brussels, Belgium; ex-Belgian Communications Flight; not airworthy.
Mark IIC (Tac R)	*LD619 (5285)*	Saxonwold Museum, Johannesburg, South Africa; believed not airworthy.
Canadian Mark XII	*5584*	War Museum, Ottawa, Canada; Canadian-built aircraft; believed not airworthy. At least two other aircraft being restored to flying condition.

The Hurricane IIC LF363 *as it has appeared at air displays during the past twenty years as part of the Battle of Britain Memorial Flights.* Left, above, *as the late Douglas Bader's aircraft on No 242 Squadron, displayed at Wethersfield on 24th May 1969 (Neg Ref X13/21).* Left, below, *as above but with the code letters corrected in style, displayed at Yeovilton on 5th August 1978 (Neg Ref B75/7/13).* Above, *in the night fighter markings of No 85 Squadron (Neg Ref C165/6/36; all photos by courtesy of R. L. Ward, Farnborough)*

although recent reports suggest that a number of other Hurricanes will complete restoration in the near future in Britain, America and elsewhere.

In conclusion a list is shown opposite of Hurricanes believed to have survived at least into the 1980s. Unfortunately it cannot be claimed to be complete (in most instances on account of conflicting reports of aircraft being either scrapped or awaiting restoration). It is to be hoped that, by the time the fiftieth anniversary of the Battle of Britain falls due in 1990 there will once more be a sizeable number of Hurricanes straining to go aloft to recall those years of great endeavour and achievement.

15

ANATOMY OF A STORM

The Hurricane Described—General

The Hawker Hurricane was a single-engine, single-seat, low-wing monoplane powered by a Rolls-Royce Merlin supercharged V-12 liquid-cooled in-line engine. It possessed retractable undercarriage and was of all-metal construction with fabric-covered rear fuselage and flying control surfaces. (Early aircraft also featured fabric-covered outer wings.) Gun armament was carried in or under the outer wings.

Fuselage

Structure of the fuselage comprised a metal primary framework of round tubes, swaged to square section at their ends and bolted together to form a box structure whose sides formed Warren trusses; additional strength in the rear fuselage was provided by diagonal wires between the tubular joints, each with screw tensioners. In the nose of the aircraft the side structure was modified to triangular part-truss with four main engine bearer pads on the upper components. Welded to the forward primary structure were a number of thump-stud sockets with which fasteners for the external metal panels engaged. Attached to the rear fuselage primary framework were 11 secondary metal frames, tapering rearwards, into which were slotted closely spaced multiple stringers; on to these were attached doped fabric. Longerons as such were not included, the longtidunal strength being provided by the fore-and-aft members of the Warren truss primary structure. An armoured bulkhead was located forward of the cockpit and a sheet of armour was provided for the pilot's protection immediately behind his seat. An emergency break-out panel was provided in the starboard side of the fuselage below the sliding cockpit canopy.

Wings

The all-metal wing centre-section comprised a basic two-spar structure attached to the lower members of the fuselage primary Warren truss components. Fuel and oil tanks were accommodated between the spars and (on the port side) forward of the front mainspar. Wheelbays were located in the lower part of the centre-section between the mainspars. The landing flaps were hinge-mounted on the lower rear face of the outer portions of the centre-section rear-spar. Metal skinning, with radiused fillet joint, was integral with that of the front fuselage.

The outer wings comprised a two-spar structure with diagonal Warren truss between the spars and primary nose frames for the leading edge. Secondary chordwise metal frames provided the aerofoil section, with metal skin attached. In later cannon-armed aircraft the Warren truss was discarded and replaced by secondary (intermediate) spanwise spars so as to provide unrestricted gun bays and magazine stowage. A pair of strongpoint attachment lugs were provided on front and rear mainspars inboard of the gun bays to which could be bolted auxiliary fuel tank pylons or bomb racks. On later Mark IIs and all Mark IVs four further strongpoints were provided under the spars to which a contoured pack fairing, each with four rails for rocket projectiles, could be attached. The ailerons were hinged to the rear face of the rear spar.

Powerplant

The Rolls-Royce Merlin was a supercharged (single-stage on Marks I–III engines, two-stage thereafter) upright V-12 liquid-cooled in-line engine. The exhaust manifolds comprised stub-ejectors grouped for pairs of cylinders. Each cylinder incorporated two plugs and four valves, the overhead camshafts being driven at the rear. The propeller reduction gear, located at the front, transmitted power to a splined universal propeller shaft capable of accommodating Rotol, de Havilland or Hamilton Standard three-blade metal variable-pitch or constant-speed propellers. On Rotol propeller-equipped aircraft the constant-speed unit was located at the front of the engine. The coolant header tank (water-with-methanol) was located in the upper starboard side of the nose, and the radiator in a fairing on the aircraft's centreline under the wing centre-section immediately aft of the landing gear wheel recesses. The engine oil reservoir tank was located in the port wing centre-section. Carburettor air was introduced by means of up-draught trunk from an intake fairing below and to the rear of the engine.

Landing Gear

The mainwheel undercarriage comprised single-oleo pneumatic units mounting the wheels inboard and hinged at the outer extremities of the wing centre-section to retract inwards, being drawn upwards by an hydraulically operated jack. A shortening drag strut drew the main oleo aft through approximately seven degrees to allow the wheels to clear the mainspar during retraction into the wheel-bays. Lockheed or Dunlop wheel brakes were provided on the mainwheels and metal fairing panels, attached to the mainwheel oleos, enclosed the landing gear (except for a segment of tyre) when retracted. On all but the very early Mark I Hurricanes the tailwheel, comprising an oleo-sprung levered-suspension unit, was non-retractable.

Equipment

Radio equipment (VHF transmitter/receiver) was located behind a detachable panel in the starboard side of the fuselage immediately aft of the cockpit; access to the aerial mast was through a breakable patch below the mast on the port side. IFF equipment, when incorporated in northern Europe, was located in the radio bay, its aerial wires being passed out through the sides of the rear fuselage to the leading edges of the tailplane.

The pilot's oxygen cylinder was mounted below and behind the cockpit, and a first aid kit in the lower port side of the fuselage above the wing walkway behind a break-in panel.

Gun armament was pneumatically cocked, and fired by a two-position ("safe-fire") button on the pilot's control column. Gun aiming (except on early aircraft which had ring-and-bead sights) was by means of reflector sight; most aircraft retained the bead foresight even when equipped with the reflector sight. Very late production Hurricane Mark IICs incorporated stadiametric ranging and in these the bead foresight was always omitted. A camera "gun" was located in the starboard wing inboard of the normal gun armament and exposed automatically when the guns were fired.

Geometric Data, Weights and Loading

HURRICANE PROTOTYPE

Geometric Data. Wing span 40 ft 0 in.; overall length 31 ft 6 in.; maximum height (propeller vertical) 13 ft 6 in.

Weights. Aircraft tare weight (with 18 gallons of coolant) 4,129 lb. Pilot and parachute 200 lb. Armament ballast 400 lb. Instruments 52 lb. Fuel (107.5 gallons at 7.7 lb/gallon) 828 lb. Oil (7.0 gallons at 9 lb/gallon) 63 lb. Aircraft Normal Loaded Weight 5,672 lb.

Loadings. Wing loading at Aircraft Normal Loaded Weight (5,672 lb), 22 lb/sq ft. Power loading (take-off at 5,672 lb), 5.5 lb/bhp.

HURRICANE MARK I

Geometric Data. Wing span 40 ft 0 in.; overall length 31 ft 4 in.; maximum height (Watts propeller, blades vertical) 13 ft 2 in. (Rotol propeller, top blade vertical 12 ft 11½ in.) *Wing*. Root chord 8 ft 1 in.; tip chord 3 ft 11¼ in.; gross wing area 258.0 sq ft; aspect ratio 6.2; wing incidence +2 degrees; dihedral 3.5 degrees on datum; sweep-back 3 degrees on front spar; aileron span 7 ft 9 in.; aileron root chord 1 ft 7¼ in.; aileron tip chord 10.5 in.; aileron area (both) 19.64 sq ft; aileron movement 22 degrees up, 21 degrees down; landing flap centre-section span (each) 4 ft 6¾ in.; landing flap outboard section span (each) 6 ft 4 in.; landing flap chord (constant), 1 ft 2¾ in.; total landing flap area 25.11 sq ft; landing flap movement, 80 degrees down. *Tail*. Tailplane span 11 ft 0 in.; tailplane root chord 4 ft 2in.; tailplane area 19.6 sq ft; tailplane incidence 1.5 degrees; elevator span 11 ft 0 in.; elevator area (including tabs) 13.65 sq ft; elevator movement 28.5 degrees up, 25.5 degrees down; elevator tab range 23 degrees up and down. Fin height 3 ft 1⅞ in.; maximum fin chord 3 ft 7 in.; fin area 8.82 sq ft; rudder height (early aircraft) 5 ft 11¼ in.; (modified aircraft) 6 ft 5⅜ in.; maximum rudder chord 2 ft 3⅜ in.; rudder area (early aircraft) 12.68 sq ft, (modified aircraft) 13.06 sq ft; rudder movement 28 degrees left and right. *Undercarriage*. Track 7 ft 7 in.; mainwheels 800 × 10 in.; ground angle 10° 19′; propeller ground clearance (static, thrust line horizontal) 11 in.

Weights. Merlin II version. Aircraft tare weight (with 18 gallons coolant) 4,743 lb; pilot and parachute 200 lb; eight Browning guns and accessories, 212 lb; case and link chutes, 9 lb; ammunition and boxes (2,660 rounds) 202 lb; instruments and gunsight 79.5 lb; G.45 gun camera, 9 lb; pyrotechnics 48.5 lb; oxygen equipment 15 lb; First Aid 3 lb; radio 57 lb; fuel (77 gallons at 7.5 lb/

gallon) 577 lb; oil (7.0 gallons at 9 lb/gallon) 63 lb. Aircraft Normal Loaded Weight 6,218 lb.

Merlin III version. Aircraft tare weight (with 18 gallons coolant) 4,982 lb with Rotol propeller, 5,034 lb with DH 2-position propeller. Equipment and fuel as Merlin II version. Aircraft Normal Loaded Weight 6,447 lb with Rotol propeller, 6,499 lb with DH 2-position ropeller.

Mark I Overload. (Tropical aircraft, Rotol propeller, two 44-gallon fixed ferry tanks and full ammunition). Aircraft Overload Weight 7,490 lb. Sea Hurricane Mark Is. Aircraft Normal Loaded Weights. Mark IA 6,589 lb; Mark IB 7,410 lb; Mark IC 7,605 lb; Tropical Mark IC 8,210 lb.

Datum Point. 21.2 inches below thrust line and 28 inches forward of the wing leading edge extended to the centre line.

Loadings and Centre of Gravity. Wing loading at Aircraft Normal Loaded Weight (6,218 lb) 24.1 lb/sq ft. Power loading (take-off at 6,218 lb) 6.0 lb/bhp. CG at normal loaded weight 57.3 inches aft of Datum Point; CG limits, 54.9 to 58.7 inches aft of Datum Point.

HURRICANE MARK II

Geometric Data. All figures as for Mark I except overall length 32 ft 2¼ in.

Weights. Mark IIB (Temperate). Measured on aircraft *Z3067* (14 March, 1941). Aircraft tare weight (with 18 gallons coolant) 5,467 lb; pilot and parachute 200 lb; twelve Browning guns and accessories 318 lb; case and link chutes 14 lb; ammunition and boxes (3,990 rounds) 302 lb; gunsight 17 lb; G.45 gun camera 9 lb; pyrotechnics 18 lb; oxygen equipment 15 lb; First Aid 3 lb; TR1133 radio 79 lb; R3002 radio 24 lb; fuel (main, 69 gallons) 497 lb; fuel (reserve, 28 gallons) 202 lb; oil (7.5 gallons) 68 lb. Aircraft Normal Loaded Weight 7,233 lb.

Mark IIB (Tropical). Measured on aircraft *V7480* (23 January, 1941). Aircraft Tare Weight (with 18 gallons coolant) 5,594 lb; pilot and parachute 200 lb; twelve Browning guns and accessories 295 lb; case and link chutes 14 lb; ammunition and boxes (3,990 rounds) 302 lb; gunsight 18 lb; G.45 gun camera 9 lb; pyrotechnics 26 lb; oxygen equipment 15 lb; First Aid 3 lb; desert equipment 50 lb; TR1133 radio 79 lb; R3002 radio 24 lb; fuel (main, 69 gallons) 497 lb; fuel (reserve, 28 gallons) 202 lb; oil (7.5 gallons) 68 lb. Aircraft Normal Loaded Weight 7,396 lb. Equipped with 44-gallon auxiliary (ferry or combat) drop tanks: Normal ferry weight 7,594 lb; overload combat weight 7,896 lb.

Mark IIC (Temperate). Measured on aircraft *Z2891* (14 March, 1941). Aircraft Tare Weight (with 18 gallons coolant), 5,658 lb; pilot and parachute 200 lb; four 20-mm Oerlikon cannon 425 lb; ammunition boxes and belt feeds (364 rounds) 327 lb; gunsight 17 lb; G.45 gun camera 9 lb; pyrotechnics 18 lb; oxygen equipment 15 lb; First Aid 3 lb; TR1133 radio 79 lb; R3002 radio 24 lb; fuel (main, 69 gallons) 497 lb; fuel (reserve, 28 gallons) 202 lb; oil (7.5 gallons) 68 lb. Aircraft Normal Loaded Weight 7,544 lb. Equipped with 44-gallon auxiliary (ferry or combat) drop tanks: Normal ferry weight 7,619 lb; overload combat weight 8,044 lb.

Mark IIC (Tropical). Aircraft Tare Weight 5,785 lb. Aircraft Normal Loaded Weight, 7,707 lb. Equipped with 44-gallon auxiliary (ferry or combat) drop tanks: Normal ferry weight 7,782 lb; overload combat weight 8,207 lb.

Mark IID (Tropical). Measured on aircraft *BP173/G* (28 July, 1942). Aircraft Tare Weight (with 18 gallons coolant) 5,550 lb. Pilot and parachute 200 lb. Two Vickers "S" 40-mm guns and two Browning 0.303-in. guns, 893 lb; ammunition (660 rounds of 0.303-in. and 30 rounds of 40-mm) 230 lb; gunsight (gyro) 54 lb; G.45 gun camera 9 lb; pyrotechnics 26 lb; oxygen equipment 15 lb; First Aid 3 lb; TR1133 radio 79 lb; R3002 radio 24 lb; fuel (main, 69 gallons) 497 lb; fuel (reserve, 28 gallons) 202 lb; oil (7.5 gallons) 68 lb. Aircraft Normal Loaded Weight 7,850 lb.

Sea Hurricane Mark IIC (Temperate). Aircraft Tare Weight (with 18 gallons coolant) 5,738 lb; pilot and parachute 200 lb; four 20-mm cannon 425 lb; ammunition boxes and belt feeds (364 rounds) 327 lb; gunsight (gyro) 54 lb; oxygen equipment 15 lb; naval radio 92 lb; fuel (main, 69 gallons) 497 lb; fuel (reserve, 28 gallons) 202 lb; oil (7.5 gallons) 68 lb. Aircraft Normal Loaded Weight 7,618 lb. (Tropical Aircraft Normal Loaded Weight 8,278 lb).

Mark II Maximum Ferry Overload Weight (Tropical mark IIC carrying front and back armour, full ammunition and two 90-gallon ferry tanks) 9,145 lb.

Datum Point. 21.6 inches below thrust line and 30 inches forward of wing leading edge extended to centreline.

Centre of Gravity. CG at Tare Weight, 9.9 in. above and 55.8 in. aft of Datum Point. CG at Normal Loaded Weight, 9.45 in. above and 59.5 in. aft of Datum Point. CG limits: 57–60 in. aft of Datum Point.

HURRICANE MARK IV

The Hurricane IV was similar in most respects to the Mark IIC, being distributed in the same production line and using the same assembly jigs. The provision of universal "low attack" wings and attachment points, together with additional armour protection, resulted in greater weights and therefore reduced performance. The following figures are therefore quoted for the Mark IV with two Vickers "S" 40-mm guns for ease of comparison with the Mark IID.

Weights. Measured on Tropical aircraft *KZ198*. Aircraft Tare Weight (with 18 gallons coolant) 6,150 lb; pilot and parachute 200 lb; two Vickers and two Browning guns, 905 lb; ammunition 230 lb; equipment 210 lb; fuel (main, 69 gallons) 497 lb; fuel (reserve, 28 gallons) 202 lb; oil (7.5 gallons) 68 lb. Aircraft Normal Loaded Weight 8,462 lb.

Performance

(Maximum speeds and climb performance, all versions, see accompanying table)

HURRICANE PROTOTYPE

Stalling speeds (sea level): wheels and flaps up 70 mph IAS; wheels and flaps down 57 mph IAS. Airfield performance (grass surface): take-off ground run 265 yards (time 11.5 seconds), take-off distance to clear 50 feet, 430 yards; landing ground run with flaps and wheelbrakes 220 yards; landing distance from 50 feet with flaps and wheelbrakes 475 yards.

HURRICANE MARK I

(a) Range. Aircraft flying at optimum range speed, 190 mph TAS, mean flying weight 5,830 lb, mean ICAN altitude 15,000 ft. Mark I with Merlin II and wooden propeller, 525 miles maximum or 440 miles with 20-minute reserve. Mark I with Merlin III and Rotol propeller, 505 miles maximum or 425 miles with 20-minute reserve. Mark I tropical with Rotol propeller, 460 miles maximum or 380 miles with 20-minute reserve. Mark I tropical with Merlin III, Rotol propeller and two 44-gallon auxiliary tanks, 935 miles maximum or 840 miles with 20-minute reserve.

(b) Stalling speed. Clean aircraft, wheels and flaps up 72–80 mph IAS; clean aircraft, wheels and flaps down 60–75 mph IAS.

(c) Aerobatics. The following are the recommended minimum entry speeds: 270 mph IAS for a loop; 210 mph IAS for a roll; 290 mph IAS for a half roll off a loop; 300 mph IAS for an upward roll.

(d) Airfield Performance (grass surface). Take-off ground run (wooden propeller) 370 yards; distance to 50 feet (wooden propeller) 580 yards. Take-off ground run (Rotol propeller) 350 yards; distance to 50 feet (Rotol propeller) 540 yards. Landing ground run (either propeller) using flaps and brakes 205 yards; landing distance from 50 feet (either propeller) using flaps and brakes 420 yards.

HURRICANE MARK II

(a) Range.

Version	*Optimum Range Speed TAS (mph)*	*Range (statute miles)* Clean Aircraft	*Two 44-gall Tanks*	*Two 90-gall Tanks*
Mark IIA	177	468	946	1,090
Mark IIA (Trop)	185	440	900	1,015
Mark IIB	177	465	935	1,080
Mark IIB (Trop)	185	436	880	1,010
Mark IIC	178	460	920	1,086
Mark IIC (Trop)	188	426	908	1,022
Mark IID	186	420	895	1,020
Mark IID (Trop)	192	404	870	995
Sea Hurricane IIC	180	452	908	1,062
Sea Hurricane IIC (Trop)	190	415	895	998

(b) Stalling speed (sea level). Clean aircraft, wheels and flaps up, 75–85 mph IAS; aircraft with stores, wheels and flaps up, 80–90 mph IAS; clean aircraft, wheels and flaps down, 60–75 mph IAS; aircraft with stores, wheels and flaps down, 65–80 mph IAS. At the stall one wing tends to drop sharply with flaps either up or down.

(c) Aerobatics. The following are the recommended minimun entry speeds: 280 mph IAS for a loop; 220 mph IAS for a roll; 300 mph for a half roll off a loop; 300 mph IAS for an upward roll.

Powerplant: Rolls-Royce Merlin

Hurricane Prototype (at time of preliminary evaluation, March 1936) Rolls-Royce Merlin "C" No. 19. Engine developed 1,025 bhp at 3,000 rpm at 11,000 feet at +6 pounds boost, and 905 bhp at 2,400 rpm at 9,800 feet. Propeller, Watts two-blade right-hand wooden Type Z33; diameter 11 ft 6 in.; weight 96.5 lb.

Hurricane Mark I (early aircraft). Rolls-Royce Merlin II. Engine developed 1,030 bhp at 3,000 rpm at 16,250 feet at +6¼ pounds boost, and 990 bhp at 2,600 rpm at 12,250 feet at +6¼ pounds boost. Propeller, Watts two-blade right-hand wooden Type Z38; diameter 11 ft 3 in.; weight 79 lb.

Hurricane Mark I (late aircraft). Rolls-Royce Merlin III. Engine developed 1,029 bhp at 3,000 rpm at 16,250 feet at +6¾ pounds boost, and 971 bhp at 12,250 feet at +5.9 pounds boost. Propeller, Rotol three-blade constant-speed right-hand Type RMS.7; pitch range 35 degrees; diameter 10 ft 9 in. Also fitted with de Havilland two-position three-blade propeller.

Hurricane Mark II. Rolls-Royce Merlin XX. Engine developed 1,260 bhp at 3,000 rpm at 11,750 feet in MS gear, and 1,160 bhp at 3,000 rpm at 20,750 feet in S-gear. Sea level take-off power 1,300 bhp at 3,000 rpm. Propeller, either three-blade Rotol RS5/2 with Swarz blades or Rotol RS5/3 with Jablo blades; gear ratio 0.42; diameter 11 ft 3 in.

Rolls-Royce Merlin XX fuel consumption.

(a) Weak mixture (gallons/hour)

Boost lb/sq in.	*MS Gear 8,000–20,000 ft* 2,650 rpm	2,300 rpm	2,000 rpm	*S Gear 14,000–30,000 ft* 2,650 rpm	2,300 rpm	2,000 rpm
+ 4	56	50	46	57	51	47
+ 2	52	46	42	53	47	43
0	47	42	38	48	43	39
– 2	42	37	34	43	39	35
– 4	37	33	30	38	34	31

(b) Rich mixture (gallons/hour)

Boost	*Engine speed*	*Fuel Consumption*
+ 12	3,000	115
+ 9	3,000	100
+ 9	2,850	95
+ 7	2,650	80

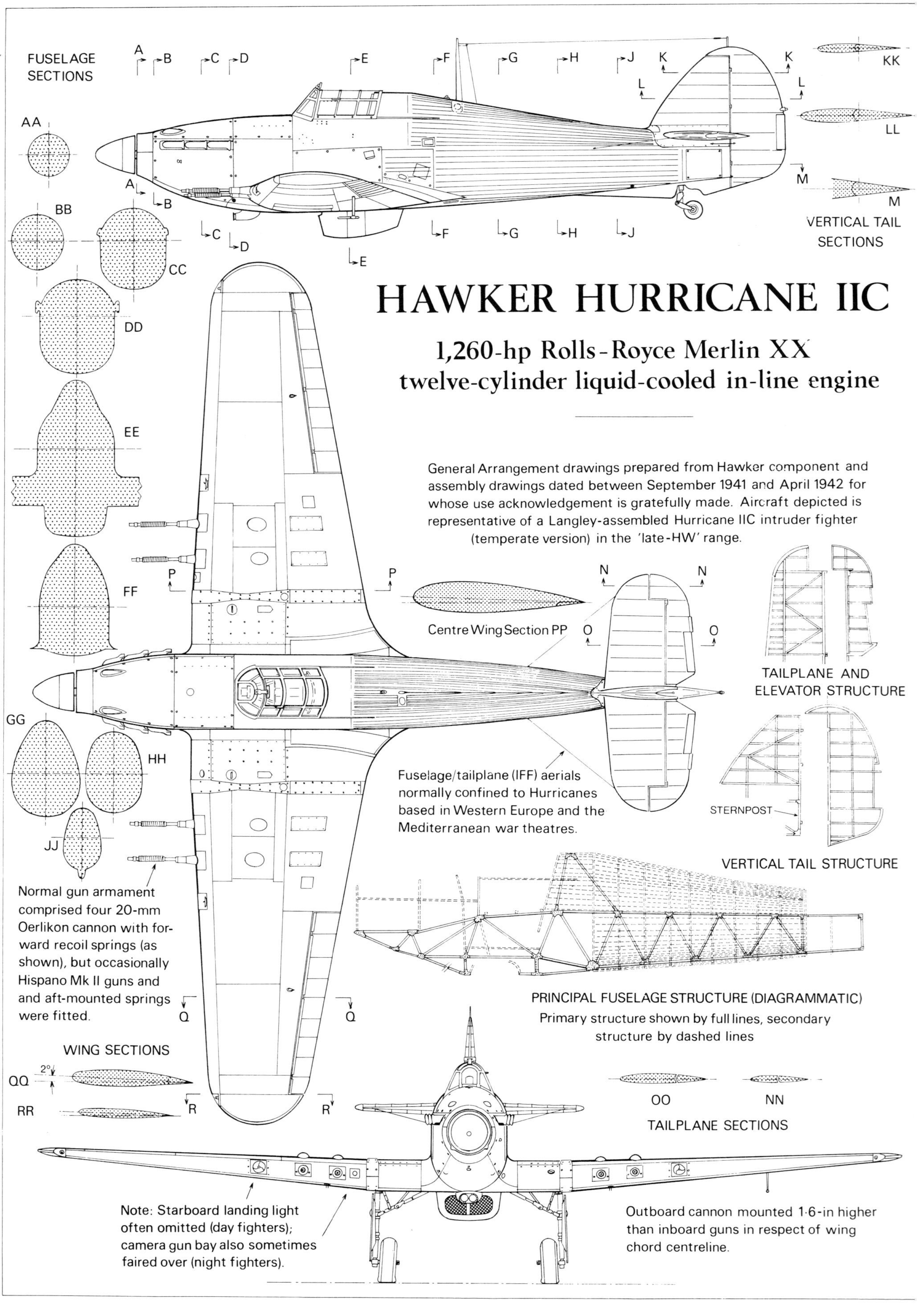

HAWKER HURRICANE IIC
1,260-hp Rolls-Royce Merlin XX
twelve-cylinder liquid-cooled in-line engine
General Arrangement drawings prepared from Hawker component and assembly drawings dated between September 1941 and April 1942 for whose use acknowledgement is gratefully made. Aircraft depicted is representative of a Langley-assembled Hurricane IIC intruder fighter (temperate version) in the 'late-HW' range.
FUSELAGE SECTIONS
AA
BB
CC
DD
EE
FF
GG
HH
JJ
VERTICAL TAIL SECTIONS
KK
LL
M
Centre Wing Section PP
TAILPLANE AND ELEVATOR STRUCTURE
STERNPOST
VERTICAL TAIL STRUCTURE
Fuselage/tailplane (IFF) aerials normally confined to Hurricanes based in Western Europe and the Mediterranean war theatres.
Normal gun armament comprised four 20-mm Oerlikon cannon with forward recoil springs (as shown), but occasionally Hispano Mk II guns and and aft-mounted springs were fitted.
PRINCIPAL FUSELAGE STRUCTURE (DIAGRAMMATIC)
Primary structure shown by full lines, secondary structure by dashed lines
WING SECTIONS
QQ
RR
2°
OO
NN
TAILPLANE SECTIONS
Note: Starboard landing light often omitted (day fighters); camera gun bay also sometimes faired over (night fighters).
Outboard cannon mounted 1·6-in higher than inboard guns in respect of wing chord centreline.

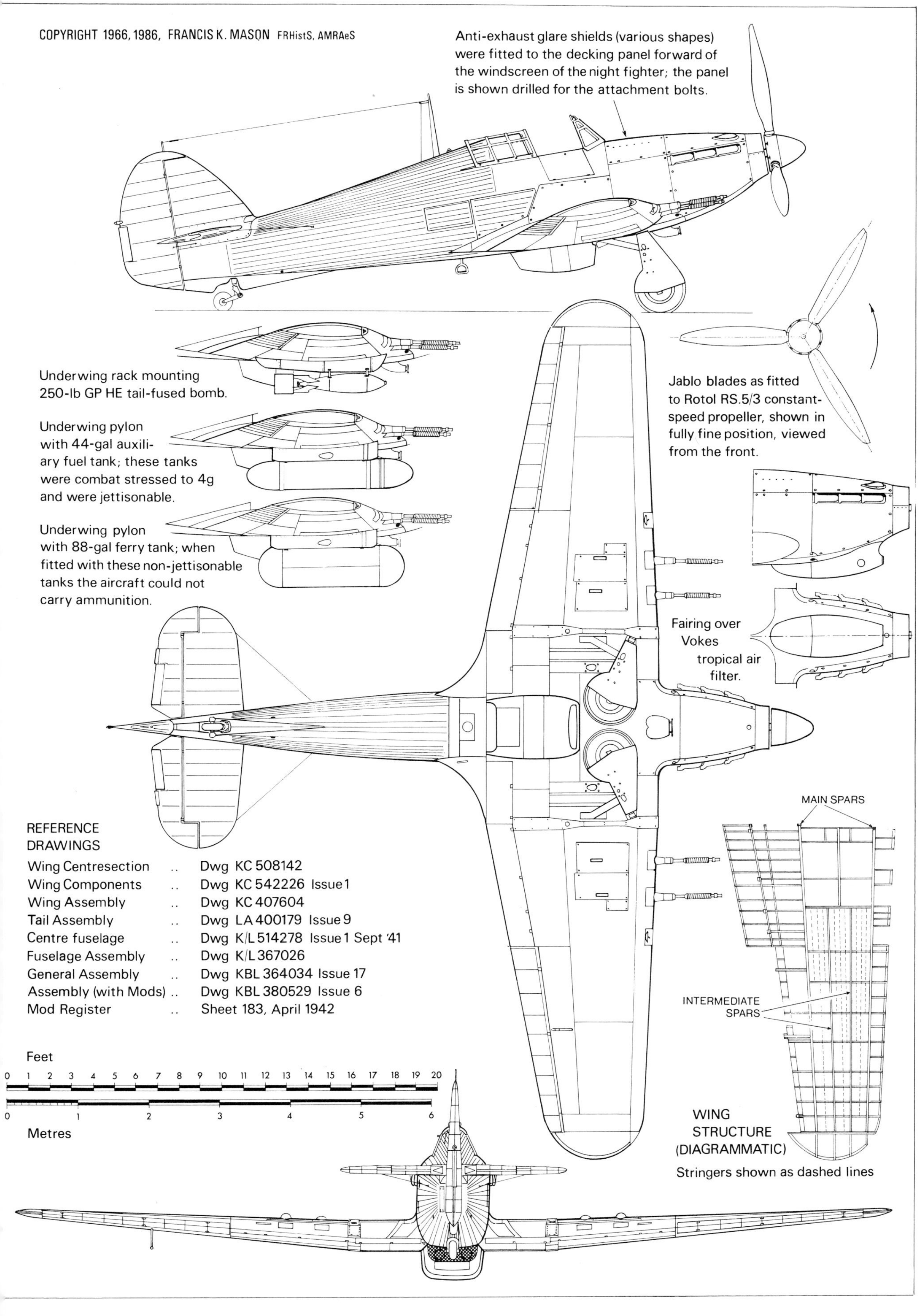
COPYRIGHT 1966, 1986, FRANCIS K. MASON FRHistS, AMRAeS
Anti-exhaust glare shields (various shapes) were fitted to the decking panel forward of the windscreen of the night fighter; the panel is shown drilled for the attachment bolts.
Underwing rack mounting 250-lb GP HE tail-fused bomb.
Underwing pylon with 44-gal auxiliary fuel tank; these tanks were combat stressed to 4g and were jettisonable.
Underwing pylon with 88-gal ferry tank; when fitted with these non-jettisonable tanks the aircraft could not carry ammunition.
Jablo blades as fitted to Rotol RS.5/3 constant-speed propeller, shown in fully fine position, viewed from the front.
Fairing over Vokes tropical air filter.
REFERENCE DRAWINGS
Wing Centresection .. Dwg KC 508142
Wing Components .. Dwg KC 542226 Issue 1
Wing Assembly .. Dwg KC 407604
Tail Assembly .. Dwg LA 400179 Issue 9
Centre fuselage .. Dwg K/L 514278 Issue 1 Sept '41
Fuselage Assembly .. Dwg K/L 367026
General Assembly .. Dwg KBL 364034 Issue 17
Assembly (with Mods) .. Dwg KBL 380529 Issue 6
Mod Register .. Sheet 183, April 1942
Feet
0 1 2 3 4 5 6 7 8 9 10 11 12 13 14 15 16 17 18 19 20
0 1 2 3 4 5 6
Metres
MAIN SPARS
INTERMEDIATE SPARS
WING STRUCTURE (DIAGRAMMATIC)
Stringers shown as dashed lines

Hawker Hurricane maximum speed and climb performance

(a) Maximum speed, mph (TAS) (b) Rate of Climb (ft/min) (c) Time to Height (minutes)

Version		*Sea Level*	*5,000 ft*	*10,000 ft*	*15,000 ft*	*20,000 ft*	*25,000 ft*	*30,000 ft*	*35,000 ft*	*Maximum Speed*	*Service Ceiling*	*Absolute Ceiling*
Hurricane Prototype	(a)	270	286	301	316	304	284	252	—	316 mph at 15,000 ft	29,000 ft	33,000 ft
	(b)	2,400	2,100	1,650	1,500	1,100	750	350	—			
	(c)	—	2.1	4.5	7.45	10.4	14.6	22.7	—			
Mark I Merlin II Watts propeller	(a)	258	274	287	300	295	277	248	—	305 mph at 17,000 ft	30,000 ft	35,000 ft
	(b)	2,500	2,250	1,990	1,600	1,290	880	500	0			
	(c)	—	1.9	3.9	6.8	8.9	13.4	20.8	—			
Mark I Merlin III Rotol propeller	(a)	280	300	312	320	321	310	290	—	324 mph at 17,800 ft	31,000 ft	35,400 ft
	(b)	2,560	2,300	1,950	1,640	1,340	920	560	70			
	(c)	—	1.7	3.6	6.1	8.1	11.9	18.2	27.5			
Mark I (Trop) Merlin III, Rotol propeller	(a)	238	265	280	290	286	268	(200)	—	295 mph at 17,800 ft	26,500 ft	30,000 ft
	(b)	2,200	1,920	1,640	1,300	980	610	0	—			
	(c)	—	2.6	5.4	8.0	11.5	16.5	27.5	—			
Mark IIA Series 2 (Clean)	(a)	272	287	304	317	340	332	316	270	342 mph at 17,500 ft	33,000 ft	36,300 ft
	(b)	3,050	2,710	2,360	1,920	1,620	1,240	810	380			
	(c)	—	2.1	3.8	6.2	8.2	12.5	15.8	23.2			
Mark IIA Series 2 Trop (Clean)	(a)	265	280	296	310	333	324	300	240	334 mph at 17,500 ft	31,800 ft	34,000 ft
	(b)	2,800	2,480	2,150	1,710	1,510	1,120	680	170			
	(c)	—	2.4	4.7	7.4	10.0	13.2	17.2	25.4			
Mark IIA Series 2 (RPs)	(a)	247	258	268	305	290	250	—	—	308 mph at 12,700 ft	23,900 ft	27,000 ft
	(b)	2,200	1,910	1,595	1,510	1,010	380	—	—			
	(c)	—	4.6	9.1	13.7	18.0	24.9	—	—			
Mark IIB (Clean)	(a)	256	280	295	303	328	320	301	250	330 mph at 17,800 ft	34,500 ft	36,000 ft
	(b)	2,960	2,610	2,390	1,910	1,690	1,350	980	470			
	(c)	—	1.7	3.4	5.5	7.5	9.6	12.7	21.0			
Mark IIB Two 250-lb bombs	(a)	217	237	260	274	285	270	225	—	287 mph at 17,800 ft	32,500 ft	35,600 ft
	(b)	2,830	2,500	2,100	1,610	1,480	1,150	750	120			
	(c)	—	2.1	4.0	6.4	8.6	11.5	14.5	24.9			
Mark IIB (Trop) Two 250-lb bombs	(a)	200	217	227	236	242	226	160	—	247 mph at 17,800 ft	27,400 ft	29,900 ft
	(b)	2,410	2,190	1,750	1,200	1,010	760	60	—			
	(c)	—	2.6	5.7	8.7	11.9	16.9	24.9	—			
Mark IIC (Clean)	(a)	260	279	290	302	328	321	300	210	329 mph at 17,800 ft	32,400 ft	35,600 ft
	(b)	2,760	2,430	2,080	1,670	1,490	1,170	680	190			
	(c)	—	1.7	3.4	5.7	7.7	10.1	14.2	24.6			
Mark IIC (Trop) Two 250-lb bombs	(a)	203	223	241	258	272	209	175	—	275 mph at 17,800 ft	25,500 ft	30,800 ft
	(b)	2,280	1,930	1,600	1,210	880	510	80	—			
	(c)	—	2.8	5.7	8.6	11.5	15.0	22.5	—			
Sea Hurricane Mk IIC	(a)	260	275	286	296	311	307	285	—	317 mph at 17,500 ft	31,700 ft	33,000 ft
	(b)	2,010	1,760	1,520	1,210	920	610	350	—			
	(c)	—	2.1	3.8	6.2	8.1	10.6	15.8	—			

HURRICANE PROJECTS

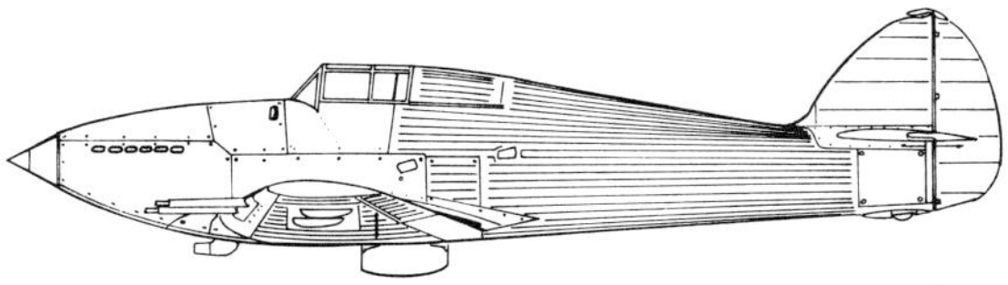

F.37/35 FOUR-CANNON DESIGN. Proposal based on Hurricane prototype with four Oerlikon 20-mm guns. Tendered 23 April 1936 but rejected. (Westland Whirlwind was the successful contender.)

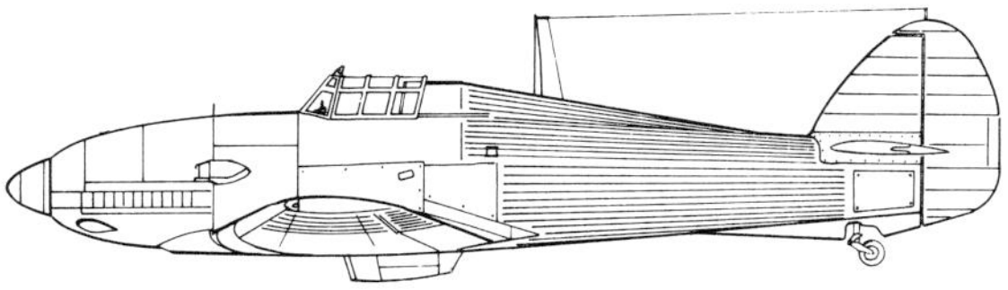

YUGOSLAV DAIMLER-BENZ HURRICANE. DB601A installation undertaken in Yugoslavia, 1940-41. At least one completed in licence-built airframe before the German invasion of April 1941.

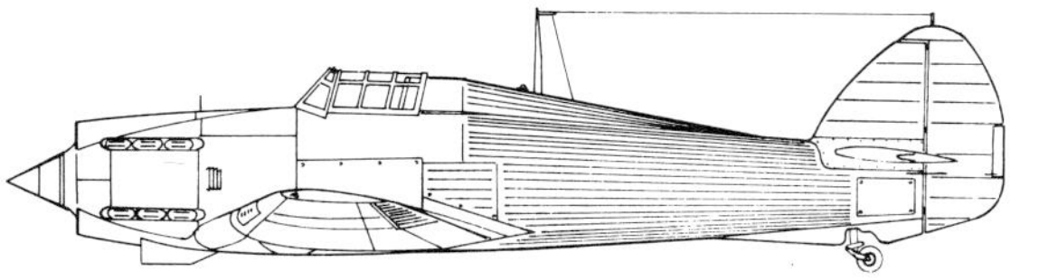

DAGGER HURRICANE. Simplified operational trainer project with Napier Dagger, studied during Battle of Britain as a means of easing pressures on Merlin production. Discontinued, November 1940.

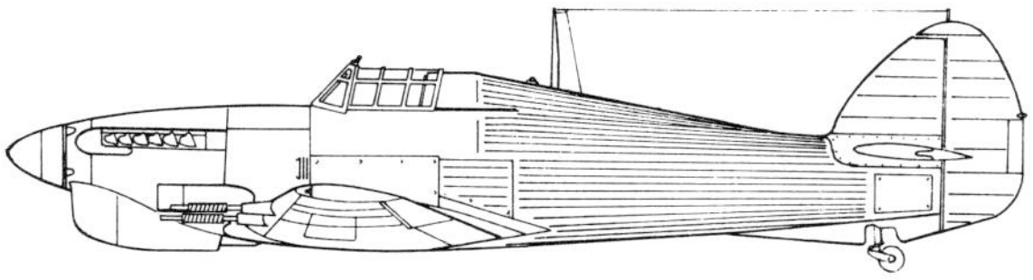

GRIFFON HURRICANE. One of several schemes submitted for the development of a four-cannon Hurricane with Rolls-Royce Griffon IIA, 1939-41. Discontinued when Typhoon entered production.

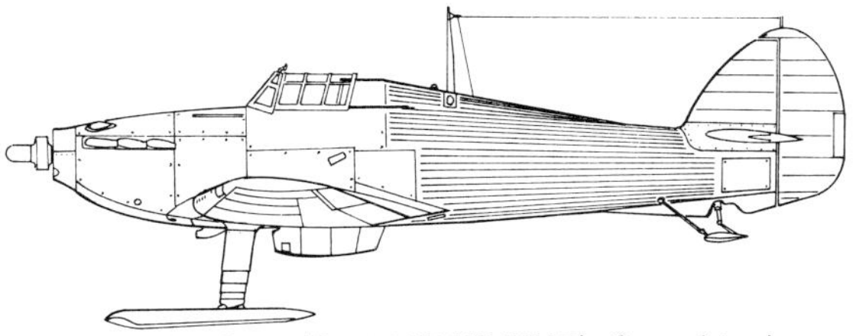

CANADIAN HURRICANE (SKI LANDING GEAR). Several twelve-gun Canadian Hurricane Mark XIs modified with fixed-ski main landing gear and 'snow-shoe' tailskid; wheel gear deleted and wheel wells faired over; Packard-built Merlin 28 and Hamilton Standard propeller. For service with RCAF in Canada, 1941-43.

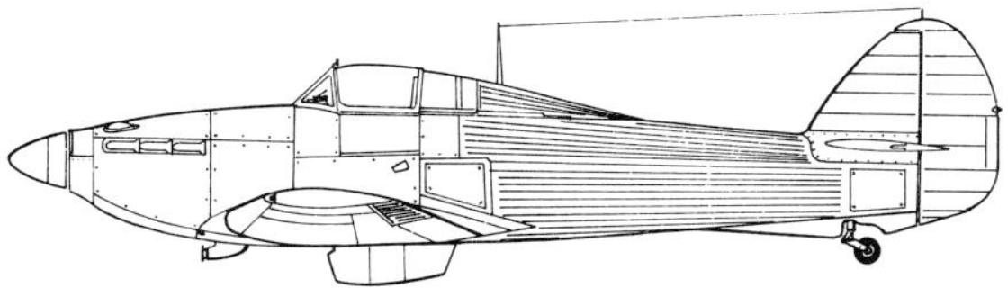

HURRICANE (IMPROVED CANOPY) PROJECT. Reduced rear fuselage secondary structure. Intended to increase field of view for intruder operations. Prototype started but discontinued in March 1942.

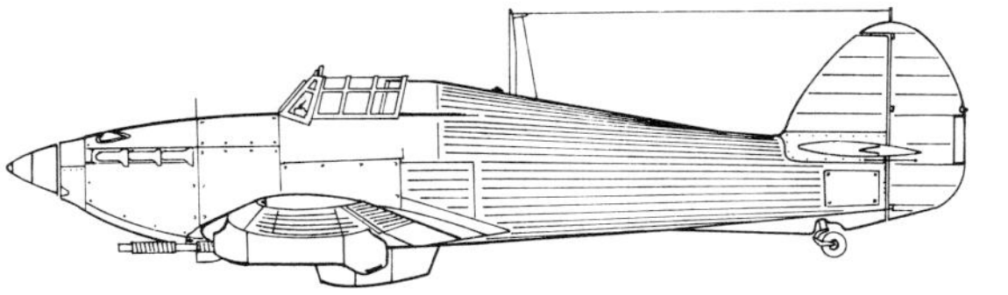

TWO-CANNON HURRICANE. Originated as trial installation of two Oerlikon 20-mm guns under the wings for Service trials in 1939. Fought in the Battle of Britain with No 151 Squadron, 1940.

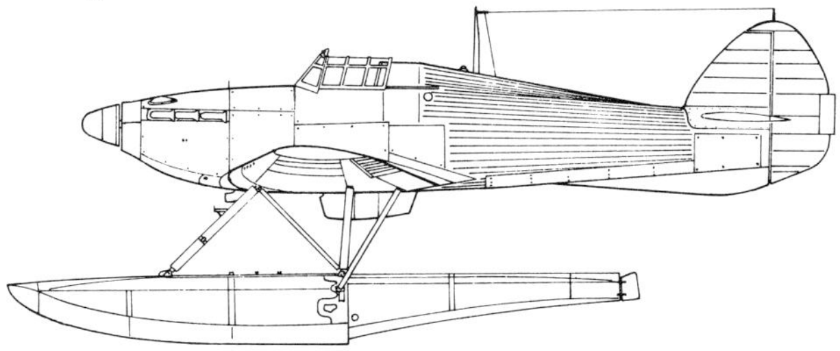

HURRICANE FLOATPLANE. One airframe allocated and part modified (Dwg No. 13440). Modified Blackburn Roc floats delivered to Kingston. Conceived during Norwegian campaign but abandoned in June 1940. Design maximum speed 210 mph at 10,000 ft.

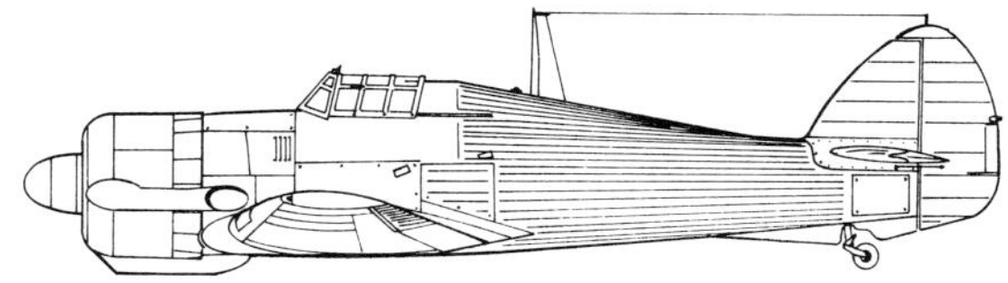

HERCULES HURRICANE. One of several schemes (1941) investigating alternative powerplants for Hurricanes in second-line duties to alleviate possible shortages of Merlin engines.

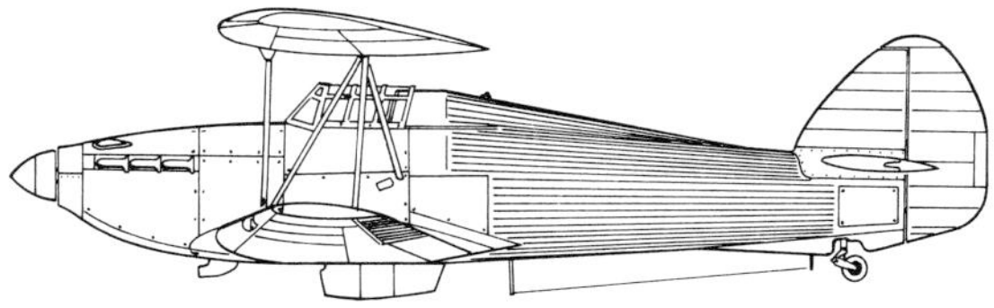

HILLSON FH.40 SLIP-WING HURRICANE. Hawker-built Canadian aircraft modified in the UK with jettisonable auxiliary wing to assist short take-off. Trials discontinued in January 1944.

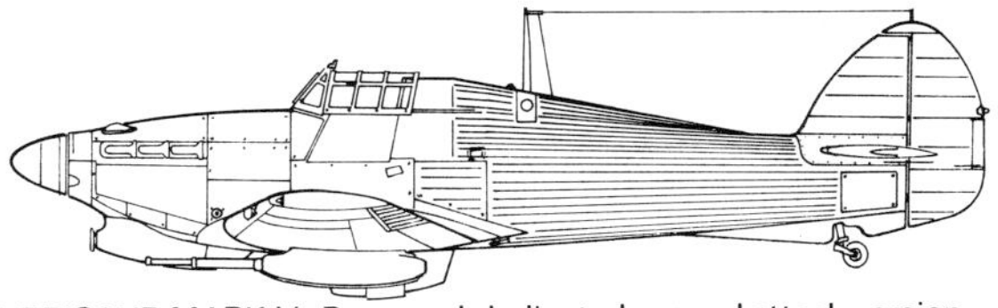

HURRICANE MARK V. Proposed dedicated ground attack version for the Far East. Ground boosted Merlin, four-blade propeller, much-increased armour and universal wing. 3 prototypes built, 1943.

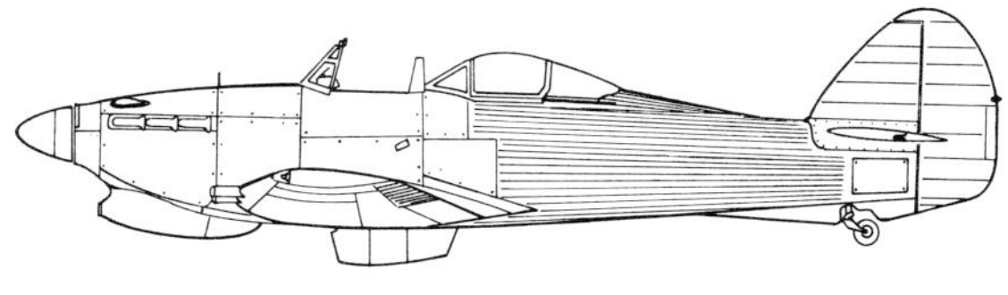

PERSIAN HURRICANE 2-SEAT TRAINER. Two examples delivered. Original design started in 1939; completed 1945. First flown with both cockpits open but delivered with Tempest hood on rear cockpit.

REFERENCES

1 Two RAF Squadrons, Nos. 3 and 17 at Upavon, had been officially regarded as night fighter squadrons between 1925 and 1928 while flying Woodcocks, but this distinction lapsed when they were re-equipped with Gamecocks and Bulldogs, as neither aircraft proved entirely suitable for night flying. Thereafter all squadrons were required to perform a limited proportion of night flying. The suggestion that they represented any sort of night defence fooled no one.

2 Another Hawker product, the Nimrod naval fighter, was also under development, not as is so often portrayed as a development of the Fury but as an entirely independent derivative of the naval Specifications N.21/26 and 16/30.

3 This South African-born officer had formed and commanded the RAF High Speed Flight that had won the 1927 Schneider Trophy. He then commanded Nos. 19, 111 and 43 Squadrons before being appointed senior RAF Officer aboard the carrier HMS *Courageous* from 1932 until 1935. In the Second World War he commanded the RAF in Eritrea/Abyssinia during the successful campaign of 1940–41.

4 "The bomber will always get through" . . . "England's frontier on the Rhine", etc.

5 Major (later Sqn Ldr Sir John) Buchanan, CBE, became Deputy Director of Production at the Department for Development and Production at the Air Ministry, and later Director General of Aircraft Production in 1941.

6 Although the fixed landing gear in Camm's "Fury Monoplane" was soon discarded, the Gladiator's cantilever undercarriage came to be employed on Hawker Fury biplanes sold to Yugoslavia and Spain, aircraft which ironically possessed top speeds within an ace of F.7/30's 250 mph target!

7 It almost certainly gave rise to some observations published very recently that stated quite erroneously that "the Hurricane was not originally designed to mount the eight-gun battery and only when the Spitfire appeared with this armament did the Hawker designers cobble-up hurried modifications to accommodate the extra guns". Delays in the licence negotiations, as well as problems with the Colt's ammunition feed—disclosed during trials using a Parnall Hendy Heck II—affected the Supermarine design no more nor less than that of the Hawker project, except in so far as the Spitfire was running roughly six months later. The facts remain that in April 1935 both designs still incorporated provision for four guns only, and that by November, when the Hawker prototype first flew, it was ballasted for eight wing guns, as was the Supermarine aeroplane when it made its maiden flight on 5 March, 1936. If anything, the irregular spacing of the Spitfire's wing guns—when they were eventually fitted—suggests greater installation inconvenience than in the Hurricane, whose guns were grouped together. It is also necessary to record that in fact it was the Hurricane prototype which first flew with guns fitted, on 21 August, 1936.

8 The Hurricane had a span of exactly 40 ft. The much larger Horsley (and Harrier) was not fully assembled at Kingston, and they were too large to be loaded on to a lorry; each had to be towed backwards on a jury undercarriage all the way to Brooklands on the King's highway at walking pace.

9 The prototype Spitfire nevertheless also made its first flight with a Merlin C.

10 Not 18 February as previously believed. It was formerly understood that only flight testing was undertaken during this first visit, but the full report, filed at a rather later date, indicates otherwise.

11 Sammy Wroath, to whom further references are made later, had been one of Trenchard's earliest Halton "Brats" at the age of 16. He was now a highly experienced pilot, having recently served for three years with No. 1 (Fighter) Squadron at Tangmere on Hawker Furies, and was aged 27 when *K5083* arrived at the A&AEE. He was commissioned in February 1938 and continued to fly with the A&AEE until 1943, moving to Boscombe Down at the outbreak of war. During that period he undertook a tremendous amount of Hurricane testing and evaluation before he was appointed the first Commandant of the Empire Test Pilots' School, also at Boscombe Down in 1943. In 1944 he was appointed Chief Test Pilot of the British Air Commission at Wright Field, Dayton, Ohio, in 1944, and Superintendent of Flying at the A&AEE, Boscombe Down, from 1945 until 1947. He then served in the Operational Requirements Branch at the Air Ministry in 1947–48. Uniquely he was appointed Commandant of the Empire Test Pilots' School for a second time, now at Farnborough, from 1952 till 1957. He retired from the RAF as Group Captain in 1957 with a CBE and two AFCs (all awarded in respect of his services to test flying), and in the 1970s was the Military Sales Manager (Aero Engine Division), Rolls-Royce Ltd. The author was fortunate to meet this remarkable gentleman during the celebrations on the 50th Anniversary of the First Flight of the Hurricane on 6 November, 1985 at Brooklands.

12 Who shortly afterwards left the A&AEE on posting to the Air Ministry's Directorate of Intelligence.

13 This venerable aeroplane did spend a few weeks on the strength of No. 111 Squadron towards the end of 1938, but was finally pressed into operational service with one of the newly formed "Free Czech" squadrons of Fighter Command towards the end of the Battle of Britain. Both it and its pilot, Sergeant O. Hanzlicek, were to die in action, shot down over Merseyside on 10 October, 1940, just two days short of the aeroplane's "third birthday".

14 By June, however, four Hurricanes, which had suffered accidents and whose repair was beyond the resources of the new squadrons, had been returned to Brooklands; three of these repaired aircraft were also modified with the "spin fairing" and with this were the first to reach the Service in July.

15 Henry Charles Watts, MBE, was probably Britain's foremost authority on aeroplane propellers at the end of the First World War and became Technical Director of Airscrew Co Ltd in 1932. His book *Design of Screw Propellers for Aircraft* came to be regarded as the standard work of reference on the subject.

16 Rotol Limited had been formed as a jointly-owned company by Rolls-Royce and Bristol Engines to take over and develop the old Hele-Shaw-Beecham patents and projects.

17 Later Air Cdre, CB, CBE, DSO, AFC and Bar. "Teddy" Donaldson continued to command No. 151 Squadron until well into the Battle of Britain. He had served on No. 3 Squadron from 1932 until 1936 and twice won the Fighter Command Brooke-Popham Air Firing Trophy. Later in the war he commanded the RAF's first jet fighter station at RAF Colerne, and in 1946 he established a new World Air Speed Record of 616 mph in a Gloster Meteor jet fighter. After retiring from the RAF in 1961 he was appointed Air Correspondent to the *Daily Telegraph*.

18 Much confusion has arisen as to how the Romanian aircraft were replaced in the Air Ministry's contract. It transpired that the airframes were selected from the production line *after* RAF serial numbers had been allotted; the aircraft were then re-allotted Romanian numbers and new Hurricanes laid down at the end of the production batch, reverting to the original RAF serial numbers. This seems to explain the oft-quoted appearance of a "Romanian" Hurricane in France in 1940!

19 The pilot of this aircraft was Graf Schack, the famous German flying-boat and seaplane pilot of pre-war years.

20 Some small consolation could be gleaned from the tragedy. The gallantry of HMS *Acasta* and *Ardent* resulted in a torpedo hit being scored by the former on the *Scharnhorst* before both the British destroyers were overwhelmed and sunk. The torpedo strike so damaged the German battle cruiser that her captain decided to set course for home (with the *Gneisenau*) immediately—thereby saving from almost certain destruc-

tion two lightly escorted British convoys returning from Narvik and routed almost exactly through the same area.

21 The first Auxiliary Air Force officer to take command of a Regular fighter Squadron.

22 Although history generally records that the German attack in the West of 10 May, 1940, achieved complete tactical surprise, fairly powerful evidence suggests that not only had British photographic reconnaissance disclosed the considerable preparatory build-up by German forces facing the Low Countries, but also that Dowding was privy to the Intelligence being gleaned through the interpretation of the German Enigma code network immediately prior to 10 May. Though Dowding was expressly prevented from acting tactically on receipt of such information (on security grounds), it is worth noting that on those four squadrons that were ordered to France that day all leave had been cancelled 24 hours previously.

23 The figure of 11 Hurricanes, so often quoted as the maximum available to the *Aéronautique Militaire*, is evidently based on a figure quoted in Belgium in January referring only to the British-built aircraft (of which one had been shot down when it tried to intercept a German reconnaissance aircraft in Belgian airspace the previous October with the loss of its pilot, another aircraft which had been lost in an accident and seven aircraft which were undergoing modification). At that time no Belgian-built Hurricanes had actually reached the Service, but by 10 May at least a dozen (and perhaps as many as 17), some with the latest Rotol propellers, were on Service charge.

24 Later to become *Geschwaderkommodore* of *Jagdgeschwader 26 "Schlageter"* during the Battle of Britain, a holder of the Knight's Cross with Diamonds and, before the end of the war, General of Fighters in the *Luftwaffe*; his final victory score of 104 Allied aircraft destroyed was huge by RAF standards—yet relatively modest in comparison with many other German *Experten*.

25 Loel Guinness, who also held a commission in the Irish Guards, was one of no fewer than 12 Members of Parliament who were commissioned in the Auxiliary Air Force at the time of the Dunkirk evacuation; five of them flew Hurricanes during the Battle of France.

26 No. 17 Sqn (Sqn Ldr Geoffrey Donald Emms); No. 43 Sqn (Sqn Ldr Charles George Lott, later Air Vice-Marshal, CB, CBE, DSO, DFC); No. 56 Sqn (Sqn Ldr Edward Vincent Knowles); No. 145 Sqn (Sqn Ldr John Douglas Miller, later Air Cdre, CBE); No. 242 Sqn (Sqn Ldr Fowler M. Gobeil, RCAF); No. 245 Sqn (Sqn Ldr Eric William Whitley); and No. 605 Sqn (Sqn Ldr Vivian Perry, AAFRO).

27 As far as can be discovered this was the first aircraft to be destroyed by the RAF using 20-mm cannon as no record exists of any other success achieved prior to this date by No. 19 Squadron's cannon-armed Spitfires, which were still giving considerable trouble up at Fowlmere. Exactly how *L1750* came to be flown by a line pilot on No. 151 Squadron has never been authoritatively explained, although one account, probably apocryphal, suggests that the aircraft had been purloined at Martlesham Heath (where it had been flown by the A&AEE the previous year, as well as being one of No. 151's forward airfields) to provide a training "hack". While this is entirely in character with RAF squadrons of the day, it does not explain how 20-mm ammunition had become available to No. 151 Squadron—unless this had also been purloined from the airfield defence's Oerlikon guns! A more likely explanation is that some degree of informal authority was obtained for an experienced Hurricane pilot to "try his hand" with the old aeroplane to discover what effects cannon fire might have on German aircraft. No trace of any formal authority to bring *L1750* on to No. 151 Squadron's charge can be found. One senses the hand of the indomitable Wing Commander Victor Beamish, station commander at North Weald, somewhere in this little saga!

28 It is worth passing comment here on the line command structure of the *Luftwaffe*. The largest autonomous combat formation was the *Gruppe*, roughly equivalent to the RAF's Wing, commanded by an Oberstleutnant (Lieutenant-Colonel) in the bomber arm, or a Major or Hauptmann (Captain) in the fighter and *Zerstörer* arms. The normal combat formation was the *Staffel* of about 10 or 12 aircraft (and therefore roughly a Squadron, though rather smaller), commanded by a Hauptmann, or, increasingly, by an Oberleutnant (Senior Lieutenant). *Staffeln* were almost invariably closely administered by, and were components of, a *Gruppe*—unlike RAF squadrons, which were generally autonomous, though later became *ad hoc* components of Wings. A *Geschwader*, commanded by an *Oberst* (full colonel), usually comprised three or four *Gruppen* but was not itself a combat formation.

29 The first Canadian Squadron, No. 1 Squadron RCAF (soon to be renumbered No. 401) would be declared operational at Northolt with Hurricanes in a day or so; the first Polish Squadron, No. 302, was declared operational on Hurricanes at Leconfield on the 19th, and No. 303 (Polish) Squadron would follow suit within a week, also on Hurricanes at Northolt. No. 310 (Czech) Squadron had become operational at Duxford on the 17th, again with Hurricanes; another Czech Squadron would be formed by the end of the month. The fact that all these new squadrons flew Hurricanes reflected the far greater stocks than of Spitfires—despite the enormous losses in France—as well as the relative ease with which pilots could be trained on the Hawker aeroplane and the greater availability of Hurricane flying instructors, a number of whom were veterans of France, being "rested" for a few months.

30 The Defiants did, however, destroy a Bf 109 of JG 51 and five Ju 88s of II./KG 76 on this occasion, including the bomber of the *Gruppenkommandeur*, Major Moricke, who was killed.

31 The recalcitrant cannons on No. 19 Squadron so frustrated the pilots that the commanding officer pleaded to be allowed to revert to the standard eight-gun Spitfires. His prayers were answered in September, but the replacement aircraft turned out to be relatively old and tired. Nevertheless they had eight guns, and they worked.

32 The discovery only relatively recently of some *Luftwaffe* records has indicated that German losses on this day were much greater than had been thought previously, particularly among the Heinkels of KG 53 and the Bf 109s of JG 54. Loss returns by these units had not been filed with the Quartermaster General and therefore did not appear in the records held by the British Air Ministry before being returned to Germany in 1969, and today held at the *Bundesarchiv*.

33 On this occasion Gleave was shot down while flying alone near Biggin Hill but never saw his attacker. He remained unaware for 27 years of whence the enemy aircraft came; only in 1967 was the wreck of his Hurricane found, examination of which showed cannon shell penetration of the main spar and fuselage stern post, indicating an attack by a Bf 109E from below and astern. He was badly burned and became one of the first patients in Archibald McIndoe's Masonic Hospital at East Grinstead for seriously burned victims—the famous Guinea Pigs. The second patient was to be a Czech Hurricane pilot, Sergeant Josef Koukal, who was shot down over the Isle of Sheppey on 7 September. Both recovered from their injuries, the former to become Station Commander at Manston and later the President of the Battle of Britain Pilots' Association in recent years, and the latter—whose burns had been truly horrific—a State Test Pilot in Czechoslovakia after the war.

34 Even a very new and experimental Hurricane with an armament of four 20-mm cannon, which at that time was being flown for a short evaluation by No. 46 Squadron at Stapleford, was flown into combat by Flt Lt Alexander Coullate Rabagliati (son of a famous pilot of the RFC's pioneer years). Originally the aircraft, *V7360*, had been delivered to No. 151 Squadron at North Weald for evaluation on 3 September, but that squadron had just been ordered north to rest, and Rabagliati, who had been shot down without injury to himself, gained permission to take over the new aeroplane, and on the 5th had blown a Bf 109 of I./JG 54 to pieces. On

the 7th, however, he only succeeded in damaging a Do 17. He was to be killed on 6th July, 1943.

35 Flt Lt Howard Peter ("Cowboy") Blatchford, DFC (Canadian), Plt Off G. North, RAFVR, Plt Off P. A. Mortimer, RAFVR, Plt Off B. Davey, RAFVR, Plt Off K. Pniak (Polish), Sgt L. D. Barnes, Sgt S. E. Lucas, Plt Off J. K. Kay, RAFVR, Plt Off S. E. Andrews, DFM.

36 A month earlier, on 9 May, Lucas had been flying the prototype Typhoon when failure of the monocoque structure occurred just aft of the cockpit, threatening disintegration of the rear fuselage. Instead of abandoning the aircraft he returned to Langley and made a safe landing, enabling an examination to be made of this important aeroplane. For his courage and skill, Lucas was awarded the George Medal, the first such award to a member of the Royal Air Force (he held the rank of Flight Lieutenant in the RAF Reserve of Officers).

37 The maximum speed of a standard Hurricane I with Rotol propeller was 324 mph in full fighting trim. On one occasion Dowding complained that the Hurricane possessed a speed of "only 316 mph"; his observation has since been quoted out of context, for he himself was quoting a report by the A&AEE on the evaluation of "a typical repaired aircraft". The aeroplane was one that had seen considerable service in France, and its engine, with DH propeller, had flown more than 200 hours. One must assume that this specimen was indeed rather "tired", as all other performance measurements on Rotol-equipped Hurricane Is showed maximum speeds between 324 and 332 mph.

38 Although no mention of the gun armament is made in Hawker flight test reports (being no more than a performance and handling check flight), the stated all-up weight of this aircraft on this day coincides almost exactly with that of the known four-cannon Hurricane *V7360*, subsequently flown by the A&AEE—making allowance for the heavier Rotol propeller.

39 Whether this occurred during Sammy Wroath's one and only flight in *V7360* on 13 August is not known (see Appendix II).

40 Sqn Ldr "Hettie" Rosier had flown with No. 229 Squadron in France as a flight commander and was with the squadron once more at the end of the Battle of Britain, being appointed its CO. In 1941 he led Hurricane IICs off HMS *Furious* for the Middle East. After a long and distinguished career he was appointed the last Air Officer Commanding-in-Chief, Fighter Command, from 1966 to 1968.

41 Such as Small Bomb Carriers (SBCs) and Smoke Curtain Installations (SCIs).

42 Rapidly increasing production of the Packard-built Merlin in the United States prompted the Ministry of Aircraft Production at the end of 1941 to issue instructions for the introduction of the Packard Merlin 28 into the Langley production line, the aircraft to be known as the Hurricane Mark III. Though the necessary modifications were drawn up and retained for possible use in the future, adequate supplies of Rolls-Royce-built engines were maintained and no Hurricane III ever came to be built as such. The Packard Merlin 28 had, however, been introduced in the Canadian Hurricane Marks X and XI.

43 Later Air Cdre, CB, DFC. Charlie Widdows, though never to become one of the most famous and high-scoring pilots of the war, was a confirmed and dedicated night fighter pilot of long standing, who, in the early fifties as Sector Commander of Fighter Command's vital Eastern Sector, could seldom resist the temptation to jump into a Vampire or Venom jet night fighter at a moment's notice to participate in any convenient exercise.

44 The Auxiliary Air Force officer who had been joint Commanding Officer of No. 303 (Polish) Squadron on its formation with Hurricanes at the height of the Battle of Britain. He was awarded the DSO, two DFCs and the Polish *Virtuti Militari*.

45 Stevens, who had joined No. 151 Squadron as a sergeant pilot in September, was commissioned *after* his victory, but the Commission was backdated to 4 January, 1940. He was to be killed on 15 December the same year, having been awarded the DSO and two DFCs.

46 One of the most highly decorated of any Royal Air Force officer.

47 Vasatko had escaped from Czechoslovakia and joined the French *Armée de l'Air*, flying Curtiss Hawks with *Groupe de Chasse* I/5 as a *Capitaine*. With a score of 12 German aircraft shot down (among the highest in the French Air Force), he accompanied the *Groupe* when it flew to Algeria on 20 June, 1940, but then made his way to England, where he joined No. 312 Squadron on 5 September to fly Hurricanes, claiming a share in the destruction of a Ju 88A in October. Awarded the DFC, he was to be killed on 23 June, 1942.

48 The *Luftwaffe*, even less prepared for night fighting than the RAF at the beginning of the war, had in August 1940 started flying Junkers Ju 88C-2 intruder fighters of II./NJG 1 over British bomber bases in East Anglia and Lincolnshire.

49 It was normal practice with RAF fighters for groundcrew personnel to hold the tail down by draping themselves over the rear fuselage and tailplane while the pilot ran up the engine to full power to check mag drop. There were at least a dozen other known instances of similar accidents occurring with Hurricanes, Spitfires and other fighters during the war. On one occasion the pilot succeeded in completing a circuit and landing safely with an unwelcome passenger, cold and frightened but otherwise unhurt.

50 Most, if not all, of these losses can be reconciled with German records, although some doubt remains in the instances of Finnish casualties. The Finnish records are less explicit in times and locations of combats and losses, but at least one Finnish veteran who flew Hurricane Is—formerly supplied by Britain early in 1940 (see page 54)—recollects at least one combat in which he fought against Soviet-flown Hurricanes (after the date of the RAF's departure from Vaenga) on the northern sector of the Eastern Front.

51 The Blackburn Roc was to the Skua roughly what the Defiant was to the Hurricane or Spitfire—underpowered and overweight with a heavy four-gun power-operated turret which was largely useless in the mêlée of fighter-versus-fighter dogfighting.

52 It has been incorrectly suggested that the Hurricane I was selected as it was "being phased out of service". It was not; indeed more squadrons were being equipped with this version in Fighter Command at the time, the operational training units were crying out for it, and it was being shipped out to Middle East squadrons in fast-growing numbers. The Hurricane was selected on account of it already being in use as a trainer in the Royal Navy, and more pilots were therefore available in the Fleet Air Arm with Hurricane hours behind them if called on to fly the catapult fighters. The Spitfire I—which *was* beginning to disappear from Squadron service in the RAF—was not considered owing to its flap system interfering with the only otherwise suitable position for catapult spools. A small number of Fulmars was also employed, however.

53 Petty Officer Shaw had flown Fulmars alongside Fighter Command with No. 804 Squadron, Fleet Air Arm, during the Battle of Britain, but was to lose his life later in the war.

54 Both Davidson and Campbell had fought in the Battle of Britain, the former as a sergeant pilot flying Hurricanes with No. 249 Squadron and shooting down three German aircraft, and the latter, a Canadian, flying Spitfires with No. 54 Squadron.

55 But was posted away without seeing action in the battle.

56 HMS *Furious* made two further trips into the Mediterranean, bringing 58 Spitfires for Malta before the Torch landings in North Africa.

57 One of the Sea Hurricane pilots of No. 880 Squadron, Lieut Richard J. Cork, DSC, was credited with destroying three German and three Italian aircraft. Cork had flown Hurricanes as an Acting Sub-Lieutenant in the Battle of Britain as one of the original Fleet Air Arm volunteers to join Fighter Command. He joined No. 242 Squadron on 1 July, 1940, shooting down five enemy aircraft—for which he was awarded the DFC, later changed to the DSC. For his actions in August 1942 over the Pedestal convoy he was awarded the

DSO, but was to lose his life on 14 April, 1944, a Corsair accident in Ceylon while leading the fighter Wing of HMS *Illustrious*.

58 The most distinguished Canadian naval scout pilot who, with 60 victories to his credit, had been the third-highest scoring British Commonwealth pilot during the First World War.

59 Later Air Vice-Marshal, CB, CBE, DSC, DFC, AFC.

60 Later Air Marshal Sir Patrick Dunn, KBE, CB, DFC. Sqn Ldr Dunn had served with the Long Range Development Unit on Wellesley bombers just prior to the war. At the end of a long and distinguished career in the RAF he was appointed Commander-in-Chief, RAF Flying Training Command, from 1964 to 1966.

61 For a number of years after the war the belief persisted that Gp Capt J. E. Johnson, CBE, DSO and two Bars, DFC and Bar, was the highest-scoring RAF fighter pilot. At that time little was known of the achievements of the early desert pilots, largely owing to loss of so many squadrons' records in Greece and elsewhere. When, however, accounts were pieced together from various squadrons and individual pilots, and detailed examination of German and Italian records carried out, Pattle's record emerged. His final score, now generally accepted as 40 destroyed (solo), 4 destroyed (shared), 5 destroyed on the ground, 6 probably destroyed and 6 damaged, was gained in a period of nine months—of which seven were spent flying Gladiators. Far more significant was the fact that, unlike so many other high-scoring pilots, whose victories were gained in conditions of air superiority, if not air supremacy, Pattle's fighting career occurred at a time when the RAF faced heavy odds. All this South African's combats were fought at the age of 26, and he was awarded a single DFC.

62 One of three famous Irish brothers in the Royal Air Force, Victor Beamish had been station commander at North Weald during the Battle of Britain (see page 75).

63 Sir Roderick was the second of three brothers to be killed flying with the Royal Air Force. Their mother, Lady Rachel MacRobert of Douneside and Cromar, and widow of the 1st Baronet Sir Alexander MacRobert, was wartime President of the Spitfire-Memorial Fund, and she herself donated the cost of a Stirling bomber and three Hurricane IICs in memory of her sons, each of the latter named *The MacRobert Fighter* and inscribed with the name of one of the sons. (See page 140).

64 Promoted squadron leader, Whittingham (then aged over 40) took over command of No. 261 Squadron in April, but only one month later, due to continuing heavy losses, it was disbanded and the survivors absorbed into a new unit, No. 185 Squadron.

65 Although both these Axis fighters possessed slightly higher maximum speeds (345 mph at 18,000 feet and 338 mph at 18,000 feet, respectively, in their tropicalized configuration, compared with 334 mph at 17,250 feet of the Hurricane IIA Series 2 Trop), the advantage of initial height and less concern about use of full throttle (*vis-à-vis* fuel consumption) usually gave the intercepting fighters some small performance advantage.

66 It is perhaps of interest to note that the above-listed squadron commanders (other than those of Nos. 94, 213, 335 (Greek), 1 (SAAF) and 451 (RAAF) Squadrons, whose details are not known, and of No. 2 PRU) had an average age of 23 years 7 months; all had been pilot officers or acting pilot officers only three years previously. By contrast, Squadron Leader Hugh Macphail of No. 2 PRU, who had been a distinguished pilot in the Kaiser's War, was more than twice the age of any of these officers!

67 A small number of unarmed reconnaissance Spitfires had from time to time visited the Mediterranean during the previous six months.

68 No. 238 Squadron had just reverted to Hurricanes.

69 On returning to Libya in March the Squadron had supported General LeClerc's Free French forces on the western flank of the Eighth Army in Tunisia, and suffered very heavy losses to German *flak*. In one action on the 6th six out of ten Hurricanes were shot down. On the other hand, in an attack on an *Afrika Korps* concentration at Zamlet-el-Hadid on the 10th, the squadron destroyed six tanks, three half-tracks, 15 other armoured vehicles and ten lorries without loss.

70 As a postscript to the Balkan campaign it only remains to record that the two Greek Squadron, Nos 335 and 336, had moved across to Hassani in Greece in November 1944 and took part in the final operations against Crete and the Dodecanese islands. These two Squadrons were re-equipped with Spitfires and finally disbanded at Salonika on 31st July 1946. No. 6 Squadron of the RAF returned to Palestine in July 1945 for army co-operation duties at Megiddo with its Hurricane IVs, the last examples of which were finally retired in January 1947.

71 Frank Carey had been a sergeant pilot with No. 43 Squadron before the war. After being awarded the DFM he was commissioned, fought with No. 3 Squadron in France, with No. 43 Squadron in the Battle of Britain and, as a Squadron Leader with two DFCs and a victory tally of 18 enemy aircraft destroyed, formed No. 135 Squadron at Baginton on 15 August, 1941. He ultimately attained the rank of Group Captain with CBE, DFC and two Bars, AFC, DFM, and a score of 28 victories—all of which were gained while flying Hurricanes.

72 Count Czernin, an English national who had been a pre-war member of the RAF Reserve of Officers, had fought with great distinction during the Battle of Britain in Hurricanes with No 17 Squadron (destroying ten enemy aircraft). During the Second World War he was to be awarded the DSO, MC and DFC. He died in 1962.

73 Both "Fatty" Pearson and Freddie Proctor had been on the pre-war RAF Reserve of Officers, the former entering the Reserve with the rank of flight lieutenant in July 1929.

74 "Bill" Wise had been one of the RAF's earliest PR pilots of the war, having flown reconnaissance Spitfires in France and Britain in 1940.

75 Owing to the unpredictable behaviour of the Japanese air force No. 28 Squadron was ordered to retain the full cannon armament, but the pilots were enjoined 'not to go looking for trouble'; they also carried the 44-gallon drop tanks in case their landing was delayed for any reason. In the event, during their seven-month stay at Imphal, none of the pilots ever saw a Japanese aircraft.

76 Mark Is: *107* (ex-*P2968*), *108* (ex-*P3416*), *109* (ex-*V7173*), *110* (ex-*V7158*), *111*, *112* and *114*. Mark IICs: *115*, *116* (ex-*LF541*), *117* (crashed July 1947), *118* (ex-*LF624*), *119* and *120* (ex-*PZ796*).

APPENDIX I Summary of Hurricane Development Test Flights

Summary of Experimental Flying by Hurricanes with Hawker Aircraft Ltd at Brooklands and Langley, 1935–1947

I. BROOKLANDS

Date	*Aircraft*	*No.*	*Nature of Test*	*Engine*	*Propeller*	*Weight (lb)*
6.11.35	Prototype	K5083	First flight; handling	Merlin C No. 11	Watts Z2390	5,270
11.11.35	Proto.	K5083	Second handling	Merlin C No. 11	Watts Z2390	5,270
23.11.35	Proto.	K5083	Third handling	Merlin C No. 11	Watts Z2390	5,270
26.11.35	Proto.	K5083	Fourth handling	Merlin C No. 11	Watts Z2390	5,270
29.11.35	Proto.	K5083	Engine and under-carriage tests	Merlin C No. 11	Watts Z2390	5,270
3.12.35	Proto.	K5083	Engine handling	Merlin C No. 11	Watts Z2390	5,270
15.12.35	Proto.	K5083	Handling at increased weight	Merlin C No. 11	Watts Z2390	5,628
26.1.36	Proto.	K5083	Engine handling (new propeller)	Merlin C No. 11	Watts Z3150	5,660
5.2.36	Proto.	K5083	Engine handling (new engine)	Merlin C No. 15	Watts Z2390	5,670
7.2.36	Proto.	K5083	Engine test	Merlin C No. 15	Watts Z2390	5,676
26.5.36	Proto.	K5083	Aileron test	Merlin C No. 19	Watts Z2390	5,500
27.5.36	Proto.	K5083	Aileron test and cockpit pressures	Merlin C No. 19	Watts Z2390	5,500
27.5.36	Proto.	K5083	Diving and fuel system tests	Merlin C No. 19	Watts Z2390	5,500
16.7.36	Proto.	K5083	Landing flap with cut-out	Merlin C No. 19	Watts Z2390	5,500
17.8.36	Proto.	K5083	8-gun wing. Performance measurements	Merlin C No. 17	Watts Z3550 (no spinner)	5,660
21.8.36	Proto.	K5083	8 guns. Performance. New propeller	Merlin C No. 17	Watts Z3300 (no spinner)	5,660
25.8.36	Proto.	K5083	8 guns. Aileron tests	Merlin C No. 17	Watts Z3300 (no spinner)	5,660
26.8.36	Proto.	K5083	8 guns. Performance comparison	Merlin C No. 17	Watts Z2390 (no spinner	5,660
26.8.36	Proto.	K5083	Sliding hood test	Merlin C No. 17	Watts Z3300 (no spinner)	5,660
26.8.36	Proto.	K5083	Take-off tests	Merlin C No. 17	Various	5,660
27.10.36	Proto.	K5083	Climb and level speed measurement	Merlin C No. 17	Watts Z3551	5,638
29.10.36	Proto.	K5083	Fuel system tests	Merlin C No. 17	Watts Z3551	5,638
29.10.36	Proto.	K5083	Take-off tests	Merlin C No. 17	Watts Z3551	5,400
6.11.36	Proto.	K5083	First spinning test	Merlin C No. 17	Watts Z3551	5,685
20.11.36	Proto.	K5083	Aileron tests	Merlin C No. 17	Watts Z3551	5,685
3.3.37	Proto.	K5083	New radiator fairing and electric under-carriage indicator	Merlin C No. 17	Watts Z3551	5,697
20.3.37	Proto.	K5083	Performance with fixed tailwheel	Merlin C No. 17	Watts Z3300	5,697
12.10.37	Mk.I	L1547	1st production air-craft. Handling	Merlin II No.G.7	Watts Z3890	5,459

Date	Aircraft	No.	Nature of Test	Engine	Propeller	Weight (lb)
16.10.37	Mk.I	L1547	Handling with cg in forward position	Merlin II No.G.7	Watts Z3890	5,255
20.10.37	Mk.I	L1547	Ditto and under-carriage test	Merlin II No.G.7	Watts Z3890	5,255
23.10.37	Mk.I	L1547	Handling at full load	Merlin II No.G.7	Watts Z3890	5,993
26.10.37	Mk.I	L1547	Performance. Hood stiffened	Merlin II No.G.7	Watts Z2390	5,707
28.10.37	Mk.I	L1547	Stability with cg position normal. No aerial mast fitted	Merlin II No.G.7	Watts Z2390	5,993
28.10.37	Mk.I	L1547	Ditto. Climb and level speeds	Merlin II No.G.7	Watts Z2390	5,993
30.10.37	Mk.I	L1547	Handling with the hood removed	Merlin II No.G.7	Watts Z3892	5,707
11.11.37	Mk.I	L1547	Handling with new engine and ejector exhaust manifolds	Merlin II No. 463	Watts Z3892	5,690
12.11.37	Mk.I	L1547	As above. Airscrew tests	Merlin II No. 463	Watts Z3890	5,700
13.11.37	Mk.I	L1547	As above. Take-off measurements	Merlin II No. 463	Watts Z3890, Z3892, Z3893	5,993
23.11.37	Mk.I	L1547	Kidney exhausts. Performance measurements	Merlin II No. 463	Watts Z3895	5,993
26.11.37	Mk.I	L1547	Aerial mast replaced. Kidney exhausts	Merlin II No. 463	Watts Z3895	5,993
29.11.37	Mk.I	L1547	Oil cooling at rated altitude	Merlin II No. 463	Watts Z3895	Not stated
1.12.37	Mk.I	L1547	Aerobatics with cg at aft position	Merlin II No. 463	Watts Z3895	5,876
6.12.37	Mk.I	L1547	Dives with cg at aft position	Merlin II No. 463	Watts Z3895	5,876
19.1.38	Mk.I	L1547	Spinning, cg forward; rear underfin fitted	Merlin II No. 463	Watts Z3895	5,570
24.1.38	Mk.I	L1547	Ditto; spin parachute fitted	Merlin II No. 463	Watts Z3895	5,570
26.1.38	Mk.I	L1547	Ditto, at full load	Merlin II No. 463	Watts Z3895	6,017
1.2.38	Mk.I	L1547	Ditto, at full load and cg fully aft	Merlin II No. 463	Watts Z3895	6,017
21.4.38	Mk.I	L1547	Modified exit panel	Merlin II No. 463	Watts Z3896	5,900
4.5.38	Mk.I	L1547	Dives with cg normal	Merlin II No. 463	Watts Z3896	5,876
10.8.38	Mk.I	L1625	Tests on modified fuel vent system	Merlin II	Not stated	Not stated
12.8.38	Mk.I	L1562	Automatic landing gear retraction	Merlin II No. 431	Watts Z3895	Light load
26.8.38	Mk.I	L1638	Flap pressure measurements	Merlin II	Not stated	Not stated
29.8.38	Mk.I	L1562	DH Hamilton 2-pitch prop; cg forward limited	Merlin II	DH 54598 11 ft dia.	Not stated
13.9.38	Mk.I	L1654	Standard production performance check	Merlin II No. 583	Watts Z3897	5,670
16.9.38	Mk.I	L1562	Automatic undercart and flap control	Merlin II No. 431	DH 54598 11 ft dia.	Not stated
22.9.38	Mk.I	L1661	Standard production performance check	Merlin II No. 589	Watts Z3897	5,670
6.10.38	Mk.I	L1562	Speed performance with 2-pitch prop.	Merlin II No. 431	DH 54598 11 ft dia.	5,950
14.10.38	Mk.I	L1562	Climb performance with 2-pitch prop. (PGL)	Merlin II No. 431	DH 54598 11 ft dia.	6,300
15.10.38	Mk.I	L1562	Take-off tests with 2-pitch prop. (PGL)	Merlin II No. 431	DH 54598 1 ft dia.	6,300

Date	Aircraft	No.	Nature of Test	Engine	Propeller	Weight (lb)
15.10.38	Mk.I	L1562	Climb tests with 2-pitch prop. (RCR)	Merlin II No. 431	DH 54598 11 ft dia.	6,300
11.11.38	Mk.I	L1562	Modified tailwheel and 2-pitch prop. (PGL)	Merlin II No. 431	DH 54598 11 ft dia.	6,300
24.1.39	Mk.I	G-AFKX	1st flight. Handling with Rotol c.s. prop.	Merlin III No.11111	Rotol 10ft 6in dia.	6,130
31.1.39	Mk.I	G-AFKX	Performance with Rotol c.s. prop. (PGL)	Merlin III No. 11111	Rotol 10ft 6in dia.	6,402
6.2.39	Mk.I	L1562	Scheme B bullet-proof windscreen. (PGL)	Merlin II No. 431	DH 54598 11 ft dia.	Not stated
7.2.39	Mk.I	G-AFKX	Rotol prop. Level speeds (PWSB)	Merlin III No. 11111	Rotol 10ft 6in dia.	6,402
9.2.39	Mk.I	L1547	Spinning with DH 2-pitch prop. (PGL)	Merlin II No. 431	DH 54598 11 ft dia.	6,396
9.2.39	Mk.I	L1547	Diving with DH 2-pitch prop. (PGL)	Merlin II No. 431	DH 54598 11ft dia.	6,396
23.2.39	Mk.I	L1852	Failure of lower engine cowling in dive (KGS-S)	Merlin II	Watts	Not stated
27.2.39	Mk.I	G-AFKX	Performance with Watts prop. (PGL)	Merlin III No. 11111	Watts Z3897	6,163
14.3.39	Mk.I	G-AFKX	Performance with Rotol prop. (PGL)	Merlin III No. 11111	Rotol 10ft 6in dia.	6,402
13.3.39	Mk.I	G-AFKX	Watts prop with nose diaphragm. (RCR)	Merlin III No. 11111	Watts Z3897	6,163
5.4.39	Mk.I	L1750	Scheme A armoured windscreen. (PGL)	Merlin II	Watts	Not stated
25.3.39	Mk.I Yugoslav	No. 11	Handling and performance (RCR)	Merlin II	Watts Z3897	6,120
12.4.39	Mk.I Yugoslav	No. 11	Contract performance check (KGS-S)	Merlin II	Watts	Not stated
14.4.39	Mk.I	G-AFKX	1st flight with Rotol prop with 150mm blade roots (PGL)	Merlin III No. 11111	Rotol 150mm blade roots	6,210
15.4.39	Mk.I	G-AFKX	Ditto; performance measurements (PGL)	Merlin III No. 11111	Rotol 150mm blade roots	6,210
18.4.39	Mk.I	G-AFKX	Ditto; climb and level speeds (RCR)	Merlin III No. 11111	Rotol 150mm blade roots	6,402
18.4.39	Mk.I	G-AFKX	Ditto; climbs at 2,600 rpm (KGS-S)	Merlin III No. 11111	Rotol 150mm blade roots	6,210
21.4.39	Mk.I	L1562	Climb to 36,000ft with DH prop. (RCR)	Merlin II	DH54598 11ft dia.	6,200
28.4.39	Mk.I	L1877	First flight with stressed-skin wings; light load (PGL)	Merlin II No.1711	DH P2004	Not stated
4.5.39	Mk.I	L1696	Handling with slotted wings (RCR & PGL)	Merlin II	Not stated	Light load
13.5.39	Mk.I Belgian	No. 18	Contract performance check (PWSB)	Merlin III No. 14165	Watts Z3897	6,122
17.5.39	Mk.I Tropical	L1669	Performance and handling (PGL)	Merlin III	Rotol	Not stated
24.5.39	Mk.I	L1750	Handling and performance with two 20mm cannon (PGL)	Merlin II No. 118411	Watts Z3897	6,166
26.6.39	Mk.I Belgian	L1993	Performance check (KGS-S)	Merlin III No. 14169	Watts Z5370	Light load
4.7.39	Mk.I	G-AFKX	Metal wings fitted; performance (KGS-S)	Merlin III No. 11111	Rotol 150mm blade roots	6,130
6.7.39	Mk.I	L1856	Performance with metal wings and 100-octane fuel (RCR)	Merlin IIIS	DH 2-pitch 11ft dia.	6,449
7.7.39	Mk.I Tropical	L1893	Performance and handling (2nd aircraft) (RCR)	Merlin III	Rotol	Not stated
13.7.39	Mk.I	L2026	1st flight with Merlin XII (RCR)	Merlin XII	Rotol 10ft 9in dia.	Not stated

Date	*Aircraft*	*No.*	*Nature of Test*	*Engine*	*Propeller*	*Weight (lb)*
15.8.39	Mk.I	G-AFKX	1st flight with new Rotol prop. (RCR)	Merlin III No. 11111	Rotol 10ft 9in No. 2571	6,402
11.10.39	Mk.I	L2026	Interconnected throttle and constant speed control. (KGS-S)	Merlin XII	Rotol 10ft 9in dia.	Not stated
30.10.39	Mk.I	L1877	Rolls-Royce tropical air intake (EGR-S)	Merlin II No. 1711	DH 2-pitch 11ft dia.	6,380
15.11.39	Mk.I	L1562	Windscreen de-icing operation (KGS-S)	Merlin II No. 431	DH 54598 11ft dia.	6,300
21.12.39	Mk.I	L1877	Metal port wing, and fabric starboard wing (RCR)	Merlin II No. 1711	DH 2-pitch 11ft dia.	6,380
22.2.40	Mk.I	L1562	Carbon monoxide in cockpit (RCR)	Merlin II No. 431	DH 54598 11ft dia.	Not stated
4.3.40	Mk.I	P3265	Windscreen de-icing on A Scheme screen. (RCR)	Merlin (type not stated)	Not stated	Not stated
8.3.40	Mk.I	N2541	Windscreen de-icing on B Scheme screen	Merlin (type not stated)	Not stated	Not stated
30.3.40	Mk.I	P3345	Performance with improved external finish (RCR)	Merlin III No. 148094	Rotol CS No. 4907	Light load
16.4.40	Mk.I	P3265	Performance at high AUW (RCR)	Merlin III	Rotol CS RX5/2	6,727
7.5.40	Mk.I	P3462	Mod 169. Long-range fuel load. (RCR)	Merlin III	Rotol CS	6,950
11.5.40	Mk.I	N2485	Performance checks (RCR)	Merlin III	DH 2-pitch	6,585
15.5.40	Mk.I	P3462	Long-range fuel load performance (RCR)	Merlin III	DH 2-pitch	7,300
16.5.40	Mk.I Persian	P3720 (No. 252)	Performance checks Tropical filter (RCR)	Merlin III	DH 2-pitch	6,550
27.5.40	Mk.I	P2640	Maximum fuel overload consumption tests (RCR)	Merlin III	DH 2-pitch	7,428
9.6.40	Mk.I	G-AFKX	First flight with Merlin IV RM4S (RCR)	Merlin RM4S	Rotol CS RX5/2	6,132
5.7.40	Mk.I	G-AFKX	Dowty levered suspension tailwheel (RCR)	Merlin R4MS	Rotol CS	Not stated
6.7.40	Mk.I	G-AFKX	Lockheed tailwheel comparison (ER-S)	Merlin R4MS	Rotol CS	Not stated
11.7.40	Canadian Mk.I	P5170	Performance checks (ER-S)	Merlin III	DH 2-pitch	Light load
9.8.40	Mk.I	G-AFKX	Climb to 36,000 ft (RCR)	Merlin RM4S	Rotol CS RX5/2	6,132
19.8.40	Mk.IIA	Z2314	Production performance check (RCR)	Merlin XX	Rotol CS RX5/5	Light load
30.8.40	Mk.I	G-AFKX	Performance with new Rotol prop. (KGS-S)	Merlin RM4S	Rotol RX5/2 11ft dia.	6,655

II. LANGLEY

13.11.39	Mk.I	N2318	Speed performance with prop diaphragm (PGL)	Merlin III No. 5485	DH 2-pitch No. 500486	Light load
11.6.40	Mk.IIA	P3269	Prototype, 1st flight and handling test (PGL)	Merlin XX No. C9873	Rotol CS RX5/2	6,689
17.6.40	Mk.I	P3830	Desmo car mirror test (KGS-S)	Merlin III	Not stated	Not stated
17.6.40	Mk.IIA	P3269	Performance with enlarged prop. (PGL)	Merlin XX No. C9873	Rotol CS 11ft 6in dia.	6,738
18.6.40	Mk.I	P3925	Enlarged Desmo car mirror (KGS-S)	Merlin III	Not stated	Not stated
21.6.40	Mk.IIA	P3269	Modified radiator fairing (PGL)	Merlin XX No. C9873	Rotol CS 11ft 6in dia.	6,738
27.6.40	Mk.IIA	P3269	Performance check with Spitfire-type air intake (PGL)	Merlin XX No. C9873	Rotol CS 11ft 6in dia.	6,738

Date	Aircraft	No.	Nature of Test	Engine	Propeller	Weight (lb)
29.6.40	Mk.IIA	P3269	Fitted with Dowty tailwheel (PGL)	Merlin XX No. C9873	Rotol CS 11ft 6in dia.	6,738
1.7.40	Mk.I	P3811	Production performance check (HSB)	Merlin III	Rotol (Standard)	Not stated
11.7.40	Mk.I	R2689	Production performance check (KGS-S)	Merlin III	Rotol (Jablo)	Not stated
11.7.40	Mk.I	R2689	Production performance check (KGS-S)	Merlin III	Rotol (Schwarz)	Not stated
3.8.40	Mk.IIA	P3269	Fuel check at 35,000 feet (PGL)	Merlin XX	Rotol CS 11ft 3in dia.	6,738
20.8.40	Mk.IIA	Z2312	Measurement of full-throttle ceiling (PGL)	Merlin XX	Rotol CS RX5/5	Not stated
31.8.40	Mk.IIA	P3269	Climb to 37,000ft (PGL)	Merlin XX	Rotol Jablo 11ft 3in dia.	6,738
26.10.40	Mk.I	P3899	Sliding hood with side blisters (HSB)	Merlin III	Not stated	Not stated
5.12.40	Mk.IIC	V7360	Drum-fed 4-cannon; gun bay heating test (PGL)	Merlin XX	Not stated	Full load
8.12.40	Mk.IIA	P3269	Performance with Rotol 4-blade prop (PGL)	Merlin XX	Rotol Jablo 11ft 6in dia.	6,968
6.2.41	Mk.IIC	V2461	4-cannon, Chatellerault feed; gun bay heating test (KGS-S)	Merlin XX No. 25295	Rotol CS No. 17400	Full load
8.2.41	Mk.II Tropical	V7480	Tropical filter and extra fuel (PGL)	Merlin XX	Rotol CS RS5/3	7,059
16.4.41	Mk.IIB	Z2399	Gun heating in 12-gun wing (HSB)	Merlin XX	Rotol CS RS5/5	Not stated
3.5.41	Mk.I	G-AFKX	First flight with Merlin 45 (WH)	Merlin 45 No. 11111	Rotol CS RX5/2	6,760
5.5.41	Mk.II	AP517	Performance check on Austin-built aircraft (KGS-S)	Merlin XX	Rotol CS RS5/5	Not stated
6.5.41	Mk.IIA	P3269	Metal-covered ailerons (PGL)	Merlin XX	Not stated	Not stated
29.5.41	Mk.IIA	P3269	Full tear-drop hood with large mirrors (PGL)	Merlin XX	Not stated	Not stated
11.6.41	Mk.IIC Tropical	Z3521	Performance with 4 cannon and ferry tanks (KGS-S)	Merlin XX No. C10225	Rotol CS	8,040
11.6.41	Mk.II	Z4940	Performance at 36,000ft (JACW)	Merlin XX	Rotol CS	6,734
11.6.41	Mk.IIA	P3269	Performance with full tear-drop hood (WH)	Merlin XX No. C10225	Rotol CS	Not stated
13.6.41	Mk.IIC	Z3564	Performance with 4 cannon and ferry tanks (WH)	Merlin XX No. 26687	Rotol CS RS5/2	8,070
13.6.41	Mk.IIC	Z3521	Four cannon, ammunition and ferry tanks (WH)	Merlin XX No. C10225	Rotol CS RS5/2	8,323
23.6.41	Sea Hurricane Mk.I	P5187	Performance measurements and handling (KGS-S)	Merlin III No. 5815	DH CS No. 59700	6,801
11.7.41	Mk.IIA	P3269	Extra-bulged blister hood (PGL)	Merlin XX	Not stated	Not stated
9.8.41	Mk.II	Z2326	Jettison trials of 44-gal drop tanks (KGS-S)	Merlin XX	Not stated	Not stated
14.8.41	Mk.II	Z2326	Jettison trials of 88-gal ferry tanks (KGS-S)	Merlin XX	Not stated	Not stated
9.9.41	Mk.II	Z2326	Jettison of full 44-gal drop tanks (DMB)	Merlin XX	Not stated	Not stated
18.9.41	Mk.IID	Z2326	First flight of 40mm anti-tank guns; handling (KGS-S)	Merlin XX	Not stated	Not stated
29.9.41	Mk.II	BE225	Force landing on drop tanks (DMB)	Merlin XX	Not stated	Not stated

Date	*Aircraft*	*No.*	*Nature of Test*	*Engine*	*Propeller*	*Weight (lb)*
25.10.41	Mk.IIC	Z2905	Take-off with full 88-gal ferry tanks and ammunition (KGS-S)	Merlin XX	Rotol CS RS5/3	9,245
22.2.42	Mk.IIB	BN114	Dives to 390 mph ASI at high AUW (JAC-W)	Merlin XX	Rotol CS	8,260
23.6.42	Mk.IIB	HL953	Production performance check (TBF)	Merlin XX No. 64539	Rotol RS5/11 No. 38418	7,257
28.7.42	Mk.IID	BP173/G	Handling with 40mm anti-tank guns (HSB)	Merlin XX	Not stated	Not stated
14.3.43	Mk.IV Tropical	KX405	First flight; general handling (PGL)	Merlin 32 No. 66303	Rotol R/5/4 4-blade	7,215
16.3.43	Mk.IV Tropical	KX405	Take-off performance with Spitfire prop. (HSB)	Merlin 32 No. 66303	Rotol R/4FS 4-blade	7,215
15.4.43	Mk.IV Tropical	KX405	Performance with 3-blade prop. (HSB)	Merlin 32 No. 66303	Rotol RS5/11 3-blade	7,240
20.7.43	Mk.V Tropical	KZ193	First flight; general handling (HSB)	Merlin 27 No. 118001	Rotol R/4FS 4-blade	7,440
20.7.43	Mk.V Tropical	KZ193	Cruise performance measurements (RPB)	Merlin 27 No. 118001	Rotol R/4FS 4-blade	7,440
27.9.46	Persian 2-seater	2/31	Investigation of two-hood arrangement (WH)	Merlin XX	Rotol CS	Not stated
10.11.46	Persian 2-seater	KZ232 (2/31)	Initial spinning trials (WH)	Merlin 22	Rotol CS	Not stated
29.11.46	Portuguese Mk.IIC	LF422	Tests of tropical equipment (WH)	Merlin 22	Rotol CS RS5/10	Not stated
4.12.46	Portuguese Mk.IIC	PG538	Tests of tropical air intake	Merlin 22 No. 169927	Rotol CS RS5/10	Not stated
4.12.46	Portuguese Mk.IIC	PG453	Tests of tropical air intake (FM)	Merlin 22 No. 166867	Rotol CS RS5/10	Not stated
9.1.47	Portuguese Mk.IIC	PG538	Improved tropical air intake (FM)	Merlin 22 No. 169927	Rotol CS RS5/10	Not stated

Abbreviations of pilots' initials:

DMB	D. M. Bay
EGR-S	E. G. Russell-Stacey
FM	Sqn Ldr F. Murphy, DFC
HSB	Capt Hubert Broad, MBE, AFC
JAC-W	J. A. Crosby-Warren
KGS-S	K. G. Seth-Smith
PGL	P. G. Lucas, GM
PWSB	Gp Capt P. W. S. Bulman, CBE, MC, AFC
RCR	R. C. Reynell
RPB	Sqn Ldr R. P. Beamont, DSO, OBE, DFC
RSM	Flt Lt R. S. Munday
TBF	T. B. Fitzgerald
WH	W. Humble, MBE

APPENDIX II Extracts from a Service Test Pilot's Log Books

Transcript from the Log Books of Gp Capt S. Wroath, CBE, AFC and Bar, listing his Hurricane flying while a test pilot with the Aircraft & Armament Establishment, Martlesham Heath and Boscombe Down, 1936–43.

Date	*Aircraft*	*Test or Flight Details*	*Flight Time*	*Maximum Height*
16.3.36	K5083	Prototype—handling	:20	
24.3.36	K5083	Level speeds	1:25	28,000
24.3.36	K5083	Position error, speed course	1:25	
31.3.36	K5083	Level speeds	:20	10,000
4.4.36	K5083	Level speeds	:30	15,000
7.4.36	K5083	Climb and level speeds	1:15	27,000
3.4.37	K5083	Handling—second Phase	:15	
7.4.37	K5083	R/T tests	:40	
19.4.37	K5083	Compass tests	:25	
30.4.37	K5083	Handling	:40	
10.5.37	K5083	Aerobatics	:25	
29.5.37	K5083	Aerobatics—Empire Air Day	:20	
		Display, Martlesham and Felixstowe	:40	
26.8.37	K5083	Handling	:20	
27.8.37	K5083		1:00	
28.8.37	K5083		:40	
30.8.37	K5083		1:10	
31.8.37	K5083		1:10	
1.9.37	K5083	Flying for MGM Film at Martlesham	1:05	
2.9.37	K5083	Heath *Shadow of the Wing*	:40	
2.9.37	K5083	(starring Clarke Gable and	:55	
2.9.37	K5083	Myrna Loy); film eventually	:50	
2.9.37	K5083	issued as *Test Pilot*	:45	
2.9.37	K5083	(Air shots, etc)	:30	
2.9.37	K5083		:25	
2.9.37	K5083		:25	
14.10.37	K5083		:30	
15.10.37	K5083		:45	
21.3.38	L1562	Radiator suitability	1:25	26,000
13.4.38	L1562	Ceiling climb	1:00	33,000
20.4.38	L1562	Ceiling climb	:55	33,000
16.5.38	L1562	Air compressor test	1:10	15,000
19.5.38	L1562	Partials	:30	
21.5.38	L1562	Partials	1:25	26,000
23.5.38	L1562	Position error—speed course	1:40	
26.5.38	L1562	Air Day practice	:35	
28.8.38	L1562	Empire Air Day displays, 1938	:30	
			:40	
			:20	
			:10	
14.7.38	L1574	"Sticks"	:30	
17.8.38	L1574	Handling	:25	
6.10.38	L1574	Spinning with aft cg	:40	18,000
17.10.38	L1574	"Sticks"	:40	
20.10.38	L1574	"Sticks"	:15	
8.11.38	L1574	Handling—variable pitch airscrew	:15	
9.11.38	L1574	"Sticks"—variable pitch airscrew	:35	
18.11.38	L1574	Handling—variable pitch airscrew	:25	
22.11.38	L1574	Level speeds—variable pitch airscrew	1:00	25,000
1.12.38	L1574	Level speeds—variable pitch airscrew	:40	20,000
2.12.38	L1696	Level speeds	:25	20,000
3.1.39	L1696	Dives	:30	26,000
3.1.39	L1696	Dives	:20	26,000
31.1.39	L1696	To Hendon: Prime Minister's Panel demonstration	1.00	
1.2.39	L1696	Demonstration at Hendon	:10	
		Return from Hendon	:50	

Date	*Aircraft*	*Test or Flight Details*	*Flight Time*	*Maximum Height*
13.2.39	L1547	Spinning, 3-blade prop (cg normal)	:40	18,000
13.2.39	L1547	Spinning, 3-blade prop (cg extreme aft)	:45	
17.2.39	L1696	Night flying tests	:20	
17.2.39	L1547	Night flying tests, 3-blade prop	:25	
17.2.39	L1574	Night flying tests; exhaust manifold trials	:30	
17.2.39	L1696	Night flying tests: exhaust manifold trials	:30	
21.2.39	L1696	Handling	:30	
1.3.39	L1696	Air test	:15	
8.3.39	L1696	Climb—oil cooling	:40	28,000
9.3.39	L1696	Climb and level speeds	1:05	26,000
14.3.39	L1696	Air test	:20	
14.3.39	L1547	Take-off using flaps	:20	
16.3.39	L1547	Determination of best take-off flap angles	:50	
17.3.39	L1547	Handling	:30	
21.3.39	L1696	Climb	:45	26,000
21.3.39	L1547	Chase plane for Seversky NX2586	:45	20,000
30.3.39	L1547	Chase plane climb	:55	25,000
26.4.39	L1547	Climb abandoned—leg unlocked	:15	
27.4.39	L1547	Climb and levels—normal fuel	1:05	28,000
20.6.39	L1750	Handling with cannon installation	1:00	
8.10.39	L1750	Formations—position error	:40	
19.10.39	L1547	Handling	:45	
8.11.39	L1547	Navigation lights—test	:40	
19.11.39	L2026	Level speeds—Rotol propeller	1:10	21,000
28.11.39	L1547	Speed conversion—position error	1:20	
10.12.39	L2026	Partial climbs	1:20	30,000
10.12.39	L2026	Partial climbs	1:05	30,000
20.12.39	L1547	Handling	:50	
21.12.39	L2026	Partial climbs	:55	7,000
25.2.40	L1547	Handling	:20	
9.4.40	L2026	Handling	:30	
10.4.40	L2026	Position error—aneroid method	:45	
19.4.40	L2026	Handling	:30	
21.5.40	L2026	Handling	:25	
29.5.40	L1547	Handling	:20	
18.6.40	P3811	Handling	1:00	
17.7.40	P5170	First Canadian Hurricane; handling	:45	
22.7.40	P5170	First Canadian Hurricane; climb and level speeds	1:40	21,000
25.7.40	P5170	First Canadian Hurricane; climb and level speeds	1:20	25,000
30.7.40	P5170	First Canadian Hurricane; climb and level speeds	:35	30,000
3.8.40	P5170	First Canadian Hurricane; climb and level speeds	1:15	30,000
13.8.40	V7360	Level speeds; 4-cannon Mark I	1:00	
26.9.40	Mk II	Experience at Langley	:30	
24.11.40	Z2346	Mark II. Climb	:50	35,000
5.12.40	Z2346	Handling and "sticks"	:40	
9.12.40	V7709	Partials	1:05	29/30,000
11.12.40	V7709	Partials	1:25	29/30,000
20.12.40	V7709	Partials	1:20	29/30,000
27.12.40	Z3157	Climb and level speeds	1:15	
2.1.41	Z2415	Handling	:40	
14.1.41	Z3157	Climb and level speeds	1:15	
16.1.41	Z3157	Take-off accident—con rod through sump. "Bang!"	—	
10.2.41	Z3157	Air test after repair	:10	
23.2.41	T9526	Mk I. Climbs. Tropical filter	:30	25,000
1.3.41	T9526	Climbs. Tropical filter	:40	26,000
3.3.41	Z3157	Oil cooling (wash-out)	:50	18,000
9.3.41	Z2885	Mark IIC. Handling	:30	
14.3.41	Z3157	Oil cooling	:50	18,000
31.3.41	Z2905	Mark II. Fuel consumptions	2:50	15,000
3.4.41	Z2905	Mark II. Fuel consumptions	1:50	15,000
3.4.41	Z2905	Mark II. Fuel consumptions	2:20	15,000
5.4.41	Z2905	Mark II. Fuel consumptions	2:15	2,000
8.4.41	Z2905	Mark II. Ranges	6:00	2,000

Date	*Aircraft*	*Test or Flight Details*	*Flight Time*	*Maximum Height*
29.5.41	Z2905	Mark II. Dives	1:00	
18.6.41	Z3564	Overload tanks—handling	:30	
19.6.41	Z3564	Overload tanks—handling	:50	
19.6.41	Z3564	Overload tanks—handling	:25	
30.6.41	Z3564	Dives	:30	
30.6.41	Z3564	Dives	:30	
2.7.41	V7480	Mark I tropical. Level speeds	1:05	
12.7.41	Z3888	Climb—Mark IIC	2:00	32,000
12.7.41	Z3888	Gun firing—Lyme Regis	:50	
14.7.41	Z3888	Handling	1:05	
19.7.41	Z3888	Dives	:45	
20.7.41	Z3888	Dives	:55	
22.7.41	Z3564	Longitudinal stability test	1:00	
25.7.41	Z3564	Oil cooling during level speeds	1:20	
27.8.41	Z3564	To Langley—delivery	:40	
3.8.41	Z2346	"ADM–293" (significance unknown)	1:25	
2.9.41	Z2346	"Sticks"	:10	
8.9.41	Z2346	"Sticks"	:30	
17.9.41	Z2346	Climb and level speeds	2:20	35,000
29.9.41	Z2346	Climb and level speeds	1:40	35,000
30.9.41	Z2346	Climb and level speeds	1:15	35,000
1.10.41	Z2346	Level speeds	1:00	
7.10.41	Z2346	Level speeds	1:00	
10.10.41	V6786	Mark I. Single lever control	:55	
16.10.41	Z3888	Mark IIC. Climb and level speeds	1:00	35,000
17.10.41	V6786	Formation, single lever control	1:10	
18.10.41	Z2419	Negative g trial	:50	
20.10.41	Z2419	Climb and level speeds	1:15	35,000
20.10.41	Z3888	Mark IIC. Level speeds	:55	30,000
21.10.41	Z3888	Mark IIC. Level speeds	:25	20,000
25.10.41	Z3888	Mark IIC at overload: 9,150 lb	:20	
27.10.41	Z3888	Mark IIC. Spinning—cg normal	:30	
29.10.41	Z3888	Mark IIC Spinning—cg normal	1:00	
29.10.41	Z3888	Mark IIC. Spinning—cg extreme aft	:45	
30.10.41	V6786	Single-lever control; fuel consumption measurements	1:50	5,000
31.10.41	V6987	Negative g trial	—	
5.11.41	V6786	Single-lever control	:35	
6.11.41	V6786	Single-lever control; fuel consumption measurements	1:20	
7.11.41	Z3888	Climb and level speed performance with four 20mm cannon	1:20	35,000
7.11.41	Z3888	Climb and level speed performance with four 20mm cannon	1:00	25,000
12.11.41	Z2691	Handling	:45	
15.11.41	V6786	Consumptions; single lever	2:10	
15.11.41	V6786	Consumptions; single lever	1:05	
21.11.41	Z2691	Negative g trial	:35	
21.11.41	Z2691	Negative g trial	:35	
23.11.41	Z2691	Negative g trial	1:00	
25.11.41	Z2691	Negative g trial	:50	
7.12.41	Z2326	Mark IID prototype. Climb and level speed performance measurement	1:15	33,500
7.12.41	Z2326	Mark IID prototype. Climb and level speed performance measurement	:15	
8.12.41	Z2326	Level speeds; oil cooling check	1:10	20,000
8.12.41	Z2326	Level speeds; oil cooling check	1:10	11,000
10.2.42	BN526/G	Mark IID production. Handling	:20	
9.3.42	BN526/G	Mark IID production. Level speeds	:50	
13.3.42	BN526/G	Mark IID. Oil cooling check	1:05	
19.3.42	Z2905	Mark IIC in ferry configuration; level speed measurement	1:00	

Date	*Aircraft*	*Test or Flight Details*	*Flight Time*	*Maximum Height*
19.3.42	Z2905	Mark IIC in ferry configuration; level speed measurement	1:10	
13.4.32	Z2905	Mark IIC. Handling	:40	
16.4.42	Z2905	Long distance flight at 190 ASI	5:45	15,000
4.5.42	Z2905	Oil cooling check	:15	
4.5.42	Z2905	Oil cooling check	:40	3,000
29.5.42	Z2905	Climb and level speed with DH prop	1:15	33,500
9.6.42	Z3236	Mark IID. Further handling test	:25	
9.6.42	Z2326	Mark IID. Level speed measurement	1:25	
9.6.42	Z2326	Mark IID. Level speed measurement	1:00	
30.7.42	BP173/G	Mark IID. Handling check	1:00	
31.7.42	BP173/G	Mark IID. Dive performance	:50	
31.7.42	BP173/G	Mark IID. Aircraft to Langley	:20	
17.12.42	Z3451	Handling with cg extreme aft	:10	
19.10.42	Z3451	Handling with cg extreme aft	:20	
10.11.42	BP173/G	Mark IID. Level speed measurement	:50	
11.11.42	BP173/G	Mark IID. Level speed measurement	:35	
11.11.42	BP173/G	Mark IID. Level speed measurement	:50	
11.11.42	BP173/G	Mark IID. Level speed measurement	1:00	
9.1.43	BP173/G	Mark IID. Dive performance	:25	
13.1.43	BP173/G	Mark IID. Level speed measurement	:50	
26.1.43	HW747	Tropical Mark IIC. Handling	:45	
26.1.43	HW747	To and from Farnborough escorting captured Focke-Wulf Fw 190	1:00	
19.5.43	KZ232	Mark IIC. Climb and level speed performance	1:15	35,000
21.5.43	KZ232	Mark IIC. Climb and level speed performance	1:05	35,000
9.6.43	KZ232	Mark IIC. Position error test	:55	
3.7.43	Z2399	Mark IIC. Modified oil cooler. Handling check	:30	
24.8.43	LD264	Mark IIC bomb TIs. Handling check	:50	
2.9.43	Z2399	Mark IIC. Handling check.	:10	
14.9.43	LD264	Mark IIC bomb TIs. Handling check	:30	
21.9.43	LD264	Mark IIC bomb TIs. Handling check	:40	

APPENDIX III Highest-scoring RAF pilots who fought in Hurricanes

THE HIGHEST-SCORING ROYAL AIR FORCE PILOTS WHO FOUGHT IN HURRICANES

(Solo victories only)

Name	*Nationality*	*Total Victory Score*	*Remarks*
PATTLE, Marmaduke Thomas St John	South African	41	26 on Hurricanes (Nos. 80 and 33 Sqns) and 15 on Gladiators
TUCK, Robert Roland Stanford	British	29	12 on Hurricanes (No. 257 Sqn) and 17 on Spitfires
CAREY, Frank Reginald	British	28+	All while flying Hurricanes
LACEY, James Harry	British	28	23 on Hurricanes (No. 501 Sqn) and 5 on Spitfires
WADE, Lance C.	American	25	15 on Hurricanes (No. 33 Sqn) and 10 on Spitfires
VALE, William	British	24+	15 on Hurricanes (No. 80 Sqn) and 9 on Gladiators
DRAKE, Billy	British	23	3 on Hurricanes (No. 1 Sqn), 14 on Kittyhawks and 6 on Spitfires
ALLARD, Geoffrey	British	23	All while flying Hurricanes
BADER, Douglas Robert Stewart	British	23	11 on Hurricanes (No. 242 Sqn) and 12 on Spitfires
CROSSLEY, Michael Nicholson	British	22	All while flying Hurricanes
DALTON-MORGAN, Thomas Frederick	British	22	All while flying Hurricanes
HUGO, Petrus Hendrik	South African	22	6 on Hurricanes (No. 615 Sqn) and 16 on Spitfires
STEPHENS, Maurice Michael	British	22	11 on Hurricanes (Nos. 3, 232, 274 and 80 Sqns) and 11 on Spitfires
WOODWARD, Vernon Crompton	Canadian	21	15 on Hurricanes (Nos. 33, 80 and 274 Sqns) and 6 on Gladiators
HALLOWES, Herbert James Lampriere	British	21+	20 on Hurricanes (No. 43 Sqn) and 1+ on Spitfires
DEMOZAY, Jean E. F.	French	21	7 on Hurricanes (Nos. 1 and 242 Sqns) and 14 on Spitfires
HEWETT, Edward William Foott	British	21	10 on Hurricanes (No. 80 Sqn), 5 on Gladiators and 6 on other aircraft
McKELLAR, Archie Ashmore	British	21	20 on Hurricanes (No. 605 Sqn) and one on Spitfires
DAVID, William Dennis	British	20	All while flying Hurricanes
MARSHALL, Alfred Ernest	British	19	15 on Hurricanes (No. 73 Sqn) and 4 on Spitfires and Mosquitoes
ROBINSON, Michael Lister	British	19	7 on Hurricanes (No. 601 Sqn) 12 on Spitfires
DUTTON, Roy Gilbert	British	19	All while flying Hurricanes
BROWN, Mark Henry	Canadian	18+	All while flying Hurricanes
BOYD, Adrian Hope	British	18	14 on Hurricanes (No. 145 Sqn) and 4 on Spitfires
KUTTELWASCHER, Karel	Czech	18	All while flying Hurricanes
LEWIS, Albert Gerald	South African	18	All while flying Hurricanes
MASON, Ernest Mitchelson	British	18	All while flying Hurricanes
FRANTISEK, Jozef	Czech	17	All while flying Hurricanes
KANE, Edgar James	New Zealander	17	All while flying Hurricanes
NEIL, Thomas Francis	British	17	All while flying Hurricanes
ORTON, Newell	British	17	15 on Hurricanes (No. 73 Sqn) and 2 on Spitfires
URBANOWICZ, Witold	Polish	17	All while flying Hurricanes (plus 3 on USAAFP-40s)
CULLEN, Richard Nigel	Australian	16+	9 on Hurricanes (No. 80 Sqn) and 7+ on Gladiators
MacLACHLAN, James Archibald Findlay	British	16+	13 on Hurricanes (Nos. 73, 145, 261 and 1 Sqns) and 3 on other aircraft
McKNIGHT, William Lidstone	Canadian	16+	All while flying Hurricanes (No. 615 Sqn)
AITKEN, John William Maxwell	British	16	7 on Hurricanes (No. 601 Sqn) and 9 on other aircraft
McKAY, Donald Alistair Stewart	British	16	8 on Hurricanes (No. 501 Sqn and 421 Flt) and 8 on Spitfires
CLISBY, Leslie Redford	Australian	16	All while flying Hurricanes (No. 1 Sqn)
LLEWELLYN, Reginald Thomas	British	16	All while flying Hurricanes (No. 213 Sqn)
NOWELL, Gareth Leofric	British	16	14 on Hurricanes (Nos. 87 and 32 Sqns) and 2 on other aircraft
SANDERS, James Gilbert	British	16	6 on Hurricanes (No. 615 Sqn), 3 on Gladiators and 7 on other aircraft
SIMPSON, Peter James	British	16	4 on Hurricanes (No. 111 Sqn) and 12 on Spitfires

Name	*Nationality*	*Total Victory Score*	*Remarks*
BROTHERS, Peter Malam	British	15	9 on Hurricanes (Nos. 32 and 257 Sqns) and 6 on Spitfires
CURRANT, Christopher Frederick	British	15	All while flying Hurricanes (Nos. 151 and 501 Sqns)
CZERNIN, Count Manfred Beckett	British	15	All while flying Hurricanes (Nos. 85 and 17 Sqns)
DOE, Robert Francis Thomas	British	15	4 on Hurricanes (No. 238 Sqn) and 11 on Spitfires
FROST, John Everitt	South African	15	8 on Hurricanes (No. 3 Sqn, SAAF) and 7 on Tomahawks
GLEED, Ian Richard	British	15	11 on Hurricanes (No. 87 Sqn) and 4 on Spitfires
HIGGINSON, Frederick William	British	15	11 on Hurricanes (No. 56 Sqn) and 4 on Typhoons
KILMARTIN, John Ignatius	British	15	14 on Hurricanes (No. 1 Sqn) and 1 on Typhoons
MILNE, Richard Maxwell	British	15	8 on Hurricanes (No. 151 Sqn) and 7 on Spitfires
PAGE, Alan Geoffrey	British	15	2 on Hurricanes (No. 56 Sqn) and 13 on other aircraft
SCOULAR, John Evelyn	British	15	12 on Hurricanes (No. 73 Sqn) and 3 on Gladiators and Tomahawks
STORRAR, James Eric	British	15	All while flying Hurricanes (Nos. 145 and 73 Sqns)
WYKEHAM-BARNES, Peter Guy	British	15	7 on Hurricanes (Nos. 80, 33, 274 and 73 Sqns), 5 on Gladiators and 3 on other aircraft

The above figures, reflecting the claims by 55 of the RAF's 109 highest-scoring fighter pilots, total 1,044 enemy aircraft claimed shot down, of which 759 (72.7 per cent) were claimed by Hurricane pilots, 161 (15.4 per cent) by Spitfire pilots and 124 (11.9 per cent) by pilots of other fighter aircraft. Compared with the claims recorded in 11,400 traceable air-to-air combat reports (Forms 1151), covering all RAF fighter pilots' claims, 55 per cent were by Hurricane pilots, 33 per cent by Spitfire pilots and 12 per cent by pilots of other fighters. If claims by bomber crews are taken into account the figures are modified to become 51.5, 30.5 and 11.0 per cent respectively, with approximately 7 per cent claimed by the bomber crews.

THE COUNTERFEIT HURRICANES

ACCORDING TO HAWKER RECORDS there was a total of 394 'presentation' Hurricanes, that is aircraft subscribed by individual persons, families, bodies, villages, towns, cities and States who requested that their presentation aircraft be inscribed accordingly. As far as can be discovered roughly half of these aeroplanes did leave the Brooklands, Langley, Gloster and Austin factories duly inscribed; others may have been 'dedicated' and inscribed while in service (see, for instance pages XX, XX and XX).

It is known however that at least 60 'presentation' inscriptions were applied at Langley to just five aircraft by the simple expedient of changing the serial number and re-painting the side of the fuselage below the cockpit sill on the port side and re-applying a new inscription. The purpose was obviously so that photographs might be sent to the subscribers as 'evidence' of the dedications. Three such photographs are reproduced above.

In the following instances the spurious nature of these dedications is detectable by the choice of counterfeit serial numbers which did not apply to the correct version of the Hurricane (for instance none of the BP or HL serials were applicable to Hurricane IVs); in other instances there are clear indications that serial numbers have been repeatedly altered.

Z2705	*Mark IIA*	'BAHAMAS'
Z2730	*Mark IIA*	'FEN TIGER'
Z3773	*Mark IIB*	*(Dedication illegible*
BP352	*Mark IIC*	'MOHLOMI'
BP390	*Mark IV*	'THE COTSWOLD QUEEN'
BP433	*Mark IV*	'S.R.C.D. No ONE'
BP441	*Mark IV*	'CITY OF INDORE'
BP444	*Mark IV*	'FIJI CIVIL SERVICE'
BP445	*Mark IV*	'JODHPUR JAGIRDARS'
BP452	*Mark IV*	'KENYA WEEKLY NEWS'
BP471	*Mark IV*	'PALESTINE & TRANSJORDAN VI'
HL670	*Mark IV*	'BASTAR'
HL676	*Mark IV*	'BRITISH SPLENDOUR'
HL677	*Mark IV*	'BRITISH RESOURCE'
HL678	*Mark IV*	'CAMBAY I'
HL679	*Mark IV*	'ORISSA VII'
HW660	*Mark IV*	'SWAZILAND II'
KW922	*Mark IIC*	'ORISSA VIII'
KW924	*Mark IIC*	'BRITISH PRUDENCE'

APPENDIX IV Production, Allocation and History of Hurricanes

Notes of Explanation

1. While all Hurricanes built and converted are annotated in this Appendix in the periodic introductory paragraphs, greatest emphasis on historical detail is laid upon aircraft flown by operational units, particularly prior to and early in the Second World War, as well as those flown in the Mediterranean, Middle and Far Eastern theatres.
2. The widely quoted figure of 14,231 as being the total number of Hurricanes produced must be regarded with considerable scepticism following recent research, although it is the figure that has been perpetuated by the manufacturers down the years. At least 150 "new" aircraft were delivered by Hawker (and a similar number by Gloster) employing major spare parts, as well as cannibalized components from damaged aircraft; retrospective adjustments were of course made to contract terms. Moreover, almost 3,000 Hurricanes, which were struck off Royal Air Force charge (as being beyond Service capabilities to repair) were made good by the extensive Repair Organization and taken back on charge "as new" by the Service, in some instances with new serial numbers. (This also, of course, complicates the generally accepted aircraft casualty figures issued for such periods as the Battle of Britain, when more than 400 Hurricanes, admitted as having been shot down, lost and struck off charge, were subsequently salvaged, repaired and returned to the Service.) In all, the civilian repair agencies returned about 4,500 damaged aircraft to the RAF, though many of them had not been struck off charge. A further 1,400 repaired aircraft were returned to the Service overseas and to the Fleet Air Arm. It is therefore impossible (and misleading) to quote an exact number of wholly new Hurricanes built—the true figure for the RAF is probably about 14,100, compared with about 14,380 "new" aircraft taken on charge by the Service, and these figures do not include unquestionably new aircraft sold overseas before the war, some of which were taken from the Air Ministry's original order and then replaced for the RAF, reverting to their original serial numbers.
3. Much confusion has also been created by the practice of painting spurious serial numbers on "presentation" aircraft for photographic purposes, the great majority of presentation inscriptions being removed prior to delivery to the Service. Such presentation aircraft are not listed as only likely to compound the confusion (See however p. 212).
4. Dates in the Appendix are shown in the "British" fashion, i.e. day-month-year (e.g., 3-9-40, 3 September, 1940), or month-year (9-40).
5. Unless otherwise stated, all squadrons referred to are Royal Air Force Squadrons. The nationality of pilots is given, where known; however, the absence of nationality does not necessarily indicate that the pilot is of British or British Commonwealth nationality.
6. The statement that a Hurricane has been shot down or crashed cannot be taken to indicate that it was necessarily destroyed or "struck off charge", although if an accident or crash resulted in the death of the pilot it was extremely rare for the aircraft to be salvaged, repaired and returned to flying duties. (See also Para 2 above.)
7. Squadron code letters. These are annotated as "*NO-B*", "*US-A*", etc. In many instances, however, particularly at times of considerable operational activity, the squadron simply identified its aircraft by a single letter. There are many instances in this Appendix where only the aircraft individual letter is known (as being its reference in Squadron Forms 541); it does not imply that the full code letters were not painted on the aircraft.
8. Sources of material. The bulk of material in this Appendix (particularly that relating to the years 1937–1941) originated in Squadron Forms 541 (as distinct from the history Forms 540), computerized and cross-referred to extracts from surviving pilots' log books. This has been reinforced by reference to manufacturers' Service record cards. Theoretically these record cards should be identical to the record cards now held at the Public Record Office, but a random check on some 100 cards has disclosed an astonishing number of discrepancies; only by checking a third, independent source (photographs, pilot's log book, Form 541, etc) has it been possible to come closer to accuracy.
9. It must be stated that material here presented supersedes anything that appeared in this Author's former work *THE HAWKER HURRICANE*, originally published in 1962 (and subsequent works by other authors which used this book to present such material), and does so as the result of continuing research.

HAWKER F.36/34 ("INTERCEPTOR MONOPLANE") HURRICANE PROTOTYPE. One aircraft, *K5083*, developed and designed to Air Ministry Specification F.36/34 and ordered under Contract No. 357483/34. Powered by Rolls-Royce Merlin "C" (Nos. 11, 15, 17 and 19) engines driving Watts wooden two-blade fixed-pitch propellers (No. Z.2390, Z3150, etc.). First flown on 6th November 1935 at Brooklands by Flt. Lt. P.W.S. Bulman. Trials at Brooklands, Martlesham Heath, Farnborough, and Hucknall, 1935-37. Eight-gun wings first fitted and flown, 17th August 1936. Employed in filming of "*Shadow of the Wing*" at Martlesham Heath, September-October 1937, flown by F/Sgt. S. Wroath, R.A.F.

HAWKER HURRICANE MARK I (Hawker-built). First production batch of 600 aircraft built by Hawker Aircraft Limited, Kingston-upon-Thames and Brooklands, during 1937-39 to Air Ministry Specification 15/36, and ordered under Contract No. 527112/36, dated 3rd June 12936. *L1547-L2146*. First flight by *L1547*, 12th October 1937, flown by P.G. Lucas (with Merlin II No. G.7, driving Watts Type Z.38 wooden fixed-pitch propeller). Deliveries commenced (to No. 111 (Fighter) Sqradron, Northolt), 15th December 1937. Delivery of entire batch completed on 6th October 1939. Average rate of production, approximately two aircraft per day. Rolls-Royce Merlin II engines and Watts wooden propellers fitted initially but many later replaced by Merlin IIIs and Rotol or D.H. variable-pitch and constant-speed three-blade propellers. Early aircraft did not feature ventral spine fairings; fabric-covered wing fitted on almost all aircraft but some were later modified with metal stressed-skin wings at Maintenance Units.

L1547 *Production trials* at Brooklands, Martlesham Heath and Hucknall, 1937-38; No. 111 Sqn., Northolt, 10-38; No. 312 (Czech) Sqn., Speke, 10-40; shot down beside Mersey, 10-10-40; Sgt. O. Hanzlicek (Czech) killed.

L1548 No. 111 Sqn., Northolt, 1-38; No. 6 O.T.U., became ***3273M***, 7-42.

L1549 No. 111 Sqn., Northolt, 1-38; crashed on approach to Northolt, Hillingdon, 20-7-38.

L1550 No. 111 Sqn., Northolt, 1-38; crashed in forced landing, Colnbrook, Bucks, 18-7-38.

L1551 No. 111 Sqn., Northolt, 1-38; crashed in forced landing, Ickenham, Middlesex, 15-5-38. Became ***2307M.***

L1552 No. 111 Sqn., Northolt, 1-38; No. 56 O.T.U.; crashed in forced landing, Terrington Marsh, Norfolk, 17-12-40; became ***2643M.***

L1553 No. 111 Sqn., Northolt, 1-38; wheels-up landing at Northolt, 6-10-38; became ***1430M.***

L1554 No. 111 Sqn., Northolt, 1-38; crashed while landing at Northolt, 24-4-39; became ***1493M.***

L1555 No. 111 Sqn., Northolt, 1-38; No. 6 O.T.U.; No. 56 O.T.U.; crashed at Long Sutton, Norfolk, 17-4-41.

L1556 No. 111 Sqn., Northolt, 2-38; crashed at Uxbridge, 1-2-39.

L1557 No. 111 Sqn., Northolt, 2-38; crashed after take-off 2 miles SW of Biggin Hill, 9-8-39.

L1558 No. 111 Sqn., Northolt, 2-38; crashed near Alton, Hants, 17-1-39.

L1559 No. 111 Sqn., Northolt, 2-38; crashed near Dorking, Surrey, 17-1-39. Became ***1539M.***

L1560 No. 111 Sqn., Northolt, 2-38. To R.A.E., Farnborough. Became ***1191M.***

L1561 No. 111 Sqn., Northolt, 2-38; force landed on Harrow golf course, Middlesex, 17-2-39. Became ***1368M.***

L1562 Production trials, Martlesham Heath, 1938; fitted with metal wings. Special Duties Flt. *Converted to Mark IIA and shipped to Russia* as ***DR344***, 1941.

L1563 No. 111 Sqn., Northolt, 2-38. A.F.D.U. No. 52 O.T.U. No. 55 O.T.U. No. 41 O.T.U.; crashed while landing at Andover, 4-3-44.

L1564 No. 111 Sqn., Northolt, 2-38; **TM-P**, 9-38; crashed in sea, 2-6-40.

L1565 No. 3 Sqn., Biggin Hill, 3-38. No. 73 Sqn. No. 56 Sqn. No. 3 Sqn. No. 253 Sqn.; Missing, 1-6-40.

L1566 No. 3 Sqn., Biggin Hill, 3-38. No. 73 Sqn.; crashed while landing at Sutton Bridge, 9-5-39.

L1567 No. 3 Sqn., Biggin Hill, 3-38. No. 32 Sqn., Biggin Hill. S.O.C., 8-39.

L1568 No. 3 Sqn., Biggin Hill, 3-38. No. 73 Sqn. No. 56 O.T.U. No. 8 F.T.S. No. 51 O.T.U. Became ***4534M***, 2-44.

L1569 No. 3 Sqn., Biggin Hill, 3-38. No. 73 Sqn., Digby; crashed while landing at Norrent-Fontes, 8-10-39; assumed abandoned in France, 5-40, while still under repair.

L1570 No. 3 Sqn., Biggin Hill, 3-38. No. 73 Sqn., Digby; crashed while taking off at Digby, 21-4-39.

L1571 No. 3 Sqn., Biggin Hill, 3-38. No. 73 Sqn., Digby. No. 5 O.T.U. No. 5 F.T.S. No. 55 O.T.U. No. 41 O.T.U. S.O.C., 6-7-44.

L1572 No. 3 Sqn., Biggin Hill, 3-38. No. 73 Sqn., Digby. No. 32 Sqn., Biggin Hill. No. 242 Sqn., Coltishall. No. 501 Sqn., A.A.F. No. 5 O.T.U. No. 8 F.T.S. No. 318 (Polish) Sqn.; crashed at Detling after engine failure, 2-7-43.

L1573 No. 3 Sqn., Biggin Hill, 3-38. No. 73 Sqn., Digby; crashed near Newark, Notts, 23-6-39.

L1574 *Production trials*, Martlesham Heath, 1938. No. 6 O.T.U. No. 56 O.T.U. A.T.A. No. 59 O.T.U. No. 41 O.T.U. S.O.C., 23-4-44.

L1575 *Retained by manufacturers as exhibition aircraft*, 1938. No. 85 Sqn., Debden; crashed while landing at Debden, 3-1-39. Became ***1380M.***

L1576 No. 3 Sqn., Biggin Hill, 4-38. No. 73 Sqn., Digby; crashed while landing at Digby, 9-3-39.

L1577 No. 3 Sqn., Biggin Hill, 4-38. No. 73 Sqn., Digby. No. 43 Sqn. No. 607 Sqn., A.A.F.; crashed at Middle Moneynut, East Lothian, 1-2-41.

L1578 No. 3 Sqn., Biggin Hill, 4-38. No. 73 Sqn., Digby. No. 501 Sqn., A.A.F.; shot down near Ashford, Kent, 2-9-40; P/O A.T. Rose-Price killed.

L1579 No. 3 Sqn., Biggin Hill, 4-38; crashed while landing at Kenley, 10-5-38.

L1580 No. 3 Sqn., Biggin Hill, 4-38. No. 73 Sqn., Digby; crashed while landing at Digby, 25-7-39.

L1581 No. 111 Sqn., Northolt, 4-38, **TM-Q**. No. 56 O.T.U. *Converted to Mark IIA*, ***BV157***, 1940.

L1582 No. 3 Sqn., Biggin Hill, 4-38. No. 73 Sqn., Digby; crashed while landing at Digby, 4-8-39.

L1583 No. 111 Sqn., Northolt, 4-38. No. 263 Sqn. No. 3 Sqn. No. 504 Sqn., A.A.F. A.T.A. S.O.C., 22-12-41.

L1584 No. 111 Sqn., Northolt, 4-38. No. 213 Sqn. No. 111 Sqn. No. 242 Sqn. No. 56 Sqn. No. 615 Sqn., A.A.F.; shot down by Bf 109s off Dover, 14-7-40; P/O M.R. Mudie died after rescue.

L1585 No. 3 Sqn., Biggin Hill, 4-38. No. 73 Sqn., Digby. No. 79 Sqn., Biggin Hill. No. 257 Sqn.; shot down near Billericay, 3-9-40; pilot baled out safely.

L1586 No. 3 Sqn., Biggin Hill, 5-38. No. 73 Sqn., Digby. No. 79 Sqn., Biggin Hill; crashed at Pett, Sussex, 21-11-39.

L1587 No. 3 Sqn., Biggin Hill, 5-38. No. 73 Sqn., Digby. S.O.C., 27-2-40.

L1588 No. 3 Sqn., Biggin Hill, 5-38. No. 73 Sqn., Digby; crashed on beach, 29-9-39.

L1589 No. 111 Sqn., Northolt, 5-38, **TM-R**. S.O.C., 5-40.

L1590 No. 56 Sqn., North Weald, 5-38. No. 17 Sqn. No. 85 Sqn. No. 1 Sqn. S.O.C., 30-11-39.

L1591 No. 56 Sqn., North Weald, 5-38, **LR-B**. No. 17 Sqn. No. 3 Sqn.; Missing, 14-5-40.

L1592 No. 56 Sqn., North Weald, 5-38. No. 17 Sqn. No. 87 Sqn. No. 43 Sqn., **FT-C**. No. 17 Sqn. No. 152 Sqn. No. 43 Sqn. No. 615 Sqn., A.A.F. Special Duties Flt. No. 9 Air Observers' School. No. 5 P.A.F.U. No. 9 P.A.F.U. *Restored and preserved as museum display aircraft.*

L1593 No. 56 Sqn., North Weald, 5-38, LR-C. No. 79 Sqn., Biggin Hill; crashed near Ditchling Common, Sussex, 20-6-39.

L1594 No. 56 Sqn., North Weald, 5-38. No. 17 Sqn. No. 79 Sqn. No. 56 Sqn. No. 43 Sqn. No. 56 O.T.U. Service Pilots' Ferry Pool. No. 5 F.T.S. No. 9 F.T.S. No. 9 P.A.F.U. Crashed near Castle Combe, 24-7-42.

L1595 No. 56 Sqn., North Weald, 5-38. No. 504 Sqn., A.A.F. No. 242 Sqn., Coltishall. No. 249 Sqn.; crashed near Bulford Camp, Amesbury, Wilts, 20-9-40.

L1596 No. 56 Sqn., North Weald, 5-38; damaged during delivery but repaired. No. 32 Sqn. No. 55 O.T.U.; crashed at Aston Down, 27-12-40. Repaired and fitted with metal wings and *converted to Mark IIA*, ***DG618***, 1941.

L1597 No. 56 Sqn., North Weald, 5-38; wheels-up landing at North Weald, 6-2-39. Became ***1242M.***

L1598 No. 56 Sqn., North Weald, 5-38; collided with Hurricane ***L1611*** and crashed near North Weald, 12-6-39.

L1599 No. 56 Sqn., North Weald, 5-38; crashed near Chelmsford, Essex, 24-4-39.

L1600 No. 56 Sqn., North Weald, 5-38. No. 17 Sqn. No. 213 Sqn. No. 501 Sqn., A.A.F. No. 253 Sqn. No. 55 O.T.U. Became ***4862M.***

L1601 No. 56 Sqn., North Weald, 6-38. No. 17 Sqn. No. 605 Sqn., A.A.F. No. 151 Sqn. No. 46 Sqn. No. 6 O.T.U. No. 9 F.T.S. R.A.F. College, Cranwell. No. 56 O.T.U.; collided with Hurricane ***V7081*** and crashed near Tealing, 4-7-43.

L1602 No. 56 Sqn., North Weald, 6-38; crashed while landing at Filton, 2-6-39. Became ***1703M.***

L1603 No. 56 Sqn., North Weald, 6-38; crashed while landing at night at Northolt, 29-9-38. Became ***1181M.***

L1604 No. 85 Sqn., Debden, 8-38; crashed while landing at Debden, 12-12-38. Became ***1468M.***

L1605 No. 56 Sqn., North Weald, 6-38. No. 17 Sqn. No. 213 Sqn. No. 501 Sqn., A.A.F. No. 87 Sqn.; written off, 30-5-40.

L1606 No. 151 Sqn., North Weald. No. 56 Sqn., North Weald; damaged in accident while landing at North Weald. *Returned to H.A.L. and repaired; purchased by H.A.L. and registered* **G-AFKX;** *armament removed and employed for T.I.s, including Rotol propeller.*

L1607 No. 56 Sqn., North Weald. No. 17 Sqn. No. 111 Sqn.; shot down by Bf 110 over France, 18-5-40.

L1608 No. 56 Sqn., North Weald. No. 17 Sqn. No. 152 Sqn. No. 43 Sqn.; shot down, 7-6-40.

L1609 No. 56 Sqn., North Weald, **LR-D.** No. 17 Sqn, **UV-D.** No. 501 Sqn., A.A.F. No. 253 Sqn. No. 3 Sqn.; abandoned over Merville, France, 17-5-40.

L1610 No. 56 Sqn., North Weald. No. 17 Sqn. No. 3 Sqn.; force landed at Wevelghem, 15-5-40, and abandoned.

L1611 No. 56 Sqn., North Weald, 6-38. No. 17 Sqn. No. 605 Sqn., A.A.F. No. 253 Sqn. S.O.C., 5-40.

L1612 No. 87 Sqn., Debden, 7-38. S.O.C., 5-40.

L1613 No. 87 Sqn., Debden, 7-38; crashed at Plechatel, France, 12-2-40.

L1614 No. 87 Sqn., Debden, 7-38. S.O.C., 5-40.

L1615 No. 87 Sqn., Debden, 7-38. No. 253 Sqn. No. 504 Sqn., A.A.F.; shot down at Graveney, near Faversham, Kent, 7-9-40; P/O K.V. Wendle killed.

L1616 No. 87 Sqn., Debden, 8-38. S.O.C., 5-40.

L1617 No. 87 Sqn., Debden, 8-38. No. 79 Sqn., Biggin Hill. No. 56 O.T.U. S.O.C., 7-1-42.

L1618 No. 87 Sqn., Debden, 8-38; pilot lost control after being dazzled by searchlights and abandoned aircraft over Steeple Morden, Cambs, 18-8-39.

L1619 No. 87 Sqn., Debden, 8-38; force landed at Courtrai, Belgium, 10-11-39, and interned.

L1620 No. 87 Sqn., Debden, 8-38; crashed into sea off Holbeach, Lincs, 14-9-38.

L1621 No. 87 Sqn., Debden, 9-38; crashed while landing at Debden, 6-2-39. Became ***1431M.***

L1622 No. 87 Sqn., Debden, 9-38; wheels-up landing at Debden, 6-2-39. Became ***1237M.***

L1623 No. 87 Sqn., Debden, 9-38; abandoned over sea

off Felixstowe, 17-7-39.

L1624 No. 87 Sqn., Debden, 9-38. No. 79 Sqn., Biggin Hill. No. 501 Sqn., A.A.F.; written off, 21-6-40.

L1625 No. 87 Sqn., Debden, 9-38; crashed on take-off at Bury St. Edmunds L.G., 11-11-39. Became ***1370M.***

L1626 No. 87 Sqn., Debden, 9-38; crashed while taking off at Debden, 19-11-38.

L1627 No. 87 Sqn., Debden, 9-38; crashed while landing at Debden, 11-7-39.

L1628 No. 87 Sqn., Debden, 9-38; force landed at La Panne, Belgium, 14-11-39, and interned.

L1629 No. 87 Sqn., Debden, 9-38; crashed near Debden, 2-2-39.

L1630 No. 87 Sqn., Debden, 9-38; lost or abandoned in France, 5-40.

L1631 No. 3 Sqn., Biggin Hill, 9-38. No. 111 Sqn., Northolt, TM-S; crashed during night landing at Northolt, 8-9-39.

L1632 No. 85 Sqn., Debden, 9-38; lost in France, 5-40.

L1633 No. 73 Sqn., Digby, 9-38; crashed during night landing at Digby, 18-4-39.

L1634 No. 85 Sqn., Debden, 9-38; crashed during night landing at Debden, 20-12-38. Became ***1358M.***

L1635 No. 85 Sqn., Debden, 9-38, **NO-B**; lost in France, 5-40.

L1636 No. 85 Sqn., Debden, 9-38. No. 17 Sqn. No. 501 Sqn., A.A.F. No. 87 Sqn. No. 4 F.P.P. Service Pilots' Ferry Pool. Converted to Mark IIA, ***DG640.***

L1637 No. 85 Sqn., Debden, 9-38; force landed in France and abandoned, 5-40.

L1638 Hydraulic trials, H.A.L., Brooklands, 1938. No. 111 Sqn., Northolt, 2-39. No. 504 Sqn., A.A.F. No. 242 Sqn., Coltishall. No. 56 O.T.U. No. 5 F.T.S. No. 6 F.P.P.; crashed at Kirkbride, 6-2-42.

L1639 No. 85 Sqn., Debden, 9-38. No. 504 Sqn., A.A.F., Hucknall; lost in France, 5-40.

L1640 No. 85 Sqn., Debden, 9-38; lost in France, 5-40.

L1641 No. 85 Sqn., Debden, 9-38; lost in France, 5-40.

L1642 No. 85 Sqn., Debden, 9-38. S.O.C., 6-12-39.

L1643 No. 85 Sqn., Debden, 9-38; crashed on take-off at Debden, 12-4-39. Became ***1474M.***

L1644 No. 85 Sqn., Debden, 9-38. No. 3 Sqn. No. 312 (Czech) Sqn.; abandoned after fire in the air near Cambridge, 10-9-40.

L1645 No. 56 Sqn., North Weald, 9-38. No. 17 Sqn. No. 253 Sqn. No. 3 Sqn.; Missing in France, 15-5-40.

L1646 No. 87 Sqn., Debden, 9-38; lost in France, 5-40.

L1647 No. 32 Sqn., Biggin Hill, 9-38; taxied into tractor at Sutton Bridge, 2-5-39.

L1648 No. 85 Sqn., Debden, 9-38; crashed while landing at Debden, 6-10-38.

L1649 No. 85 Sqn., Debden, 9-38; lost in France, 5-40.

L1650 No. 85 Sqn., Debden, 9-38; crashed on take-off at Debden, 12-1-39. Became ***1365M.***

L1651 No. 85 Sqn., Debden, 9-38; crashed while landing at Aldergrove, 27-10-38. Became ***1215M.***

L1652 Crashed on test at H.A.L., Brooklands, 9-38; test pilot John Hindmarsh killed; aircraft to No. 4 M.U., Ruislip, for disposal.

L1653 No. 85 Sqn., Debden, 9-38. No. 253 Sqn. No. 7 O.T.U. No. 5 O.T.U. No. 5 F.T.S. No. 52 O.T.U. No. 55 O.T.U. No. 5 F.T.S. No. 5 P.A.F.U. A.T.A. Disposal details not known.

L1654 No. 111 Sqn., Northolt, 9-38. No. 151 Sqn., North Weald. No. 242 Sqn., Coltishall. No. 6 O.T.U., Sutton Bridge; collided with Hurricane ***L1833*** and crashed at Saddlebow, near Kings Lynn, 3-9-40; Sgt. F.J. Howarth killed.

L1655 No. 32 Sqn., Biggin Hill, 9-38. No. 253 Sqn.; lost in France, 5-40.

L1656 No. 85 Sqn., Debden, 9-38; crashed while landing at Debden, 9-11-38. Became ***1232M.***

L1657 No. 73 Sqn., Digby, 9-38. No. 501 Sqn., A.A.F.; shot down by Bf 109Es at Pembury, 30-9-40; F/O N.J.M. Barry unhurt. Aircraft repaired. No. 52 O.T.U. Became ***2834M***, 12-40.

L1658 No. 32 Sqn., Biggin Hill, 9-38. No. 55 O.T.U.; crashed near Aston Down, 1-11-40; repaired and *converted to Mark IIA*, ***DG622***, 1941.

L1659 No. 32 Sqn., Biggin Hill, 9-38. No. 501 Sqn., A.A.F. No. 257 Sqn. No. 56 O.T.U.; crashed while landing at Sutton Bridge, 19-11-40. Became ***3222M***, 7-42.

L1660 No. 32 Sqn., Biggin Hill, 9-38. No. 253 Sqn. No. 111 Sqn. No. 6 O.T.U. No. 55 O.T.U. No. 8 F.T.S. Became ***3587M.***

L1661 No. 32 Sqn., Biggin Hill, 9-38; pilot abandoned aircraft 5 miles south of Herne Bay, Kent, 9-7-39.

L1662 No. 32 Sqn., Biggin Hill, 10-38. Crashed at Tatsfield, Kent, 11-8-39.

L1663 No. 32 Sqn., Biggin Hill, 10-38. No. 253 Sqn. No. 56 O.T.U. No. 8 F.T.S. Became ***4501M***, 1-44.

L1664 No. 32 Sqn., Biggin Hill, 10-38. No. 601 Sqn., A.A.F. No. 5 O.T.U. No. 56 O.T.U. No. 1422 Flt. No. 59 O.T.U. No. 63 O.T.U. No. 4 Tactical Exercise Unit. S.O.C., 27-5-44.

L1665 No. 32 Sqn., Biggin Hill, 10-38. No. 242 Sqn., Coltishall; Missing in action, 18-5-40.

L1666 No. 32 Sqn., Biggin Hill, 10-38. No. 242 Sqn. No. 253 Sqn. No. 56 O.T.U. No. 9 F.T.S. A.T.A.; crashed 5-2-44.

L1667 No. 32 Sqn., Biggin Hill 10-38. No. 253 Sqn.; Missing in action, 18-5-40.

L1668 No. 32 Sqn., Biggin Hill, 10-38. No. 253 Sqn., Manston, 1-40; pilot abandoned aircraft near Rickmansworth, Herts, 26-4-40.

L1669 *First tropicalised aircraft;* Rolls-Royce Ltd., 12-38; A. & A.E.E.; *to Khartoum for tropical trials*, 1939; No. 80 Sqn., Egypt. No. 274 Sqn., Egypt, 1940. Crashed while landing at Amriya, 30-9-40.

L1670 No. 32 Sqn., Biggin Hill, 10-38. No. 601 Sqn., A.A.F. No. 4 F.P.P. No. 55 O.T.U.; crashed at Keld, Yorks, after fire in the air, 10-4-41.

L1671 No. 1 Sqn., Tangmere, 10-38. No. 43 Sqn., Tangmere. No. 1 Sqn.; lost in France, 5-40.

L1672 No. 32 Sqn., Biggin Hill, 10-38; crashed while landing at Biggin Hill, 6-4-39. Became ***1466M.***

L1673 No. 1 Sqn., Tangmere, 10-38. No. 73 Sqn., Digby, 4-39; shot down at Betheniville, France, 13-5-40.

L1674 No. 32 Sqn., Biggin Hill, 10-38; Missing over France, 19-5-40.

L1675 No. 32 Sqn., Biggin Hill, 10-38; crashed while landing at Biggin Hill, 26-2-39. Became ***1426M.***

L1676 No. 1 Sqn., Tangmere, 10-38; lost in France, 5-40.

L1677 No. 1 Sqn., Tangmere, 10-38; crashed while landing at Tangmere, 24-11-38. Became ***1226M.***

L1678 No. 1 Sqn., Tangmere, 10-38; crashed while landing at Tangmere, 16-2-39.

L1679 No. 1 Sqn., Tangmere, 10-38; lost in France, 5-40.

L1680 No. 1 Sqn., Tangmere, 10-38; crashed on beach at Hayling Island, Hants, 4-7-39.

L1681 No. 1 Sqn., Tangmere, 10-38; lost in France, 5-40.

L1682 No. 1 Sqn., Tangmere, 10-38; crashed at night 4 miles SE of Debden, 7-2-39.

L1683 No. 73 Sqn., Digby, 10-38. No. 5 O.T.U. No. 5 F.T.S. No. 9 F.T.S. Empire Central Flying School. Became ***3589M***, 3-43.

L1684 Northolt Stn. Flt., 10-38. *Converted to Mark IIA*, ***DR354***, 1940.

L1685 No. 1 Sqn., Tangmere, 10-38. No. 43 Sqn., Tangmere. No. 1 Sqn.; shot down one German aircraft over France, 2-4-40. No. 43 Sqn. Lost in France, 5-40.

L1686 No. 1 Sqn., Tangmere, 10-38. No. 43 Sqn. No. 1 Sqn.; lost in France, 5-40.

L1687 No. 1 Sqn., Tangmere, 10-38. No. 43 Sqn. No. 73 Sqn., Digby. No. 306 (Polish) Sqn. No. 9 F.T.S.; crashed while landing at Hullavington, 20-6-41.

L1688 No. 1 Sqn., Tangmere, 11-38; lost in France, 5-40.

L1689 No. 1 Sqn., Tangmere, 11-38. No. 43 Sqn., Tangmere. No. 1 Sqn.; lost in France, 5-40.

L1690 No. 1 Sqn., Tangmere, 11-38; crashed at night 2 miles NW of Tangmere, 26-6-39.

L1691 No. 1 Sqn., Tangmere, 11-38; crashed while landing at Tangmere, 5-1-39. Became ***1373M.***

L1692 No. 1 Sqn., Tangmere, 11-38; crashed while landing at Tangmere, 13-3-39.

L1693 No. 1 Sqn., Tangmere, 11-38. No. 73 Sqn., Digby; lost in France, 5-40.

L1694 No. 1 Sqn., Tangmere, 11-38, **NA-F**; crashed on take-off at Tangmere, 4-4-39.

L1695 *Trials with Rotol and D.H. propellers* (Merlin III engine); Brooklands, Martlesham and Farnborough, 1939. No. 56 O.T.U. No. 9 F.T.S. No. 5 F.T.S.; crashed at Eaton Constantine, Salop, 3-1-42.

L1696 *Trials with slotted wings*, Martlesham and Farnborough, 1939. No. 303 (Polish) Sqn., 1940; S.O.C., 27-9-40.

L1697 No. 79 Sqn., Biggin Hill, 11-38, **AL-A**. Rolls-Royce Ltd., 1940. Became ***3202M***, 7-42.

L1698 No. 79 Sqn., Biggin Hill, 11-38, **NV-R**. No. 7 O.T.U. No. 5 O.T.U. No. 55 O.T.U. Became ***3174M***, 7-42.

L1699 No. 79 Sqn., Biggin Hill, 11-38. No. 32 Sqn., Biggin Hill, **KT-G**. No. 79 Sqn.; crashed in sea off Reculver, Kent, 16-2-40.

L1700 No. 79 Sqn., Biggin Hill, 11-38. No. 253 Sqn. No. 312 (Czech) Sqn., 1940. No. 55 O.T.U.; crashed at Saul, Glos, 28-12-40.

L1701 No. 79 Sqn., Biggin Hill, 11-38. No. 253 Sqn. No. 312 (Czech) Sqn. No. 55 O.T.U. No. 9 F.T.S. No. 9 P.A.F.U. Became ***3586M***, 3-43.

L1702 *Position error assessment*, R.A.E. and A. & A.E.E., 1939. No. 238 Sqn., 1940; collided with Hurricane ***N2474*** and crashed near Shaftesbury, Dorset, 30-9-40; P/O V.C. Simmonds baled out unhurt.

L1703 No. 9 F.T.S. No. 257 Sqn., Hendon, 1-40; crashed at Watford Way, Edgware, Middx., after fire in the air, 15-8-40; P/O C.G. Frizell baled out unhurt.

L1704 No. 43 Sqn., Tangmere, 11-38. No. 111 Sqn., **TM-T**. No. 3 Sqn. No. 7 O.T.U. No. 6 O.T.U. No. 5 F.T.S. No. 56 O.T.U. S.O.C., 21-11-44.

L1705 No. 79 Sqn., Biggin Hill, 11-38. No. 6 O.T.U.; crashed near Sutton Bridge, 4-10-40.

L1706 No. 9 F.T.S. No. 257 Sqn. No. 56 O.T.U. No. 1622 Flt. No. 667 Sqn. S.O.C., 4-9-44.

L1707 No. 79 Sqn., Biggin Hill, 11-38; crashed at Chelsham, Surrey, 11-9-39.

L1708 No. 36 M.U. Shipped direct to *South African Air Force*, 11-38.

L1709 No. 79 Sqn., Biggin Hill, 11-38; crashed 3 miles NE of Three Bridges, Sussex, 26-4-40.

L1710 No. 36 M.U. Shipped direct to *South African Air Force*, 11-38.

L1711 No. 36 M.U. Shipped direct to *South African Air Force*, 11-38.

L1712 No. 79 Sqn., Biggin Hill, 11-38. No. 253 Sqn. No. 8 F.T.S. No. 17 P.A.F.U. No. 5 P.A.F.U. No. 56 O.T.U. S.O.C., 23-5-44.

L1713 *Merlin III trials*; Rolls-Royce Ltd. R.A.E., Farnborough. No. 7 O.T.U. No. 56 O.T.U.; crashed near Sutton Bridge, 15-10-40.

L1714 No. 79 Sqn., Biggin Hill, 12-38, **AL-O**. No. 6 O.T.U.; crashed near Wisbech, Lincs, 29-7-40.

L1715 No. 79 Sqn., Biggin Hill, 12-38. No. 249 Sqn. No. 56 Sqn. No. 85 Sqn. No. 71 Sqn. No. 2 Sqn., R.C.A.F. No. 59 O.T.U. No. 1623 Flt. No. 691 Sqn.; damaged beyond repair, 17-4-44.

L1716 No. 79 Sqn., Biggin Hill, 12-38, **AL-D**. No. 111 Sqn. No. 79 Sqn. No. 7 O.T.U. No. 5 O.T.U. No. 55 O.T.U. No. 5 F.T.S. No. 1 A.A.S. S.O.C., 29-7-44.

L1717 *Balloon cable cutting trials*, R.A.E., Farnborough, 1939. No. 306 (Polish) Sqn.; crashed 3 miles south of Shrewsbury, 26-11-40.

L1718 No. 79 Sqn., Biggin Hill, 12-38, **AL-T**. No. 111 Sqn.; lost in France, 5-40.

L1719 No. 79 Sqn., Biggin Hill, 12-38, **AL-F**. wheels-up landing at Biggin Hill, 13-4-40.

L1720 No. 79 Sqn., Biggin Hill, 12-38. No. 111 Sqn.; shot down by Bf 110 over France, 19-5-40.

L1721 No. 79 Sqn., Biggin Hill, 12-38. No. 7 O.T.U. No. 55 O.T.U. No. 5 F.T.S. No. 9 P.A.F.U. No. 7

P.A.F.U.; crashed at Eye, Cambs, 14-10-44.

L1722 No. 79 Sqn., Biggin Hill, 12-38. No. 3 Sqn. No. 43 Sqn. No. 87 Sqn.; collided with Hurricane on ground in France, 20-4-40, and abandoned, 5-40.

L1723 No. 43 Sqn., Tangmere, 12-38. No. 3 Sqn. No. 8 F.T.S. No. 17 P.A.F.U. No. 318 (Polish) Sqn. S.O.C., 12-42.

L1724 No. 151 Sqn., North Weald, 12-38, **GG-M**; crashed at Waltham Abbey, Herts, 18-2-40.

L1725 No. 43 Sqn., Tangmere, 12-38; abandoned over Northumberland, 5-12-39.

L1726 No. 43 Sqn., Tangmere, 12-38, **NQ-R**; abandoned over France, 7-6-40.

L1727 No. 43 Sqn., Tangmere, 12-38, **FT-R**. No. 17 Sqn. No. 59 O.T.U.; crashed at Gedney Dye, Lincs, 8-9-40; became ***3368M***.

L1728 No. 43 Sqn., Tangmere, 12-38, **NQ-B**. No. 607 Sqn., A.A.F. No. 43 Sqn. No. 607 Sqn., A.A.F.; collided with Hurricane, 7-10-40; F/O I.B. Difford killed.

L1729 No. 43 Sqn., Tangmere, 12-38; crashed on take-off at Acklington, 21-2-40.

L1730 No. 43 Sqn., Tangmere, 12-38. No. 111 Sqn. S.O.C., 6-40.

L1731 No. 43 Sqn., Tangmere, 12-38. No. 1 Sqn., R.C.A.F. No. 1 Sqn. No. 56 O.T.U. No. 8 F.T.S; crashed while landing at Montrose, 13-9-41; became ***2797M***.

L1732 No. 43 Sqn., Tangmere, 12-38, **NQ-E**. No. 7 O.T.U. No. 6 O.T.U. No. 286 Sqn.; crashed at Torcross, Devon, 14-5-43.

L1733 No. 43 Sqn., Tangmere, 12-38. No. 111 Sqn.; abandoned in France, 19-5-40.

L1734 No. 43 Sqn., Tangmere, 12-38, **NQ-G** and **FT-G**; S.O.C., 28-1-40.

L1735 No. 43 Sqn., Tangmere, 12-38; crashed while landing at Tangmere, 24-1-39; became ***1363M***.

L1736 No. 43 Sqn., Tangmere, 12-38; damaged in combat near Tangmere, 16-8-40; Sgt. J.L. Crisp baled out but broke thigh.

L1737 No. 43 Sqn., Tangmere, 12-38; crashed while landing at Rouen/Boos, 7-6-40.

L1738 No. 43 Sqn., Tangmere, 12-38; crashed while landing at Tangmere, 22-4-39.

L1739 No. 43 Sqn., Tangmere, 12-38; shot down by He 111H off Beachy Head, 14-8-40; Sgt. H.F. Montgomery killed.

L1740 No. 111 Sqn., Northolt, 12-38. No. 312 (Czech) Sqn. No. 315 (Polish) Sqn. No. 56 O.T.U. No. 9 Group Comms. Flt. No. 55 O.T.U. No. 41 O.T.U. S.O.C., 18-5-44.

L1741 No. 111 Sqn., Northolt, 12-38, **TM-W**. No. 6 O.T.U. No. 56 O.T.U.; crashed 3 miles south of Downham Market, 4-1-41.

L1742 No. 56 Sqn., North Weald, 12-38. No. 17 Sqn. No. 43 Sqn. No. 9 F.T.S. No. 5 P.A.F.U. No. 318 (Polish) Sqn. No. 3 Sqn. No. 55 O.T.U. No. 41 O.T.U. S.O.C., 1944.

L1743 No. 87 Sqn., Debden, 12-38. S.O.C., 6-12-39.

L1744 No. 43 Sqn., Tangmere, 12-38, **NQ-A**; crashed in sea off Northumberland coast, 9-2-40.

L1745 No. 151 Sqn., North Weald, 12-38; crashed while landing at North Weald, 20-3-39; became ***1439M***.

L1746 No. 151 Sqn., North Weald, 12-38. No. 17 Sqn. No. 242 Sqn.; Missing over France, 28-5-40.

L1747 No. 151 Sqn., North Weald, 12-38. No. 242 Sqn. No. 32 Sqn. Special Duties Flt. No. 55 O.T.U. No. 5 F.T.S. No. 9 F.T.S. No. 9 P.A.F.U. No. 318 (Polish) Sqn. No. 55 O.T.U. S.O.C., 28-9-44.

L1748 No. 151 Sqn., North Weald, 12-38. No. 242 Sqn. No. 56 Sqn. No. 312 (Czech) Sqn. No. 52 O.T.U. No. 55 O.T.U.; crashed at Whatton, Northumberland, 3-1-42.

L1749 No. 151 Sqn., North Weald, 12-38. No. 242 Sqn.; Missing over France, 5-40.

L1750 *Equipped with additional cockpit armour and two 20-mm Oerlikon cannon under wings*; trials, A. & A.E.E., 1939. No. 151 Sqn. No. 46 Sqn. No. 601 Sqn., A.A.F. No. 1 A.A.S.; damaged beyond repair, 31-5-41.

L1751 *Shipped to Yugoslav Air Force*, 15-12-38, as "***1-205***".

L1752 *Shipped to Yugoslav Air Force*, 15-12-38, as "***2-206***".

L1753 No. 151 Sqn., North Weald, 12-38; crashed during night landing at North Weald, 15-4-39.

L1754 No. 151 Sqn., North Weald, 12-38; crashed while landing at North Weald, 29-2-39; became ***1424M***.

L1755 No. 151 Sqn., North Weald, 12-38; lost in France, 5-40.

L1756 No. 151 Sqn., North Weald, 12-38. No. 242 Sqn.; crashed while taking off at Manston, 29-5-40.

L1757 No. 151 Sqn., North Weald, 12-38. No. 242 Sqn. No. 1 Sqn.; damaged in forced landing, Chateau Bougon, France, 29-5-40, and abandoned, 18-6-40.

L1758 No. 151 Sqn., North Weald, 12-38. No. 43 Sqn.; shot down over Dunkirk, 1-6-40.

L1759 *Shipped to R.C.A.F. in Canada*, 10-38, as "***310***".

L1760 *Shipped to R.C.A.F. in Canada*, 10-38, as "***311***".

L1761 *Shipped to R.C.A.F. in Canada*, 10-38, as "***312***".

L1762 *Shipped to R.C.A.F. in Canada*, 10-38, as "***313***"; No. 401 Sqn., R.C.A.F., Middle Wallop, 6-40, **YO-L**.

L1763 *Shipped to R.C.A.F. in Canada*, 10-38, as "***314***".

L1764 No. 151 Sqn., North Weald, 12-38. No. 56 Sqn. No. 249 Sqn. No. 56 Sqn.; shot down by Bf 110s near Portland, 30-9-40; Sgt. P.H. Fox unhurt.

L1765 No. 85 Sqn., Debden, 12-38; crashed at Le Touquet, 23-12-39.

L1766 No. 151 Sqn., North Weald, 12-38. No. 242 Sqn. No. 73 Sqn. No. 6 O.T.U.; crashed at Walpole St. Andrew, Lincs, 5-10-40.

L1767 No. 151 Sqn., North Weald, 12-38; crashed while landing at North Weald, 14-4-39.

L1768 No. 151 Sqn., North Weald, 12-38, **GG-K**. No. 87 Sqn. No. 55 O.T.U. No. 5 F.T.S. T.A.F. Comms. Flt. No. 41 O.T.U. No. 2 Tactical Exercise Unit. No. 81 O.T.U. No. 1665 Heavy Conversion Unit. S.O.C., 18-9-44.

L1769 No. 151 Sqn., North Weald, 12-38. No. 6 O.T.U. *Converted to Mark IIA*, 1940, as ***DR359*** and *shipped to Russia*, 1941.

L1770 No. 213 Sqn., Wittering, 1-39, **AK-A**. No. 229 Sqn. No. 303 (Polish) Sqn. No. 5 F.T.S. Transferred to Admiralty Charge, 17-9-42, for *conversion to Sea Hurricane Mark IB*.

L1771 No. 213 Sqn., Wittering, 1-39. No. 253 Sqn. No. 306 (Polish) Sqn. No. 54 O.T.U. No. 79 Sqn. No. 59 O.T.U. Shipped to India; became ground instruction airframe, 4-10-44.

L1772 No. 213 Sqn., Wittering, 1-39. No. 601 Sqn., A.A.F.; crash landed at Rose Green, near Pagham, Sussex, 22-7-40, after engine failure; P/O J.K.U.B. McGrath unhurt.

L1773 No. 85 Sqn., Debden, 1-39, **NO-G**. S.O.C., 2-1-40.

L1774 No. 85 Sqn., Debden, 1-39. No. 111 Sqn.; shot down by Bf 110 over France, 19-5-40.

L1775 No. 85 Sqn., Debden, 1-39; later **LK-D**; lost in France, 5-40.

L1776 No. 87 Sqn., Debden, 1-39; crashed at Forêt de Nieppe, France, 5-10-39.

L1777 No. 87 Sqn., Debden, 1-39. No. 213 Sqn. No. 151 Sqn. No. 56 O.T.U. No. 8 F.T.S. No. 17 P.A.F.U. No. 9 P.A.F.U. S.O.C., 14-12-43.

L1778 No. 85 Sqn., Debden, 1-39; lost in France, 5-40.

L1779 No. 85 Sqn., Debden, 1-39; lost in France, 10-5-40.

L1780 No. 213 Sqn., Wittering, 1-39. No. 229 Sqn. R.A.E., Farnborough. A. & A.E.E. R.A.E. A. & A.E.E. Became ***3441M***, 11-42.

L1781 No. 79 Sqn., Biggin Hill, 1-39. No. 3 Sqn. S.O.C., 3-7-40.

L1782 No. 79 Sqn., Biggin Hill, 1-39; abandoned one mile north of Bekesbourne, Kent, 27-2-39.

L1783 No. 213 Sqn., Wittering, 1-39. No. 229 Sqn. No. 145 Sqn. No. 229 Sqn. No. 56 O.T.U. Became ***3084M***, 5-42.

L1784 No. 213 Sqn., Wittering, 1-39. No. 79 Sqn. No. 9 F.T.S. No. 9 P.A.F.U. Became ***3285M***, 5-42.

L1785 No. 213 Sqn., Wittering, 1-39; crashed near Wittering, 20-5-39; became ***2141M***.

L1786 No. 213 Sqn., Wittering, 1-39. No. 229 Sqn. No. 7 O.T.U. No. 5 O.T.U. No. 55 O.T.U.; crashed at Usworth, 2-3-41; became ***2741M***.

L1787 No. 213 Sqn., Wittering, 2-39; crashed while landing at Wittering, 13-4-39.

L1788 Trials at Brooklands and Farnborough, 1939. No. 5 F.T.S.; crashed on take-off at Ternhill, 30-9-41.

L1789 No. 213 Sqn., Wittering, 2-39. No. 601 Sqn., A.A.F. No. 605 Sqn., A.A.F. No. 6 O.T.U. No. 55 O.T.U. No. 9 F.T.S.; crashed near Mere, Somerset, 9-10-41.

L1790 No. 213 Sqn., Wittering, 2-39. No. 229 Sqn.; crashed in sea 30 miles off Grimsby, Lincs, 9-4-40.

L1791 No. 46 Sqn., Digby, 2-39. No. 7 O.T.U.; crashed at Holt, near Wrexham, 25-7-40; became ***2172M***.

L1792 No. 46 Sqn., Digby, 2-39; crashed near Corby, Northants, at night, 29-3-39.

L1793 No. 46 Sqn., Digby, 2-39; lost in H.M.S. *Glorious* on return from Norway, 8-6-40.

L1794 No. 46 Sqn., Digby, 2-39; shot down by Ju 88 near Narvik, Norway, 29-5-40.

L1795 No. 46 Sqn., Digby, 2-39; crashed while landing at Digby, 24-2-39; became ***1388M***.

L1796 No. 46 Sqn., Digby, 2-39. No. 85 Sqn. No. 71 Sqn. No. 2 Sqn., R.C.A.F. No. 59 O.T.U. No. 5 P.A.F.U. S.O.C. 3-1-45.

L1797 No. 46 Sqn., Digby, 2-39; crashed while landing at Digby, 19-6-39.

L1798 No. 151 Sqn., North Weald, 2-39. No. 7 O.T.U. No. 5 O.T.U. No. 55 O.T.U.; crashed at Combe Down, near Yatesbury, 10-9-40; became ***3576M***.

L1799 No. 151 Sqn., North Weald, 2-39; crashed into the North Sea, 2-4-40.

L1800 No. 213 Sqn., Wittering, 3-39; crashed while landing at Wittering, 4-7-39.

L1801 No. 46 Sqn., Digby, 3-39; pilot lost control and abandoned aircraft 2 miles north of Leadenham, Lincs, 18-4-40.

L1802 No. 46 Sqn., Digby, 3-39. No. 229 Sqn.; assumed abandoned in France, 5-40.

L1803 No. 46 Sqn., Digby, 3-39. No. 229 Sqn. No. 263 Sqn.; pilot baled out after aircraft caught fire near Falkirk, 24-8-40.

L1804 No. 46 Sqn., Digby, 3-39; lost in H.M.S. *Glorious* on return from Norway, 8-6-40.

L1805 No. 46 Sqn., Digby, 3-39; lost in H.M.S. *Glorious* on return from Norway, 8-6-40.

L1806 No. 46 Sqn., Digby, 3-39; lost in H.M.S. *Glorious* on return from Norway, 8-6-40.

L1807 No. 46 Sqn., Digby, 3-39. No. 312 (Czech) Sqn.; aircraft twice damaged in action, 10-40. Converted to Mark IIA, ***DG628***, 1-41: No. 55 O.T.U.; crashed at Usworth, 8-3-41.

L1808 No. 213 Sqn., Wittering, 3-39. No. 229 Sqn. No. 46 Sqn. No. 229 Sqn. No. 17 Sqn. No. 73 Sqn. No. 5 O.T.U. No. 55 O.T.U. No. 59 O.T.U. No. 56 O.T.U. No. 2 Tactical Exercise Unit. S.O.C., 18-5-44.

L1809 No. 213 Sqn., Wittering, 3-39; abandoned one miles NE of Grantham, 10-3-39; became ***1442M***.

L1810 No. 213 Sqn., Wittering, 3-39; crashed while landing at Wittering, 29-3-39; became ***1454M***.

L1811 No. 213 Sqn., Wittering, 3-39; crashed on take-off at Wittering, 3-8-39.

L1812 No. 213 Sqn., Wittering, 3-39. No. 229 Sqn. No. 46 Sqn. S.O.C., 5-40.

L1813 No. 46 Sqn., Digby, 4-39. No. 43 Sqn. No. 1 Sqn. No. 87 Sqn.; force landed at Coxyde, Belgium, 14-11-39, and interned.

L1814 No. 46 Sqn., Digby, 4-39. No. 6 O.T.U. No. 56 O.T.U. Became ***3579M***, 3-43.

L1815 No. 46 Sqn., Digby, 4-39; lost in H.M.S. *Glorious* on return from Norway, 8-6-40.

L1816 No. 46 Sqn., Digby, 4-39; shot down by Ju 88 near Narvik, Norway, 29-5-40.

L1817 No. 46 Sqn., Digby, 4-39. No. 229 Sqn. No. 213 Sqn; lost over France, 5-40.
L1818 No. 213 Sqn., Wittering, 4-39. No. 253 Sqn. No. 59 O.T.U.; crashed near Longtown, 5-4-41; became ***2577M***.
L1819 No. 213 Sqn., Wittering, 4-39. No. 601 Sqn., A.A.F. No. 55 O.T.U. No. 5 F.T.S. No. 5 P.A.F.U. S.O.C., 20-3-43.
L1820 No. 111 Sqn., Northolt, 4-39, **TM-V**. Rolls-Royce Ltd. No. 6 O.T.U. No. 56 O.T.U.; crashed while landing at Sutton Bridge, 17-12-40.
L1821 No. 111 Sqn., Northolt, 4-39, **TM-L**. No. 7 O.T.U. No. 5 O.T.U. No. 9 F.T.S. No. 41 O.T.U.; crashed while landing at Andover, 22-4-44.
L1822 No. 111 Sqn., Northolt, 4-39, **TM-A**, later **JU-K**; F/O H.M. Ferris shot down four Bf 110s over Dunkirk, 18-5-40. No. 312 (Czech) Sqn. No. 9 F.T.S.; abondoned after fire in the air at Dursley, Glos, 10-9-41.
L1823 No. 111 Sqn., Northolt, 4-39, **TM-X**. No. 43 Sqn. S.O.C., 24-8-40.
L1824 No. 43 Sqn., Tangmere, 4-39, **NO-F**; crashed while landing at Tangmere, 9-7-40; P/O J. Cruttenden unhurt.
L1825 No. 43 Sqn., Tangmere, 4-39. No. 7 O.T.U. No. 303 (Polish) Sqn. No. 9 F.T.S. To India, 1943. S.O.C., 30-6-44.
L1826 No. 73 Sqn., Digby. 3-39; lost in France, 7-6-40.
L1827 No. 73 Sqn., Digby, 3-39. No. 238 Sqn. No. 5 O.T.U. No. 8 F.T.S.; crashed at Perth, 12-9-41.
L1828 No. 56 Sqn., North Weald, 3-39; crashed while landing at North Weald, 23-3-39.
L1829 No. 56 Sqn., North Weald, 3-39. No. 17 Sqn. No. 501 Sqn., A.A.F. No. 213 Sqn. No. 229 Sqn. S.O.C., 15-8-42.
L1830 No. 56 Sqn., North Weald, 3-39. No. 17 Sqn. No. 605 Sqn., A.A.F. No. 111 Sqn. No. 253 Sqn.; shot down by Bf 109E near Biggin Hill, 31-8-40; S/L T.P. Gleave baled out wounded.
L1831 No. 87 Sqn., Debden, 4-39; wheels-up landing at Debden, 23-5-39.
L1832 No. 87 Sqn., Debden, 4-39. No. 249 Sqn. Special Duties Flt. No. 55 O.T.U. No. 9 F.T.S.; crashed while landing at Castle Combe, 8-7-41.
L1833 No. 85 Sqn., Debden, 3-39, **NO-J**. No. 111 Sqn. No. 7 O.T.U. No. 6 O.T.U.; collided with Hurricane ***L1654***, 3-9-40, and crashed at Saddlebow, near Kings Lynn; Sgt. K. Stibor (Czech) killed.
L1834 No. 85 Sqn., Debden, 3-39. No. 87 Sqn.; assumed lost in France, 5-40.
L1835 No. 85 Sqn., Debden, 3-39. No. 43 Sqn. No. 85 Sqn.; S.O.C., 2-1-40.
L1836 No. 504 Sqn., Hucknall, 3-39. No. 32 Sqn. No. 5 O.T.U. *Converted to Mark IIA*, ***DG636***. No. 55 O.T.U.; crashed at Bournmore, Co. Durham, 28-4-41.
L1837 *Shipped to Yugoslav Air Force*, 4-39, as "***3-291***".
L1838 *Shipped to Yugoslav Air Force*, 4-39, as "***4-292***".
L1839 *Shipped to Yugoslav Air Force*, 4-39, as "***5-293***".
L1840 *Shipped to Yugoslav Air Force*, 4-39, as "***6-294***".
L1841 No. 32 Sqn., Biggin Hill, 3-39. No. 253 Sqn. No. 79 Sqn. No. 312 (Czech) Sqn., **DU-H**. No. 55 O.T.U.; crashed at Great Stainton, 1-5-41.
L1842 No. 1 Sqn., Tangmere, 3-39. No. 310 (Czech) Sqn.; abandoned after fire in the air over the Isle of Sheppey, 2-11-40.
L1843 No. 1 Sqn., Tangmere, 3-39; assumed lost over France, 5-40.
L1844 No. 1 Sqn., Tangmere, 3-39. No. 73 Sqn. S.O.C., 1-7-40.
L1845 No. 79 Sqn., Biggin Hill, 3-39; crashed during night landing at Biggin Hill, 4-4-39.
L1846 No. 79 Sqn., Biggin Hill, 3-39. No. 3 Sqn. Sumburgh Stn. Flt. No. 9 F.T.S. R.A.F. College, Cranwell. No. 6 F.T.S. No. 1623 Flt. No. 691 Sqn. S.O.C., 24-4-44.
L1847 No. 43 Sqn., Tangmere, 4-39, **NQ-J**; shot down over France, 7-6-40.
L1848 *Shipped to Canadian Car & Foundry as pattern aircraft*, 2-3-39. Returned to U.K., 9-40. No. 310 (Czech) Sqn. No. 5 F.T.S. To India, No. 151 O.T.U.; S.O.C., 31-7-44.
L1849 No. 43 Sqn., Tangmere, 4-39; abandoned after fire in the air 4 miles SE of Tangmere, 7-7-40; pilot unhurt.
L1850 No. 151 Sqn., North Weald, 4-39; assumed lost over France, 5-40, and S.O.C.
L1851 No. 213 Sqn., Wittering, 4-39. No. 1 Sqn., R.C.A.F. No. 6 O.T.U. No. 56 O.T.U.; crashed at Tydd St. Mary, Norfolk, 1-11-40.
L1852 No. 213 Sqn., Wittering, 4-39, **AK-E**. No. 229 Sqn. No. 5 O.T.U. No. 55 O.T.U.; crashed while taking off at Moreton-in-Marsh, 2-1-41.
L1853 No. 46 Sqn., Digby, 2-39; lost in H.M.S. *Glorious* while returning from Norway, 8-6-40.
L1854 No. 46 Sqn., Digby, 2-39. No. 229 Sqn. No. 213 Sqn. No. 85 Sqn.; crashed near Church Fenton, 25-9-40.
L1855 No. 1 Sqn., Tangmere, 4-39; crashed during night landing at Tangmere, 26-6-39.
L1856 No. 1 Sqn., Tangmere, 4-39; shot down by flak over St. Quentin, France, 18-5-40.
L1857 No. 46 Sqn., Digby, 3-39; crashed on take-off at Digby, 6-3-40.
L1858 *Supplied to Yugoslav Air Force*, 4-39, as "***7-312***".
L1859 *Supplied to Yugoslav Air Force*, 4-39, as "***8-313***".
L1860 *Supplied to Yugoslav Air Force*, 4-39, as "***9-314***".
L1861 *Supplied to Yugoslav Air Force*, 4-39, as "***10-315***".
L1862 *Supplied to Yugoslav Air Force*, 4-39, as "***11-316***".
L1863 *Supplied to Yugoslav Air Force*, 4-39, as "***12-317***".
L1864 No. 73 Sqn., Digby, 3-39. No. 501 Sqn., A.A.F. No. 6 O.T.U. No. 5 F.T.S. No. 1480 Flt. No. 55 O.T.U. No. 263 Sqn. No. 56 O.T.U.; crashed while landing at Sutton Bridge, 12-12-40.
L1865 No. 501 Sqn., A.A.F., Filton, 2-39; shot down by Bf 109E over Dover, 24-8-40; P/O K.R. Aldridge baled out at Ryarth but sustained a broken arm.
L1866 No. 501 Sqn., A.A.F., Filton, 2-39, **ZH-B**; abandoned in France, 5-40.
L1867 No. 501 Sqn., A.A.F., Filton, 2-39; crashed during night landing at Tangmere, 18-1-40; became ***1843M***.
L1868 No. 501 Sqn., A.A.F., Filton, 2-39; later **SD-D**. No. 257 Sqn. No. 56 O.T.U.; crashed while landing at Sutton Bridge, 17-1-41.
L1869 No. 501 Sqn., A.A.F., Filton, 2-39; crashed while landing at Filton, 26-3-39; became ***1467M***.
L1870 No. 501 Sqn., A.A.F., Filton, 2-39. No. 11 Group Pool. No. 7 O.T.U. No. 306 (Polish) Sqn. No. 59 O.T.U.; crashed at Watch Hill, Aspatria, Cumberland, 29-7-41.
L1871 No. 501 Sqn., A.A.F., Filton, 2-39. No. 11 Group Pool. No. 6 O.T.U.; crashed while landing at Sutton Bridge, 1-10-40.
L1872 No. 501 Sqn., A.A.F., Filton, 3-39. No. 11 Group Pool; crashed while landing at Hanworth, 20-5-39.
L1873 No. 501 Sqn., A.A.F., Filton, 3-39. Central Flying School. Became 3244M, 7-42.
L1874 *Shipped to South African Air Force*, 4-39.
L1875 *Shipped to South African Air Force*, 4-39.
L1876 *Shipped to South African Air Force*, 4-39.
L1877 *D.T.D. aircraft, fitted with metal wings and tropical filter*; trials with H.A.L. and Rolls-Royce Ltd., 1939. No. 601 Sqn., A.A.F., Tangmere, 3-40. No. 504 Sqn., A.A.F. No. 59 O.T.U. No. 81 Group Comms. Flt. No. 56 O.T.U. No. 2 Tactical Exercise Unit. No. 81 O.T.U. No. 1665 H.C.U. S.O.C., 18-9-44.
L1878 *Shipped to R.C.A.F. in Canada*, 2-39, as "***315***". Returned to U.K., 1940. No. 402 Sqn., R.C.A.F., **YO-M**.
L1879 *Shipped to R.C.A.F. in Canada*, 2-39, as "***316***".
L1880 *Shipped to R.C.A.F. in Canada*, 2-39, as "***317***".
L1881 *Shipped to R.C.A.F. in Canada*, 2-39, as "***318***".
L1882 *Shipped to R.C.A.F. in Canada*, 2-39, as "***319***". Returned to U.K., 1940. No. 402 Sqn., R.C.A.F. **YO-N**.
L1883 *Shipped to R.C.A.F. in Canada*, 2-39, as "***320***".
L1884 *Shipped to R.C.A.F. in Canada*, 3-39, as "***321***". Returned to U.K., 1940. *Became Hillson F.H.40 slip-wing Hurricane bi-mono*, 1943-44.
L1885 *Shipped to R.C.A.F. in Canada*, 3-39, as "***322***".
L1886 *Shipped to R.C.A.F. in Canada*, 3-39, as "***323***".
L1887 *Shipped to R.C.A.F. in Canada*, 3-39, as "***324***". *(Was the first production aircraft completed with metal wings)*. Returned to U.K., 1940. No. 402 Sqn., R.C.A.F., 8-40; collided with Hurricane ***L2082***, 18-8-40, and crashed near Sutton Bridge.
L1888 *Shipped to R.C.A.F. in Canada*, 3-39, as "***325***".
L1889 No. 85 Sqn., Debden, 3-39. No. 79 Sqn., Biggin Hill, 4-39, **AL-E**. No. 213 Sqn. No. 229 Sqn. No. 85 Sqn. No. 238 Sqn. No. 55 O.T.U. No. 5 P.A.F.U. No. 56 O.T.U. S.O.C., 5-4-45.
L1890 *Shipped to R.C.A.F. in Canada*, 3-39, as "***326***".
L1891 No. 73 Sqn., Digby, 3-39; assumed lost in France, 5-40.
L1892 No. 46 Sqn., Digby, 3-39. No. 111 Sqn.; shot down by Ju 88s near Kenley, 6-9-40; Sgt. L.J. Tweed wounded and baled out.
L1893 *Second tropical trials aircraft; trials at Brooklands and A. & A.E.E.. To Middle East*. No. 33 Sqn. No. 112 Sqn. S.O.C., 18-3-40.
L1894 No. 213 Sqn., Wittering, 4-39. No. 601 Sqn., A.A.F.; hit machine gun post on take-off at Exeter, 21-9-40
L1895 No. 12 Group Pool. No. 6 O.T.U. No. 306 (Polish) Sqn. No. 6 O.T.U.; crashed while landing at Sutton Bridge, 12-6-40.
L1896 No. 12 Group Pool. No. 6 O.T.U. No. 7 O.T.U. No. 5 O.T.U. No. 55 O.T.U. Ferry Training Unit. Became ***2984M***, 6-42.
L1897 No. 12 Group Pool. No. 6 O.T.U.; crashed at Upwell, Norfolk, 25-6-40.
L1898 No. 3 Sqn., Kenley, 4-39. No. 43 Sqn. No. 85 Sqn.; lost in France, 5-40.
L1899 No. 3 Sqn., Kenley, 4-39; force landed at Vitry-en-Artois, France, 17-5-40, and abandoned.
L1900 No. 85 Sqn., Debden. S.O.C., 6-12-39.
L1901 No. 3 Sqn., Kenley, 4-39; Missing over France, 13-5-40.
L1902 No. 3 Sqn., Kenley, 4-39. No. 5 O.T.U. No. 55 O.T.U.; crashed at Andoversford, Glos, 17-12-40.
L1903 No. 3 Sqn., Kenley, 4-39; crashed after tyre burst on take-off at Kenley, 25-3-40; became ***1884M***.
L1904 No. 3 Sqn., Kenley, 4-39; crashed on take-off at Kenley, 24-3-40.
L1905 No. 1 Sqn., Tangmere, 4-39; lost in France, 5-40.
L1906 No. 79 Sqn., Biggin Hill, 4-39; crashed on take-off at Manston, 25-11-39.
L1907 No. 3 Sqn., Kenley, 4-39; crashed in sea, 1-2-40.
L1908 No. 3 Sqn., Kenley, 4-39; abandoned in France, 14-5-40.
L1909 *Shipped to South African Air Force*, 4-39.
L1910 No. 501 Sqn., A.A.F., Filton, 4-39. No. 6 O.T.U. No. 59 O.T.U. Became ***4321M***, 11-43.
L1911 No. 504 Sqn., A.A.F., Hucknall, 3-39. No. 501 Sqn., A.A.F.; lost over France, 21-6-40.
L1912 No. 504 Sqn., A.A.F., Hucknall, 4-39; assumed lost in France, 5-40.
L1913 No. 504 Sqn., A.A.F., Hucknall, 4-39; damaged by British A.A. and abandoned near Nuneaton, 29-9-40.
L1914 No. 213 Sqn., Wittering, 4-39. No. 601 Sqn., A.A.F.; assumed lost in France, 5-40.
L1915 No. 504 Sqn., A.A.F., Hucknall, 4-39. No. 17 Sqn. No. 85 Sqn.; shot down by Bf 109Es over Kent, 29-8-40; F/L H.R. Hamilton killed.
L1916 No. 504 Sqn., A.A.F., Hucknall, 4-39; assumed lost in France, 5-40.

L1917 No. 3 Sqn., Kenley, 4-39. No. 601 Sqn., A.A.F. No. 56 O.T.U. No. 1480 Flt. No. 55 O.T.U. No. 3 Tactical Exercise Unit; crashed on beach north of Jurby, Isle of Man, 10-5-44.

L1918 *Supplied to Belgium*, 4-39 as "***1***", *Aéronautique Militaire.*

L1919 *Supplied to Belgium*, 4-39 as "***2***", *Aéronautique Militaire.*

L1920 *Supplied to Belgium*, 4-39 as "***3***", *Aéronautique Militaire.*

L1921 No. 17 Sqn., North Weald, 6-39; shot down in combat near Dover, 18-8-40; P/O N.D. Soloman missing.

L1922 No. 504 Sqn., A.A.F., Hucknall, 5-39. No. 242 Sqn.; assumed lost in France, 5-40.

L1923 No. 3 Sqn., Kenley, 5-39; shot down near Fiefs, France, 10-5-40.

L1924 No. 3 Sqn., Kenley, 5-39. No. 6 O.T.U. No. 59 O.T.U. Fate not known.

L1925 No. 1 Sqn., Tangmere, 5-39; assumed lost in France, 5-40.

L1926 No. 3 Sqn., Kenley, 5-39. No. 312 (Czech) Sqn. No. 55 O.T.U.; crashed while landing at Ouston, 15-4-41.

L1927 No. 1 Sqn., Tangmere, 5-39. No. 73 Sqn. No. 6 O.T.U. No. 8 F.T.S.; crashed while landing at Montrose, 23-12-41.

L1928 No. 3 Sqn., Kenley, 5-39. No. 253 Sqn.; crashed while on patrol at Maidstone, Kent, 10-10-40; pilot, Sgt. H.H. Allgood, suffered oxygen failure and was killed.

L1929 No. 79 Sqn., Biggin Hill, 5-39; crashed, 10-10-39.

L1930 No. 87 Sqn., Debden, 5-39; Missing over France, 13-5-40.

L1931 No. 504 Sqn., A.A.F., Hucknall, 5-39. No. 43 Sqn.; shot down by Bf 109Es near Abbeville, France, 7-6-40.

L1932 No. 3 Sqn., Kenley, 5-39, **OP-S**; force landed near Louvain, 14-5-40, and abandoned.

L1933 No. 3 Sqn., Kenley, 5-39. No. 85 Sqn.; hit by British A.A. and crash landed at Hawkinge, 24-8-40; P/O J. Lockhart unhurt.

L1934 No. 3 Sqn., Kenley, 5-39, **OP-D**. No. 5 O.T.U. No. 55 O.T.U. No. 8 F.T.S. No. 17 P.A.F.U. No. 1622 Flt. No. 667 Sqn. S.O.C., 30-10-44.

L1935 No. 3 Sqn., Kenley, 5-39. No. 85 Sqn. No. 71 Sqn., 11-40. No. 56 O.T.U. N. 8 F.T.S. No. 1 A.A.S. *To India*, 1943. No. 151 O.T.U.; crashed at Risalpur, 11-12-43.

L1936 No. 3 Sqn., Kenley, 5-39. No. 601 Sqn., A.A.F.; crashed near Lewes, Sussex, 4-7-40, when pilot was overcome by glycol fumes, but was not hurt.

L1937 No. 3 Sqn., Kenley, 5-39, **OP-T**, later **QO-T**; pilot lost control and abandoned aircraft 6 miles south of Dorking, Surrey, 10-10-39.

L1938 No. 3 Sqn., Kenley, 5-39; crashed while approaching to land at Biggin Hill, 30-6-39.

L1939 No. 3 Sqn., Kenley, 5-39; crashed in bad visibility near Sittingbourne, Kent, 10-9-39.

L1940 No. 3 Sqn., Kenley, 5-39. S.O.C., 3-7-40.

L1941 No. 504 Sqn., A.A.F., Hucknall, 6-39; Missing over France, 14-5-40.

L1942 No. 504 Sqn., A.A.F., Hucknall, 5-39. No. 79 Sqn. No. 6 O.T.U. No. 9 F.T.S. No. 9 P.A.F.U. A.T.A. S.O.C., 18-5-44.

L1943 No. 504 Sqn., A.A.F., Hucknall, 5-39. No. 1 Sqn.; shot down by Bf 110s over France, 15-5-40.

L1944 No. 504 Sqn., A.A.F., Hucknall, 5-39; assumed lost in France, 5-40.

L1945 No. 504 Sqn., A.A.F., Hucknall, 5-39. No. 79 Sqn. No. 52 O.T.U. A.T.A.; crashed, 5-7-42.

L1946 No. 504 Sqn., A.A.F., Hucknall, 5-39. No. 7 O.T.U. No. 5 O.T.U.; crashed near Beachley, Glos., 1-10-40.

L1947 No. 504 Sqn., A.A.F., Hucknall, 5-39; crashed one mile north of Bungay, Suffolk, 30-4-40.

L1948 No. 504 Sqn., A.A.F., Hucknall, 5-39. No. 242 Sqn.; Missing in action, 1-6-40.

L1949 No. 501 Sqn., A.A.F., Filton, 4-39, **ZH-O**. S.O.C., 5-40.

L1950 No. 504 Sqn., A.A.F., Hucknall, 5-39. S.O.C., 5-40.

L1951 No. 504 Sqn., A.A.F., Hucknall, 5-39. No. 601 Sqn., A.A.F. No. 229 Sqn. No. 56 O.T.U. No. 5 F.T.S. No. 9 F.T.S.; crashed on take-off at Park Farm, Chipping Sodbury, Glos., 11-2-42.

L1952 No. 504 Sqn., A.A.F., Hucknall, 5-39. No. 232 Sqn. No. 59 O.T.U. Became ***3369M***, 1-43.

L1953 No. 501 Sqn., A.A.F., Filton, 4-39; later **SD-F**. S.O.C., 5-40.

L1954 No. 504 Sqn., A.A.F., Hucknall, 5-39; crashed while landing at Metheringham L.G., 9-9-39.

L1955 No. 43 Sqn., Tangmere, 5-39; crashed near Ashford, Kent, 29-7-40, following engine failure; P/O K.C. Campbell killed.

L1956 No. 504 Sqn., A.A.F., Hucknall, 5-39. No. 607 Sqn. No. 306 (Polish) Sqn. S.F.P.P. S.O.C., 29-12-41.

L1957 No. 504 Sqn., A.A.F., Hucknall, 5-39. No. 55 O.T.U. Became ***3274M***, 7-42.

L1958 No. 43 Sqn., Tangmere, 5-39. No. 5 O.T.U. No. 8 F.T.S. R.A.F. College, Cranwell. No. 41 O.T.U. S.O.C., 12-6-44.

L1959 No. 1 Sqn., Tangmere, 5-39. No. 151 Sqn. No. 43 Sqn. No. 1 Sqn. No. 73 Sqn.; force landed in Luxembourg and interned, 9-11-39.

L1960 No. 1 Sqn., Tangmere, 5-39. No. 73 Sqn. S.O.C., 3-6-42.

L1961 No. 1 Sqn., Tangmere, 5-39. No. 151 Sqn. No. 229 Sqn. No. 46 Sqn.; lost in H.M.S. *Glorious* on return from Norway, 8-6-40.

L1962 No. 1 Sqn., Tangmere, 5-39. No. 151 Sqn. No. 1 Sqn. No. 73 Sqn.; crashed at St. Privat, France, 12-3-40.

L1963 No. 1 Sqn., Tangmere, 5-39. No. 87 Sqn. No. 43 Sqn.; crashed during aerobatics at Cragburn Dean, near Usworth, 27-10-40; Sgt. L.V. Toogood killed.

L1964 No. 1 Sqn., Tangmere, 5-39. No. 87 Sqn.; assumed lost in France, 5-40.

L1965 No. 1 Sqn., Tangmere, 5-39. No. 87 Sqn. No. 73 Sqn. No. 253 Sqn.; shot down by Bf 109Es south of Maidstone, 30-8-40; P/O C.D. Francis killed.

L1966 No. 1 Sqn., Tangmere, 5-39. No. 73 Sqn. S.O.C., 6-8-40.

L1967 No. 1 Sqn., Tangmere, 5-39. No. 73 Sqn.; shot down by Bf 109Es near Metz, 22-12-39.

L1968 No. 1 Sqn., Tangmere, 5-39. No. 73 Sqn. No. 607 Sqn., A.A.F. No. 43 Sqn., A.A.F.; crashed in sea off Acklington, 4-2-41.

L1969 No. 1 Sqn., Tangmere, 5-39. No. 306 (Polish) Sqn. No. 315 (Polish) Sqn. No. 317 (Polish) Sqn. Became ***3672M***.

L1970 No. 1 Sqn., Tangmere, 5-39. No. 32 Sqn. No. 43 Sqn. No. 87 Sqn.; Missing in action, 12-5-40.

L1971 No. 1 Sqn., Tangmere, 5-39; crashed at Fenetrange, France, 2-3-40.

L1972 No. 1 Sqn., Tangmere, 5-39. No. 32 Sqn. No. 242 Sqn. No. 56 Sqn.; Missing over France, 29-5-40.

L1973 No. 1 Sqn., Tangmere, 5-39. No. 111 Sqn. No. 1 Sqn. No. 1 Sqn., R.C.A.F. No. 5 O.T.U. No. 1 A.S.S. No. 56 O.T.U. No. 1 Tactical Exercise Unit. S.O.C., 7-7-44.

L1974 No. 1 Sqn., Tangmere, 5-39. No. 43 Sqn. No. 1 Sqn.; burnt on evacuation, Château Bougon, France, 18-6-40.

L1975 No. 1 Sqn., Tangmere, 5-39. No. 56 Sqn. No. 17 Sqn. No. 73 Sqn. No. 151 Sqn. No. 73 Sqn. No. 5 O.T.U. No. 55 O.T.U. Empire Central Flying School. No. 7 P.A.F.U. S.O.C., 1-10-44.

L1976 No. 1 Sqn., Tangmere, 5-39. No. 56 Sqn. No. 17 Sqn.; crashed while landing at Kenley, 8-9-39.

L1977 No. 1 Sqn., Tangmere, 5-39. No. 151 Sqn. No. 5 O.T.U. No. 55 O.T.U.; crashed near Stroud, Glos., after take-off at Aston Down, 9-10-40.

L1978 No. 1 Sqn., Tangmere, 5-39. No. 85 Sqn.; crashed, 6-3-40.

L1979 No. 1 Sqn., Tangmere, 5-39. No. 85 Sqn.; Missing over France, 13-5-40.

L1980 No. 56 Sqn., North Weald, 5-39. No. 229 Sqn. No. 46 Sqn.; lost in H.M.S. *Glorious* on return from Norway, 8-6-40.

L1981 No. 56 Sqn., North Weald, 5-39. No. 242 Sqn. No. 73 Sqn. No. 5 F.T.S. No. 8 S.F.T.S. No. 9 P.A.F.U. R.A.F. College, Cranwell. No. 3 Tactical Exercise Unit. S.O.C., 18-5-44.

L1982 No. 56 Sqn., North Weald, 5-39. No. 229 Sqn. No. 213 Sqn. No. 229 Sqn.; Missing over France, 31-5-40.

L1983 No. 56 Sqn., North Weald, 5-39, **LR-N**. No. 242 Sqn. No. 56 Sqn. No. 615 Sqn., A.A.F. No. 43 Sqn. No. 5 F.T.S. No. 55 O.T.U. No. 41 O.T.U. S.O.C., 30-5-44.

L1984 No. 56 Sqn., North Weald, 5-39; crashed at Playford, Suffolk, 29-1-40.

L1985 No. 56 Sqn., North Weald, 5-39; shot down by Spitfires near Ipswich, 6-9-39.

L1986 No. 56 Sqn., North Weald, 5-39. No. 79 Sqn. No. 7 O.T.U. No. 6 O.T.U.; abandoned near Marholm, Northants, 30-9-40.

L1987 No. 56 Sqn., North Weald, 5-39, **LR-Q**, later **US-S**. No. 601 Sqn., A.A.F. S.O.C., 3-7-40.

L1988 No. 56 Sqn., North Weald, 5-39. No. 229 Sqn. No. 46 Sqn., Missing from patrol near Harstad, Norway, 29-5-40.

L1989 No. 56 Sqn., North Weald, 5-39. No. 229 Sqn. Hucknall Stn. Flt. Rolls-Royce Ltd. No. 7 O.T.U. Rolls-Royce Ltd. No. 85 Sqn. No. 71 Sqn., 11-40. No. 56 O.T.U. *Converted to Mark IIA*, ***DG649***.

L1990 No. 56 Sqn., North Weald, 5-39. No. 601 Sqn., A.A.F.; shot down by Bf 109Es near Portsmouth, 18-8-40; Sgt. R.P. Hawkings killed.

L1991 No. 56 Sqn., North Weald, 5-39. No. 501 Sqn., A.A.F.; abandoned in France, 5-40.

L1992 No. 56 Sqn., North Weald, 5-39. No. 242 Sqn. No. 56 Sqn. No. 615 Sqn., A.A.F. No. 55 O.T.U. No. 1 A.A.S. S.O.C., 20-11-41.

L1993 *Supplied to Belgium*, 5-39, as "***4***", *Aéronautique Militaire.*

L1994 *Supplied to Belgium*, 5-39, as "***5***", *Aéronautique Militaire.*

L1995 *Supplied to Belgium*, 5-39, as "***6***", *Aéronautique Militaire.*

L1996 *Supplied to Belgium*, 5-39, as "***7***", *Aéronautique Militaire.*

L1997 *Supplied to Belgium*, 5-39, as "***8***", *Aéronautique Militaire.*

L1998 No. 56 Sqn., North Weald, 6-39. No. 229 Sqn. No. 249 Sqn. No.238 Sqn. No. 601 Sqn., A.A.F. No. 236 Sqn. No. 56 O.T.U. Transferred to Admiralty Charge, 6-9-42, and *converted to Sea Hurricane IB.*

L1999 No. 56 Sqn., North Weald, 6-39. No. 504 Sqn., A.A.F. No. 55 O.T.U.; crashed at Tetbury, Glos., 29-11-40; became ***2466M.***

L2000 No. 56 Sqn., North Weald, 6-39. No. 229 Sqn.; S.O.C., 16-5-40.

L2001 No. 56 Sqn., North Weald, 6-39. No. 111 Sqn., **JU-B**; crashed while landing at Hatfield, 19-6-40.

L2002 No. 56 Sqn., North Weald, 6-39. No. 242 Sqn.; crashed at night near Bolton Percy, Tadcaster, Yorks, 3-3-40.

L2003 No. 56 Sqn., North Weald, 6-39. No. 242 Sqn. No. 615 Sqn., A.A.F. No. 6 O.T.U.; crashed while landing at Sutton Bridge, 16-10-40.

L2004 No. 56 Sqn., North Weald, 6-39. No. 242 Sqn.; Missing in action, France, 1-6-40.

L2005 No. 56 Sqn., North Weald, 6-39. No. 151 Sqn., **DZ-D**; shot down by Bf 109Es, 28-8-40; P/O J.W.E. Alexander baled out severely burned.

L2006 No. 11 Group Pool. No. 6 O.T.U. No. 56 O.T.U. A. & A.E.E. Became ***4343M***, 11-43.

L2007 No. 11 Group Pool; crashed in sea after take-off at St. Athan, 11-11-39.

L2008 No. 11 Group Pool; collided with Hurricane ***L2069*** while taking off at St. Athan, 15-11-39.

L2009 No. 11 Group Pool; crashed in fog 6 miles west of Ripon, Yorks, 22-4-40.

L2010 No. 11 Group Pool; crashed while landing at St. Athan, 5-7-39; became ***1611M.***

L2011 No. 11 Group Pool. No. 6 O.T.U. No. 306

(Polish) Sqn. No. 56 O.T.U. S.O.C., 14-8-44.
L2012 No. 605 Sqn., A.A.F., Castle Bromwich, 8-39; collided with Do 17Z near Marden, Kent, 15-9-40; P/O T.P.M. Cooper-Slipper baled out unhurt.
L2013 No. 605 Sqn., A.A.F., Castle Bromwich, 8-39. S.O.C., 6-5-40.
L2014 No. 605 Sqn., A.A.F., Castle Bromwich, 8-39. Transferred to Admiralty Charge, 21-4-41, and *converted to Sea Hurricane IB*.
L2015 *Supplied to Turkish Air Force*, 26-8-39.
L2016 *Supplied to Turkish Air Force*, 26-8-39.
L2017 *Supplied to Turkish Air Force*, 26-8-39.
L2018 No. 605 Sqn., A.A.F., Castle Bromwich, 8-39. Became ***3194M***, 2-41.
L2019 *Supplied to Turkish Air Force*, 26-8-39.
L2020 No. 605 Sqn., A.A.F., Castle Bromwich, 8-39. No. 253 Sqn. No. 7 O.T.U.; crashed while landing at Hawarden, 22-7-40.
L2021 *Shipped to R.C.A.F. in Canada*, 6-39, as "***327***".
L2022 *Shipped to R.C.A.F. in Canada*, 6-39, as "***328***".
L2023 *Shipped to R.C.A.F. in Canada*, 6-39, as "***329***".
L2024 *Supplied to Turkish Air Force*, 26-8-39.
L2025 *Supplied to Turkish Air Force*, 26-8-39.
L2026 A. & A.E.E., 11-39. No. 303 (Polish) Sqn. No. 56 O.T.U. No. 9 P.A.F.U. No. 16 F.P.P.; crashed 5 miles NE of Cupar, Fife, 11-10-43.
L2027 *Supplied to Turkish Air Force*, 3-9-39.
L2028 *Supplied to Turkish Air Force*, 3-9-39.
L2029 *Supplied to Turkish Air Force*, 3-9-39.
L2030 *Supplied to Turkish Air Force*, 3-9-39.
L2031 *Supplied to Turkish Air Force*, 3-9-39.
L2032 *Supplied to Turkish Air Force*, 3-9-39.
L2033 *Supplied to Turkish Air Force*, 3-9-39.
L2034 No. 17 Sqn., North Weald, 7-39. No. 601 Sqn., A.A.F., **UF-L**; Missing in action, 6-40.
L2035 No. 17 Sqn., North Weald, 7-39. No. 601 Sqn., A.A.F.; S.O.C., 5-40.
L2036 No. 87 Sqn., Debden, 8-39. No. 73 Sqn.; shot down by Bf 109Es over Thames Estuary, 23-9-40; P/O N.G. Langham-Hobart ditched and was rescued with severe burns.
L2037 No. 501 Sqn., A.A.F., Filton, 8-39; assumed lost in France, 5-40.
L2038 No. 501 Sqn., A.A.F., Filton, 8-39, **SD-B**. No. 9 F.T.S.; crashed at Rudloe, Somerset, 31-10-41.
L2039 No. 501 Sqn., A.A.F., Filton, 8-39. No. 242 Sqn. No. 73 Sqn. Transferred to Admiralty charge, 11-42, and *converted to Sea Hurricane Mark IA*.
L2040 *Supplied to Belgium*, 7-39, as "***9***", *Aéronautique Militaire*.
L2041 *Supplied to Belgium*, 7-39, as "***10***", *Aéronautique Militaire*.
L2042 *Supplied to Belgium*, 7-39, as "***11***", *Aéronautique Militaire*.
L2043 *Supplied to Belgium*, 7-39, as "***12***", *Aéronautique Militaire*.
L2044 *Supplied to Belgium*, 7-39, as "***13***", *Aéronautique Militaire*.
L2045 No. 501 Sqn., A.A.F., Filton, 8-39. No. 6 O.T.U. No. 9 F.T.S. To Admiralty Charge as instructional airframe, 15-5-43.
L2046 No. 501 Sqn., A.A.F., Filton, 7-39. Became ***3573M***, 3-43.
L2047 No. 43 Sqn., Tangmere, 8-39. No. 87 Sqn. No. 73 Sqn. No. 151 Sqn.; crashed while landing at Digby, 25-10-40; Sgt. Grant unhurt.
L2048 *Shipped to Poland*, 24-7-39; *re-shipped back to U.K.*, c.26-8-39. No. 29 Sqn., Debden, 11-39. S.O.C., 26-1-40.
L2049 No. 32 Sqn., Biggin Hill, 8-39; later Gravesend. No. 79 Sqn., Biggin Hill; assumed lost in France, 5-40.
L2050 No. 32 Sqn., Biggin Hill, 8-39; later Gravesend. No. 79 Sqn., Biggin Hill. No. 501 Sqn., A.A.F.; assumed lost in France, 5-40.
L2051 No. 111 Sqn., Wick, 9-39; later Northolt; shot down by Bf 109Es over France, 18-5-40.
L2052 No. 501 Sqn., A.A.F., Filton, 8-39. No. 111 Sqn. No. 3 F.P.P. No. 111 Sqn. No. 6 O.T.U. No. 5 F.T.S. No. 59 O.T.U. S.O.C., 5-4-45.
L2053 No. 501 Sqn., A.A.F., Filton, 8-39; crashed at Mezières, France, 12-5-40.
L2054 No. 501 Sqn., A.A.F., Filton, 8-39, **SD-E**; crashed at Beauvillers, France, 12-5-40.
L2055 No. 501 Sqn., A.A.F., Filton, 8-39, **SD-F**. No. 1 Sqn. No. 111 Sqn. No. 56 O.T.U.; crashed at West Walton, Norfolk, 11-6-41.
L2056 No. 501 Sqn., A.A.F., Filton, 8-39, **SD-G**; crashed while landing at Anglure, France, 31-5-40.
L2057 No. 213 Sqn., Wittering, 9-39. No. 601 Sqn., A.A.F.; shot down off Portland, 11-8-40; P/O W.G. Dickie killed.
L2058 No. 605 Sqn., A.A.F., Castle Bromwich, 8-39; Missing in action, 22-5-40.
L2059 No. 605 Sqn., A.A.F., Castle Bromwich, 8-39; shot down near Odiham, 9-9-40; P/O G.M. Forrester killed.
L2060 No. 213 Sqn., Wittering, 8-39, **AK-G**. No. 229 Sqn. No. 213 Sqn.; lost in France, 5-40.
L2061 No. 1 Sqn., Tangmere, 8-39. No. 605 Sqn., A.A.F.; shot down by Bf 109E near Tunbridge Wells, Kent, 8-9-40; P/O J. Fleming baled out badly burned and wounded.
L2062 No. 213 Sqn., Wittering, 8-39. No. 263 Sqn. No. 32 Sqn.; Missing, 1-9-40 (circumstances not known).
L2063 No. 32 Sqn., Biggin Hill, 8-39. No. 7 O.T.U. No. 6 O.T.U.; crashed at Holbeach, Lincs, 30-8-40.
L2064 No. 11 Group Pool, 8-39. No. 6 O.T.U. No. 5 F.T.S. No. 1623 Flt. No. 691 Sqn. S.O.C., 4-5-44.
L2065 No. 79 Sqn., Biggin Hill, 8-39; S.O.C., 5-40.
L2066 No. 43 Sqn., Tangmere, 9-39; collided with Hurricane ***L1734*** and crashed, 18-1-40.
L2067 No. 3 Sqn., Croydon, 9-39. No. 249 Sqn. No. 5 O.T.U. No. 55 O.T.U. Ferry Pilots Pool. Became ***3581M***, 2-43.
L2068 No. 79 Sqn., Biggin Hill, 8-39; S.O.C., 5-40.
L2069 No. 11 Group Pool, 8-39; collided with Hurricane ***L2008*** while taking off at St. Athan, 15-11-39.
L2070 No. 11 Group Poll, 8-39. No. 6 O.T.U. No. 56 O.T.U. No. 135 Sqn., Baginton, 8-41. No. 56 O.T.U. No. 116 Sqn., Hendon, 1-42. No. 55 O.T.U.; crashed near Annan, 11-3-43.
L2071 No. 46 Sqn., Digby, 8-39. No. 229 Sqn. No. 253 Sqn. No. 229 Sqn. No. 85 Sqn.; shot down by Bf 109E near Kenley, 1-9-40; Sgt. J.H.M. Ellis killed.
L2072 No. 11 Group Pool, 9-39. No. 6 O.T.U.; crashed near Sutton Bridge, 22-3-40.
L2073 No. 11 Group Pool, 9-39. No. 6 O.T.U. No. 8 F.T.S. No. 2 Flying Instructors' School. No. 56 O.T.U.; collided with Hurricane ***P3650***, 23-6-43, and crashed in sea off Leuchars.
L2074 No. 11 Group Pool, 9-39; crashed into mountain in cloud, Nant-y-Moel, Glamorgan, 7-1-40.
L2075 No. 11 Group Pool, 9-39. No. 32 Sqn. No. 615 Sqn., A.A.F. No. 55 O.T.U. No. 5 F.T.S. No. 5 P.A.F.U. No. 59 O.T.U. No. 5 P.A.F.U. S.O.C., 10-9-44.
L2076 No. 73 Sqn, Digby, 8-39. No. 56 Sqn. No. 7 O.T.U. No. 5 O.T.U. No. 55 O.T.U.; crashed while taking off at Aston Down, 22-2-41.
L2077 *Supplied to Romanian Air Force*, 28-8-39.
L2078 *Supplied to Romanian Air Force*, 28-8-39.
L2079 *Supplied to Iranian Air Force*, 8-39.
L2080 No. 29 Sqn., Debden, 9-39. No. 17 Sqn. No. 601 Sqn., A.A.F. No. 5 O.T.U. No. 55 O.T.U. No. 9 F.T.S.; crashed at Wootton Bassett, Wiltshire, 25-6-41.
L2081 No. 29 Sqn., Debden, 9-39. No. 17 Sqn. No. 601 Sqn., A.A.F.; Missing over France, 16-5-40.
L2082 No. 29 Sqn., Debden, 9-39. No. 17 Sqn. No. 7 O.T.U. No. 6 O.T.U.; collided with Hurricane ***324*** of R.C.A.F., 18-8-40, and crashed near Sutton Bridge.
L2083 No. 29 Sqn., Debden, 9-39. No. 17 Sqn. No. 46 Sqn. No. 6 O.T.U. No. 56 O.T.U.; crashed near Sutton Bridge following fire in the air, 8-10-40.
L2084 No. 29 Sqn., Debden, 9-39. No. 17 Sqn. No. 601 Sqn., A.A.F. No. 6 O.T.U. Became ***3575M***, 3-43.
L2085 *Supplied to Romanian Air Force*, 2-9-39.
L2086 No. 29 Sqn., Debden, 9-39. No. 17 Sqn. No. 32 Sqn. Transferred to Admiralty Charge, 22-4-41, *for conversion to Sea Hurricane IA*.
L2087 No. 29 Sqn., Debden, 9-39. No. 17 Sqn. No. 151 Sqn. No. 242 Sqn. No. 52 O.T.U. No. 9 F.T.S. No. 7 P.A.F.U.; damaged beyond repair, 9-11-44.
L2088 No. 29 Sqn., Debden, 9-39. No. 17 Sqn. No. 601 Sqn., A.A.F.; Missing over France, 21-5-40.
L2089 No. 29 Sqn., Debden, 9-39. No. 17 Sqn. No. 238 Sqn. No. 55 O.T.U. No. 8 F.T.S. No. 2 Flying Instructors' School. No. 59 O.T.U. No. 7 P.A.F.U. S.O.C., 13-2-44.
L2090 No. 29 Sqn., Debden, 9-39. No. 242 Sqn; crashed, 30-9-40.
L2091 No. 29 Sqn., Debden, 9-39. No. 17 Sqn. No. 6 O.T.U. No. 56 O.T.U. S.O.C., 21-11-44.
L2092 No. 29 Sqn., Debden, 9-39. No. 17 Sqn. No. 151 Sqn. No. 308 (Polish) Sqn. No. 55 O.T.U. No. 8 F.T.S. S.O.C., 15-11-41.
L2093 *Supplied to Romanian Air Force*, 2-9-39.
L2094 *Supplied to Romanian Air Force*, 2-9-39.
L2095 *Supplied to Romanian Air Force*, 2-9-39.
L2096 *Supplied to Romanian Air Force*, 2-9-39.
L2097 *Supplied to Romanian Air Force*, 2-9-39.
L2098 No. 616 Sqn., A.A.F., Leconfield, 10-39. No. 605 Sqn., A.A.F. No. 5 O.T.U. No. 55 O.T.U.; crashed at Aston Down, 26-12-40.
L2099 No. 601 Sqn., A.A.F., Tangmere, 3-40; crashed near Middle Wallop, 1-6-40.
L2100 No. 29 Sqn., Debden, 9-39. No. 17 Sqn. No. 605 Sqn., A.A.F. No. 7 O.T.U. No. 5 O.T.U. No. 56 O.T.U. No. 9 F.T.S. S.O.C., 3-9-44.
L2101 No. 616 Sqn., A.A.F., Leconfield, 10-39. No. 605 Sqn., A.A.F. No. 257 Sqn. No. 55 O.T.U. No. 9 F.T.S. Became ***3582M***, 3-43.
L2102 No. 616 Sqn., A.A.F., Leconfield, 10-39. No. 17 Sqn. No. 601 Sqn., A.A.F. No. 257 Sqn. No. 55 O.T.U. No. 9 F.T.S. Became ***3592M***, 3-43.
L2103 No. 616 Sqn., A.A.F., Leconfield, 10-39. No. 605 Sqn., A.A.F.; crashed in sea off Dunbar, East Lothian, 9-8-40; Sgt. R.D. Ritchie killed, believed overcome by glycol fumes.
L2104 *Supplied to Romanian Air Force*, 4-9-39.
L2105 *Supplied to Belgium*, 9-39, as "***14***", *Aéronautique Militaire*.
L2106 *Supplied to Belgium*, 9-39, as "***15***", *Aéronautique Militaire*.
L2107 *Supplied to Belgium*, 9-39, as "***16***", *Aéronautique Militaire*.
L2108 *Supplied to Belgium*, 9-39, as "***17***", *Aéronautique Militaire*.
L2109 *Supplied to Belgium*, 9-39, as "***18***", *Aéronautique Militaire*.
L2110 *Supplied to Belgium*, 9-39, as "***19***", *Aéronautique Militaire*.
L2111 *Supplied to Belgium*, 9-39, as "***20***", *Aéronautique Militaire*.
L2112 *Supplied to Romanian Air Force*, 4-9-39.
L2113 *Supplied to Romanian Air Force*, 4-9-39.
L2114 *Supplied to Romanian Air Force*, 4-9-39.
L2115 No. 610 Sqn., A.A.F., Hooton Park, 9-39. No. 605 Sqn., A.A.F.; aircraft crashed 5 miles south of Dunbar, East Lothian, 24-6-40, following loss of gun panel.
L2116 No. 610 Sqn., A.A.F., Hooton Park, 9-39. No. 43 Sqn.; shot down near Abbeville, France, 7-6-40.
L2117 No. 610 Sqn., A.A.F., Hooton Park, 9-39. No. 605 Sqn., A.A.F.; crashed 6 miles north of Folkestone, Kent, 31-5-40.
L2118 No. 610 Sqn., A.A.F., Hooton Park, 9-39. No. 605 Sqn., A.A.F., Croydon; Missing in action, 14-9-40 (pilot and circumstances unknown).
L2119 No. 610 Sqn., A.A.F., Hooton Park, 9-39. No. 605 Sqn., A.A.F.; Missing in action over France, 27-5-40.
L2120 No. 610 Sqn., A.A.F., Hooton Park, 9-39. No. 605 Sqn., A.A.F.; Missing in action over France, 22-5-40.
L2121 No. 610 Sqn., A.A.F., Hooton Park, 9-39. No. 605 Sqn., A.A.F.; Missing in action over France, 23-5-40.
L2122 No. 610 Sqn., A.A.F., Hooton Park, 9-39. No.

605 Sqn., A.A.F., Croydon; shot down by Bf 109Es over West Malling, Kent, 15-9-40; P/O R.E. Jones baled out with slight wounds.

L2123 No. 3 Sqn., Croydon, 9-39. No. 615 Sqn., A.A.F. No. 3 Sqn.; crashed from spin on Folkestone golf course, 11-3-40.

L2124 No. 501 Sqn., Kenley, 9-39. No. 7 O.T.U. No. 5 O.T.U. No. 55 O.T.U.; crashed at Moreton-in-Marsh, Glos., 5-12-40.

L2125 *Supplied to Turkish Air Force*, 14-9-39.

L2126 *Supplied to Turkish Air Force*, 14-9-39.

L2127 *Supplied to Turkish Air Force*, 14-9-39.

L2128 *Supplied to Turkish Air Force*, 14-9-39.

L2129 *Supplied to Turkish Air Force*, 21-9-39.

L2130 *Supplied to Turkish Air Force*, 21-9-39.

L2131 *Supplied to Turkish Air Force*, 21-9-39.

L2132 *Supplied to Turkish Air Force*, 21-9-39.

L2133 *Supplied to Turkish Air Force*, 28-9-39.

L2134 *Supplied to Turkish Air Force*, 28-9-39.

L2135 *Supplied to Turkish Air Force*, 28-9-39.

L2136 *Supplied to Turkish Air Force*, 5-10-39.

L2137 *Supplied to Turkish Air Force*, 5-10-39.

L2138 *Supplied to Turkish Air Force*, 5-10-39.

L2139 *Supplied to Turkish Air Force*, 5-10-39.

L2140 No. 79 Sqn., Manston, 11-39; Missing over France, 17-5-40.

L2141 No. 213 Sqn., Wittering, 10-39. No. 601 Sqn.; S.O.C., 3-7-40.

L2142 No. 213 Sqn., Wittering, 10-39. No. 229 Sqn. No. 213 Sqn.; S.O.C., 5-40.

L2143 No. 43 Sqn., Tangmere, 10-39. No. 601 Sqn., A.A.F. No. 43 Sqn. No. 59 O.T.U. No. 41 O.T.U. S.O.C., 13-10-44.

L2144 *Shipped to R.C.A.F. in Canada*, 28-9-39, as "***330***", but said not to have arrived.

L2145 No. 79 Sqn., Manston, 11-39; Missing over France, 20-5-40.

L2146 No. 151 Sqn., North Weald, 11-39. No. 229 Sqn. No. 213 Sqn.; assumed lost in France, 6-40.

HAWKER HURRICANE MARK I (Hawker built). Second production batch of 300 aircraft built by Hawker Aircraft Ltd., Kingston-upon-Thames and Brooklands, under Contract No. 751458/38 during 1939 and 1940, and delivered between September 1939 and May 1940. First 80 aircraft completed with fabric-covered wings (most later modified with metal stressed-skin wings); remainder completed with metal wings from outset. Rolls-Royce III engines driving Rotol or D.H. constant speed or variable pitch three-blade propellers. *N2318-N2367, N2380-N2409, N2422-N2441, N2453-N2502, N2520-N2559, N2582-N2631,* and *N2645-N2729*. Deliveries commenced 29-9-39; completed 1-5-40; average rate of production, approximately two aircraft per day.

N2318 No. 1 Sqn., Vassincourt, France, 10-39. No. 73 Sqn.; assumed lost in France, 5-40.

N2319 No. 1 Sqn., Vassincourt, France, 10-39. No. 85 Sqn., Lille, France; assumed lost in France, 5-40.

N2320 No. 56 Sqn. No. 242 Sqn.; lost in France, 5-40.

N2321 No. 43 Sqn., 12-39. No. 5 O.T.U. No. 55 O.T.U.; crashed at Hetton-le-Hole, Co. Durham, 7-5-41.

N2322 *Made ready for shipment to Poland*, 9-39, *but cancelled; remained packed and shipped to Finland*, 2-2-40.

N2323 *Made ready for shipment to Poland*, 9-39, *but cancelled; remained packed and shipped to Finland*, 2-2-40.

N2324 *Made ready for shipment to Poland*, 9-39, *but cancelled; remained packed and shipped to Finland*, 2-2-40.

N2325 No. 11 E.F.T.S. No. 59 O.T.U. No. 2 Tactical Air Force Comms. Sqn. No. 5 P.A.F.U.; S.O.C., 3-1-45.

N2326 No. 85 Sqn. No. 1 Sqn.; abandoned in France, 5-40.

N2327 *Made ready for shipment to Poland*, 9-39, *but cancelled; remained packed and shipped to Finland*, 2-2-40.

N2328 No. 615 Sqn., A.A.F., France. Flown to U.K. by No. 501 Sqn., 5-40. No. 257 Sqn. No. 56 O.T.U. No. 3 F.T.S. Became ***3590M***, 3-43.

N2329 No. 238 Sqn. No. 501 Sqn. No. 6 O.T.U. Ferry Training Unit. Lyneham Stn. Flt. Heston Stn. Flt. Technical Training Command Comms. Flt. No. 41 O.T.U.; S.O.C., 18-5-44.

N2330 No. 615 Sqn., A.A.F.; lost in France, 5-40.

N2331 No. 615 Sqn., A.A.F.; lost in France, 5-40.

N2332 Shipped to Takoradi, West Africa, 1941; crashed near Takoradi during delivery flight to Middle East, 5-8-41.

N2333 No. 1 Sqn., Vassincourt, France, 12-39. No. 3 Sqn., Kenley, 1-40; abandoned at night near Dover, 10-5-40.

N2334 No. 85 Sqn., France. No. 1 Sqn., France. No. 73 Sqn., France; assumed lost in France, 5-40.

N2335 No. 615 Sqn., A.A.F., France; assumed lost in France, 5-40.

N2336 No. 213 Sqn.; aircraft struck sea (English Channel) during patrol, 27-8-40; Sub-Lt. W.J.M. Moss assumed killed.

N2337 No. 615 Sqn., A.A.F.; damaged in landing accident at Hawkinge, 11-8-40; P/O J.A.P. McClintock unhurt. Aircraft repaired. No. 73 Sqn. No. 55 O.T.U.; collided with Hurricane ***V7059*** and crashed, 19-4-41.

N2338 No. 242 Sqn. No. 7 O.T.U. No. 6 O.T.U. No. 56 O.T.U. No. 56 O.T.U. Ferry Pilots' Pool. Ferry Training Unit. No. 1622 Flt. No. 667 Sqn. S.O.C., 21-11-44.

N2339 No. 605 Sqn., A.A.F. No. 3 Sqn.; lost over France, 6-40.

N2340 No. 111 Sqn., Drem, 11-39; S/L H. Broadhurst destroyed He 111H, 29-11-39 (Squadron's first victory of the War); shot down near Kenley, 18-8-40; F/L S.D.P. Connors killed.

N2341 No. 242 Sqn. No. 6 O.T.U. No. 56 O.T.U. No. 8 F.T.S. No. 17 P.A.F.U. No. 9 P.A.F.U. Became ***3588M***, 3-43.

N2342 No. 242 Sqn. No. 32 Sqn. No. 257 Sqn.; Missing in action, 17-11-40.

N2343 No. 242 Sqn. No. 6 O.T.U. No. 56 O.T.U. No. 52 O.T.U. Became ***2836M***, 12-41.

N2344 No. 242 Sqn. No. 56 Sqn. No. 1 Sqn., R.C.A.F. No. 213 Sqn. No. 52 O.T.U. No. 8 F.T.S. No. 9 F.T.S. No. 9 P.A.F.U. R.A.F. College, Cranwell. No. 1622 Flt. No. 667 Sqn. S.O.C., 1-1-45.

N2345 No. 242 Sqn. No. 46 Sqn. No. 32 Sqn., Acklington; lost in accident, 31-8-40; circumstances not known.

N2346 *Performance check trials*, Brooklands, 11-39. No. 605 Sqn., A.A.F., Hawkinge, 5-40; Missing in action, 26-5-40.

N2347 *Shipped to Finland*, 2-2-40.

N2348 *Shipped to Finland*, 2-2-40.

N2349 No. 605 Sqn., A.A.F., Hawkinge, 5-40; Missing in action, 22-5-40.

N2350 *Work started to convert to two-seat trainer*, 10-39, but cancelled 1-40. Reverted to standard and flown to France as replacement, but abandoned before being allocated to Squadron, 5-40.

N2351 No. 605 Sqn., A.A.F. No. 3 Sqn. No. 249 Sqn. No. 85 Sqn. No. 615 Sqn., A.A.F. No. 229 Sqn. No. 55 O.T.U.; crashed, 20-5-42.

N2352 No. 605 Sqn., A.A.F. No. 302 (Polish) Sqn. No. 55 O.T.U. *Converted to Sea Hurricane IA* and transferred to Admiralty Charge, 18-7-41.

N2353 No. 43 Sqn. No. 87 Sqn.; shot down in France, 18-5-40.

N2354 No. 11 Group Pool. No. 6 O.T.U. No. 79 Sqn. Became ***2646M***, 3-41.

N2355 No. 43 Sqn.; Missing over France, 5-40.

N2356 No. 11 Group Pool. No. 6 O.T.U. No. 55 O.T.U.; crashed near Silkworth, Co. Durham, 28-2-41.

N2357 No. 11 Group Pool. No. 6 O.T.U.; crashed while landing at Sutton Bridge, 27-9-40.

N2358 No. 43 Sqn., Tangmere, 11-39. No. 79 Sqn., Manston, 12-39. Packing Depot, Sealand, 1-40: *Shipped to Finland*, 2-2-40.

N2359 No. 17 Sqn. No. 6 O.T.U. No. 56 O.T.U.; crashed, 11-6-41.

N2360 No. 43 Sqn., Tangmere, 11-39. No. 87 Sqn. S.O.C., 21-6-40.

N2361 No. 43 Sqn., Acklington, 12-39. Aircraft interned (Belgium?), 12-39.

N2362 No. 43 Sqn., Acklington, 12-39. No. 87 Sqn.; crashed near Rethel, France, 9-5-40.

N2363 No. 43 Sqn., Acklington, 12-39. No. 85 Sqn.; damaged in accident in France, 21-4-40, and abandoned, 5-40.

N2364 No. 501 Sqn., A.A.F. No. 43 Sqn. No. 73 Sqn.; crashed near St. Privat la Montagne, Metz, 12-3-40.

N2365 No. 11 Group Pool. No. 6 O.T.U. No. 56 O.T.U. No. 9 F.T.S. R.A.F. College, Cranwell. No. 5 P.A.F.U.; S.O.C., 6-9-44.

N2366 No. 501 Sqn., A.A.F. No. 43 Sqn. No. 73 Sqn.; lost in France, 5-40.

N2367 No. 11 Group Pool. No. 6 O.T.U. No. 56 O.T.U. *Converted to Sea Hurricane IA*, 2-41, and transferred to Admiralty Charge, 27-8-43.

N2380 No. 501 Sqn., A.A.F. No. 1 Sqn.; lost in France, 5-40.

N2381 No. 501 Sqn., A.A.F. No. 1 Sqn. No. 242 Sqn.; destroyed on evacuation, Nantes, 18-6-40.

N2382 No. 1 Sqn.; lost in France, 5-40.

N2383 No. 1 Sqn., France. No. 43 Sqn.; lost in France, 5-40.

N2384 No. 79 Sqn., Hawkinge; shot down at Temple Ewell, Kent, 8-7-40; P/O J.E.R. Wood killed.

N2385 No. 1 Sqn., 11-39. No. 43 Sqn., 12-39. No. 73 Sqn., Rouvres, France; shot down by Bf 109Es near Metz, 22-12-39.

N2386 No. 73 Sqn. No. 43 Sqn. No. 73 Sqn. No. 249 Sqn. No. 56 Sqn. No. 55 O.T.U.; crashed at Usworth after fire in the air, 8-4-41.

N2387 *Supplied to Turkish Air Force*, 9-1-40.

N2388 No. 1 Sqn. No. 43 Sqn. No. 85 Sqn., France, 4-40; Missing in action, 11-5-40.

N2389 No. 43 Sqn. No. 85 Sqn.; lost in France, 5-40.

N2390 No. 87 Sqn. No. 43 Sqn. No. 87 Sqn.; lost in France, 5-40.

N2391 No. 1 Sqn. No. 43 Sqn. No. 73 Sqn.; crashed at Metz, 23-4-40.

N2392 *Made ready for shipment to Poland*, 9-39, *but cancelled. Shipped to Finland*, 2-2-40.

N2393 *Made ready for shipment to Poland*, 9-39, *but cancelled. Shipped to Finland*, 2-2-40.

N2394 *Made ready for shipment to Poland*, 9-39, *but cancelled. Shipped to Finland*, 2-2-40.

N2395 *Made ready for shipment to Poland*, 9-39, *but cancelled. Shipped to Finland*, 2-2-40.

N2396 No. 151 Sqn. No. 229 Sqn. No. 213 Sqn.; lost in France, 5-40.

N2397 No. 17 Sqn.; lost in France, 5-40.

N2398 No. 56 Sqn. No. 6 O.T.U. No. 56 O.T.U.; became ***4759M***, 4-44.

N2399 No. 56 Sqn. No. 615 Sqn., A.A.F. No. 6 O.T.U. No. 56 O.T.U. R.A.E., Farnborough. Became ***4661M***, 3-44.

N2400 No. 56 Sqn. No. 238 Sqn.; shot down by Bf 110s over Isle of Wight, 27-9-40; Sgt. E.S. Bann baled out but killed by enemy fighters while descending by parachute.

N2401 No. 213 Sqn., Tangmere, 9-40; believed lost in flying accident, 27-9-40; circumstances and pilot not known.

N2402 No. 56 Sqn. No. 55 O.T.U. No. 9 F.T.S. S.O.C., 29-12-41.

N2403 No. 17 Sqn.; lost in France, 5-40.

N2404 No. 87 Sqn. No. 73 Sqn.; abandoned in France, 5-40.

N2405 No. 17 Sqn.; lost in France, 5-40.

N2406 No. 32 Sqn.; Missing over English Channel, 8-6-40.

N2407 No. 32 Sqn. No. 17 Sqn.; lost over France, 5-40.

N2408 No. 17 Sqn.; lost over Northern France, 19-5-40.

N2409 No. 32 Sqn. No. 55 O.T.U.; crashed at Urchfont,

Wiltshire, 19-12-40.

N2422 No. 32 Sqn., Biggin Hill, 12-39. No. 3 Sqn., Merville, France, 5-40; Missing in action, 15-5-40.
N2423 No. 32 Sqn., Biggin Hill, 12-39. No. 17 Sqn. No. 229 Sqn. Flown to North Africa, via France and Tunisia, 7-40. No. 33 Sqn., Helwan, Egypt, 9-40. To India, 1943. S.O.C., 1-4-44.
N2424 No. 43 Sqn. No. 253 Sqn. No. 242 Sqn.; lost in France, 19-5-40.
N2425 No. 87 Sqn., Lille, France, 12-39. No. 85 Sqn., Lille, France; abandoned in France, 5-40.
N2426 No. 79 Sqn., Manston, 12-39; Missing in action over France, 5-40.
N2427 No. 17 Sqn. No. 85 Sqn. No. 71 Sqn., 11-40. No. 56 O.T.U. No. 87 Sqn. No. 197 Sqn. No. 195 Sqn. No. 55 O.T.U.; S.O.C., 23-5-44.
N2428 No. 56 Sqn., Martlesham Heath, 12-39. No. 5 O.T.U. No. 308 (Polish) Sqn. No. 55 O.T.U. No. 59 O.T.U.; crashed 3 miles south of Shankend, Roxburgh, 12-6-42.
N2429 No. 56 Sqn., Martlesham Heath, 12-39. No. 315 (Polish) Sqn. No. 245 Sqn. *Converted to Sea Hurricane IA*, early 1941; transferred to Admiralty Charge, 7-12-41.
N2430 No. 56 Sqn., Martlesham Heath, 12-39; Missing in action, 19-5-40.
N2431 No. 56 Sqn., Martlesham Heath, 1-40; Missing in action, 22-5-40.
N2432 No. 56 Sqn., Martlesham Heath, 12-39; shot down over the Straits of Dover, 13-7-40; Sgt. J.J. Whitfield killed.
N2433 No. 601 Sqn., A.A.F., Tangmere, 1-40. No. 32 Sqn. No. 6 O.T.U. No. 1 Sqn. No. 55 O.T.U.; crashed at Ouston, 16-4-41.
N2434 No. 601 Sqn., A.A.F., Tangmere, 1-40. No. 249 Sqn. No. 56 Sqn., Boscombe Down, 9-40, **US-H**; shot down by Bf 110s near Portland, 30-9-40; P/O M.H. Constable-Maxwell unhurt.
N2435 No. 601 Sqn., A.A.F., Tangmere, 1-40. Transferred to F.A.A. Became ***4577M***, 2-44.
N2436 No. 56 O.T.U. No. 253 Sqn. No. 55 O.T.U. No. 253 Sqn. No. 229 Sqn. No. 43 Sqn. No. 121 Sqn. Shipped to India, 1943. S.O.C., 4-10-44.
N2437 No. 56 Sqn., Martlesham Heath, 12-39; Missing in action, 17-5-40.
N2438 No. 17 Sqn., Debden, 1-40. No. 5 O.T.U. No. 501 Sqn., A.A.F., Kenley, 10-40; shot down by Bf 109Es near Cranbrook, 25-10-40; P/O V.R. Snell killed.
N2439 No. 56 Sqn., Martlesham Heath, 1-40; Missing in action, 17-5-40.
N2440 No. 56 Sqn., Martlesham Heath, **US-H**, 1-40. No. 249 Sqn., North Weald, 9-40; shot down by London A.A. defences, 7-9-40; Sgt. J.M.B. Beard baled out unhurt.
N2441 No. 56 Sqn., Martlesham Heath, 1-40. No. 3 Sqn.; lost over France, 5-40.

N2453 No. 245 Sqn., Hawkinge, 5-40; Missing in action, c.29-5-40.
N2454 No. 17 Sqn., Debden, 1-40; S.O.C., 13-5-40.
N2455 No. 245 Sqn., Hawkinge, 5-40. No. 615 Sqn., A.A.F. No. 253 Sqn. Transferred to the F.A.A. Became ***4693M***, 3-44.
N2456 No. 17 Sqn., Debden, 1-40; crashed in Debden Park during air test, 6-8-40; P/O H.W.A. Britton killed.
N2457 No. 17 Sqn., Debden, 1-40. No. 85 Sqn. No. 310 (Czech) Sqn. No. 73 Sqn. No. 85 Sqn. No. 56 O.T.U. Merchant Ship Fighter Unit. No. 55 O.T.U.; crashed at Langtown, Cumberland, 14-6-43.
N2458 No. 32 Sqn., Gravesend, 1-40; crashed near Dunchurch, Rugby, 27-12-40.
N2459 No. 32 Sqn., Gravesend, 1-40; shot down 15 miles off Harwich, 15-8-40; P/O D.H. Grice rescued from sea with severe burns.
N2460 No. 32 Sqn., Gravesend, 1-40. No. 303 (Polish) Sqn. No. 253 Sqn. No. 56 O.T.U.; crashed one miles south of Wiggenhall, Norfolk, 25-2-41.
N2461 No. 32 Sqn., Gravesend, 1-40; shot down by Bf 109Es near Detling, 18-8-40; F/L N.M. Crossley baled out unhurt.
N2462 No. 32 Sqn., Gravesend, 1-40; shot down near Le Cateau, France, 19-5-40.
N2463 No. 32 Sqn., Gravesend, 1-40. No. 56 O.T.U. S.O.C., 7-3-41.
N2464 No. 32 Sqn., Gravesend, 1-40; shot down near Douai, France, 18-5-40.
N2465 No. 229 Sqn., Digby, 12-39. *Converted to Mark IIA*, ***BV162***, 9-41. To Malta, 1941; damaged beyond repair.
N2466 No. 229 Sqn., Digby, 12-39; shot down by Bf 109Es, 11-9-40; P/O K.M. Carver baled out with burns.
N2467 No. 7 O.T.U. No. 6 O.T.U. No. 56 O.T.U. *Converted to Sea Hurricane IA*, 10-40; transferred to Admiralty Charge, 14-2-42.
N2468 No. 6 O.T.U. *Converted to Sea Hurricane IA*, 11-40. (Ultimate disposal unknown).
N2469 No. 6 O.T.U. No. 56 O.T.U. *Converted to Sea Hurricane IA*, 11-40; transferred to Admiralty Charge, 16-4-42.
N2470 No. 245 Sqn., Leconfield, 1-40; crashed at Leconfield, 18-4-40.
N2471 No. 504 Sqn., A.A.F.; damaged in forced landing, 11-9-40; P/O J.V. Gurteen unhurt. No. 605 Sqn., A.A.F. No. 312 (Czech) Sqn. No. 59 O.T.U. No. 312 (Czech) Sqn. No. 56 O.T.U. Northolt Stn. Flt. No. 59 O.T.U. No. 63 O.T.U. No. 4 Tactical Exercise Unit. S.O.C. 27-5-44.
N2472 No. 43 Sqn., Acklington, 1-40. No. 85 Sqn.; force landed and abandoned in Belgium, 10-5-40.
N2473 No. 213 Sqn., Wittering, 1-40. No. 229 Sqn.; Missing over France, 29-5-40.
N2474 No. 17 Sqn., Martlesham Heath, 1-40. No. 238 Sqn.; collided with Hurricane ***L1702*** and crashed near Shaftesbury, Dorset, 30-9-40; P/O R.A. Kings baled out unhurt.
N2475 No. 17 Sqn., Martlesham Heath, 1-40; lost, 5-40.
N2476 No. 213 Sqn., Wittering, 1-40. No. 85 Sqn. No. 73 Sqn. No. 85 Sqn. No. 310 (Czech) Sqn. No. 242 Sqn.; crashed at Grange Farm, Alderton, Suffolk, 21-2-41.
N2477 No. 79 Sqn., Manston, 1-40. No. 85 Sqn. No. 59 O.T.U. No. 55 O.T.U. No. 56 O.T.U. To India, 1943. To Southern Rhodesia, c.1945. S.O.C., 5-9-46.
N2478 No. 7 O.T.U.; crashed at Broughton, Cheshire, 18-7-40.
N2479 No. 56 Sqn. No. 213 Sqn. No. 6 O.T.U. *Converted to Mark IIA*, ***BV168***, 10-41. To Middle East, 1942. No. 208 Sqn. No. 1 Aircraft Delivery Unit; collided with Liberator while landing at Lydda, Palestine, 18-11-43.
N2480 No. 46 Sqn., Stapleford Tawney; shot down by Bf 109Es at Little Thurrock, Essex, 15-10-40; P/O P.S. Gunning killed.
N2481 No. 504 Sqn., A.A.F.; shot down by Do 17Zs over Kent, 15-9-40; P/O J.V. Gurteen killed.
N2482 No. 111 Sqn. No. 6 O.T.U. No. 8 F.T.S. No. 9 F.T.S. No. 9 P.A.F.U. R.A.F. College, Cranwell; crashed near Grantham, 10-5-42.
N2483 To the Middle East, c.9-40. No. 33 Sqn. No. 71 O.T.U.; S.O.C., 1-1-44.
N2484 No. 418 Flt.; to Malta, c.10-40. No. 71 O.T.U. No. 1 Middle East Training School; collided with Hurricane ***BP391***, 14-11-42, and crashed near El Ballah.
N2485 No. 501 Sqn., Middle Wallop; shot down off Portland, 11-7-40; Sgt. F.J.P. Dixon baled out but drowned.
N2487 No. 245 Sqn.; crashed while landing at Aldergrove, 7-11-40; damaged but not repaired.
N2488 No. 245 Sqn. No. 605 Sqn., A.A.F. No. 6 O.T.U. No. 56 O.T.U. *Converted to Sea Hurricane IA*. Merchant Ship Fighter Unit. No. 53 O.T.U. No. 41 O.T.U. S.O.C., 18-9-44.
N2489 No. 213 Sqn. No. 229 Sqn. No. 5 O.T.U. *Converted to Sea Hurricane IA*; transferred to Admiralty Charge, 12-5-41.
N2490 No. 213 Sqn., Wittering, 2-40. No. 79 Sqn.; lost over France, 5-40.
N2491 No. 245 Sqn., Leconfield, 2-40; lost over North France, 5-40.
N2492 No. 504 Sqn., A.A.F., Martlesham Heath, 2-40; lost over France, 5-40.
N2493 No. 145 Sqn., Croydon, 3-40. No. 263 Sqn. No. 258 Sqn. No. 615 Sqn., A.A.F. No. 9 F.T.S. No. 3 Sqn. No. 55 O.T.U. No. 59 O.T.U. Became ***4516M***, 2-44.
N2494 No. 145 Sqn., Croydon, 3-40. No. 55 O.T.U.; struck HT cables and crashed at Coxhoe, Durham, 4-6-41.
N2495 No. 145 Sqn., Croydon, 3-40. No. 56 O.T.U.; S.O.C., 27-7-41.
N2496 No. 145 Sqn., Croydon, 3-40. No. 56 O.T.U. No. 5 F.T.S. To the Middle East, 1942. S.O.C., 28-8-44.
N2497 No. 145 Sqn., Croydon, 3-40. No. 46 Sqn.; crashed 4-12-40.
N2498 To the Middle East, c.10-40. No. 274 Sqn.; Missing over Iraq, 21-5-41.
N2499 To the Middle East, c.10-40. No. 33 Sqn. No. 94 Sqn.; crashed near Ismailia, 24-4-41.
N2500 No. 145 Sqn., Croydon, 3-40; crashed near Cowfold, Sussex, 21-4-40, during aerobatics.
N2501 No. 245 Sqn., Leconfield, 4-40; lost over North France, 5-40.
N2502 No. 6 O.T.U. No. 56 O.T.U.; crashed while landing at Sutton Bridge, 30-3-41.

N2520 No. 213 Sqn., Wittering, 2-40. Northolt Stn. Flt. No. 3 F.T.S. South Cerney Stn. Flt. No. 55 O.T.U. No. 41 O.T.U. S.O.C., 23-5-44.
N2521 No. 213 Sqn., Wittering, 2-40. No. 229 Sqn.; S.O.C., 12-6-40.
N2522 No. 56 Sqn. Hucknall. No. 5 O.T.U. No. 41 O.T.U.; crashed from spin near Amble, Northumberland, 25-4-41.
N2523 No. 56 Sqn., **US-S**. No. 249 Sqn., Boscombe Down; lost (probably in accident), 28-8-40.
N2524 No. 32 Sqn., Manston, 3-40. Northolt Stn. Flt. No. 56 O.T.U. No. 41 O.T.U. S.O.C., 17-4-44.
N2525 No. 17 Sqn., Martlesham Heath, 4-40; lost over France, 19-5-40.
N2526 No. 17 Sqn., Martlesham Heath, 4-40. No. 5 O.T.U. No. 245 Sqn. No. 55 O.T.U. To the Middle East, 1942. S.O.C., 27-4-44.
N2527 No. 32 Sqn., Manston, 3-40; lost over France, 23-5-40.
N2528 No. 32 Sqn., Manston, 3-40; lost over France, 20-5-40.
N2529 No. 17 Sqn., Martlesham Heath, 4-40. No. 111 Sqn. No. 3 F.P.P. No. 6 O.T.U. No. 56 O.T.U.; crashed, 21-3-41.
N2530 No. 145 Sqn., Croydon, 3-40. No. 1 Sqn., R.C.A.F.; shot down by Bf 109Es near Dover, 31-8-40; F/O Sprenger, RCAF, baled out unhurt.
N2531 No. 32 Sqn., Manston, 3-40; crashed in sea 2 miles off Folkestone, Kent, 24-3-40.
N2532 No. 32 Sqn., Manston, 3-40; shot down by Bf 109Es 5 miles NE of Dover, 20-7-40.
N2533 No. 32 Sqn., Manston, 3-40; Missing in action, 11-6-40.
N2534 No. 3 Sqn., Merville, France, 5-40; Missing in action over France, 15-5-40.
N2535 No. 32 Sqn., Manston, 3-40; S.O.C., 3-7-40.
N2536 No. 213 Sqn., Wittering, 2-40. No. 85 Sqn.; crashed 2 miles north of Debden, 31-5-40.
N2537 No. 213 Sqn., Wittering, 2-40. No. 229 Sqn., Northolt, 9-40; shot down by Do 17Z and crashed on Staplehurst railway station, 15-9-40; P/O G.L.J. Doutrepont (Belgian) killed.
N2538 No. 213 Sqn., Wittering, 2-40; Missing in action, 19-5-40.
N2539 No. 213 Sqn., Wittering, 2-40; crashed at Ingoldisthorpe, Norfolk, 5-3-40.
N2540 No. 213 Sqn., Wittering, 2-40. No. 229 Sqn. No. 32 Sqn., Biggin Hill, 8-40; destroyed in enemy raid

on Biggin Hill, 30-8-40.

N2541 No. 213 Sqn., Wittering, 2-40; shot down near Dartmouth, Devon, 15-7-40; Sub-Lt. H.G.K. Bramah survived.

N2542 No. 253 Sqn., Northolt, 3-40; Missing over France, 19-5-40.

N2543 No. 46 Sqn., Digby, 3-40; crashed while landing at Bardufoss, Norway, 2-6-40.

N2544 No. 213 Sqn., Wittering, 3-40. No. 17 Sqn. No. 213 Sqn. No. 85 Sqn. No. 55 O.T.U. No. 229 Sqn. *Converted to Mark IIA* by Rolls-Royce Ltd., 3-41, ***DG616***. To the Middle East, 8-41. No. 274 Sqn.; crashed into sea off Tobruk, 12-2-42.

N2545 No. 253 Sqn., Kenley, 5-40; Missing in action, 18-5-40.

N2546 No. 3 Sqn. No. 238 Sqn. No. 605 Sqn., A.A.F.; shot down by Bf 109Es near Maidstone, Kent, 15-10-40; P/O I.J. Muirhead killed.

N2547 No. 17 Sqn., Hawkinge, 4-40; S.O.C., 5-40.

N2548 No. 213 Sqn., Wittering, 3-40. No. 85 Sqn. No. 5 O.T.U. No. 56 O.T.U. No. 9 F.T.S. Ferry Training Unit. No. 41 O.T.U.; S.O.C., 21-11-44.

N2549 No. 504 Sqn., A.A.F., Debden, 4-40. No. 111 Sqn.; S.O.C., 5-40.

N2550 No. 213 Sqn., Wittering, 3-40; crashed into sea 40 miles east of Wick, 16-4-40.

N2551 No. 43 Sqn., Tangmere. No. 213 Sqn. No. 229 Sqn.; Missing over France, 28-5-40.

N2552 No. 70 O.T.U.; became ***2835M***, 12-41.

N2553 No. 56 Sqn., North Weald, 5-40; Missing in action, 18-5-40.

N2554 No. 52 O.T.U.; became ***2835M***, 12-41.

N2555 No. 9 E.F.T.S. No. 59 O.T.U. No. 63 O.T.U. No. 4 Tactical Exercise Unit. S.O.C., 11-12-44.

N2556 No. 32 Sqn., Manston, 3-40. S.O.C., 5-40.

N2557 No. 245 Sqn. No. 605 Sqn., A.A.F. No. 85 Sqn. No. 605 Sqn., A.A.F. No. 312 (Czech) Sqn. No. 56 O.T.U.; crashed near Sutton Bridge in poor visibility, 18-2-41.

N2558 No. 245 Sqn. No. 13 Group Anti-aircraft Co-operation Flt. No. 289 Sqn.; crashed while taking off at Ayr, 8-5-42.

N2559 No. 245 Sqn.; crashed while taking off at Drem, 16-5-40.

N2582 No. 32 Sqn., Biggin Hill, 3-40; Missing in action, 8-6-40.

N2583 No. 32 Sqn., Biggin Hill, 3-40; Missing in action, 20-5-40.

N2584 No. 43 Sqn., Tangmere; shot down near Dunkirk, 1-6-40.

N2585 No. 43 Sqn., Tangmere; shot down near Dunkirk, 7-6-40.

N2586 No. 501 Sqn., A.A.F. No. 607 Sqn., A.A.F., Usworth; crashed near Usworth, 1-9-40.

N2587 No. 504 Sqn., A.A.F. No. 32 Sqn., Acklington; abandoned 3 miles north of Berwick, 22-11-40, after fire in the air.

N2588 No. 32 Sqn., Biggin Hill, 3-40. No. 253 Sqn. No. 55 O.T.U. To the Middle East, 1942. S.O.C., 6-7-44.

N2589 No. 145 Sqn. No. 605 Sqn., A.A.F. No. 55 O.T.U. No. 9 F.T.S.; crashed at Keevil, 11-2-42, after fire in the air.

N2590 No. 213 Sqn. No. 43 Sqn. No. 253 Sqn. No. 1 Sqn., R.C.A.F. *Converted to Sea Hurricane IA*, c.1-41; transferred to Admiralty charge, 28-8-41.

N2591 No. 6 O.T.U. No. 56 O.T.U. *Converted to Sea Hurricane IA*, c-4-41; transferred to Admiralty charge, 29-9-41; became ***4725M***, 3-44.

N2592 No. 229 Sqn. No. 55 O.T.U. *Converted to Mark II*, ***BV172***, 2-41. No. 52 O.T.U. No. 136 Sqn. No. 615 Sqn., A.A.F. No. 486 (NZ) Sqn. No. 253 Sqn. No. 245 Sqn. No. 55 O.T.U. S.O.C., 16-10-44.

N2593 No. 245 Sqn. No. 605 Sqn., A.A.F., Turnhouse; lost (probably in accident), 28-7-40.

N2594 No. 245 Sqn. No. 8 F.T.S. No. 2 Flying Instructors' School. No. 56 O.T.U. No. 41 O.T.U. S.O.C., 21-5-44.

N2595 No. 245 Sqn., Leconfield, 3-40; S.O.C., 5-40.

N2596 No. 245 Sqn., Leconfield, 3-40. No. 501 Sqn., A.A.F. No. 32 Sqn., Biggin Hill; shot down and crashed near Hawkinge, 12-8-40; P/O A.R.H. Barton unhurt.

N2597 No. 245 Sqn., Leconfield, 3-40. No. 249 Sqn. No. 238 Sqn. No. 9 F.T.S. Became ***3577M***, 3-43.

N2598 No. 145 Sqn., Croydon, 4-40; Missing over Belgium, 19-5-40.

N2599 No. 145 Sqn., Croydon, 4-40. No. 46 Sqn. No. 55 O.T.U. *Converted to Sea Hurricane Mk. IA*. Merchant Ship Fighter Unit. No. 59 O.T.U. No. 7 Observers' Advance Flying Unit. S.O.C., 8-6-44.

N2600 No. 145 Sqn., Croydon, 4-40; shot down near Brussels, 18-5-40.

N2601 No. 145 Sqn., Croydon, 4-40. S.O.C., 5-40.

N2602 No. 145 Sqn., Croydon, 4-40. No. 601 Sqn., Debden, 8-40; shot down by Bf 109Es near Colchester, 31-8-40; Sgt. A.W. Woolley baled out with slight burns.

N2603 No. 145 Sqn., Croydon, 4-40. No. 5 O.T.U. No. 55 O.T.U.; crashed at Chewton Mendip, Somerset, 16-10-40.

N2604 No. 145 Sqn., Croydon, 4-40. No. 3 Sqn. No. 9 F.T.S. No. 9 P.A.F.U. No. 59 O.T.U. No. 1 Tactical Exercise Unit. No. 2 T.E.U.; crashed at Cumbernauld, Dumbarton, 7-5-44.

N2605 No. 145 Sqn., Croydon, 4-40; S.O.C., 5-40.

N2606 No. 7 O.T.U. No. 5 O.T.U.; crashed at South Cerney, 26-8-40.

N2607 No. 7 O.T.U. No. 5 O.T.U. Wittering Stn. Flt. No. 1 Sqn. No. 229 Sqn. Northolt Stn. Flt. *Converted to Mark IIA*, ***DG633***, 4-41. *Shipped to Russia*, 24-9-42.

N2608 No. 1 Sqn., R.C.A.F. No. 213 Sqn.; lost, 1-11-40.

N2609 No. 79 Sqn., Sealand; collided with Miles Master at Sealand, 12-7-40; pilot unhurt.

N2610 No. 145 Sqn., Croydon, 4-40. To the Middle East. S.O.C., 19-5-41.

N2611 To the Middle East. No. 208 Sqn.; Missing, 29-1-41.

N2612 To the Middle East. S.O.C., 5-5-41.

N2613 To the Middle East. Training and Reserve Pool. No. 70 O.T.U. S.O.C., 28-2-45.

N2614 No. 253 Sqn., Kenley, 4-40; Missing in action, 23-4-40.

N2615 No. 43 Sqn., Tangmere, 6-40; crashed in sea 5 miles east of Shoreham, 15-6-40.

N2616 No. 6 O.T.U. No. 56 O.T.U. No. 2 T.E.U. S.O.C., 17-7-44.

N2617 No. 6 O.T.U. No. 501 Sqn., A.A.F., Hawkinge, 8-40; shot down by Bf 109Es near Canterbury, 18-8-40; F/Sgt. P.F. Morfill unhurt.

N2618 No. 6 O.T.U. No. 1 Sqn. No. 55 O.T.U. *Converted to Sea Hurricane IA*; transferred to Admiralty Charge, 9-1-42.

N2619 No. 79 Sqn., Hawkinge, 7-40; shot down by Bf 109Es over St. Margaret's Bay; Sgt. H. Cartwright killed.

N2620 No. 610 Sqn., A.A.F. No. 213 Sqn. No. 79 Sqn. No. 55 O.T.U. No. 59 O.T.U. No. 7 P.A.F.U. S.O.C., 10-10-44.

N2621 No. 6 O.T.U. No. 53 O.T.U. No. 316 (Polish) Sqn. No. 56 O.T.U.

N2622 *Trop. Mk. I.* No. 418 Flt. To Mediterranean and Malta. No. 261 Sqn.; crashed 4 miles NW of Luqa, Malta, 11-1-41.

N2623 *Trop. Mk. I.* To the Middle East, 1940. No. 33 Sqn. No. 70 O.T.U. S.O.C., 25-5-44.

N2624 *Trop. Mk. I.* To the Middle East, 1940. No. 94 Sqn.; destroyed in air raid on Malta, 28-9-41.

N2625 *Trop. Mk. I.* To the Middle East, 1940. No. 274 Sqn.; Missing in action, 4-1-41.

N2626 *Trop. Mk. I.* To the Middle East, 1940. T.U.R.P. No. 70 O.T.U. No. 208 Sqn.; Missing in action, 15-6-41.

N2627 *Trop. Mk. I.* To the Middle East, 1940. No. 70 O.T.U.; crashed on take-off, Nakuru, 10-3-41.

N2628 *Trop. Mk. I.* To the Middle East, 1940. No. 94 Sqn. No. 274 Sqn.; destroyed in air raid on Malta, 28-9-41.

N2629 *Trop. Mk. I.* To the Middle East, 1940. No. 274 Sqn. No. 73 Sqn. No. 208 Sqn. No. 1 Middle East Training School. S.O.C., 21-1-41.

N2630 No. 213 Sqn. *Converted to Sea Hurricane IA*. Merchant Ship Fighter Unit. No. 59 O.T.U. No. 41 O.T.U. S.O.C., 25-5-44.

N2631 No. 213 Sqn. No. 229 Sqn. *Converted to Sea Hurricane IA*. Transferred to Admiralty Charge, 28-2-42.

N2645 No. 213 Sqn. No. 85 Sqn. No. 229 Sqn. No. 615 Sqn., A.A.F. Digby Stn. Flt. No. 56 O.T.U.; crashed while landing at Leuchars, 8-5-42.

N2646 No. 213 Sqn., Exeter, 8-40; shot down near Portland, 25-8-40; P/O H.D Atkinson killed.

N2647 No. 6 O.T.U. No. 229 Sqn. No. 9 F.T.S. No. 59 O.T.U. *Converted to Sea Hurricane IA*. Merchant Ship Fighter Unit. No. 318 (Polish) Sqn. No. 245 Sqn. S.O.C., 7-11-44.

N2648 No. 229 Sqn. No. 111 Sqn. No. 6 O.T.U. No. 5 O.T.U. Converted to Sea Hurricane IA. Transferred to Admiralty Charge, 8-11-41.

N2649 No. 213 Sqn. No. 242 Sqn. No. 605 Sqn., A.A.F., Croydon; crashed, 8-11-40.

N2650 No. 213 Sqn., Exeter; shot down by Bf 109E off Portland, 11-8-40; Sgt. S.L. Butterfield killed.

N2651 No. 151 Sqn. No. 242 Sqn.; Missing in action, 28-5-40.

N2652 No. 46 Sqn. No. 229 Sqn., Northolt, 9-40; shot down by Bf 109Es near Edenbridge, Kent, 30-9-40; P/O N.K. Stansfeld (Canadian) baled out, wounded in leg.

N2653 No. 3 Sqn., Merville, France, 5-40; collided with Hurricane ***N2654*** near Merville, 13-5-40.

N2654 No. 3 Sqn., Merville, France, 5-40; collided with Hurricane ***N2653*** near Merville, 13-5-40.

N2655 No. 213 Sqn., Merville, France, 5-40; lost, 5-40.

N2656 No. 213 Sqn., Merville, France, 5-40; lost, 5-40.

N2657 No. 32 Sqn., Biggin Hill, 4-40; Missing in action, 22-5-40.

N2658 No. 245 Sqn., Hawkinge, 5-40; shot down near Dunkirk, 1-6-40.

N2659 No. 56 Sqn., North Weald, 5-40; Missing in action, 29-5-40.

N2660 No. 229 Sqn. No. 111 Sqn. No. 6 O.T.U. No. 257 Sqn. *Converted to Sea Hurricane IA*. Merchant Ship Fighter Unit. Became ***4560M***, 2-44.

N2661 No. 213 Sqn. No. 303 (Polish) Sqn. No. 253 Sqn. No. 8 F.T.S.; crashed, 13-7-41.

N2662 No. 17 Sqn. No. 59 O.T.U. No. 52 O.T.U. No. 55 O.T.U.; abandoned and crashed at Pelton, Co. Durham, 5-12-41.

N2663 No. 17 Sqn. No. 10 M.U., Hullavington; crashed while landing at Hullavington, 15-7-40.

N2664 No. 56 Sqn.; North Weald; crashed, 7-6-40.

N2665 No. 213 Sqn. No. 43 Sqn. No. 145 Sqn. No. 56 O.T.U. *Converted to Mark IIA*, ***DR367***, 8-41. *Shipped to Russia*, 4-4-42.

N2666 No. 56 Sqn., North Weald, 6-40. No. 17 Sqn. No. 5 O.T.U. No. 55 O.T.U.; crashed near Drumburgh, Cumberland, 25-6-42.

N2667 No. 56 Sqn., North Weald, 6-40; reported to have been shot down by Spitfires while on convoy patrol, 11-8-40; Sgt. R.D. Baker killed.

N2668 No. 213 Sqn. No. 5 O.T.U. No. 56 Sqn.; Shot down, 30-8-40; F/O R.E.P. Brooker, unhurt.

N2669 No. 504 Sqn., A.A.F. No. 3 Sqn. No. 504 Sqn., A.A.F. No. 133 Sqn. No. 52 O.T.U. No. 59 O.T.U. Transferred to Admiralty Charge, 15-1-41. Became ***2876M***.

N2670 No. 32 Sqn., Hawkinge, 7-40; shot down by Bf 109Es 5 miles NE of Dover, 20-7-40; Sub-Lt. G.G.R. Bulmer baled out but drowned.

N2671 No. 32 Sqn., Hawkinge, 7-40. No. 79 Sqn. *Converted to Sea Hurricane IA*, c.4-41; transferred to Admiralty Charge, 7-41. Became ***4664M***, 2-44.

N2672 *Trop. Mk. I.* No. 418 Flt. To Malta, 8-40; Missing in action, 10-4-42.

N2673 *Trop. Mk. I.* No. 418 Flt. To Malta, 8-40; S.O.C., 9-6-41.

N2674 *Trop. Mk. I.* To the Middle East. T.U.R.P. No. 71 O.T.U. No. 73 O.T.U. S.O.C., 28-2-43.

N2700 *Trop. Mk. I.* No. 418 Flt. To Malta, 8-40. Crashed at Luqa, *2-8-40.*
N2701 *Trop. Mk. I.* No. 418 Flt. To Malta, 8-40. Lost, 26-11-40.
N2702 No. 245 Sqn., Hawkinge, 5-40; S.O.C., 5-40.
N2703 No. 245 Sqn., Hawkinge, 5-40. No. 145 Sqn., Tangmere, 7-40; crashed near Ringwood, Hants, 12-7-40; pilot believed unhurt.
N2704 No. 17 Sqn. No. 607 Sqn., A.A.F.; crashed near Sedgefield, Durham, 26-6-40.
N2705 No. 504 Sqn., A.A.F., Hendon, 9-40; shot down by Do 17Zs at Dartford, 15-9-40; F/O M. Jebb baled out grievously wounded.
N2706 No. 615 Sqn., A.A.F. No. 55 O.T.U. *Converted to Sea Hurricane IA*; transferred to Admiralty Charge, 25-7-41.
N2707 No. 245 Sqn.; crashed on landing at Aldergrove, 7-10-40, following engine failure.
N2708 No. 213 Sqn. No. 79 Sqn.; crashed at Carew Cheriton, 25-10-40.
N2709 No. 245 Sqn., Hawkinge, 5-40; lost in action, 1-6-40.
N2710 No. 145 Sqn., Tangmere, 5-40; lost in action, 27-5-40.
N2711 No. 145 Sqn., Tangmere, 5-40; lost in action, 27-5-40.
N2712 No. 145 Sqn., Tangmere, 5-40. No. 85 Sqn. No. 56 Sqn. No. 52 O.T.U.; crashed at Chafford, Glos., 13-9-41.
N2713 No. 145 Sqn., Tangmere, 5-40; lost in action, 27-5-40.
N2714 No. 145 Sqn., Tangmere, 5-40; lost in action, 30-5-40.
N2715 *Trop. Mk. I.* No. 418 Flt. To Malta, 8-40. Crashed in sea off Malta, 12-2-41.
N2716 *Trop. Mk. I.* No. 418 Flt. To Malta, 8-40. Lost in action, 1-8-40.
N2717 *Trop. Mk. I.* No. 418 Flt. To Malta, 8-40. S.O.C., 9-10-40.
N2718 *Shipped to Yugoslavia,* 3-40.
N2719 *Shipped to Yugoslavia,* 3-40.
N2720 *Shipped to Yugoslavia,* 3-40.
N2721 *Shipped to Yugoslavia,* 3-40.
N2722 *Shipped to Yugoslavia,* 3-40.
N2723 *Shipped to Yugoslavia,* 3-40.
N2724 *Shipped to Yugoslavia,* 3-40.
N2725 *Shipped to Yugoslavia,* 3-40.
N2726 *Shipped to Yugoslavia,* 3-40.
N2727 *Shipped to Yugoslavia,* 3-40.
N2728 *Shipped to Yugoslavia,* 3-40.
N2729 *Shipped to Yugoslavia,* 3-40.

HAWKER HURRICANE MARK I (Gloster-built). First production batch of 500 aircraft built by Gloster Aircraft Co., Ltd., Brockworth, Glos., during 1939-40 under Contract No. 962371/38/C.23a. Rolls-Royce Merlin III engines and de Havilland variable-pitch or Rotol constant-speed propellers. First flight, 20-10-39. *P2535-P2584, P2614-P2653, P2672-P2701, P2713-P2732, P2751-P2770, P2792-P2836, P2854-P2888, P2900-P2924, P2946-P2995, P3030-P3069, P3080-P3124, P3140-P3179, P3200-P3234, P3250-P3264.* Deliveries commenced, 12-39; completed 4-40; average rate of production, approximately three aircraft per day.
P2535 No. 73 Sqn., Rouvres, France, "**K**", 3-40.
P2544 *Trop. Mk. I.* No. 418 Flt. To the Middle East, c.8-40. No. 274 Sqn., Amriya, **YK-T**, 9-40.
P2546 No. 1 Sqn., Vassincourt, France, 3-40.
P2548 No. 1 Sqn., Vassincourt, France, 3-40.
P2552 No. 85 Sqn., Lille/Seclin, France, 3-40.
P2556 No. 56 Sqn., North Weald, 3-40.
P2559 No. 73 Sqn., Le Mans, France, "**D**", 6-40.
P2562 No. 87 Sqn., Le Touquet, France, 4-40.
P2564 No. 615 Sqn., A.A.F., Kenley, 6-40.
P2571 No. 73 Sqn., Echemines, France, "**X**", 6-40. No. 1 Sqn., Northolt, 7-40; damaged in combat with He 111H over Sussex, 16-8-40; S/L D.A. Pemberton unhurt.
P2573 No. 601 Sqn., A.A.F., Tangmere, 3-40.
P2575 No. 312 (Czech) Sqn., Duxford, 8-40.
P2578 No. 615 Sqn., A.A.F., Abbeville, France, 4-40; Kenley, 6-40.
P2579 No. 73 Sqn., Echemines, France, "**J**", 6-40.
P2617 No. 607 Sqn., A.A.F., Usworth, 6-40. No. 9 F.T.S., 8-41.
P2624 *Trop. Mk. I.* No. 418 Flt. To the Middle East, c.8-40. No. 33 Sqn., Fuka, 10-40.
P2627 *Trop. Mk. I.* No. 418 Flt. To the Middle East, c.8-40. No. 274 Sqn., Amriya, 9-40.
P2630 No. 59 O.T.U., c.1942.
P2631 No. 253 Sqn., Northolt, 3-40.
P2632 No. 46 Sqn., Digby, 4-40; lost in H.M.S. *Glorious* on return from Norway, 8-6-40.
P2638 To the Middle East via Takoradi, 9-40. No. 274 Sqn., Sidi Haneish, 11-40. *Converted to Trop. P.R. Mk. I.* No. 208 Sqn., Heliopolis, 7-42; shot down by Bf 109Fs, 24-7-42.
P2639 *Trop. Mk. I.* To the Middle East via Takoradi, 9-40. No. 274 Sqn., Sidi Haneish, Egypt, 11-40. No. 80 Sqn., Maleme, Crete, 4-41.
P2640 *Trop. Mk. I.* To the Middle East via Takoradi, 9-40. No. 274 Sqn., Sidi Haneish, Egypt, 11-40. No. 80 Sqn., Maleme, Crete, 4-41. No. 33 Sqn., Eleusis, Greece, 3-41.
P2641 *Trop. Mk. I.* No. 4 F.P.P. To the Middle East via Takoradi, 9-40. No. 274 Sqn., Sidi Haneish, Egypt, 11-40. No. 80 Sqn., Maleme, Creet, 4-41. No. 94 Sqn., Ismailia, 5-41.
P2643 *Trop. Mk. I.* To the Middle East via Takoradi, 9-40. No. 274 Sqn., Sidi Haneish, Egypt, 11-40.
P2649 No. 1 Sqn., Northolt, 7-40.
P2651 *Trop. Mk. I.* To the Middle East via Takoradi, 9-40. No. 274 Sqn., Sidi Haneish, Egypt, 11-40.
P2652 No. 46 Sqn., Digby, 4-40; lost in H.M.S. *Glorious* on return from Norway, 8-6-40.
P2674 No. 601 Sqn., A.A.F., Tangmere, "**N**", 3-40. *Converted to Trop. Mk. IIA, **BV171***, 12-40. No. 185 Sqn., Malta; crashed 3 miles NE of Imtarfa, Malta, after night take-off, 20-7-41.
P2677 No. 56 Sqn., North Weald, 30-40. No. 253 Sqn., Kenley, 9-40; shot down by Bf 109E, 29-9-40; Sgt. A. Edgley baled out unhurt.
P2679 No. 245 Sqn., Leconfield, 3-40, **DX-A**. No. 59 O.T.U., c.1941.
P2680 No. 607 Sqn., A.A.F., Tangmere, 9-40; shot down by Bf 109Es, 9-9-40; Sgt. R.A. Spyer wounded.
P2682 *Converted to Mark IIA* as ***DG641*** by Rolls-Royce Ltd., 4-41; *shipped to Russia*, 1-10-41.
P2685 No. 46 Sqn., Digby, 7-40; destroyed in accident, 24-7-40; P/O A.M. Cooper-Slipper killed.
P2686 No. 1 Sqn., Northolt, 7-40.
P2687 No. 87 Sqn., Exeter, 8-40; aircraft badly damaged in combat off Portland, 15-8-40; P/O D.T. Jay unhurt. Aircraft repaired and despatched to the Middle East via Takoradi, 10-40. No. 80 Sqn., Yanina, Greece, 3-41.
P2691 No. 501 Sqn., A.A.F., Middle Wallop, 7-40.
P2692 No. 56 Sqn., North Weald, **US-T**, 4-40. No. 253 Sqn., Kenley, 9-40.
P2693 No. 3 Sqn., Turnhouse, 9-40; damaged in taxying accident; P/O A.M.W. Scott unhurt.
P2695 *Trop. Mk. I.* To the Middle East, 9-40. No. 274 Sqn., Amriya, 10-40.
P2696 No. 146 Sqn., Tangmere, **SO-P**, 10-40; damaged in forced landing following combat, 23-10-40; P/O B.M. de Hemptinne (Belgian) unhurt.
P2714 No. 501 Sqn., A.A.F., Anglure, France, "**F**", 5-40.
P2716 No. 85 Sqn., Martlesham Heath, 7-40; shot down by Do 17 off Harwich, 11-7-40; S/L P.W. Townsend safe.
P2725 No. 504 Sqn., A.A.F., Hendon, 9-40; Sgt. R.T. Holmes collided with He 111H over London, 15-9-40, but baled out unhurt.
P2728 No. 617 Sqn., A.A.F., Tangmere, 9-40; shot down by Bf 109Es, 9-9-40; P/O G.J. Drake killed.
P2731 *Converted to Sea Hurricane IA*, 1941, and transferred to Admiralty Charge.
P2751 No. 1 Sqn., Northolt, 7-40.
P2752 No. 302 (Polish) Sqn., Duxford, 10-40; shot down by Bf 109Es near Chatham, Kent, 16-10-40; Sgt. M. Wedzik (Polish) unhurt.
P2753 No. 601 Sqn., A.A.F., Tangmere, 7-40; shot down by Bf 109Es off St. Catherine's Point, 26-7-40; P/O P.C. Lindsey killed.
P2754 No. 617 (Polish) Sqn., Acklington, 2-41.
P2755 No. 32 Sqn., Biggin Hill, 5-40; F/L R.V. Jeff shot down one Bf 109E, 22-5-40.
P2756 No. 79 Sqn., Hawkinge, 7-40; aircraft crashed near Folkestone (cause unknown), 7-7-40; S/L J.D.C. Joslin killed.
P2760 No. 501 Sqn., A.A.F., Anglure, France, 5-40, "**B**"; shot down by Bf 109Es over Kent, 15-9-40; P/O A.E.D.J.V. Van den Hove d'Ertsenryck (Belgian) killed.
P2765 No. 605 Sqn., A.A.F., Croydon, 9-40; shot down by Bf 110, 9-9-40; P/O J.S. Humphreys slightly hurt.
P2768 No. 501 Sqn., A.A.F., Anglure, France, 5-40, "**E**". No. 615 Sqn., A.A.F., Kenley, 8-40; shot down by Bf 109Es over Surrey, 18-8-40; Sgt. P.K. Walley killed.
P2796 No. 73 Sqn., Debden, 9-40; shot down by Bf 110 at Detling, 11-9-40; Sgt. H.G. Webster unhurt.
P2798 No. 87 Sqn., Merville, France, **LK-A**, 4-40.
P2806 No. 111 Sqn., Croydon, 6-40.
P2815 No. 73 Sqn., Castle Camps, 9-40. No. 229 Sqn., Northolt, 9-40; shot down by Bf 109Es over Kent, 30-9-40; P/O M. Ravenhill killed.
P2822 No. 56 Sqn., North Weald, 5-40.
P2823 *Converted to Mark IIA* as ***BV161***, 10-40. No. 56 Sqn. No. 253 Sqn. *Shipped to Russia*, 8-4-42.
P2826 No. 151 Sqn., Digby, 9-40; damaged by Ju 88A off Lincolnshire coast, 30-9-40; F/O K.H. Blair unhurt. *Converted to Sea Hurricane IA*, 3-41.
P2829 No. 87 Sqn., Merville, France, 5-40, **LK-G**. *Converted to Mark IIA* as ***DR355***, 8-41, and shipped to Russia, 12-12-41.
P2831 No. 242 Sqn., Coltishall, 9-40; shot down by Bf 109Es, 9-9-40; Sgt. R.V.H. Lonsdale unhurt.
P2835 No. 257 Sqn., North Weald, 11-40; P/O P.A. Mortimer shot down one Fiat BR.20, 11-11-40. *Converted to Mark IIA* as ***DR353***, 8-41, and *shipped to Russia*, 5-12-41.
P2855 No. 308 (Polish) Sqn., Baginton, 11-40.
P2857 No. 56 Sqn., North Weald, "**H**", 5-40. No. 258 Sqn., Duxford and Drem, 12-40.
P2861 No. 232 Sqn., Sumburgh, 7-40; force landed in sea off Shetland Islands following engine failure, 23-7-40; Sgt. A.F. Butteride unhurt.
P2901 No. 607 Sqn., A.A.F., Norrent Fontes, France, 5-40. No. 213 Sqn., Wittering, 6-40.
P2902 No. 56 Sqn., North Weald, 7-40; shot down off Dover, 13-7-40; Sgt. J.R. Cowsill missing.
P2903 No. 501 Sqn., A.A.F., Kenley, 10-41; collided with Hurricane ***V6806*** during combat with Bf 109Es, 25-10-40; P/O V. Göth (Czech) killed.
P2904 *Converted to Mark IIA* as ***DR357***, 8-41, and *shipped to Russia*, 15-12-41.
P2908 No. 504 Sqn., A.A.F., Hendon, 9-40. *Converted to Mark IIA, **DR369***, 9-41, and *shipped to Russia*, 25-3-42.
P2909 No. 232 Sqn., Castletown, 9-40.
P2910 No. 56 Sqn., North Weald, 5-40; damaged in combat with Bf 110s near Portsmouth, 30-9-40; F/L H.M. Pinfold unhurt.
P2911 No. 232 Sqn., Sumburgh; damaged in taxying accident, 4-8-40; pilot unhurt.
P2912 No. 607 Sqn., A.A.F., Tangmere, 9-40; shot down by Bf 109Es, 9-9-40; Sgt. P.A. Burnell-Phillips wounded.
P2915 *Trop. Mk. I.* To Middle East. No. 680 Sqn., Matariya, 2-43.
P2919 No. 615 Sqn., A.A.F., Kenley, 8-40.
P2920 No. 238 Sqn., Middle Wallop, 9-40; damaged in combat with Bf 110s, 26-9-40; S/L H.A. Fenton unhurt.

P2921 No. 315 (Polish) Sqn., Acklington, 2-41.
P2922 No. 56 Sqn., North Weald, 5-40.
P2924 No. 145 Sqn., Tangmere, 6-40.
P2946 No. 253 Sqn., 8-40; shot down by Bf 109Es over Kent, 30-8-40; Sgt. J.H. Dickenson shot dead while parachuting down.
P2948 No. 4 F.P.P., 9-40. *Converted to Sea Hurricane IA*, c.11-40, and transferred to Admiralty Charge, 1941.
P2949 No. 239 Sqn., Gatwick, 1-42.
P2950 No. 238 Sqn., Middle Wallop, 7-40; crashed at Warmwell after combat, 13-7-40; F/L J.C. Kennedy killed.
P2953 *Converted to Sea Hurricane IA*, 12-40, and later transferred to Admiralty Charge.
P2956 No. 239 Sqn., Gatwick, 1-42.
P2958 No. 111 Sqn., Croydon, 7-40; damaged in take-off accident, 14-7-40; P/O B.M. Fisher unhurt.
P2960 No. 257 Sqn., North Weald, 11-40.
P2963 *Converted to Sea Hurricane IA*, c.1-41, and later transferred to Admiralty Charge.
P2965 No. 242 Sqn., Coltishall, **LE-X**, 8-40.
P2966 No. 615 Sqn., A.A.F., Kenley, 8-40; shot down by Bf 109Es over Kent, 18-8-40; F/L L.M. Gaunce unhurt.
P2967 No. 242 Sqn., Coltishall, 9-40; shot down by Bf 109Es near Dover, 27-9-40; F/O M.G. Homer killed.
P2968 No. 9 F.T.S., 8-41. *Supplied to the Irish Air Corps*, 29-11-43, as "***107***".
P2970 No. 56 Sqn., North Weald, **US-X**, 5-40.
P2972 *Converted to Sea Hurricane IA*, 12-41, and later transferred to Admiralty Charge.
P2975 No. 73 Sqn., Castle Camps, 9-40. "**Q**". *Converted to Mark IIA* as ***DR372***, 9-41, and *shipped to Russia*, 6-3-42.
P2976 No. 242 Sqn., Coltishall, 8-40; crashed off Norfolk coast during patrol, 20-8-40; Midshipman P.J. Patterson killed.
P2979 No. 111 Sqn., Croydon, 7-40.
P2980 No. 1 Sqn., Northolt, 7-40.
P2981 No. 257 Sqn., Tangmere, 8-40; shot down by Bf 109Es off St. Catherine's Point, 8-8-40; F/L N.M. Hall killed.
P2984 No. 73 Sqn., Castle Camps, 9-40.
P2985 No. 56 Sqn., North Weald, 5-40. No. 303 (Polish) Sqn., 8-40.
P2986 *Converted to Sea Hurricane IA*, 3-41, and later transferred to Admiralty Charge.
P2987 No. 504 Sqn., A.A.F., Hendon, 9-40; damaged in action near Yeovil, 30-9-40; P/O E.M. Frisby unhurt. No. 4 F.P.P., 10-40.
P2989 *Trials at A. & A.E.E., Boscombe Down, with 250-lb. bombs*, 1941.
P2991 No. 263 Sqn., Grangemouth, 7-40; destroyed in night accident; F/L W.O.L. Smith unhurt.
P2992 No. 258 Sqn., Duxford, 12-40. No. 331 (Norwegian) Sqn., Catterick, 7-41. No. 527 Sqn., Castle Camps, 6-43.
P2993 No. 501 Sqn., A.A.F., Kenley, 9-40; shot down by He 111H, 13-9-40; Sgt. J.H. Lacey baled out unhurt.
P2994 No. 605 Sqn., A.A.F., Drem, 7-40. *Converted to Sea Hurricane IA*, 2-41, and later transferred to Admiralty Charge.
P3020 No. 3 Sqn., Turnhouse, 9-40; damaged in accident, 18-9-40; P/O P. Kennett unhurt. No. 402 Sqn., R.C.A.F., Digby, "X", 12-40. *Converted to Sea Hurricane IA*, 2-41, and later transferred to Admiralty Charge.
P3021 No. 504 Sqn., A.A.F., Hendon, 9-40; damaged in combat over Kent, 7-9-40; Sgt. B.M. Bush unhurt; shot down over Soverset, 30-9-40; Sgt. B.M. Bush unhurt.
P3022 No. 605 Sqn., A.A.F., Drem, 7-40.
P3023 *Converted to Mark IIA* as ***DR342***, 7-41, and *shipped to Russia*, 15-10-41.
P3024 No. 46 Sqn., Digby, 6-40; shot down off Essex coast, 3-9-40; Sgt. E. Bloor unhurt.
P3026 No. 46 Sqn., Digby, 6-40; shot down by Bf 109Es near Southend, 4-9-40; P/O C.F. Ambrose unhurt.
P3028 No. 56 Sqn., North Weald, 5-40.
P3029 No. 111 Sqn., Croydon, 7-40.
P3030 No. 46 Sqn., Digby, 6-40. No. 601 Sqn., A.A.F., Tangmere, 8-40.
P3031 No. 46 Sqn., Digby, 6-40.
P3032 No. 253 Sqn., Kenley, 9-40.
P3034 No. 111 Sqn., Croydon, 7-40. No. 73 Sqn., Castle Camps, 9-40.
P3036 *Converted to Sea Hurricane IA*, c.3-41, and later transferred to Admiralty Charge.
P3037 No. 229 Sqn., Northolt, 9-40; shot down, 30-9-40; P/O L.B.R. Way baled out unhurt.
P3038 No. 229 Sqn., Northolt, 9-40; shot down by Bf 109Es, 11-9-40; P/O M. Ravenhill unhurt.
P3040 No. 501 Sqn., A.A.F., Middle Wallop, 7-40.
P3041 No. 501 Sqn., A.A.F., Middle Wallop, 7-40. No. 247 Sqn., Roborough, **HP-P**, 12-40.
P3042 No. 1 Sqn., Northolt, 7-40.
P3043 No. 1 Sqn., Northolt, 7-40; shot down south of Harwich, 15-8-40; P/O D.O.M. Browne killed.
P3044 No. 111 Sqn., Croydon, 6-40. No. 1 Sqn., Northolt, 7-40; lost on patrol, 3-9-40; F/L H.B.L. Hillcoat missing.
P3046 No. 111 Sqn., Croydon, 7-40; Montrose, 10-40; destroyed in take-off accident, 24-10-40; Sgt. M.J. Mansfield (Czech) unhurt.
P3047 No. 1 Sqn., Northolt, 7-40; shot down off Harwich, 15-8-40; F/L M.H. Brown rescued but wounded.
P3049 No. 257 Sqn., Martlesham Heath, 9-40; shot down over the Isle of Sheppey, 7-9-40; F/L H.R.A. Beresford killed.
P3050 No. 257 Sqn., Martlesham and North Weald, 1940.
P3052 No. 46 Sqn., Digby, 6-40; shot down by Bf 109Es near Southend, 4-9-40; P/O R.P. Plummer died of wounds, 15-9-40.
P3053 No. 46 Sqn., Digby, 6-40.
P3054 No. 111 Sqn., Croydon, 7-40. No. 242 Sqn., Coltishall, **LE-N**, 9-40.
P3055 No. 56 Sqn., North Weald, **US-P**, 6-40.
P3056 No. 310 (Czech) Sqn., Duxford, **NN-J**, 7-40. *Converted to Sea Hurricane IA*, c.4-41, and later transferred to Admiralty Charge.
P3057 *Converted to Mark IIA*, as ***BV169***, 8-41. No. 59 O.T.U. No. 232 Sqn. No. 615 Sqn., A.A.F. No. 486 (N.Z.) Sqn. No. 3 Sqn. No. 245 Sqn. No. 184 Sqn. No. 56 O.T.U. S.O.C., 30-11-45.
P3058 No. 257 Sqn., Tangmere, 8-40; shot down by Bf 109Es off St. Catherine's Point, 8-8-40; F/O J.L.W. D'Arcy-Irvine killed.
P3062 No. 46 Sqn., Digby, 6-40.
P3063 No. 46 Sqn., Digby, 6-40; shot down near Rochford, 3-9-40; P/O H. Morgan-Gray unhurt.
P3064 No. 46 Sqn., Digby, 6-40; shot down near Southend, 3-9-40; Sgt. G.H. Edgworthy killed.
P3065 No. 151 Sqn., North Weald, "G", 6-40; shot down over Kent, 15-8-40; Sub-Lt. H.W. Beggs wounded.
P3066 No. 46 Sqn., Digby, 6-40.
P3067 No. 46 Sqn., Digby, 6-40; shot down and badly damaged by Bf 109E over Kent, 2-9-40; P/O J.C.L.D. Bailey killed. Aircraft repaired and *converted to Trop. Mk. I*, 10-40. To Middle East, 1941. No. 6 Sqn., Helwan, Egypt, 2-42.
P3068 No. 1 Sqn., R.C.A.F., Northolt, 8-40; damaged in combat with Bf 109Es, 1-9-40; F/O E.W.B. Beard, RCAF, unhurt. *Converted on repair to Mark IIA* by Rolls-Royce Ltd., as ***DG615***, 3-41; shipped or flown to Malta; lost from enemy action, 21-12-41.
P3069 No. 303 (Polish) Sqn., Northolt, "C", 8-40.
P3080 No. 401 Sqn., R.C.A.F., Croydon, "C", 8-40; shot down by Bf 109E, 15-9-40; F/O A.D. Nesbitt wounded.
P3082 No. 501 Sqn., A.A.F., Middle Wallop, 7-40; shot down over Lyme Bay, 20-7-40; P/O E.J.H.H. Sylvester killed.
P3083 No. 501 Sqn., A.A.F., Middle Wallop, **SD-E**, 7-40.
P3084 No. 501 Sqn., A.A.F., Middle Wallop, 7-40; crashed off Portland, 12-7-40; P/O D.A. Hewitt killed.
P3085 No. 302 (Polish) Sqn., Duxford, 10-40; collided with Hurricane ***V6923***, 29-10-40; Sgt. Thomson baled out unhurt.
P3086 No. 302 (Polish) Sqn., Duxford, "**Z**", 10-40.
P3087 No. 242 Sqn., Coltishall, 9-40; shot down by Bf 109Es, 9-9-40; P/O K.M. Sclanders, RCAF, killed.
P3088 No. 249 sqn. North Weald, **GN-G**, 9-40.
P3090 *Converted to Sea Hurricane IA*, c.4-41, and later transferred to Admiralty Charge.
P3092 *Converted to Sea Hurricane IA*, c.4-41, and later transferred to Admiralty Charge.
P3093 No. 87 Sqn., Exeter, 8-40; shot down off Portsmouth, 25-8-40; Sgt. S.R.E. Wakeling killed.
P3094 No. 46 Sqn., Stapleford Tawney, 9-40; shot down near Dungeness, 11-9-40; P/O P.R. McGregor wounded.
P3096 No. 238 Sqn., Middle Wallop, 9-40; shot down by Ju 88A near Rye, 11-9-40; P/O W. Tower-Perkins wounded.
P3103 No. 71 Sqn., Kirton-in-Lindsey, 11-40. *Converted to Mark IIA*, 7-41, as ***DR340***, and *shipped to Russia*, 2-10-41.
P3104 No. 232 Sqn., Sumburgh, 8-40; damaged in combat with He 111H, 23-8-40; F/L M.M. Stephens unhurt. Repaired and *converted to Sea Hurricane IA*, 1-41, and later transferred to Admiralty Charge.
P3105 No. 111 Sqn., Croydon, 6-40. No. 1 Sqn., Northolt, 7-40.
P3106 No. 111 Sqn., Croydon, 6-40. *Converted to Mark IIA* as ***DR370***, 8-41, and *shipped to Russia*, 4-3-42.
P3107 No. 605 Sqnm., A.A.F., Croydon, 10-40; aircraft probably hit balloon cable during combat over London, 14-10-40; P/O R. Hope killed.
P3111 *Converted to Sea Hurricane IA*, c.1-41, and transferred later to Admiralty Charge.
P3112 No. 32 Sqn., Biggin Hill, 5-40; F/O J.B.W. Humpherson shot down one Ju 87, 20-7-40. No. 315 (Polish) Sqn., Speke, 3-41.
P3114 No. 46 Sqn., Digby, 5-40. *Converted to Sea Hurricane IA*, c. 11-40.
P3115 No. 253 Sqn., Kenley, 8-40; shot down by Bf 109E near Biggin Hill, 31-8-40; S/L T.P. Gleave baled out wounded.
P3117 No. 607 Sqn., A.A.F., Tangmere, 9-40; shot down by Bf 109Es, 9-9-40; P/O S.B. Parnall killed.
P3119 No. 85 Sqn., Debden, **VY-X**, 5-40. No. 151 Sqn., North Weald, 7-40; damaged in combat with Bf 110, 29-7-40; P/O C.D. Whittingham unhurt; damaged again in combat with Bf 110s, 30-8-40; P/O J.L.W. Ellacombe unhurt.
P3120 No. 303 (Polish) Sqn., Northolt, **RF-D**, 8-40.
P3121 *Converted to Mark IIA* as ***DR350***, 7-41, and *shipped to Russia*, 5-11-41.
P3122 No. 79 Sqn., Biggin Hill, 6-40.
P3124 No. 85 Sqn., Debden, "L", 5-40. No. 238 Sqn., Middle Wallop, 6-40.
P3140 No. 43 Sqn., Tangmere, 6-40; shot down by Bf 109Es over South Coast, 19-7-40; F/L J.W.C. Simpson wounded.
P3141 No. 501 Sqn., A.A.F., Middle Wallop, ***SD-W***, 7-40.
P3142 No. 310 (Czech) Sqn., Duxford, **NN-M**, 9-40; crashed near Oxted after running out of fuel, 9-9-40; P/O Rypl (Czech) unhurt.
P3143 No. 3 Sqn., Croydon, **QO-Z**, 3-40. No. 145 Sqn., Croydon, **SO-Z**, 4-40.
P3144 No. 32 Sqn., Hawkinge, **GZ-B**, 7-40; shot down by Bf 109Es near Dover, 19-7-40; Sgt. G. Turner wounded.
P3145 No. 247 Sqn., Roborough, **HP-L**, 12-40.
P3149 No. 87 Sqn., Church Fenton, **LK-P**, 6-40.
P3152 No. 56 Sqn., North Weald, 6-40. No. 151 Sqn., North Weald, 7-40; damaged in action, 12-7-40; S/L E.M. Donaldson unhurt. *Converted to Sea Hurricane IA*, 2-41, and transferred later to Admiralty Charge.

P3155 No. 1456 Sqn., Westhampnett; shot down by Hs 126 south of Hastings, 1-8-40; Sub-Lt. I.H. Kestin killed.

P3157 *Minor trial installations and performance trials*, A. & A.E.E., 12-40; engine failure on take-off, 16-1-41; F/L Sammy Wroath unhurt. Aircraft repaired.

P3160 No. 79 Sqn., Biggin Hill, 6-40.

P3162 No. 56 O.T.U., Sutton Bridge, 6-41; collided with Hurricane ***W9114*** and crashed at Walpole St. Peter, 2-6-41; Sgt. Bisgood killed.

P3165 No. 245 Sqn., Aldergrove, **DX-X**, 7-40. *Converted to Sea Hurricane IA*, 3-41, and transferred to Admiralty Charge.

P3167 No. 1 Sqn., Northolt, 7-40.

P3168 *Converted to Sea Hurricane IA*, 2-41, and transferred to Admiralty Charge.

P3169 No. 1 Sqn., Northolt, **JX-T**, 7-40. No. 151 Sqn., Digby, **DZ-P**, 9-40.

P3170 No. 1 Sqn., Northolt, 7-40.

P3172 No. 1 Sqn., Northolt, 7-40; shot down at Sandown, Isle of Wight, by Bf 109Es, 11-8-40; P/O J.A.J. Davey killed.

P3173 No. 1 Sqn., Northolt, 8-40; shot down by Portsmouth A.A. guns, 16-8-40; P/O J.F.D. Elkington wounded.

P3174 No. 257 Sqn., Northolt, **DT-S**, 7-40.

P3200 No. 32 Sqn., Biggin Hill, 5-40.

P3201 No. 46 Sqn., Stapleford Tawney, 9-40; Missing after combat over Sheerness, 8-9-40; Sub-Lt. J.C. Carpenter Missing.

P3205 No. 32 Sqn., Hawkinge, 8-40; destroyed in landing accident, 22-8-40; P/O J. Pfeiffer unhurt.

P3206 *Converted to Sea Hurricane IA*, c.4-41, and transferred to Admiralty Charge.

P3207 No. 242 Sqn., Coltishall, 10-40; slightly damaged in combat with Do 17 near Great Yarmouth, 17-10-40; P/O M.K. Brown unhurt. Repaired and *converted to Mark IIA* by Rolls-Royce Ltd., as ***DG631***, 4-41. No. 56 U.T.U. *Converted to Trop. Mk. IIB* and shipped to the Middle East, c.11-41. No. 274 Sqn.; shot down by flak near Martuba, 21-3-42.

P3209 No. 73 Sqn., Castle Camps, 9-40; shot down by Spitfire, 14-9-40; Sgt. M.E. Leng unhurt.

P3212 No. 116 Sqn., Hendon, 11-41.

P3213 No. 253 Sqn., Kenley, 9-40. No. 213 Sqn., Northolt, 11-40.

P3214 No. 32 Sqn., Biggin Hill, 5-40. No. 229 Sqn., Northolt, 10-40; shot down by Bf 109Es, 15-10-40; F/L A.J. Banham baled out wounded.

P3215 No. 87 Sqn., Exeter, 8-40; shot down off Portland, 15-8-40; S/L T.G. Lovell-Gregg killed.

P3219 No. 32 Sqn., Biggin Hill, 5-40.

P3223 No. 238 Sqn., Middle Wallop, 9-40; damaged in landing accident, 25-9-40; P/O D.S. Harrison unhurt. Repaired and *converted to Mark IIA* as ***DG614*** by Rolls-Royce Ltd., 3-41; shipped to the Far East. S.O.C., 1-1-47.

P3226 No. 73 Sqn., Debden, 9-40; shot down by Bf 109Es, 23-9-40; P/O D.S. Kinder wounded.

P3229 No. 1 Sqn., Northolt, 7-40. *Converted to Sea Hurricane IA*, 3-41, and transferred to Admiralty Charge.

P3230 No. 601 Sqn., A.A.F., Tangmere, 7-40.

P3232 No. 601 Sqn., A.A.F., Tangmere, 8-40; shot down over Winchester, 15-8-40; P/O G.N.S. Cleaver wounded.

P3255 No. 85 Sqn., Castle Camps, **VY-H**, 9-40.

P3256 *Converted to Mark IIA* as ***DR365***, 8-41; *shipped to Russia, but lost at sea*, c.2-42.

P3260 No. 3 Sqn., Castletown, 10-40; crashed during aerobatics, 19-10-40; F/O G.F. McAvity, RCAF, killed.

P3261 No. 3 Sqn., Turnhouse, 9-90; damaged in forced landing (not combat), 1-10-40; P/O J. Lonsdale unhurt; damaged in taxying accident, 18-10-40; P/O J. Lonsdale unhurt.

HAWKER HURRICANE MARK I (Hawker-built). Third production batch of 500 aircraft (plus 44 attrition replacements), built by Hawker Aircraft Ltd., Kingston-upon-Thamnes, Brooklands and Langley, under Contract No. 962371/38. Rolls-Royce Merlin III engines; majority with metal wings from new. *P3265-P3279, P3300-P3324, P3345-P3364, P3380-P3429, P3448-P3492, P3515-P3554, P3574-P3623, P3640-P3684, P3700-P3739, P3755-P3789, P3802-P3836, P3854-P3903, P3920-P3944, P3960-P3984.* Replacement aircraft: *P8809-P8818; R2680-R2689; T9519-T9538; W6667-W6670.* Deliveries commenced, 21-2-40; completed 20-7-40; average rate of production, approximately three aircraft per day.

P3265 *Performance trials*, Brooklands, 2-40 to 4-40. No. 229 Sqn., Northolt, 9-40.

P3268 No. 303 (Polish) Sqn., Northolt, 9-40, **RF-J**. No. 312 (Czech) Sqn., Speke, 11-40.

P3269 *Prototype Hurricane Mark II with Merlin XX engine. Tests with rear-view hood*, 1941, Brooklands. Ground instruction airframe, No. 3 S. of T.T., 12-10-42.

P3270 *Trop. Mk. I*. To the Middle East. No. 208 Sqn., El Khanka, Egypt, 11-41.

P3273 No. 151 Sqn., North Weald, 8-40; damaged in combat near Dover, 15-8-40; P/O K.B.L. Debenham unhurt; shot down by Bf 109Es, 24-8-40; Sgt. G.T. Clarke killed.

P3275 No. 151 Sqn., North Weald, 7-40; shot down by Do 17Zs off Ordfordness, 12-7-40; F/O J.H.L. Allan believed drowned.

P3276 No. 1 Sqn., Northolt, 8-40; aircraft lost in flying accident, 1-9-40; Sgt. G.F. Berry unhurt.

P3301 No. 151 Sqn., Stapleford Tawney, 8-40; damaged in action with Bf 109Es near Shoeburyness, 31-8-40; P/O Czajkowsli (Polish) wounded. Repaired and *converted to Sea Hurricane IA*, 11-40.

P3302 No. 151 Sqn., North Weald, 8-40; shot down off North Foreland, 12-8-40; P/O R.W.G. Beley died of wounds.

P3304 No. 151 Sqn., North Weald, 7-40; damaged in combat off Orfordness, 12-7-40; W/C F.V. Beamish unhurt.

P3306 No. 151 Sqn., Digby, 9-40; collided with Hurricane ***V7432***, 24-9-40; Sgt. J. McPhee baled out unhurt.

P3307 No. 151 Sqn., North Weald, 7-40; damaged in combat wirh Bf 110s over Thames Estuary, 29-7-40; F/O R.M. Milne unhurt. *Converted to Mark IIA* as ***DR364***, 8-41, and *shipped to Russia*, 23-2-42.

P3309 No. 151 Sqn., North Weald, 7-40; damaged in combat, 9-7-40; repaired by Rollasons. No. 46 Sqn., Sherburn-in-Elmet, 4-41.

P3310 No. 151 Sqn., North Weald, 8-40; shot down off South Coast, 13-8-40; Sgt. G. Atkinson unhurt.

P3312 No. 151 Sqn., Stapleford Tawney, 8-40; shot down by Do 17Zs, 31-8-40; P/O J.L.W. Ellacombe wounded.

P3316 No. 151 Sqn., North Weald, 7-40; destroyed in flying accident, 24-7-40; P/O J.R. Hamar killed.

P3317 No. 87 Sqn., Church Fenton, **LK-Q**, 7-40.

P3318 No. 1 Sqn., Northolt, 7-40; Wittering, 10-40; damaged in flying accident, 16-10-40; Sgt. J. Prihoda (Czech) unhurt.

P3320 No. 151 Sqn., North Weald, 8-40; damaged in combat, 28-8-40; Sgt. L. Davies wounded.

P3345 *Trials with various paint and colour schemes*, Brooklands, 2-40 to 5-40.

P3351 No. 73 Sqn., Gaye, France, 6-40. No. 32 Sqn., Acklington, 10-40. *Converted to Mark IIA*, ***DR393***, 9-41; *shipped to Russia*, 26-3-42.

P3356 No. 56 Sqn., North Weald, 5-40.

P3357 No. 253 Sqn., Kirton-in-Lindsey, 7-40.

P3358 No. 601 Sqn., Tangmere, 8-40; aircraft landed on fire at Tangmere while bombing raid was in progress, 16-8-40; P/O W.M.L. Fiske (American) died of burns.

P3359 No. 253 Sqn., Kirton-in-Lindsey, 7-40; crashed near Humber, 10-7-40; Sgt. I.C.C. Clenshaw killed.

P3362 *Converted to Sea Hurricane IA*, 2-41, and transferred to Admiralty Charge.

P3363 No. 601 Sqn., A.A.F., Tangmere, 9-40; shot down over Kent, 6-9-40; F/O C.R. Davis killed.

P3381 No. 145 Sqn., Tangmere, 7-40; damaged in combat with He 111H off Bognor Regis, 18-7-40; F/L A.H.Mc.N. Boyd unhurt.

P3382 No. 601 Sqn., A.A.F., Tangmere, 9-40; shot down by Bf 109Es over Kent, 6-9-40; F/O J. Topolnicki (Polish) slightly wounded.

P3383 No. 601 Sqn., Debden, 8-40; shot down by Bf 109Es near Colchester, 31-8-40; F/O M.D. Doulton killed.

P3386 No. 43 Sqn., Tangmere, **FT-Y**, 9-40.

P3388 No. 504 Sqn., A.A.F., Hendon, 9-40.

P3393 No. 601 Sqn., A.A.F., Tangmere, 8-40; damaged in combat near Tangmere, 13-8-40; F/O W.P. Clyde unhurt; damaged in landing accident at Exeter, 14-10-40; Sgt. R.A. Milburn unhurt.

P3394 *Converted to Sea Hurricane IA*, c.1-41, and transferred to Admiralty Charge.

P3395 No. 1 Sqn., Northolt, **JX-B**, 9-40; shot down by Bf 109Es over Kent, 1-9-40.

P3396 No. 1 Sqn., Northolt, 7-40.

P3398 *Converted to Sea Hurricane IA*, c.2-41, and transferred to Admiralty Charge.

P3399 No. 56 Sqn., North Weald, 5-40. No. 111 Sqn., North Weald, 6-40.

P3402 *Converted to Mark IIA* by Rolls-Royce Ltd., 11-40, as ***BV160***. No. 59 O.T.U. No. 232 Sqn. No. 615 Sqn., A.A.F. No. 486 (N.Z.) Sqn. No. 43 Sqn. No. 245 Sqn. West Malling Stn. Flt. No. 55 O.T.U. S.O.C., 11-8-44.

P3404 No. 87 Sqn., Church Fenton, **LK-J**, 8-40.

P3405 No. 1 Sqn., Northolt, 7-40. No. 504 Sqn., A.A.F., Filton, 9-40; force landed after combat at Axminster, 27-9-40; Sgt. C. Haw unhurt. Aircraft repaired by Rollasons.

P3406 No. 1 Sqn., Northolt, 7-40; shot down by Bf 109E over Kent, 1-9-40.

P3407 No. 85 Sqn., Debden, 7-40.

P3408 No. 85 Sqn., Debden, 7-40.

P3409 No. 85 Sqn., Debden, **VY-K**, 7-40.

P3410 No. 331 (Norwegian) Sqn., Catterick, 7-41.

P3411 No. 501 Sqn., A.A.F., Middle Wallop, **SD-N**, 7-40. No. 232 Sqn., Sumburgh, 7-40; damaged in accident, 27-7-40; pilot unhurt.

P3412 No. 257 Sqn., Northolt, 8-40. *Converted to Trop. Mark IIA* by Rolls-Royce Ltd., 3-41, as ***DG613***; shipped to the Middle East, 1941. No. 79 Sqn. No. 2 P.R.U.; crashed on landing at Beirut, 26-10-42.

P3414 No. 504 Sqn., A.A.F., Hendon, 9-40; shot down south of Weymouth, 30-9-40; F/O J.R. Hardacre killed.

P3415 No. 504 Sqn., A.A.F., Hendon, 9-40. No. 151 Sqn., Digby, DZ-V, 10-40.

P3416 No. 9 P.A.F.U., 1941. *Supplied to Irish Air Corps*, 29-11-43 as "***108***".

P3617 No. 501 Sqn., A.A.F., Kenley, 9-450; shot down by Bf 109Es near Deal, Kent, 28-9-40; F/O F.C. Harrold killed.

P3421 No. 56 Sqn., North Weald, 5-40; Warmwell, 10-40; shot down by Bf 109Es, 10-10-40; Sgt. J. Hlavac (Czech) killed.

P2422 No. 229 Sqn., Northolt, 9-40; damaged in combat with Bf 109Es over Kent, 30-9-40; P/O R.A.L. du Vivier unhurt.

P3428 No. 245 Sqn., Aldergrove, **DX-N**, 9-40.

P3429 No. 504 Sqn., A.A.F., Hendon, 9-40; damaged in take-off accident, 11-9-40; P/O M. Rook unhurt.

P3449 Converted to Mark IIA as ***DR362***, 8-41, and *shipped to Russia*, 7-4-42.

P3451 Damaged in combat and repaired by Rollasons, late 1940.

P3456 No. 73 Sqn., Gaye, France, 6-40. No. 229 Sqn., Northolt, 10-40; damaged in combat with Bf 109Es, 15-10-40; F/L W.A. Smith unhurt.

P3457 No. 253 Sqn., Turnhouse, 8-40; damaged in night landing, 7-8-40; P/O D.N.O. Jenkins unhurt.

P3459 No. 111 Sqn., North Weald, 6-40.

P3460 No. 32 Sqn., Acklington, 10-40. No. 71 Sqn., Kirton-in-Lindsey, 11-40. *Converted to Sea Hurricane IA*, c.1-41, and transferred to Admiralty Charge.

P3461 No. 79 Sqn., Hawkinge, 7-40; shot down off

Dover, 8-7-40; P/O J.E.R. Wood killed.
P3462 Tests with long range fuel tanks, Brooklands, 8-40. No. 238 Sqn., Middle Wallop, 9-40; damaged in combat, 15-9-40; pilot unhurt.
P3463 No. 229 Sqn., Northolt, 9-40; damaged in combat with Bf 109E, 11-9-40; F/L R.F. Rimmer wounded. No. 249 Sqn., North Weald, 10-40; damaged in flying accident, 18-10-40; Adjutant H. Bouquillard (French) unhurt. No. 59 O.T.U.
P3464 No. 43 Sqn., Tangmere, 7-40; S/L C.G. Lott baled out after being wounded in the eye in combat near Southampton, 9-7-40.
P3465 No. 87 Sqn., Exeter, 8-40; shot down off Portland, 15-8-40; P/O P.W. Comely killed.
P3466 *Converted to Sea Hurricane IA*, c.1-41, and transferred to Admiralty Charge.
P3467 *Converted to Sea Hurricane IA*, c.1-41, and transferred to Admiralty Charge.
P3468 No. 45 Sqn., Wick, 3-40. No. 17 Sqn., Tangmere, 8-40.
P3470 No. 111 Sqn., North Weald, 6-40.
P3471 No. 1 Sqn., Northolt, 7-40; shot down, 19-7-40; P/O D.O.M. Browne unhurt.
P3473 No. 56 Sqn., North Weald, **US-K**, 5-40.
P3474 No. 56 Sqn., North Weald, 5-40.
P3478 No. 56 Sqn., North Weald, 5-40.
P3479 No. 56 Sqn., North Weald, 5-40.
P3482 No. 17 Sqn., Tangmere, 8-40; crashed during patrol, 15-7-40; P/O D.L. Dawbarn unhurt.
P3485 No. 242 Sqn., Coltishall, **LE-Y**, 9-40.
P3487 No. 615 Sqn., A.A.F., Prestwick, 9-40.
P3489 Damaged in action, 1940; repaired by Rollasons.
P3515 No. 56 Sqn., North Weald, 5-40.
P3516 No. 501 Sqn., A.A.F., Gravesend, 9-40; shot down over Ashford, Kent, 6-9-40; Sgt. G.W. Pearson killed.
P3521 Damaged in action, 1940; repaired by Rollasons. *Converted to Trop. Mark IIA* as ***BV167*** by Rolls-Royce Ltd., 1-41. Shipped and flown to Malta, 1942; Missing in action, 4-2-43.
P3522 No. 32 Sqn., Biggin Hill, **GZ-H**, 6-40.
P3524 No. 111 Sqn., North Weald, 6-40.
P3525 No. 249 Sqn., Boscombe Down, 8-40. No. 46 Sqn., Stapleford Tawney, 9-40; destroyed in flying accident, 12-9-40; Sgt. S. Andrew killed.
P3527 No. 32 Sqn., Biggin Hill, **GZ-V**, 6-40. No. 43 Sqn., Tangmere, **FT-O**, 9-40.
P3530 Damaged in action, 1940; repaired by Rollasons. *Converted to Sea Hurricane IA*, c.12-41, and transferred to Admiralty Charge.
P3531 No. 43 Sqn., Wick, 3-40; shot down off Shoreham, 19-70-40; Sgt. J.A. Buck drowned.
P3534 No. 1 Sqn., R.C.A.F., Northolt, 9-40; shot down by Bf 109E, 11-9-40; F/O T.B. Little, RCAF, wounded.
P3536 No. 17 Sqn., Martlesham Heath, 10-40; shot down by Chatham A.A. guns, 13-10-40; P/O J.H. Ross baled out unhurt.
P3537 No. 253 Sqn., Kenley, 10-40; destroyed in flying accident, 17-10-40; P/O T. Nowak (Polish) unhurt.
P3538 No. 302 (Polish) Sqn., Northolt, "**J**", 10-40.
P3539 *Converted to Trop. Mark IIA* as ***DG634*** by Rolls-Royce Ltd., 4-41, and shipped to the Middle East. No. 274 Sqn. No. 229 Sqn.; shot down by Bf 109Fs over Sicily, 9-1-42.
P3544 *Converted to Sea Hurricane IA*, c.2-41, and transferred to Admiralty Charge.
P3545 No. 145 Sqn., Tangmere, 7-40; damaged in taxying accident, 7-7-40; P/O D.N. Forde unhurt.
P3547 No. 56 Sqn., North Weald, 4-40.
P3548 No. 111 Sqn., North Weald, 6-40.
P3551 No. 71 Sqwn., Kirton-in-Lindsey, 11-41. *Converted to Mark IIA* as ***DR343***, 7-41, and shipped to Russia, 3-11-41.
P3554 No. 56 Sqn., North Weald, 4-40.
P3576 No. 249 Sqn., Boscombe Down, 8-40; shot down by Bf 110 near Southampton, 16-8-40; F/L J.B. Nicolson baled out with burns but survived and awarded the Victoria Cross.
P3578 No. 257 Sqn., Northolt, 8-40; shot down by Bf 110s, 3-9-40; P/O C.A. Bon-Seigneur, RCAF, killed.
P3579 No. 56 Sqn., North Weald, 5-40. No. 249 Sqn., Boscombe Down, 8-40.
P3580 No. 605 Sqn., A.A.F., Croydon, 9-40.
P3582 No. 501 Sqn., A.A.F., Middle Wallop, 7-40.
P3585 No. 213 Sqn., Wittering, **AK-Q**, 8-40.
P3587 No. 56 Sqn., North Weald, 5-40.
P3588 No. 605 Sqn., A.A.F., Croydon, 9-40.
P3593 No. 87 Sqn., Church Fenton, "**O**", 6-40.
P3594 No. 249 Sqn., Boscombe Down, 8-40; shot down by Bf 109Es over Kent,, 7-9-40; F/O P.H.V. Wells wounded.
P3595 No. 111 Sqn., North Weald, 6-40.
P3596 No. 87 Sqn., Exeter, 7-40; destroyed in night landing accident at Hullavington, 26-7-40; Sgt. J.H. Culverwell killed.
P3597 No. 46 Sqn., Stapleford Tawney, 9-40; forced landed after combat, 2-9-40; F/L A.C. Rabagliati unhurt. No. 46 Sqn., Sherburn-in-Elmet, 4-41. *Converted to Sea Hurricane IA*, 5-41.
P3598 No. 308 (Polish) Sqn., Baginton, 11-40.
P3599 No. 238 Sqn., Middle Wallop, 9-40; shot down by Bf 110s over Poole, 1-10-40; Sgt. F.A. Sibley killed.
P3603 No. 229 Sqn., Northolt, 9-40; shot down by Bf 109Es, 27-9-40; F/L W.A. Smith unhurt.
P3604 No. 501 Sqn., A.A.F., Middle Wallop, 7-40.
P3605 No. 501 Sqn., A.A.F., Kenley, 9-40; crashed on landing after combat, 28-9-40. F/O D.A.E. Jones unhurt.
P3606 No. 263 Sqn., Drem, 9-40.
P3608 No. 229 Sqn., Northolt, 9-40.
P3609 No. 245 Sqn., Aldergrove, **DX-F**, 9-40.
P3610 No. 253 Sqn., Kenley, 8-40; aircraft destroyed in accident, 2-9-40; pilot unhurt.
P3611 No. 238 Sqn., Middle Wallop, 9-40; shot down by Bf 109Es near Middle Wallop, 5-10-40; Sgt. J.W. McLaughlin baled out with burns.
P3612 No. 56 Sqn., North Weald, 5-40.
P3614 No. 504 Sqn., A.A.F., Hendon, 9-40.
P3615 No. 249 Sqn., Boscombe Down, 8-40.
P3616 No. 249 Sqn., Boscombe Down, 8-40; shot down near Southampton, 16-8-40; P/O M.A. King killed.
P3620 No. 257 Sqn., Northolt, **DT-M**, 7-40. *Converted to Sea Hurricane IA* by General Aircraft Ltd., 2-41.
P3622 No. 257 Sqn., Northolt, 7-40; shot down by Bf 109E over Kent, 28-7-40; Sgt. F.V. Forward slightly wounded.
P3641 No. 257 Sqn., Northolt, 7-40. *Radio trials*, T.R.E., Malvern, 1941.
P3642 No. 257 Sqn., Northolt, 8-40; damaged in flying accident following engine failure, 16-9-40; Sgt. D.J. Hulbert unhurt.
P3643 No. 257 Sqn., Northolt, 8-40; Castle Camps, 9-40; shot down by Bf 109Es at Detling, 23-9-40; Sgt. D.J. Aslin wounded.
P3646 No. 501 Sqn., A.A.F., Middle Wallop, 7-40.
P3647 No. 73 Sqn., Church Fenton, 7-40. No. 401 Sqn., R.C.A.F., Northolt, 9-40.
P3650 No. 605 Sqn., A.A.F., Croydon, 9-40.
P3653 No. 1 Sqn., Northolt, 7-40; damaged in combat over Sussex, 16-8-40; F/O P.V. Boot unhurt.
P3657 No. 245 Sqn., Aldergrove, 10-40; crashed during training flight, 21-10-40; Sgt. E.G. Greenwood killed.
P3662 No. 257 Sqn., Northolt, 8-40; shot down near Portsmouth, 12-8-40; P/O J.A. Chomley killed.
P3663 No. 111 Sqn., North Weald, 6-40. No. 303 (Polish) Sqn., Northolt, 9-40.
P3664 No. 232 Sqn., Castletown, 9-40; damaged in landing accident, 23-9-40; Sgt. E.A. Redfern unhurt.
P3669 No. 111 Sqn., North Weald, 6-40.
P3670 *Converted to Mark IIA* as ***DG646*** by Rolls-Royce Ltd., 5-41, and *shipped to Russia*, 9-9-41.
P3671 No. 111 Sqn., North Weald, 6-40; collided with Do 17Z of KG 2, 10-7-40; P/O T.P.K. Higgs killed.
P3677 No. 605 Sqn., A.A.F., Croydon, 10-40; shot down by Bf 109Es, 7-10-40; P/O C.E. English killed.
P3678 No. 1 Sqn., Northolt, 7-40.
P3679 No. 501 Sqn., A.A.F., Middle Wallop, **SD-X**, 7-40.
P3681 No. 601 Sqn., A.A.F., Tangmere, 7-40; shot down by gun defences on the Isle of Wight; Sgt. A.W. Woolley baled out wounded.
P3701 No. 111 Sqn., Debden, 8-40.
P3702 No. 56 Sqn., North Weald, **US-W**, 6-40. No. 4 F.P.P., 6-40.
P3703 No. 238 Sqn., Middle Wallop, 7-40; crashed, 5-7-40; P/O B. Firminger killed.
P3704 No. 257 Sqn., Northolt, 8-40; damaged in combat with Bf 110 near Chelmsford, 3-9-40; P/O K.C. Grundy unhurt; shot down by Bf 109Es, 12-10-40; P/O J. Redman unhurt.
P3705 No. 257 Sqn., Northolt, "**B**", 8-40; damaged in accident, 17-9-40, but repaired; Sgt. R.H.B. Fraser unhurt. *Converted to Trop. Mk. I* and shipped to the Middle East, 10-40. No. 103 M.U., Aboukir, 11-40.
P3706 No. 257 Sqn., Northolt, 8-40; damaged in combat with Bf 110s, 3-9-40; Sgt. R.C. Nutter slightly wounded. *Converted to Sea Hurricane IA*, 2-41.
P3707 No. 257 Sqn., Northolt, 8-40.
P3708 No. 257 Sqn., Northolt, 8-40; P/O J.A.McD. Henderson shot down two Bf 110s of LG 1, 31-8-40, but himself shot down, unhurt.
P3709 No. 257 Sqn., Northolt, 8-40. No. 601 Sqn., A.A.F., Exeter, 10-40; collided with Hurricane ***V6917*** during training flight, 25-10-40; Sgt. Mills-Smith killed.
P3710 *Converted to Sea Hurricane IA* by General Aircraft Ltd., c.3-41, and transferred to Admiralty Charge.
P3712 No. 96 Sqn., Cranage, 12-40.
P3713 No. 316 (Polish) Sqn., Pembrey, **SZ-E**, 2-41.
P3714 *Converted to Mark IIA* as ***DR341***, 7-41, and *shipped to Russia*, 16-10-41.
P3715 No. 242 Sqn., Coltishall, 9-40; damaged in action, 7-6-40; P/O D.W. Crowley-Milling unhurt. No. 4 F.P.P. No. 17 P.A.F.U.
P3716 No. 229 Sqn., Northolt, 10-40; destroyed in flying accident, 6-10-40; F/L W.A. Smith unhurt.
P3717 *Converted to Mark IIA* as ***DR348***, 7-41, and *shipped to Russia*, 11-10-41.
P3719 *Converted to Sea Hurricane IA* by General Aircraft Ltd., c.4-41, and transferred to Admiralty Charge.
P3720 *Shipped to Persia* as "***252***", c. 11-40.
P3721 *Trop. Mk. I.* No. 418 Flt. To the Middle East, 8-40. No. 6 Sqn., Ramleh, Palestine, 3-41.
P3722 *Trop. Mk. I.* No. 418 Flt. To the Middle East, 8-40. No. 274 Sqn., Bardia, 2-41.
P3723 *Trop. Mk. I.* No. 418 Flt. To the Middle East, 8-40.
P3724 *Trop. Mk. I.* No. 418 Flt. To the Middle East, 8-40. No. 33 Sqn., Eleusis, Greece, 4-41.
P3728 No. 601 Sqn., A.A.F., Debden, **UF-R**, 8-40.
P3729 *Trop. Mk. I.* No. 418 Flt. To the Middle East, 8-40. No. 274 Sqn., Sidi Haneish, 11-40.
P3731 *Trop. Mk. I.* No. 418 Flt. To the Mediterranean abaord H.M.S. *Argus*, 2-8-40; No. 261 Sqn., Luqa, Malta, "**J**", 8-40. No. 127 Sqn., Habbaniya, Iraq, 6-41.
P3732 *Trop. Mk. I.* No. 418 Flt. To the Mediterranean aboard H.M.S. *Argus*, 2-8-40; No. 261 Sqn., Luqa, Malta, 16-8-40.
P3733 *Trop. Mk. I.* No. 418 Flt. To the Mediterranean aboard H.M.S. *Argus*, 2-8-40; No. 261 Sqn., Luqa, Malta, 16-8-40.
P3734 *Trop. Mk. I.* To the Mediterranean, 8-40. No. 33 Sqn., Eleusis, Greece, 4-41. No. 274 Sqn., Gerawla, 5-41.
P3735 No. 601 Sqn., A.A.F., Debden, 8-40; shot down by Bf 109Es near Colchester, 31-8-40; Sgt. R.N. Taylor unhurt.
P3736 Fuel consumptioon trials, Brooklands, 1940.
P3737 No. 605 Sqn., A.A.F., Croydon, 10-40; shot down by Bf 109Es, 26-10-40; F/O C.W. Passey unhurt.
P3738 No. 232 Sqn., Castletown, 9-40; damaged in landing accident, 22-9-40; F/L H.M. Stephens unhurt.
P3755 No. 87 Sqn., Church Fenton, "**Z**", 6-40.

P3756 No. 46 Sqn., Stapleford Tawney, 9-40; damaged in combat with Bf 109Es, 27-9-40; P/O K. Mräzek (Czech) unhurt. *Converted to Trop. Mark IIA* as ***DG612***, 3-41, and shipped to Malta. S.O.C., 20-4-42.

P3757 No. 32 Sqn., Biggin Hill, **GZ-L**, 6-40.

P3759 *Converted to Mark IIA* as ***DR349***, 7-41, and *shipped to Russia*, 16-10-41.

P3764 No. 238 Sqn., Warmwell, 7-40.

P3766 No. 238 Sqn., Warmwell, 7-40; shot down over Lyme Bay, 20-7-40; Sgt. C. Parkinson died from burns.

P3767 No. 257 Sqn., Northolt, 7-40; destroyed in landing accident, 12-7-40; P/O the Hon. D.A. Coke unhurt.

P3771 No. 79 Sqn., Biggin Hill, 8-40.

P3772 No. 229 Sqn., Castletown, 9-40.

P3773 No. 3 Sqn., Castletown, 9-40. *Converted to Sea Hurricane IA*, 3-41, and transferred to Admiralty Charge.

P3774 No. 504 Sqn., A.A.F., Hendon, **TM-V**, 9-40; damaged in action near Yeovil, 30-9-40; Sgt. W.H. Banks unhurt.

P3775 No. 257 Sqn., Northolt, 9-40; North Weald, 10-40; shot down by Bf 109Es over Kent, 12-10-40; P/O K.C. Grundy slightly wounded.

P3776 No. 257 Sqn., Northolt, 8-40; shot down and force landed near Portsmouth, 12-8-40; P/O the Hon. D.A. Coke wounded. Aircraft repaired and *converted to Sea Hurricane IA*, c.3-41; transferred to Admiralty Charge.

P3780 No. 151 Sqn., 8-40; damaged in combat off North Foreland, 12-8-40; P/O D.B.L. Debenham unhurt. Aircraft repaired by Rollasons.

P3781 No. 43 Sqn., Tangmere, 9-40.

P3782 No. 1 Sqn., Northolt, 7-40; Missing from patrol, 3-9-40; P/O R.H. Shaw Missing.

P3783 No. 601 Sqn., A.A.F., Tangmere, 8-40; shot down off Portland, 11-8-40; P/O J. Gillan killed.

P3784 No. 56 Sqn., North Weald, 6-40. *Converted to Sea Hurricane IA*, c.3-41, and transferred to Admiralty Charge.

P3786 Damaged in action, 1940, and repaired by Rollasons.

P3788 No. 402 Sqn., R.C.A.F., Digby, 12-40.

P3802 No. 253 Sqn., Kenley, 8-40; shot down over Kent, 30-8-40; F/L G.A. Brown wounded.

P3803 No. 501 Sqn., A.A.F., Middle Wallop, **SD-Z**, 7-40; shot down by Bf 109Es near Gravesend, 2-9-40; Sgt. W.B. Henn wounded.

P3805 *Converted to Sea Hurricane IA*, c.3-41, and transferred to Admiralty Charge.

P3806 No. 151 Sqn., North Weald, 7-40; shot down over Thames Estuary, 9-7-40; Midshipman O.M. Wightman rescued unhurt.

P3808 No. 501 Sqn., A.A.F., Middle Wallop, 7-40; shot down by Dover A.A. guns, 26-7-40; F/L P.A.N. Cox killed.

P3811 *Trial installation of 12-gun wing and propeller trials*, Brooklands, 7-40. *Converted to Mark IIA* as ***DG644,*** by Rolls-Royce Ltd., 5-41, and *shipped to Russia*, 7-9-41.

P3812 No. 302 (Polish) Sqn., Leconfield, "**L**", 8-40.

P3813 No. 242 Sqn., Coltishall, 7-40; destroyed in flying accident, 6-7-40; Sub-Lt. R.J. Cork unhurt.

P3814 *Converted to Sea Hurricane IA* by General Aircraft Ltd., 3-41, and transferred to Admiralty Charge.

P3816 No. 46 Sqn., Stapleford Tawney, 9-40; shot down by Bf 109Es near Chatham, Kent, 18-9-40; Sgt. C.A.L. Hurry slightly wounded.

P3818 *Trop. Mk. I.* Shipped to the Middle East via Takoradi, 12-40. No. 33 Sqn., Eleusis, Greece, 4-41.

P3820 *Engine handling and performance checks*, Brooklands and Langley, 8-40. No. 501 Sqn., A.A.F., Kenley, 9-40; shot down by Bf 109Es over Kent, 17-9-40; Sgt. E.J. Egan killed.

P3821 *Trop. Mk. I.* Shipped to the Middle East, 10-40. No. 274 Sqn., Sidi Haneish, 11-40.

P3822 *Trop. Mk. I.* Shipped to the Middle East, 10-40. No. 274 Sqn., Sidi Haneish, 11-40.

P3823 *Engine handling trials and performance comparison checks* with ***P3820***, Brooklands, 8-40. No. 238 Sqn., Middle Wallop, 9-40.

P3826 *Trop. Mk. I.* Shipped to the Middle East, 10-40; *modified as 2-camera Tac R. Mk. I.* No. 208 Sqn., Gambut, 1-41.

P3828 No. 605 Sqn., A.A.F., Croydon, 9-40; severely damaged in combat with Bf 109Es, 28-9-40; F/O R. Hope unhurt. Aircraft repaired and *converted to Mark IIA* as ***DR363***, 8-41, and *shipped to Russia*, 25-3-42.

P3829 Damaged in action and repaired by Rollasons, 1940. *Converted to Sea Hurricane IA*, c.2-41, and transferred to Admiralty Charge.

P3830 *Various trial installations to improve rearward field of view*, Brooklands, 7-40.

P3832 No. 605 Sqn., A.A.F., Croydon, 9-40; shot down by Bf 109Es near Boulogne, 24-9-40; P/O W.J. Glowacki (Polish) believed killed.

P3833 No. 238 Sqn., Middle Wallop, 9-40; damaged in combat over London, 15-9-40; pilot unhurt.

P3834 No. 249 Sqn., North Weald, 9-40; shot down by Ju 88A near London, 27-9-40; P/O J.R.B. Meaker killed.

P3854 No. 85 Sqn., Martlesham Heath, 7-40.

P3855 No. 56 Sqn., North Weald, 6-40.

P3861 No. 249 Sqn., North Weald, 6-40.

P3864 No. 242 Sqn., Colitshall, **LE-U**, 9-40.

P3866 No. 56 Sqn., North Weald, 6-40.

P3868 No. 73 Sqn., Debden, 9-40; damaged in action over the Isle of Sheppey, 11-9-40; Sgt. R.V. Ellis unhurt.

P3870 No. 56 Sqn., North Weald, 6-40; damaged in combat with Bf 110s near Portsmouth, 30-9-40; P/O B.J. Wicks unhurt. *Converted to Sea Hurricane IA*, c.3-41.

P3872 No. 302 (Polish) Sqn., Duxford, 10-40; crashed after running out of fuel, 18-10-40; P/O S. Wapniarek (Polish) killed.

P3873 No. 401 Sqn., R.C.A.F., Northolt, 9-40.

P3874 No. 56 Sqn., North Weald, 6-40.

P3876 No. 1 Sqn., R.C.A.F., Northolt, 9-40; shot down over South London, 15-8-40; F/O R. Smither, RCAF, killed.

P3877 *Converted to Sea Hurricane IA*, c.1-41, and transferred to Admiralty Charge.

P3878 No. 17 Sqn., Debden, **YB-W**, 10-40.

P3879 No. 56 Sqn., North Weald, 6-40; Rochford, 7-40; shot down by Bf 109E over Dover, 29-7-40; F/Sgt. C.J. Cooney killed.

P3880 No. 111 Sqn., Debden, 8-40.

P3881 No. 263 Sqn., Drem, 6-40. No. 4 F.P.P., 6-40.

P3882 No. 151 Sqn., Stapleford Tawney, 8-40; shot down over Essex, 29-8-40; P/O A.G. Wainwright wounded.

P3883 *Conversted to Sea Hurricane IA*, c.1-41, and transferred to Admiralty Charge.

P3885 No. 601 Sqn., A.A.F., Tangmere, 8-40; shot down off Portland, 11-8-40; P/O J.L. Smithers killed.

P3886 No. 601 Sqn., Exeter, 10-40; damaged in landing accident, 15-10-40, but repaired; P/O J.W. Seddon unhurt. No. 1 Sqn., Kenley, 1-41.

P3888 No. 310 (Czech) Sqn., Duxford; collided with He 111H during combat, 9-9-40; P/O J.E. Boulton killed.

P3889 No. 310 (Czech) Sqn., Duxford, **NN-S**, 9-40.

P3893 No. 257 Sqn., Northolt, 8-40; damaged on take-off during raid on North Weald, 29-10-40; P/O F. Surma (Polish) baled out unhurt.

P3895 No. 85 Sqn., Martlesham Heath, 7-40; crashed in night landing accident at Castle Camps, 22-7-40; P/O J.L. Bickerdyke killed.

P3896 No. 145 Sqn., Tangmere, 10-40; shot down by Bf 109Es, 12-10-40; Sgt. Thorpe unhurt.

P3901 No. 501 Sqn., A.A.F., Middle Wallop, 7-40 (with fabric wings). No. 253 Sqn., Kenley, 9-40 (with metal wings).

P3902 No. 56 Sqn., North Weald, 7-40.

P3921 No. 253 Sqn., Kenley, 8-40; shot down near Redhill, 30-8-40; P/O D.N.O. Jenkins killed.

P3923 *Performance trials with modified Rotol propellers*, Brooklands, 8-40. No. 302 (Polish) Sqn., Leconfield, 10-40.

P3924 No. 302 (Polish) Sqn., Leconfield, 9-40; damaged in taxying accident, 30-9-40. Repaired by de Havillands, 10-40. *Converted to Sea Hurricane IA*, c.1-41, and later transferred to Admiralty Charge.

P3925 *Converted to Sea Hurricane IA*, c. 2-41, and transferred to Admiralty Charge.

P3926 No. 145 Sqn., Tangmere, **SO-Y**, 10-40; shot down by Bf 109Es, 23-10-40; P/O R.D. Yule wounded. Aircraft recovered and repaired; *converted to Sea Hurricane IA*, c.2-41, and transferred to Admiralty Charge.

P3927 No. 302 (Polish) Sqn., Leconfield, 8-40; aircraft crashed during training flight, 17-8-40; P/O Glowczynski (Polish) badly burned.

P3928 No. 229 Sqn., Castletown, 9-40. *Converted to Mark IIA* as ***DR363***, 8-41, and *shipped to Russia*, 25-3-42.

P3930 No. 302 (Polish) Sqn., Duxford, 10-40; crashed after running out of fuel, 18-10-40; P/O J. Borowski (Polish) killed.

P3931 No. 302 (Polish) Sqn., Duxford, 10-40; crashed after running out of fuel, 18-10-40; P/O P.E.G. Carter killed.

P3932 No. 302 (Polish) Sqn., Duxford, 10-40; crashed on French coast (not combat), 25-20-40; P/O F. Jastrzebski (Polish) killed.

P3934 No. 302 (Polish) Sqn., Leconfield, 8-40; damaged in combat with Ju 88A, 24-8-40; P/O S.J. Chalupa unhurt. *Converted to Sea Hurricane IA*, c.2-41, and transferred to Admiralty Charge.

P3935 No. 302 (Polish) Sqn., Leconfield, 9-40; damaged in taxying accident, 30-9-40; Sgt. J. Zaluski (Polish) unhurt; damaged by striking balloon barrage cable, 16-10-40; Sgt. Kosarz (Polish) unhurt.

P3936 No. 315 (Polish) Sqn., Speke, 3-41.

P3938 No. 312 (Czech) Sqn., Speke, ***DU-Q***, 9-40.

P3940 No. 151 Sqn., North Weald, 8-40; S/L J.A.G. Gordon wounded.

P3941 No. 151 Sqn., North Weald, 8-40; shot down near Dover, 15-8-40; P/O J.T. Johnston killed.

P3942 No. 111 Sqn., North Weald, 6-40.

P3943 No. 111 Sqn., North Weald, 6-40.

P3944 No. 111 Sqn., North Weald, 6-40; shot down over Selsey Bill, 15-8-40; F/O B.M. Fisher killed.

P3963 No. 111 Sqn., Debden, **JU-S**, 8-40; shot down over Biggin Hill, 1-9-40; F/O B.V. Kerwin (Canadian) wounded.

P3964 No. 43 Sqn., Northolt, 7-40; shot down by He 59 seaplane off Selsey Bill, 20-7-40; F/O J.F.J. Howarth drowned.

P3967 *Trop. Mk. I.* Ferry Pool, Takoradi, 10-40. No. 6 Sqn., Barce, Libya, 3-41.

P3969 *Trop. Mk. I.* Shipped to Middle East via Takoradi, 10-40. No. 33 Sqn., Eleusis, Greece, 4-41.

P3970 *Trop. Mk. I.* Ferry Pool, Takoradi, 10-40.

P3971 No. 43 Sqn., Northolt, 7-40; damaged by Bf 109Es off the Needles, 21-7-40; S/L J.V.C. Badger unhurt.

P3972 No. 43 Sqn., Tangmere, 8-40; shot down near Petworth, 13-8-40; F/L T.P. Dalton-Morgan wounded.

P3973 No. 43 Sqn., Tangmere, 7-40; shot down by Bf 109Es south of the Needles, 21-7-40; P/O R.A. de Mancha killed.

P3974 No. 303 (Polish) Sqn., Northolt, 9-40.

P3975 *Converted to Sea Hurricane IA*, c.3-41, and transferred to Admiralty Charge.

P3977 *Trop. Mk. I.* Shipped to the Middle East via Takoradi, c.10-40. No. 274 Sqn., Sidi Haneish, 11-40.

P3978 *Trop. Mk. I.* Shipped to the Middle East via Takoradi, c.10-40. No. 274 Sqn., Sidi Haneish, 11-40.

P3979 *Converted to Sea Hurricane IA*, c.2-41, and transferred to Admiralty Charge.

P3980 *Trop. Mk. I.* Shipped to the Middle East via

Takoradi, c.10-40. No. 274 Sqn., Sidi Haneish, 11-40.

P3984 No. 238 Sqn., Middle Wallop, 10-40; shot down near Poole, 10-10-40; P/O R.F.T. Doe wounded.

Attrition Replacements

P8809 No. 310 (Czech) Sqn., Duxford, 9-40.
P8810 No. 232 Sqn., Castletown, 9-40.
P8812 No. 73 Sqn., Debden, 9-40; shot down by Bf 109Es over Kent, 23-9-40; Sgt. M.E. Leng wounded.
P8813 No. 96 Sqn., Cranage, 12-40.
P8818 No. 601 Sqn., A.A.F., Tangmere, 9-40; shot down over Kent, 6-9-40; F/O W.H. Rhodes-Moorehouse killed.

R2680 No. 238 Sqn., St. Eval, 8-40; suffered landing accident, 3-9-40; Sgt. F.A. Sibley unhurt, and aircraft repaired. No. 56 O.T.U. No. 32 Sqn. No. 183 Sqn. No. 55 O.T.U.; crashed 2 miles north of Dumfries, 19-4-43.
R2681 No. 238 Sqn., St. Eval, 8-40. No. 59 O.T.U. No. 5 F.T.S. No. 56 O.T.U. Catterick Stn. Flt. S.O.C., 27-11-44.
R2682 No. 238 Sqn., Middle Wallop, 9-40; shot down by Bf 109Es over Kent, 11-9-40; P/O J.L. Malinski (Polish) killed.
R2683 No. 145 Sqn. *Converted to Trop. Mk IIA,* ***BV163***, and shipped to Malta, c.2-41. S.O.C., 27-4-42.
R2684 No. 302 (Polish) Sqn., Duxford, 10-40; damaged in forced landing, 16-10-40; P/O J.L. Malinski (Polish) unhurt. Aircraft repaired. No. 46 Sqn. No. 121 Sqn. No. 52 O.T.U. No. 59 O.T.U.; crashed while low flying near Appleby, Cumberland, 5-7-42.
R2685 No. 303 (Polish) Sqn., Northolt, 9-40; suffered accident, 6-9-40; F/L J.A. Kent unhurt, and aircraft repaired. No. 52 O.T.U. No. 1 Air Armament School. S.O.C., 24-2-45.
R2686 No. 56 Sqn., North Weald. No. 253 Sqn., Kenley, 9-40; destroyed in accident (circumstances not known), 20-9-40.
R2687 No. 87 Sqn. No. 302 (Polish) Sqn.; crashed near Arundel, Sussex, 20-2-41.
R2688 No. 303 (Polish) Sqn., Northolt, 9-40. No. 258 Sqn., Acklington, 12-40. No. 615 Sqn., A.A.F. No. 56 O.T.U. S.O.C., 9-12-44.
R2689 No. 56 Sqn., North Weald. No. 249 Sqn.; S.O.C., 1-12-40.

T9521 No. 402 Sqn., R.C.A.F., Digby, 9-40.
T9522 *Trop. Mk. I.* No. 261 Sqn., Ta Kali, Malta, 12-40. No. 335 (Greek) Sqn., Aqir, Palestine, 10-41.
T9523 No. 316 (Polish) Sqn., Pembrey, 2-41.
T9524 No. 232 Sqn., Castletown, 9-40.
T9527 No. 253 Sqn., Kenley, 10-40.
T9530 No. 317 (Polish) Sqn., Acklington, 2-41.
T9536 *Trop. Mk. I.* To the Middle East, c.12-40. No. 33 Sqn., Eleusis, Greece, 3-41. No. 73 Sqn., Tobruk, 8-41. No. 208 Sqn., L.G.134, Western Desert; abandoned at Sollum, 18-10-41, but recaptured 5-42.

HAWKER CANADIAN HURRICANE MARK I. Pilot production batch of 40 aircraft, *P5170-P5209*, built by the Canadian Car & Foundry Corporation, Montreal, during 1939-40. Powered by Rolls-Royce Merlin IIs and IIIs with Watts two-blade fixed-pitch or D.H. three-blade variable-pitch propellers; mnost aircraft were shipped to the U.K. between March and November 1940. Note: Aircraft of this batch were not correctly re-designated Hurricane Mark Xs, and always remained "Canadian Mark Is".
P5170 *Production check trials* at Brooklands, Farnborough and Boscombe Down, 3-40 to 8-40.
P5172 No. 253 Sqn., Kenley, 9-40.
P5176 Forced landed in Eire, 1942; *transferred to the Irish Air Corps* as "***93***".
P5178 No. 43 Sqn., Tangmere, 9-40.
P5179 No. 253 Sqn., Kenley, 9-40.
P5180 No. 401 Sqn., R.C.A.F., Northolt, 9-40.
P5181 No. 253 Sqn., Kenley, 9-40.
P5182 No. 151 Sqn., Digby, 9-40; damaged by Ju 88A off the Lincolnshire coast, 30-9-40; Sgt. D.B.F. Nicholls unhurt.
P5183 *Converted to Sea Hurricane IA* by General Aircraft Ltd., 3-41. Merchant Ship Fighter Unit, Speke, c.4-41.
P5187 No. 1 Sqn., Wittering, 10-41; destroyed in landing accident, 29-10-40; P/O J. Dygryn (Czech) unhurt.
P5188 No. 43 Sqn., Usworth, 10-40.
P5189 No. 501 Sqn., A.A.F., Kenley, **SD-M**, 9-40.
P5191 No. 43 Sqn., Tangmere, 8-40.
P5193 No. 501 Sqn., A.A.F., Kenley, **SD-O**, 10-40; shot down by Bf 109Es, 25-10-40; Sgt. S.A.H. Whitehouse killed.
P5194 No. 501 Sqn., A.A.F., Kenley, 10-40; shot down by Bf 109Es at Rochford, 15-10-40; Sgt. R.W.E. Jarrett wounded.
P5195 No. 56 O.T.U., Sutton Bridge, 11-40.
P5196 No. 43 Sqn., Tangmere, 8-40.
P5200 No. 501 Sqn., A.A.F., Kenley, 9-40; shot down by Bf 109E over Kent, 11-9-40; Sgt. T.G. Pickering unhurt.
P5206 No. 249 Sqn., North Weald, 9-40.
P5208 No. 601 Sqn., A.A.F., Debden, 8-40; shot down by Bf 109Es over Debden, 31-8-40; P/O T. Grier unhurt.
P5209 No. 111 Sqn., Croydon, 8-40.

HAWKER HURRICANE MARK I (Gloster-built). Second production batch of 100 aircraft built by Gloster Aircraft Co., Ltd., Brockworth, Glos., under Contract No. 19773/39/23a. Rolls-Royce Merlin III engine and Rotol or D.H. propellers. *R4074-R4123*, *R4171-R4200* and *R4213-R4232*. Deliveries commenced, July 1940; completed, August 1940; average rate of production, approximately three aircraft per day.
R4074 No. 151 Sqn., 9-40. No. 46 Sqn., Stapleford Tawney; lost in unknown circumstances, 22-10-40.
R4075 No. 1 Sqn., Northolt; shot down south of Harwich, 15-8-40; Sgt. M.M. Shanahan killed.
R4076 No. 3 Sqn. No. 17 Sqn. No. 331 (Norwegian) Sqn., Catterick, 7-41. No. 56 O.T.U. No. 2 Tactical Exercise Unit. S.O.C., 6-6-44.
R4077 No. 3 Sqn. Sumburgh Fighter Flt. No. 17 Sqn. Transferred to Admiralty Charge, 23-12-41, for *conversion to Sea Hurricane.*
R4078 No. 3 Sqn. Sumburgh Fighter Flt. No. 17 Sqn. Transferred to Admiralty Charge, 12-12-41, for *conversion to Sea Hurricane.*
R4079 No. 3 Sqn. No. 245 Sqn.; crashed near Cushendall, Co. Antrim, 30-11-40.
R4080 No. 59 O.T.U.; crashed on training flight near Crosby, 11-11-41.
R4081 No. 32 Sqn. No. 253 Sqn. No. 303 (Polish) Sqn. No. 71 Sqn. No. 56 O.T.U. *Converted to Mark II,* ***DR358***, 8-41.
R4082 *Supplied to South African Air Force*, 20-8-40.
R4083 *Supplied to South African Air Force*, 20-8-40.
R4084 No. 310 (Czech) Sqn., Duxford; shot down by Bf 109E, 9-9-40; F/O G.L. Sinclair baled out near Purley with minor injury.
R4085 No. 310 (Czech) Sqn., Duxford; shot down over Billericay by Bf 109E, 15-9-40; S/L A. Hess baled out unhurt.
R4086 No. 213 Sqn. No. 111 Sqn. No. 59 O.T.U.; crashed near Crosby after air collision, 20-12-41.
R4087 No. 310 (Czech) Sqn., Duxford; shot down by Bf 109E near Chatham, 15-9-40; Sgt. H. Hrbacek (Czech) baled out slightly wounded.
R4088 No. 257 Sqn. No. 55 O.T.U.; Missing on training flight, 16-7-41.
R4089 No. 310 (Czech) Sqn., Duxford, 9-40. Became ***4504M***, 2-44.
R4090 No. 4 Ferry Pilots' Pool; abandoned after engine failure, Rora Moss, Longside, Aberdeen, 1-8-40.
R4091 No. 17 Sqn. No. 308 (Polish) Sqn. No. 401 Sqn., R.C.A.F. No. 56 O.T.U. *Converted to Hurricane Mark II,* ***DR373***, 9-41, and shipped to Russia.
R4092 No. 601 Sqn., A.A.F.; shot down by Messerschmitts off Portland, 11-8-40; P/O R.S. Demetriadi killed.
R4093 No. 56 Sqn., North Weald; shot down by Bf 109Es near Rochford, 13-8-40; P/O C.C.O. Joubert baled out slightly wounded.
R4094 No. 253 Sqn. No. 257 Sqn., Tangmere; shot down by Bf 109Es off St. Catherine's Point; Sgt. K.B. Smith killed.
R4095 No. 302 (Polish) Sqn. To Merchant Ship Fighter Unit and *converted to Sea Hurricane IA* (on Admiralty Charge), 30-3-42.
R4096 No. 111 Sqn., Martlesham Heath; shot down near Martlesham, 26-8-40; Sgt. R.F. Sellars slightly wounded.
R4097 No. 238 Sqn., Middle Wallop; shot down by Bf 109Es between Weymouth and Swanage, 11-8-40; F/O M. Steborowski (Polish) killed.
R4098 No. 232 Sqn. No. 59 O.T.U.; abandoned in poor visibility near Dumfries, 17-3-42.
R4099 No. 213 Sqn. No. 238 Sqn. No. 59 O.T.U.; crashed on take-off at Crosby, 25-8-41.
R4100 No. 303 (Polish) Sqn. No. 59 O.T.U.. Ultimate disposal not known.
R4101 No. 501 Sqn. No. 306 (Polish) Sqn. No. 52 O.T.U.; damaged beyond repair, 3-8-41.
R4102 No. 43 Sqn., Tangmere; shot down by enemy fighters over the Isle of Wight, 8-8-40; P/O H.C. Upton unhurt.
R4103 To the Middle East. No. 2 Sqn., S.A.A.F. No. 73 O.T.U. Aden Defence Flt. S.O.C., 1-12-43.
R4104 *Supplied to the South African Air Force* .
R4105 No. 501 Sqn., A.A.F. No. 605 Sqn., A.A.F. No. 245 Sqn. Transferred to Admiralty Charge, 4-41, for *conversion to Sea Hurricane IA.*
R4106 No. 32 Sqn., Biggin Hill; shot down by Bf 109Es at Chartham Hatch, near Canterbury, Kent, 18-8-40; Sgt. L.H.B. Pearce baled out with burns.
R4107 No. 43 Sqn. No. 1 Sqn., R.C.A.F. No. 55 O.T.U. No. 316 (Polish) Sqn. No. 87 Sqn. No. 55 O.T.U.; crashed near Annan, 28-6-43.
R4108 No. 43 Sqn., Tangmere; crashed while landing at Tangmere, 12-8-40.
R4109 No. 43 Sqn., Tangmere, 8-40. No. 1 Sqn., R.C.A.F. No. 213 Sqn; crashed near Castletown, 18-3-41, following air collision with another Hurricane.
R4110 No. 43 Sqn., Tangmere, 8-40. S.O.C., 1-9-43.
R4111 No. 615 Sqn., Kenley, 8-40; shot down by Bf 109Es and crashed on Rochester airfield, 26-8-40; P/O D.H. Hone wounded in legs.
R4112 No. 111 Sqn. No. 229 Sqn. No. 601 Sqn., A.A.F. No. 59 O.T.U.; crashed near Heathergill, Dumfries, 13-8-41.
R4113 No. 8 F.T.S. No. 56 O.T.U. To India, 1943; S.O.C., 28-9-44.
R4114 No. 56 Sqn. No. 249 Sqn., North Weald; shot down by Bf 109Es near Maidstone, 7-9-40; P/O R.D.S. Fleming killed.
R4115 No. 242 Sqn. No. 111 Sqn. No. 59 O.T.U.; crashed at Sleinsford, Northumberland, 23-9-42.
R4116 No. 615 Sqn., A.A.F., Kenley, 8-40; shot down and force landed near Ashford, Kent, 28-8-40; P/O S.J. Madle slightly injured.
R4117 No. 56 Sqn., North Weald, 8-40; shot down by Bf 109Es over Thames Estuary, 28-8-40; F/O P.S. Weaver unhurt.
R4118 No. 605 Sqn., A.A.F. No. 111 Sqn. No. 59 O.T.U. No. 56 O.T.U. S.O.C. in India, 10-44.
R4119 No. 615 Sqn., A.A.F., Kenley, 8-40. No. 5 F.T.S. Became ***3452M***, 11-42.
R4120 No. 501 Sqn., A.A.F. No. 601 Sqn., A.A.F. No. 501 Sqn., A.A.F.; crashed at Wool, Dorset, 30-4-41.
R4121 No. 615 Sqn., A.A.F., Kenley, 8-40; shot down by Bf 109E off Sheerness, 26-8-40; P/O J.A.P. McClintock baled out unhurt.
R4122 No. 32 Sqn. No. 315 (Polish) Sqn. No. 303 (Polish) Sqn. No. 55 O.T.U. No. 239 Sqn. No. 56 O.T.U. No. 2 Tactical Exercise Unit. S.O.C., 7-6-44.

R4123 No. 317 (Polish) Sqn. No. 55 O.T.U.; struck by Hurricane ***P2906*** at dispersal, Usworth, 9-3-42, and damaged beyond repair.

R4171 No. 1 Sqn., R.C.A.F., Northolt; shot down by Bf 109Es near West Malling, 1-9-40; F/O A. Yuile, RCAF, baled out unhurt.
R4172 No. 111 Sqn., Croydon, 9-40; shot down by Bf 109Es near Folkestone, 4-9-40; P/O J. Maccinski (Polish) baled out but killed by enemy fighters while descending.
R4173 No. 303 (Polish) Sqn., Northolt, 9-40; shot down by Bf 109Es over Essex, 7-9-40, and crashed near Loughton, Essex; F/O M. Pisarek (Polish) baled out unhurt.
R4174 No. 17 Sqn., Debden, 9-40; shot down (probably by Do 17Z) and crashed on Foulness Island, 3-9-40; F/O D.W.H. Hanson baled out at about 100 feet and was killed.
R4175 No. 303 (Polish) Sqn., Northolt; destroyed by bomb while taxying during raid on Northolt, 6-10-40; Sgt. A. Suidak (Polish) killed.
R4176 No. 145 Sqn., Westhampnett, 8-40; shot down off the Isle of Wight, 12-8-40; F/L W. Pankratz (Polish) killed.
R4177 No. 145 Sqn., Westhampnett, 8-40. Merchant Ship Fighter Unit; *converted to Sea Hurricane IA*, 4-41. Transferred to R.C.A.F. Charge, 4-6-42.
R4178 No. 303 (Polish) Sqn. No. 504 Sqn., A.A.F. No. 249 Sqn. No. 316 (Polish) Sqn. Transferred to Admiralty Charge, 23-10-41, *converted to Sea Hurricane IA*.
R4179 No. 303 (Polish) Sqn. No. 8 F.T.S. No. 32 M.U.; crashed while landing at St. Athan, 18-7-44.
R4180 No. 145 Sqn., Westhampnett, 8-40; shot down off the Isle of Wight, 12-8-40; Sgt. J. Kwiecinski (Polish) killed.
R4181 No. 151 Sqn., North Weald, 8-40; shot down off the Essex coast, 18-8-40; P/O J.B. Ramsay killed.
R4182 No. 151 Sqn., North Weald, 8-40; S.O.C., 9-40.
R4183 No. 151 Sqn., North Weald, 8-40. No. 52 O.T.U.; collided with Hurricane ***W9149*** and crashed, 3-8-41.
R4184 No. 151 Sqn., North Weald, 8-40; collided with Hurricane ***V7434*** during night take-off at Digby, 26-10-40; Sgt. R. Holder killed.
R4185 No. 151 Sqn., North Weald, 8-40; crashed following engine failure, 16-9-40.
R4186 No. 615 Sqn., A.A.F., Kenley, 8-40; destroyed in air raid on Kenley, 18-8-40.
R4187 No. 111 Sqn., Croydon, 8-40; shot down near Kenley, 18-8-40.
R4188 No. 111 Sqn., Croydon, 8-40. No. 238 Sqn. No. 59 O.T.U.; crashed at Cornhill-on-Tweed, Northumberland, 5-5-43.
R4189 No. 257 Sqn. No. 601 Sqn., A.A.F. No. 607 Sqn., Tangmere, 9-40; shot down by enemy fighters off Selsey, 28-9-40; F/L W.E. Gore killed.
R4190 No. 257 Sqn. No. 46 Sqn. No. 257 Sqn. No. 46 Sqn., Digby, 2-41; crashed at Endery Farm, Asterby, Lincs, 22-2-41.
R4191 No. 145 Sqn. No. 601 Sqn., A.A.F., Tangmere, 8-40; reported Missing, 18-8-40, but no details of circumstances or pilot.
R4192 No. 615 Sqn., A.A.F. No. 317 (Polish) Sqn. No. 71 O.T.U. S.O.C., 28-8-44.
R4193 No. 111 Sqn., Croydon, 8-40; aircraft abandoned after pilot experienced control difficulties, 15-8-40.
R4194 No. 615 Sqn., A.A.F., Kenley, 8-40. No. 9 F.T.S. S.O.C., 22-12-41.
R4195 No. 111 Sqn., Croydon, 8-40. No. 257 Sqn., North Weald, 10-40; shot down by British A.A. guns at Lydd, Kent, 22-10-40; P/O N.B. Heywood killed.
R4196 No. 56 Sqn. No. 43 Sqn. No. 17 Sqn. No. 55 O.T.U. S.O.C., 13-7-42.
R4197 No. 56 Sqn., North Weald, 8-40; shot down by Bf 109E near North Weald, 31-8-40; F/L P.S. Weaver killed.
R4198 No. 56 Sqn., North Weald, 8-40; shot down by Bf 109E over the Thames Estuary, 28-8-40; P/O M.C. Maxwell slightly wounded.
R4199 No. 17 Sqn., Tangmere, 8-40; shot down by Bf 109 south of Tangmere, 25-8-40; F/L A.W.A. Bayne rescued from sea unhurt.
R4200 No. 32 Sqn., 8-40. No. 315 (Polish) Sqn. No. 303 (Polish) Sqn. No. 55 O.T.U. To the Middle East. S.O.C., 1-4-44.

R4213 No. 151 Sqn., North Weald, 8-40; shot down by Bf 110s near Rochester, Kent; Sgt. F. Gmur (Polish) killed.
R4214 No. 601 Sqn., A.A.F., 8-40; damaged in combat near Worthing, 4-9-40; F/O J.S. Jankiewicz (Polish) wounded. Aircraft repaired and *converted to Sea Hurricane IA*; to Admiralty Charge, 18-3-42.
R4215 No. 601 Sqn., A.A.F., 8-40; details of disposal not known.
R4216 No. 32 Sqn. No. 317 (Polish) Sqn. No. 59 O.T.U. No. 56 O.T.U. No. 2 Tactical Exercise Unit; crashed at Dunbog, Fife, 27-3-44.
R4217 No. 303 (Polish) Sqn. No. 56 O.T.U. No. 55 O.T.U.; crashed at Southwaite Head, Cumberland, 20-7-42.
R4218 No. 145 Sqn., 8-40. No. 601 Sqn., A.A.F. *Converted to Hurricane Trop. Mk. IIA*, ***BV155***, 10-40. No. 73 Sqn., El Adem, Libya, 2-42. No. 208 Sqn.; force landed after combat with Bf 109Fs near El Amanein, 15-8-42.
R4219 No. 501 Sqn., A.A.F., Hawkinge; shot down by Bf 109Es near Canterbury, Kent, 18-8-40; P/O F. Kozlowski (Polish) seriously wounded.
R4220 No. 615 Sqn., A.A.F., Kenley, 8-40. No. 402 Sqn., R.C.A.F. No. 52 O.T.U. No. 56 O.T.U.; crashed at Chushford Toll, Fife, 27-4-42.
R4221 No. 615 Sqn., A.A.F., Kenley, 8-40; shot down by Bf 109Es and crashed near Orpington, Kent, 18-8-40; P/O P.H. Hugo (South African) wounded in the leg.
R4222 No. 501 Sqn., A.A.F., Hawkinge, 8-40. No. 245 Sqn. No. 8 F.T.S. Became ***2872M***, 1-42.
R4223 No. 501 Sqn., A.A.F., Gravesend, 8-40; shot down by Bf 109Es, 29-8-40; Sgt. W.J. Green baled out unhurt near Hawkinge.
R4224 No. 145 Sqn., 8-40. No. 17 Sqn., Debden, 9-40; shot down by Bf 110 near North Weald, 3-9-40; S/L A.G. Miller unhurt.
R4225 No. 145 Sqn., 8-40. No. 43 Sqn.; crashed at Hazeldene, Co. Durham, 10-11-40.
R4226 No. 111 Sqn., Drem, 9-40; aircraft damaged in accident, 23-9-40. Repaired and *converted to Sea Hurricane IA*, and transferred to Admiralty Charge, 20-7-41.
R4227 No. 145 Sqn., 9-40. No. 43 Sqn., 10-40; abandoned one mile off May Island, Firth of Forth, 15-12-40.
R4228 No. 111 Sqn., Drem, 9-40. No. 87 Sqn. No. 1449 Flt.; ditched 4 miles SW of St. Agnes, Cornwall, after engine failure, 1-11-42.
R4229 No. 56 Sqn., 8-40. No. 249 Sqn., North Weald, 9-40; shot down by Bf 109Es near Maidstone, Kent, 6-9-40; S/L J. Grandy baled out slightly wounded.
R4230 No. 56 Sqn., 8-40. No. 249 Sqn., North Weald, 9-40; shot down by Bf 109Es near Maidstone, Kent, 7-9-40; Sgt. F.W.G. Killingback baled out wounded.
R4231 No. 43 Sqn., 9-40. No. 56 O.T.U. No. 9 Group Comms. Flt. Netheravon Stn. Flt. No. 38 Group Comms. Flt. S.O.C., 20-12-44.
R4232 No. 56 Sqn., 9-40. No. 238 Sqn. No. 59 O.T.U. No. 55 O.T.U.; crashed in cloud 2 miles south of Langholm, Dumfries, 6-12-42.

HAWKER HURRICANE MARK I (Gloster-built). Third (main) production batch of 1,700 aircraft built by Gloster Aircraft Co., Ltd., Brockworth, Glos., during 1940-41 under Contract No. 85730/40/C.23a. All aircraft with metal wings, Merlin III engines and D.H. variable-pitch or Rotol constant-speed propellers. Production divided into four component runs:

Part 1. 500 aircraft. Delivered between July and November 1940; average rate of production, five aircraft per day. *V6533-V6582, V6600-V6649, V6665-V6704, V6722-V6761, V6776-V6825, V6840-V6889, V6913-V6962, V6979-V7028, V7042-V7081, V7099-V7138, V7156-V7195.*
V6533 No. 71 Sqn., Church Fenton, 9-40.
V6534 No. 56 Sqn., North Weald, 2-41. No. 331 (Norwegian) Sqn., Catterick, 7-41.
V6535 *Converted to Trop. Mark IIA* as ***DG630***, 4-41, and shipped to the Middle East. S.O.C., 1-1-47.
V6536 *Converted to Sea Hurricane IA*, c.1-41, and transferred to Admiralty Charge.
V6537 *Converted to Sea Hurricane IA*, c.1-41, and transferred to Admiralty Charge.
V6538 No. 111 Sqn., Debden, 8-40. *Converted to Mark IIA* as ***DR371***, 8-41, and *shipped to Russia*, 10-3-42.
V6539 No. 111 Sqn., Montrose, 10-40; suffered night landing accident, 25-10-40; Sub-Lt. T.V. Worral, RN, unhurt.
V6541 No. 43 Sqn., Tangmere, 9-40; shot down by Bf 109E over Thames Estuary, 7-9-40; S/L C.B. Hull (South African) killed.
V6542 No. 312 (Czech) Sqn., Speke, 10-40; crashed after running out of fuel, 15-10-40; F/L H.A.G. Comerford unhurt.
V6545 No. 501 Sqn., A.A.F., Kenley, 9-40. No. 317 (Polish) Sqn., Acklington, 2-41. *Converted to Sea Hurricane IA*, 4-41.
V6546 *Converted to Mark IIA* as ***DR374***, 9-42, and *shipped to Russia*, 15-3-42.
V6549 No. 46 Sqn., Stapleford Tawney, 9-40; shot down by Bf 110s over Surrey, 11-9-40; Sgt. R.E. de J'a Hamale (Belgian) unhurt.
V6551 No. 32 Sqn., Acklington, 10-40.
V6552 *Converted for training*, 1941; *armament removed.*
V6553 No. 17 Sqn., Debden, 10-40.
V6555 *Converted to Sea Hurricane IA*, 5-41, and transferred to Admiralty Charge.
V6556 *Converted to Sea Hurricane IA*, 4-41.
V6557 No. 46 Sqn., Stapleford Tawney, 10-40. *Radio trials*, T.R.E., Malvern (date not known).
V6558 No. 257 Sqn., North Weald, 11-40.
V6559 No. 249 Sqn., North Weald, 9-40; slightly damaged in combat near Gatwick, 27-9-40; P/O H.J.S. Beazley slightly wounded in foot. Aircraft repaired. No. 258 Sqn., Acklington, 12-40.
V6562 No. 111 Sqn., Debden, 9-40.
V6564 *Converted to Sea Hurricane IA*, c.4-41.
V6569 No. 302 (Polish) Sqn., Northolt, "**K**", 10-40.
V6570 No. 253 Sqn., Kenley, 10-40; shot down by Bf 109Es near Tunbridge Wells, 11-10-40; P/O L.C. Murch baled out wounded.
V6571 No. 302 (Polish) Sqn., Duxford, 10-40; crashed after running out of fuel over Surrey, 18-10-40; P/O A. Zukowski (Polish) killed.
V6574 No. 249 Sqn., North Weald, 9-40; shot down by Bf 109Es and crashed at Eastchurch, 7-9-40; Sgt. R. Smithson wounded.
V6575 No. 242 Sqn., Coltishall, 10-40; shot down by Do 17Z near Great Yarmouth, 17-10-40; P/O N.N. Campbell (Canadian) killed.
V6576 *Supplied to the Irish Air Corps*, 3-44, as "***111***".
V6577 *Converted to Sea Hurricane IA*, 5-41, and transferred to Admiralty Charge.
V6582 *Converted to Mark IIA* as ***DG639*** by Rolls-Royce Ltd., 5-41, and *shipped to Russia*, 7-9-41.
V6600 No. 501 Sqn., A.A.F., Kenley, 9-40; shot down over Kent, 18-9-40; Sgt. C.J. Saward baled out unhurt.
V6602 *Converted to Mark IIA* as ***DG638*** by Rolls-Royce Ltd., 5-41, and *shipped to Russia*, 7-9-41.
V6604 No. 257 Sqn., North Weald, **DT-T**, 10-40.
V6606 No. 111 Sqn., Debden, 9-40.
V6608 No. 310 (Czech) Sqn., Duxford, 9-40, **NN-B**; shot down over Kent, 27-9-40; F/O G.L. Sinclair baled out unhurt.
V6609 No. 1 (Canadian) Sqn., Northolt, **YO-X**, 9-40.
V6610 No. 249 Sqn., North Weald, 9-40; shot down by

Bf 109E over Kent, 7-9-40; P/O R.G.A. Barclay unhurt. Aircraft repaired and *converted to Sea Hurricane IA*, c.4-41.

V6611 No. 85 Sqn., Church Fenton, ***VY-U***, 9-40.

V6612 No. 501 Sqn., A.A.F., Gravesend, 9-40; shot down near Ashford, Kent, 6-9-40; Sgt. H.C. Adams killed.

V6613 No. 111 Sqn., Debden, 9-40. *Supplied to the Irish Air Corps*, 7-7-43, as "***103***".

V6614 No. 249 Sqn., North Weald, 9-40.

V6616 No. 229 Sqn., Northolt, 9-40; shot down over Kent, 15-9-40; P/O R.R. Smith baled out wounded.

V6617 No. 249 Sqn., North Weald, 9-40; shot down at Faversham, 28-9-40; P/O A.G. Lewis suffered burns.

V6620 No. 501 Sqn., A.A.F., Kenley, 9-40; shot down by Bf 109Es over Kent, 18-9-40; S/L H.A.V. Hogan baled out unhurt.

V6621 No. 253 Sqn., Kenley, 9-40; shot down near Haywards Heath, Sussex, 29-9-40; P/O R.C. Graves slightly wounded.

V6622 No. 249 Sqn., North Weald, 9-40, ***HP-X***; shot down and force landed at West Malling, 27-9-40; P/O R.G.A. Barclay unhurt.

V6625 No. 249 Sqn., North Weald, 9-40.

V6630 No. 601 Sqn. A.A.F., Tangmere, 9-40.

V6631 No. 46 Sqn., Stapleford Tawney, 9-40; shot down near Maidstone, 8-9-40; F/O N.W. Burnett wounded.

V6635 No. 249 Sqn., North Weald, 10-40; damaged in forced landing with engine trouble during patrol; P/O A.R.F. Thompson unhurt.

V6637 No. 253 Sqn., Kenley, 9-40.

V6638 No. 253 Sqn., Kenley, 9-40; shot down, 4-9-40; F/O A.A.G. Trueman killed.

V6644 No. 501 Sqn., A.A.F., Gravesend, 9-40; shot down by Bf 109E over Herne Bay, Kent, 5-9-40; P/O S. Skalski (Polish) baled out wounded.

V6645 No. 501 Sqn., A.A.F., Kenley, 9-40; shot down by Bf 109Es, 27-9-40; P/O E.M. Gunter killed when his parachute failed to open.

V6646 No. 501 Sqn., A.A.F., Gravesend, 9-40; shot down near Ashford, Kent, 6-9-40; Sgt. O.V. Houghton killed.

V6647 No. 601 Sqn., A.A.F., Tangmere, 9-40; shot down by Bf 109Es over Mayfield, Kent, 6-9-40; P/O H.T. Gilbert killed.

V6649 No. 601 Sqn., A.A.F., Exeter, 10-40; damaged in landing accident, 16-10-40; S/L Sir Archibald Hope Bt. unhurt. Aircraft repaired and *converted to Sea Hurricane IA*, 4-41.

V6667 No. 85 Sqn., Church Fenton, **VY-O**, 10-40.

V6669 No. 232 Sqn., Drem, 10-40.

V6670 No. 1 (Canadian) Sqn., Northolt, 9-40; shot down near Romney, 11-9-40; F/O P.W. Lochnan (Canadian) safe.

V6671 No. 257 Sqn., North Weald, 11-40.

V6672 No. 501 Sqn., A.A.F., Kenley, 9-40; shot down by Bf 110 near Godstone, 27-9-40; Sgt. V.H. Ekins baled out wounded.

V6675 No. 242 Sqn., Duxford, **LE-V**, 10-40.

V6677 No. 73 Sqn., Castle Camps, 10-40.

V6680 No. 257 Sqn., North Weald, 11-40; P/O J.K. Kay shot down one Fiat BR.20, 11-11-40.

V6683 No. 249 Sqn., North Weald, 9-40; shot down by Bf 110s at Gatwick, 27-9-40; P/O P.R.F. Burton killed.

V6684 No. 96 Sqn., Cranage, 12-40. No. 303 (Polish) Sqn., Leconfield, 1-41.

V6695 No. 504 Sqn., A.A.F., Filton, 9-40.

V6696 No. 111 Sqn., Dyce, 11-40.

V6697 *Converted to Sea Hurricane IA*, 4-41, and transferred to Admiralty Charge.

V6698 No. 402 Sqn., R.C.A.F., Digby, 12-40.

V6699 No. 605 Sqn., A.A.F., Croydon, 9-40; shot down by Bf 109Es, 28-9-40; F/O P.G. Crofts killed.

V6700 No. 504 Sqn., A.A.F., Filton, 10-40. *Converted to Sea Hurricane IA*, c.4-41, and transferred to Admiralty Charge.

V6701 No. 111 Sqn., Dyce, 10-40.

V6703 No. 615 Sqn., A.A.F., Northolt, 10-40.

V6704 No. 229 Sqn., Northolt, 10-40; shot down by Bf 109Es, 26-10-40; P/O D.B.H. McHardy rescued unhurt.

V6722 No. 605 Sqn., A.A.F., Croydon, 9-40; damaged in combat with Bf 109Es, 20-9-40. P/O W.J. Glowacki (Polish) unhurt. Aircraft repaired. No. 501 Sqn., A.A.F., Kenley, 10-40; shot down by Bf 109Es near Redhill, 15-10-40; Sgt. S.A. Fenemore killed.

V6723 *Converted to Sea Hurricane IA*, c.4-41.

V6724 No. 32 Sqn., Acklington, 10-40.

V6727 No. 238 Sqn., Middle Wallop, 9-40; destroyed in air collision with Hurricane ***V6801***, 30-9-40; P/O R.A. Kings unhurt.

V6728 No. 249 Sqn., North Weald, 10-40; damaged in landing accident, 11-10-40; P/O J.J. Solak (Polish) unhurt.

V6729 No. 249 Sqn., North Weald, 9-40; shot down by Bf 110s at Gatwick, 27-9-40; F/L R.A. Barton unhurt.

V6730 No. 85 Sqn., Gravesend, **VY-O**, 12-40.

V6731 No. 504 Sqn., A.A.F., Filton, 10-40. *Converted to Sea Hurricane IA*, 4-41.

V6732 No. 504 Sqn., A.A.F., Filton, 10-40.

V6733 No. 501 Sqn., A.A.F., Kenley, 10-40; damaged in forced landing at Cuckfield, Sussex, 4-10-40; F/O D.A.E. Jones unhurt.

V6735 No. 302 (Polish) Sqn., Duxford, 10-40; damaged in forced landing after running out of fuel; 26-10-40; P/O S. Kleczkowski (Polish) unhurt. Aircraft repaired. No. 316 Sqn., Pembrey, **SZ-B**, 2-41.

V6737 No. 310 (Czech) Sqn., Duxford, **NN-R**, 11-40.

V6738 No. 73 Sqn., Castle Camps, 9-40. *Converted to Trop. Mk. I* and shipped to the Middle East. *Converted to Trop. P.R. Mk. I.* No. 680 (PR) Sqn., Tunisia, 1943.

V6739 *Converted to Mark IIA* as ***DR352***, 7-41, and *shipped to Russia*, 7-11-41.

V6741 *Converted to Sea Hurricane IC* by H.A.L., c.1942, and transferred to Admiralty Charge.

V6745 No. 229 Sqn., Northolt, 9-40; damaged in combat with Bf 110s, 26-9-40; Sgt. S.W. Merryweather wounded.

V6747 *Trop. Mk. I.* Shipped to the Mediterranean, c.12-40. No. 261 Sqn., Ta Kali, Malta, 2-41. No. 94 Sqn., Ismailia, 6-41. No. 680 Sqn., Tunisia, 1943.

V6750 No. 504 Sqn., A.A.F., Filton, 10-40.

V6751 *Converted to Sea Hurricane IA*, 4-41.

V6755 No. 605 Sqn., A.A.F., 10-40; damaged in combat with Bf 109Es over Ashford, 20-10-40; P/O J.H. Rothwell unhurt.

V6756 No. 253 Sqn., Kenley, 10-40; shot down by Bf 109Es over Kent, 15-10-40; Sgt. E.H.C. Kee unhurt. Aircraft repaired and *converted to Sea Hurricane IA*, 1941.

V6757 No. 71 Sqn., Chruch Fenton, 10-40. *Converted to Trop. Mark IIA* as ***DG619*** by Rolls-Royce Ltd., 3-41. Shipped to the Middle East, 1941. S.O.C., 16-2-42.

V6758 No. 238 Sqn., Chilbolton, 11-40.

V6759 *Converted to Sea Hurricane IA*, c.5-41.

V6760 *Converted to Sea Hurricane IA*, c.5-41.

V6779 *Converted to Sea Hurricane IA*, 4-41.

V6781 No. 601 Sqn., A.A.F., Exeter, 10-40; damaged in landing accident, 31-10-40; Sgt. Fearn unhurt.

V6782 No. 229 Sqn., Northolt, 9-40; shot down by Bf 109Es at Burwash, 27-9-40; F/L R.F. Rimmer killed.

V6783 No. 605 Sqn., A.A.F., Croydon, 10-40; shot down by Bf 109Es over Dorking, 22-10-40; P/O J.A. Milne wounded.

V6784 No. 605 Sqn., A.A.F., Croydon, 10-40; damaged in forced landing, 4-10-40; P/O C.E. English unhurt. Aircraft repaired. No. 5 P.A.F.U., 1941.

V6785 *Converted to Trop. Mark IIA* as ***BV158*** by Rolls-Royce Ltd., 11-41. Shipped to Malta, 12-41. S.O.C., 25-1-42.

V6787 No. 501 Sqn., A.A.F., Kenley, 10-40; damaged in combat with Bf 109Es, 15-10-40; F/O R.C. Dafforn unhurt. Aircraft repaired. No. 402 Sqn., R.C.A.F., Digby, 12-40.

V6790 *Converted to Trop. Mark IIA* as ***BV156*** by Rolls-Royce Ltd., 10-41. Shipped to Malta, 11-41. S.O.C., 22-12-41.

V6792 No. 238 Sqn., Middle Wallop, 9-40; shot down over the Isle of Wight, 26-9-40; P/O R.A. Kings baled out wounded.

V6793 No. 255 Sqn., Kirton-in-Lindsey, 3-41.

V6794 *Converted to Sea Hurricane IA*, 5-41.

V6795 No. 257 Sqn., North Weald, **DT-E**, 10-40.

V6796 No. 255 Sqn., Kirton-in-Lindsey, 3-41. No. 15 P.A.F.U., 1941.

V6797 No. 310 (Czech) Sqn., Duxford, **NN-R**, 10-40.

V6798 No. 316 (Polish) Sqn., Pembrey, **SZ-T**, 2-41.

V6799 No. 501 Sqn., A.A.F., Kenley, **SD-X**, 9-40. No. 238 Sqn., Middle Wallop, 10-40; shot down by Bf 109Es near Yeovil, 7-10-40; P/O A.R. Covington slightly wounded. Aircraft salvaged and *converted to Sea Hurricane IA*, 5-41.

V6800 No. 501 Sqn., A.A.F., Kenley, 10-40; shot down by Bf 109Es north of Ashford, Kent, 7-10-40; F/O N.J.M. Barry killed.

V6801 No. 238 Sqn., Middle Wallop, 9-40; destroyed in air collision with Hurricane ***V6727***, 30-9-40; P/O V.C. Simmonds baled out unhurt.

V6802 No. 257 Sqn., North Weald, 11-40. *Converted to Sea Hurricane IA*, 5-41.

V6803 No. 46 Sqn., Stapleford Tawney, 11-40.

V6806 No. 501 Sqn., A.A.F., Kenley, 10-40; collided with Hurricane ***P2903*** near Cranbrook, 25-10-40; P/O K.W. MacKenzie killed.

V6808 No. 601 Sqn., A.A.F., Exeter, **UF-D**, 10-40.

V6811 No. 312 (Czech) Sqn., Speke, 10-40; crashed after running out of fuel, 15-10-40; P/O T. Vybiral (Czech) baled out unhurt.

V6813 *Trop. Mk. I.* To the Middle East, 1941. No. 71 O.T.U.

V6814 No. 71 Sqn., Church Fenton, **XR-C**, 10-40.

V6815 No. 253 Sqn., Kenley, 10-40. *Converted to Sea Hurricane IA*, 5-41.

V6817 *Converted to Sea Hurricane IA*, 5-41.

V6819 No. 79 Sqn., Pembrey, 10-40. No. 504 Sqn., A.A.F., Exeter, 12-40.

V6820 No. 229 Sqn., Northolt, 10-40; exploded in flight following suspected oxygen system failure, 8-10-40; Sgt. J.R. Farrow killed.

V6822 No. 229 Sqn., Northolt, 10-40.

V6843 *Converted to Sea Hurricane IA*, 5-41.

V6844 No. 605 Sqn., A.A.F., Croydon, 10-40; damaged in combat with Bf 109Es over Ashford, 20-10-40; P/O P.D. Thompson unhurt.

V6845 No. 181 Sqn., Duxford, 9-42.

V6846 No. 312 (Czech) Sqn., Speke, 10-40; crashed after running out of fuel, 15-10-40; Maj. J.K. Ambrus (Czech) unhurt.

V6848 No. 232 Sqn., Drem, 10-40; damaged in landing accident, 29-10-40; Sgt. E.A. Redfern unhurt.

V6852 No. 257 Sqn., North Weald, 10-40; struck by bomb and destroyed while taking off during raid, 29-10-40; Sgt. A.G. Girdwood killed.

V6853 No. 308 (Polish) Sqn., Baginton, 10-40. *Converted to Mark IIA* as ***DG643*** by Rolls-Royce Ltd., 5-41, and *shipped to Russia*, 9-9-41.

V6854 No. 249 Sqn., North Weald, 10-40; shot down by Bf 109Es at Eastchurch, 12-10-40; Adjutant G. Perrin (French) slightly wounded.

V6855 No. 249 Sqn., North Weald, 10-40; force landed following engine failure on patrol, 22-10-40; P/O A.R.F. Thompson unhurt. Aircraft repaired. No. 316 Sqn., Pembrey, **SZ-E**, 3-41.

V6856 No. 145 Sqn., Tangmere, 10-40; severely damaged in landing accident, 18-10-40; P/O M.A. Newling unhurt.

V6857 No. 73 Sqn., Debden, 10-40; shot down by Bf 109Es near Gravesend, 11-10-40; Sgt. R. Plenderleith wounded.

V6858 *Converted to Sea Hurricane IA*, 5-41.

V6861 *Converted to Mark IIA* as ***DG650*** by Rolls-Royce Ltd., 5-41, and *shipped to Russia*, 2-10-41.

V6864 No. 257 Sqn., North Weald, 11-40; P/O G. North shot down one Fiat BR.20, 11-11-40. No. 56 O.T.U., Sutton Bridge, 11-41; collided with Manchester of

No. 97 Sqn., 24-11-41, and crashed at Walpole St. Andrew; Sgt. G.A. Johnstone killed.
V6865 No. 56 O.T.U., Sutton Bridge, 1942; collided with Stirling of No. 7 Sqn., and crashed near Erith Bridge, Cambs, 17-1-42; P/O D.M. Browne killed.
V6867 No. 96 Sqn., Cranage, 12-40. *Converted to Sea Hurricane IA*, 5-41.
V6868 No. 111 Sqn., Dyce, 11-40.
V6873 No. 257 Sqn., North Weald, **DT-O**, 11-40.
V6878 No. 249 Sqn., North Weald, 10-40; crashed following engine failure, 10-10-40; Sgt. E.A. Bayley killed.
V6880 No. 56 Sqn., Middle Wallop, **US-V**, 11-40.
V6881 *Converted to Sea Hurricane IA*, 5-41.
V6886 *Converted to Sea Hurricane IA*, 5-41.
V6913 No. 242 Sqn., Duxford, **LE-G**, 10-40.
V6914 *Converted to Mark IIA* as ***BV165*** by Rolls-Royce Ltd., 1-41, and *shipped to Russia*, 5-9-41.
V6915 No. 87 Sqn., Church Fenton, **LK-P**, 10-40. No. 308 (Polish) Sqn., Baginton, 11-40. *Converted to Mark IIA* as ***DR351***, 7-41, and *shipped to Russia*, 24-10-41.
V6917 No. 601 Sqn., A.A.F., Exeter, 10-40; collided with Hurricane ***P3709*** off Exmouth, 25-10-40; Sgt. May killed.
V6919 No. 71 Sqn., Church Fenton, **XR-T**, 11-40.
V6921 No. 312 (Czech) Sqn., Speke, **DU-R**, 11-40.
V6923 No. 302 (Polish) Sqn., Duxford, 10-40; collided with Hurricane ***P3085***, 29-10-40; F/L H. Czerny (Polish) baled out unhurt.
V6924 *Converted to Sea Hurricane IA*, 5-41, and transferred to Admiralty Charge.
V6929 *Converted to Mark IIA* as ***DG647*** by Rolls-Royce Ltd., 5-41, and *shipped to Russia*, 25-9-41.
V6931 No. 151 Sqn., Digby, **DZ-D**, 11-40.
V6932 No. 1 Sqn., Kenley, 6-41.
V6933 No. 1 Sqn., Kenley, 1-41. *Converted to Sea Hurricane IA*, 5-41.
V6934 *Converted to Trop. Mark IIA* as ***DG629*** by Rolls-Royce Ltd., 4-41, and shipped to the Middle East. S.O.C., 1-1-47.
V6935 No. 312 (Czech) Sqn., Speke, **DU-W**, 11-40.
V6936 No. 331 (Norwegian) Sqn., Catterick, 7-41. *Converted to Mark IIA* as ***DR360***, 8-41, and *shipped to Russia*, 5-11-41.
V6940 *Trop. Mk. I.* No. 9 P.A.F.U., 1941.
V6942 *Converted to Mark IIA* as ***DR391***, 9-41, and shipped to Russia, 14-3-42.
V6943 No. 605 Sqn., A.A.F., Croydon, 10-40; shot down by Bf 109Es near Cranbrook, 26-10-40; P/O J.F.E. Hayter unhurt.
V6944 No. 56 Sqn., North Weald, 2-41.
V6945 No. 316 (Polish) Sqn., Pembrey, SZ-J, 3-41.
V6950 *Converted to Trop. Mark IIA* as ***DG624***, by Rolls-Royce Ltd., 4-41. Shipped to the Middle East, c.12-41. S.O.C., 31-3-45.
V6952 *Converted to Sea Hurricane IA*, 6-41, and transferred to Admiralty Charge.
V6955 No. 255 Sqn., Kirton-in-Lindsey, 3-41.
V6957 *Converted to Mark IIA* as ***DG627*** by Rolls-Royce Ltd., 4-41. No. 135 Sqn., Baginton, 8-41. *Shipped to Russia*, 25-10-41.
V6960 No. 87 Sqn., Charmy Down, **LK-E**, 1-41.
V6979 No. 315 (Polish) Sqn., Acklington, **PK-U**, 2-41.
V6982 No. 253 Sqn., Kenley, 10-40.
V6984 No. 111 Sqn., Dyce, 11-40.
V6985 No. 245 Sqn., Aldergrove, **DX-H**, 11-40. No. 111 Sqn., Dyce, 12-40.
V6988 *Trop. Mk. I.* To the Middle East, c.12-40. No. 30 Sqn., Amriya, 6-41.
V6989 No. 238 Sqn., Chilbolton, 11-40.
V6991 No. 316 (Polish) Sqn., Pembrey, **SZ-F**, 3-41.
V6993 No. 308 (Polish) Sqn., Baginton, 11-40.
V6997 No. 1 Sqn., Kenley, 6-41.
V6998 *Trop. Mk. I.* To the Mediterranean, c.12-41. No. 80 Sqn., Crete, 4-41.
V6999 *Converted to Mark IIA* as ***DG648*** by Rolls-Royce Ltd., 5-41, and *shipped to Russia*, 27-9-41.
V7001 Scheduled for conversion to Sea Hurricane, but crashed at Wrexham, 29-1-42; 2/Off. P.J. Collins, A.T.A., killed.
V7003 *Trop. Mk. I.* To the Middle East, c.12-40. No. 80 Sqn., Crete, 4-41.
V7005 No. 46 Sqn., Stapleford Tawney, 11-40. *Converted to Sea Hurricane IA*, 5-41.
V7006 *Converted to Mark IIA* as ***DR347***, 7-41, and *shipped to Russia*, 11-10-41.
V7009 No. 310 (Polish) Sqn., Duxford, **NN-Q**, 11-40.
V7010 No. 256 Sqn., Squire's Gate, **JT-C**, 3-41.
V7017 No. 317 (Polish) Sqn., Acklington, 2-41.
V7018 *Converted to Mark IIA* as ***DR392***, 9-41. No. 55 O.T.U., 10-41. *Shipped to Russia*, 5-3-42.
V7020 No. 247 Sqn., Roborough, **HP-R**, 12-40.
V7021 No. 238 Sqn., Chilbolton, 12-40. No. 245 Sqn., Aldergrove, **DX-M**, 2-41. *Converted to Mark IIA* as ***DR294***, 9-41, and *shipped to Russia*, 6-3-42.
V7027 *Converted to Sea Hurricane IA*, c.6-41.
V7042 *Converted to Sea Hurricane IA*, 5-41.
V7043 *Converted to Sea Hurricane IA*, 5-41.
V7046 *Converted to Sea Hurricane IA*, c.6-41.
V7049 *Converted to Sea Hurricane IA*, c.6-41.
V7050 *Converted to Sea Hurricane IA*, 6-41.
V7054 *Converted to Mark IIA* as ***DR361***, 8-41. No. 87 Sqn. No. 43 Sqn. No. 56 O.T.U. Damaged beyond repair in accident, 31-10-42.
V7061 *Converted to Trop. Mark IIA* as ***DG626*** by Rolls-Royce Ltd., 4-41. Shipped to the Middle East. S.O.C., 15-2-42.
V7063 No. 312 (Czech) Sqn., Speke, **DU-K**, 12-40. *Converted to Sea Hurricane IA*, 1941.
V7064 No. 258 Sqn., Acklington, 1-41.
V7067 No. 303 (Polish) Sqn., Leconfield, **RF-T**, 1-42.
V7069 *Converted to Mark IIA* as ***DR339***, 7-41, and *shipped to Russia*, 2-10-41.
V7070 *Converted to Sea Hurricane IA*, 1941.
V7071 *Converted to Sea Hurricane IA*, 1941.
V7073 No. 308 (Polish) Sqn., Baginton, 1-41.
V7074 No. 85 Sqn., Gravesend, 12-40,
V7075 No. 46 Sqn., Sherburn-in-Elmet, 4-41.
V7076 No. 257 Sqn., North Weald, 11-40.
V7077 No. 229 Sqn., Northolt, 11-40. *Converted to Sea Hurricane IA*, 1941.
V7079 No. 253 Sqn., Kenley, 12-40.
V7100 No. 56 Sqn., North Weald, 2-41. *Converted to Sea Hurricane IA*, 1941.
V7103 No. 258 Sqn., Acklington, 12-40. *Converted to Trop. Mk. I.* To the Middle East via Takoradi, 1941. No. 71 O.T.U.
V7104 No. 601 Sqn., A.A.F., Exeter, **UF-B**, 12-40.
V7105 No. 56 Sqn., North Weald, 2-41.
V7108 No. 331 (Norwegian) Sqn., Catterick, 7-41.
V7113 *Converted to Sea Hurricane IA*, 1941.
V7118 No. 306 (Polish) Sqn., Church Fenton, **UZ-V**, 11-40.
V7120 No. 151 Sqn., Digby, 11-40.
V7123 No. 183 Sqn., Church Fenton, 11-42.
V7125 *Converted to Sea Hurricane IA*, c.8-41.
V7127 No. 32 Sqn., Acklington, 12-40.
V7129 *Converted to Sea Hurricane IA*, 1941.
V7130 *Converted to Sea Hurricane IA*, 1941.
V7133 *Converted to Sea Hurricane IA*, 1941.
V7135 *Converted to Sea Hurricane IA*, 1941.
V7137 No. 257 Sqn., North Weald, **DT-G**, 11-40.
V7156 No. 232 Sqn., Elgin, 12-40.
V7157 *Converted to Sea Hurricane IA*, 1941.
V7158 *Supplied to the Irish Air Corps*, 21-2-44, as *"**110**"*.
V7161 No. 258 Sqn., Acklington, 12-40. *Converted to Sea Hurricane IA*, 1941, and transferred to Admiralty Charge.
V7162 No. 303 (Polish) Sqn., Leconfield, **RF-B**, 1-41. *Converted to Sea Hurricane IA*, 1941.
V7167 No. 257 Sqn., North Weald, **DT-H**, 11-40.
V7168 *Trop. Mk. I.* No. 5 P.A.F.U., 1-41.
V7170 *Converted to Sea Hurricane IA*, 1941.
V7172 *Converted to Sea Hurricane IA*, 1941.
V7173 *Supplied to the Irish Air Corps*, 29-11-43, as *"**109**"*.
V7176 No. 56 Sqn., North Weald, **US-P**, 2-41.
V7178 No. 238 Sqn., Chilbolton, 12-40.
V7179 No. 56 Sqn., North Weald, 2-41.
V7181 *Trop. Mk. I.* To the Middle East, 1-41, via Takoradi. No. 33 Sqn., Eleusis, Greece, 4-41.
V7182 *Converted to Sea Hurricane IA*, 1941.
V7183 No. 71 Sqn., Church Fenton, 11-40.
V7184 No. 96 Sqn., Cranage, 12-40.
V7186 No. 257 Sqn., North Weald, 11-40; crashed 1-1-41.
V7187 No. 315 (Polish) Sqn., Speke, 1-41.
V7189 *Converted to Sea Hurricane IA*, 1941.
V7191 *Converted to Sea Hurricane IA*, 1941.
V7094 *Converted to Sea Hurricane IA*, 1941.
V7095 *Converted to Sea Hurricane IA*, 1941.

PART 2. 200 aircraft. Delivered during November and December 1940; average rate of production, five aircraft per day. *W9110-W9159, W9170-W9209, W9215-W9244, W9260-W9279, W9290-W9329, W9340-W9359.*

W9110 No. 46 Sqn., Sherburn-in-Elmet, 3-41
W9112 No. 111 Sqn., Dyce, 2-41.
W9114 No. 111 Sqn., Dyce, 2-41. No. 56 O.T.U., Sutton Bridge, 6-41; collided with Hurricane ***P3162*** and crashed at Terrington St. John, 2-6-41; F/Sgt. J.T. Craig DFM killed.
W9115 No. 232 Sqn., Elgin, 3-41. To the Middle East without tropical equipment, 5-41; *converted to Trop. Met. Mk. I*, 1943. No. 1413 (Met.) Flt., Lydda, Palestine, 1944.
W9116 To the Middle East without tropical equipment, 2-41. *Converted to Trop. P.R. Mk. I (3-cameras)*, 6-41. No. 2 P.R.U., Western Desert, 1941; Missing over Benghazi, 3-10-41.
W9117 No. 111 Sqn., Dyce, 2-41.
W9124 No. 247 Sqn., St. Eval, **HP-K**, 4-41. *Converted to Sea Hurricane IA*, c.8-41.
W9128 *Converted to Sea Hurricane IA*, 1941, and transferred to Admiralty Charge.
W9130 No. 257 Sqn., Coltishall, **DT-K**, 3-41.
W9133 *Trop. Mk. I.* To the Middle East via Takoradi, 3-41. No. 261 Sqn., Ta Kali, Malta, 5-41.
W9136 No. 402 Sqn., R.C.A.F., Wellingore, 5-41.
W9137 No. 312 (Czech) Sqn., Jurby, 4-41. No. 331 (Norwegian) Sqn., Catterick, 7-41.
W9139 No. 87 Sqn., Charmy Down, **LK-N**, c.4-41.
W9141 To the Middle East without tropical equipment, 2-41. *Converted to Trop. Mk. I*, 4-41. No. 80 Sqn., Haifa, Palestine, 6-41.
W9150 No. 96 Sqn., Cranage, 3-41.
W9151 No. 1 Sqn., Kenley, c.2-41. No. 79 Sqn., Baginton, 3-41.
W9154 No. 87 Sqn., Colerne, **LK-D**, 3-41.
W9173 No. 87 Sqn., Colerne, **LK-V**, 4-41.
W9174 No. 96 Sqn., Cranage, 4-41. *Converted to Sea Hurricane IA*, 1941, and transferred to Admiralty Charge.
W9175 No. 402 Sqn., R.C.A.F., Wellingore, 5-41.
W9176 No. 238 Sqn., Chilbolton, 4-41.
W9179 No. 111 Sqn., Dyce, 4-41.
W9180 No. 56 O.T.U., Sutton Bridge, 1941; collided with Hurricane ***V7469***; Sgt. F. Pokorny (Czech) injured in crash landing near Walpole St. Peter.
W9181 No. 1 Sqn., Kenley, c.2-41, *Converted to Trop. Mark IIA* as ***DG635*** by Rolls-Royce Ltd., 4-41. Shipped to the Middle East, but diverted to India, c.12-41; P.R.U., Calcutta, 2-42; assumed lost in Burma, 2-42.
W9182 *Converted to Sea Hurricane IA*, 1941.
W9183 No. 317 (Polish) Sqn., Ouston, 4-41.
W9185 To the Middle East without tropical equipment, 4-41. No. 71 O.T.U.
W9188 *Converted to Sea Hurricane IA*, 1941, and transferred to Admiralty Charge.
W9191 *Converted to Mark IIA* as ***DR345***, 7-41, and *shipped to Russia*, 11-10-41.
W9192 No. 247 Sqn., St. Eval, **HP-H**, 4-41.
W9196 No. 87 Sqn., Colerne, **LK-B**, 4-41.
W9197 *Trop. Mark I.* To the Middle East, 2-41. No. 73 Sqn., Bu Amoud, 4-41. No. 274 Sqn., Gerawla, 6-41.

W9198 *Trop. Mark I.* To the Middle East, 2-41. No. 73 Sqn., Bu Amoud, 4-41.
W9199 No. 232 Sqn., Montrose, 4-41.
W9203 No. 245 Sqn., Aldergrove, **DX-T**, c.5-41.
W9205 No. 17 Sqn., Martlesham Heath, 2-41.
W9209 *Converted to Sea Hurricane I,* 11-40, and transferred to Admiralty Charge.
W9215 *Converted to Sea Hurricane I,* 11-40, and transferred to Admiralty Charge.
W9216 *Converted to Sea Hurricane I,* 11-40.
W9218 *Converted to Sea Hurricane I,* 11-40, and transferred to Admiralty Charge.
W9219 *Converted to Sea Hurricane I,* 11-40.
W9220 *Converted to Sea Hurricane I,* 11-40.
W9221 *Converted to Sea Hurricane I,* 11-40, and transferred to Admiralty Charge.
W9222 *Converted to Sea Hurricane I,* 11-40.
W9223 *Converted to Sea Hurricane I,* 11-40, and transferred to Admiralty Charge.
W9224 *Converted to Sea Hurricane I,* 11-40.
W9225 *Trop. Mk. I.* To the Middle East via Takoradi, c.2-41. No. 680 (PR) Sqn., 1943 (communications duties).
W9226 *Trop. Mk. I.* To the Middle East via Takoradi, c.2-41. No. 260 Sqn., Haifa, Palestine, "**J**", 8-41.
W9228 *Trop. Mk. I.* To the Middle East via Takoradi, c.2-41. No. 450 Sqn., R.A.A.F., Damascus, 7-41.
W9231 *Trop. Mk. I.* To the Middle East via Takoradi, c.2-41. No. 73 Sqn., Bu Amoud, 4-41.
W9233 No. 316 (Polish) Sqn., Pembrey, **SZ-H**, 2-41.
W9237 *Converted to Sea Hurricane IA,* 1941.
W9238 *Trop. Mk. I.* To the Middle East by sea, 2-41. No. 213 Sqn. Famagusta, Cyprus, 6-41. No. 30 Sqn., Heliopolis, 2-42.
W9239 No. 245 Sqn., Aldergrove, **DX-M**, 4-41.
W9242 *Trop. Mk. I.* To the Middle East by sea, 3-41. No. 680 (PR) Sqn., 1943 (communications duties).
W9244 No. 46 Sqn., Sherburn-in-Elmet, 3-41.
W9265 *Converted to Trop. Mk. IIA* as ***DR356,*** 7-41, and *shipped to Russia,* 5-11-41.
W9267 *Trop. Mk. I.* To the Middle East via Takoradi, 2-41. *Converted to Trop. Tac R Mk. I.* No. 208 Sqn., Tmimi, 1-42.
W9268 *Trop. Mk. I.* To the Middle East via Takoradi, 2-41. No. 73 Sqn., Bu Amoud, 4-41.
W9269 *Trop. Mk. I.* To the Middle East via Takoradi, 2-41. No. 274 Sqn., Gerawla, 6-41.
W9270 No. 247 Sqn., Roborough, 2-41, **HP-Y**. *Modified as Trop. Mk. I.* To the Middle East via Takoradi, 4-41. No. 213 Sqn., Famagusta, Cyprus, 6-41.
W9271 *Trop. Mk. I.* To the Middle East, 4-41. No. 94 Sqn., Ismailia, 6-41.
W9272 No. 317 (Polish) Sqn., Ouston, 4-41. *Converted to Sea Hurricane IA,* 1941.
W9274 To the Middle East without tropical equipment, via Takoradi, 3-41. No. 213 Sqn., Nicosia, Cyprus, 6-41.
W9276 *Converted to Sea Hurricane I,* 1941, and transferred to Admiralty Charge.
W9277 *Converted to Sea Hurricane I,* 1941, and transferred to Admiralty Charge.
W9279 *Converted to Sea Hurricane IA,* 1941.
W9290 To the Middle East without tropical equipment, via Takoradi, 3-41. No. 213 Sqn., Nicosia., Cyprus, 6-41, "**B**". No. 335 (Greek) Sqn., Aqir, Palestine, 10-41.
W9291 To the Middle East without tropical equipment, via Takoradi, 3-41. No. 213 Sqn., Nicosia, Cyprus, 6-41. No. 30 Sqn., Heliopolis, 2-42.
W9293 *Trop. Mk. I.* To the Middle East, c.2-41. No. 73 Sqn., Bu Amoud, 4-41.
W9299 *Trop. Mk. I.* To the Middle East via Takoradi, 3-41. No. 33 Sqn., Amriya, 6-41.
W9300 *Trop. Mk. I.* To the Middle East via Takoradi, 3-41. *Modified as Trop. Tac R. Mk. I.* No.208 Sqn., 1-42.
W9301 No. 46 Sqn., Sherburn-in-Elmet, 3-41.
W9306 No. 257 Sqn., Coltishall, 3-41.
W9307 No. 229 Sqn., Speke, 4-41.
W9308 No. 111 Sqn , Dyce, 4-41.
W9309 To the Middle East without tropical equipment, via Takoradi, 4-41. No. 213 Sqn., Nicosia, Cyprus, 6-41.
W9311 *Converted to Sea Hurricane I,* 1941.
W9312 *Converted to Sea Hurricane I,* 1941.
W9314 *Trials at H.A.L. and A. & A.E.E. with four 20-mm gun wing,* 2-41. *Became a Hurricane Mk. IIC prototype.*
W9315 *Converted to Sea Hurricane I,* 1941, and transferred to Admiralty Charge.
W9316 *Converted to Sea Hurricane I,* 1941, and transferred to Admiralty Charge.
W9318 *Converted to Sea Hurricane I,* 1941.
W9319 *Converted to Sea Hurricane IA,* 1941.
W9320 *Trop. Mk. I.* To the Middle East via Takoradi, 4-41. No. 80 Sqn., Haifa, Palestine, 5-41.
W9322 *Trop. Mk. I.* To the Middle East via Takoradi, 4-41. No. 94 Sqn., Ismailia, 6-41. No. 274 Sqn., Gerawla, 8-41.
W9324 No. 46 Sqn., Sherburn-in-Elmet, 4-41.
W9326 *Trop. Mk. I.* To the Middle East via Takoradi, 3-41. No. 73 Sqn., Sidi Haneish, 5-41.
W9328 *Trop. Mk. I.* To the Middle East via Takoradi, 3-41. *Modified as Trop. Tac R. Mk. I.* No. 208 Sqn., Antelat, 1-42.
W9342 No. 32 Sqn., Pembrey, 4-41.
W9346 *Trop. Mk. I.* No. 6 Sqn., Tobruk West, 4-41.
W9349 To the Middle East without tropical equipment, via Takoradi, c.4-41. No. 213 Sqn., Nicosia, Cyprus, 6-41.
W9350 *Trop. Mk. I.* To the Middle East via Takoradi, c.4-41. No. 213 Sqn., Nicosia, Cyprus, 6-41.
W9352 *Trop. Mk. I.* To the Middle East via Takoradi, c.4-41. No. 335 (Greek) Sqn., Aqir, Palestine, 10-41.
W9353 *Trop. Mk. I.* To the Middle East via Takoradi, c.4-41. *Converted as Trop. P.R. Mk. I (3-camera).* No. 2 P.R.U., Heliopolis, 11-41 (replacing ***W9116***).
W9354 *Trop. Mk. I.* To the Middle East via Takoradi, c.4-41. *Converted as Trop. Tac R. Mk. I.* No. 208 Sqn., Bu Amoud, 5-42.
W9359 *Trop. Mk. I.* To the Middle East via Takoradi, c.4-41. No. 274 Sqn., Gerawla, 5-41.

Part 3. 400 aircraft. Delivered between December 1940 and March 1941; average rate of production, five aircraft per day. *Z4022-Z4071, Z4085-Z4119, Z4161-Z4205, Z4223-Z4272, Z4308-Z4327, Z4347-Z4391, Z4415-Z4434, Z4482-Z4516, Z4532-Z4581, Z4603-Z4652.*

Z4029 *Trop. Mk. I.* To the Middle East, 5-41. No. 261 Sqn., Habbaniya, Iraq, 7-41. No. 127 Sqn., St. Jean, Palestine, 2-42.
Z4031 *Trop. Mk. I.* To the Middle East, 5-41. No. 80 Sqn., Nicosia, Cyprus, 7-41.
Z4035 No. 46 Sqn., Sherburn-in-Elmet, 5-41.
Z4036 No. 229 Sqn., Speke, 5-41. *Converted to Trop. Mk. I.* To the Middle East. No. 451 Sqn., R.A.A.F., Egypt.
Z4037 *Supplied to the Irish Air Corps,* 7-7-43, as "***106***".
Z4039 *Converted to Sea Hurricane I,* 1941.
Z4040 *Trop. Mk. I.* To the Middle East, 5-41. No. 33 Sqn., Amriya, 7-41.
Z4045 No. 1423 Flt., Kaldadarnes, Iceland, 7-41.
Z4047 *Trop. Mk. I.* To the Middle East, 5-41. No. 335 (Greek) Sqn., Aqir, Palestine, 10-41.
Z4051 *Converted to Sea Hurricane I,* 1941.
Z4053 *Converted to Sea Hurricane I,* 1941.
Z4055 *Converted to Sea Hurricane I,* 1941.
Z4056 *Converted to Sea Hurricane I,* 1941.
Z4057 *Converted to Sea Hurricane I,* 1941.
Z4062 *Trop. Mk. I.* To the Middle East, 6-41. *Converted to Trop. Tac R. Mk. I.* No. 237 Sqn., Benghazi, 1-42.
Z4063 *Trop. Mk. I.* To the Middle East, 6-41. *Converted to Trop. Tac R. Mk. I.* No. 208 Sqn., Gerawla, 10-41.
Z4064 *Trop. Mk. I.* To the Middle East, 6-41. No. 274 Sqn., Gerawla, 8-41.
Z4086 To the Middle East without tropical equipment, 5-41. No. 30 Sqn., Idku, 7-41.
Z4089 To the Middle East without tropical equipment, 5-41. No. 213 Sqn., Famagusta, **AK-U**, 6-43.
Z4093 To the Middle East without tropical equipment, 5-41. No. 71 O.T.U., Egypt, 1941.
Z4094 *Converted to Sea Hurricane I,* 1941.
Z4095 To the Middle East without tropical equipment, 5-41. No. 213 Sqn., Famagusta, Cyprus, **AK-W**, 6-41.
Z4096 To the Middle East without tropical equipment, 5-41.
Z4097 To the Middle East without tropical equipment, 5-41. No. 274 Sqn., Gerawla, 8-41.
Z4102 To the Middle East without tropical equipment, 5-41.
Z4107 To the Middle East without tropical equipment, 5-41. *Tropicalised,* 7-41. No. 33 Sqn., Sidi Haneish, 9-41.
Z4108 To the Middle East without tropical equipment, 5-41. *Tropicalised,* 7-41. No. 33 Sqn., Sidi Haneish, 9-41.
Z4113 To the Middle East without tropical equipment, 5-41. No. 71 O.T.U., Egypt, 1941.
Z4115 *Trop. Mk. I.* To the Middle East, 5-41. No. 261 Sqn., Habbaniya, Iraq, 7-41. No. 127 Sqn., St. Jean, Palestine, 2-42.
Z4162 *Trop. Mk. I.* To the Middle East, 5-41. No. 80 Sqn., Nicosia, Cyprus, 7-41.
Z4163 To the Middle East without tropical equipment, 5-41. No. 213 Sqn., Famagusta, Cyprus, **AK-M**, 6-41.
Z4170 *Trop. Mk. I.* To the Middle East, 5-41. No. 94 Sqn., Ismailia, 7-41.
Z4172 *Trop. Mk. I.* To the Middle East, 5-41. No. 450 Sqn., R.A.A.F., Damascus, Syria, 7-41.
Z4173 *Trop. Mk. I.* To the Middle East, 5-41. No. 73 Sqn., Sidi Haneish and Mersa Matruh, 8-41.
Z4189 *Trop. Mk. I.* To the Middle East, 5-41. No. 274 Sqn., Gerawla, 7-41.
Z4190 *Trop. Mk. I.* To the Middle East, 5-41. No. 73 Sqn., Sidi Haneish, 6-41; Missing over Tobruk, 26-6-41.
Z4203 To the Middle East without tropical equipment, 5-41. No. 213 Sqn., Famagusta, Cyprus, 6-41.
Z4205 To the Middle East without tropical equipment, 5-41. No. 213 Sqn., Famagusta, Cyrpus, 6-41; crashed 29-12-41.
Z4223 To the Middle East without tropical equipment, 5-41. No. 80 Sqn., Nicosia, Cyprus, 7-41.
Z4225 To the Middle East without tropical equipment, 5-41. No. 213 Sqn., Famagusta, Cyprus, 6-41.
Z4227 Scheduled for the Middle East without tropical equipment, but diverted to India, 5-41. No. 258 Sqn., Ratmalana, Ceylon, 3-42.
Z4229 To the Middle East without tropical equipment, 5-41. *Tropicalised,* 7-41. No. 94 Sqn., El Balla, 8-41.
Z4230 *Trop. Mk. I.* To the Middle East, 5-41. No. 30 Sqn., Idku, **RS-C**, 7-41.
Z4231 *Trop. Mk. I.* To the Middle East, 5-41. *Converted to Trop. P.R. Mk. I (3-cameras).* No. 208 Sqn., Gerawla, 10-41. No. 451 Sqn., R.A.A.F., 11-41 (*stripped of cameras*).
Z4233 *Trop. Mk. I.* To the Middle East, 5-41. No. 335 (Greek) Sqn., Bardia, 2-42. No. 127 Sqn., St. Jean, Palestine, 4-42.
Z4238 *Trop. Mk. I.* To the Middle East, 5-41. No. 73 Sqn., Sidi Haneish, 7-41.
Z4239 *Trop. Mk. I.* To the Middle East, 5-41. No. 261 Sqn., Habbaniya, Iraq, 7-41.
Z4242 To the Middle East without tropical equipment, 5-41. No. 213 Sqn., Famagusta, Cyprus, **AK-X**, 6-41.
Z4247 Scheduled for the Middle East without tropical equipment, but diverted to India, c.8-41. No. 258 Sqn., Ratmalana, Ceylon, 3-42.
Z4252 *Trop. Mk. I.* To the Middle East, 5-41. *Converted to Trop. Tac R. Mk. I.* No. 208 Sqn., Gerawla, 10-41.
Z4254 *Trop. Mk. I.* To the Middle East, 5-41. No. 450

Sqn., R.A.A.F., Damascus, Syria, 7-41.

Z4256 *Trop. Mk. I.* No. 95 (MR) Sqn., Fighter Flight, Hastings, Sierra Leone, 9-41.

Z4257 *Trop. Mk. I.* No. 95 (MR) Sqn., Fighter Flight, Hastings, Sierra Leone, 9-41; collided with DC-2, 7-9-42.

Z4266 *Trop. Mk. I.* To the Middle East, 6-41. No. 71 O.T.U., Egypt, 1941.

Z4269 *Trop. Mk. I.* To the Middle East, 6-41. No. 80 Sqn., Nicosia, Cyprus, 8-41.

Z4272 *Trop. Mk. I.* To the Middle East, 6-41. No. 274 Sqn., Gerawla, 8-41.

Z4313 *Trop. Mk. I.* To Takoradi, 5-41. No. 95 (MR) Sqn., Fighter Flight, Hastings, Sierra Leone, 9-41.

Z4322 *Trop. Mk. I.* To the Middle East, 6-41. No. 73 Sqn., Sidi Haneish, 8-41.

Z4348 *Trop. Mk. I.* To the Middle East, 6-41. No. 33 Sqn., Amriya, 8-41.

Z4350 *Trop. Mk. I.* To the Middle East, c.6-41. No. 6 Sqn., Helwan, 1-42.

Z4361 To the Middle East without tropical equipment, 5-41. No. 213 Sqn., Famagusta, Cyprus, **AK-B**, 7-41.

Z4365 *Converted to Sea Hurricane I*, 1941.

Z4366 To the Middle East without tropical equipment, 5-41. No. 213 Sqn., Famagusta, Cyrpus, 6-41. No. 73 Sqn., Sidi Haneish, 7-41.

Z4367 To the Middle East without tropical equipment, 5-41. *Tropicalised*, 6-41. No. 213 Sqn., Famagusta, Cyprus, 6-41.

Z4370 To the Middle East without tropical equipment, 5-41. *Tropicalised*, 6-41. No. 6 Sqn., Tel Aviv, Palestine, 7-41.

Z4372 Scheduled for the Middle East without tropical equipment, but diverted to India, c.11-41. No. 258 Sqn., Ratmalana, Ceylon, 3-42.

Z4373 To the Middle East without tropical equipment, 5-41. *Tropicalised*, 6-41. No. 94 Sqn., Ismailia, 8-41.

Z4374 To the Middle East without tropical equipment, 6-41. No. 213 Sqn., Famagusta, Cyprus, **AK-Y**, 6-41.

Z4375 To the Middle East without tropical equipment, 6-41. No. 450 Sqn., R.A.A.F., Damascus, Syria, 7-41.

Z4380 To the Middle East without tropical equipment, 6-41. No. 261 Sqn., Habbaniya, Iraq, 7-41. No. 71 O.T.U., 12-41.

Z4391 *Trop. Mk. I.* To the Middle East, 6-41. *Converted to Trop. Tac R. Mk. I.* No. 237 Sqn., Benghazi, Libya, 1-42.

Z4419 *Trop. Mk. I.* To the Middle East, 6-41. No. 30 Sqn., Idku, 8-41.

Z4483 *Trop. Mk. I.* To the Middle East, 6-41. *Converted to Trop. Tac R. Mk. I.* No. 237 Sqn., Benghazi, Libya, 1-42.

Z4484 *Trop. Mk. I.* To Takoradi, 6-41. No. 95 (MR) Sqn., Fighter Flight, Hastings, Sierra Leone, 10-41.

Z4486 *Trop. Mk. I.* To the Middle East, 6-41. *Converted to Trop. Tac R. Mk. I.* No. 208 Sqn., El Khanka, 10-41.

Z4489 *Trop. Mk. I.* To the Middle East, 6-41. No. 208 Sqn., 10-41. *Converted to Trop. Mk. IIA* in the Middle East, 1942.

Z4491 *Trop. Mk. I.* To the Middle East, 6-41. No. 73 Sqn., Sidi Haneish, 7-41. No. 274 Sqn., Gerawla, 9-41.

Z4494 *Trop. Mk. I.* To the Middle East, 6-41. No. 335 (Greek) Sqn., Helwan, 1-42.

Z4500 *Converted to Sea Hurricane I*, 1941.

Z4504 *Converted to Sea Hurricane I*, 1941.

Z4508 *Trop. Mk. I.* To the Middle East, 6-41. No. 33 Sqn., Amriya, 8-41.

Z4515 No. 43 Sqn., Drem, **FT-U**, 4-41.

Z4532 *Converted to Sea Hurricane I*, 1941.

Z4544 *Trop. Mk. I.* To the Middle East, via Takoradi, 6-41.

Z4550 *Converted to Sea Hurricane I*, 1941.

Z4551 *Trop. Mk. I.* To the Middle East, 6-41. *Converted to Trop. Tac R. Mk. I.* No. 237 Sqn., Benghazi, Libya, 1-42.

Z4553 *Converted to Sea Hurricane I*, 1941.

Z4554 *Trop. Mk. I.* To the Middle East, 7-41. *Converted to Trop. Tac R. Mk. I.* No. 208 Sqn., El Khanka, 10-41.

Z4555 *Trop. Mk. I.* To the Middle East, 7-41. *Converted to Trop. Tac R. Mk. I.* No. 208 Sqn., Gerawla, 10-41.

Z4557 *Trop. Mk. I.* To the Middle East, 7-41. No. 73 Sqn., Sidi Haneish, 9-41.

Z4561 *Trop. Mk. I.* To the Middle East, 7-41. No. 261 Sqn., Habbaniya, Iraq (8-41), and Mosul, Iraq (10-41).

Z4563 *Trop. Mk. I.* To the Middle East, 7-41. No. 450 Sqn., R.A.A.F., Damascus, Syria, 10-41.

Z4564 *Trop. Mk. I.* To the Middle East, 7-41.

Z4566 *Trop. Mk. I.* To the Middle East, 7-41. No. 94 Sqn., El Ballah, 9-41.

Z4568 *Converted to Sea Hurricane I*, 1941.

Z4569 *Converted to Sea Hurricane I*, 1941.

Z4574 *Trop. Mk. I.* To the Middle East, 7-41. No. 335 (Greek) Sqn., Aqir, Palestine, 10-41.

Z4576 *Trials to develop oil system for tropics*, G.A.C., c.8-41. To India as *Trop. Mk. I.* No. 258 Sqn., Ratmalana, Ceylon, 3-42.

Z4581 *Converted to Sea Hurricane I*, 1941.

Z4604 *Trop. Mk. I.* To the Middle East, 7-41. No. 335 (Greek) Sqn., Aqir, Palestine, 10-41; crashed 15-11-41. Repaired and *converted to Trop. P.R. Mk. I.* No. 680 (PR) Sqn., 2-44.

Z4605 *Converted to Sea Hurricane I*, 1941.

Z4607 No. 1423 Flt., Kaldadarnes, Iceland, 7-41; crashed, 23-9-41.

Z4609 No. 43 Sqn., Drem, **FT-T**, 4-41.

Z4616 *Trop. Mk. I.* To the Middle East, 7-41. *Converted to Trop. Tac R. Mk. I.* No. 208 Sqn., Gerawla, 10-41. No. 237 Sqn., Benghazi, Libya, 1-42.

Z4617 No. 1423 Flt., Kaldadarnes, Iceland, 7-41.

Z4619 *Trop. Mk. I.* To the Middle East, 7-41. No. 80 Sqn., Rayak, Syria, 9-41.

Z4621 *Trop. Mk. I.* To the Middle East, 7-41. No. 450 Sqn., R.A.A.F., Rayak, Syria, 9-41.

Z4624 *Converted to Sea Hurricane I*, 1941.

Z4630 No. 1423 Flt., Kaldadarnes, Iceland, 7-41.

Z4638 *Converted to Sea Hurricane I*, 1941.

Z4639 No. 1423 Flt., Kaldadarnes, Iceland, 7-41.

Z4644 *Trop. Mk. I.* To the Middle East, 7-41. No. 450 Sqn., R.A.A.F., Rayak, Syria, 9-41.

Z4646 *Trials at G.A.C. and A. & A.E.E. to develop modified tropical air filter*, c.6-41. *Converted to Sea Hurricane I*, c.8-41.

Z4649 *Converted to Sea Hurricane I*, 1941.

Z4652 *Trop. Mk. I.* To the Middle East, 7-41. No. 261 Sqn., Mosul. Iraq, 10-41. No. 335 (Greek) Sqn., Aqir, Palestine, 11-41; Missing, 14-3-42.

Part 4. 600 aircraft. Delivered between March and September 1941; average rate of production, approximately three aircraft per day. 150 Mark Is: *Z4686-Z4720, Z4670-4809, Z4832-Z4876, Z4920-Z4939.* 33 Mark IIAs: *Z4940-Z4969, Z4987-Z4989.* 417 Mark IIBs: *Z4990-Z5006, Z5038-Z5087, Z5117-Z5161, Z5202-Z5236, Z5252-Z5271, Z5302-Z5351, Z5376-Z5395, Z5434-Z5483, Z5529-Z5563, Z5580-Z5629, Z5649-Z5693.*

MARK Is.

Z4686 *Converted to Sea Hurricane I*, 1941.

Z4689 *Trop. Mk. I.* To the Middle East, 7-41. No. 6 Sqn., Kufra, Egypt, 9-41.

Z4697 *Trop. Mk. I.* To the Middle East, 8-41. No. 73 Sqn., Amriya, 9-41.

Z4698 *Trop. Mk. I.* To the Middle East, 8-41. No. 73 Sqn., Amriya, 9-41.

Z4700 *Trop. Mk. I.* To the Middle East, 8-41. No. 267 Sqn., Heliopolis (for communications duties), 4-42.

Z4702 No. 1423 Flt., Kaldadarnes, Iceland, 7-41.

Z4703 *Trop. Mk. I.* To the Middle East, 8-41. No. 274 Sqn., Maryut, 10-41.

Z4714 *Trop. Mk. I.* To the Middle East, 8-41. No. 94 Sqn., El Ballah, 10-41.

Z4718 *Trop. Mk. I.* To the Middle East, 8-41. No. 30 Sqmn., Idku, PS-T, 10-41.

Z4762 *Trop. Mk. I.* To the Middle East, 8-41. No. 261 Sqn., Shaibah, Iraq, 9-41.

Z4767 *Trop. Mk. I.* To the Middle East, 8-41. No. 237 Sqn., Western Desert, 10-41.

Z4770 *Retained by G.A.C. for various trials*, 8-41.

Z4772 *Trop. Mk. I.* To the Middle East, 8-41. No. 208 Sqn., Western Desert, 9-41. Abandoned on L.G.134, Sollum, 10-41.

Z4773 *Trop. Mk. I.* To the Middle East, 8-41. No. 73 Sqn., Amriya, 9-41. No. 229 Sqn., Msus, 1-42.

Z4775 *Trop. Mk. I.* To the Middle East, 8-41. No. 208 Sqn., Western Desert, Gaza and Ramleh, Palestine, 9-41.

Z4777 *Trop. Mk. I.* To the Middle East, 8-41, No. 237 Sqn., Western Desert, 10-41.

Z4778 *Converted to Sea Hurricane I*, 1941.

Z4783 Scheduled for the Middle East as *Trop. Mk. I*, but diverted to India, 8-41. No. 258 Sqn., Ratmalana, Ceylon, 3-42.

Z4805 *Trop. Mk. I.* To the Middle East, 8-41. No. 213 Sqn., Nicosia, Cyprus, 10-41.

Z4809 *Trials at R.A.E., Farnborough, with various "desert paint schemes"*, 8-41. *Trop. Mk. I.* To the Middle East, c.8-41. No. 335 (Greek) Sqn., Aqir, Palestine, 11-41.

Z4835 *Converted to Sea Hurricane I*, 1941.

Z4836 To the Middle East without tropical equipment, 8-41. *Tropicalised* 9-41. No. 94 Sqn., El Ballah, 10-41.

Z4837 To the Middle East without tropical equipment, 8-41. No. 71 O.T.U., Egypt, 1941.

Z4838 *Trials of night flying equipment*, R.A.E., Farnborough, 8-41; to A & A.E.E., 9-41.

Z4842 No. 43 Sqn., Drem, **FT-L**, 8-41.

Z4846 *Converted to Sea Hurricane I*, 1941.

Z4847 *Converted to Sea Hurricane I*, 1941.

Z4849 *Converted to Sea Hurricane I*, 1941.

Z4851 *Converted to Sea Hurricane I*, 1941.

Z4852 *Converted to Sea Hurricane I*, 1941.

Z4853 *Converted to Sea Hurricane I*, 1941.

Z4854 *Converted to Sea Hurricane I*, 1941.

Z4855 To the Middle East, c.8-41; *tropicalised*, 9-41. No. 237 Sqn., Western Desert, 11-41. No. 71 O.T.U., 4-42.

Z4857 To the Middle East, c.8-41; *tropicalised*, 9-41. No. 80 Sqn., El Gubbi, 12-41.

Z4862 To the Middle East, 8-41; *tropicalised*, 9-41. No. 80 Sqn., El Gubbi, 12-41.

Z4864 *Trop. Mk. I.* To the Middle East, 8-41. No. 208 Sqn., Western Desert and Palestine, 9-41.

Z4865 *Converted to Sea Hurricane I*, 1941.

Z4866 *Performance and handling trials*, Brooklands and Boscombe Down, 8-41. *Converted to Sea Hurricane I*, c.10-41.

Z4867 *Converted to Sea Hurricane I*, 1941.

Z4871 *Trop. Mk. I.* To the Middle East, 8-41. No. 30 Sqn., Idku, 10-41.

Z4873 *Converted to Sea Hurricane I*, 1941.

Z4874 *Converted to Sea Hurricane I*, 1941.

Z4876 *Converted to Sea Hurricane I*, 1941.

Z4920 *Converted to Sea Hurricane I*, 1941.

Z4921 *Converted to Sea Hurricane I*, 1941.

Z4922 *Converted to Sea Hurricane I*, 1941.

Z4923 *Converted to Sea Hurrciane I*, 1941.

Z4924 *Converted to Sea Hurricane I*, 1941.

Z4925 *Converted to Sea Hurricane I*, 1941.

Z4926 *Converted to Sea Hurricane I*, 1941.

Z4929 *Converted to Sea Hurricane I*, 1941.

Z4933 *Converted to Sea Hurricane I*, 1941.

Z4934 *Trop. Mk. I.* To the Middle East, 8-41. No. 274 Sqn., Maryut, 10-41.

Z4935 *Converted to Sea Hurricane I*, 1941.

Z4936 *Converted to Sea Hurricane I*, 1941.

Z4937 *Converted to Sea Hurricane I*, 1941.

Z4938 *Converted to Sea Hurricane I*, 1941.

Z4939 *Converted to Sea Hurricane I*, 1941.

MARK IIAs

Z4940 *Trop. Mk. IIA.* To the Middle East, 8-41. No. 33 Sqn., Gambut, Libya, 3-42.

Z4941 *Converted to Mark IIB* by H.A.L., 1941.

Z4942 *Trop. Mk. IIA.* To the Middle East, 8-41. No. 185 Sqn., Hal Far, Malta, "**Y**", 9-41.

Z4944 *Trop. Mk. IIA.* To the Middle East, 8-41. No. 274 Sqn., **YK-L**, Maryut, 10-41.

Z4950 *Trop. Mk. IIA.* To the Middle East, 8-41. No. 208 Sqn., Acroma, 2-42; shot down by Bf 109F of *JG 27*, El Adem, Libya, 7-9-42.

Z4952 *Trop. Mk. IIA.* To the Middle East, 8-41, and onward to India, 12-41. No. 273 Sqn., China Bay, Ceylon, "**K**", 7-42.

Z4953 *Trop. Mk. IIA.* To the Middle East, 8-41. No. 238 Sqn., Msus, "**L**", 12-41.

Z4954 *Trop. Mk. IIA.* To the Middle East, 8-41. No. 274 Sqn., Maryut, 10-41. No. 208 Sqn., Sidi Azeiz, 3-42.

Z4955 *Trop. Mk. IIA.* To the Middle East, 8-41. No. 274 Sqn., Maryut, **YK-P**, 10-41.

Z4958 *Trop. Mk. IIA.* To the Middle East, 8-41. No. 208 Sqn., Sidi Azeiz, 3-42.

Z4964 *Trop. Mk. IIA.* To Takoradi, 8-41. No. 128 Sqn., Hastings, Sierra Leone, **WG-D**, 10-41. No. 229 Sqn., Msus, **HB-D**, 1-42.

Z4969 No. 605 Sqn., A.A.F., Baginton, 8-41.

MARK IIBs

Z4993 *Miscellaneous trials*, R.A.E. Farnborough, c.9-41.

Z4994 No. 312 (Czech) Sqn., Ayr, 10-41.

Z4996 No. 245 Sqn., Chilbolton, **MR-A**, 10-41.

Z4999 No. 43 Sqn.,. Drem, 6-41. Shipped to Russia, 4-5-42.

Z5003 No. 136 Sqn. Shipped to Russia, 26-10-41.

Z5004 *Trop. Mk. IIB.* To the Middle East, 9-41. No. 213 Sqn., Idku, **AK-A**, 1-42.

Z5005 *Trop. Mk. IIB.* To the Middle East, 9-41. No. 213 Sqn., Idku, **AK-B**, 1-42.

Z5044 No. 257 Sqn., Coltishall, 8-41. Shipped to Russia, 24-10-41.

Z5045 No. 257 Sqn., Coltishall, 8-41. Lost in action off Happisburgh, Norfolk, 4-10-41.

Z5050 No. 257 Sqn., Coltishall, **DT-T**, 8-41. No. 401 Sqn., R.C.A.F., Digby, 9-41.

Z5052 No. 17 Sqn., Dyce, 8-41. Shipped to Russia, 12-3-42.

Z5054 No. 615 Sqn., A.A.F., Valley, 8-41. Shipped to Russia, 14-3-42.

Z5058 No. 121 Sqn., Kirton-in-Lindsey, 10-41; abandoned near Burton-on-Trent, 2-10-41.

Z5059 No. 56 Sqn., Duxford, **US-N**, 9-41. Shipped to Russia, 26-10-41.

Z5060 No. 312 (Czech) Sqn., Ayr, 10-41. Shipped to Russia, 26-10-41.

Z5064 *Trop. Mk. IIB.* To the Middle East, 10-41. No. 274 Sqn., Gazala, 12-41.

Z5072 No. 32 Sqn., Angle, 9-41. No. 247 Sqn., Predannack, 12-41. Supplied to Portugal, 15-8-43.

Z5077 No. 71 Sqn., North Weald, 9-41. Shipped to Russia, 23-5-42; lost at sea.

Z5078 No. 316 (Polish) Sqn., Church Stanton, 9-41. No. 615 Sqn., A.A.F.; shot down by flak near Dunkirk, 23-11-41.

Z5080 No. 316 (Polish) Sqn., Church Stanton, 9-41. No. 79 Sqn.; crashed 27-10-41.

Z5082 No. 504 Sqn., A.A.F., Ballyhalbert, 9-41. Shipped to Russia, 15-11-41.

Z5083 No. 257 Sqn., Coltishall, 8-41.

Z5086 *Trop. Mk. IIB.* To the Middle East, 8-41. No. 274 Sqn., Maryut, 10-41.

Z5087 *Trop. Mk. IIB.* To the Middle East, 8-41. No. 274 Sqn., Maryut, **YK-N**, 10-41. Mo. 238 Sqn., Msus, 1-42.

Z5117 *Trop. Mk. IIB.* To the Middle East, 8-41. No. 274 Sqn. To India, 2-42. No. 261 Sqn., China Bay, Ceylon, 3-42. S.O.C., 1-10-44.

Z5118 *Trop. Mk. IIB.* To the Middle East, 8-41. No. 126 Sqn., Ta Kali, Malta, 9-41. S.O.C., 16-3-42.

Z5119 *Trop. Mk. IIB.* To the Middle East, 8-41. S.O.C., 31-12-41.

Z5122 No. 81 Sqn., Vaenga, North Russia; *left in Russia*, 28-10-41.

Z5123 No. 151 Wing, Vaenga, North Russia; *left in Russia*, 28-10-41.

Z5126 No. 504 Sqn., A.A.F., Ballyhalbert, 9-41. No. 79 Sqn. No. 615 Sqn., A.A.F. *Shipped to Russia*, 18-5-42.

Z5127 No. 605 Sqn., A.A.F., Kenley, 9-41. *Shipped to Russia*, 11-10-41.

Z5132 *Trop. Mk. IIB.* To the Middle East. *Modified locally as high altitude Trop. P.R. Mk. IIB.* No. 2 P.R.U., 1942. No. 680 (PR) Sqn., Cyprus, 7-43.

Z5133 No. 331 (Norwegian) Sqn., Castletown, **PN-F**, 9-41. *Shipped to Russia*, 1-3-42.

Z5137 *Trop. Mk. IIB.* To the Middle East, 9-41. No. 274 Sqn., Maryut, **YK-O**, 10-41.

Z5140 *Trop. Mk. IIB.* To the Mediterranean, 9-41. No. 185 Sqn., Hal Far, Malta, 10-41; destroyed in air raid on Hal Far, 10-3-42.

Z5142 *Trop. Mk. IIB.* To the Mediterranean, 9-41. No. 185 Sqn., Hal Far, Malta, 10-41. No. 1 Sqn., S.A.A.F.; Missing, 27-6-42.

Z5143 *Trop. Mk. IIB.* To the Middle East, 9-41. No. 33 Sqn., Gambut, Libya, 3-42; Missing, 12-6-42.

Z5146 *Trop. Mk. IIB.* To the Middle East, 9-41. No. 238 Sqn., 10-41. To India., 1-42. No. 261 Sqn., China Bay, Ceylon, 3-42.

Z5148 *Trop. Mk. IIB.* To the Middle East, 9-41. No. 274 Sqn., Gazala, 12-41. No. 238 Sqn. No. 208 Sqn.

Z5153 No. 43 Sqn., 10-41. No. 245 Sqn.; crashed near Charmy Down, 14-11-42.

Z5157 No. 81 Sqn., Vaenga, North Russia, 10-41; *left in Russia*, 28-10-41.

Z5159 No. 134 Sqn., Vaenga, North Russia, 10-41, "**GV-33**"; *left in Russia*, 28-10-41.

Z5203 No. 504 Sqn., A.A.F., c.9-41. *Shipped to Russia*, 15-11-41.

Z5207 No. 81 Sqn., Vaenga, North Russia, 10-41; *left in Russia*, 28-10-41.

Z5208 No. 81 Sqn., Vaenga, North Russia, 10-41; *left in Russia*, 28-10-41.

Z5209 No. 81 Sqn., Vaenga, North Russia, 10-41; *left in Russia*, 28-10-41.

Z5209 No. 81 Sqn., Vaenga, North Russia, 10-41; *left in Russia*, 28-10-41.

Z5210 No. 134 Sqn., Vaenga, North Russia, 10-41; *left in Russia*, 28-10-41.

Z5217 *Trop. Mk. IIB.* To Takoradi, 9-41. No. 128 Sqn., Hastings, Sierra Leone, 10-41.

Z5224 No. 32 Sqn., Angle, 9-41. No. 615 Sqn., A.A.F. *Shipped to Russia*, 20-1-43.

Z5227 No. 81 Sqn., Vaenga, North Russia, 10-41; *left in Russia*, 28-10-41.

Z5228 No. 81 Sqn., Vaenga, North Russia, 10-41; *left in Russia*, 28-10-41.

Z5236 No. 134 Sqn., Vaenga, North Russia, 10-41; *left in Russia*, 28-10-41.

Z5256 No. 79 Sqn. No. 247 Sqn. No. 32 Sqn., Angle, 9-41; crashed in sea off Dungeness, Kent, 8-7-42.

Z5261 No. 331 (Norwegian) Sqn. *Modified to Trop. Mk. IIB.* To the Middle East. No. 71 O.T.U. S.O.C., 13-9-45.

Z5262 No. 331 (Norwegian) Sqn., Castletown, **PN-X**, 9-41; crashed at Cammachmore, Kincardine, 24-11-41.

Z5306 *Trop. Mk. IIB.* To the Middle East, 10-41. No. 335 (Greek) Sqn. No. 417 Sqn., R.C.A.F., Shandur, 9-42. S.O.C., 24-4-44.

Z5307 No. 79 Sqn., Fairwood Common, 10-41. No. 615 Sqn., A.A.F. No. 257 Sqn. No. 32 Sqn. No. 1449 Flt. S.O.C., 2-11-44.

Z5309 No. 486 (NZ) Sqn., Kirton-in-Lindsey, 3-42. *Shipped to Russia*, 7-1-43.

Z5312 *Trop. Mk. IIB.* To the Middle East, 10-41. No. 73 Sqn., Shandur, 12-41; shot down at El Adem, Libya, 8-2-42.

Z5314 *Trop. Mk. IIB.* To the Middle East, 10-41. No. 274 Sqn., 12-41. No. 335 (Greek) Sqn. No. 41 Sqn., S.A.A.F. S.O.C., 28-9-44.

Z5324 No. 331 (Norwegian) Sqn., Castletown and Skaebrae, **FN-H**, 10-41. Shipped to Russia, 15-5-42.

Z5330 *Trop. Mk. IIB.* To the Middle East, 10-41. No. 94 Sqn., Msus, Libya, 1-42. No. 208 Sqn. No. 335 (Greek) Sqn. S.O.C., 28-9-44.

Z5333 No. 486 (NZ) Sqn., Kirton-in-Lindsey, 3-42. *Shipped to Russia*, 10-2-43.

Z5346 No. 486 (NZ) Sqn., Kirton-in-Lindsey, 3-42. *Shipped to Russia*, 20-9-42.

Z5381 *Trop. Mk. IIB.* To the Middle East, 11-41. No. 274 Sqn. To India, 2-42. No. 258 Sqn., Colombo Racecourse, 3-42.

Z5387 *Trop. Mk. IIB.* To the Middle East, 11-41. No. 274 Sqn., Gambut, 3-42. *Supplied to Turkey*, 1-8-43.

Z5388 *Trop. Mk. IIB.* To the Middle East, 11-41. No. 33 Sqn., Gambut, Libya, 3-42. No. 127 Sqn., Shandur, 6-42.

Z5390 *Miscellaneous trials*, R.A.E., 9-41. *Shipped to Russia*, 24-9-41.

Z5436 *Trop. Mk. IIB.* To the Middle East, 11-41. To India, 12-41. No. 258 Sqn., Colombo Racecourse, Ceylon, 3-42; crashed at Chittagong, 21-1-43.

Z5443 *Trop. Mk. IIB.* To the Middle East, 11-41. No. 274 Sqn., Gambut, 3-42. No. 335 (Greek) Sqn., Dekheila, 8-42.

Z5444 *Trop. Mk. IIB.* To the Middle East, 11-41. No. 73 Sqn., El Adem, Libya, 2-42; shot down near El Adem, 5-4-42.

Z5451 No. 242 Sqn., Valley, 10-41. *Shipped to Russia*, 22-10-41.

Z5457 No. 17 Sqn., Tain, 9-41. *Shipped to Russia*, 16-10-41.

Z5461 *Trop. Mk. IIB.* To the Middle East, 11-41, and onwards to India, 12-41. No. 258 Sqn., Colombo Racecourse, Ceylon, 3-42.

Z5470 No. 79 Sqn., Fairwood Common, 10-41. No. 486 (NZ) Sqn. *Shipped to Russia*, 19-9-42, but lost at sea.

Z5480 *Shipped to Russia*, 12-10-41.

Z5482 *Trop. Mk. IIB.* To the Middle East, 11-41, and onwards to Singapore. No. 232 Sqn., Singapore, 1-42; crashed in sea off Kallang, 7-2-42.

Z5529 *Shipped to Russia*, 5-9-41.

Z5533 *Trop. Mk. IIB.* To the Middle East, 11-41, and onwards to India. No. 261 Sqn., China Bay, Ceylon, 2-42; shot down by A6M fighters over China Bay, 9-4-42.

Z5539 No. 504 Sqn., Ballyhalbert, 9-41. *Shipped to Russia*, 15-11-41.

Z5542 No. 253 Sqn., Hibaldstow, 10-41. *Shipped to Russia*, 15-11-41.

Z5587 *Trop. Mk. IIB.* To the Middle East, 11-41, and onwards to India. No. 258 Sqn., Colombo Racecourse, Ceylon, 3-42.

Z5592 *Trop. Mk. IIB.* To the Middle East, 11-41, and onwards to India, 12-41. No. 146 Sqn., Dum Dum, 5-42. S.O.C., 31-8-44.

Z5597 *Trop. Mk. IIB.* To the Middle East, 11-41. No. 73 Sqn., El Adem, Libya, 2-42; crashed 3 miles SE of Gambut, 14-3-42.

Z5600 *Trop. Mk. IIB.* To the Middle East, 11-41, and onwards to India, 12-41. No. 261 Sqn., China Bay, Ceylon, 3-42.

Z5604 *Trop. Mk. IIB.* To the Middle East, 11-41. No. 94 Sqn., Msus, Libya, 1-42; Missing, 14-1-42.

Z5626 *Trop. Mk. IIB.* To the Middle East, 11-41. No. 94 Sqn., Msus, Libya, 1-42.

Z5628 *Trop. Mk. IIB.* To the Middle East, 11-41, and on to India, 12-41. No. 607 Sqn., A.A.F., Chittagong, 2-43. No. 2 Sqn., I.A.F.; crashed, 3-8-44.

Z5659 *Trop. Mk. IIB.* To the Middle East, 11-41, but diverted on to Burma, 12-41. No. 135 Sqn., Mingaladon, 2-42.

Z5661 *Trop. Mk. IIB.* To the Middle East, 11-41, but diverted on to India,, 12-41. No. 261 Sqn., China Bay, Ceylon; shot down by A6M fighters over Colombo, 5-4-42.

Z5666 *Trop. Mk. IIB.* To the Middle East, 11-41. No.

238 Sqn., Msus, Libya, "**P**", 1-42.

Z5668 *Trop. Mk. IIB.* To the Middle East, 11-41, and onwards to India, 12-41. No. 258 Sqn., Colombo Racecourse, Ceylon, 3-42. No. 146 Sqn., Dum Dum, 5-42. S.O.C., 11-10-44.

Z5674 *Trop. Mk. IIB.* To the Middle East, 10-41. No. 274 Sqn., Msus, Libya, 12-41. S.O.C., 1-9-43.

HAWKER HURRICANE Mark I (Hawker-built). Fourth production batch of 500 aircraft built by Hawker Aircraft Ltd., Kingston-upon-Thames, Langley and Brooklands, between July 1940 and February 1941, under Contract No. 62305/39. Rolls-Royce Merlin III engines. First 25 aircraft delivered with fabric wings, but most re-fitted with metal wings at M.U.s. *V7200-V7209, V7221-V7260, V7276-V7318, V7337-V7386, V7400-V7446, V7461-V7510, V7533-V7572, V7588-V7627, V7644-V7690, V7705-V7737, V7741-V7780, V7795-V7838, V7851-V7862; AS987-AS990.* Deliveries commenced, 2-7-40; completed 5-2-41. Average rate of production, approximately two aircraft per day.

V7202 No. 242 Sqn., Coltishall, **LE-T**, 8-40.

V7204 No. 87 Sqn., Church Fenton, **LK-V**, 8-40.

V7207 *Converted to Sea Hurricane IA*, 1941, and fitted with metal wings.

V7208 *Converted to Sea Hurricane IA*, 1941, and fitted with metal wings,

V7209 No. 73 Sqn., Castle Camps, 9-40; slightly damaged by Spitfire, 14-9-40; F/L M.L.ff. Beytagh unhurt.

V7222 No. 151 Sqn., Digby, **DZ-X**, 9-41.

V7229 *Converted to Sea Hurricane IA*, c.3-41.

V7230 No. 501 Sqn., A.A.F., Kenley, **SD-F**, 9-40.

V7232 No. 46 Sqn., Stapleford Tawney, 9-40; shot down, probably over Sussex, 11-9-40; Sgt. W.A. Peacock presumed killed.

V7234 No. 501 Sqn., A.A.F., Gravesend, 8-40; shot down by Bf 109Es over Kent, 2-9-40; Sgt. H.C. Adams unhurt. Aircraft salvaged, repaired and converted to Trop. Mark IIA as ***DG617***. to the Middle East, 1941. Missing, 14-12-41.

V7237 No. 111 Sqn., Debden, 8-40.

V7240 No. 85 Sqn., Debden, **VY-M**, 8-40. No. 238 Sqn., Middle Wallop, 9-40; shot down over Kent, 11-9-40; F/L D.P. Hughes killed.

V7241 No. 17 Sqn., Debden, 9-40; damaged in air collision with Hurricane ***L1808***, 18-9-40; Sgt. L.H. Bartlett unhurt. Aircraft repaired and *converted to Sea Hurricane IA*, 12-40.

V7244 *Converted to Sea Hurricane IA*, 1941.

V7246 *Converted to Sea Hurricane IA*, 1941.

V7248 No. 257 Sqn., Coltishall, 1-41.

V7249 *Retained by H.A.L., Langley, for de-icing trials*, 8-40.

V7252 *Converted to Sea Hurricane IA*, 1941.

V7253 No. 601 Sqn., A.A.F., Tangmere, 8-40; shot down by Bf 109Es near Portsmouth, 18-8-40; Sgt. L.N. Guy killed.

V7254 No. 257 Sqn., Martlesham Heath, 9-40; shot down over the Isle of Sheppey, 7-9-40; F/O L.R.G. Mitchell killed.

V7256 No. 1 Sqn., North Weald, 9-40; destroyed one Bf 109E over Tonbridge, 1-9-40.

V7257 No. 43 Sqn., Tangmere, 9-40; shot down by Bf 109Es over Thames Estuary, 7-9-40; F/L R.C. Reynell (Hawker Test Pilot) killed.

V7258 No. 1 Sqn., Northolt, 9-40. *Converted to Mark IIA* as ***DG621***, 3-41, by Rolls-Royce Ltd. No. 59 O.T.U. No. 79 Sqn. No. 486 (NZ) Sqn. No. 9 P.A.F.U. No. 4 T.E.U. S.O.C., 11-8-44.

V7259 No. 43 Sqn., Tangmere, 8-40; shot down near Portsmouth, 26-8-40; P/O H.L. North baled out wounded.

V7260 *Trials with H.A.L. and A. & A.E.E. with four 20-mm. cannon wing*, 7/8-40.

V7286 *Converted to Mark IIA* as ***DR346***, 7-41, and *shipped to Russia*, 11-10-41.

V7288 No. 401 Sqn., R.C.A.F., Prestwick, 10-40.

V7291 No. 601 Sqn., A.A.F., Exeter, **UF-P**, 10-40.

V7295 To the Middle East without tropical equipment, c.9-40. No. 208 Sqn., Halfaya, 11-40.

V7296 No. 257 Sqn., North Weald, **DT-Z**, 10-40; P/O K. Pniak (Polish) shot down one Fiat BR.20, 11-11-40.

V7297 To the Middle East without tropical equipment, 10-40. No. 33 Sqn., Fuka, 12-40.

V7298 No. 257 Sqn., North Weald, 10-40; shot down by Bf 109Es near Dungeness, 12-10-40; P/O C.F.A. Capon baled out wounded.

V7299 *Trop. Mk. I.* To the Middle East, c.12-40. No. 94 Sqn., Ismailia, 5-41.

V7300 *Trop. Mk. I.* To the Middle East, c.12-40. No. 335 (Greek) Sqn., Aqir, Palestine, 10-41.

V7301 No. 253 Sqn., Kenley, 10-40; believed shot down and damaged, 30-10-40; Sgt. P.J. Moore unhurt. Aircraft salvaged and *converted to Sea Hurricane IA*, 1941.

V7302 No. 1 Sqn., Wittering, 10-40; damaged on landing after combat with Do 17Z, 29-10-40; Sgt. J. Dygryn (Czech) unhurt. Aircraft salvaged and *converted to Mk. IIA* as ***BV164***, 1941.

V7303 No. 43 Sqn., Usworth, 10-40.

V7304 No. 255 Sqn., Hibaldstow, 5-41.

V7305 No. 605 Sqn., A.A.F., Croydon, 10-40; shot down by Bf 109E over London, 7-10-40; P/O I.J. Muirhead baled out unhurt.

V7307 No. 43 Sqn., Usworth, 10-40; dusk landing accident, 24-10-40; Sgt. D.R. Stoodley killed.

V7311 No. 3 Sqn., Dyce, 10-40. No. 17 Sqn., Martlesham Heath, 12-40, **YB-P**. *Converted to Sea Hurricane IA*, 1941.

V7313 No. 249 Sqn., North Weald, 9-40.

V7315 No. 56 Sqn., Boscombe Down, **US-L**, 10-40.

V7317 No. 257 Sqn., Martlesham Heath, 9-40; damaged in forced landing after combat, 7-9-40; Sgt. D.J. Hulbert unhurt.

V7337 No. 145 Sqn., Tangmere, 10-40; shot down by Bf 109Es over Christchurch Bay, 15-10-40; P/O Machacek (Czech) unhurt.

V7338 Silloth Stn. Flt., c.10-40. No. 232 Sqn., Drem, 11-40.

V7339 No. 317 (Polish) Sqn., Acklington, **JH-X**, 2-41. *Converted to Sea Hurricane I*, 1941.

V7340 No. 56 Sqn., Boscombe Down, 10-40.

V7342 No. 56 Sqn., Boscombe Down, 10-40.

V7348 To the Middle East without tropical equipment, 1940; *tropicalised* 12-40. No. 274 Sqn., Bardia, 1-41.

V7349 No. 402 Sqn., R.C.A.F., Digby, 12-40. *Converted to Sea Hurricane I*, 1941.

V7351 No. 257 Sqn., North Weald, 10-41; shot down by Bf 109Es near Hawkinge, 15-10-40; P/O G. North unhurt. Aircraft salvaged and *converted to Trop. Mark IIA* as ***BV173***, 3-41. Shipped to Malta. No. 126 Sqn. S.O.C., 18-9-41.

V7352 No. 56 Sqn., Boscombe Down, 10-40. *Converted to Sea Hurricane I*, 1941.

V7353 *Trop. Mk. I.* To the Middle East, 12-40. No. 73 Sqn., Sidi Haneish, 3-41; 2/Lt. Littolff (South African) destroyed one Bf 109E over Tobruk, 22-4-41.

V7354 *Trop. Mk. I.* To the Middle East, 12-40. No. 247 Sqn., Gerawla, Egypt, 5-41.

V7357 No. 501 Sqn., A.A.F., Kenley, 9-40; shot down by Bf 109Es near Ashford, Kent, 17-9-40; Sgt. J.H. Lacey baled out unhurt.

V7360 *First aircraft to be fitted with four-cannon wings.* To A. & A.E.E., 7-40. No. 46 Sqn., Stapleford Tawney, **PO-B**, 9-40. F/L A.C. Rabagliati shot down one Bf 109E, 5-9-40.

V7361 No. 111 Sqn., Dyce, 10-40.

V7368 No. 501 Sqn., A.A.F., Kenley, 9-40.

V7369 No. 151 Sqn., Stapleford Tawney, 8-40; shot down by Bf 109Es near Rochester, Kent, 30-8-40. S/L E.B. King killed.

V7370 *Trop. Mk. I.* To the Middle East, c.12-40. No. 94 Sqn., Ismailia, 5-41. No. 127 Sqn., Habbaniya, Iraq, 6-41.

V7372 *Trop. Mk. I.* To the Middle East, 11-40. No. 73 Sqn., Sidi Haneish, 3-41.

V7375 No. 1 Sqn., Northolt, 8-40; shot down by Bf 109Es over Chelmsford, 31-8-40; Sgt. H.J. Marchant baled out unwounded.

V7376 No. 1 Sqn., Wittering, 10-40; Missing from patrol, 9-10-40; Sgt. S. Warren presumed killed.

V7377 No. 1 Sqn., Northolt, 9-40.

V7379 No. 1 Sqn., Northolt, 9-40. *Converted to Sea Hurricane*, 1941.

V7384 No. 253 Sqn., Kenley, 10-40.

V7386 *Converted to Sea Hurricane I*, 1941.

V7400 No. 111 Sqn., Dyce, 10-40.

V7402 *Converted to Sea Hurricane I*, 1941.

V7409 No. 249 Sqn., North Weald, 10-41; shot down by Bf 109Es and force landed on Rochester airfield, 25-10-40. Adjutant H. Bouquillard (French) wounded.

V7411 No. 229 Sqn., Northolt, 9-40; damaged in forced landing after combat, 30-9-40; Sgt. C.G. Hodson slightly wounded. Aircraft repaired and *supplied to the Irish Air Corps*, 7-7-43, as "***104***".

V7416 *Converted to Sea Hurricane IA*, 1941.

V7417 No. 302 (Polish) Sqn., Leconfield, **WX-T**, 10-40.

V7421 *Converted to Sea Hurricane IA*, 1941.

V7422 No. 145 Sqn., Drem, **SO-P**, 9-40. No. 247 Sqn., Roborough and St. Eval, **HP-O**, 1-41.

V7423 *Trop. Mk. I.* To the Middle East, 11-40. No. 274 Sqn., Bardia, 1-41. *Converted to Trop. P.R. Mk. I (2-camera).* No. 2 P.R.U., Heliopolis, 6-41.

V7425 No. 32 Sqn., Acklington, 10-40.

V7426 No. 145 Sqn., Tangmere, 10-40; shot down by Bf 109Es near Cranbrook, 12-10-40; Sgt. J. Wadham killed.

V7428 *Trop. Mk. I.* To the Middle East, 11-40. *Converted to Trop. P.R. Mk. I (2-camera).* No. 2 P.R.U., Heliopolis, 6-41.

V7431 *Trop. Mk. I.* To the Middle East, c.2-41. No. 208 Sqn., El Khanka, 10-41.

V7432 No. 151 Sqn., Digby, 9-40; force landed after collision with Hurricane ***P3306***, 24-9-40. P/O J.K. Haviland (American) unhurt.

V7433 No. 501 Sqn., A.A.F., Kenley, 9-40; shot down by Bf 109E near Maidstone, 15-9-40; S/L H.A.V. Hogan unhurt.

V7434 No. 151 Sqn., Digby, 10-40; air collision at night with Hurricane ***R4184***, 26-10-40; Sgt. D.O. Stanley killed.

V7435 *Supplied to the Iriah Air Corps*, 30-3-44, as "***112***".

V7438 *Converted to Sea Hurricane I*, 1941.

V7439 *Converted to Sea Hurricane I*, 1941.

V7440 No. 85 Sqn., Castle Camps, 9-40. No. 43 Sqn., Usworth, 10-40.

V7442 No. 46 Sqn., Stapleford Tawney, 9-40; shot down by Bf 109Es over Kent, 18-9-40; Sgt. J.W. Jeffreys killed when his parachute failed to open.

V7443 No. 46 Sqn., Digby, 1-41; Missing after combat over Calais, 10-2-41.

V7461 To the Middle East without tropical equipment, 1940. No. 30 Sqn., Fuka, Egypt, 12-40.

V7463 *Supplied to the Irish Air Corps*, 30-3-44, as "***114***".

V7464 No. 1 Sqn., Wittering, 10-40.

V7465 *Converted to Sea Hurricane I*, 1941.

V7467 No. 111 Sqn., North Weald, 10-40. No. 242 Sqn., Duxford, **LE-D**, 12-40.

V7469 No. 56 O.T.U., Sutton Bridge, 1941; collided with Hurricane ***W9180***; P/O J.F. Zerovnicky (Czech) killed in crash near Walpole St. Peter.

V7477 *Trop. Mk. I.* To the Middle East via Takoradi, 12-40.

V7479 *Trop. Mk. I.* To the Middle East, 12-40. No. 94 Sqn., Ismailia, "**U**", 5-41.

V7480 *Miscellaneous trials*, A. & A.E.E., from 3-41. To Flight Refuelling Ltd., Staverton, Glos., for *towed-fighter trials with Halifaxes*, from 25-3-41.

V7482 *Trop. Mk. I.* To the Middle East, 12-40.

V7490 *Trop. Mk. I.* To the Middle East, 11-40. No. 261 Sqn., Ta Kali, Malta, 12-40.

V7491 *Trop. Mk. I.* To the Middle East, 11-40. No. 73 Sqn., Sidi Haneish and Bu Amoud, 3-41.

V7492 *Trop. Mk. I.* To the Middle East, 11-40. No. 73 Sqn., Sidi Haneish and Bu Amoud, 3-41.
V7497 No. 501 Sqn., A.A.F., Kenley, 9-40; shot down by Bf 109Es near Deal, 28-9-40; P/O E.B. Rogers baled out unhurt.
V7498 No. 501 Sqn., A.A.F., Kenley, 9-40; damaged in forced landing after combat, 4-10-40; Sgt. J.H. Lacey unhurt. Aircraft salvaged and *converted to Sea Hurricane IA*, 1941.
V7501 No. 73 Sqn., Debden and Hornchurch, 10-40. *Converted to Sea Hurricane*, 1941.
V7502 No. 73 Sqn., Debden, 10-40. No. 79 Sqn., Pembrey, 12-40. *Converted to Sea Hurricane*, 1941.
V7503 *Converted to Sea Hurricane*, 1941.
V7504 No. 253 Sqn., Kenley, 10-40. *Converted to Sea Hurricane*, 1941.
V7505 *Converted to Sea Hurricane*, 1941.
V7506 *Converted to Sea Hurricane*, 1941.
V7534 No. 1 Sqn., Kenley, 1-41.
V7540 *Supplied to the Irish Air Corps*, 7-7-43, as "***105***".
V7541 *Trop. Mk. I.* To the Middle East, 11-40. No. 335 (Greek) Sqn., Helwan, 1-42.
V7543 *Trop. Mk. I.* To the Middle East, 11-40. No. 127 Sqn., Habbaniya, Iraq, 6-41.
V7545 *Trop. Mk. I.* To the Middle East, 11-40. No. 73 Sqn., Sidi Haneish and Bu Amoud, 3-41.
V7546 *Trop. Mk. I.* To the Middle East, 11-40. No. 73 Sqn., Sidi Haneish and Bu Amoud, 3-41.
V7547 *Trop. Mk. I.* To the Middle East, 11-40. No. 261 Sqn., Ta Kali, Malta, 12-40.
V7550 *Trop. Mk. I.* To the Middle East, 11-40. No. 73 Sqn., Sidi Haneish and Bu Amoud, 3-41.
V7551 *Trop. Mk. I.* To the Middle East, 11-40. No. 73 Sqn., Sidi Haneish, 3-41.
V7558 *Trop. Mk. I.* To the Middle East, 11-40. No. 274 Sqn., Bardia, 2-41.
V7559 *Trop. Mk. I.* To the Middle East, 11-40. No. 73 Sqn., Sidi Haneish and Bu Amoud, 3-41.
V7561 *Trop. Mk. I.* To the Middle East, 11-40. No. 73 Sqn., Sidi Haneish and Bu Amoud, 3-41.
V7568 No. 17 Sqn., Martlesham Heath, 12-40.
V7571 *Trop. Mk. I.* To the Middle East, 11-40. No. 335 (Greek) Sqn., Aqir, Palestine, 10-41.
V7572 No. 73 Sqn., Debden and Hornchurch, 9-9-40.
V7588 *Converted to Sea Hurricane IA*, 1941.
V7589 No. 87 Sqn., Colerne, **LK-T**, 11-40.
V7591 No. 615 Sqn., A.A.F., Northolt, 12-40.
V7592 No. 145 Sqn., Tangmere, **SO-V**, 10-40; shot down off the Isle of Wight by Bf 109Es, 27-10-40; Sgt. J. Weber unhurt.
V7600 *Converted to Sea Hurricane IA*, 1941.
V7601 No. 601 Sqn., A.A.F., Northolt, 2-41.
V7603 No. 46 Sqn., Sherburn-in-Elmet, 4-41.
V7607 No. 257 Sqn., North Weald, **DT-H**, 11-40; P/O B. Davey shot down one Fiat BR.20, 11-11-40.
V7608 No. 71 Sqn., Kirton-in-Lindsey, **XR-J**, 11-40.
V7623 *Converted to Sea Hurricane IA*, 1941.
V7644 No. 238 Sqn., Middle Wallop, 1-41.
V7646 No. 87 Sqn., Charmy Down, **LK-R**, 1-41. *Converted to Sea Hurricane IA*, 1941.
V7647 *Converted to Sea Hurricane IA*, 1941.
V7648 No. 145 Sqn., Tangmere, 11-40.
V7650 *Converted to Sea Hurricane IA*, 1941.
V7654 *Trop. Mk. I.* To the Middle East, 1-41. No. 127 Sqn., Habbaniya, Iraq, 6-41.
V7656 No. 315 (Polish) Sqn., Acklington, **PK-M**, 1-41.
V7657 *Converted to Mark IIA* as ***DG651*** by Rolls-Royce Ltd., 5-41. *Shipped to Russia*, 2-10-41.
V7659 No. 310 (Czech) Sqn., Duxford, **NN-E**, 1-41.
V7665 No. 232 Sqn., Skitten, 12-40. *Converted to Sea Hurricane IA*, 1941.
V7667 No. 257 Sqn., Coltishall, 1-41.
V7670 *Trop. Mk. I.* To the Middle East, c.1-41. Captured intact by German forces, 3-41; recaptured later at Gambut.
V7675 No. 145 Sqn., Tangmere, 1-41. *Converted to Sea Hurricane IA*, 1941.
V7677 No. 249 Sqn., North Weald, 1-41.
V7681 *Converted to Sea Hurricane IA*, 1941.
V7683 No. 258 Sqn., Acklington, 1-41.
V7684 *Converted to Mark IIA* as ***DG645*** by Rolls-Royce Ltd., 5-41. *Shipped to Russia*, 7-9-41.
V7685 *Converted to Sea Hurricane IA*, 1941.
V7687 No. 258 Sqn., Acklington, 1-41.
V7716 *Trop. Mk. I.* To the Middle East, 12-40. No. 73 Sqn., Sidi Haneish and Bu Amoud, 3-41.
V7717 *Trop. Mk. I.* To the Middle East, 12-40. No. 274 Sqn., Gerawla, Egypt, 5-41.
V7726 No. 615 Sqn., A.A.F., Kenley, 2-41.
V7745 No. 402 Sqn., R.C.A.F., Digby, 1-41. *Converted to Sea Hurricane IA*, 1941.
V7752 No. 96 Sqn., Cranage, 2-41.
V7753 *Trop. Mk. I.* To the Middle East, 12-40. No. 73 Sqn., Sidi Haneish, 3-41.
V7754 No. 245 Sqn., Aldergrove, **DX-R**, c.12-40.
V7757 *Trop. Mk. I.* To the Middle East, 12-40. No. 73 Sqn., Sidi Haneish, 3-41.
V7763 *Trop. Mk. I.* To the Middle East, 12-40. No. 274 Sqn., Gerawla, Egypt, 5-41.
V7770 *Trop. Mk. I.* To the Middle East, 12-40. No. 274 Sqn., Gerawla, Egypt, 5-41.
V7772 *Trop. Mk. I.* To the Middle East, c.2-41. No. 208 Sqn., Tmimi, 1-42.
V7777 *Trop. Mk. I.* To the Middle East, c.2-41. No. 6 Sqn., Tobruk West, "**D**",4-41.
V7816 No. 71 Sqn., Kirton-in-Lindsey, **XR-Z**, 2-41.
V7817 *Trop. Mk. I.* To the Middle East, 1-41. No. 33 Sqn., Larissa, Greece, 3-41. No. 208 Sqn., Ramleh, Palestine, c.6-41.
V7820 *Trop. Mk. I.* To the Middle East, 1-41. No. 274 Sqn., Gerawla, 5-41; shot down at Mersa Matruh, 12-5-41; F/O English Missing.
V7822 *Trop. Mk. I.* To the Middle East, 1-41. No. 73 Sqn., Sidi Haneish, 3-41. No. 250 Sqn., El Gamil, 2-42.
V7824 *Converted to Sea Hurricane IA*, 1941.
V7828 *Trop. Mk. I.* To the Middle East, 1-41. No. 73 Sqn., Sidi Haneish, 5-41. No. 274 Sqn., Gerawla.

AS987 *Trop. Mk. I.* To the Middle East, 1-41. No. 73 Sqn., Sidi Haneish, 4-41. No. 213 Sqn. No. 73 O.T.U. Aden Defence Flt. S.O.C., 28-8-44.
AS988 *Trop. Mk. I.* To the Middle East, c.1-41. No. 94 Sqn.; Missing in action, 20-4-41.
AS989 *Trop. Mk. I.* To the Middle East, c.1-41. No. 6 Sqn., 1942. S.O.C., 1-9-43.
AS990 *Trop. Mk. I.* To the Middle East, 2-41. No. 3 Sqn., R.A.A.F. No. 73 Sqn., Mersa Matruh, 5-41; S.O.C., 15-5-41.

HAWKER HURRICANE Mark IIA, IIB and IIC (Hawker-built). Fifth production batch of 1,000 aircraft built by Hawker Aircraft Ltd., Kingston-upon-Thames and Langley, under Contract No. 62305/39. Rolls-Royce Merlin XX (and mostly Rotol constant-speed propellers). ***Z2308-Z2357, Z2382-Z2426, Z2446-Z2465, Z2479-Z2528, Z2560-Z2594, Z2624-Z2643, Z2661-Z2705, Z2741-Z2775, Z2791-Z2840, Z2882-Z2931, Z2959-Z2999, Z3017-Z3036, Z3050-Z3099, Z3143-Z3187, Z3221-Z3276, Z3310-Z3359, Z3385-Z3404, Z3421-Z3470, Z3489-Z3523, Z3554-Z3598, Z3642-Z3691, Z3740-Z3784, Z3826-Z3845, Z3885-Z3919, Z3969-Z4018.*** **Deliveries commenced, 14-1-41; completed 28-7-41. Average rate of production, five aircraft per day.**
Z2308 *Mark IIA.* No. 111 Sqn., Croydon, 9-40. No. 605 Sqn., A.A.F.; Missing on patrol, 2-2-41.
Z2309 *Mark IIA.* No. 111 Sqn., Croydon, 9-40; shot down by Bf 109Es near Folkestone, 4-9-40; F/L D.C. Bruce killed. (*The first Hurricane II lost in action.*)
Z2314 *Trop. Mk. IIB.* No. 127 Sqn., Shandur, 6-42.
Z2317 *Mark IIA.* No. 605 Sqn., A.A.F., Croydon, 1-41.
Z2320 *Mark IIA. Armament trials, Boscombe Down*, as ***Z2320/G***, 2-41.
Z2326 *Mark IIA. Armament trials with Rolls-Royce BF and Vickers "S" 40-mm anti-tank guns*, A. & A.E.E. and H.A.L., 1941-42.
Z2328 *Trop. Mk. IIA.* To the Middle East. *Converted to Trop. P.R. Mk. IIA.* No. 208 Sqn., Heliopolis, 7-42; shot down, 28-7-42.
Z2334 *Mark IIA.* No. 605 Sqn., A.A.F., Croydon, 1-41.
Z2340 *Mark IIA.* No. 310 (Czech) Sqn., Duxford, 3-41.
Z2341 *Mark IIA.* No. 310 (Czech) Sqn., Duxford, 3-41.
Z2342 *Mark IIA.* No. 302 (Polish) Sqn., Westhampnett, "**F**", 3-41.
Z2343 *Mark IIA.* No. 257 Sqn., Coltishall, 3-41.
Z2346 *Mark IIA. Cockpit heating trials*, Boscombe Down, 4-41.
Z2347 *Mark IIA.* No. 605 Sqn., A.A.F., Croydon, 2-41.
Z2349 *Mark IIA.* No. 249 Sqn., North Weald, 2-41.
Z2351 *Mark IIA.* No. 605 Sqn., A.A.F., Croydon, 2-41.
Z2353 *Mark IIB.* No. 56 Sqn., North Weald, **US-L**, 2-41. No. 258 Sqn., Kenley, 4-41.
Z2355 *Mark IIB.* No. 56 Sqn., North Weald, 2-41.
Z2383 *Mark IIB.* No. 253 Sqn., Skaebrae, 7-41.
Z2384 *Mark IIA.* No. 605 Sqn., A.A.F., Croydon, 2-41.
Z2386 *Mark IIA.* No. 302 (Polish) Sqn., Westhampnett, "**C**", 3-41.
Z2388 *Mark IIA.* No. 249 Sqn., North Weald, 2-41. No. 43 Sqn., Drem, 4-41.
Z2389 *Mark IIA.* No. 136 Sqn., Kirton-in-Lindsey, 8-41; No. 253 Sqn., Hibaldstow, 10-41. *Shipped to Russia*, 4-5-42.
Z2390 *Mark IIA.* No. 1 Sqn., Kenley, 2-41. No. 247 Sqn., Predannack, 6-41. No. 317 (Polish) Sqn., Exeter, 7-41. *Shipped to Russia*, 5-11-41.
Z2391 *Mark IIA.* No. 615 Sqn., A.A.F., Kenley, 2-41. No. 258 Sqn., Kenley, 4-41. *Shipped to Russia*, 28-9-41.
Z2396 *Trop. Mark IIA.* No. 185 Sqn., Hal Far, Malta, 7-41. S.O.C., 7-7-42.
Z2399 *Converted to Mark IIB. Trials with modified oil cooler*, H.A.L., Langley, 2-41. S.O.C., 14-10-44.
Z2401 *Mark IIB.* No. 32 Sqn., Angle, 7-41. No. 242 Sqn. *Shipped to Russia*, 29-11-41.
Z2405 *Mark IIB.* No. 56 Sqn., North Weald, 7-41. No. 316 (Polish) Sqn. *Shipped to Russia*, 27-1-42.
Z2410 *Mark IIA.* No. 258 Sqn., Kenley, 4-41; shot down by Bf 109Es off Dover, 15-4-41.
Z2411 *Mark IIA.* No. 249 Sqn., North Weald, 3-41. No. 247 Sqn.; collided with Do 17Z off Lizard Point, Cornwall, 31-7-41.
Z2414 *Trop. Mk. IIB.* No. 185 Sqn., Hal Far, Malta, "**E**", 7-41. *Converted to Trop. Mk. IIC*, and transferred to Admiralty Charge, 1-7-43.
Z2415 *Trop. Mk. IIB. High altitude trials and performance measurement*, Langley, 12-40; Boscombe Down and Farnborough, 1-42. Aircraft exploded and crashed near Sutton Bridge, 1-7-42.
Z4216 *Trop. Mk. IIB.* No. 73 Sqn., Sidi Haneish, 5-41. No. 208 Sqn., Sidi Azeiz, 5-42; shot down, 2-8-42.
Z2426 *Mark IIA.* No. 402 Sqn., R.C.A.F., Wellingore, 5-41. No. 257 Sqn., Honiley, 11-41. *Shipped to Russia*, but lost at sea, 20-7-42.
Z2446 *Mark IIA.* No. 615 Sqn., A.A.F., Kenley, 4-41. No. 135 Sqn., Baginton, 8-41. *Shipped to Russia*, but lost at sea, 21-7-42.
Z2448 *Mark IIA.* No. 56 Sqn., North Weald, **US-Y**, 4-41. *Shipped to Russia*, but lost at sea, 29-12-42.
Z2449 *Mark IIA.* No. 56 Sqn., North Weald, **US-M**, 4-41. No. 247 Sqn., Predannack, 6-41.
Z2454 *Mark IIA.* No. 253 Sqn., Hibaldstow, 10-41. *Shipped to Russia*, 16-2-42.
Z2455 *Mark IIA.* No. 247 Sqn., North Weald, 3-41. No. 316 (Polish) Sqn., Colerne, 6-41.
Z2457 *Mark IIA.* No. 1. Sqn., Kenley and Hawkinge, convoy patrols, 3-41. R.A.E., 1942. S.O.C., 28-5-45.
Z2459 *Mark IIA.* No. 402 Sqn., R.C.A.F., Wellingore, 5-41.
Z2461 *Mark IIA. Hood jettison trials*, A. & A.E.E., 2-41. *Shipped to Russia*, 20-1-43.
Z2462 *Mark IIA.* No. 253 Sqn., Hibaldstow, 10-41. *Shipped to Russia*, but lost at sea, 21-7-42.
Z2463 *Mark IIA.* No. 43 Sqn., **FT-B**, Drem, 4-41. No. 71 Sqn., **XP-X**, North Weald, 6-41. No. 317 (Polish) Sqn., Exeter.
Z2482 *Mark IIA.* No. 1 Sqn., Kenley and Hawkinge, 3-41; convoy patrols. No. 79 Sqn., Fairwood Common, 4-42.

Z2484 *Mark IIA*. No. 1 Sqn., Kenley and Hawkinge, 3-41; damaged in action and repaired by David Rosenfields Ltd., 1942.
Z2485 *Mark IIA*. No. 302 (Polish) Sqn., Westhampnett, "**U**", 3-41. No. 312 (Czech) Sqn., Kenley, 5-41.
Z2488 *Mark IIA*. No. 310 (Czech) Sqn., Duxford, 3-41.
Z2501 *Mark IIA*. No. 1 Sqn., Kenley and Hawkinge, 3-41; convoy patrols. S.O.C., 24-4-41.
Z2502 *Trop. Mk. IIA*. Lost at sea en route for the Middle East, 4-41.
Z2505 *Mark IIA*. No. 310 (Czech) Sqn., Duxford, 3-41. Crashed at Loch Oich, Inverness, 31-8-41.
Z2509 *Trop. Mark IIB*. No. 605 Sqn., A.A.F., Hal Far, Malta, 1-42; bombed and destroyed by Ju 88 at Hal Far, 2-2-42.
Z2513 *Mark IIB*. No. 242 Sqn., Martlesham Heath, **LE-A**, 4-41; Missing from patrol, 23-4-41.
Z2521 *Mark IIA*. No. 247 Sqn., Predannack, 6-41.
Z2522 *Mark IIA*. No. 249 Sqn., North Weald, 3-41; lost, 18-4-41.
Z2567 *Mark IIB*. No. 56 Sqn., North Weald, **US-R**, 3-41. Lost en route to the Middle East, 4-41.
Z2570 *Mark IIA*. No. 617 Sqn., A.A.F., Kenley, 4-41.
Z2572 *Mark IIA*. No. 56 Sqn., North Weald, 4-41. No. 247 Sqn., Predannack, 6-41; crashed off Land's End, 6-9-41.
Z2573 *Mark IIA*. No. 56 Sqn., North Weald, 4-41. *Converted to Trop. Mark IIB* and shipped to the Far East, 12-41. No. 261 Sqn., China Bay, Ceylon, 3-42. Shot down by A5Ms over China Bay, 9-4-42.
Z2575 *Mark IIA*. No. 56 Sqn., North Weald, **US-L**, 4-41; Missing, 17-6-41.
Z7578 *Mark IIA*. No. 249 Sqn., North Weald, 4-41. No. 402 Sqn., R.C.A.F., Wellingore, 5-41.
Z2579 *Mark IIA*. No. 601 Sqn., A.A.F., Northolt, **UF-N**, 4-41.
Z2582 *Mark IIB*. No. 43 Sqn., Drem, **FT-S**, 4-41. No. 242 Sqn., Manston, 7-41.
Z2585 *Mark IIA*. No. 56 Sqn., North Weald, 4-41.
Z2586 *Mark IIA*. No. 56 Sqn., North Weald, **US-P**, 4-41. No. 316 (Polish) Sqn., Colerne, 6-41.
Z2587 *Mark IIA*. No. 56 Sqn., North Weald, 4-41; shot down over the Channel, 21-5-41.
Z2589 *Temporarily fitted with four-cannon wing for tests by H.A.L.*; delivered to R.A.F. as *Mark IIA*. No. 615 Sqn., A.A.F. No. 258 Sqn., Kenley, 4-41; crashed at Lingfield, Surrey, 16-5-41.
Z2591 *Trop. Mark IIA*. To the Middle East. S.O.C., 26-11-41.
Z2628 *Mark IIA*. No. 1 Sqn., Kenley and Hawkinge, 3-41. *Shipped to Russia*, 11-10-41.
Z2630 *Mark IIA*. No. 615 Sqn., A.A.F., Kenley, 4-41.
Z2632 *Mark IIB*. No. 242 Sqn., Manston, **LE-A**, 7-41.
Z2633 *Mark IIB*. No. 79 Sqn., Pembrey, **NV-M**, 4-41.
Z2635 *Mark IIA*. No. 56 Sqn., North Weald, 4-41. *Shipped to Russia*, 7-1-42.
Z2636 *Mark IIA*. No. 56 Sqn., North Weald, US-U, 4-41. *Shipped to Russia*, 25-9-41.
Z2639 *Mark IIA*. No. 249 Sqn., North Weald, 4-41. No. 402 Sqn., R.C.A.F., Wellingore, 5-41.
Z2663 *Mark IIA*. No. 249 Sqn., North Weald, 4-41; crashed near Ongar, Essex, 7-4-41.
Z2664 *Mark IIA*. No. 56 Sqn., North Weald, **US-O**, 4-41; Missing over the Channel, 17-6-41.
Z2667 *Mark IIA*. No. 302 (Polish) Sqn., Westhampnett, "**E**", 4-41.
Z2670 *Mark IIA*. No. 601 Sqn., A.A.F., Northolt, **UF-J**, 4-41.
Z2671 *Mark IIA*. No. 310 (Czech) Sqn., Duxford, 4-41.
Z2674 *Mark IIA*. No. 79 Sqn., Pembrey, **NV-M**, 4-41. No. 56 Sqn., North Weald, **US-M**, 5-41.
Z2676 *Mark IIA*. No. 402 Sqn., R.C.A.F., Wellingore, 5-41.
Z2677 *Mark IIA*. No. 56 Sqn., North Weald, **US-N**, 5-41.
Z2679 *Trop. Mark IIB*. No. 80 Sqn., El Adem, 1941. No. 335 (Greek) Sqn., 1943; crashed 26-2-43.
Z2681 *Mark IIB*. No. 312 (Czech) Sqn., Kenley, 5-41.
Z2682 *Mark IIB*. No. 247 Sqn., Predannack, **HP-R**, 6-41.
Z2683 *Mark IIB*. No. 310 (Czech) Sqn., Duxford, 4-41.
Z2684 *Mark IIB*. No. 43 Sqn., Drem, 4-41. No. 136 Sqn., Kirton-in-Lindsey, 8-41.
Z2687 *Mark IIA*. No. 257 Sqn., Coltishall, 3-41. No. 1 Sqn., Kenley and Hawkinge, 4-41; convoy patrols.
Z2688 *Mark IIA*. No. 56 Sqn., North Weald, **US-S**, 4-41.
Z2689 *Mark IIA*. No. 258 Sqn., Kenley, 4-41.
Z2690 *Mark IIA*. No. 1 Sqn., Kenley and Hawkinge, 4-41; convoy patrols. *Shipped to Russia*, 9-9-41.
Z2693 *Mark IIA*. No. 310 (Czech) Sqn., Duxford, 4-41.
Z2696 *Mark IIA*. No. 317 (Polish) Sqn., Exeter, 7-41. S.O.C., 15-11-44.
Z2697 *Mark IIA*. No. 56 Sqn., North Weald, 4-41.
Z2700 *Mark IIA*. No. 258 Sqn., Kenley, 4-41. No. 258 Sqn.; crashed in sea off Shoreham, Sussex, 18-5-41.
Z2702 *Mark IIA*. No. 56 Sqn., North Weald, 4-41. No. 316 (Polish) Sqn. *Shipped to Russia*, 11-10-41.
Z2703 *Mark IIA*. No. 615 Sqn., A.A.F., Kenley, **KW-M**, 4-41.
Z2705 *Mark IIA*. No. 316 (Polish) Sqn., Colerne, 6-41.
Z2744 *Mark IIA*. No. 71 Sqn., North Weald, 6-41.
Z2747 *Mark IIB*. No. 242 Sqn., Manston, 7-41. No. 79 Sqn.
Z2752 *Mark IIA*. No. 257 Sqn., Honiley, 11-41.
Z2755 *Mark IIA*. No. 56 Sqn., North Weald, 5-41.
Z2758 *Mark IIA*. No. 258 Sqn., Kenley, 4-41. No. 615 Sqn., A.A.F., Kenley, 4-41.
Z2759 *Mark IIA*. No. 1 Sqn., Kenley and Hawkinge, 4-41; convoy patrols.
Z2763 *Mark IIA*. No. 56 Sqn., North Weald, 4-41; Missing from patrol, 26-4-41.
Z2764 *Mark IIA*. No. 1 Sqn., Kenley and Hawkinge, 4-41; shot down by Bf 109Es near Calais, 21-5-41.
Z2767 *Mark IIA*. No. 56 Sqn., North Weald, 4-41. Shipped to the Middle East.
Z2769 *Mark IIA*. No. 56 Sqn., North Weald, **US-W**, 4-41. *Shipped to Russia*, but lost at sea, 20-5-42.
Z2770 *Mark IIA*. No. 310 (Czech) Sqn., Duxford, 4-41.
Z2772 *Mark IIA*. No. 302 (Polish) Sqn., Westhampnett, "**B**", 4-41.
Z2774 *Mark IIA*. No. 253 Sqn., Hibaldstow, 10-41.
Z2792 *Mark IIA*. No. 316 (Polish) Sqn., Colerne, 6-41.
Z2795 *Mark IIA*. *Radio trials*, T.R.E., Malvern, 8-41. Telecommunications Flying Unit, 3-42; crashed north of Hurn, 27-4-42.
Z2799 *Mark IIA*. No. 17 Sqn., Castletown, **YB-P**, 4-41.
Z2801 *Mark IIA*. No. 17 Sqn., Castletown, **YB-S**, 4-41. No. 43 Sqn., Drem, **FT-R**, 5-41.
Z2802 *Mark IIA*. No. 1 Sqn., Kenley and Hawkinge, 4-41. No. 316 (Polish) Sqn., Colerne, 6-41. No. 253 Sqn., Hibaldstow, 10-41.
Z2804 *Mark IIA*. No. 402 Sqn., R.C.A.F., Wellingore, 5-41.
Z2806 *Mark IIA*. No. 302 (Polish) Sqn., Kenley, "**A**", 4-41.
Z2807 *Mark IIA*. No. 1 Sqn., Kenley and Hawkinge, 4-41.
Z2808 *Mark IIA*. No. 257 Sqn., Honiley, 11-41. *Shipped to Russia*, 5-2-43.
Z2810 *Mark IIA*. No. 1 Sqn., Kenley and Hawkinge, 3-41; damaged by Bf 109Es, 19-3-41, and S.O.C. on return.
Z2814 *Mark IIA*. No. 302 (Polish) Sqn., Kenley, "**K**", 4-41; crashed in sea off Dungeness, 26-4-41.
Z2815 *Trop. Mark IIA*. No. 605 Sqn., A.A.F., Hal Far, Malta; S.O.C., 7-3-42.
Z2821 *Mark IIA*. No. 135 Sqn., Baginton, 8-41. *Shipped to Russia*, 25-3-42.
Z2825 *Trop. Mark IIA*. No. 126 Sqn., Ta Kali, Malta, 6-41.
Z2828 *Mark IIA*. No. 1 Sqn., Croydon, 4-41. No. 1 T.E.U. S.O.C., 31-5-41.
Z2832 *Mark IIA*. No. 32 Sqn., 5-41; force landed in Eire, 10-6-41; *flown temporarily by Irish Air Corps* as "***94***"; returned to R.A.F., 7-43. S.O.C., 31-5-45.
Z2884 *Mark IIA*. No. 306 (Polish) Sqn., Northolt, **UZ-Z**, 4-41.
Z2885 *Trials with four 20-mm. Hispano cannon in production Mark IIC wing*, A. & A.E.E., 3-41.
Z2890 *Mark IIC*. No. 537 (Turbinlite) Sqn., Middle Wallop, "**G**" 12-41.
Z2891 *Mark IIB*. No. 3 Sqn., Martlesham Heath, **QO-R**, 4-41.
Z2893 *Mark IIB*. No. 601 Sqn., A.A.F., Manston, **UF-I**, 5-41.
Z2895 *Trials with modified fuel system*, A. & A.E.E., 4-41.
Z2903 *Mark IIB*. Northolt Stn. Flt., 7-41. *Shipped to Russia*, 7-9-41.
Z2905 *Trials with 90-gallon ferry tanks on Mark IIC wing*, A. & A.E.E., 13-3-41.
Z2906 *Mark IIB*. No. 257 Sqn., Coltishall, 6-41.
Z2907 *Mark IIB*. No. 257 Sqn., Coltishall, 4-41.
Z2909 *Mark IIB*. No. 1 Sqn., Croydon, 4-41.
Z2916 *Mark IIB*. No. 331 (Norwegian) Sqn., Castletown, **FN-U**, 8-41.
Z2918 *Mark IIB*. No. 601 Sqn., A.A.F., Manston, 5-41. *Shipped to Russia*, 19-1-42.
Z2920 *Mark IIB*. No. 317 (Polish) Sqn., Exeter, 7-41. *Shipped to Russia*, but lost at sea, 17-12-42.
Z2926 *Mark IIB*. No. 257 Sqn., Coltishall, 4-41. *Shipped to Russia*, 23-1-42.
Z2928 *Mark IIA*. No. 402 Sqn., R.C.A.F., Wellingore, 5-41.
Z2960 *Mk. IIB*. No. 245 Sqn., Ballyhalbert, **MR-P**, 8-41.
Z2961 *Trop. Mark IIB*. No. 185 Sqn., Hal Far, Malta, "**K**", 8-41.
Z2962 *Mark IIA*. No. 316 (Polish) Sqn., Colerne, 6-41; crashed at Wolverhampton, 1-10-41.
Z2966 *Mark IIA*. No. 257 Sqn., Honiley. No. 55 O.T.U. S.O.C., 11-8-44.
Z2967 *Mark IIA*. No. 253 Sqn., Hibaldstow, 10-41. S.O.C., 31-5-45.
Z2985 *Mark IIC*. No. 3 Sqn., Stapleford Tawney, **QO-F**, 6-41. No. 1449 Flt. S.O.C., 29-9-44.
Z2987 *Mark IIB*. No. 312 (Czech) Sqn., Kenley, 5-41. *Shipped to Russia*, 23-10-41.
Z2991 *Mark IIB*. No. 253 Sqn., Skaebrae, 7-41. *Shipped to Russia*. 2-2-42.
Z2992 *Mark IIB*. No. 401 Sqn., R.C.A.F., Digby, 6-41.
Z3018 *Mark IIB*. No. 401 Sqn., R.C.A.F., Digby, 6-41. To India, 1943.
Z3022 *Mark IIB*. No. 56 Sqn., Martlesham Heath, **US-C**, 6-41.
Z3025 *Mark IIB*. No. 3 Sqn., Martlesham Heath, **QO-C**, 4-41. No. 257 Sqn., Coltishall, 6-41. *Shipped to Russia*, 29-4-42.
Z3030 *Mark IIB*. No. 601 Sqn., A.A.F., Manston, 5-41.
Z3031 *Mark IIB*. No. 43 Sqn., Drem, **FT-A**, 6-41. *Shipped to Russia*, but lost at sea, 22-10-42.
Z3036 *Mark IIB*. Northolt Stn. Flt., 4-41. *Tropicalised* and shipped to the Mediterranean.
Z3051 *Mark IIC*. No. 257 Sqn., Coltishall, 5-41. No. 247 Sqn.; crashed near Predannack, 5-11-41.
Z3056 *Mark IIC*. Northolt Stn. Flt., 4-41. No. 249 Sqn.; Missing, 4-9-41.
Z3058 *Mark IIC*. Northolt Stn. Flt., 4-41. *Tropicalised*, and shipped to the Middle East, but lost at sea, 5-41.
Z3069 *Mark IIC*. No. 3 Sqn., Stapleford Tawney, **QO-F**, 6-41.
Z3070 *Mark IIC*. No. 257 Sqn., Coltishall, 6-41. No. 615 Sqn., A.A.F., Manston, 10-41. *Tropicalised*, 1942. *Supplied to French Armée de l'Air*, 9-8-45.
Z3075 *Mark IIB*. No. 242 Sqn., Manston, 7-41. No. 245 Sqn.
Z3076 *Mark IIB*. No. 121 Sqn., Kirton-in-Lindsey, 7-41.
Z3078 *Mark IIB*. No. 135 Sqn., Baginton, 8-41. *Shipped to Russia*, 12-2-42.
Z3081 *Mark IIB*. No. 43 Sqn., Drem, **FT-C**, 6-41. *Converted to Mark IIC*. No. 534 (Turbinlite) Sqn.; collided with Boston near Arundel, 21-10-42.
Z3084 *Mark IIC*. No. 247 Sqn., Predannack, 8-41. *Tropicalised* and shipped to the Middle East.
Z3086 *Mark IIC*. No. 3 Sqn., Stapleford Tawney, **QO-P**, 6-41.
Z3088 *Mark IIC*. No. 257 Sqn., Coltishall, 6-41. No. 247 Sqn.

Z3091 *Mark IIB*. No. 312 (Czech) Sqn., Kenley, 6-41. Collided with Hurricane and abandoned near Westerham, Kent, 29-6-41.
Z3092 *Mark IIB*. *Trials with three-inch R.P.s*, A. & A.E.E., 4-41, as ***Z3092/G.***
Z3095 *Mark IIA*. No. 302 (Polish) Sqn., "**N**", Kenley, c.4-41.
Z3099 *Mark IIB*. No. 605 Sqn., A.A.F., Baginton, 5-41. *Shipped to Russia*, 11-10-41.
Z3148 *Mark IIA*. No. 249 Sqn., North Weald, 6-41. No. 601 Sqn., A.A.F., Matlaske, 7-41.
Z3150 *Mark IIB*. No. 43 Sqn., Drem, **FT-Y**, 6-41; crashed at Peel Fell, Roxburgh, 3-11-41.
Z3151 *Mark IIB*. No. 253 Sqn., Skaebrae, 7-41. No. 402 Sqn., R.C.A.F., Rochford, 8-41. No. 79 Sqn., Fairwood Common, **NV-F**, 10-41.
Z3156 *Mark IIB*. No. 79 Sqn., Pembrey, **NV-H**, 6-41. No. 242 Sqn., Manston, 7-41.
Z3157 *Trials with "universal" wing*, A. & A.E.E. and R.A.E., 1941.
Z3160 *Mark IIB*. No. 1 Sqn. No. 247 Sqn., Predannack, 8-41. *Shipped to Russia*, 5-4-42.
Z3161 *Mark IIB (modified to Mark IIC)*. No. 539 (Turbinlite) Sqn., Acklington, 9-42. Shipped to the Far East. S.O.C., 28-9-44.
Z3164 *Mark IIB*. No. 257 Sqn., Coltishall, 7-41.
Z3165 *Mark IIB*. No. 302 (Polish) Sqn., Jurby, "**K**", 7-41. No. 1 Sqn., Tangmere. *Shipped to Russia*, 13-3-42.
Z3171 *Mark IIB*. No. 121 Sqn., Kirton-in-Lindsey, 7-41.
Z3174 *Mark IIA*. No. 71 Sqn., North Weald, **XR-B**, 7-41.
Z3175 *Mark IIC*. No. 257 Sqn., Coltishall, 7-41. *Shipped to Russia*, 17-6-42, but lost at sea.
Z3176 *Mark IIA*. No. 249 Sqn., North Weald, 6-41.
Z3177 *Mark IIA*. No. 601 Sqn., A.A.F., Manston, 7-41.
Z3181 *Mark IIB*. No. 312 (Czech) Sqn., Kenley, 7-41. No. 615 Sqn., A.A.F.
Z3182 *Mark IIB*. No. 133 Sqn., Duxford, 8-41; crashed at Roslarkin, Ulster, 27-10-41.
Z3222 *Mark IIB*. No. 331 (Norwegian) Sqn., Castletown, **FN-J**, 8-41.
Z3225 *Mark IIB*. No. 3 Sqn., Stapleford Tawney, 6-41. No. 601 Sqn., A.A.F.
Z3227 *Mark IIB*. No. 56 Sqn., Martlesham Heath, **US-V**, 6-41. No. 331 (Norwegian) Sqn.
Z3230 *Mark IIA*. No. 402 Sqn., R.C.A.F., Rochford, 8-41.
Z3238 *Mark IIB*. No. 136 Sqn., Kirton-in-Lindsey, "**P**", 8-41.
Z3241 *Mark IIB*. No. 257 Sqn., Coltishall, 6-41. *Lost at sea en route to Russia*, 19-7-42.
Z3257 *Mark IIB*. No. 601 Sqn., A.A.F., Manston, **UF-A**, 6-41.
Z3261 *Mark IIC*. No. 151 Sqn., Wittering, 6-41. No. 253 Sqn., Hibaldstow, 1-42; crashed south of Grimsby, 14-8-42.
Z3263 *Mark IIB*. No. 253 Sqn., Skaebrae, 7-41.
Z3265 *Mark IIC*. No. 3 Sqn., Stapleford Tawney, **QO-Z**, 6-41.
Z3271 *Mark IIC*. No. 253 Sqn., Hibaldstow, **SW-P**, 1-42.
Z3314 *Mark IIB*. No. 312 (Czech) Sqn., Kenley, 7-41.
Z3316 *Mark IIB*. No. 43 Sqn., Drem, **FT-E**, 6-41; crashed near Bowes, Yorks, 1-5-42.
Z3319 *Mark IIB*. No. 402 Sqn., R.C.A.F., Rochford, 8-41.
Z3322 *Mark IIB*. No. 257 Sqn., Coltishall, 6-41; shot down by enemy fighters over Holland, 15-9-41.
Z3323 *Mark IIC*. No. 245 Sqn., Middle Wallop, c.3-42. *Tropicalised* and shipped to the Middle East. Middle East Central Gunnery School; crashed while landing at El Ballah, 16-1-45.
Z3324 *Mark IIB*. No. 56 Sqn., Duxford, **US-F**, 7-41.
Z3332 *Mark IIB*. No. 1 Sqn., Redhill, 6-41.
Z3333 *Mark IIB*. No. 401 Sqn., R.C.A.F. Digby Stn. Flt. No. 253 Sqn. *Shipped to Russia*, 19-8-42.
Z3341 *Mark IIB*. No. 1 Sqn., Tangmere, Channel patrols, 7-41.
Z3345 *Mark IIA*. No. 71 Sqn., North Weald, 7-41. No. 133 Sqn.
Z3347 *Mark IIA*. No. 133 Sqn., Duxford, 8-41. No. 134 Sqn., Eglinton, 1-42.
Z3353 *Mark IIB*. No. 317 (Polish) Sqn., Exeter, 7-41. Shipped to India. S.O.C., 29-12-45.
Z3355 *Mark IIB* No. 1 Sqn., Tangmere, 7-41, Channel patrols.
Z3356 *Mark IIB*. No. 601 Sqn., A.A.F., Matlaske, **UF-O**, 7-41. No. 515 Sqn., A.A.F., Manston, 9-41. *Lost at sea during shipment to Russia*, 20-5-42.
Z3387 *Mark IIB*. No. 257 Sqn., Coltishall, 7-41. S.O.C., 27-2-42.
Z3390 *Mark IIB*. No. 257 Sqn., Coltishall, 7-41.
Z3395 *Mark IIB* No. 402 Sqn., R.C.A.F., Rochford, 8-41.
Z3397 *Mark IIB*. No. 601 Sqn., A.A.F., Matlaske, **UF-T**, 7-41.
Z3399 *Mark IIB*. No. 121 Sqn., Kirton-in-Lindsey, 7-41.
Z3402 *Mark IIB*. No. 302 (Polish) Sqn., Jurby, "**Z**", 7-41.
Z3422 *Mark IIB*. No. 121 Sqn., Kirton-in-Lindsey, 7-41; collided with Hurricane ***Z3317*** over Lincoln and abandoned, 27-7-41.
Z3447 *Mark IIB* No. 3 Sqn., Stapleford Tawney, 7-41.
Z3448 *Mark IIB*. No. 257 Sqn., Coltishall, 7-41; crashed 3 miles NE of Coltisall, 31-8-41, during aerobatics.
Z3451 *TI aircraft for various equipment trials*, A. & A.E.E., 1941-43.
Z3454 *Mark IIB* No. 601 Sqn., A.A.F., Matlaske, **UF-S**, 7-41.
Z3458 *Mark IIA* No. 71 Sqn., North Weald, 7-41. No. 615 Sqn., A.A.F.
Z3465 *Mark IIC*. No. 151 Sqn., Wittering, 7-41. No. 253 Sqn.
Z3467 *Mark IIC*. No. 151 Sqn., Wittering, 7-41. No. 3 Sqn.
Z3496 *Mark IIB*. No. 1 Sqn., Redhill, 7-41. No. 121 Sqn.
Z3501 *Mark IIB*. No. 312 (Czech) Sqn., Martlesham Heath, 7-41.
Z3502 *Mark IIC*. No. 87 Sqn., Charmy Down, **LK-J**, 7-41. No. 486 (NZ) Sqn.
Z3504 *Mark IIB*. No. 242 Sqn., Manston, 8-41. No. 331 (Norwegian) Sqn, 9-41.
Z3511 *Mark IIB*. No. 257 Sqn., Coltishall, 8-41. *Shipped to Russia*, 19-5-42.
Z3513 *Mark IIB*. No. 56 Sqn., Duxford, **US-S**, 8-41.
Z3514 *Trop. Mark IIC*. To the Middle East. No. 213 Sqn., Western Desert. *Supplied to Turkey*, 31-1-43.
Z3516 *Mark IIB*. No. 257 Sqn., Coltishall, 8-41.
Z3554 *Trop. Mark IIC*. No. 73 Sqn. No. 250 Sqn., El Gamil, 2-42.
Z3559 *Mark IIB* No. 317 (Polish) Sqn., Exeter, 8-41.
Z3564 *Armament trials with Mark IIB wings*, H.A.L. and A. & A.E.E., 1941-42. S.O.C., 15-5-42.
Z3573 *Mark IIB*. No. 316 (Polish) Sqn., Colerne, 8-41. No. 615 Sqn., A.A.F., Manston, 9-41.
Z3583 *Mark IIC*. No. 3 Sqn., Stapleford Tawney, 8-41. Missing from intruder sortie to Laon, 28-8-42.
Z3589 *Mark IIB*. No. 401 Sqn., R.C.A.F. Digby, 8-41. No. 257 Sqn. shot down by enemy fighters over Dutch coast, 12-9-41.
Z3590 *Trop. Mark IIC*. No. 213 Sqn., Idku, **AK-R**, 1-42. No. 250 Sqn., El Gamil, 2-42. S.O.C., 25-6-42.
Z3593 *Mark IIB*. No. 121 Sqn., Kirton-in-Lindsey, **AV-F**, 8-41.
Z3595 *Mark IIB*. No. 1 Sqn., Tangmere, 8-41. *Tropicalised* and shipped to the Middle East. *Supplied to the French Armée de L'Air*, 2-8-45.
Z3596 *Mark IIB*. No. 253 Sqn., Skaebrae, 8-41. No. 4 T.E.U. S.O.C., 28-5-45.
Z3654 *Mark IIB*. No. 56 Sqn., Duxford, **US-P**, 8-41.
Z3659 *Mark IIB*. No. 401 Sqn., R.C.A.F., Digby, 8-41.
Z3662 *Mark IIB*. No. 247 Sqn., Predannack, 8-41. No. 79 Sqn.; crashed 3 miles north of Treherbert, Monmouth, 26-9-41.
Z3665 *Mark IIB*. No. 133 Sqn., Duxford, 8-41.
Z3666 *Mark IIB*. No. 121 Sqn., Kirton-in-Lindsey, **AV-J**, 8-41. *Shipped to Russia*, 22-10-41.
Z3668 *Mark IIB*. No. 302 (Polish) Sqn., Jurby, "**W**", 8-41.
Z3669 *Mark IIB*. No. 121 Sqn., Kirton-in-Lindsey, **AV-X**, 8-41.
Z3670 *Mark IIB*. No. 253 Sqn., Skaebrae, 8-41; crashed in sea off Spurn Head, 12-12-41.
Z3672 *Mark IIB*. No. 43 Sqn., Drem, **FT-T**, 8-41.
Z3675 *Mark IIB*. No. 302 (Polish) Sqn., Jurby, "**B**", 8-41.
Z3677 *Mark IIA*. No. 71 Sqn., North Weald, 8-41. No. 133 Sqn.; crashed at Ramsey, Isle of Man, 8-10-41.
Z3684 *Mark IIB*. No. 331 (Norwegian) Sqn., Castletown, **FN-C**, 8-41. *Converted to Mark IIC*. No. 245 Sqn., Middle Wallop, 3-42.
Z3686 *Mark IIB*. No. 136 Sqn., Kirton-in-Lindsey, 8-41. Shipped to Russia, 5-11-41.
Z3687 *Mark IIB*. No. 17 Sqn. No. 123 Sqn. No. 245 Sqn. To the R.A.E., Aerodynamics Dept.; *trials with A.W.A. laminar flow wings*, 1946-48. S.O.C., 9-4-51.
Z3740 *Mark IIB*. No. 317 (Polish) Sqn., Exeter, 8-41.
Z3744 *Mark IIB*. No. 257 Sqn., Coltishall, 8-41. No. 601 Sqn., A.A.F., Duxford, **UF-P**, 9-41.
Z3745 *Mark IIB*. No. 79 Sqn., Fairwood Common, **NV-B**, 7-41. No. 133 Sqn. No. 134 Sqn.
Z3746 *Mark IIB*. No. 81 Sqn., Vaenga, North Russia, 9-41; shot down by flak, North Russia, 12-9-41; Sgt. N. Smith killed.
Z3748 *Mark IIC*. *Shipped to Russia*, 8-10-41.
Z3760 *Trop. Mark IIB*. No. 127 Sqn., Shandur, 6-42.
Z3763 *Trop. Mark IIB*. No. 134 Sqn., Vaenga, North Russia, 9-41. *Left in Russia*, 28-10-41.
Z3766 *Trop. Mark IIB*. No. 126 Sqn., Ta Kali, Malta, 10-41; damaged by Bf 109Fs and abandoned off Malta, 10-4-42.
Z3768 *Trop. Mark IIB*. No. 134 Sqn., Vaenga, North Russia, 9-41, "**FK-49**". *Left in Russia*, 28-10-41.
Z3770 *Mark IIB*. No. 121 Sqn., Kirton-in-Lindsey, 8-41.
Z3773 *Mark IIB*. No. 245 Sqn., Ballyhalbert, MR-D, 8-41.
Z3774 *Mark IIC*. No. 1 Sqn., Tangmere, 8-41; Missing after attacks on destroyers during escape of *Scharnhorst* and *Gneisenau* in English Channel, 12-2-42.
Z3775 *Mark IIC*. No. 87 Sqn., Charmy Down, **LK-B**, 8-41. No. 533 (Turbinlite) Sqn., Colerne, 11-41.
Z3776 *Mark IIC*. No. 87 Sqn., Charmy Down, **LK-N**, 8-41; crashed near Northleach, Glos., 24-2-42.
Z3778 *Mark IIC*. No. 1 Sqn., Tangmere, **JX-Y**, 2-42; crashed while landing at Acklington, 14-8-42.
Z3779 *Mark IIC*. No. 87 Sqn., Colerne, **LK-Y**, 10-41; crashed near Dundry, Somerset, 1-4-42.
Z3781 *Mark IIA*. No. 71 Sqn., North Weald, 9-41. No. 133 Sqn., Colly Weston, 9-41.
Z3782 *Mark IIB*. No. 253 Sqn., Coltishall, 9-41. No. 257 Sqn., Coltishall, 9-41.
Z3826 *Mark IIC*. No. 1 Sqn., Tangmere, **JX-E**, 9-41; shot down by flak near Ostend, 27-10-41.
Z3830 *Mark IIC*. No. 532 (Turbinlite) Sqn., Wittering, 9-41. No. 615 Sqn., A.A.F., Manston, 10-41.
Z3841 *Mark IIC*. No. 1 Sqn., Tangmere, 8-41. No. 615 Sqn., A.A.F., Manston, 10-41.
Z3842 *Mark IIC*. No. 1 Sqn., Tangmere, 8-41. No. 32 Sqn.; collided with Havoc over Farleigh, Kent, 2-6-42.
Z3843 *Mark IIC*. No. 1 Sqn., Tangmere, 8-41; abandoned 2 miles north of Horsham, Sussex, 27-8-41.
Z3844 *Mark IIC*. No. 1 Sqn., Tangmere, 7-41; crashed while landing at Langley, 2-10-41.
Z3845 *Mark IIC*. No. 245 Sqn., 8-41; Missing after attack on flak ships off French coast, 17-8-41.
Z3885 *Mark IIC*. No. 1 Sqn., Redhill, 8-41. No. 615 Sqn., A.A.F.
Z3888 *Miscellaneous external store trials with production Mark IIC wing*, A. & A.E.E., 7-41 to 1-42. Shipped to India; crashed at Ranchi, 28-3-45.
Z3893 *Mark IIB*. No. 43 Sqn., Drem, 8-41. *Modified to*

Mark IIC. No. 532 (Turbinlite) Sqn., Wittering, 11-41.

Z3894 *Mark IIC*. No. 3 Sqn., Hunsdon, **QO-R**, 8-41. *Shipped to Russia*, 15-1-43.

Z3897 *Mark IIC*. No. 1 Sqn., Tangmere, **JX-N**, 8-41; crashed at Bersted, Sussex, 3-6-42.

Z3899 *Mark IIC*. No. 1 Sqn., Tangmere, 7-41; collided with Hurricane ***BD940*** over the Isle of Wight, 22-11-41.

Z3900 *Mark IIB*. No. 17 Sqn. Tain Stn. Flt. *Shipped to Russia*, but lost at sea, 7-6-42.

Z3902 *Mark IIC*. No. 1 Sqn., Tangmere, 7-41; crashed near Petworth, Sussex, 16-7-41.

Z3903 *Mark IIC*. No. 1 Sqn., Tangmere, 7-41.

Z3919 *Trials at R.A.E. with various rocket projectiles*, 1942-44.

Z3969 *Mark IIB*. No. 401 Sqn., R.C.A.F., Digby, 8-41.

Z3970 *Mark IIC*. No. 1 Sqn., Tangmere, 7-41; took part in attack on enemy destroyers during escape of German fleet up Channel, 12-2-42; crashed near Bognor, Sussex, 10-4-42, during low flying.

Z3971 *Mark IIC*. No. 253 Sqn., Hibaldstow, **SW-S**, 1-42.

Z3975 *Mark IIB*. No. 317 (Polish) Sqn., Exeter, 9-41.

Z3976 *Mark IIB*. No. 134 Sqn., Vaenga, North Russia, 9-41. *Left in Russia*, 28-10-41.

Z3977 *Mark IIB*. No. 134 Sqn., Vaenga, North Russia, 9-41, "**FK-55**"; *left in Russia*, 28-10-41.

Z3979 *Mark IIB*. No. 253 Sqn., Skaebrae, 8-41. *Shipped to Russia*, 15-11-41.

Z3981 *Performance check trials*, H.A.L., 8-41. *Shipped to Russia*, 5-9-41.

Z3982 *Mark IIB*. No. 302 (Polish) Sqn., Jurby, "**S**", 8-41. *Shipped to Russia*, 12-10-41.

Z3987 *Mark IIB*. No. 331 (Norwegian) Sqn., Castletown, 8-41. *Shipped to Russia*, 21-3-42.

Z3988 *Mark IIB*. No. 504 Sqn., A.A.F., Fairwood Common, 8-41. No. 79 Sqn.

Z3993 *Trop. Mark IIB*. No. 185 Sqn., Hal Far, Malta, "**X**", 10-41. S.O.C., 9-6-42.

Z4006 *Trop. Mark IIB*. No. 81 Sqn., Vaenga, North Russia, 9-41. *Left in Russia*, 28-10-41.

Z4007 *Trop. Mark IIB*. No. 335 (Greek) Sqn., Dekheila, Egypt, 1942; crashed while landing at L.G.08, Western Desert, 21-8-43.

Z4009 *Trop. Mark IIB*. No. 127 Sqn., Shandur, 6-42; crashed at Ramat David, 11-2-43.

Z4011 *Trop. Mark IIB*. No. 185 Sqn., Hal Far, Malta, "**B**", 10-41; crashed into Hurricane ***Z2904*** while landing at Ta Kali, 12-2-42.

Z4014 *Trop. Mark IIB*. No. 605 Sqn., A.A.F., Hal Far, Malta, 1-42. S.O.C., 2-9-42.

Z4017 *Trop. Mark IIB*. No. 81 Sqn., Vaenga, North Russia, 9-41. *Left in Russia*, 28-10-41.

Z4018 *Trop. Mark IIB*. No. 81 Sqn., Vaenga, North Russia, 9-41. *Left in Russia*, 28-10-41.

HAWKER CANADIAN HURRICANE Mark I. First series production batch of 100 aircraft built by Canadian Car & Foundry Corporation, Montreal, Canada, and delivered between November 1940 and April 1941. *Z6983-Z7017, Z7049-Z7093, Z7143-Z7162*. Rolls-Royce Merlin XX engines.

Z6983 *Trop. Mk. I*. Shipped to the Middle East but lost at sea, 5-41.

Z6984 *Trop. Mk. I*. Shipped to the Middle East. Lost, 23-6-41.

Z6985 *Trop. Mk. I*. Shipped to the Middle East. No. 30 Sqn. Royal Navy Fighter Sqn., R.A.F.; lost, 23-6-41.

Z6986 *Trop. Mk. I*. Shipped to the Middle East. No. 74 O.T.U. S.O.C., 12-44.

Z6987 *Converted to Sea Hurricane I* and transferred to Admiralty charge, 17-7-41.

Z6988 *Trop. Mk. I*. Shipped to the Middle East. No. 30 Sqn., Idku; crashed during night landing at Idku, 23-7-41.

Z6989 *Trop. Mk. I*. Shipped to the Middle East. No. 74 O.T.U.

Z6990 *Trop. Mk. I*. Shipped to the Middle East but lost at sea, 5-41.

Z6991 *Trop. Mk. I*. Shipped to the Middle East. S.O.C., 12-6-41.

Z6992 *Trop. Mk. I*. Shipped to the Middle East, 1-41. No. 73 Sqn.

Z6993 *Trop. Mk. I*. Shipped to the Middle East, 1941. S.O.C., 9-8-41.

Z6994 *Trop. Mk. I*. Shipped to the Middle East but lost at sea, 5-41.

Z6995 *Converted to Sea Hurricane I* and transferred to Admiralty Charge, 1-11-41.

Z6996 *Trop. Mk. I*. Shipped to the Middle East. No. 74 O.T.U.

Z6997 *Converted to Sea Hurricane I* and transferred to Admiralty Charge, 7-41.

Z6998 *Trop. Mk. I*. Shipped to the Middle East. No. 213 Sqn., Idku, 1-42. No. 1564 Flt. S.O.C., 25-5-44.

Z6999 *Trop. Mk. I*. Shipped to the Middle East. No. 127 Sqn. No. 451 Sqn., R.A.A.F. No. 335 (Greek) Sqn. S.O.C., 1-12-43.

Z7000 *Trop. Mk. I*. Shipped to the Middle East. No. 80 Sqn. No. 3 Sqn., R.A.A.F. No. 30 Sqn.; Missing, 8-7-42.

Z7001 No. 59 O.T.U.; crashed at Dovenby, Cumberland, 23-6-42.

Z7002 *Trop. Mk. I*. Shipped to the Middle East, but lost at sea, 5-41.

Z7003 *Trop. Mk. I*. Shipped to the Middle East. No. 213 Sqn., Idku, 1-42. No. 74 O.T.U. No. 1413 Flt. Rhodesian Air Training Group. S.O.C., 22-10-45.

Z7004 *Trop. Mk. I*. Shipped to the Middle East. No. 30 Sqn.; crashed near Idku, 31-8-41.

Z7005 *Trop. Mk. I*. Shipped to the Middle East. No. 30 Sqn. No. 71 O.T.U. S.O.C., 1-1-44.

Z7006 *Trop. Mk. I*. Shipped to the Middle East, but lost at sea, 5-41.

Z7007 *Trop. Mk. I*. Shipped to the Middle East. No. 74 O.T.U.; crashed while landing at Rayak, Syria, 7-8-42.

Z7008 *Converted to Sea Hurricane I* and transferred to Admiralty Charge, 7-41.

Z7009 *Trop. Mk. I*. Shipped to the Middle East. No. 213 Sqn., Nicosia, Cyprus; crashed while landing at Nicosia, 4-12-41.

Z7010 No. 1 Ferry Pilots' Pool; crashed at Bledloe, Bucks, 17-3-41.

Z7011 No. 232 Sqn. No. 55 O.T.U. *Tropicalised* and shipped to the Middle East. S.O.C., 1-4-44.

Z7012 *Trop. Mk. I*. Shipped to the Middle East. No. 30 Sqn. No. 335 (Greek) Sqn. No. 71 O.T.U. S.O.C., 1-12-43.

Z7013 *Trop. Mk. I*. Shipped to the Middle East. No. 213 Sqn. No. 7 Sqn., S.A.A.F. S.O.C., 28-8-44.

Z7014 *Trop. Mk. I*. Shipped to the Middle East. No. 450 Sqn., R.A.A.F. No. 335 (Greek) Sqn.

Z7015 *Converted to Sea Hurricane I*, and transferred to Admiralty Charge, 7-41.

Z7016 *Converted to Sea Hurricane I*, and transferred to Admiralty Charge, 7-41.

Z7017 *Trop. Mk. I*. Shipped to the Middle East. No. 94 Sqn. No. 26 Anti-Aircraft Co-operation Unit. S.O.C., 28-8-44.

Z7049 No. 232 Sqn. No. 8 F.T.S. No. 55 O.T.U. No. 41 O.T.U. S.O.C., 21-5-44.

Z7050 *Converted to Sea Hurricane I* and transferred to Admiralty Charge, 7-41.

Z7051 Crashed while on test with No. 5 M.U., 3-8-41.

Z7052 No. 232 Sqn. No. 55 O.T.U.; crashed in snowstorm, 6 miles NW of Horncastle, Lincs, 17-2-42.

Z7053 No. 232 Sqn.; abandoned in bad weather over Yorkshire, 31-7-41.

Z7054 Nothing known.

Z7055 *Converted to Sea Hurricane I* and transferred to Admiralty Charge, 10-8-41.

Z7056 No. 55 O.T.U. No. 1624 Flt. No. 567 Sqn. S.O.C., 18-5-44.

Z7057 *Converted to Sea Hurricane I* and transferred to Admiralty Charge, 22-8-41.

Z7058 *Trop. Mk. I*. Shipped to the Middle East but lost at sea, 1-43.

Z7059 No. 59 O.T.U. *Tropicalised* and shipped to the Far East. S.O.C., 30-6-44.

Z7060 No. 59 O.T.U. *Tropicalised* and shipped to the Far East. Rhodesian Training Group; S.O.C., 3-5-46.

Z7061 *Converted to Sea Hurricane I* and transferred to Admiralty Charge, 8-8-41.

Z7062 No. 232 Sqn.; crashed at Consett, Co. Durham, 30-8-41.

Z7063 No. 55 O.T.U. S.O.C., 29-12-41.

Z7064 *Converted to Sea Hurricane I* and transferred to Admiralty Charge, 28-8-41.

Z7065 *Converted to Sea Hurricane I* and transferred to Admiralty Charge, 21-6-41.

Z7066 R.A.E., Farnborough. S.O.C., 18-5-44.

Z7067 *Converted to Sea Hurricane I* and transferred to Admiralty Charge, 7-41.

Z7068 *Converted to Sea Hurricane I* and transferred to Admiralty Charge, 7-41.

Z7069 *Converted to Sea Hurricane I* and transferred to Admiralty Charge, 7-41.

Z7070 No. 55 O.T.U. S.O.C., 11-7-44.

Z7071 *Converted to Sea Hurricane I* and transferred to Admiralty Charge, 10-9-41.

Z7072 *No. 55 O.T.U.* No. 232 Sqn., Ouston, 9-41; crashed near Ouston, 25-10-41.

Z7073 *Converted to Sea Hurricane IA*. Merchant Ship Fighter Unit, 8-41. Transferred to Admiralty Charge, 5-6-43.

Z7074 No. 55 O.T.U. *Tropicalised* and shipped to the Far East. S.O.C., 30-6-44.

Z7075 No. 55 O.T.U. No. 41 O.T.U. S.O.C., 18-5-44.

Z7076 Crashed near Henlow, 27-3-41, following control failure.

Z7077 No. 55 O.T.U.; collided with Canadian Hurricane ***AG125*** and crashed in sea off Drumburgh, Cumberland, 8-7-42.

Z7078 *Converted to Sea Hurricane I* and transferred to Admiralty Charge, 7-41; became ***4537M***, 2-44.

Z7079 *Converted to Sea Hurricane I* and transferred to Admiralty Charge, 23-11-41.

Z7080 *Converted to Sea Hurricane I* and transferred to Admiralty Charge, 17-7-41.

Z7081 No. 55 O.T.U. *Tropicalised* and shipped to the Far East. S.O.C., 1-3-44.

Z7082 *Converted to Sea Hurricane I* and transferred to Admiralty Charge, 15-8-41.

Z7083 Merchant Ship Fighter Unit. No. 59 O.T.U.; crashed near Milfield, 29-11-43.

Z7084 *Trop. Mk. I*. To the Middle East. No. 1 Sqn., S.A.A.F.

Z7085 *Converted to Sea Hurricane I* and transferred to Admiralty Charge, 7-41; became ***4660M***, 3-44.

Z7086 *Converted to Sea Hurricane I* and transferred to Admiralty Charge, 7-41; became ***4688M***, 3-44.

Z7087 *Converted to Sea Hurricane I* and transferred to Admiralty Charge, 7-41.

Z7088 *Converted to Sea Hurricane I* and transferred to Admiralty Charge, 16-10-41.

Z7089 *Converted to Sea Hurricane I* and transferred to Admiralty Charge, 28-8-41.

Z7090 *Converted to Sea Hurricane I* and transferred to Admiralty Charge, 21-6-41.

Z7091 *Converted to Sea Hurricane I* and transferred to Admiralty Charge, 21-6-41; became ***4665M***, 2-44.

Z7092 No. 55 O.T.U.; collided with Canadian Hurricane ***AG274*** and abandoned near Newtyle, Angus, 23-2-43.

Z7093 *Converted to Sea Hurricane I* and transferred to Admiralty Charge, 19-8-41.

Z7143 No. 615 Sqn., A.A.F. No. 256 Sqn. No. 55 O.T.U. No. 9 Group Comms. Flt. No. 41 O.T.U. S.O.C., 23-5-44.

Z7144 *Converted to Sea Hurricane I* and transferred to Admiralty Charge, 6-41; became ***4746M***, 3-44.

Z7145 Merchant Ship Fighter Unit. No. 59 O.T.U. Empire Central Flying School. Became ***5042M***, c.6-44.

Z7146 No. 55 O.T.U. *Tropicalised* and shipped to the Far East. S.O.C., 31-8-44.
Z7147 *Converted to Sea Hurricane* and transferred to Admiralty Charge, 6-41; became ***4507M***, 2-44.
Z7148 *Converted to Sea Hurricane I* and transferred to Admiralty Charge, 7-41.
Z7149 *Converted to Sea Hurricane I* and transferred to Admiralty Charge, 14-10-41.
Z7150 No. 59 O.T.U.; collided with Hurricane ***Z4103*** and crashed near Kirkbride, 13-4-42.
Z7151 *Converted to Sea Hurricane I* and transferred to Admiralty Charge, 7-41.
Z7152 *Converted to Sea Hurricane I* and transferred to Admiralty Charge, 21-6-41.
Z7153 *Converted to Sea Hurricane I* and transferred to Admiralty Charge, 15-8-41.
Z7154 *Converted to Sea Hurricane I* and transferred to Admiralty Charge, 23-7-41.
Z7155 *Converted to Sea Hurricane I* and transferred to Admiralty Charge, 15-8-41.
Z7156 No. 59 O.T.U.; crashed, 23-4-42; became ***3603M***.
Z7157 No. 56 O.T.U.; crashed while taking off at Kinnell, 2-10-42.
Z7158 No. 56 O.T.U. Newtownards Stn. Flt.
Z7159 No. 615 Sqn., A.A.F. No. 59 O.T.U.; crashed at Dalmally, Argyll, 27-11-41.
Z7160 *Converted to Sea Hurricane I* and transferred to Admiralty Charge, 21-6-41.
Z7161 *Converted to Sea Hurricane I* and transferred at Admiralty Charge, 21-6-41.
Z7162 *Converted to Sea Hurricane I* and transferred to Admiralty Charge, 31-7-41.

HAWKER (CANADIAN) HURRICANE Mark I (re-designated Mark X). Second series production batch of 340 aircraft, in three parts, built by Canadian Car & Foundry Corporation, Ontario, Canada, and delivered between March 1941 and May 1942; average rate of production, slightly less than one aircraft per day. Part 1 (20 aircraft): *AE958-AE977*. Part 2 (300 aircraft): *AF945-AG344*. Part 3 (20 aircraft): *AG665-AG684*. All aircraft in Parts 1 and 2 originally built with eight-gun wings and Packard Merlin 28 engines; some later modified (by No. 13 M.U., Henlow) with 12-gun or four-cannon wings, but remaining Mark Xs; other fitted with Merlin XX engines to become Mark IIAs, IIBs and IICs. (Dates given beside Sea Hurricane conversions are those on which they were taken on charge by the Admiralty.)

Part 1.
AE958 *Converted to Sea Hurricane IB*, 7-41.
AE959 *Converted to Sea Hurricane IB*, 7-41.
AE960 No. 401 Sqn., R.C.A.F., **YO-W**, 8-41. *Converted to Sea Hurricane IC*, 27-9-41.
AE961 *Converted to Sea Hurricane IB*, 7-41.
AE962 *Converted to Sea Hurricane IB*, 24-10-42.
AE963 No. 401 Sqn., R.C.A.F. No. 615 Sqn., A.A.F. No. 331 (Norwegian) Sqn., 7-41.
AE964 No. 401 Sqn., R.C.A.F., **YO-C**. *Converted to Sea Hurricane IC*, 15-8-41.
AE965 Merchant Ship Fighter Unit. No. 55 O.T.U. No. 41 O.T.U. S.O.C., 29-12-44.
AE966 No. 401 Sqn., R.C.A.F., **YO-A**. *Converted to Sea Hurricane IC*, 15-8-41.
AE967 *Converted to Sea Hurricane IB*, 7-41.
AE968 *Converted to Sea Hurricane IB*, 22-7-41.
AE969 *Converted to Sea Hurricane IB*, 7-41.
AE970 S.O.C. on arrival in U.K., 8-5-41.
AE971 Lost at sea during delivery to U.K., 4-41.
AE972 Lost at sea during delivery to U.K., 4-41.
AE973 Lost at sea during delivery to U.K., 4-41.
AE974 Lost at sea during delivery to U.K., 4-41.
AE975 *Converted to Sea Hurricane IB*, 9-8-41.
AE976 No. 55 O.T.U.; collided with Hurricane ***V6915***, Tudhoe, Co. Durham, 14-2-42.
AE977 *Converted to Sea Hurricane IB*, 17-7-42.

Part 2.
AF945 *Converted to Sea Hurricane IB*, 21-6-41; became ***4758M***.
AF946 *Converted to Sea Hurricane IB*, 28-1-42.
AF947 *Converted to Sea Hurricane IB*, 15-8-41.
AF948 *Tropicalised* and shipped to India. No. 1 Sqn., I.A.F. S.O.C., 30-11-43.
AF949 *Converted to Sea Hurricane IB*, 17-7-41.
AF950 *Converted to Sea Hurricane IB*, 17-7-41; became ***4694M***.
AF951 *Converted to Sea Hurricane IB*, 7-41.
AF952 *Converted to Sea Hurricane IB*, 15-8-41.
AF953 *Converted to Sea Hurricane IB*, 9-41.
AF954 *Tropicalised* and shipped to India. No. 1 Sqn., I.A.F. S.O.C., 10-44.
AF955 *Converted to Sea Hurricane IB*, 7-41.
AF956 No. 59 O.T.U.; crashed on take-off at Milfield, 14-6-43, following engine failure.
AF957 Aircraft declared rogue. Became ***3082M***.
AF958 No. 59 O.T.U. No. 56 O.T.U. No. 2 T.E.U. S.O.C., 23-6-44.
AF959 No. 225 Sqn. No. 55 O.T.U.; crashed near Keswick, 21-1-43.
AF960 *Tropicalised* and shipped to India. No. 1 Sqn., I.A.F.
AF961 No. 43 Sqn., Tangmere, 7-42; believed ditched in English Channel during training, 11-7-42.
AF962 *Converted to Sea Hurricane IB*, 2-8-42.
AF963 *Converted to Sea Hurricane IB*, 6-41.
AF964 No. 56 O.T.U. No. 43 Sqn. No. 32 Sqn. No. 59 O.T.U. S.O.C., 28-12-44.
AF965 Merchant Ship Fighter Unit. *Converted to Sea Hurricane IB*, 30-8-43.
AF966 *Converted to Sea Hurricane IB*, 15-7-41.
AF967 *Converted to Sea Hurricane IB*, 7-41.
AF968 No. 55 O.T.U.; collided with Hurricane ***V6798*** and crashed near Stanley, Co. Durham, 12-4-42.
AF969 *Converted to Sea Hurricane IB*, 7-41.
AF970 No. 55 O.T.U. No. 59 O.T.U. No. 63 O.T.U. No. 4 T.E.U. No. 2 T.E.U.; crashed near Castle Corroch, Cumberland, 20-3-44.
AF971 *Converted to Sea Hurricane IB*, 6-41.
AF972 No. 59 O.T.U. *Tropicalised* and shipped to the Far East.
AF973 *Converted to Sea Hurricane IB*, 1-10-41.
AF974 *Converted to Sea Hurricane IB*, 19-9-41.
AF975 Telecommunications Flying Unit. No. 41 O.T.U.
AF976 Merchant Ship Fighter Unit. No. 56 Fighter Unit; crashed 4 miles east of Rattray, Perthshire, 24-8-43.
AF977 *Tropicalised* and shipped to the Middle East; later West Africa. S.O.C., 21-6-45.
AF978 No. 56 O.T.U. Damaged beyond repair, 9-10-42.
AF979 R.A.E., Farnborough. No. 1441 Flt. No. 197 Sqn., Drem, 11-42. No. 7 P.A.F.U. S.O.C., 9-12-44.
AF980 No. 1 Sqn. No. 55 O.T.U. Shipped to the Far East. S.O.C., 30-4-44.
AF981 *Converted to Sea Hurricane IB*, 10-10-41; became ***4696M***.
AF982 *Converted to Sea Hurricane IB*, 25-9-41.
AF983 Shipped to the Far East. S.O.C., 1-3-44.
AF984 No. 32 Sqn. No. 55 O.T.U.; crashed at night 8 miles NE of Longtown, 15-4-43.
AF985 Crashed in sea near Skinburnness, Solway Firth, 3-12-41.
AF986 No. 59 O.T.U. No. 55 O.T.U. No. 41 O.T.U. No. 7 P.A.F.U.; crashed at Pinchbeck, Lincs, 12-9-44.
AF987 Ferry Training Unit. No. 55 O.T.U. S.O.C., 27-5-44.
AF988 *Trop. Mark X*. To the Middle East. No. 71 O.T.U.; S.O.C., 1-4-44.
AF989 *Trop. Mark X*. To India. No. 151 O.T.U.; S.O.C., 28-9-44.
AF990 No. 247 Sqn. No. 534 (Turbinlite) Sqn. No. 10 Group Comms. Flt. S.O.C., 24-11-44.
AF991 *Trop. Mark X*. To the Far East. S.O.C., 31-7-44.
AF992 *Trop. Mark X*. To the Far East. S.O.C., 9-44.
AF993 *Trop. Mark X*. To the Middle East. No. 71 O.T.U., Ismailia, 2-43. Rhodesia Air Training Group. S.O.C., 22-10-45.
AF995 No. 225 Sqn. No. 87 Sqn. S.O.C., 23-5-44.
AF999 *Trop. Mark X*. To India. No. 151 O.T.U. S.O.C., 28-9-44.
AG100 *Trop. Mark X*. To India. No. 151 O.T.U. S.O.C., 28-9-44.
AG101 No. 286 Sqn., Lulsgate Bottom, 2-42. No. 318 (Polish) Sqn., 3-43. No. 2 T.E.U. S.O.C., 27-5-44.
AG106 No. 247 Sqn., Predannack, 6-41. No. 2 T.E.U. S.O.C., 23-5-44.
AG109 *Trop. Mark X*. Shipped to India. No. 151 O.T.U.; crashed near Risalpur, 22-4-43.
AG111 No. 57 O.T.U.; collided with Spitfire ***P7902*** and crashed near Wooler, Northumberland, 5-5-43.
AG112 *Trop. Mark X*. Shipped to India. No. 151 O.T.U.; collided with Canadian Hurricane ***AG155***, 24-11-42.
AG118 No. 1 Sqn., Hawkinge, 5-41. No. 55 O.T.U. S.O.C., 3-1-45.
AG122 No. 55 O.T.U. Fitted with 12-gun wings. *Converted to Mark IIB* with Merlin XX by Rolls-Royce Ltd. S.O.C. 14-6-45.
AG123 No. 59 O.T.U.; crashed at Witches Knowe, Berwick, 24-6-43.
AG124 No. 56 O.T.U.; collided with Hurricane ***P2799*** and crashed near Forfar, Angus, 11-9-42.
AG125 No. 55 O.T.U.; collided with Hurricane ***Z7077*** and crashed in sea of Drumburgh, Cumberland, 8-7-42.
AG128 *Trop. Mark X*. Shipped to India. No. 151 O.T.U.; crashed while landing at Risalpur, 12-2-43.
AG129 *Trop. Mark X*. Shipped to India. No. 151 O.T.U.; crashed while landing at Risalpur, 19-11-42.
AG131 *Trop. Mark X*. Shipped to India. No. 1 Sqn., I.A.F.; crashed at Ragbunathpur, 24-10-43.
AG136 *Trop. Mark X*. Shipped to India. No. 151 O.T.U.; collided with Hurricane ***Z4229*** near Peshawar, 13-5-40.
AG141 No. 245 Sqn. No. 181 Sqn., Duxford, 9-42. Shipped to the Far East. S.O.C., 12-43.
AG146 No. 527 Sqn., Hornchurch; calibration of East Coast radar, 10-43. S.O.C., 21-11-4.
AG149 *Trop. Mark X*. Shipped to the Middle East. No. 71 O.T.U., Ismailia. S.O.C., 1-3-44.
AG153 *Trop. Mark X*. Shipped to the Mediterranean. No. 680 (PR) Sqn., Cyprus, 8-43. Rhodesian Air Training Group. S.O.C., 22-10-45.
AG159 No. 182 Sqn., Martlesham Heath. To the Far East. S.O.C., 30-4-44.
AG161 *Trop. Mark X*. Shipped to India. No. 151 O.T.U.; crashed near Risalpur, 12-11-42.
AG164 No. 56 O.T.U.; crashed at Loch Rannoch, Perthshire, 9-8-42.
AG169 *Trop. Mark X*. Shipped to India. No. 151 O.T.U.; crashed near Khunda, Peshawar, 5-2-44.
AG170 *Trop. Mark X*. Shipped to the Middle East. No. 71 O.T.U., Ismailia, 11-42. S.O.C., 28-8-44.
AG171 No. 56 O.T.U.; crashed near Lauder, Berwick, 29-6-43.
AG177 *Trop. Mark X*. No. 1432 (Army Co-operation) Flt., Oshogbo, Nigeria; crashed north of Kano, 12-12-42.
AG178 *Trop. Mark X*. No. 1432 (Army Co-operation) Flt., Oshogbo, Nigeria; crashed in the Abwa Hills, Nigeria, 19-6-43..
AG181 No. 59 O.T.U.; crashed while landing at Milfield, 16-1-43, following engine failure.
AG187 No. 253 Sqn., Skaebrae, 8-42; coastal shipping protection off the Orkneys.
AG190 No. 1449 Flt.; crashed while landing at St. Mary's, Scillies, 25-7-42.
AG191 No. 257 Sqn., Coltishall, 6-41; coastal shipping protection. S.O.C., 27-5-44.
AG195 No. 55 O.T.U.; collided with Hurricane ***W9151*** and crashed near Ecclefechan, Dumfies, 11-11-42.
AG196 No. 247 Sqn. No. 56 Sqn., North Weald, coastal shipping protection.
AG198 *Trop. Mark X*. Shipped to the Middle East. No.

71 O.T.U., Ismailia, 3-43. S.O.C., 28-8-44.

AG216 *Converted to Mark IIB*. No. 486 (NZ) Sqn. No. 1 Sqn., Tangmere, **JX-O**. Crashed near Collaton, Devon, 22-5-44.

AG223 *Trop. Mark X*. Shipped to the Middle East. No. 71 O.T.U., Ismailia, 3-43.

AG232 No. 182 Sqn., Martlesham Heath, **XM-P**, 9-42.

AG236 *Converted to Mark IIC*. No. 43 Sqn., Tangmere, 6-42.

AG237 *No. 247 Sqn*., Predannnack, c.6-41. No. 55 O.T.U.

AG249 *Trop. Mark X*. Shipped to the Middle East. No. 71 O.T.U.; crashed near Moascar, 25-5-43.

AG264 No. 32 Sqn. No. 55 O.T.U.; crashed near Coniston, Cumberland, 25-4-43.

AG265 No. 253 Sqn. No. 609 Sqn., A.A.F.; crashed on landing at Manston, 27-5-43.

AG274 No. 56 O.T.U.; collided with Hurricane ***Z7092*** and crashed near Auchterhouse, Angus, 23-2-43.

AG280 No. 245 Sqn. No. 181 Sqn., Duxford, 9-42. No. 56 O.T.U.; crashed near Tealing, 5-5-43.

AG283 *Trop. Mark X*. Shipped to India. No. 1 Sqn., I.A.F.; crashed at Bangalore, 2-10-42.

AG342 *Trop. Mark X*. Shipped to India. No. 20 Sqn., Madhaibunia, India; Missing from tactical reconnaissance, 18-2-44.

[Note: The following aircraft were transferred to the R.C.A.F. in Canada: AG287, AG293-AG296, AG299, AG300, AG302-AG319, AG323, AG325-AG327, AG330, AG332. The following aircraft were converted to Mark IIBs in Britain and shipped to Russia between july and September 1942: AG298, AG301, AG320, AG321, AG324, AG328, AG329, AG333, AG336, AG339, AG343, AG344.]

Part 3.

AG665 *Mark IIB*. No. 3 Sqn. *Shipped to Russia*, 6-1-43.

AG666 *Mark IIB*. *Converted to Sea Hurricane*, 14-9-42.

AG667 *Mark IIB*. *Converted to Sea Hurricane*, 10-9-42.

AG668 *Mark IIB*. *Shipped to Russia*, 19-8-42.

AG669 *Mark IIB*. *Converted to Sea Hurricane*, 12-9-42.

AG670 *Mark IIB*. *Shipped to Russia*, 28-12-42.

AG671 *Converted to Mark IIC*. Shipped to the Far East, 1942.

AG672 *Mark IIB*. *Shipped to Russia*, 24-8-42.

AG673 *Mark IIB*. *Shipped to Russia*, 20-9-42.

AG674 *Mark IIB*. *Shipped to Russia*, 22-9-42.

AG675 *Mark IIB*. *Shipped to Russia*, 24-8-42.

AG676 *Mark IIB*. No. 3 Sqn. *Shipped to Russia*, 12-1-43.

AG677 *Mark IIB*. *Shipped to Russia*, 19-8-42.

AG678 *Mark IIB*. *Shipped to Russia*, 20-8-42, but lost at sea.

AG679 *Mark IIB*. *Shipped to Russia*, 22-9-42.

AG680 *Mark IIB*. Crashed 12-6-42.

AG681 *Mark IIB*. *Shipped to Russia*, 20-8-42, but lost at sea.

AG682 *Mark IIB*. *Shipped to Russia*, 26-1-43.

AG683 *Mark IIB*. *Shipped to Russia*, 19-8-42.

AG684 *Mark IIB*. *Shipped to Russia*, 12-1-43.

HAWKER CANADIAN HURRICANE Mark X (Rebuilt as Mark IIBs and IICs in U.K.). Third production batch of 100 aircraft built by Canadian Car & Foundry Corporation, Ontario, Canada, between March 1942 and February 1943. *AM270-AM369*. (Aircraft not listed below were shipped to Russia either from the U.K. or direct from Canada).

AM275 No. 247 Sqn., Predannack. No. 1449 Flt. S.O.C., 18-5-44.

AM277 *Converted to Sea Hurricane*, 12-10-42.

AM280 No. 1 Sqn., Tangmere. No. 3 Sqn., Stapleford Tawney; collided with Hurricane near Debden, 26-11-42.

AM282 No. 3 Sqn., Stapleford Tawney. No. 539 (Turbinlite) Sqn., Acklington; crashed while landing at Acklington, 4-11-42.

AM283 *Trop. Mark IIB*. Shipped to India. No. 2 Sqn., I.A.F. No. 3 Refresher Unit; crashed 20-5-44.

AM286 No. 3 Sqn., Stapleford Tawney; shot down by Fw 190 and crashed into cliffs at Dieppe, 19-8-42.

AM288 *Converted to Sea Hurricane*, 2-9-42.

AM289 *Mark IIC*. No. 534 (Turbinlite) Sqn. *Supplied to Portugal*, 4-9-43.

AM293 No. 3 Sqn., Stapleford Tawney. *Tropicalised* and shipped to the Far East. S.O.C., 31-8-44.

AM294 *Mark IIC*. *Supplied to Portugal*, 14-8-43.

AM295 No. 247 Sqn., Predannack. No. 1449 Flt.; abandoned over the sea south of the Scillies, 14-6-43.

AM311 *Mark IIC*. No. 43 Sqn., **FT-X**. Telecommunications Flying Unit. S.O.C., 12-8-44.

AM315 No. 43 Sqn. No. 247 Sqn. *Tropicalised* and shipped to the Middle East. Air Bombing & Gunnery School (Middle East); crashed near Kantara, 21-8-44.

AM347 No. 1 Sqn., Tangmere. No. 32 Sqn.; crashed near West Malling, Kent, during low attack exercise, 23-8-42.

AM353 No. 32 Sqn. No. 247 Sqn. No. 3 Sqn. *Supplied to Portugal*, 15-8-43.

AM358 No. 1 Sqn. No. 32 Sqn., No. 247 Sqn. *Tropicalised* and shipped to the Middle East. S.O.C., 24-7-45.

HAWKER CANADIAN HURRICANE Mark IIB. Fourth production batch of 26 aircraft (all with 12-gun wings and Rolls-Royce Merlin XX engines), *AP138-AP163*. *AP138* shipped to Russia from Canada but lost at sea. All the remaining aircraft retained in Canada and delivered to the R.C.A.F. for training purposes.

HAWKER HURRICANE Mark IIB and IIC (Austin-built). Single production batch of 300 aircraft built by the Austin Motor Co., Longbridge, between February 1941 and October 1942. *AP516-AP550, AP564-AP613, AP629-AP648, AP670-AP714, AP732-AP781, AP801-AP825, AP849-AP898, AP912-AP936*. (A further 100 aircraft, *AP937-AP956, AR113-AR162* and *AR178-AR207*, cancelled).

AP516 *Mark IIB*. *Performance trials*, A. & A.E.E., 1941. No. 306 (Polish) Sqn.; Missing from bomber escort to Comines, 28-6-41.

AP517 *Mark IIB*. *Performance trials*, H.A.L. and A. & A.E.E. *Shipped to Russia*, 1942.

AP518 *Mark IIB*. No. 312 (Czech) Sqn., Ayr, 10-41. *Shipped to Russia*, 23-10-41.

AP519 *Mark IIB*. No. 312 (Czech) Sqn., Ayr, 10-41. *Shipped to Russia*, 22-10-41.

AP520 *Mark IIB*. *Shipped to Russia*.

AP521 *Mark IIB*. No. 121 Sqn. *Shipped to Russia*, 15-11-41.

AP522 *Mark IIB*. No. 245 Sqn. *Shipped to Russia*, 27-11-41.

AP523 *Mark IIB*. No. 245 Sqn. *Shipped to Russia*, 22-10-41.

AP524 *Mark IIC*. No. 245 Sqn.; collided with Hurricane ***BD738*** and crashed near Chilbolton, 25-9-41.

AP525 *Mark IIB*. No. 17 Sqn. *Shipped to Russia*, 25-10-41.

AP529 *Mark IIB*. No. 242 Sqn. *Shipped to Russia*, 12-10-41.

AP530 *Mark IIB*. No. 242 Sqn. No. 615 Sqn., A.A.F. No. 32 Sqn.; crashed at Bexley Hill, Maidstone, 29-5-42.

AP532 *Mark IIC*. No. 601 Sqn., A.A.F. *Shipped to Russia*, 12-10-41.

AP533 *Mark IIB*. No. 242 Sqn. *Shipped to Russia*, 10-10-41.

AP534 *Mark IIB*. No. 242 Sqn. *Shipped to Russia*, 12-10-41.

AP849 *Trop. Mk. IIC*. Shipped to the Middle East. No. 208 Sqn. No. 241 Sqn.; damaged beyond repair, 15-12-43.

AP850 *Trop. Mk. IIC*. Shipped to the Middle East. No. 889 Sqn., F.A.A., L.G.104, El Daba, 12-42. No. 335 (Greek) Sqn.

AP851 *Trop. Mk. IIB. Shipped to the Middle East. Converted to Trop. Tac R. Mk. IIB*. No. 208 Sqn., 1942. S.O.C., 1-4-44.

AP852 *Trop. Mk. IIB. Shipped to the Middle East. Converted to Trop. Tac R. Mk. IIB*. No. 208 Sqn., 1942; crashed near L.G.202, 29-9-42.

AP854 *Trop. Mk. IIB. Shipped to the Middle East*. S.O.C., 31-12-42.

AP855 *Trop. Mk. IIB*. Shipped to the Middle East. S.O.C., 1-7-43.

AP856 *Trop. Mk. IIB*. Shipped to the Mediterranean. No. 127 Sqn. No. 261 Sqn.

AP857 *Trop. Mk. IIB*. Shipped to the Far East. No. 20 Sqn. No. 261 Sqn.

AP858 *Trop. Mk. IIB*. Shipped to the Far East. S.O.C., 26-9-44.

AP881 *Trop. Mk. IIC*. Shipped to India. Crashed near Allahabad, 18-11-43.

AP882 *Trop. Mk. IIB*. No. 1 Sqn., I.A.F.; crashed 18-11-43.

AP885 *Trop. Mk. IIB*. Shipped to the Middle East. No. 336 (Greek) Sqn.

AP888 *Trop. Mk. IIC*. No. 335 (Greek) Sqn. S.O.C., 3-10-42.

AP889 *Trop. Mk. IIB*. Shipped to India. No. 607 Sqn., Chittagong, 2-43.

AP892 *Trop. Mk. IIB*. No. 261 Sqn., China Bay, Ceylon, 6-42. No. 146 Sqn., Dum Dum, 7-42.

AP894 *Trop. Mk. IIB*. No. 135 Sqn., Akyab, Burma, 3-42. S.O.C., 28-9-44.

AP896 *Trop. Mk. IIB*. No. 261 Sqn., Chittagong; shot down by Ki 43s near Chittagong, 20-10-43.

AP916 *Trop. Mk. IIB*. No. 261 Sqn., China Bay, Ceylon, 5-42.

AP920 *Trop. Met Mk. IIC*. No. 1414 (Met.) Flt., Mogadishu, Italian Somaliland; weather reconnaissance, 1943. S.O.C., 26-4-45.

AP925 *Trop. Mk. IIB*. No. 335 (Greek) Sqn.; collided with Hurricane ***HV581*** during take-off at L.G.121, 12-6-43.

AP929 *Trop. Mk. IIB*. No. 146 Sqn., Dum Dum, 8-42. S.O.C., 27-9-44.

AP930 *Trop. Mk. IIB*. No. 261 Sqn., China Bay, Ceylon, 6-42; Missing from combat operation, 23-10-43.

AP936 *Trop. Mk. IIB*. No. 261 Sqn., Chittagong; shot down by Ki 43s near Chittagong, 20-10-43.

[Note: The following aircraft were shipped to Russia from the U.K. without any prior service with the R.A.F.: AP528, AP535-AP550, AP564-AP613, AP629-AP648, AP670-AP714, AP732-AP781, AP801-AP825, AP859-AP879.]

HAWKER HURRICANE Mark IIB, IIC and IID (Hawker-built). Sixth production batch of 1,350 aircraft built by Hawker Aircraft Ltd., Kingston-upon-Thames and Langley. Rolls-Royce Merlin XX engines. *BD696-BD745, BD818-BD837, BD855-BD899, BD914-BD963, BD980-BD986, BE105-BE117, BE130-BE174, BE193-BE242, BE274-BE308, BE323-BE372, BE394-BE428, BE468-BE517, BE546-BE590, BE632-BE651, BE667-BE716; BM898-BM936, BM947-BM996, BN103-BN142, BN155-BN189, BN203-BN242, BN265-BN298, BN311-BN337, BN346-BN389, BN399-BN435, BN449-BN497, BN512-BN547, BN559-BN603, BN624-BN654, BN667-BN705, BN719-BN759, BN773-BN802, BN818-BN846, BN859-BN882, BN896-BN940, BN953-BN987*. Deliveries commenced 24-7-41; completed 18-3-42; average rate of production, six aircraft per day.

BD696 *Mk. IIC*. No. 3 Sqn., Hunsdon; night intruder operations, 9-41. *Tropicalised* and shipped to the Middle East. No. 229 Sqn., Bu Amoud, 12-41.

BD697 *Mk. IIB*. No. 81 Sqn., Vaenga, North Russia, 9-41.

BD699 *Mk. IIB*. No. 134 Sqn., Vaenga, North Russia,

9-41; defensive patrols.

BD700 *Mk. IIB (later tropicalised).* No. 335 (Greek) Sqn., Dekheila; patrols over Mersa Matruh, 8-42.

BD701 *Mk. IIB (later tropicalised).* No. 258 Sqn., Ratmalana and Colombo, Ceylon; defensive patrols, 3-42; shot down by A6M2s over Colombo, 5-4-42.

BD704 *Mk. IIB.* No. 134 Sqn., Vaenga, North Russia; defensive patrols, 9-41.

BD707 *Mk. IIB.* No. 402 Sqn., R.C.A.F., Rochford; bomber escorts, 8-41.

BD709 *Mk. IIB.* No. 401 Sqn., R.C.A.F., Digby; offensive sweeps, 8-41. *Shipped to Russia*, 26-10-41.

BD712 *Mk. IIB.* No. 402 Sqn., R.C.A.F., Rochford; bomber escorts, 8-41. No. 601 Sqn., A.A.F., Duxford, **UF-Y**, 9-41. No. 111 Sqn.; shot down during Dieppe combined operations, 19-8-42.

BD714 *Mk. IIB.* No. 331 (Norwegian) Sqn., Skaebrae, **FN-O**; shipping patrols, 9-41.

BD715 *N.F. Mk. IIB.* No. 43 Sqn., Drem; Turbinlite patrols, **FT-M**, 9-41.

BD716 *Mk. IIB.* No. 401 Sqn., R.C.A.F., Digby; offensive sweeps, 8-41.

BD717 *N.F. Mk. IIB.* No. 43 Sqn., Drem; Turbinlite patrols, 9-41.

BD719 *Mk. IIB.* No. 317 (Polish) Sqn., Exeter; shipping patrols, 9-41.

BD727 *Trop. Mk. IIB.* No. 136 Sqn., Alipore, India; night interception patrols, 3-42.

BD728 *N.F. Mk. IIB.* No. 486 (N.Z.) Sqn., Kirton-in-Lindsey; Turbinlite patrols, 9-41.

BD729 *N.F. Mk. IIC.* No. 3 Sqn., Hunsdon; night interception patrols, 3-42.

BD730 *Trop. Mk. IIB.* No. 136, Alipore, India; night interception patrols, 3-42.

BD731 *Mk. IIB.* No. 605 Sqn., A.A.F., Kenley; fighter sweeps, 9-41. Shipped to Russia, 16-2-42.

BD734 *Mk. IIB.* No. 331 (Norwegian) Sqn., Skaebrae, **FN-D**; shipping patrols, 9-41.

BD737 *Mk. IIB.* No. 504 Sqn., A.A.F., Ballyhalbert; operational training, 9-41.

BD741 *Mk. IIB.* No. 17 Sqn., Catterick, 11-41. *Shipped to Russia*, 14-11-41.

BD742 *Mk. IIB.* No. 605 Sqn., A.A.F., Kenley; fighter sweeps, 9-41. *Shipped to Russia*, 10-10-41.

BD744 *N.F. Mk. IIB.* No. 253 Sqn., Hibaldstow; night defensive operations, 9-41.

BD761 *N.F. Mk. IIB.* No. 253 Sqn., Hibaldstow; night defensive operations, 9-41.

BD762 *N.F. Mk. IIB.* No. 43 Sqn., Drem; Turbinlite patrols, 9-41. No. 331 (Norwegian) Sqn., Skaebrae; **FN-S**; shipping escorts, 11-41.

BD764 *Mk. IIB.* No. 402 Sqn., R.C.A.F., Rochford; bomber escorts, 9-41.

BD765 *Mk. IIB.* No. 402 Sqn., R.C.A.F., Rochford; bomber escorts, 9-41.

BD766 *Mk. IIB (A.I.-equipped).* No. 245 Sqn., Chilbolton; night defensive patrols, 9-41; shot down during Dieppe combined operatrions, 19-8-42.

BD768 *Mk. IIB.* No. 32 Sqn., Manston; daylight sweeps, 11-41.

BD770 *N.F. Mk. IIB.* No. 1 Sqn., Tangmere; intruder operations, 2-42. No. 539 (Turbinlite) Sqn., Acklington, c.6-42; crashed 2 miles south of Ashington, Northumberland, 30-11-42.

BD772 *Trop. Mk. IIB.* Shipped to Egypt. Lost through enemy action, 22-2-42.

BD774 *Trop. Mk. IIB.* No. 73 Sqn., El Adem; desert patrols, 2-43; lost through enemy action, 28-5-42.

BD775 *Trop. Mk. IIB.* No. 94 Sqn., Msus; desert patrols, 1-42.

BD776 *Trop. Mk. IIB.* No. 128 Sqn., Hastings, Sierra Leone; **WG-F**; base patrols, 1-42. *Supplied to Turkey*, 1-7-43.

BD777 *Trop. Mk. IIB.* No. 238 Sqn., Gambut; desert offensive sweeps, 2-42.

BD779 *Trop. Mk. IIB.* No. 417 Sqn., R.C.A.F., Shandur; air defence of the Suez Canal, 9-42.

BD782 *Trop. Mk. IIB.* No. 73 Sqn., El Adem, 2-42. No. 208 Sqn.

BD787 *Mk. IIC.* No. 242 Sqn., Manston, anti-shipping sweeps, 9-41. No. 615 Sqn., A.A.F.; shot down by Bf 109Fs off Blankenberge, 18-9-41.

BD791 *Trop. Mk. IIB.* No. 126 Sqn., Ta Kali, Malta; defensive operations, 9-41.

BD792 *Trop. Mk. IIB.* No. 81 Sqn., Vaenga, North Russia; defensive patrols, 9-41.

BD793 *Trop. Mk. IIB.* No. 127 Sqn., Shandur; desert patrols, 9-41. Converted to *Trop. Tac R Mk. IIC*, 8-42. No. 208 Sqn., Western Desert, c.9-42.

BD820 *Trop. Mk. IIB.* No. 274 Sqn., Maryut; shipping escorts, 10-41.

BD822 *Mk. IIB.* No. 81 Sqn., Vaenga, North Russia; defensive patrols, 9-41. *Left in Russia*, 28-10-41.

BD823 *Mk. IIB.* No. 134 Sqn., Vaenga, North Russia; defensive patrols, 9-41. *Left in Russia*, 29-10-41.

BD825 *Mk. IIB.* No. 134 Sqn., Vaenga, North Russia; crashed, 27-9-41, with two airmen on the tail; both killed.

BD831 *Mk. IIC.* No. 242 Sqn., Manston, anti-shipping sweeps, 9-41.

BD833 *Mk. IIC.* No. 87 Sqn., Charmy Down; night interception patrols, **LK-Q**, 2-42. No. 533 (Turbinlite) Sqn., Charmy Down, c.4-42.

BD834 *N.F. Mk. IIC.* No. 247 Sqn., Exeter; night anti-shipping sweeps, **ZY-V**, 8-42

BD836 *N.F. Mk. IIC.* No. 3 Sqn., Hunsdon; night interception operations, 9-41.

BD855 *N.F. Mk. IIC.* No. 605 Sqn., A.A.F., Kenley; day/night intruder operations, 10-41.

BD859 *N.F. Mk. IIC.* No. 247 Sqn., Exeter; night anti-shipping sweeps, 9-42.

BD860 *N.F. Mk. IIC.* No. 3 Sqn., Hunsdon; night interception operations, **QO-Y**, 9-41.

BD863 *N.F. Mk. IIC.* No. 43 Sqn., Tangmere; night intruder operations, 7-42.

BD866 *Trop. Mk. IIC.* No. 238 Sqn., Gambut; desert offensive operations, "**F**", 3-42.

BD867 *N.F. Mk. IIC.* No. 3 Sqn., Hunsdon; night interception operations, **QO-W**, 9-41.

BD868 *N.F. Mk. IIC.* No. 3 Sqn., Hundson; night interception operations, **QO-P**, 9-41.

BD871 *Mk. IIC. Shipped to Russia*, 7-9-41.

BD872 *Mk. IIC.* No. 242 Sqn., Manston; anti-shipping sweeps, 9-41. No. 539 (Turbinlite) Sqn. Shipped to the Far East.

BD874 *Mk. IIC.* No. 331 (Norwegian) Sqn., Skaebrae; shipping escorts, **FN-Z**, 9-41.

BD875 *Mk. IIC.* No. 242 Sqn., Manston; anti-shipping sweeps, 9-41.

BD881 *Trop. Mk. IIB.* No. 258 Sqn., Colombo Racecourse, Ceylon; defensive operations, 4-42; crashed near Bakori, 15-11-44.

BD884 *Trop. Mk. IIB.* No. 335 (Greek) Sqn., Dekheila; defensive patrols over Mersa Matruh, 8-42.

BD887 *Trop. Mk. IIB.* No. 94 Sqn., Msus; desert patrols, 1-42. No. 73 Sqn., El Adem, Libya; desert patrols, 2-41.

BD893 *N.F. Mk. IIB.* No. 3 Sqn., Hunsdon; night interception operations, **QO-G**, 9-41.

BD894 *Trop. Mk. IIB.* No. 274 Sqn., Maryut; shipping escorts. "**A**", 10-41.

BD897 *Trop. Mk. IIB.* No. 128 Sqn., Hastings, Sierra Leone; base patrols, "**M**", 1-42.

BD916 *Trop. Mk. IIB.* No. 73 Sqn., El Adem, Libya; desert patrols, 2-42; lost through enemy action, 28-5-42.

BD919 *Trop. Mk. IIB.* No. 94 Sqn., Msus; desert patrols, 1-42; Missing on operations, 2-1-42.

BD920 *Trop. Mk. IIB.* No. 73 Sqn., El Adem, Libya; desert patrols, 2-42. No. 134 Sqn., Helwan, 6-42.

BD930 *Trop. Mk. IIB.* No. 73 Sqn., El Adem, Libya; desert patrols, "**R**", 2-42. No. 335 (Greek) Sqn.

BD931 *Trop. Mk. IIB.* No. 73 Sqn., El Adem, Libya; desert patrols, 2-42.

BD935 *N.F. Mk. IIC.* No. 1 Sqn., Tangmere; intruder operations, 2-42. *Shipped to Russia*, 21-5-43.

BD936 *N.F. Mk. IIC.* No. 247 Sqn., Exeter; night anti-shipping sweeps, **ZY-S**, 8-42.

BD937 *N.F. Mk. IIC.* No. 1 Sqn., Tangmere; intruder operations, 2-42. No. 615 Sqn., A.A.F. No. 32 Sqn.; shot down by Ju 88 while on convoy escort, 25-3-42.

BD940 *N.F. Mk. IIC.* No. 1 Sqn., Tangmere; 11-41; collided with Hurricane **Z3899** over the Isle of Wight, 22-11-41, and crashed.

BD945 *N.F. Mk. IIC.* No. 1 Sqn., Tangmere; intruder operations, 2-42; crashed while landing at night at Tangmere, 11-2-42.

BD946 *N.F. Mk. IIC.* No. 1 Sqn., Tangmere; intruder operations, **JX-H**, 2-42. No. 532 (Turbinlite) Sqn., Wittering, c.4-42.

BD947 *N.F. Mk. IIC.* No. 1 Sqn., Tangmere; intruder operations, 2-42.

BD948 *N.F. Mk. IIC.* No. 3 Sqn., Hunsdon; night interception operations, **QO-X**, 10-41.

BD949 *N.F. Mk. IIC.* No. 1 Sqn., Tangmere; intruder operations, 2-42; lost in action against *Scharnhorst* and *Gneisenau*, 12-2-42.

BD950 *N.F. Mk. IIC.* No. 1 Sqn., Tangmere; intruder operations, 9-41; ditched in sea at night off Bognor, Sussex, 11-9-41.

BD956 *N.F. Mk. IIC.* No. 3 Sqn., Hunsdon; night interception operations; 12-41; crashed at Brabourne, Kent, 31-5-42.

BD957 *Trop. Mk. IIB.* No. 73 Sqn., El Adem, Libya, 2-42; F/L G.R.A.M. Johnston shot down one Bf 109F, 9-2-42.

BD959 *N.F. Mk. IIC.* No. 537 (Turbinlite) Sqn., Middle Wallop, c.6-42. Aircraft abandoned near Wooton, Oxon, 4-2-43, after engine failure.

BD980 *N.F. Mk. IIB (A.I.-equipped).* No. 3 Sqn., Hunsdon, 9-41. No. 245 Sqn., Chilbolton; night defensive patrols, *MR-J*, 10-41.

BD981 *Trop. Mk. IIB.* No. 127 Sqn., Shandur, desert patrols, 6-42. S.O.C., 27-10-44.

BD982 *N.F. Mk. IIC.* No. 3 Sqn., Hunsdon; night interception duties, **QO-L**, 10-41. Became ***4223M***, 10-43.

BD983 *N.F. Mk. IIC.* No. 1 Sqn., Tangmere; intruder operations, 2-42. No. 539 (Turbinlite) Sqn.; crashed 13-10-42.

BE115 *N.F. Mk. IIB.* No. 232 Sqn., Ouston, 9-41; embarked for Far East, 11-41; shot down over Palembang I, 8-2-42.

BE116 *N.F. Mk. IIC.* No. 3 Sqn., Hunsdon, night interception operations, **QO-K**, 10-41. *Tropicalised* and shipped to Malta, 11-41. No. 229 Sqn., Hal Far, 1-43; shot down by Bf 109Gs over Sicily, 9-1-43.

BE131 *Trop. Mk. IIB.* No. 33 Sqn., Gambut; ground support operations, 3-42.

BE141 *Trop. Mk. IIB.* No. 80 Sqn., El Adem, Libya; desert patrols, 1-42.

BE150 *N.F. Mk. IIC.* No. 1 Sqn., Tangmere; night intruder operations, **JX-F**, 2-42. No. §35 (Turbinlite) Sqn. Shipped to Far East, 1943.

BE155 *Trop. Mk. IIB.* No. 261 Sqn., China Bay, Ceylon; defensive operations, 3-42.

BE157 *Trop. Mk. IIB.* Missing on operations, 6-2-42 (Unit not known).

BE162 *Mk. IIB.* No. 32 Sqn. No. 615 Sqn., A.A.F. No. 486 (N.Z.) Sqn. *Shipped to Russia*, 24-9-42.

BE167 *Trop. Mark IIB.* No. 94 Sqn., Msus; desert patrols, 2-42; lost through enemy action, 23-10-42.

BE169 *Trop. Mk. IIB.* No. 73 Sqn., El Adem; desert patrols, 2-42; lost through enemy action, 29-5-42.

BE193 *Trop. Mk. IIB.* No. 238 Sqn., Gambut; desert offensive sweeps, "**V**", 3-42. No. 274 Sqn. S.O.C., 29-3-45.

BE197 *Trop. Mk. IIB.* No. 146 Sqn., Dum Dum, India; defence of Calcutta, 5-42.

BE200 *Trop. N.F. Mk. IIC.* No. 213 Sqn., Idku; night defensive patrols, **AK-M**, 10-41. S.O.C., 6-10-42.

BE213 *Mk. IIB.* No. 247 Sqn. No. 32 Sqn., Manston; daylight sweeps, 11-41; force landed at Manston on return from patrol, 22-2-42, and S.O.C.

BE215 *N.F. Mk. IIC.* No. 1 Sqn., Tangmere, 1-42, **JX-I**; in action against German warships, *Scharnhorst* and *Gneisenau*, 12-2-42; crashed 2 miles SW of Worthy Down, 2-5-42.

BE219 *N.F. Mk. IIB.* No. 232 Sqn., Ouston; night

patrols, 10-41; aircraft possibly shipped for the Far East.

BE221 *Mark IIE (sic).* No. 402 Sqn., R.C.A.F., Rochford; offensive fighter-bomber sweeps, 9-41. No. 607 Sqn., A.A.F.; Missing from sweep near St. Valery, 11-11-41.

BE222 *Mark IIE (sic).* No. 607 Sqn., A.A.F., Manston; offensive sweeps; Missing from shipping strike off Le Touquet, 12-2-42.

BE223 *Trop. Mk. IIB.* Shipped to India. No. 146 Sqn., Dum Dum; defence of Calcutta, 6-42. No. 2 Sqn., I.A.F.; caught fire and crashed near Valadi, 19-7-42.

BE224 *Trop. Mk. IIB.* No. 127 Sqn., Shandur; desert patrols, 6-42.

BE227 *Trop. Mk. IIB.* No. 261 Sqn., China Bay, Ceylon; defensive operations, 3-42; shot down by A6M2s over China Bay, 9-4-42.

BE231 *Trop. Mk. IIC.* No. 238 Sqn., Gambut; desert offensive sweeps, "**T**", 3-42. No. 335 (Greek) Sqn.

BE232 *Trop. Mk. IIB.* No. 261 Sqn., China Bay, Ceylon; defensive operations, "**G**", 3-42. No. 151 O.T.U.

BE281 *Trop. Mk. IIB.* No. 274 Sqn., Sidi Haneish; bomber escorts, "**T**", 4-42; collided with Hurricane ***HL738*** near Mellaha, 26-2-43.

BE299 *Mk. IIB bomber.* No. 174 Sqn., Manston; fighter-bomber sweeps, 3-42. Shipped to Far East.

BE301 *Mk. IIB. bomber.* No. 175 Sqn., Warmwell, 4-42; took part in attack which sank three E-boats in Channel, 15-5-42.

BE338 *Trop. Mk. IIC.* No. 237 Sqn., Shandur; coastal shipping patrols, 2-43. Converted to Trop. Mk. IIB.

BE340 *Trop. N.F. Mk. IIC.* No. 213 Sqn., Idku; night defensive patrols, **AK-W**, 3-42.

BE342 *Trop. Mk. IIC.* No. 80 Sqn., El Adem; desert patrols, 2-42. Lost through enemy action, 21-5-42.

BE353 *N.F. Mk. IIC.* No. 151 Sqn., Wittering; night defensive patrols, 1-41. No. 3 Sqn. Shipped to the Far East.

BE354 *N.F. Mk. IIC (A.I.-equipped).* No. 245 Sqn., Chilbolton; night defensive patrols, **MR-J**, 10-41.

BE355 *Trop. N.F. Mk. IIC.* No. 213 Sqn., Idku; night defensive patrols, **AK-Q**, 4-42. No. 6 Sqn., Idku, 12-42; crashed from spin, north of Aboukir, 17-12-42.

BE369 *Trop. N.F. Mk. IIC.* No. 213 Sqn., Idku; night defensive patrols, **AK-P**, 4-42. No. 335 (Greek) Sqn.

BE372 *Trop. N.F. Mk. IIC.* No. 73 Sqn., Gambut; night intruder operations, "**H**", 6-42. No. 127 Sqn., L.G.92, Amriya, 7-42.

BE394 *Mk. IIC bomber.* No. 607 Sqn., A.A.F., Manston; fighter-bomber sweeps, 12-41. No. 174 Sqn. No. 175 Sqn.

BE395 *Trop. Tac R Mk. IIC.* No. 80 Sqn., L.G.92, El Alamein, 8-42. No. 274 Sqn. No. 336 (Greek) Sqn.; crashed near Bug Bug, 17-7-43.

BE397 *Trop. Mk. IIE (sic).* No. 274 Sqn., Sidi Haneish; bomber escorts, "**H**", 4-42. Lost in action, 1-9-43.

BE398 *Mk. IIB bomber.* No. 607 Sqn., A.A.F., Manston; fighter-bomber sweeps, 12-41.

BE400 *Mk. IIB bomber.* No. 607 Sqn., A.A.F., Manston; fighter-bomber sweeps, 12-41.

BE401 *Mk. IIB bomber.* No. 607 Sqn., A.A.F., Manston; fighter-bomber sweeps, 12-41.

BE402 *Trop. Mk. IIB.* No. 242 Sqn., Palembang, Sumatra; defensive operations, 2-42.

BE403 *Mk. IIE (sic).* No. 607 Sqn., Manston; fighter-bomber sweeps, 10-41; Missing from shipping strike near Dunkirk, 3-10-41.

BE404 *Mk. IIE (sic).* No. 607 Sqn., Manston; fighter-bomber sweeps, 10-41. No. 174 Sqn. No. 175 Sqn. *Supplied to Portugal*, 29-8-43.

BE407 *Trop. Mk. IIC.* No. 33 Sqn., Gambut; ground support operations, 6-42. No. 33 Sqn. No. 238 Sqn.

BE408 *Trop. Mk. IIC.* No. 33 Sqn., Gambut, 1-42. No. 229 Sqn., Gazala; ground support operations, 2-42.

BE417 *Mk. IIE (sic).* No. 402 Sqn., R.C.A.F., Warmwell; fighter-bomber sweeps, **AE-K**, 11-41. No. 175 Sqn., Warmwell; fighter-bomber sweeps, 3-42. Shipped to the Middle East.

BE418 *Mk. IIE (sic).* No. 607 Sqn., A.A.F., Manston; fighter-bomber sweeps, 11-41; shot down by flak near Le Touquet, 4-11-41.

BE419 *Mk. IIE (sic).* No. 402 Sqn., R.C.A.F., Warmwell; fighter-bomber sweeps, 11-41. No. 175 Sqn., Warmwell; ditched in English Channel, 2-6-42.

BE420 *Mk. IIE (sic).* No. 607 Sqn., A.A.F., Manston; fighter-bomber sweeps, 11-41; shot down by Bf 109Fs off Middelkerke, 6-11-41.

BE421 *Mk. IIE (sic).* No. 607 Sqn., A.A.F. No. 174 Sqn., Warmwell; fighter-bomber sweeps; Missing from sweep, 2-6-42.

BE422 *Mk. IIE (sic).* No. 607 Sqn., A.A.F., Manston; fighter-bomber sweeps; Missing in action, 4-1-42.

BE423 *Mk. IIE (sic).* No. 607 Sqn., A.A.F., Manston; fighter-bomber sweeps, 11-41. No. 174 Sqn., Warmwell; collided with Hurricane ***BP754*** over Goodwin Sands, 5-6-43.

BE424 *Mk. IIE (sic).* No. 402 Sqn., R.C.A.F., Warmwell; fighter-bomber sweeps, 11-41. No. 175 Sqn., Warmwell; abandoned over Channel, 14-6-42, after engine failure.

BE425 *Mk. IIE (sic).* No. 607 Sqn., A.A.F., Manston; fighter-bomber sweeps, 11-41; lost during shipping strike off Ostend, 2-11-41.

BE426 *Mk. IIE (sic).* No. 402 Sqn., R.C.A.F., Warmwell, 11-42. *Shipped to Russia*, 13-1-42.

BE470 *Mk. IIE (sic).* No. 402 Sqn., R.C.A.F., Warmwell; fighter-bomber sweeps, 11-41.

BE471 *Mk. IIE (sic).* No. 402 Sqn., R.C.A.F., Warmwell; fighter-bomber sweeps, 11-41.

BE472 *Mk. IIE (sic).* No. 402 Sqn., R.C.A.F., Warmwell; Missing from sweep over Forêt de St. Saens, France, 11-11-41.

BE473 *Mk. IIE (sic).* No. 402 Sqn., R.C.A.F., Warmwell. No. 175 Sqn., Warmwell; crashed in sea while attacking ships off Alderney, 18-7-42.

BE474 *Mk. IIE (sic).* No. 607 Sqn., A.A.F., Manston; fighter-bomber sweeps, 11-41; crashed at Lympne Castle, Kent, 7-11-41.

BE475 *Mk. IIE (sic).* No. 607 Sqn., A.A.F., Manston; lost during shipping strike off Le Havre, 5-12-41.

BE476 *Mk. IIE (sic).* No. 607 Sqn., A.A.F., Manston; lost during shipping strike off Le Touquet, 12-2-42.

BE477 *Mk. IIE (sic).* No. 402 Sqn., R.C.A.F., Warmwell. No. 175 Sqn., Warmwell; crashed while landing at Croydon, 18-8-42.

BE478 *Mk. IIE (sic).* No. 402 Sqn., R.C.A.F., Warmwell. No. 175 Sqn., Warmwell, **HH-S**; took part in attack which sank three E-boats in the English Channel, 15-5-42. Brize Norton Stn. Flt.

BE479 *Mk. IIE (sic).* No. 402 Sqn., R.C.A.F., Warmwell, fighter-bomber sweeps, 12-41; crashed near Hurn, 23-2-42.

BE481 *Trop. Mk. IIC.* No. 80 Sqn., El Adem, Libya; desert patrols, 2-42. No. 274 Sqn.; lost in action, 1-4-42.

BE483 *Mk. IIE (sic).* No. 402 Sqn., R.C.A.F., Warmwell, fighter-bomber sweeps, 12-41; shot down by Bf 109Fs off Cherbourg, 2-1-42.

BE484 *Mk. IIE (sic).* No. 175 Sqn., Warmwell; fighter-bomber sweeps; shot down by flak ships off Cherbourg, 28-6-42.

BE485 *Mk. IIE (sic).* No. 402 Sqn., R.C.A.F., Warmwell, **AE-W**, 12-41. No. 175 Sqn., Warmwell; lost in action, 17-4-42.

BE486 *Mk. IIE (sic).* No. 402 Sqn., R.C.A.F., Warmwell. No. 175 Sqn., Warmwell; shot down by flak off Ile de Batz, 30-7-42.

BE487 *Trop. Mk. IIB bomber.* No. 274 Sqn., Sidi Haneish; desert offensive sweeps, "**F**", 6-42. *Modified as Trop. Met Mk. IIC.* No. 1415 (Met.) Flt., Habbaniya, 1943-45. S.O.C., 31-6-45.

BE488 *Mk. IIE (sic). Converted to Trop. Mk. IIB* and shipped to the Far East. No. 20 Sqn. S.O.C., 31-8-44.

BE489 *Mk. IIE (sic).* No. 175 Sqn., Warmwell; took part in attach which sank three E-boats in the English Channel, 15-5-42. No. 55 O.T.U.; collided with Hurricane ***Z2687*** and crashed at Brockworth, Cumberland, 23-6-43.

BE490 *Trop. Mk. IIC.* No. 274 Sqn., Idku; defence of the Nile Delta, "**Y**", 9-42. No. 1555 Flt.

BE492 *Mk. IIE (sic).* No. 402 Sqn., R.C.A.F., Warmwell; fighter-bomber sweeps, 12-41. No. 175 Sqn., Warmwell.

BE494 *Trop. Mk. IIC.* No. 80 Sqn. No. 7 Sqn., S.A.A.F. No. 71 O.T.U.

BE496 *N.F. Mk. IIB (A.I.-equipped).* No. 245 Sqn., Chilbolton, **MR-M**, 11-41. No. 537 (Turbinlite) Sqn., Middle Wallop, c.6-42. Shipped to the Far East.

BE500 *N.F. Mk. IIC.* No. 87 Sqn., Charmy Down; night interception patrols, **LK-B**, 2-42. Shipped to the Far East.

BE502 *Mk. IIE (sic).* No. 402 Sqn., R.C.A.F., Warmwell; fighter-bomber sweeps, 1-42. *Supplied to Portugal*, 15-8-43.

BE503 *Mk. IIE (sic).* No. 175 Sqn., Warmwell; fighter-bomber sweeps, 3-42. *Shipped to Russia*, 4-3-43.

BE506 *Mk. IIE (sic).* No. 174 Sqn., Warmwell; fighter-bomber sweeps, 3-42. Abandoned over the Channel with flak damage, 19-5-42.

BE507 *Trop. Mk. IIE (sic).* No. 274 Sqn., Sidi Haneish; desert offensive sweeps, "**D**", 6-42.

BE514 *N.F. Mk. IIC (A.I.-equipped).* No. 87 Sqn., Charmy Down, 2-42. No. 533 (Turbinlite) Sqn., Charmy Down, 4-42.

BE516 *N.F. Mk. IIC (A.I.-equipped),* No. 245 Sqn., Chilbolton; night defensive patrols, **MR-W**, 1-42; crashed near Chilbolton, 23-2-42.

BE550 *Trop. Mk. IIC.* No. 128 Sqn., Hastings, Sierra Leone, 2-42.

BE553 *Trop. Mk. IIC.* No. 80 Sqn., El Adem, Libya; desert partrols, 2-42.

BE557 *Trop. N.F. Mk. IIC.* No. 73 Sqn., Gambut; night intruder operations, 6-42.

BE565 *Trop. Mk. IIE (sic). Converted to Trop. Mk. IIA*, Malta, c.2-42.

BE567 *Trop. Tac R Mk. IIC.* No. 208 Sqn., Western Desert, 8-42; Missing from Tac R patrol, 24-8-42.

BE569 *Trop. N.F. Mk. IIC.* No. 213 Sqn., Idku; night defensive operations, **AK-P**, 3-42.

BE570 *Trop. N.F. Mk. IIC.* No. 73 Sqn., Gambut; night intruder operations, 6-42. No. 40 Sqn., S.A.A.F., 1-43.

BE571 *Trop. N.F. Mk. IIC.* No. 87 Sqn., Philippeville, Algeria; convoy protection, 12-42.

BE572 *N.F. Mk. IIC (A.I.-equipped).* No. 538 (Turbinlite) Sqn., Hibaldstow, c.6-42.

BE574 *N.F. Mk. IIC.* No. 615 Sqn., A.A.F. No. 247 Sqn., Exeter; night anti-shipping operations, 8-42.

BE580 *Mk. IIB.* No. 79 Sqn., Beginton, 12-41. No. 530 (Turbinlite) Sqn., Hunsdon, 2-42.

BE581 *N.F. Mk. IIC.* No. 1 Sqn., Tangmere; intruder operations, **JX-E**, 2-42. No. 532 (Turbinlite) Sqn., Wittering, c.4-42.

BE583 *Trop. N.F. Mk. IIC.* No. 185 Sqn., "**T**", Hal Far, Malta; defensive operations, 3-42.

BE641 *Trop. Mk. IIB.* No. 232 Sqn., Singapore, 1-42; Missing on defensive patrol over Singapore, 25-1-42.

BE643 *Trop. Mk. IIC.* No. 213 Sqn., Idku; night defensive patrols, **AK-U**, 3-42. Lost through enemy action, 3-7-42.

BE645 *N.F. Mk. IIC.* No. 247 Sqn., Exeter; night anti-shipping operations, 8-42.

BE648 *Trop. Mk. IIC.* No. 238 Sqn., Gambut; desert offensive sweeps, "**M**", 3-42.

BE650 *Mk. IIE (sic).* No. 175 Sqn., Warmwell; fighter-bomber sweeps, 3-42. *Shipped to Russia*, 12-1-43.

BE667 *Mk. IIE (sic).* No. 175 Sqn., Warmwell; took part in attack which sank three E-boats in the English Channel, 5-5-42. *Tropicalised and supplied to the South African Air Force.* No. 41 Sqn., S.A.A.F., Aksum and Debarec, Abyssinia, 11-42.

BE668 *Mk. IIE (sic).* No. 175 Sqn., Warmwell; took part in attack which sank three E-boats in the English Channel, 5-5-42. *Supplied to Portugal*, 14-8-43.

BE669 *Trop. Mk. IIE (sic).* No. 274 Sqn., Sidi Haneish,

"**G**", 6-42. No. 1414 Flt. *Supplied to Turkey*, 1-5-43.
BE670 *Mk. IIE (sic).* No. 607 Sqn., A.A.F., Manston; Missing from shipping strike off Le Touquet, 12-2-42.
BE681 *Trop. Mk. IIE (sic).* No. 238 Sqn., Gambut; desert offensive operations, "**Z**", 3-42. No. 335 (Greek) Sqn., Dekheila, 1943.
BE684 *Mk. IIE (sic).* No. 174 Sqn., Manston; fighter-bomber sweeps; shot down by flak near Cap Gris Nez, 30-7-42.
BE687 *Mk. IIE (sic).* No. 175 Sqn., Warmwell; hit by flak over Dieppe and abandoned off Portsmouth, 19-8-42.
BE688 *Trop. Mk. IIE.* No. 128 Sqn., Hastings, Sierra Leone; base patrols, 2-42.
BE689 *Trop. Mk. IIE (sic).* No. 335 (Greek) Sqn.; defensive patrols over Mersa Matruh, 8-42. Missing on tac. recce sortie, 25-12-42.
BE701 *Trop. Mk. IIE (sic).* No. 335 (Greek) Sqn. S.O.C., 20-9-45.
BE702 *Trop. N.F. Mk. IIC.* No. 213 Sqn., Idku; night defensive patrols, **AK-V**, 3-42.
BE709 *Trop. Mk. IIC.* No. 208 Sqn., Western Desert, 9-42; shot down by fighters near Burg-el-Arab, 28-9-42.
BE713 *Trop. Mk. IIC.* No. 80 Sqn., El Adem, Libya; desert patrols, 2-42. S.O.C., 29-3-45.
BE715 *Trop. Mk. IIC.* No. 250 Sqn., El Gamil; night desert patrols, 2-42.
BE716 *Trop. Mk. IIC.* No. 229 Sqn., Gazala; desert patrols, 2-42; lost through enemy action, 15-5-42.

BM899 *Trop. Mk. IIB.* No. 232 Sqn., Palembang, Sumatra; defensive operations, 1-42; crashed in sea off Kallang, 23-1-42.
BM903 *Trop. Mk. IIB.* No. 232 Sqn., Palembang, Sumatra; defensive operations, 1-42; damaged and abandoned, 22-1-42.
BM906 *Trop. Mk. IIB.* No. 232 Sqn., Palembang, Sumatra; defence of Singapore, 1-42; Missing over Singapore, 20-1-42.
BM921 *Trop. Mk. IIB.* No. 136 Sqn., Alipore, India; shipping protection patrols, 4-42; crashed 60 miles east of Calcutta, 27-5-42.
BM927 *Trop. Mk. IIB.* No. 146 Sqn., Dum Dum, India; defence of Calcutta, "**D**", 5-42.
BM933 *Trop. Mk. IIB.* No. 261 Sqn., China Bay, Ceylon; defensive operations, "**M**", 4-42. No. 151 O.T.U.
BM935 *Trop. N.F. Mk. IIB.* No. 135 Sqn., Dum Dum, India; shot down by Ki 43s near Buthidaung, 31-3-43.
BM936 *Trop. N.F. Mk. IIB.* No. 136 Sqn., Alipore, 6-42; assumed shot down by Ki 43s, 15-3-43.
BM948 *Trop. N.F. Mk. IIB.* No. 135 Sqn., Dum Dum, India. No. 607 Sqn., A.A.F., Dum Dum; crashed after engine fire near Dum Dum, 7-8-43.
BM952 *Trop. Mk. IIB.* No. 146 Sqn., Dum Dum, India; defence of Calcutta, 7-42. No. 20 Sqn. S.O.C., 30-6-44.
BM964 *Trop. Mk. IIC.* No. 229 Sqn., Hal Far, Malta. S.O.C., 6-4-42.
BM966 *Trop. Mk. IIC.* No. 213 Sqn., El Gamil; M.T. column escorts, **AK-T**, 6-42. S.O.C., 23-10-42.
BM967 *Trop. Mk. IIC.* No. 73 Sqn., Shandur; defence of the Suez Canal, 6-42. Lost through enemy action, 17-6-42.
BM968 *Trop. Mk. IIC.* No. 67 Sqn., Alipore, India; defence of Calcutta, 6-42.
BM974 *Trop. Mk. IIC.* No. 238 Sqn., Gambut; coastal convoy protection, "**D**", 2-42. No. 80 Sqn.; shot down by Bf 109s near El Adem, 23-5-42.
BM975 *Trop. Mk. IIC.* No. 73 Sqn., Gambut; night intruder operations, "**G**", 5-42. S.O.C., 8-3-44.
BM976 *Trop. Tac R Mk. IIC.* No. 80 Sqn., Amriya; desert tactical reconnaissance, 7-42. To India, 1943. No. 67 Sqn. S.O.C., 29-3-45.
BM979 *Trop. Mk. IIC.* No. 127 Sqn., Western Desert; patrols in El Alamein area, 9-42.
BM987 *Trop. Mk. IIC.* No. 134 Sqn.; desert defensive patrols, 1-43.
BM989 *Trop. Mk. IIC.* No. 238 Sqn., desert defensive patrols, "**M**", 6-42.
BM991 *Trop. Tac R Mk. IIC.* No. 274 Sqn., Sidi Haneish; tactical reconnaissance, 4-42.
BM995 *Trop. Mk. IIB.* No. 258 Sqn., Ratmalana and Colombo Racecourse; tactical training, 3-42.

BN110 *Trop. Mk. IIC.* No. 238 Sqn., Gambut; desert defensive patrols, "**B**", 6-42; crashed in desert, 27-10-42.
BN113 *Trop. Mk. IIB.* No. 274 Sqn., Sidi Haneish, "**B**", 4-42.
BN114 *Mk. IIE (sic).* No. 174 Sqn., Warmwell; fighter-bomber sweeps, 9-42.
BN115 *Trop. Mk. IIC.* No. 73 Sqn., Burg-el-Arab; night desert patrols, 7-42. No. 451 Sqn., R.A.A.F.
BN117 *Trop. Mk. IIC.* No. 213 Sqn., El Gamil; M.T. column escorts, **AK-X**, 6-43. No. 80 Sqn.
BN121 *Trop. N.F. Mk. IIC.* No. 73 Sqn., Burg-el-Arab; night desert patrols, 6-42; shot down, 17-6-42.
BN122 *Trop. Mk. IIC.* No. 250 Sqn., El Gamil; desert fighter sweeps, 2-42. No. 229 Sqn., Hal Far, Malta; daylight defensive operations, 4-42; destroyed in air raid, Hal Far, 11-4-42.
BN125 *Trop. Mk. IIC.* No. 258 Sqn., Colombo Racecourse, Ceylon; tactical training, 4-42. No. 146 Sqn. No. 261 Sqn. S.O.C., 8-11-43.
BN126 *Trop. Tac R Mk. IIC.* No. 80 Sqn., Amriya; tactical reconnaissance, 7-42; assumed shot down by Bf 109Fs near El Alamein, 30-8-42.
BN131 *Trop. N.F. Mk. IIC.* No. 73 Sqn., Gambut; night intruder operations, "**P**", 6-43. No. 335 (Greek) Sqn.
BN132 *Trop. Mk. IIC.* No. 213 Sqn., El Gamil; M.T. column escorts, **AK-X**, 6-43.
BN133 *Trop. Mk. IIC.* No. 213 Sqn., El Gamil; M.T. column escorts, **AK-Y**, 6-43. No. 335 (Greek) Sqn.
BN134 *Trop. Mk. IIC.* No. 213 Sqn., El Gamil; M.T. column escorts, **AK-Z**, 6-43. No. 33 Sqn., 7-43. S.O.C., 23-7-42.
BN136 *Trop. Mk. IIC.* No. 213 Sqn., El Gamil; M.T. column escorts, AK-S, 6-43.
BN137 *Trop. Mk. IIC.* No. 213 Sqn., El Gamil; M.T. column escorts, 6-43.
BN155 *Trop. Mk. IIC.* No. 73 Sqn., Gambut; night intruder operations, 5-42. No. 208 Sqn.; crashed near Bierut, 3-7-43.
BN156 *Trop. Mk. IIC.* No. 73 Sqn., Gambut; night intruder operations, 5-42. No. 208 Sqn., L.G.100; Missing on tactical reconnaissance, 24-8-42.
BN159 *Trop. Mk. IIC.* No. 213 Sqn., El Gamil; M.T. column escorts, **AK-J**, 6-43.
BN162 *Trop. Mk. IIC.* No. 451 Sqn., R.A.A.F., Idku; offensive patrols, 4-42; ditched off Egyptian coast after engine failure, 24-4-43.
BN163 *Trop. N.F. Mk. IIB.* Shipped to India. No. 135 Sqn., Dum Dum; night defensive patrols, 6-42. No. 28 Sqn.; crashed on landing, Imphal, 24-9-43.
BN167 *Trop. N.F. Mk. IIB.* Shipped to India. No. 136 Sqn., Alipore; shipping protection patrols, 6-42; crashed at Alipore, 10-6-42.
BN184 *Trop. Mk. IIC.* No. 213 Sqn., Western Desert; night defensive patrols, **AK-W**, 5-42.
BN185 *N.F. Mk. IIC.* No. 3 Sqn., Hunsdon; night intruder operations, **QO-A**, 3-42. Missing, 13-1-43.
BN188 *N.F. Mk. IIC.* No. 3 Sqn., Hunsdon, **QO-B.** No. 247 Sqn. No. 536 (Turbinlite) Sqn. Tropicalised and shipped to India.
BN205 *N.F. Mk. IIC.* No. 1 Sqn., Tangmere; intruder operations, 2-42; flew in operations against the *Scharnhorst* and *Gneisenau*, 12-2-42. No. 539 (Turbinlite) Sqn., Acklington, 7-42.
BN206 *N.F. Mk. IIC.* No. 537 (Turbinlite) Sqn., Middle Wallop, c.7-42.
BN208 *Trop. Mk. IIC.* No. 258 Sqn., Colombo Racecourse, Ceylon; defensive operations, 4-42. No. 1 Sqn., I.A.F.
BN212 *Trop. N.F. Mk. IIC.* No. 135 Sqn., Dum Dum, India; night defensive patrols, 8-42. No. 2 Sqn., I.A.F.
BN229 *N.F. Mk. IIC.* No. 43 Sqn., Tangmere; night intruder operations, 8-42. No. 111 Sqn. S.O.C., 8-3-44.
BN230 *N.F. Mk. IIC.* No. 43 Sqn., Tangmere; night intruder operations, 8-42, **FT-A.** No. 534 (Turbinlite) Sqn., Tangmere, 9-42.
BN232 *N.F. Mk. IIC.* No. 1 Sqn., Tangmere; night intruder operations, 2-42, **JX-R**; took part in operations against *Scharnhorst* and *Gneisenau*, 12-2-42. No. 486 (N.Z.) Sqn.
BN234 *N.F. Mk. IIC.* No. 43 Sqn., Tangmere; night intruder operations, 8-42; was in action over Dieppe landings, 19-8-42. *Shipped to Russia*, 10-2-43.
BN235 *N.F. Mk. IIC.* No. 43 Sqn., Tangmere; night intruder operations, 8-42. No. 532 (Turbinlite) Sqn., Hibaldstow.
BN236 *N.F. Mk. IIC.* No. 247 Sqn., Exeter; night intruder operations, 5-42. Shipped to the Far East.
BN241 *Trop. Mk. IIB.* No. 261 Sqn., China Bay, Ceylon; defensive operations, "**T**". No. 151 O.T.U.; crashed at Hazahai, 29-12-43.
BN270 *Trop. Mk. IIB.* No. 274 Sqn., Sidi Haneish, 4-42.
BN274 *Trop. Mk. IIB.* No. 146 Sqn., Dum Dum; defence of Calcutta, "**V**", 7-42; crashed following engine failure, 27-10-43.
BN277 *Trop. Mk. IIC.* No. 73 Sqn., Gambut, 5-42; shot down, 17-6-42; S/L D.H. Ward RNZAF, Missing.
BN279 *Trop. Mk. IIC.* No. 128 Sqn., Hastings, Sierra Leone; base patrols, 5-42.
BN285 *Trop. Mk. IIC.* No. 213 Sqn., El Gamil; M.T. column escorts, **AK-M**, 6-43.
BN286 *Trop. N.F. Mk. IIC.* No. 213 Sqn., Western Desert, **AK-O**, 6-42.
BN287 *Trop. Mk. IIC.* No. 238 Sqn., L.G.92, Western Desert; defensive operations, "**V**", 7-42.
BN289 *N.F. Mk. IIC.* No. 538 (Turbinlite) Sqn., Hibaldstow, "**S**", c.7-42.
BN290 *Trop. Mk. IIC.* No. 451 Sqn., R.A.A.F., Idku; offensive patrols, 3-43.
BN298 *Trop. Mk. IIC.* No. 258 Sqn., Colombo Racecourse, Ceylon; defensive operations, 4-42. S.O.C., 1-12-42.
BN315 *Trop. N.F. Mk. IIB.* No. 135 Sqn., Dum Dum; night defence of Calcutta, 6-42.
BN325 *Trop. Mk. IIB.* No. 146 Sqn., Dum Dum; daylight defence of Calcutta, 7-42. No. 261 Sqn.; destroyed in air raid on Imphal, 9-11-43.
BN331 *Trop. Mk. IIC.* No. 67 Sqn., Alipore; defence of Calcutta, 6-42; crashed while landing, Acorn strip, 26-1-43.
BN335 *Trop. Tac R Mk. IIC.* No. 80 Sqn., Amriya; desert tactical reconnaissance, 7-42. *Supplied to Turkey*, 1-7-43.
BN347 *Trop. Met Mk. IIC.* No. 1414 (Met.) Flt., Mogadishu and Eastleigh, East Africa, 1943-45.
BN354 *Trop. N.F. Mk. IIC.* No. 213 Sqn., Western Desert; night defensive patrols, "**S**", 7-42.
BN355 *Trop. Tac R Mk. IIC.* No. 80 Sqn., L.G.192; desert tactical reconnaissance, 8-42.
BN356 *Trop. Tac R Mk. IIC.* No. 4521 Sqn., R.A.A.F., Idku; desert tactical reconnaissance, 8-42.
BN360 *N.F. Mk. IIC.* No. 533 (Turbinlite) Sqn., Charmy Down, c.6-42. Shipped to the Far East.
BN368 *Trop. Mark IIC.* No. 213 Sqn., El Gamil; M.T. column escorts, **AK-Z**, 6-43.
BN372 *N.F. Mk. IIC.* No. 87 Sqn., Charmy Down; night intruder operations, 5-42.
BN373 *N.F. Mk. IIC.* No. 1 Sqn., Tangmere; intruder operations; took part in operations against *Scharnhorst* and *Gneisenau*, 12-2-42. No. 531 (Turbinlite) Sqn., Debden, "**E**", 10-42.
BN388 *Trop. Mk. IIB.* No. 136 Sqn., Alipore; shipping patrols, 7-42; shot down by Ki43s over the Arakan, 15-3-43.
BN404 *Trop. Mk. IIC.* No. 451 Sqn., R.A.A.F., Idku; offensive patrols, 3-43.
BN406 *Trop. Mk. IIC.* No. 127 Sqn., Western Desert; patrols in El Alamein area, 9-42.
BN410 *Trop. Mk. IIC.* No. 73 Sqn., Heliopolis; defence

of Cairo, 6-42.
BN415 *Trop. Mk. IIC.* No. 73 Sqn., Gambut; night intruder operations, 6-42; crashed near Suez, 6-8-42, while performing low level aerobatics.
BN463 *Trop. Mk. IIC.* No. 17 Sqn., Alipore; defence of Calcutta, 8-42.
BN466 *Trop. Mk. IIC.* No. 30 Sqn., Dambulla, Ceylon; defensive patrols, 8-42.
BN526 *Armament trials* at A. & A.E.E., Boscombe Down, as ***BN526/G***, 1942. S.O.C., 7-7-45.
BN538 *Trop. Mk. IIC.* No. 73 Sqn., Heliopolis; defence of Cairo, 7-42; shot down over Cairo, 29-8-42.
BN540 *Trop. Mk. IIC.* No. 17 Sqn., Alipore; defence of Calcutta, 8-42; crashed, 1-1-43, following engine failure.
BN560 *Trop. Mk. IIC.* No. 73 Sqn., Shandur; desert patrols, 6-42; Missing from patrol, 16-6-42.
BN564 *Trop. Mk. IIC.* No. 17 Sqn., Alipore; defence of Calcutta, 8-42.
BN566 *Trop. Mk. IIC.* No. 73 Sqn., Shandur; defence of the Suez Canal, 7-42.
BN569 *Trop. Mk. IIC.* No. 79 Sqn., Bombay and Kanchrapara; operational training, 7-42.
BN571 *Mk. IID. Armament TI aircraft; trials at A. & A.E.E. with 40-mm anti-tank guns as* ***BN571/G***, 1942.
BN581 *Trop. Mk. IIC.* No. 607 Sqn., A.A.F., Alipore, India; offensive operations, Burma Front, 6-42.
BN596 *Trop. Mk. IIC.* No. 79 Sqn., Chittagong; defence of Chittagong, 12-42. No. 30 Sqn.
BN603 *Trop. Mk. IIC.* No. 128 Sqn., Hastings, Sierra Leone; base patrols, 7-42. No. 74 O.T.U.
BN627 *Trop. Mk. IIB.* No. 71 O.T.U.; collided with Hurricane ***W9354*** and crashed 10 miles east of Ismailia, 20-12-43.
BN672 *Trop. Mk. IIC.* No. 67 Sqn., Alipore; defence of Calcutta, 6-42. No. 17 Sqn.
BN676 *Trop. Mk. IIC.* No. 607 Sqn., A.A.F., Alipore; offensive operations, Burma Front, 6-42; crashed one mile east of Alipore, 5-11-42.
BN678 *Trop. Mk. IIC.* No. 889 Sqn., F.A.A., Western Desert. No. 134 Sqn., L.G.121, Western Desert; coastal convoy patrols, 3-43.
BN696 *Trop. Mk. IIC.* No. 607 Sqn., A.A.F., Alipore; offensive operations, Burma Front, 6-42.
BN701 *Trop. Mk. IIC.* No. 261 Sqn., Chiringa; ground attack operations, Burma Front, "**K**", 10-43; abandoned after engine failure near Mowdok, 20-1-44.
BN703 *Trop. Mk. IIC.* No. 17 Sqn., Alipore; defence of Calcutta, 8-42.
BN704 *Trop. Mk. IIC.* No. 615 Sqn., A.A.F., Fenny; offensive operation in the Arakan, 1-43.
BN719 *Trop. Mk. IIC.* No. 67 Sqn., Alipore; defence of Calcutta, 6-42. Crashed while taking off at Kanchrapara, 25-1-44.
BN780 *Trop. Mk. IIC.* No. 30 Sqn., Dambulla, Ceylon; defence of naval base, 8-42.
BN781 *Trop. Mk. IIC.* No. 607 Sqn., A.A.F., Alipore; offensive operations, Burma Front, 7-42.
BN797 *Trop. Mk. IID.* No. 6 Sqn., Shandur; anti-tank operations in Western Desert, 5-42; hit by flak and crash landed in desert, 15-6-42.
BN841 *Trop. Mk. IID.* No. 6 Sqn., Shandur; anti-tank operations in Western Desert, 5-42; hit by flak and crash landed in desert, 13-7-42.
BN842 *Trop. Mk. IID.* No. 6 Sqn., Shandur; anti-tank operations in Western Desert, 5-42; Missing from anti-tank sweep, 14-7-42.
BN845 *Trop. Mk. IID.* No. 6 Sqn., Shandur; anti-tank operations in Western Desert, 5-42.
BN846 *Trop. Mk. IID.* No. 6 Sqn., Shandur; anti-tank operations in Western Desert, 5-42; crashed during gunnery practice near Kabrit, 14-9-42.
BN860 *Trop. Mk. IID.* No. 6 Sqn., Shandur; anti-tank operations in Western Desert, 5-42.
BN861 *Trop. Mk. IID.* No. 6 Sqn., Shandur; anti-tank operations in Western Desert, 5-42; hit by flak and abandoned near Bir Hakim, 8-6-42.
BN868 *Trop. Mk. IIC.* No. 615 Sqn., A.A.F., Fenny, India; offensive operations in the Arakan, 1-43.
BN870 *Trop. Tac R Mk. IIC.* No. 80 Sqn., Amriya; desert tactical reconnaissance, 7-42; crashed near Ismailia, 17-12-43.
BN896 *Trop. Mk. IIC.* No. 67 Sqn., Alipore; defence of Calcutta, 6-42.
BN906 *Trop. Mk. IIC.* No. 607 Sqn., A.A.F., Alipore; offensive operations, Burma Front, 7-42.
BN959 *Trop. Mk. IIC.* No. 67 Sqn., Alipore; defence of Calcutta, 6-42.
BN960 *Trop. Mk. IIC.* No. 335 (Greek) Sqn., Dekheila; desert offensive operations, 8-42.
BN961 *Trop. Mk. IID.* No. 71 O.T.U., 4-42. No. 6 Sqn., Shandur, 5-42; anti-tank operations in Western Desert; shot down by flak and abandoned near Bir Hakim, 8-6-42.
BN970 *Trop. Mk. IIC.* No. 30 Sqn., Dambulla, Ceylon; defence of naval bases, 8-42.
BN974 *Trop. Met. Mk. IIC.* No. 1413 (Met.) Flt., Rayak, Damascus, Aqir and Lydda, 1943-45; aircraft damaged when it flew into a flock of storks, 7-3-44; W/O Lavallee unhurt.

HAWKER HURRICANE Mark IIB (Gloster-built). Fourth production batch of 450 aircraft built by Gloster Aircraft Co. Ltd., Brockworth, Glos. Rolls-Royce Merlin XX. (Large proportion of batch shipped to Russia, including almost all the last 100 aircraft). ***BG674-BG723, BG737-BG771, BG783-BG832, BG844-BG888, BG901-BG920, BG933-BG977, BG990-BG999, BH115-BH154, BH167-BH201, BH215-BH264, BH277-BH296, BH312-BH361.*** **Deliveries commenced, November 1941; completed March 1942; average rate of production, approximately four aircraft per day.**
BG674 Shipped to India. No. 151 O.T.U.; wheels-up landing at Risalpur, 19-8-44.
BG675 No. 258 Sqn., Colombo Racecourse, Ceylon; defence of Colombo, 6-42.
BG676 No. 261 Sqn., China Bay, Ceylon; shot down by A6M2s over China Bay, 9-4-42.
BG688 No. 135 Sqn., Dum Dum, India; offensive sweeps, Northern Burma, 1-43.
BG689 *Trop. N.F. Mk. IIB.* No. 73 Sqn., El Gamil; night defence of Port Said, 1-42.
BG691 No. 33 Sqn., Gambut, Libya; offensive fighter operations, 3-42.
BG692 No. 273 Sqn., Katukurunda, Ceylon; coastal shipping protection, Ceylon, "**D**", 8-42.
BG693 No. 232 Sqn., Tjililitan, Java; defence against Japanese invasion forces, 2-42; shot down by Japanese fighters near Palembang, 13-2-42.
BG697 No. 146 Sqn., Alipore, India; defence of Calcutta, 9-42.
BG705 No. 258 Sqn., Colombo Racecourse, Ceylon; defence of Colombo, 6-42.
BG707 No. 127 Sqn., Shandur; defensive operations, Western Desert, 6-42. No. 417 Sqn., R.C.A.F., Shandur; defence of the Suez Canal, 9-42.
BG745 No. 605 Sqn., A.A.F., Ta Kali, Malta; defensive operations, 2-42; lost through enemy action, 7-6-42.
BG750 *Converted to Trop. Mk. IIC.* No. 73 Sqn., El Gamil; night defence of Port Said, 1-42.
BG751 *Converted to Trop. Mk. IIC.* No. 73 Sqn., El Gamil; night defence of Port Said, 1-42.
BG753 No. 605 Sqn., A.A.F., Ta Kali, Malta; defensive operations, 2-42. No. 134 Sqn., Shandur, Egypt; air defence of the Suez Canal, 1-43.
BG760 No. 261 Sqn., China Bay, Ceylon; coastal shipping protection, Ceylon, "**P**", 9-42.
BG770 No. 605 Sqn., A.A.F., Ta Kali, Malta; defensive operations, 2-42. No. 185 Sqn., Hal Far, Malta; defensive operations, 5-42.
BG784 No. 605 Sqn., A.A.F., Ta Kali, Malta; defensive operations, 2-42.
BG785 *Trop. Tac R Mk. IIB.* No. 208 Sqn., L.G.100, Western Desert; ground support in Bir Hakim region, 8-42.
BG801 No. 258 Sqn., Colombo Racecourse, Ceylon; air defence of Colombo, 5-42.
BG810 No. 232 Sqn., Tjilititan, Java; air defence of Singapore, 1-42; shot down by Japanese fighters off Singapore, 22-1-42.
BG812 No. 146 Sqn., Alipore, India; defence of Calcutta, 9-42; crashed at Barascat, 8-3-43.
BG815 No. 261 Sqn., Ratmalana, Ceylon; coastal shipping protection, Ceylon, "**F**", 10-42.
BG827 No. 273 Sqn., Katukurunda, Ceylon; coastal shipping protection, Ceylon, "**W**", 8-42.
BG828 No. 232 Sqn., Tjililitan, Java; air defence of Singapore, 1-42; crash landed at Seletar, Singapore, 19-1-42.
BG854 No. 273 Sqn., Katukurunda, Ceylon; coastal shipping protection, Ceylon, "**B**", 8-42.
BG857 No. 135 Sqn., Dum Dum, India; offensive sweeps, Northern Burma, 1-43.
BG858 No. 136 Sqn., Chittagong; defence of Chittagong, 12-42; crashed at Ritz airstrip, 2-3-43.
BG859 No. 335 (Greek) Sqn., L.G.37, Western Desert; ground support operations, El Alamein, 10-42.
BG864 No. 232 Sqn., Tjililitan, Java; air defence of Singapore, 1-42; crash landed at Seletar, Singapore, 21-1-42.
BG867 *Converted to Trop. N.F. Mk. IIC.* No. 73 Sqn., El Gamil; night defence of Port Said, 2-42.
BG872 No. 261 Sqn., China Bay, Ceylon; coastal shipping protection, Ceylon, 8-42, "**L**". No. 20 Sqn., Imphal.
BG877 *Converted to Trop. N.F. Mk. IIC.* No. 73 Sqn., El Gamil; night defence of Port Said, 2-42. No. 134 Sqn., Shandur, 1-43.
BG887 No. 273 Sqn., Katukurunda, Ceylon; coastal shipping protection, Ceylon, "**P**", 8-42.
BG902 *Converted to Trop. N.F. Mk. IIC.* No. 73 Sqn., El Gamil; night defence of Port Said, 2-42. No. 238 Sqn., 6-42.
BG913 No. 261 Sqn., China Bay, Ceylon; coastal shipping protection, "**S**", 8-42.
BG916 No. 30 Sqn., Ratmalana, Ceylon; coastal shipping protection, Ceylon; crashed, 20-4-42.
BG936 No. 261 Sqn., China Bay, Ceylon, coastal shipping protection, Ceylon; "**M**", 9-42.
BG942 *Converted to Trop. Mk. IIC.* No. 607 Sqn., A.A.F., Alipore, India; local air training exercises, 6-42.
BG946 No. 146 Sqn., Alipore, India; defence of Calcutta. No. 607 Sqn., A.A.F., Alipore; local training air exercies, 6-42.
BG949 No. 274 Sqn., Sidi Haneish; escorts for medium bombers, "**Y**", 4-42. No. 336 (Greek) Sqn. No. 451 Sqn., R.A.A.F.
BG950 No. 238 Sqn., L.G.92, Western Desert; escorts for ground attack Hurricane squadrons, 8-42. No. 225 Sqn.; crashed near Souk el Khemis, 2-3-43.
BG961 No. 146 Sqn., Alipore, India; defence of Calcutta, "**E**", 12-42.
BG963 No. 258 Sqn., Colombo Racecourse, Ceylon; air defence of Colombo, 7-43. No. 135 Sqn.
BG966 No. 274 Sqn., Sidi Haneish; escorts for medium bombers, 4-42. No. 134 Sqn., Shandur; air defence of the Suez Canal, 1-43.
BG971 No. 335 (Greek) Sqn., L.G.121, Western Desert; cover for fighter-bomber operations; crashed at L.G.08, 24-8-43.
BG974 *Converted to Trop. N.F. Mk. IIC.* No. 73 Sqn., Shandur; night air defence of the Cnal Zone, 7-42. No. 208 Sqn.
BG992 *Trop. Tac R Mk. IIB.* No. 208 Sqn., L.G.100, Western Desert; ground support operations, El Alamein, 9-42.
BG994 No. 135 Sqn., Dum Dum, India; offensive sweeps, Northern Burma, "**D**", 1-43; believed shot down by Ki 43s near Buthidoung, 31-3-43.
BG998 *Trop. Tac R Mk. IIB.* No. 208 Sqn., L.G.100, Western Desert; Missing from patrol over Qattara Depression, 29-8-42.

BH115 No. 607 Sqn., A.A.F., Alipore; local training exercises, 6-42. No. 20 Sqn., Imphal; destroyed in raid on Imphal, 9-11-43.
BH126 No. 128 Sqn., Hastings, Sierra Leone; area

defence operations, 9-42.

BH127 No. 258 Sqn., Colombo Racecourse, Ceylon; air defence of Colombo, 8-42. No. 261 Sqn., China Bay, Ceylon, "**G**", 10-42.

BH131 No. 417 Sqn., R.C.A.F., Shandur; air defence of the Suez Canal.

BH132 No. 135 Sqn., Dum Dum, India; offensive operations over Northern Burma, 1-43.

BH133 No. 134 Sqn., Shandur; air defence of the Suez Canal, 1-43. No. 335 (Greek) Sqn.

BH135 No. 261 Sqn., China Bay, Ceylon, 9-42; Baigachi, India, 2-43; Missing from offensive sweep over Akyab, 14-2-43.

BH151 No. 146 Sqn., Alipore; defence of Calcutta, "**U**", 1-43.

BH217 No. 128 Sqn., Hastings, Sierra Leone; area defence operations, 10-42. No. 1571 Flt. S.O.C., 27-10-44.

BH230 No. 258 Sqn., Colombo Racecourse, Ceylon; air defence of Colombo, 8-42. No. 146 Sqn., Alipore, India; air defence of Calcutta, "**Z**", 2-43.

HAWKER HURRICANE MARK IIB, IIC AND IID (Hawker-built). Seventh production batch of 1,888 aircraft built by Hawker Aircraft Ltd., Kingston, Langley and Brooklands, during 1942. Rolls-Royce Merlin XX engines and Rotol or D.H. propellers. ***BN988-BN992, BP109-BP141, BP154-BP200, BP217-BP245, BP259-BP302, BP316-BP362, BP378-BP416, BP430-BP479, BP493-BP526, BP538-BP566, BP579-BP614, BP628-BP675, BP692-BP711, BP734-BP772; HL544-HL591, HL603-HL634, HL654-HL683, HL698-HL747, HL767-HL809, HL828-HL867, HL879-HL913, HL925-HL941, HL953-HL997, HM110-HM157; HV275-HV317, HV333-HV370, HV396-HV445, HV468-HV516, HV534-HV560, HV577-HV612, HV634-HV674, HV696-HV745, HV768-HV799, HV815-HV858, HV873-HV921, HV943-HV989, HW115-HW146, HW167-HW207, HW229-HW278, HW291-HW323, HW345-HW373, HW399-HW444, HW467-HW501, HW533-HW572, HW596-HW624, HW651-HW686, HW713-HW757, HW779-HW808, HW834-HW881.*** **Deliveries commenced, 17-3-42; completed 23-11-42; average rate of production, eight aircraft per day.**

BP110 *Trop. Mk. IIC.* No. 30 Sqn., Dambulla, Ceylon; defence of naval bases, **RS-K**, 9-42.

BP123 *Trop. Mk. IIC.* No. 213 Sqn., L.G.85, Western Desert; offensive patrols, El Alamein, **AK-S**, 8-42.

BP126 *Trop. Mk. IID.* No. 6 Sqn., Shandur; anti-tank operations, Western Desert, 5-42.

BP127 *Trop. Mk. IIC.* No. 213 Sqn., L.G.106, Western Desert; offensive patrols, El Alamein, **AK-W**, 8-42.

BP128 *Trop. Mk. IIC.* No. 213 Sqn., L.G.106, Western Desert; offensive patrols, El Alamein, 8-42.

BP131 *Trop. Mk. IID.* No. 6 Sqn., Shandur; anti-tank operations, Western Desert, 5-42.

BP136 *Trop. Mk. IID.* No. 6 Sqn., Shandur; anti-tank operations, Western Desert, 5-42.

BP157 *Trop. Mk. IIB.* No. 238 Sqn., L.G.92, Western Desert; defensive patrols, Canal Zone, "**H**", 7-42.

BP167 *Trop. N.F. Mk. IIC.* No. 73 Sqn., Shandur; night intruder operations, 8-42; destroyed one Ju 88A, Burg-el-Arab, 31-8-42.

BP173 *Mk. IID. Armament trials* (sometime as ***BP173/G***), A. & A.E.E., Boscombe Down, from 29-7-42. *Later converted to Mark IV.*

BP175 *Trop. N.F. Mk. IIC.* No. 73 Sqn., Shandur; night intruder operations, 8-42.

BP177 *Trop. N.F. Mk. IIC.* No. 73 Sqn., Gambut; night intruder operations, "**L**", 6-42.

BP183 *Trop. Mk. IID.* No. 6 Sqn., Shandur; anti-tank operations, Western Desert, **JV-X**, 5-42.

BP186 *Trop. N.F. Mk. IIC.* No. 73 Sqn., Shandur; night intruder operations, 8-42.

BP187 *Trop Mk. IIC bomber.* No. 80 Sqn., El Bassa; anti-tank support, 9-42.

BP188 *Trop. Mk. IID.* No. 6 Sqn., Shandur; anti-tank operations, Western Desert, **JV-Z**, 5-42.

BP193 *Trop. Mk. IID.* No. 6 Sqn., Shandur; anti-tank operations, Western Desert, **JV-A** (later **JV-Z**), 5-42.

BP219 *Trop. Mk. IIC.* No. 213 Sqn., L.G.85, Western Desert; offensive patrols, El Alamein, 8-42. No. 6 Sqn., Idku,; off-shore convoy patrols, 12-42.

BP224 *Trop. Met. Mk. IIC.* No. 1413 (Met.) Flt., Lydda, Palestine; weather reconnaissance, 3-44.

BP231 *Trop. Mk. IIC.* No. 213 Sqn., L.G.85, Western Desert; offensive patrols, El Alamein, **AK-Y**, 8-42.

BP232 *Trop. Mk. IIC.* No. 336 (Greek) Sqn., L.G.219, Western Desert; coastal shipping protection, 3-43.

BP237 *Trop. Mk. IIC.* No. 94 Sqn., El Gamil; shipping protection, Nile Delta, 6-42, **GO-C**. No. 213 Sqn., L.G.85; offensive patrols, El Alamein, **AK-X**, 8-42.

BP240 *Trop. Mk. IIC.* No. 607 Sqn., Chittagong, India; offensive patrols over Irrawaddy river, 1-43.

BP279 *Trop. Mk. IIB.* No. 335 (Greek) Sqn., Dekheila; defensive patrols over Mersa Matruh, 8-42.

BP282 *Trop. Mk. IIB.* No. 26 A.A.C.U., El Firdan, Canal Zone, Egypt, 2-43.

BP287 *Trop. Mk. IIC.* No. 72 Sqn., Shandur; night intruder operations, 8-42.

BP288 *Trop. Met Mk. IIC.* No. 1413 (Met.) Flt., Palestine; weather reconnaissance from 3-44.

BP289 *Trop. Mk. IIC.* No. 127 Sqn., St. Jean, Palestine; coastal convoy escorts, 8-43.

BP290 *Trop. Mk. IIB.* No. 335 (Greek) Sqn., L.G.85, Western Desert; bomber escorts, 10-42.

BP295 *Mk. IIB bomber.* No. 175 Sqn., Warmwell; fighter-bomber sweeps, 6-42.

BP317 *Trop. Mk. IIB.* No. 335 (Greek) Sqn., L.G.85, Western Desert; bomber escorts, 10-42.

BP324 *Trop. Mk. IIB bomber.* No. 274 Sqn., Gambut; offensive patrols, "**R**", 5-42.

BP329 *Trop. Mk. IIB.* No. 238 Sqn., L.G.92, Western Desert; defensive patrols, Canal Zone, "**X**", 7-42.

BP337 *Trop. Tac R Mk. IIC bomber.* No. 80 Sqn., El Bassa; tactical reconnaissance and anti-tank support.

BP340 *Trop. Tac R Mk. IIC bomber.* No. 80 Sqn., El Bassa; tactical reconnaissance and anti-tank support.

BP341 *Trop. Mk. IIC bomber.* No. 213 Sqn., L.G.85, Western Desert; offensive patrols, El Alamein, 8-42, **AK-J**.

BP342 *Trop. Mk. IIC bomber.* No. 213 Sqn., L.G.85, Western Desert; offensive patrols, El Alamein, 8-42.

BP344 *Trop. N.F. Mk. IIC.* No. 73 Sqn., Shandur; night intruder operations, 8-42.

BP346 *Trop Mk. IIC.* No. 336 (Greek) Sqn., L.G.219, Western Desert; coastal shipping protection, 3-43.

BP348 *Trop. Mk. IIC.* No. 238 Sqn., LG.172, Western Desert; offensive sweeps, "**L**", 10-42.

BP358 *Trop. Mk. IIC bomber.* No. 80 Sqn., El Bassa; anti-tank support, 9-42.

BP359 *Trop. Mk. IIC.* No. 237 Sqn., L.G.106, Western Desert; coastal shipping protection, **DV-P**, 3-43.

BP380 *Trop. N.F. Mk. IIC.* No. 73 Sqn., Shandur; night intruder operations, 8-42.

BP381 *Trop. Mk. IIC.* No. 94 Sqn., El Gamil; shipping protection, Nile Delta, **GO-A**, 6-42.

BP384 *Trop. Mk. IIC.* No. 237 Sqn., LG.106, Western Desert; coastal shipping protection, 3-43.

BP387 *Trop. Mk. IIC.* No. 94 Sqn., El Gamil; shipping protection, Nile Delta, **GO-J**, 6-42.

BP389 *Trop. Mk. IIC.* No. 94 Sqn., El Gamil; shipping protection, Nile Delta, **GO-G**, 6-42.

BP391 *Trop. Mk. IIC.* Central Gunnery School, Middle East (El Ballah), 3-43; *converted for Met. Duties*, 1-44. No. 1413 (Met.) Flt., Lydda, Palestine; weather reconnaissance, 3-44 to 9-45.

BP397 *Trop. Mk. IIC.* No. 94 Sqn., El Gamil; shipping protection, Nile Delta, **GO-J**, 6-42. No., 237 Sqn., L.G.106, Western Desert; coastal shipping protection, **DV-J**, 3-43.

BP398 *Trop. N.F. Mk. IIC.* No. 73 Sqn., Gambut; night intruder operations, 11-42.

BP409 *Trop. Mk. IIC.* No. 213 Sqn., L.G.85, Western Desert; offensive patrols, El Alamein, 8-42.

BP410 *Trop. Mk. IIC.* No. 33 Sqn., LG-172, Western Desert; offensive patrols, El Alamein, 7-42.

BP414 *Trop. Tac R Mk. IIC bomber.* No. 80 Sqn., El Bassa; tactical reconnaissance and anti-tank support.

BP440 *Trop. Mk. IIB bomber.* No. 274 Sqn., Gambut; offensive patrols, "**U**", 6-42.

BP446 *Trop. Tac R Mk. IIC bomber.* No. 208 Sqn., Habbaniya, Iraq; armed tactical reconnaissance, 1-43. *Converted to Met. Mk. IIC.* No. 1415 (Met.) Flt., Habbaniya, Iraq; weather reconnaissance, "**G**", later "**A**", 9-43 to 11-45.

BP459 *Trop. Mk. IIC bomber.* No. 80 Sqn., El Bassa; anti-tank support, 9-42. No. 336 (Greek) Sqn., LG.219, Western Desert; coastal shipping escort, 3-43.

BP462 *Trop. Mk. IIC bomber.* No. 213 Sqn., L.G.85, Western Desert; offensive patrols, El Alamein, **AK-Z**, 8-42.

BP465 *Trop. Mk. IIC bomber.* To the Middle East by sea.

BP466 *Trop. N.F. Mk. IIC.* To the Middle East via Takoradi.

BP467 *Trop. Mk. IIC bomber.* To the Middle East by sea.

BP468 *Trop. Mk. IIC bomber.* To the Middle East by sea.

BP469 *Trop. Mk. IIC bomber.* To the Middle East by sea.

BP470 *Trop. Mk. IIC.* To the Middle East via Takoradi.

BP471 *Trop. Mk. IIC.* To the Middle East via Takoradi.

BP472 *Trop. Mk. IIC.* To the Middle East via Takoradi.

BP473 *Trop. Mk. IIC.* No. 33 Sqn., L.G.172, Western Desert; desert line patrols, 7-42.

BP510 *Trop. Mk. IIC.* No. 30 Sqn., Dambulla, Ceylon; coastal shipping protection, **RS-H**, 10-42.

BP512 *Trop. Mk. IIC.* No. 238 Sqn., L.G.172, Western Desert; offensive patrols, "**Z**", 10-42.

BP515 *Trop. Mk. IIC.* No. 213 Sqn., L.G.85, Western Desert; offensive patrols, El Alamein, 8-42.

BP518 *Trop. N.F. Mk. IIC.* No. 73 Sqn., Shandur; night intruder operations, 8-42; shot down one Ju 88A near El Alamein, 31-8-42.

BP521 *Trop. N.F. Mk. IIC.* No. 73 Sqn., Shandur; night intruder operations, 8-42.

BP541 *Trop. Mk. IIC.* No. 417 Sqn., R.C.A.F., Shandur; offensive patrols, 9-42.

BP550 *Trop. Mk. IID.* No. 6 Sqn., Shandur; anti-tank operations, Western Desert, 6-42.

BP566 *Trop. N.F. Mk. IIC.* No. 73 Sqn., L.G.85, Western Desert; night intruder operations, 9-42.

BP580 *Trop. Mk. IIC.* No. 213 Sqn., L.G.85, Western Desert; offensive patrols, El Alamein, 8-42.

BP584 *Trop. N.F. Mk. IIC.* No. 73 Sqn., L.G.85, Western Desert; night intruder operations, 9-42.

BP585 *Trop. Mk. IIC.* No. 94 Sqn., El Gamil; shipping protection, Nile Delta, **GO-R**, 6-42.

BP586 *Trop. Mk. IIC bomber.* No. 80 Sqn., El Bassa; support of anti-tank aircraft, 9-42.

BP592 *Trop. Mk. IIC.* No. 213 Sqn., L.G.85, Western Desert; offensive patrols, El Alamein, 8-42; shot down three Ju 88As over El Alamein, 1-9-42.

BP595 *Trop. Mk. IIC.* No. 615 Sqn., A.A.F., Jessore, India; offensive patrols over the Arakan, 9-42.

BP604 *Trop. Tac R Mk. IIB bomber.* No. 208 Sqn., L.G.100, Western Desert; armed reconnaissance, 10-42.

BP610 *Trop. Tac R Mk. IIB bomber.* No. 208 Sqn., L.G.100, Western Desert; armed reconnaissance; crashed during low-flying sortie, 16-1-43.

BP645 *Trop. Mk. IIC.* No. 127 Sqn., St. Jean, Palestine; coastal shipping protection, 8-43.

BP649 *N.F. Mk. IIC.* No. 174 Sqn., Manston; night intruder operations, 9-42.

BP653 *Mk. IIC bomber.* No. 174 Sqn., Manston; night intruder operations, 9-42.

BP656 *Trop. Mk. IIC.* No. 336 (Greek) Sqn., Dekheila; defensive patrols over Mersa Matruh, 8-42.

BP657 *N.F. Mk. IIC.* No. 174 Sqn., Manston; night intruder operations, 9-42.

BP662 *Trop. Mk. IIC bomber.* No. 274 Sqn., Idku;

offensive patrols, "**X**", 9-42.
BP666 *Trop. Mk. IIC.* No. 237 Sqn., L.G.106, Western Desert; coastal shipping protection, 3-43.
BP668 *Mk. IIC.* No. 257 Sqn., High Ercall; ground support training, 8-42.
BP672 *Mk. IIC bomber.* No. 174 Sqn., Manston; night intruder operations, 9-42. No. 527 (Calibration) Sqn.; radar calibration in the U.K., 1944-45.
BP700 *Mk. IIB.* No. 43 Sqn., Kirton-in-Lindsey; operational training, **FT-C**, 10-42.
BP703 *Mk. IIB.* No. 43 Sqn., Tangmere, 8-42; took part in combined operations, Dieppe, 19-8-42.
BP704 *N.F. Mk. IIC.* No. 538 (Turbinlite) Sqn., Hibaldstow, "**R**", 8-42.
BP706 *N.F. Mk. IIC.* No. 538 (Turbinlite) Sqn., Hibaldstow, "**M**", 8-42.
BP734 *Trop. Mk. IIC.* No. 213 Sqn., L.G.85, Western Desert; offensive patrols, El Alamein, 8-42.
BP737 *Mk. IIB bomber.* No. 175 Sqn., Stoney Cross; fighter-bomber sweeps, 3-43.
BP742 *Trop. Mk. IIB bomber.* No. 274 Sqn., Gambut; offensive patrols, "**X**", 6-42.
BP746 *Mk. IIC bomber.* No. 174 Sqn., Manston; night intruder operations, 9-42.
BP756 *Trop. Mk. IIC.* No. 67 Sqn., Alipore, India; daylight defence of Calcutta, 9-42.
BP758 *Trop. Mk. IIB.* No. 238 Sqn., L.G.92, Western Desert; defence of the Suez Canal, "**K**", 8-42.
BP760 *N.F. Mk. IIC.* No. 534 (Turbinlite) Sqn., Tangmere, 9-42, "**L**".
BP763 *Trop. Met Mk. IIC.* No. 1415 (Met.) Flt., Habbaniya, Iraq; weather reconnaissance, Iraq, 9-43 to 11-45.
BP769 *N.F. Mk. IIC.* No. 253 Sqn., Friston; night defensive operations; participated in combined operations, Dieppe, 19-8-42.

HL560 *N.F. Mk. IIC.* No. 43 Sqn., Tangmere; intruder operations; in action over Dieppe, 19-8-42.
HL562 *N.F. Mk. IIC.* No. 43 Sqn., Tangmere; intruder operations; in action over Dieppe, 19-8-42. No. 532 (Turbinlite) Sqn., Wittering, 10-42.
HL563 *N.F. Mk. IIC.* No. 43 Sqn., Tangmere; intruder operations; in action over Dieppe, 19-8-42.
HL564 *Trop. Mk. IIC.* No. 74 Sqn., Aqir, Palestine, 6-43.
HL565 *Trop. Mk. IIC.* No. 127 Sqn., St. Jean, Palestine; patrols and training, 8-43.
HL569 *Trop. Mk. IIB.* No. 335 (Greek) Sqn., Mersa Matruh; coastal shipping protection, 7-43.
HL570 *N.F. Mk. IIC.* No. 538 (Turbinlite) Sqn., Hibaldstow, 10-42.
HL584 *N.F. Mk. IIC (A.I.-equipped).* No. 245 Sqn., Middle Wallop; night interception operations, 9-42. No. 534 (Turbinlite) Sqn., Middle Wallop, 10-42.
HL589 *N.F. Mk. IIC.* No. 1 Sqn., Acklington; operational training, 9-42.
HL603 *N.F. Mk. IIC.* No. 1 Sqn., Acklington; operational training, 9-42, **JX-I**. No. 539 (Turbinlite) Sqn., Acklington, 10-42.
HL604 *N.F. Mk. IIC.* No. 32 Sqn., West Malling; night intruder operations, **GZ-U**, 8-42. No. 531 (Turbinlite) Sqn., West Malling, "**U**", 10-42.
HL605 *N.F. Mk. IIC.* No. 531 (Turbinlite) Sqn., West Malling, "**A**", 10-42.
HL607 *Trop. Mk. IIC.* No. 336 (Greek) Sqn., Sidi Barrani; coastal shipping protection, 6-43.
HL609 *Trop. Mk. IIC.* No. 213 Sqn., Misurata, Libya; MT column escorts, 1-43. No. 238 Sqn., El Gamil; defence of the Nile Delta, "**F**", 3-43.
HL611 *Trop. Mk. IIC.* No. 451 Sqn., R.A.A.F., Idku; defence of the Nile Delta, 2-43.
HL612 *Trop. Mk. IIB.* No. 71 O.T.U., North Africa, 1942.
HL627 *Trop. Mk. IIC.* No. 33 Sqn., Dekheila; desert line patrols, 10-42.
HL629 *Trop. Mk. IIB.* No. 71 O.T.U., North Africa, 1942.
HL632 *Trop. Mk. IIC.* No. 80 Sqn., Bu Amoud; shipping protection, Eastern Mediterranean, 1-43.
HL654 *Trop. Mk. IIC.* No. 123 Sqn., Doshan Teppeh, Persia; defence of Persian oilfields, "**S**", 11-42.
HL656 *N.F. Mk. IIC.* No. 43 Sqn., Tangmere; night intruder operations, 7-42.
HL658 *N.F. Mk. IIC.* No. 531 (Turbinlite) Sqn., West Malling, "**L**", 10-42.
HL660 *N.F. Mk. IIC.* No. 531 (Turbinlite) Sqn., West Malling, "**S**", 10-42.
HL664 *Trop. N.F. Mk. IIC.* No. 73 Sqn., L.G.85, Western Desert; night defence of Canal Zone, 8-42.
HL665 *Trop. Mk. IIC bomber.* To Russia; reported to have been converted to two-seater in Russia.
HL669 *N.F. Mk. IIC (A.I.-equipped).* No. 245 Sqn., Middle Wallop; night interception operations, 9-42.
HL678 *Trop Tac R Mk. IIC.* No. 208 Sqn., Rayak, Syria; tactical reconnaissance duties, 7-43.
HL683 *Trop. Mk. IIC.* No. 451 Sqn., R.A.A.F., Idku; defence of the Nile Delta, 2-43.
HL699 *Trop. Mk. IIB.* No. 335 (Greek) Sqn., Mersa Matruh; coastal shipping protection, 7-43.
HL700 *Trop. Mk. IIC.* No. 127 Sqn., St. Jean, Palestine; standing patrols and operational training, 7-43.
HL701 *Trop. Mk. IIC bomber.* No. 274 Sqn., Martuba, Libya; ground support operations, "**C**", 11-42.
HL705 *Mk. IIB bomber.* No. 174 Sqn., Odiham; fighter-bomber sweeps, 3-43.
HL707 *Trop. N.F. Mk. IIB.* No. 73 Sqn., L.G.85, Western Desert; night defence of the Canal Zone, 8-42.
HL715 *Mk. IIB bomber.* No. 174 Sqn., Odiham; fighter-bomber sweeps, 3-43.
HL716 *Trop. Mk. IIB bomber.* No. 335 (Greek) Sqn., Mersa Matruh; coastal shipping protection, 7-43.
HL721 *Trop. Mk. IIC.* No. 451 Sqn., R.A.A.F., Idku; defence of the Nile Delta, 2-43.
HL723 *Mk. IIB bomber.* No. 175 Sqn., Harrowbeer; anti-shipping strikes, 10-42.
HL728 *Mk. IIB bomber.* No. 175 Sqn., Harrowbeer; anti-shipping strikes, 10-42.
HL733 *Trop. Mk. IIB bomber.* No. 274 Sqn., L.G.88, Western Desert; desert line patrols, "**E**", 8-42.
HL735 *Trop. Mk. IIC.* No. 237 Sqn., Kirkuk, Iraq; defence of Iraqi oilfields, 12-42. No. 26 A.A.C.U., El Firdan, Canal Zone, Egypt, 1-44.
HL737 *Trop. Mk. IIC.* No. 237 Sqn., Kirkuk, Iraq; defence of Iraqi oilfields, 12-42.
HL739 *Trop. Tac R Mk. IIB.* No. 208 Sqn., Burg-el-Arab; tactical reconnaissance duties, 12-42.
HL772 *Trop. Mk. IIB.* No. 258 Sqn., Dambulla, Ceylon; defence of Colombo, 2-43.
HL773 *Trop. Mk. IIC.* No. 336 (Greek) Sqn., Sidi Barrani; coastal shipping protection, 6-43.
HL779 *Trop. N.F. Mk. IIC.* No. 87 Sqn., Philippeville; night defence of Torch supply ports, 12-42.
HL783 *Trop. Mk. IIB.* No. 607 Sqn., A.A.F., Chittagong; defence of Chittagong, 3-43.
HL785 *Trop. Mk. IIB.* No. 335 (Greek) Sqn., Mersa Matruh; coastal shipping protection, 7-43.
HL790 *Trop. Met. Mk. IIC.* No. 1413 (Met.) Flt., Lydda, Palestine; weather reconnaissance, 3-44 to 10-45.
HL791 *Trop. Mk. IIB.* No. 135 Sqn., Dum Dum, India; bomber escorts, Burma Front, 1-43.
HL795 *Trop. Mk. IIC bomber.* No. 274 Sqn., Martuba, Libya; ground support operations, "**V**", 11-42.
HL796 *Trop. N.F. Mk. IIC.* No. 73 Sqn., L.G.85, Western Desert; night defence of the Canal Zone, 8-42.
HL797 *Trop. Mk. IIC.* No. 451 Sqn., R.A.A.F., Idku; defence of the Nile Delta, 2-43.
HL799 *Trop. N.F. Mk. IIC.* No. 73 Sqn., L.G.85, Western Desert; night defence of the Canal Zone, 8-42.
HL800 *Trop Tac R Mk. IIC.* No. 255 Sqn., Maison Blanche, Algeria; tactical reconnaissance, Torch landings, 11-42.
HL801 *Trop. N.F. Mk. IIC.* No. 73 Sqn., L.G.85., Western Desert; night defence of the Canal Zone, 8-42.
HL802 *Trop. N.F. Mk. IIB.* No. 146 Sqn., Alipore, India; night railway patrols, Burma Front, "**J**", 12-42.
HL804 *Trop. Mk. IIB.* No. 258 Sqn., Dambulla, Ceylon; defence of Colombo, 2-43.
HL805 *Trop. Mk. IIC.* No. 451 Sqn., R.A.A.F., Idku; defence of the Nile Delta, 2-43.
HL830 *Trop. Tac R Mk. IIC.* No. 208 Sqn., El Bassa, Palestine; tactical reconnaissance duties, 11-*43*.
HL831 *Trop. N.F. Mk. IIC.* No. 73 Sqn., L.G.85, Western Desert; night defence of the Canal Zone, 8-42.
HL832 *Trop. Mk. IIC.* No. 6 Sqn., Bu Amoud; coastal shipping protection, 1-43.
HL833 *Trop. Mk. IIC.* No. 213 Sqn., Misurata, Libya; M.T. column escorts, **AK-W**, 2-43.
HL834 *Trop. Mk. IIB.* No. 335 (Greek) Sqn., Mersa Matruh; coastal shipping protection, 7-43.
HL835 *Trop. Mk. IIC.* No. 451 Sqn., R.A.A.F., Idku; defence of the Nile Delta, 2-43.
HL839 *Trop. N.F. Mk. IIC.* No. 73 Sqn., L.G.85, Western Desert; night defence of the Canal Zone, 8-42.
HL841 *Trop. N.F. Mk. IIC.* No. 94 Sqn., El Gamil; defence of Alexandria, **GO-W**, 9-42. No. 80 Sqn., Bu Amoud; shipping protection, Eastern Mediterranean, 1-43.
HL844 *Trop. Mk. IIC.* No. 237 Sqn., Kirkuk, Iraq; defence of Iraqi oilfields, 12-42.
HL846 *Trop. Mk. IIC.* No. 238 Sqn., El Gamil; defence of the Nile Delta, "**X**", 3-43.
HL849 *Trop. Tac R Mk. IIC.* No. 208 Sqn., El Bassa, Palestine; tactical reconnaissance duties 11-43.
HL851 *Trop. Mk. IIC.* No. 237 Sqn., Kirkuk, Iraq; defence of Iraqi oilfields, 12-42.
HL852 *Trop. N.F. Mk. IIC.* No. 73 Sqn., L.G.85, Western Desert; night defence of the Canal Zone, 8-42.
HL855 *Trop. Tac R Mk. IIC.* No. 208 Sqn., El Bassa, Palestine; tactical reconnaissance duties, 11-43.
HL857 *Trop. Mk. IIB.* No. 135 Sqn., Dum Dum, India; bomber escorts, Burma Front, 1-43.
HL859 *N.F. Mk. IIC.* No. 32 Sqn., West Malling; intruder operations, **GZ-F**. No. 531 (Turbinlite) Sqn., West Malling, "**F**", 10-42.
HL861 *N.F. Mk. IIC.* No. 32 Sqn., West Malling; intruder operations, **GZ-N**. No. 531 (Turbinlite) Sqn., West Malling, "**N**", 10-42.
HL862 *N.F. Mk. IIC.* No. 247 Sqn., Exeter; night anti-shipping operations, 8-42.
HL863 *N.F. Mk. IIC.* No. 43 Sqn., Tangmere; intruder operations, 7-42. Missing after sweep over Fécamp, 16-7-42.
HL864 *Trop. N.F. Mk. IIC.* No. 87 Sqn., Philippeville; night defence of Torch supply ports, 12-42.
HL867 *Trop. Mk. IIB.* No. 607 Sqn., A.A.F.; Chittagong, India; defence of Chittagong, 3-43.
HL884 *Trop. Mk. IIC.* No. 238 Sqn., El Gamil; defence of the Nile Delta, "**Y**", 4-43.
HL886 *Trop. Mk. IIC.* No. 113 Sqn., Yelahanka and St. Thomas Mount, India; defence of Madras, 10-43.
HL887 *Trop. Mk. IIC.* No. 213 Sqn., Misurata, Libya; M.T. column escorts, **AK-W**, 2-43.
HL891 *Trop. Mk. IIC.* No. 417 Sqn., R.C.A.F., Shandur; defence of Suez Canal, 9-42; F/Sgt. Leguerrier shot down one Ju 88A over Suez, 26-9-42.
HL892 *Trop. Mk. IIC.* No. 237 Sqn., Kirkuk, Iraq; defence of Iraqi oilfields, 12-42.
HL900 *Trop. Mk. IIC.* No. 417 Sqn., R.C.A.F., Shandur; defence of the Suez Canal, 9-42.
HL901 *Trop. Mk. IIC.* No. 417 Sqn., R.C.A.F., Shandur; defence of the Suez Canal, 9-42.
HL904 *Trop. Mk. IIC.* No. 80 Sqn., Bu Amoud; shipping protection, Eastern Mediterranean, 1-43.
HL905 *Trop. Mk. IIC.* No. 33 Sqn., El Adem; offensive sweeps, 11-42.
HL908 *Trop. Mk. IIC.* No. 335 (Greek) Sqn., Mersa Matruh; coastal shipping protection, 7-43.
HL925 *Trop. Mk. IIC bomber.* No. 274 Sqn., Martuba, Libya; ground support operations, "**O**", 11-42.
HL926 *Trop. Mk. IIC.* No. 237 Sqn., Kirkuk, Iraq;

defence of Iraqi oilfields, 12-42.
HL933 *Trop. N.F. Mk. IIC.* No. 73 Sqn., L.G.85, Western Desert; night defence of the Canal Zone, 8-42.
HL941 *Trop. Mk. IIC.* No. 213 Sqn., Misurata, Libya; M.T. column escorts, **AK-V**, 2-43.
HL956 *Trop. N.F. Mk. IIC.* No. 73 Sqn., L.G.85, Western Desert; night defence of the Canal Zone, 8-42.
HL958 *Trop. Mk. IIC.* No. 237 Sqn., Kirkuk, Iraq; defence of the Iraqi oilfields,12-42.
HL965 *Trop. Mk. IIC.* No. 451 Sqn., R.A.A.F., Idku; defence of the Nile Delta, 2-43.
HL991 *Trop. Mk. IIC.* No. 123 Sqn., Doshan Tappeh, Persia; defence of Persian oilfields, 11-42.
HL994 *Trop. Mk. IIC.* No. 336 (Greek) Sqn., Sidi Barrani; coastal shipping protection, 6-43.
HL995 *Trop. Mk. IIC.* No. 94 Sqn., El Gamil; defence of Alexandria, **GO-N**, 9-42.

HM110 *Trop. Mk. IIC.* No. 261 Chiringa, India; defence of Chittagong, "**J**", 10-43.
HM111 *Trop. Mk. IIB.* No. 335 (Greek) Sqn., Mersa Matruh; coastal shipping protection, 7-43.
HM114 *Trop. Mk. IIC.* No. 127 Sqn., St. Jean, Palestine; operational training, 8-43.
HM118 *Trop. Mk. IIC.* No. 6 Sqn., Bu Amoud; coastal shipping protection, 1-43.
HM123 *Trop. Mk. IIB.* No. 258 Sqn., Dambulla, Ceylon; defence of Colombo, 2-43.
HM131 *Trop. Mk. IIC.* No. 213 Sqn., Misurata, Libya; M.T. column escorts, **AK-Y**. 3-43.
HM133 *Trop. Mk. IIB.* No. 135 Sqn., Dum Dum, India; bomber escorts, Burma Front, 1-43.
HM135 *Trop. N.F. Mk. IIC.* No. 73 Sqn., L.G.85, Western Desert; night defence of the Canal Zone, 10-42.
HM136 *Trop. N.F. Mk. IIC.* No. 73 Sqn., L.G.85, Western Desert; night defence of the Canal Zone, 10-42. No. 274 Sqn., Martuba, Libya; ground support, 11-42.
HM139 *Trop. Mk. IIC.* No. 609 Sqn., A.A.F., Chittagong, India; defence of Chittagong, 3-43.
HM145 *Trop. Mk. IIC.* No. 237 Sqn., L.G.106, Western Desert; coastal shipping protection, 3-43.

HV288 *Trop. Mk. IIC.* No. 94 Sqn., Martuba, Libya; offensive sweeps, **GO-Z**, 2-43.
HV290 *Trop. Mk. IIC.* No. 213 Sqn., Martuba, Libya; offensive sweeps, **AK-B**, 1-43.
HV294 *Trop. Mk. IIC.* No. 451 Sqn., R.A.A.F., Idku; air defence operations, Western Desert, 3-43.
HV295 *Trop. Mk. IIB.* No. 238 Sqn., Martuba, Libya; offensive sweeps while based behind Axis lines, 1-43.
HV297 *Trop. Mk. IIB bomber.* No. 261 Sqn., Baigachi, India; fighter-bomber sweeps over Akyab Island, "**V**", 2-43.
HV299 *Trop. N.F. Mk. IIC.* No. 73 Sqn., El Adem; night intruder operations, 11-42.
HV305 *Trop. Mk. IIC.* No. 213 Sqn., Martuba, Libya; offensive sweeps while based behind Axis lines, 1-43.
HV314 *Trop. Mk. IIC.* No. 33 Sqn., Benina, Libya; desert lines patrols, 12-42.
HV315 *Trop. Mk. IIC.* No. 213 Sqn., Martuba, Libya; offensive sweeps while based behind Axis lines, 1-43. No. 238 Sqn., Martuba, Libya; offensive sweeps, 1-43.
HV317 *Trop. N.F. Mk. IIC bomber.* No. 73 Sqn., Merduma, Libya; night intruder operations, 12-42.
HV334 *Trop. Mk. IIC.* No. 336 (Greek) Sqn., Sidi Barrani; coastal shipping protection, 4-43.
HV335 *Trop. Mk. IIC.* No. 451 Sqn., R.A.A.F., Idku; air defence operations, Western Desert, 2-43.
HV336 *Trop. Mk. IIC.* No. 134 Sqn., L.G.121, Western Desert; coastal shipping protection, "**S**", 3-43.
HV350 *Trop. Mk. IIC.* No. 123 Sqn., Abadan, Persia; defence of oil refinery, 2-43.
HV352 *Trop. Mk. IIC.* No. 261 Sqn., Baigachi, India; offensive sweeps over Akyab Island, 2-43.
HV357 *Trop. Mk. IIC.* No. 274 Sqn., Mellaha, Libya; coastal shipping protection, "**A**", 3-43.
HV360 *Trop. Mk. IIC.* No. 32 Sqn., Philippeville, Algeria; defence of Torch supply ports, 12-42.
HV363 *Mk. IIB bomber.* No. 174 Sqn., Odiham; offensive fighter-bomber sweeps, 2-43.
HV366 *Trop. Mk. IIC.* R.A.F. Cranwell Stn. Flt., 12-42 to 4-43.
HV370 *Trop. Met. Mk. IIC.* No. 1414 (Met.) Flt., Mogadishu, Italian Somaliland; weather reconnaissance, 9-43 to 7-45.
HV399 *Trop. Mk. IIC.* No. 43 Sqn., Maison Blanche, Algeria; support of Torch landings, 11-42.
HV400 *Trop. N.F. Mk. IIC bomber.* No. 73 Sqn., Merduma, Libya; night intruder operations, 12-42.
HV402 *Trop. Mk. IIC.* No. 43 Sqn., Maison Blanche, Algeria; support of Torch landings, 11-42.
HV403 *Trop. Mk. IIC.* No. 43 Sqn., Maison Blanche, Algeria; support of Torch landings, 11-42.
HV405 *Trop. Tac R Mk. IIC.* No. 28 Sqn., Battle of Imphal, 4-44.
HV406 *Trop. Mk. IIC.* No. 43 Sqn., Maison Blanche, Algeria; support of Torch landings, 11-42.
HV407 *Trop. Mk. IIC.* No. 43 Sqn., Maison Blanche, Algeria; support of Torch landings, 11-42.
HV408 *Trop. Mk. IIC.* No. 43 Sqn., Maison Blanche, Algeria; support of Torch landings, 11-42.
HV409 *Trop. Mk. IIC.* No. 43 Sqn., Maison Blanche, Algeria; support of Torch landings, 11-42.
HV412 *Trop. Mk. IIC.* No. 17 Sqn., Alipore, India; offensive sweeps over Akyab Island, 2-43.
HV417 *Trop. Mk. IIC.* No. 43 Sqn., Maison Blanche, Algeria; support of Torch landings, 11-42.
HV421 *Trop. Mk. IIC.* No. 43 Sqn., Maison Blanche, Algeria; support of Torch landings, 11-42.
HV422 *Trop. Mk. IIB.* No. 146 Sqn., Alipore, India; offensive sweeps, Burma Front, 2-43.
HV426 *Trop. Mk. IIC.* No. 73 Sqn., El Adem, Libya; night intruder operations, 11-42.
HV427 *Trop. Mk. IIC.* No. 60 Sqn., St. Thomas Mount, India; defensive fighter operations, 1043.
HV428 *Trop. Mk. IIB bomber.* No. 607 Sqn., A.A.F., Chittagong, India; fighter-bomber operations, Burma Front, 2-43.
HV437 *Trop. Mk. IIB bomber.* No. 607 Sqn., A.A.F., Chittagong,
India; fighter-bomber operations, Burma Front, 2-43.
HV440 *Trop. Mk. IIC bomber.* No. 213 Sqn., Martuba, Libya; offensive sweeps while based behind Axis lines, **AK-U**, 1-43.
HV441 *Trop. Mk. IIC bomber.* No. 73 Sqn., Merduma, Libya; night intruder operations, 12-42.
HV468 *Trop. Mk. IIC bomber.* No. 213 Sqn., Martuba, Libya; offensive sweeps while based behind Axis lines, **AK-P**, 1-43.
HV473 *Trop. Mk. IIC.* No. 67 Sqn., Alipore, India; escorts for fighter-bombers, Burma Front, 2-43.
HV474 *Trop. Mk. IIC.* No. 213 Sqn., Martuba, Libya; offensive sweeps while based behind Axis lines, 1-43.
HV475 *Trop. Mk. IIB bomber.* No. 607 Sqn., A.A.F., Chittagong, India; fighter-bomber sweeps, Burma Front, 2-43.
HV479 *Trop. P.R. Mk. IIC.* No. 680 (PR) Sqn., Tocra, Libya; communications duties, 7-44.
HV480 *Trop. Mk. IIB bomber.* No. 41 Sqn., S.A.A.F., Bu Amoud; coastal shipping protection, 8-43.
HV483 *Trop. Mk. IIC.* No. 213 Sqn., Martuba, Libya; offensive sweeps while based behind Axis lines, 1-43.
HV484 *Trop. Mk. IIC.* No. 274 Sqn., Mellaha, Libya; coastal shipping protection, "**Z**", 3-43.
HV490 *Trop. Mk. IIB bomber.* No. 41 Sqn., S.A.A.F., Bu Amoud; coastal shipping protection, 8-43.
HV493 *Trop. Mk. IIB bomber.* No. 458 Sqn., Dambulla, Ceylon; coastal shipping protection, 2-43.
HV497 *Trop. Mk. IIB bomber.* No. 607 Sqn., A.A.F., Chittagong, India; fighter-bomber sweeps, Burma coast, 2-43.
HV500 *Trop. Met. Mk. IIC.* No. 1414 (Met.) Flt., Mogadishu, Italian Somaliland; weather reconnaissance, 9-43 to 7-45.
HV502 *Trop. Mk. IIB bomber.* No. 607 Sqn., A.A.F., Chittagong, India; fighter-bomber sweeps, Burma coast, 2-43.
HV505 *Mk. IIB bomber.* No. 175 Sqn., Odiham; offensive sweeps, Channel coast, **HH-S**, 2-43.
HV511 *Trop. Mk. IIC bomber.* No. 213 Sqn., Martuba, Libya; offensive sweeps while based behind Axis lines, 1-43.
HV513 *Trop. Mk. IIC. Supplied to Turkey*, 11-42, from R.A.F. stocks in the Middle East.
HV516 *Trop. N.F. Mk. IIC bomber.* No. 73 Sqn., Merduma, Libya; night intruder operations, 11-42.
HV536 *Trop. Mk. IIC.* No. 43 Sqn., Maison Blanche, Algeria; support of Torch landings, 11-42.
HV539 *Trop. Mk. IIC.* No. 213 Sqn., Martuba, Libya; offensive sweeps while based behind Axis lines, 1-43.
HV540 *Trop. Mk. IIC.* Nos. 213 and 238 Sqns., Martuba, Libya; offensive sweeps while based behind Axis lines, 1-43.
HV541 *Trop. Mk. IIC.* No. 43 Sqn., Maison Blanche, Algeria; support of Torch landings, 11-42.
HV542 *Trop. Mk. IIC bomber.* No. 335 (Greek) Sqn., Mersa Matruh; fighter-bomber operations, 2-43.
HV546 *Trop. Mk. IIC bomber.* No. 79 Sqn., Ramu, Burma; offensive ground support, **NV-L**, 2-43.
HV548 *Trop. Mk. IIC bomber.* No. 33 Sqn., Benina, Libya; desert line patrols, 12-42.
HV551 *Trop. Mk. IIC.* Supplied to Turkey, 112-42, from R.A.F. stocks in the Middle East.
HV555 *Mk. IIB bomber.* No. 175 Sqn., Odiham; offensive fighter-bomber sweeps, Channel coast, 2-43.
HV559 *Trop. Mk. IIB bomber.* Air Fighting Training Unit, Alipore, India, 1944.
HV579 *Trop. Mk. IIB bomber.* No. 261 Sqn., Baigachi, India; fighter-bomber sweeps over Akyab Island, "**B**", 2-43.
HV580 *Trop. Mk. IIC.* No. 43 Sqn., Maison Blanche, Algeria; support of Torch landings, 11-42.
HV583 *Trop. Met. Mk. IIC.* No. 1414 (Met.) Flt., Mogadishu, Italian Somaliland; weather reconnaissance, 9-43 to 7-45.
HV585 *Trop. N.F. Mk. IIC bomber.* No. 73 Sqn., Merduma, Libya; night intruder operations, 12-42.
HV587 *Trop. Mk. IIC bomber.* No. 213 Sqn., Martuba, Libya; offensive sweeps while based behind Axis lines, **AK-N**, 1-43.
HV594 *Trop. Mk. IID.* No. 6 Sqn., L.G.89, Western Desert; anti-tank operations, **JV-P**, 8-42.
HV608 *Trop. Met Mk. IIC.* No. 1414 (Met.) Flt., Mogadishu, Italian Somaliland; weather reconnaissance, 9-43 to 7-45.
HV609 *Trop. Mk. IIC.* No. 213 Sqn., Martuba, Libya; offensive sweeps, **AK-S**, 1-43. No. 274 Sqn., Mellaha, Libya; coastal shipping protection, "**J**", 3-43.
HV635 *Trop. Mk. IIC.* No. 67 Sqn., Alipore, India; escorts for fighter-bombers, Burma Front, 2-43.
HV636 *Trop. Mk. IIC.* No. 615 Sqn., A.A.F., Fenny, India; armed reconnaissance, Burma Front, 2-43.
HV640 *Trop. Mk. IIC.* No. 67 Sqn., Alipore, India; escorts of fighter-bombers, Burma Front, 2-43.
HV644 *Trop. Mk. IIC.* No. 113 Sqn., St. Thomas Mount; defence of Madras, "**D**", 11-43.
HV652 *Trop. Mk. IIB bomber.* No. 607 Sqn., A.A.F., Chittagong, India; fighter-bomber sweeps, Burma coast, 2-43.
HV660 *Trop. Mk. IIB.* No. 74 Sqn., Mehrabad and Abadan, Persia; defence of Persian oil installations, 1-43.
HV661 *Trop. Mk. IIC bomber.* No. 134 Sqn., Matariyah and Sousse, Tunisia; anti-tank support, **GQ-R**, 4-43.
HV662 *Trop. Mk. IIC bomber.* No. 79 Sqn., Ramu, Burma; offensive ground support, **NV-V**, 4-43.
HV663 *Trop. Mk. IID.* No. 71 O.T.U., Carthago, Sudan, 2-43.
HV664 *Trop. Mk. IIC.* No. 71 O.T.U., Carthago, Sudan,

2-43.
HV666 *Trop. Mk. IIC.* No. 253 Sqn., Maison Blanche, Algeria; support for Torch landings, 11-42.
HV669 *Trop. Mk. IID.* No. 6 Sqn., L.G.89, Western Desert; anti-tank operations, **JV-E**, 8-42.
HV673 *Trop. Mk. IIB.* No. 71 O.T.U., Carthago, Sudan, 2-43.
HV674 *Trop. Mk. IIC.* No. 43 Sqn., Maison Blanche, Algeria; support for Torch landings, 11-42.
HV696 *Trop. Mk. IIC.* No. 32 Sqn., Phillippeville, Algeria; defence of Torch supply ports, 12-42.
HV710 *N.F. Mk. IIC.* No. 247 Sqn., High Ercall; night intruder operations, 12-42. To the Far East, 6-43, as *Trop Tac. R. Mk. IIC.* No. 28 Sqn., Battle of Imphal, 4-44.
HV711 *Trop. Met. Mk. IIC.* No. 1413 (Met.) Flt., Lydda, Palestine; weather reconnaissance, 3-44.
HV712 *Trop. Mk. IIC.* No. 213 Sqn., Martuba, Libya; offensive sweeps while based behind Axis lines, 1-43.
HV714 *Trop. Mk. IIB bomber.* No. 335 (Greek) Sqn., Mersa Matruh; fighter-bomber operations, 2-43.
HV718 *Trop. Mk. IIC.* No. 87 Sqn., Djidjelli, Algeria; coastal shipping protection, 1-43.
HV722 *Trop. Mk. IIC.* No. 231 Group Communications Flt., 1944.
HV723 *Trop. Mk. IIC.* No. 67 Sqn., Alipore, India; escorts for fighter-bomber squadrons, Burma, 2-43.
HV735 *Trop. Mk. IIC.* No. 237 Sqn., Kermanshah, Persia; protection of Persian oil installations, **DV-P**.
HV739 *Trop. Mk. IIC bomber.* No. 34 Sqn., Cholavarum, India; fighter-bomber sweeps, Burma Front, 9-43.
HV740 *Trop. Mk. IIC.* No. 43 Sqn., Maison Blanche, Algeria; support of Torch landings, 11-42.
HV742 *Trop. Mk. IIC.* No. 253 Sqn., Maison Blanche, Algeria; support of Torch landings, 11-42.
HV743 *Trop. Mk. IIC.* No. 261 Sqn., Baigachi, India; offensive sweeps over Akyab Island, 2-43.
HV744 *Trop. Mk. IIC.* No. 11 Sqn., Yelahanka, India; bomber escorts, Burma Front, "A", 8-43.
HV745 *Trop. Mk. IIC.* No. 127 Sqn., St. Jean, Palestine; coastal shipping protection, 8-43.
HV780 *Trop. Met. Mk. IIC.* No. 1414 (Met.) Flt., Mogadishu, Italian Somaliland; weather reconnaissance, 9-43 to 7-45.
HV783 *Trop. Mk. IIB.* No. 135 Sqn., Yelahanka, India; operational training, 8-43.
HV785 *Trop. Mk. IIC.* No. 128 Sqn., Hastings, Sierra Leone; local air defence patrols, 1-43.
HV786 *Trop. Mk. IIB.* No. 146 Sqn., Alipore, India; offensive fighter sweeps, Burma Front, "L", 2-43.
HV793 *Trop. Mk. IIC bomber.* No. 79 Sqn., Ramu, Burma; offensive ground support, **NV-T**, 2-43.
HV796 *Trop. Mk. IIC.* No. 615 Sqn., A.A.F., Fenny, India; armed reconnaissance, Burma Front, 3-43.
HV798 *Trop. Mk. IIC.* No. 17 Sqn., Alipore, India; offensive fighter sweeps, Burma Front, 4-43.
HV815 *Trop. Mk. IIC.* No. 30 Sqn., Colombo Racecourse, Ceylon; defensive patrols, **RS-W**, 3-43.
HV817 *Trop. Mk. IIC.* No. 43 Sqn., Maison Blanche, Algeria; support of Torch landings, **FT-C**, 11-42.
HV818 *Trop. N.F. Mk. IIC.* No. 73 Sqn., Merduma, Libya; night intruder operations, 12-42.
HV828 *Trop. Mk. IIC.* No. 615 Sqn., A.A.F., Fenny, India; armed reconnaissance, Burma Front, 3-43.
HV830 *Trop. Mk. IIC.* No. 213 Sqn., Martuba, Libya; offensive sweeps while based behind Axis lines, 1-43.
HV834 *Trop. Mk. IIC.* No. 237 Sqn., Kermanshah, Persia; defence of Persian oil installations, 1-43.
HV836 *Trop. Mk. IIB bomber.* No. 261 Sqn., Baigachi, India; fighter-bomber sweeps over Akyab, "**K**", 3-43.
HV838 *Trop. Mk. IIC.* No. 94 Sqn., various Libyan bases, 4-43 to 5-43; coastal patrols, **GO-V**.
HV843 *Trop. Mk. IIC.* No. 451 Sqn., R.A.A.F., Mersa Matruh; air defence operations, Western Desert, 1-43.
HV844 *Mk. IIB bomber.* No. 175 Sqn., Odiham; offensive fighter-bomber sweeps, 2-43.
HV884 *Mk. IIB bomber.* No. 175 Sqn., Odiham; offensive fighter-bomber sweeps, 2-43.
HV887 *Trop. Mk. IIC.* No. 615 Sqn., A.A.F., Fenny, India; armed reconnaissance, Burma Front, 3-43.
HV890 *Trop. Met. Mk. IIC.* No. 1415 (Met.) Flt., Habbaniya, Iraq; weather reconnaissance, 9-43 to 11-45.
HV891 *Trop. Mk. IIC.* No. 128 Sqn., Hastings, Sierra Leone; local air defence patrols, 1-43.
HV901 *Trop. Mk. IIC.* No. 128 Sqn., Hastings, Sierra Leone; local air defence patrols, 1-43.
HV902 *Trop. Mk. IIC.* No. 87 Sqn., Djidjelli, Algeria; coastal shipping protection, 1-43.
HV911 *Trop. Mk. IIB bomber.* No. 41 Sqn., S.A.A.F.; coastal shipping protection, 8-43.
HV947 *Trop. Mk. IIC bomber.* No. 607 Sqn., A.A.F., Chittagong, India; fighter-bomber operations, Burma Front, 1943.
HV953 *Trop. Mk. IIC.* No. 43 Sqn., Maison Blanche, Algeria; support of Torch landings, 11-42.
HV956 *Trop. Mk. IIC.* No. 67 Sqn., Alipore, India; escorts for fighter-bombers, Burma Front, 2-43.
HV967 *Trop. Mk. IIC bomber.* No. 79 Sqn., Ramu, Burma; offensive ground support, **NV-M**, 2-43.
HV970 *Trop. Mk. IIC.* No. 43 Sqn., Maison Blanche, Algeria; support of Torch landings, 11-42.
HV973 *N.F. Mk. IIC.* No. 247 Sqn., High Ercall; night intruder operations, 12-42.
HV983 *Trop. Mk. IIB bomber.* No. 146 Sqn., Alipore, India; offensive sweeps, Burma Front, "Y", 2-43.
HV984 *Trop. Mk. IIC.* No. 43 Sqn., Maison Blanche, Algeria; support of Torch landings, 11-42.
HV985 *Trop. Mk. IIC.* No. 336 (Greek) Sqn., Sidi Barrani; coastal shipping protection, 4-43.
HV988 *Trop. Mk. IIC.* No. 253 Sqn., Maison Blanche, Algeria; support of Torch landings, 11-42.

HW115 *Production oil system check trials*, H.A.L., Langley, 9-42.
HW116 *Trop. N.F. Mk. IIC.* No. 73 Sqn., Nefatia, Libya; night intruder operations, 3-43.
HW118 *Mk. IIB bomber.* No. 175 Sqn., Stoney Cross; anti-shipping strikes, 3-43.
HW121 *Trop. Mk. IIC.* No. 253 Sqn., Philippeville, Algeria; defence of Torch supply ports, 1-43.
HW122 *Trop. Mk. IIC.* No. 43 Sqn., Philippeville, Algeria; defence of Torch supply ports, 1-43.
HW128 *Trop. Mk. IIC.* No., 127 Sqn., Nicosia, Cyprus; offensive sweeps during Dodecanese campaign, 11-43.
HW129 *N.F. Mk. IIC.* No. 530 (Turbinlite) Sqn., Hunsdon, 2-43.
HW130 *N.F. Mk. IIC.* No. 530 (Turbinlite) Sqn., Hunsdon, 2-43.
HW131 *N.F. Mk. IIC.* No. 534 (Turbinlite) Sqn., Tangmere, 2-43.
HW137 *Trop. Mk. IIC.* No. 43 Sqn., Philippeville, Algeria; defence of Torch supply ports, 1-43.
HW140 *Mk. IIB bomber.* No. 175 Sqn., Stoney Cross and Lasham; anti-shipping strikes, 3-43.
HW167 *Trop. Mk. IIB.* No. 87 Sqn., Djidjelli, Algeria; coastal shipping protection, 1-43.
HW168 *Trop. Mk. IIC.* No. 32 Sqn., Maison Blanche, Algeria; defence of Torch supply ports, 1-43.
HW173 *Trop. Mk. IIB bomber.* No. 134 Sqn., Bersis, Libya; anti-tank support operations, 9-43.
HW178 *Trop. Mk. IIB bomber.* No. 335 (Greek) Sqn., Mersa Matruh; coastal shipping protection, 7-43.
HW182 *Armament trials as HW182/G*, A. & A.E.E., Boscombe Down, from 15-10-42.
HW183 *Trop. Mk. IIC.* No. 128 Sqn., Hastings, Sierra Leone; defence of West African ports, 3-43.
HW187 *Armament trials as HW187/G*, A. & A.E.E., Boscombe Down, from 12-10-42.
HW189 *Trop. Mk. IIC.* No. 253 Sqn., Philippeville, Algeria; protection of Torch supply ports, 2-43.
HW194 *Trop. Mk. IIC.* No. 274 Sqn., Mellaha, Libya; coastal shipping protection, "E", 6-43.
HW197 *Trop. Mk. IIC.* No. 43 Sqn., Maison Blanche, Algeria; protection of Torch supply ports, 1-43.
HW199 *Trop. Mk. IIC.* No. 67 Sqn., Chittagong, India; defence of Calcutta, 11-43.
HW203 *Trials with drop tanks on universal wings*, H.A.L., Langley, 9-42.
HW204 *Trop. Mk. IIC.* No. 43 Sqn., Maison Blanche, Algeria; protection of Torch supply ports, 1-43.
HW206 *Mk. IIC (guns removed).* No. 527 (Calibration) Sqn., Hornchurch; calibration of U.K. East Coast radar, "**L**", 10-43.
HW207 *Mk. IIC (guns removed).* No. 527 (Calibration) Sqn., Hornchurch; calibration of U.K. East Coast radar, "**A**", 10-43.
HW235 *Trop. Mk. IIC.* No. 94 Sqn., Martuba, Libya; offensive sweeps, **GO-C**, 3-45.
HW239 *Trop. Mk. IIC.* No. 87 Sqn., Setif and Taher Algeria; coastal shipping protection, 2-43.
HW242 *Trop. N.F. Mk. IIC.* No. 73 Sqn., Nefatia, Libya; night intruder operations, 3-43.
HW247 *Trop. Mk. IIC.* No. 336 (Greek) Sqn., Sidi Barrani; coastal Shipping protection, 5-43.
HW257 *Trop. Mk. IIC.* No. 253 Sqn., Philippeville, Algeria; protection of Torch supply ports, 1-43.
HW267 *Trop. Mk. IIB.* No. 146 Sqn., Chittagong, India; defence of Chittagong, 11-43.
HW270 *Trop. Mk. IIB.* No. 607 Sqn., A.A.F., Alipore, India; operational training, 9-43.
HW271 *Trop. Mk. IID.* No. 6 Sqn., Sorman, Libya; anti-tank operations, 3-43; in action against Axis armour, El Hadid, 10-3-43.
HW298 *Trop. Mk. IID.* No. 6 Sqn., Sorman, Libya; anti-tank operations, 3-43; in action against Axis armour, El Hadid, 10-3-43.
HW303 *Trop. Mk. IID.* No. 6 Sqn., Sorman, Libya; anti-tank operations, 3-43; in action against Axis armour, El Hadid, 10-3-43.
HW323 *Trop. Mk. IID.* No. 6 Sqn., Bu Amoud, Egypt; anti-tank operations, **JV-N**, 1-43.
HW359 *Trop. Mk. IID.* No. 6 Sqn., Bu Anoud, Egypt; anti-tank operations, **JV-S**, 1-43.
HW361 *Trop. Mk. IIC.* No. 127 Sqn., Nicosia, Cyprus; participated in the Dodecanese campaign, 11-43.
HW371 *Trop. Mk. IIB.* No. 261 Sqn., Chittagong, India; defence of Chittagong, 10-43.
HW404 *Trop. Mk. IIC.* No. 451 Sqn., R.A.A.F., Idku; air defence of the Nile Delta, 2-43.
HW407 *Trop. Mk. IIC.* No. 67 Sqn., Chittagong, India; defence of Chittagong, 11-43.
HW413 *Trop. N.F. Mk. IIC.* No. 73 Sqn., Nefatia, Libya; night intruder operations, 3-43.
HW415 *Trop. N.F. Mk. IIC (A.I.-equipped).* No. 176 Sqn., Baigachi, India; night defence of Calcutta, 12-43.
HW421 *Trop. Mk. IIC.* No. 43 Sqn., Maison Blanche, Algeria; protection of supply ports, 1-43.
HW423 *Trop. Mk. IIC.* No. 79 Sqn., Ramu, Burma; offensive sweeps in Northern Burma, **NV-C**, 1-43.
HW431 *N.F. Mk. IIC.* No. 247 Sqn., Middle Wallop; night attacks on Axis shipping, 2-43.
HW433 *Trop. Mk. IIC.* No. 335 (Greek) Sqn., Mersa Matruh; coastal shipping protection, 6-43.
HW435 *Trop. Mk. IIC.* No. 176 Sqn., Baigachi, India; defence of Calcutta, "**N**", 12-43.
HW436 *Trop. Mk. IIC.* No. 32 Sqn., Maison Blanche, Algeria; protection of supply ports, 1-43.
HW437 *Trop. Mk. IIC.* No. 253 Sqn., Philippeville, Algeria; protection of supply ports, 1-43.
HW438 *Trop. Mk. IID.* No. 20 Sqn., Nidania, India; river shipping strikes, Burma, 1-44.
HW439 *Trop. Mk. IID.* No. 6 Sqn., Sorman, Libya; anti-tank operations, 3-43; in action against Axis armour, El Hadid, Tunisia, 10-3-43.
HW443 *Trop. Mk. IIC.* No. 87 Sqn., Djidjelli, Algeria; coastal shipping protection, 2-43.
HW474 *Trop. Mk. IIC.* No. 238 Sqn., Martuba, Libya; offensive sweeps, "**N**", 1-43.
HW483 *Trop. Mk. IIC.* No. 213 Sqn., El Gamil; M.T. column escorts, 5-43.
HW485 *N.F. Mk. IIC.* No. 247 Sqn., High Ercall, night attacks on Axis shipping, 1-43.

HW489 *Trop. Mk. IIB bomber.* No. 607 Sqn., A.A.F., Alipore, India; shipping strikes off Burma coast, 5-43.
HW538 *Trop. Mk. IIC.* No. 451 Sqn., R.A.A.F., Idku; air defence of the Nile Delta, 2-43.
HW539 *Trop. Tac R Mk. IIC.* No. 28 Sqn., Battle of Imphal, 4-44.
HW551 *N.F. Mk. IIC.* No. 534 (Turbinlite) Sqn., Tangmere, 2-43.
HW554 *N.F. Mk. IIC.* No. 530 (Turbinlite) Sqn., Hunsdon, 3-43.
HW558 *Trop. Mk. IIC bomber.* No. 60 Sqn., Agartala, India; ground support at Imphal, **MU-W**, 3-44.
HW561 *Trop. Mk. IIC.* No. 253 Sqn., Philippeville, Algeria; protection of supply ports, 1-43.
HW569 *Trop. Mk. IIC.* No. 71 O.T.U., Carthago, Sudan, 4-43.
HW571 *Trop. Mk. IIC.* No. 213 Sqn., El Gamil; M.T. column escorts, 5-43.
HW602 *Trop. Mk. IIC bomber.* No. 60 Sqn., Ramu, Burma; ground support at Imphal, **MU-Z**, 3-44.
HW608 *Trop. Mk. IIC.* No. 336 (Greek) Sqn., Sidi Barrani; coastal shipping protection, 6-43.
HW619 *Trop. Mk. IIC.* No. 87 Sqn., Djidjelli, Algeria; coastal shipping protection, 3-43.
HW655 *Trop. Mk. IIC bomber.* No. 34 Sqn., Palel, India; attacks on Japanese river traffic, Burma, 10-43.
HW660 *Trop. Mk. IIC bomber.* No. 34 Sqn., Palel, India; attacks on Japanese river traffic, Burma, 10-43.
HW663 *Trop. P.R. Mk. IIC.* No. 680 (P.R.) Sqn., Tocra, Libya; used for communications duties, 7-44.
HW666 *Trop. Mk. IIC.* No. 113 Sqn., St. Thomas Mount, India; defence of Madras, 10-43.
HW673 *Trop. Mk. IID.* No. 20 Sqn., Nidania, India; attacks on Japanese river traffic, Burma, 1-44.
HW684 *Mk. IID.* No. 184 Sqn., Colerne; tactical training with 40-mm. anti-tank guns, 1-43.
HW716 *Mk. IID.* No. 184 Sqn., Colerne; tactical training with 40-mm. anti-tank guns, 1-43.
HW719 *Mk. IID.* No. 1 School of Specialised Low Attack, Milfield, 1-43.
HW723 *Mk. IID.* No. 184 Sqn., Colerne; tactical training with 40-mm. anti-tank guns, 1-43.
HW728 *Mk. IID.* No. 184 Sqn., Colerne; tactical training with 40-mm. anti-tank guns, 1-43.
HW737 *Trop. Mk. IIC.* No. 238 Sqn., Martuba, Libya; offensive sweeps, "**U**", 1-43.
HW738 *Trop. Mk. IIC.* No. 94 Sqn., Savoia, Libya; air defence operations over Tunisia, **GO-G**, 5-43.
HW747 *Miscellaneous armament trials*, A. & A.E.E., from 24-12-42.
HW756 *Trop. Mk. IIC.* No. 60 Sqn., Ramu, Burma; ground support operations at Imphal, **MU-L**, 3-44.
HW794 *Trop. Mk. IIC bomber.* No. 34 Sqn., Palel, India; attacks on Japanese river traffic, Burma, 10-43.
HW800 *Trop. Mk. IIC.* No. 238 Sqn., Martuba, Libya; offensive sweeps in support of the 8th Army, "**X**", 1-43.
HW803 *Trop. Mk. IIC.* No. 261 Sqn., Chiringa, India; defence of Chittagong, "**B**", 10-43.
HW808 *Trop. Mk. IIC bomber.* No. 60 Sqn., Ramu, Burma; ground support strikes at Imphal, **MU-B**, 3-44.
HW848 *Trop. N.F. Mk. IIC.* No. 73 Sqn., Nefatia, Libya; night intruder operations, 3-43.
HW855 *Trop. Mk. IIC.* No. 11 Sqn., Ranchi, India; operational training, 8-43.
HW857 *Trop. Mk. IIC.* No. 17 Sqn., Minneriya, Ceylon; defence of Colombo, 5-44.
HW859 *Trop. Mk. IIC bomber.* No. 34 Sqn., Palel, India; attacks on Japanese river traffic, Burma, 10-43.
HW662 *Trop. Mk. IID.* No. 20 Sqn., Nidania, India; attacks on Japanese river traffic, Burma, 1-44.
HW668 *Trop. Mk. IIC.* No. 32 Sqn., Maison Blanche, Algeria; defence of supply ports, 1-43.
HW671 *Trop. Mk. IIC bomber.* No. 60 Sqn., Ramu, Burma; ground support operations at Imphal, **MU-G**, 3-44.
HW878 *Trop. Mk. IID.* No. 5 Sqn., Sapam, India; attacks on Japanese road vehicles, Burma, 1-44.

HAWKER HURRICANE Mark IIB, IIC, IID and IV (Hawker-built). Eighth production batch of 1,200 aircraft built by Hawker Aircraft Ltd., Kingston-upon-Thames and Langley, during 1942-43. Contract No. 62305/39/C Parts 1 to 6: *KW725-KW777, KW791-KW832, KW846-KW881, KW893-KW936, KW949-KW982, KX101-KX146, KX161-KX202, KX220-KX261, KX280-KX307, KX321-KX369, KX382-KX425, KX452-KX491, KX521-KX567, KX579-KX621, KX691-KX736, KX749-KX784, KX796-KX838, KX851-KX892, KX922-KX967, KZ111-KZ156, KZ169-KZ201, KZ216-KZ250, KZ266-KZ301, KZ319-KZ356, KZ370-KZ412, KZ424-KZ470, KZ483-KZ526, KZ540-KZ582, KZ597-KZ612.* Deliveries commenced, 20-11-42; completed, 19-4-43 (excluding some Sea Hurricane conversions). Average rate of production, approximately eight aircraft per day.
KW697 *Trop. Mk. IIC bomber.* No. 33 Sqn., Bersis, Libya; desert line patrols, 2-43.
KW699 *Trop. Mk. IIB.* No. 261 Sqn., Chittagong, India; defence of Chittagong, 10-43.
KW705 *Trop. Mk. IIB.* No. 87 Sqn., Djidjelli, Algeria; coastal shipping protection, 3-43.
KW709 *Trop. Mk. IIB.* No. 60 Sqn., Ramu, Burma; escort for fighter-bombers at Imphal, **MU-R**, 3-44.
KW714 *Trop. Mk. IIB.* No. 60 Sqn., Ramu, Burma; escort for fighter-bombers at Imphal, **MU-S**, 3-44.
KW716 *Trop. Mk. IID.* No. 6 Sqn., Grottaglie, Italy; anti-tank support for 8th Army, 3-44.
KW719 *Trop. Mk. IIC bomber.* No. 34 Sqn., Palel, India; attacks on Japanese river traffic, Burma, 11-43.
KW720 *Trop. Mk. IID.* No. 20 Sqn., Nidania, India; attacks on Japanese fuel installations, Burma, 12-43.
KW752 *Mk. IIC bomber.* No. 127 Sqn., Paphos, Cyprus; offensive sweeps during Dodecanese campaign, 11-43.
KW756 *Trop. Mk. IIC bomber.* No. 274 Sqn., Derna, Libya; coastal shipping protection, "**Z**", 8-43.
KW770 *Mk. IIC bomber.* Delivery delayed; *converted to Sea Hurricane Mk. IIC*, as **NF668**, 5-43.
KW774 *Trop. Mk. IIC bomber.* No. 67 Sqn., Ramu, Burma; offensive sweeps over Burma front, 5-43.
KW791 *Trop. Mk. IIC bomber.* No. 273 Sqn., Ratmalana, Ceylon; coastal shipping protection, 12-43.
KW792 *Mk. IIC.* Delivery delayed; converted to *Sea Hurricane Mk. IIC*, as **NF670**, 5-43.
KW794 *Trop. Mk. IID.* No. 5 Sqn., Sapam, India; attacks on Japanese raod traffic, Burma, "**J**", 1-44.
KW796 *Trop. Mk. IIC bomber.* No. 60 Sqn., Ramu, Burma; ground support operations, Imphal, **MU-J**, 3-44.
KW798 *Trop. Mk. IID.* No. 20 Sqn., Nidania, India; attacks on Japanese fuel installations, Burma, 12-43.
KW799 *Converted to Sea Hurricane Mk. IIC* ***NF672***, 5-43.
KW800 *Mk. IV.* Air Fighting Development Unit, West Raynham, 11-43; collided with Stirling III of No. 90 Sqn., 9-11-43, near Ely; F/Sgt. R.H. Brown slightly injured.
KW801 *Trop. Mk. IIC bomber.* No. 136 Sqn., Baigachi, India; offensive sweeps, Burma, 7-43.
KW804 *Converted to Sea Hurricane Mk. IIC* ***NF674***, 5-43.
KW807 *Mk. IV.* No. 186 Sqn., Ayr; rocket training, 8-43.
KW808 *Converted to Sea Hurricane Mk. IIC* ***NF675***, 5-43.
KW809 *Converted to Sea Hurricane Mk. IIC* ***NF678***, 5-43.
KW810 *Mk. IV.* No. 186 Sqn., Ayr; rocket training, 8-43.
KW816 *Converted to Sea Hurricane Mk. IIC* ***NF679***, 5-43.
KW817 *Converted to Sea Hurricane Mk. IIC* ***NF680***, 5-43.
KW818 *Trop. Mk. IIC bomber.* No. 34 Sqn., Palel, India; attacks on Japanese river traffic, Burma, 11-443.
KW827 *Trop. Mk. IIC bomber.* No. 30 Sqn., Fazilpur, India; attacks on Japanese river traffic, Burma, **RS-T**, 3-44.
KW828 *Trop. Mk. IIC bomber.* No. 261 Sqn., Baigachi, India; night offensive patrols, Burma, 2-44.
KW829 *Trop. Mk. IIC bomber.* No. 113 Sqn., Palel, India; armed reconnaissance, Burma Front, 5-44.
KW830 *Trop. Mk. IIC bomber.* No. 253 Sqn., Jemappes, Algeria; coastal shipping protection, 3-43.
KW849 *Converted to Sea Hurricane Mk. IIC* ***NF683***, 5-43.
KW850 *Converted to Sea Hurricane Mk. IIC* ***NF684***, 5-43.
KW860 *Converted to Sea Hurricane Mk. IIC* ***NF685***, 5-43.
KW862 *Converted to Sea Hurricane Mk. IIC* ***NF686***, 5-43.
KW863 *Trop. Mk. IID.* No. 20 Sqn., Nidania, India; attacks on Japanese fuel installations, Burma, 12-43.
KW864 *Trop. Mk. IIC bomber.* No. 336 (Greek) Sqn., Sidi Barrani; offensive sweeps over Crete, 7-43.
KW965 *Trop. Mk. IID.* No. 5 Sqn., Sapam, India; attacks on Japanese road traffic, Burma, "**Q**", 1-44.
KW866 *Trop. Mk. IIC bomber.* No. 60 Sqn., Ramu, Burma; ground support operations at Imphal, **MU-Y**, 3-44.
KW868 *Converted to Sea Hurricane Mk. IIC* ***NF687***, 5-43.
KW870 *Converted to Sea Hurricane Mk. IIC* ***NF688***, 5-43.
KW878 *Converted to Sea Hurricane Mk. IIC* ***NF689***, 5-43.
KW880 *Converted to Sea Hurricane Mk. IIC* **NF690**, 5-43.
KW897 *Trop. Mk. IV.* No. 42 Sqn., Palel, India; attacks on Japanese supply targets, Burma, **AW-T**, 12-43.
KW898 *Trop. Mk. IID.* No. 5 Sqn., Sapam, India; attacks on Japanese road traffic, Burma, "**R**", 1-44.
KW899 *Converted to Sea Hurricane Mk. IIC* ***NF692***, 5-43.
KW908 *Converted to Sea Hurricane Mk. IIC* ***NF693***, 5-43.
KW910 *Trop. Mk. IV.* No. 42 Sqn., Palel, India; attacks on Japanese supply targets, Burma, **AW-Q**, 12-43.
KW911 *Mk. IV.* No. 186 Sqn., Ayr; rocket training, 8-43.
KW915 *Trop. Mk. IIC bomber.* No. 33 Sqn., Bersis, Libya; desert line patrols, 3-43.
KW918 *Mk. IV.* No. 137 Sqn., Rochford and Southend; strikes with 40-mm. guns; 7-43; F/O G.S. Chalmers destroyed train at Statiestrate, Belgium, 23-7-43.
KW919 *N.F. Mk. IV.* No. 164 Sqn., Fairlop; night anti-shipping intruder operations, 9-45.
KW920 *Converted to Sea Hurricane Mk. IIC* ***NF699***, 5-43.
KW921 *Converted to Sea Hurricane Mk. IIC* ***NF700***, 5-43.
KW926 *Trop. Mk. IIC bomber.* No. 253 Sqn., Jemappes, Algeria; coastal shipping protection, 3-43.
KW928 *Converted to Sea Hurricane Mk. IIC* ***NF701***, 5-43.
KW929 *Converted to Sea Hurricane Mk. IIC* ***NF702***, 5-43.
KW930 *Converted to Sea Hurricane Mk. IIC* ***NF703***, 5-43.
KW934 *Trop. Mk. IIC bomber.* No. 213 Sqn., Idku; coastal shipping protection, 8-43.
KW935 *Trop. Mk. IIC bomber.* No. 94 Sqn., Savoia, Libya; ground attack operations over Crete, **GO-A**, 7-43.
KW950 *Trop. Mk. IIC bomber.* No. 274 Sqn., Derna, Libya; coastal shipping protection, "**P**", 8-43.
KW965 *Trop. Mk. IIC bomber.* No. 32 Sqn., Tingley, Algeria; coastal shipping protection, 5-43.
KW981 *Trop. Mk. IIC bomber.* No. 87 Sqn., Djidjelli, Algeria; coastal shipping protection, 4-43.

KX106 *Trop. Mk. IIC bomber.* No. 34 Sqn., Palel, India; attacks on Japanese river traffic, Burma, 11-43.
KX121 *Trop. Mk. IID.* No. 20 Sqn., Sapam, India; attacks on Japanese fuel installations, Burma, 12-43. No. 5 Sqn., Sapam; attacks on Japanese raod traffic, Burma, 1-44.
KX127 *Trop. Mk. IIC bomber.* No. 123 Sqn., Fenny, India; defence of Chittagong, "**B**", 12-43.
KX142 *Mk. IID.* No. 184 Sqn., Eastchurch; anti-tank trials, 3-43.
KX146 *Trop. Mk. IIC bomber.* No. 32 Sqn., Tingley, Algeria; shipping protection, 4-43. No. 87 Sqn., Monastir, Algeria; shipping protection, 7-43.
KX178 *Trop. Mk. IV.* No. 6 Sqn., Gottaglie, Italy; anti-tank operations in support of the 8th Army, **JV-B**, 3-44.
KX180 *Mk. IV.* Trials with rockets at A. &. A.E.E., c.2-43.
KX229 *Trop. Mk. IID.* No. 20 Sqn., Sapam, India; attacks on Japanese fuel installations, Burma, 12-43.
KX247 *Trop. Mk. IID.* Shipped to India for trials with 40-mm. guns.
KX249 *Trop. Mk. IID.* No. 20 Sqn., Sapam, India; attacks on Japanese fuel installations, Burma, 12-43.
KX304 *Mk. IID.* No. 184 Sqn., Eastchurch; anti-tank tactics trials, 3-43.
KX359 *Trop. Mk. IIC bomber.* No. 176 Sqn., Fenny, India; defence of Calcutta, "**Q**", 12-43.
KX401 *Mk. IIC bomber.* No. 184 Sqn., Manston; anti-shipping operations, **BR-G**, 6-43.
KX405 *Completed to Mark IV standard, but converted to prototype Mark V with Merlin 32.* Trials with H.A.L. and A. & A.E.E.. Ultimately returned to Mark IV standard.
KX407 *Mk. IIC bomber.* No. 184 Sqn., Manston; anti-shipping operations, **BR-A**, 6-43.
KX409 *Mk. IIC bomber.* No. 164 Sqn., Middle Wallop; armed shipping reconnaissance, 4-43.
KX412 *Mk. IIC bomber. Comparative trials with KX 405 in both its Mark IV and Mark V configurations,* H.A.L., c.1-43.
KX413 *Mk. IIC bomber.* No. 164 Sqn., Middle Wallop; armed shipping reconnaissance, **FJ-M**, 4-43.
KX525 *Mk. IIC bomber.* No. 137 Sqn., Rochford; anti-shipping strikes, 6-43.
KX536 *Mk. IV (rocket-armed).* No. 164 Sqn., Warmwell; anti-shipping strikes, English Channel, 8-43.
KX540 *Mk. IV (rocket-armed).* No. 164 Sqn., Warmwell and Middle Wallop; anti-shipping strikes, 6-43.
KX541 *Mk. IV (rocket-armed).* No. 164 Sqn., Middle Wallop; anti-shipping strikes, 6-43.
KX542 *Mk. IV (rocket-armed).* No. 164 Sqn., Middle Wallop; anti-shipping strikes, 6-43.
KX561 *Mk. IIC bomber.* No. 164 Sqn., Middle Wallop; armed shipping reconnaissance, **FJ-G**, 5-43.
KX580 *Mk. IV (rocket-armed).* No. 164 Sqn., Warmwell; armed shipping reconnaissance, 7-43.
KX582 *Mk. IV (rocket-armed).* No. 164 Sqn., Warmwell and Manston; took part in successful attack on Zuid Beveland lock gates, 2-9-43.
KX584 *Mk. IV (rocket-armed).* No. 184 Sqn., Manston; anti-shipping strikes off Belgian and Dutch coasts, **BR-T**, 6-43.
KX585 *Mk. IV (rocket-armed).* No. 137 Sqn., Manston; took part in successful attack on Hansweert lock gates, Holland, 2-9-43.
KX596 *Mk. IIC bomber.* No. 164 Sqn., Manston; anti-shipping sweeps, 8-43.
KX605 *Trop. Mk. IIC bomber.* No. 42 Sqn., Palel, India; attacks on Japanese river traffic, Burma, **AW-G**; took part in attacks on Hponnzeik bridge, 12-43.
KX696 *Mk. IIC bomber.* No. 164 Sqn., Manston; anti-shipping strikes, 8-43.
KX697 *Mk. IV (rocket-armed).* No. 184 Sqn., Manston; anti-shipping sweeps off Belgian and Dutch coasts, **BR-Y**, 6-43.
KX702 *Mk. IV (rocket-armed).* No. 164 Sqn., Middle Wallop; anti-shipping strikes, 7-43.
KX754 *Trop. Mk. IIC bomber.* No. 176 Sqn., Fenny, India; defence of Calcutta, "**N**", 12-43.
KX778 *Trop. Mk. IIC bomber.* No. 94 Sqn., El Adem, Libya; offensive sweeps over Crete, **GO-Y**, 1943.
KX800 *Trop. Mk. IV (rocket-armed).* No. 351 (Yugoslav) Sqn., Vis, Adriatic; attacks on German road transport, Yugoslavia, 10-44.
KX802 *Trop. Mk. IV bomber.* No. 42 Sqn., Palel, India; attacks on Japanese river traffic, Burma, **AW-B**; took part in attacks on Hponnzeik bridge, 12-43.
KX805 *Trop. Mk. IV (40-mm. guns).* No. 6 Sqn., Grottaglie, Italy; anti-armour attacks in support of the 8th Army, **JV-V**, 3-44.
KX807 *Mark IV (rocket-armed).* No. 184 Sqn., Manston, 6-43; anti-shipping strikes off Belgian and Dutch coasts, **BR-R**, 7-43.
KX813 *Trop. Mk. IIC bomber.* No. 274 Sqn., Derna, Libya; coastal shipping protection, "**Y**", 8-43.
KX826 *Mk. IV (40-mm. guns).* No. 6 Sqn., Grottaglie, Italy; anti-armour attack in support of 8th Army, **JV-R**, 3-44.
KX827 *Mk. IV (40-mm. guns).* No. 137 Sqn., Southend and Manston; offensive sweeps, 7-43. F/L J.M. Bryan DFC led attack which destroyed two trains and other targets in Belgium, 23-7-43.
KX829 *Mk. IV (40-mm. guns).* No. 137 Sqn., Manston; offensive sweeps, 9-43.
KX835 *Trop. Mk. IIC bomber.* No. 237 Sqn., Idku; coastal shipping protection, 9-43.
KX838 *Trop. Mk. IIC bomber.* No. 253 Sqn., Sousse, Tunisia; covered landings on Lampedusa, 6-43.
KX862 *Mk. IV. TI aircraft for stores trials, asymmetric armament,* etc., A. & A.E.E., c.6-43.
KX863 *Trop. Mk. IIC bomber.* No. 134 Sqn., Fazilpur, India; ground support operations, **GQ-T**; 1-44.
KX869 *Trop. Mk. IIC bomber.* No. 127 Sqn., Paphos, Cyprus; ground attack sweeps during the Dodecanese campaign, 11-43.
KX876 *Trop. Mk. IV (40-mm. guns).* No. 6 Sqn., Grottaglie, Italy; anti-tank operations in support of the 8th Army, **JV-F**, 1-44.
KX877 *Trop. Mk. IV. Temporarily modified as a Mark V with Merlin 32 engine*; trials with H.A.L. and A. & A.E.E., 4-43.
KX879 *Mk. IV (rocket-armed).* No. 164 Sqn., Manston; anti-shipping sweeps off Dutch and Belgian coasts, 9-43.
KX881 *Trop. Mk. IV (rocket-armed).* No. 351 (Yugoslav) Sqn., Vis, Adriatic; attacks on German road transport, Yuoslavia, 1-44.
KX884 *Mk. IV (rocket-armed).* No. 184 Sqn., Manston; anti-shipping sweeps off Dutch and Belgian coasts, **BR-T**, 9-43.
KX885 *Trop. Mk. IV (40-mm. guns).* No. 6 Sqn., Grottaglie, Italy; anti-armour operations in support of the 8th Army, **JV-Z**, 3-44.
KX886 *Trop. Mk. IIC bomber.* No. 87 Sqn., Palermo, Sicily; armed reconnaissance and interdiction operations, 12-43.
KX889 *Trop. Mk. IIC bomber.* No. 123 Sqn., Fenny, India; defence of Chittagong, "**X**", 12-43.
KX927 *Trop. Mk. IIC.* No. 336 (Greek) Sqn., Sidi Barrani; coastal shipping protection, 11-43.
KX932 *Trop. Mk. IIC bomber.* No. 335 (Greek) Sqn., Mersa Matruh; coastal shipping protection, 10-43.
KX936 *Trop. Mk. IIC bomber.* No. 274 Sqn., Derna, Libya; coastal shipping protection, "**X**", 8-43.
KX938 *Trop. Mk. IIC bomber.* No. 351 (Yugoslav) Sqn., Vis, Adriatic; attacks on German road traffic, Yugoslavia, 10-44.
KX951 *Trop. Mk. IIC bomber.* No. 60 Sqn., Fenny, India; ground attack sorties, Akyab island, **MU-R**, 12-43.
KX954 *Trop. Mk. IIC bomber.* No. 335 (Greek) Sqn., Mersa Matruh; coastal shipping protection, 11-43.
KX957 *Trop. Mk. IIC bomber.* No. 123 Sqn., Fenny, India; defence of Chittagong, **XE-P**, 12-43.
KX963 *Trop. Mk. IIC bomber.* No. 33 Sqn., Bersis, Libya; air defence of Benghazi, 9-43.
KX967 *Trop. Mk. IIC. bomber.* No. 336 (Greek) Sqn., Sidi Barrani; coastal shipping protection, 11-43.
KZ111 *Trop. Mk. IIC bomber.* No. 87 Sqn., Palermo, Sicily; armed reconnaissance and interdiction, 12-43.
KZ113 *Trop. Mk. IIC bomber.* No. 127 Sqn., Paphos, Cyprus; ground strikes during Dodecanese campaign, 11-43.
KZ114 *Trop. Mk. IIC bomber.* No. 451 Sqn., R.A.A.F., Idku; air defence of the Nile Delta, 4-43.
KZ115 *Trop. Mk. IIC bomber.* No. 451 Sqn., R.A.A.F., Idku; air defence of the Nile Delta, 4-43.
KZ118 *Trop. Mk. IIC bomber.* No. 451 Sqn., R.A.A.F., Idku; air defence of the Nile Delta, 4-43.
KZ126 *Trop. Mk. IIC bomber.* No. 123 Sqn., Patharkandi, India; offensive strikes over Burma, "**R**", 3-44.
KZ130 *Trop. Mk. IIC bomber.* No. 213 Sqn., El Gamil; M.T. column escorts, 6-43. No. 238 Sqn., El Gamil; coastal shipping protection, 9-43. No. 335 (Greek) Sqn., Mersa Matruh, 10-43.
KZ142 *Trop. Mk. IIC bomber.* No. 335 (Greek) Sqn., Mersa Matruh; coastal shipping protection, 10-43.
KZ144 *Trop. Mk. IIC bomber.* No. 94 Sqn., El Aden, Libya; coastal shipping protection, **GO-N**, 3-44.
KZ185 *Mk. IV (40-mm. guns).* No. 184 Sqn., Manston; anti-shipping strikes, **BR-K**, 6-43.
KZ187 *Trop. Mk. IV (40-mm. guns).* No. 6 Sqn., Grottaglie, Italy; anti-armour support for the 8th Army, **JV-X**, 1-44.
KZ188 *Trop. Mk. IV (40-mm. guns).* No. 6 Sqn., Grottaglie, Italy; anti-armour support for the 8th Army, 4-44; later based at Prkos, armed with rockets.
KZ189 *Mk. IV (40-mm. guns).* No. 184 Sqn., Manston; anti-shipping strikes, **BR-F**, 6-43.
KZ190 *Mk. IV (unarmed).* No. 290 Sqn., Newtownards; anti-aircraft co-operation duties, 1-44.
KZ193 *Hurricane Mark V prototype.* After performance trials with H.A.L., 3-43, *converted to Mark IV.* No. 164 Sqn., Warmwell (with 40-mm. guns); anti-shipping strikes, **FJ-O**, 7-43.
KZ194 *Mk. IV (40-mm. guns).* No. 184 Sqn., Eastchurch; operational trials with 40-mm. guns; **BR-J**, 3-43.
KZ218 *Trop. Mk. IIC bomber.* No. 134 Sqn., Parashuram, India; attacks on Japanese river traffic, Burma, **GQ-J**, 12-43.
KZ222 *Mk. IV (rocket-armed).* No. 186 Sqn., Ayr; ground support training exercises, 9-43.
KZ228 *Mk. IV (40-mm. guns).* No. 186 Sqn., Ayr; ground support training exercises, 9-43.
KZ232 *Mk. IIC bomber. Stability trials,* H.A.L. and A & A.E.E., 1943.
KZ299 *Trop. Mk. IIC bomber.* No. 123 Sqn., Patharkandi, India; offensive strikes over Burma, "**A**", 3-44.
KZ321 *Trop. Mk. IV (40-mm. guns).* No. 6 Sqn., Grottaglie, Italy; anti-armour support for the 8th Army, **JV-N**, 4-44.
KZ325 *Mk. IV (unarmed).* No. 577 Sqn., Castle Bromwich; anti-aircraft co-operation duties, 12-43..
KZ335 *Trop. Mk. IIC bomber.* No. 335 (Greek) Sqn., Mersa Matruh; coastal shipping protection, 10-43.
KZ352 *Trop. Mk. IIC bomber.* Ground Attack Training Unit, India, 6-45.
KZ356 *Trop. Mk. IIC bomber.* No. 113 Sqn., Johat and Tulihal, India; armed reconnaissance over Burma, 4-44.
KZ378 *Mk. IV (rocket-armed).* No. 184 Sqn., Manston; rocket attacks on coastal shipping, **BR-V**; Missing after shipping strike off Dutch coast, 28-6-43.
KZ381 *Trials aircraft, A. & A.E.E. and R.A.E.; nature of trials unknown; aircraft fitted with "D.W.I." ring* at Hullavington, 4-43, and flown by A.T.A. to Hatfield, 18-4-43, for inspection by Prime Minister; retuned to Hullavington, 19-4-43.
KZ382 *Trop. Mk. IV (rocket-armed).* No. 351 (Yugoslav) Sqn., Prkos, Yugoslavia; air support for Yugoslav National Army, 2-45.
KZ396 *Mk. IV (rocket armed).* No. 137 Sqn., Rochford; took part in successful attack on Hansweert lock gates, Holland, 2-9-43.

KZ397 *Trop. Mk. IV (mixed rocket and 40-mm gun armament).* No. 6 Sqn., Fayid, Egypt, 11-43.
KZ398 *Mk. IV (rocket-armed).* No. 186 Sqn., Ayr; ground support training exercises, 8-43.
KZ399 *Mk. IV (rocket-armed).* No. 137 Sqn., Manston, anti-shipping strikes, 9-43.
KZ400 *Mk. IV (rocket-armed).* No. 137 Sqn., Southend and Manston, anti-shipping strikes, 6-43.
KZ405 *Mk. IIC bomber.* No. 164 Sqan., Tangmere; offensive sweeps, 1-43; Fairlop, intruder operations, 9-43.
KZ406 *Mk. IV (40-mm. guns).* No. 164 Sqn., Middle Wallop; armed reconnaissance and shipping strikes, 6-43.
KZ435 *Trop. Mk. IIC bomber.* No. 335 (Greek) Sqn., Mersa Matruh, coastal shipping protection, 10-43.
KZ446 *Trop. Mk. IIC bomber.* No. 451 Sqn., R.A.A.F., Idku; air defence of the Nile Delta, 6-43.
KZ448 *Trop. Mk. IIC bomber.* No. 17 Sqn., Minneriya, Ceylon; defence of Colombo, 6-43.
KZ449 *Mk. IIC bomber.* No. 351 (Yugoslav) Sqn., Vis, Adriatic; attacks on German road traffic, Yugoslavia, 9-44.
KZ460 *Trop. Mk. IIC bomber.* No. 34 Sqn., Palel, India; offensive sweeps over Burma, 3-44.
KZ465 *Trop. Mk. IIC bomber.* No. 335 (Greek) Sqn., Mersa Matruh; coastal shipping protection, 10-43.
KZ488 *Trop. Mk. IIC bomber.* No. 256 Sqn., Alghero, Sardinia; long-range intruder sorties over Southern France, 8-44.
KZ497 *Trop. Mk. IIC bomber.* No. 134 Sqn., Parashuram, India; attacks on Japanese river traffic, Burma, **GQ-B**, 12-43.
KZ513 *Trop. Mk. IIC bomber.* No. 127 Sqn., St. Jean, Palestine; coastal shipping protection, 2-44.
KZ520 *Trop. Mk. IIC bomber.* No. 134 Sqn., Parashuram, India; attacks on Japanese river traffic, Burma, **GR-Z**, 12-43.
KZ526 *Trop. Mk. IIC bomber.* No. 11 Sqn., Lalmai, India; ground attack operations, Burma, "**X**", 1-44.
KZ543 *Trop. Mk. IIC bomber.* No. 261 Sqn., Chittagong, India; defence of Chittagong, 10-43.
KZ550 *Mk. IV bomber (rocket-armed).* No. 164 Sqn., Fairlop; offensive strikes, Channel coast, 9-43.
KZ553 *Trop. Mk. IV (40-mm. guns).* No. 6 Sqn., Grottaglie, Italy; anti-armour operations in support of the 8th Army, **JV-B**, 1-44.
KZ554 *Mk. IV (rocket-armed).* No. 184 Sqn., Manston; rocket attacks on flying bomb sites, **BR-S**, 9-43.
KZ569 *Trop. Mk. IIC bomber.* Tactical Support Trials Unit, India, 1944-45.
KZ571 *Mk. IV.* No. 279 Sqn., Bircham Newton, Norfolk; cover for air-sea rescue operations, 1943.]
KZ572 *Mk. IV (rocket-armed).* No. 184 Sqn., Manston; rocket attacks on flying bomb sites, **BR-B**, 9-43.
KZ576 *Mk. IV (rocket-armed).* No. 137 Sqn., Manston; F/O J.L. DeHoux missing after successful attack on Hansweert lock gates, Holland, 2-9-43.
KZ579 *Mk. IV (rocket-armed).* No. 184 Sqn., Manston; rocket attacks on flying bomb sites, **BR-X**, 9-43.
KZ606 *Mk. IV (rocket-armed).* No. 184 Sqn., Manston; rocket attacks on flying bomb sites, **BR-L**, 9-43.
KZ607 *Mk. IV (rocket-armed).* No. 184 Sqn., Manston; rocket attacks on flying bomb sites, **BR-F**, 9-43.
KZ609 *Mk. IV (rocket-armed).* No. 164 Sqn., Fairlop; offensive strikes, Northern France, 9-43.
KZ611 *Mk. IV (rocket-armed).* No. 184 Sqn., Manston; rocket attacks on flying bomb sites, **BR-B**, 9-43.

HAWKER HURRICANE Mark IIC and IV (Hawker-built). Ninth production batch of 1,205 aircraft built by Hawker Aircraft Ltd., Kingston-upon-Thames and Langley, during 1943. Contract No. 62305/39/C, Parts 7-12. *KZ613-KZ632, KZ646-KZ689, KZ702-KZ750, KZ766-KZ801, KZ817-KZ862, KZ877-KZ920, KZ933-KZ949, LA101-LA144; LB542-LB575, LB588-LB624, LB639-LB687, LB707-LB744, LB769-LB801, LB827-LB862, LB873-LB913, LB927-LB973, LB986-LB999; LD100-LD131; LD157-LD185, LD199-LD219, LD232-LD266, LD287-LD315, LD334-LD351, LD369-LD416, LD435-LD470, LD487-LD508, LD524-LD539, LD557-LD580, LD594-LD632, LD651-LD695, LD723-LD749, LD772-LD809, LD827-LD866, LD885-LD905, LD931-LD979, LD993-LD999.* Deliveries commenced, 18-4-43; completed 29-9-43; average rate of production, slightly over seven aircraft per day.

KZ620 *Mk. IV (rocket-armed).* No. 137 Sqn., Southend; offensive sweeps over Belgium, 7-43.
KZ622 *Trop. Mk. IIC bomber.* No. 335 (Greek) Sqn., Mersa Matruh; coastal shipping protection, 10-43.
KZ629 *Trop. Mk. IIC bomber.* No. 237 Sqn., Idku; coastal shipping protection, 11-43.
KZ647 *Trop. Tac R Mk. IIC.* No. 28 Sqn.; ground support during the Battle of Imphal, 4-44.
KZ655 *Mk. IV (40-mm. guns).* No. 137 Sqn., Southend; offensive sweeps over Belgium, 7-43.
KZ655 *Mk. IV (40-mm. guns).* No. 137 Sqn., Manston; strikes over Belgium, 7-43; P/O A.G. Brunet destroyed two trains in Belgium, 23-7-43.
KZ662 *Mk. IV (40-mm. guns).* No. 137 Sqn., Manston; strikes over Belgian coast, 7-43; F/O J.T. Davidson destroyed two trains at Cotemark and Statistrate, Belgium, 23-7-43.
KZ669 *Trop. Mk. IIC bomber.* No. 87 Sqn., Palermo; armed reconnaissance and interdiction, 12-43.
KZ674 *Mk. IV (rocket-armed).* No. 186 Sqn., Ayr; ground support training exercises, 9-43.
KZ676 *Mk. IV (rocket-armed).* No. 137 Sqn., Southend; offensive sweeps over Belgium, 7-43.
KZ678 *Mk. IV (rocket-armed).* No. 184 Sqn., Manston; rocket attacks on flying bomb sites, **BR-D**, 9-43.
KZ679 *Mk. IV (rocket-armed).* Rocket-firing trials as ***KZ679/G*** with A. & A.E.E., 1943.
KZ735 *Trop. Mk. IIC bomber.* No. 336 (Greek) Sqn., Sidi Barrani; coastal shipping protection, 11-43.
KZ742 *Trop. Mk. IIC bomber.* No. 123 Sqn., Patharkandi, India; offensive strikes over Burma, "**R**", 3-44.
KZ770 *Trop. Mk. IIC bomber.* No. 34 Sqn., Palel, India; offensive sweeps over Burma, 3-44.
KZ784 *Trop. Mk. IIC bomber.* No. 94 Sqn., Bu Amoud, Egypt; offensive sweeps over Crete, **GO-Y**, 4-44.
KZ785 *Trop. Mk. IIC bomber.* No. 113 Sqn., Torhat and Tulihal, India; armed reconnaissance over Burma, "**K**", 4-44.
KZ794 *Trop. Mk. IIC bomber.* No. 127 Sqn., St. Jean, Palestine; coastal shipping protection, 3-44.
KZ827 *Mk. IV (40-mm. guns).* No. 137 Sqn., Southend; offensive sweeps over Belgium, 7-43.
KZ829 *Mk. IV (40-mm. guns).* No. 137 Sqn., Southend; offensive sweeps over Belgium, 7-43.
KZ831 *Trop. Mk. IIC bomber.* No. 134 Sqn., Parashuram, India; attacks on Japanese river traffic, Burma, **GQ-F**, 12-43.
KZ888 *Trop. Mk. IIC bomber.* No. 67 Sqn., Ramu, Burma; defence of Calcutta, 12-43.
KZ893 *Trop. Mk. IIC bomber.* No. 336 (Greek) Sqn., Sidi Barrani; coastal shipping protection, 11-43.
KZ894 *Trop. Mk. IIC bomber.* No. 11 Sqn., Lalmai, India; ground attack operations over Burma, "**L**", 1-44.
KZ896 *Trop. Mk. IIC bomber.* No. 237 Sqn., Idku; coastal shipping protection, 11-43.
KZ906 *Mk. IV (rocket-armed).* No. 186 Sqn., Ayr; ground support training exercises, 10-43.
KZ909 *Trop. Mk. IV bomber.* No. 42 Sqn., Kangla, India; ground support operations, Imphal, **AW-Z**, 5-44.
KZ912 *Mk. IV (rocket-armed).* No. 164 Sqn., Manston, 9-43; carried out rocket attack on Abbeville airfield, 15-9-43.
KZ917 *Trop. Mk. IIC bomber.* No. 261 Sqn., Chittagong, India; defence of Chittagong, 10-43.
KZ918 *Mk. IV (40-mm guns).* No. 137 Sqn., Southend; offensive sweeps over Belgium, 7-43. No. 184 Sqn., Manston; offensive sweeps over Pas de Calais, 9-43.
KZ934 *Trop. Mk. IIC bomber.* No. 30 Sqn., Fenny, India; attacks on Japanese river traffic, Burma, **RS-W**, 3-44.
KZ935 *Trop. Mk. IIC bomber.* No. 79 Sqn., Dohazari, India; ground attack operations, Burma, **NV-N**, 3-44.
KZ940 *Trop. Mk. IIC bomber.* No. 135 Sqn., Minneriya, Ceylon; coastal shipping protection, Bay of Bengal, "**L**", 2-44.
KZ943 *Trop. Mk. IIC bomber.* No. 273 Sqn., Ratmalana, Ceylon; coastal shipping protection, Bay of Bengal, "**G**", 8-43.

LA108 *Trop. Mk. IIC bomber.* No. 135 Sqn., Minneriya, Ceylon; coastal shipping protection, Bay of Bengal, "**A**", 2-44.
LA111 *Trop. Mk. IIC bomber.* No. 261 Sqn., Chittagong, India; defence of Chittagong, 10-43.
LA119 *Trop. Mk. IIC bomber.* No. 60 Sqn., Kangla, India; ground support operations at Imphal, 9-44.
LA124 *Trop. Mk. IIC bomber.* No. 34 Sqn., Palel, India; offensive sweeps over North Burma, 3-44.
LA129 *Trop. Mk. IIC bomber.* No. 67 Sqn., Ramu, Burma; defence of Calcutta, 12-43.
LA131 *Trop. Mk. IIC bomber.* No. 113 Sqn., Tulihal, India; offensive patrols over Burma, "**A**", 4-44.
LA140 *Trop. Mk. IIC bomber.* No. 135 Sqn., Minneriya, Ceylon; coastal shipping protection, Bay of Bengal, "**N**", 2-44.

LB545 *Trop. Mk. IIC.* No. 135 Sqn., Minneriya, Ceylon; coastal shipping protection, Bay of Bengal, "**D**", 4-44.
LB551 *Trop. Mk. IIC; converted to Trop. Mk. IIB bomber.* No. 113 Sqn., Palel, India; fighter-bomber escorts over Burma, 7-44.
LB557 *Trop. Mk. IIC bomber.* No. 34 Sqn., Dergaon, India; ground support operations, Imphal, 5-44. No. 113 Sqn., Palel, India; ground attacks beyond the bomb lines, Burma, "**F**", 7-44.
LB569 *Trop. Mk. IIC bomber.* No. 11 Sqn., Lanka, India; ground attack operations, Imphal, "**N**", 4-44.
LB602 *Trop. Mk. IIB bomber. Transferred to the Indian Air Force.* No. 10 Sqn., I.A.F., 1944.
LB614 *Trop. Mk. IIC bomber.* No. 60 Sqn., Kumbhirgram, India; ground support operations, Imphal, **MU-N**, 7-44.
LB615 *Trop. Tac R Mk. IIC.* No. 28 Sqn., Cox's Bazaar; Battle of Imphal, 4-44.
LB618 *Trop. Mk. IIC bomber.* No. 135 Sqn., Minneriya, Ceylon; coastal shipping protection, Bay of Bengal, "**P**", 4-44.
LB619 *Trop. Mk. IIC bomber.* No. 42 Sqn., Kangla, India; ground support operations, Imphal, 6-44.
LB648 *Trop. Mk. IV bomber.* No. 42 Sqn., Kanlga, India; ground support operations, Imphal, **AW-Z**, 6-44.
LB649 *Trop. Mk. IV (rocket-armed).* No. 6 Sqn., Grottaglie, Italy; air support for the 8th Army, Italy, "**T**", 4-44.
LB650 *Mk. IV (unarmed).* No. 595 Sqn., Aberporth, Wales; anti-aircraft co-operation duties, 12-43.
LB658 *Trop. Mk. IIC bomber.* No. 261 Sqn., Yelahanka, India; escorts for Dakota transports on supply drops, Burma, 4-44.
LB664 *Trop. Mk. IIC bomber. Transferred to the Indian Air Force.* No. 10 Sqn., I.A.F., 1944.
LB672 *Trop. Mk. IIC bomber.* No. 273 Sqn., Ratmalana, Ceylon; coastal shipping protection, Bay of Bengal, "**L**", 3-44.
LB677 *Trop. N.F. Mk. IIC bomber.* No. 153 Sqn., Reghaia, Sardinia; night intruder operations over Southern France, "**U**", 9-44.
LB683 *Trop. Mk. IV (rocket-armed).* No. 6 Sqn., Grottaglie, Italy; air support for the 8th Army, Italy, "**Y**", 3-44.
LB718 *Trop. Mk. IIC.* No. 30 Sqn., Comilla, India; escorts for Dakota transports on supply drops, Burma, **RS-X**, 4-44.
LB727 *Trop. Mk. IIC bomber.* No. 123 Sqn., Patharkandi, India; ground attack operations, Burma, "**Y**", 5-44.
LB732 *Trop. Mk. IIC bomber. Transferred to the*

Indian Air Force. No. 10 Sqn., I.A.F., 1944.

LB734 *Trop. Mk. IIC.* No. 1344 Flt. No. 261 Sqn., Yelahanka, India; escorts for Dakota transports on supply drops, Burma, 4-44.

LB740 *Trop. Mk. IIC bomber.* No. 273 Sqn., Ratmalana, Ceylon; coastal shipping protection, Bay of Bengal, "**F**", 3-44.

LB774 *Trop. Mk. IV (rocket-armed).* No. 6 Sqn., Falconara, Italy; air support for the 8th Army, Italy, "**E**", 10-44.

LB776 *Trop. Mk. IV bomber.* No. 11 Sqn., Lanka, India; air support in Imphal area, "**T**", 4-44.

LB790 *Trop. Mk. IIC bomber.* No. 261 Sqn., Yelahanka, India; escort for Dakota transports on supply drops, Northern Burma, 4-44.

LB795 *Trop. Mk. IIC bomber.* No. 336 (Greek) Sqn., El Adem, Libya; coastal shipping protection, 7-44.

LB833 *Trop. Mk. IIC bomber.* No. 261 Sqn., Yelahanka, India; escort for Dakota transports on supply drops, Northern Burma, 4-44.

LB848 *Trop. Mk. IIC bomber.* No. 11 Sqn., Lanka, India; air support operations, Imphal, "**G**", 4-44.

LB852 *Trop. Mk. IV bomber.* No. 42 Sqn., Kangla, India; air support operations, Imphal, **AW-K**, 6-44.

LB854 *Trop. Mk. IIC bomber.* No. 273 Sqn., Ratmalana, Ceylon; coastal shipping protection, Bay of Bengal, "**S**", 4-44.

LB857 *Trop. Mk. IIC bomber.* No. 135 Sqn., Ratmalana, Ceylon; coastal shipping protection, Bay of Bengal, "**K**", 4-44.

LB875 *Trop. Mk. IIC bomber.* No. 123 Sqn., Patharkandi, India; ground attack operations, Burma, "**Z**", 5-44.

LB876 *Trop. Mk. IIC bomber.* No. 273 Sqn., Ratmalana, Ceylon; coastal shipping protection, Bay of Bengal, "**V**", 4-44.

LB879 *Trop. Mk. IIC bomber.* No. 261 Sqn., Yelahanka, India; escort for Dakota transports on supply drops, Northern Burma, 4-44.

LB880 *Trop. Mk. IIC bomber.* No. 79 Sqn., Dohazari, India; escort for Dakota transports on supply drops, North Burma, **NV-L**, 4-44.

LB883 *Trop. Mk. IIC bomber.* No. 261 Sqn., Yelahanka, India; escort for Dakota transports on supply drops, Northern Burma, 4-44.

LB885 *Trop. Mk. IIC bomber.* No. 134 Sqn., Arkonam, India; ground support operations, Burma, **GQ-V**, 5-44.

LB887 *Trop. Mk. IIC bomber.* No. 60 Sqn., Kumbhirgram, India; air support operations, Imphal, **MU-N**, 7-44.

LB891 *Trop. Mk. IIC (target tug conversion; guns removed).* No. 73 O.T.U., 1944.

LB893 *Trop. Mk. IIC (target tug conversion; guns removed).* No. 73 O.T.U., 1944.

LB931 *Trop. Mk. IIC bomber.* No. 273 Sqn., Ratmalana, Ceylon; coastal shipping protection, Bay of Bengal, "**K**", 4-44.

LB932 *Trop. Mk. IIC bomber.* No. 11 Sqn., Lanka, India; ground support operations, Imphal, "**H**", 4-44.

LB935 *Trop. Mk. IIC bomber.* No. 34 Sqn., Dergaon, India; ground support operations, Imphal, "**L**", 5-44.

LB938 *Trop. Mk. IIC.* No. 451 Sqn., R.A.A.F., Idku; air defence of the Suez Canal Zone, 10-43.

LB939 *Trop. Mk. IIC.* No. 451 Sqn., R.A.A.F., Idku; air defence of the Suez Canal Zone, 10-43.

LB957 *Trop. Mk. IIC bomber.* No. 34 Sqn., Dergaon, India; ground support operations, Imphal, "**N**", 5-44.

LB966 *Trop. Mk. IIC bomber.* No. 87 Sqn., Palermo, Sicily; armed reconnaissance and interdiction, Italy, 2-44.

LB990 *Trop. Mk. IIC bomber.* No. 113 Sqn., Yazagyo, Burma; air support for the 14th Army, 12-44.

LB992 *Trop. Tac R Mk. IIC.* No. 28 Sqn., Cox's Bazaar; ground support during the Battle of Imphal, 4-44.

LB995 *Trop. Mk. IV (rocket-armed).* No. 6 Sqn., Grottaglie, Italy; air support for the 8th Army in Italy, "**Y**", 4-44.

LB999 *Trop. Mk. IV bomber.* No. 34 Sqn., Palel, India; support operations at Imphal, 7-44.

LD101 *Trop. Mk. IV bomber.* No. 42 Sqn., Kangla; fighter-bomber attacks, Imphal, **AW-D**, 5-44.

LD107 *Trop. Mk. IIC bomber.* No. 113 Sqn., Yazagyo, Burma; air support of the 14th Army, Burma, "**C**", 12-44.

LD122 *Trop. Tac R Mk. IIC.* No. 28 Sqn., Cox's Bazaar; Battle of Imphal, 4-44.

LD162 *Trop. Mk. IV (rocket-armed).* No. 6 Sqn., Brindisi, Italy; anti-shipping attacks in the Adriatic, "**B**", 8-44.

LD163 *Trop. Mk. IV bomber.* No. 34 Sqn., Palel, India; ground attack operations, Imphal, 7-44.

LD168 *Trop. Mk. IV (rocket-armed).* No. 6 Sqn., Italy; coastal rocket strikes, Northern Italy, "**N**", 10-44.

LD172 *Trop. Mk. IIC bomber.* No. 28 Sqn., Dalbhumgarh, India; air support of the 14th Army, Burma, 11-43. No. 67 Sqn., Ramu, Burma; defence of Calcutta, 1-44. No. 17 Sqn., Minneriya, Ceylon; shipping protection, Bay of Bengal, 5-44.

LD182 *Mk. IIC bomber.* Crashed at Slough, Bucks, on test flight before delivery, 16-7-43, and not repaired.

LD185 *Trop. Mk. IIC bomber.* No. 11 Sqn., Tamu, Burma; ground support operations, Northern Burma, 12-44.

LD206 *Trop. Mk. IIC bomber.* No. 60 Sqn., Taukkyan, Burma; ground support for the 14th Army, **MU-L**, 1-45.

LD208 *Trop. Mk. IIC bomber.* No. 352 (Yugoslav) Sqn., Vis, Adriatic; attacks on German road and rail traffic, Yugoslavia, 9-44.

LD215 *Trop. Tac R Mk. IIC.* No. 28 Sqn.; ground support during the Battle of Imphal, 4-44.

LD237 *Trop. Mk. IV bomber.* No. 42 Sqn., Kangla, India; fighter-bomber attacks, Imphal, AW-H, 5-44.

LD264 *Mk. IIC bomber. Armament trials*, A. & A.E.E., 7-43.

LD265 *Trop. Mk. IIC bomber.* No. 11 Sqn., Tamu, Burma; ground support operations, "**N**", 12-44.

LD293 *Trop. IV (40-mm. guns).* No. 20 Sqn., Monywa, Burma; air support for the Irrawaddy crossing, 2-45.

LD294 *Trop. Mk. IV bomber.* No. 42 Sqn., Kangla, India; fighter-bomber attacks, Imphal, **AW-X**, 5-44.

LD299 *Trop. Tac R Mk. IIC.* No. 28 Sqn., Battle of Imphal, 3-44; later at Ye-U, Burma; support of the 14th Army, Burma, 2-45.

LD300 *Trop. Tac R Mk. IIC.* No. 28 Sqn., Battle of Imphal, 3-44; later at Ye-U, Burma; support of the 14th Army, Burma, 2-45.

LD346 *Trop. Mk. IIC bomber.* No. 60 Sqn., Taukkyan, Burma; ground support for the 14th Army, Burma, **MU-T**, 1-45.

LD387 *Trop. Tac R Mk. IIC.* No. 28 Sqn.; Battle of Imphal, 4-44.

LD395 *Trop. Mk. IIC bomber.* No. 136 Sqn., Baigachi, India; operational training, 9-43.

LD403 *Trop. Mk. IIC bomber.* No. 60 Sqn., Taukkyan, Burma; ground support for the 14th Army, Burma, **MU-X**, 1-45.

LD404 *Trop. Mk. IIC bomber.* No. 113 Sqn., Yazagyo, Burma; ground support for the 14th Army, Burma, "**A**", 1-44.

LD412 *Trop. Mk. IIC bomber.* Groud Attack Training Unit, India, 2-44.

LD442 *Trop. Mk. IV bomber.* No. 42 Sqn., Kangle, India; fighter-bomber attacks, Imphal, **AW-Q**, 5-44.

LD447 *Trop. Mk. IV (40-mm guns).* No. 20 Sqn., Monywa, Burma; air support for the Irrawaddy crossing, 2-45.

LD453 *Trop. Mk. IIC bomber.* No. 123 Sqn., St. Thomas Mount, India; second line patrols, 8-44.

LD564 *Mk. IV (rocket-armed).* No. 439 Sqn., R.C.A.F., Ayr; crashed near Loch Doon, 13-3-44.

LD570 *Mk. IV (rocket-armed).* No. 439 Sqn., R.C.A.F., Ayr; operational training with rockets, **5V-Z**, 1-44.

LD571 *Trop. Mk. IV (rocket-armed).* No. 6 Sqn., Brindisi, Italy; anti-shipping attacks in the Adriatic, 8-44.

LD605 *Trop. Mk. IV bomber.* No. 42 Sqn., Kangla, India; fighter-bomber attacks, Imphal, **AW-N**, 5-44.

LD627 *Trop. Mk. IIC bomber.* No. 34 Sqn., Palel, India; ground attack operations, Imphal, "**A**", 7-44.

LD675 *Trop. Mk. IIC bomber.* No. 42 Sqn., Kangla, India; ground attack operations, Imphal, **AW-Z**, 5-44.

LD726 *Trop. Mk. IIC bomber.* No. 60 Sqn., Taukkyan, Burma; air support for the 14th Army, Burma, **MU-Y**, 1-45.

LD774 *Trop. Mk. IIC bomber.* No. 34 Sqn., Palel, India; ground attack operations, Imphal, "**E**", 7-44.

LD780 *Trop. Mk. IIC bomber.* No. 30 Sqn., Fenny, India; attacks on Japanese river traffic, Burma, **RS-I**, 4-44.

LD798 *Trop. Mk. IIC bomber.* No. 42 Sqn., Kangla, India; fighter-bomber attacks, Imphal, 6-44.

LD859 *Trop. Mk. IIC bomber.* No. 11 Sqn., Kau, Burma; "cab-rank" operations, Burma Front, "**V**", 1-45.

LD865 *Trop. Mk. IV (rocket-armed).* No. 351 (Yugoslav) Sqn., Canne, Italy; anti-shipping strikes over the Adriatic, 10-44.

LD890 *Trop. Mk. IIC bomber.* No. 34 Sqn., Palel; India; ground attack operations, Imphal, "**T**", 7-44.

LD964 *Trop. Mk. IIC bomber.* No. 113 Sqn., Yazagyo, Burma; "cab-rank" operations in support of the 14th Army, Burma, "**B**", 1-45.

LD972 *Mk. IV (rocket-armed).* No. 439 Sqn., R.C.A.F., Ayr; operational training with rockets, 1-44.

LD973 *Mk. IV (rocket-armed).* No. 439 Sqn., R.C.A.F., Ayr; operational training with rockets, **F3-O**, 11-43.

LD975 *Trop. Mk. IV (rocket-armed).* No. 351 (Yugoslav) Sqn., Canne, Italy; anti-shipping strikes over the Adriatic, "**O**", 10-44.

LD976 *Mk. IV (target-towing conversion; no armament).* No. 639 Sqn., Cleave, Cornwall; anti-aircraft co-operation duties, 9-44.

LD977 *Mk. IV (armament removed).* No. 1688 (Bomber Defence) Training Flt.; Newmarket, 4-44.

LD997 *Trop. Tac R. Mk. IIC.* No. 28 Sqn., Dalbhumgahr, Calcutta, India, c.8-44.

LD998 *Trop. Mk. IIC bomber.* No. 60 Sqn., Taukkyan, Burma; air support of the 14th Army, Burma, **MU-F**, 1-45.

HAWKER HURRICANE Mark IIB, IIC and IV (Hawker-built). Tenth and final production batch of 1,357 aircraft built by Hawker Aircraft Ltd., Kingston-upon-Thames and Langley, during 1943-44. Rolls-Royce Merlin XX, 24 or 27 engines. Contract No. 62305/39/C, Parts 13 to 19. (Part 20 was for 143 Hurricane IVs and Vs, but was cancelled, 1-12-43). ***LE121-LE146, LE163-LE183, LE201-LE214, LE247-LE273, LE291-LE309, LE334-LE368, LE387-LE405, LE432-LE449, LE456-LE484, LE499-LE535, LE552-LE593, LE617-LE665, LE679-LE713, LE737-LE769, LE784-LE816, LE829-LE867, LE885-LE925, LE938-LE966, LE979-LE999; LF101-LF135, LF153-LF184, LF197-LF237, LF256-LF298, LF313-LF346, LF359-LF405, LF418-LF435, LF451-LF482, LF494-LF516, LF529-LF542, LF559-LG601, LF620-LF660, LF674-LF721, LF737-LF774; MW335-MW373; PG425-PG456, PG469-PG499, PG512-PG554; PG567-PG610; PZ730-PZ778, PZ791-PZ835, PZ848-PZ865.*** **Deliveries commenced, 29-9-43; completed, 24-5-44 (excluding *PZ865*); average rate of production, approxaimately six aircraft per day.**

LE166 *Trop. Mk. IIC bomber.* No. 34 Sqn., Yazagyo, Burma; air support for 14th Army on Tiddim Front, Burma, 12-44.

LE181 *Trop. Mk. IIC target tug.* No. 22 A.A.C.U., Drigh Road, Karachi, India, 6-46.

LE248 *Trop. Mk. IIC bomber.* No. 136 Sqn., Rumkhapalong, Burma; armed reconnaissance and air escorts, North Burma, 1-45.

LE263 *Trop. Mk. IIC bomber.* No. 60 Sqn., Kalewa, Burma; "cab-rank" operations in support of 14th Army, Tiddim—Chindwin Front, **MU-J**, 4-45.

LE268 *Trop. Mk. IV (rocket-armed).* No. 6 Sqn., Prkos, Yugoslavia; interdiction attacks, "**J**", 4-45.

LE291 *Trop. Mk. IV (rocket-armed).* No. 6 Sqn., Vis, Adriatic, 12-44; attacked German H.Q. at Zegar,

Yugoslavia, with rockets, 18-12-44.

LE297 *Trop. Mk. IIC bomber.* No. 79 Sqn., Yelahanka, India; second-line patrols, **NV-L**, 6-44.

LE303 *Trop. Tac R Mk. IIC.* No. 28 Sqn., Battle of Imphal, 4-44.

LE334 *Trop. Mk. IIC bomber.* No. 34 Sqn., Yazagyo, Burma; air support of the 14th Army, Tiddim Front, Burma, "**J**", 12-44.

LE342 *Trop. Mk. IIC.* No. 261 Sqn., Yelahanka, India; long-range armed reconnaissance, Burma, 5-44.

LE346 *Trop. Mk. IIC bomber.* No. 113 Sqn., Yazagyo, Burma; "cab-rank" operations in support of the 14th Army, Tiddim Front, Burma, 1-45.

LE353 *Mark IIC fighter (armament removed).* No. 231 Group Communications Flt.

LE395 *Mk. IV (armament removed; underwing winch for target towing).* No. 587 Sqn., Culmhead; anti-aircraft co-operation duties, 5-44.

LE398 *Trop. Mk. IV (rocket-armed).* Ground Attack Training Unit, Ranchi, India, 5-44.

LE400 *Trop. Mk. IV (rocket-armed).* No. 6 Sqn., Prkos, Yugoslavia; interdiction attacks, "**D**", 4-45.

LE432 *Trop. Mk. IIC bomber.* No. 11 Sqn., Magwe, Burma; air support for the 14th Army, Burma, "**Z**", 5-45.

LE440 *Trop. Mk. IIC bomber.* No. 30 Sqn., Yelahanka, India; attacks on Japanese river traffic, Burma, **RS-U**, 8-44.

LE502 *Trop. Mk. IIC bomber.* Ground Attack Training Unit, Ranchi, India, 5-44.

LE514 *Mark IV (armament removed).* No. 650 Sqn., Cark; anti-aircraft co-operation duties, Irish Sea, 3-44.

LE525 *Trop. Mk. IIC bomber.* No. 34 Sqn., Yazagyo, Burma; support for the 14th Army, Tiddim Front, Burma, 1-44.

LE527 *Trop. Mk. IIC bomber.* No. 34 Sqn., Yazagyo, Burma; support for the 14th Army, Tiddim Front, Burma, 1-44.

LE570 *Trop. Mk. IV (rocket-armed).* No. 351 (Yugoslav) Sqn., Prkos, Yugoslavia; operations in support of the Yugoslav National Army of Liberation, 3-45.

LE623 *Trop. Mk. IIC bomber.* No. 42 Sqn., Ondaw, Burma; air support for the 14th Army, Irrawaddy Front, Burma, **AW-S**, 3-45.

LE368 *Mk. IIC (guns removed).* No. 691 Sqn., Roborough; anti-aircraft co-operation duties, S.W. England, 7-44.

LE643 *Trop. Mk. IIC bomber.* No. 34 Sqn., Yazagyo, Burma; air support for the 14th Army, Tiddim Front, Burma, "**K**", 12-44.

LE646 *Trop. Mk. IIC bomber.* Ground Attack Training Unit, Ranchi, India, 6-44.

LE749 *Mk. IV (12-gun wing).* No. 309 (Polish) Sqn., Drem; coastal shipping protection, 4-44.

LE795 *Trop. Mk. IIC bomber.* No. 34 Sqn., Yazagyo, Burma; air support for the 14th Army, Tiddim Front, Burma, "**R**", 1-45.

LE796 *Trop. Mk. IIC bomber.* "D" Flight, No. 22 A.A.C.U., Meghaon, India, 1944. Ground Attack Training Unit, Ranchi, India, 4-45.

LE798 *Trop. Mk. IIC bomber.* Ground Attack Training Unit, Ranchi. India, 4-45.

LE815 *Trop. Mk. IIC bomber.* Ground Attack Training Unit, Ranchi, India, 6-44.

LE833 *Trop. Mk. IIC.* No. 261 Sqn., Yelahanka, India; long-range armed reconnaissance, North Burma, 5-44.

LE836 *Mk. IV (armament removed).* No. 288 Sqn., Collyweston; anti-aircraft co-operation duties (high-speed gun-laying training), **RP-W**, 3-44.

LE839 *Mk. IV (armament removed; underwing target winch).* No. 598 Sqn., Peterhead; anti-aircraft co-operation duties, 7-44.

LE991 *Trop. Mk. IIC bomber.* No. 11 Sqn., Magwe, Burma; air support for the 14th Army, 5-45.

LE993 *Trop. Mk. IIC bomber.* Ground Attack Training Unit, Ranchi, India, 8-44.

LE999 *Mk. IIC bomber.* No. 516 Sqn., Dundonald; combined operations training exercises, 3-44.

LF113 *Trop. Mk. IV (40-mm. guns).* No. 20 Sqn., India; attacks on Japanese road traffic, Burma, 10-44.

LF118 *Mk. IIC fighter.* No. 1681 (Bomber Defence) Training Flt., Long Marston, 7-44.

LF133 *Mk. IIC bomber.* No. 516 Sqn., Dundonald; combined operations training exercises, 4-44. *Supplied to Portugal, 1945.*

LF156 *Trop. Mk. IIC bomber.* No. 30 Sqn., Yelahanka, India; attacks on Japanese river traffic, Burma, **RS-T**, 8-44.

LF157 *Trop. Mk. IIC bomber.* Ground Attack Training Unit, Ranchi, India, 6-44.

LF160 *Mk. IIC bomber.* No. 516 Sqn., Dundonald; combined operations training exercises on Ayrshire coast, 3-44.

LF167 *Trop. Mk. IIC bomber.* No. 134 Sqn., Yazagyo, Burma; offensive air support for 14th Army, Burma, Tiddim Front, "**U**", 1-45.

LF180 *Mk. IIC bomber.* No. 516 Sqn., Dundonald; combined operations training exercises on Ayrshire coast, 3-44.

LF197 *Trop. Mk. IIC bomber.* No. 11 Sqn., Magwe, Burma; air support for 14th Army, Burma, "**S**", 5-45.

LF203 *Trop. Mk. IIC bomber.* Ground Attack Training Unit, Ranchi, India, 5-44.

LF207 *Mk. IIC bomber.* No. 516 Sqn., Dundonald; combined operations training exercises on Ayrshire coast, 3-44.

LF284 *Trop. Mk. IIC bomber.* No. 11 Sqn., Magwe, Burma; air support for 14th Army, Burma, "**Z**", 5-45.

LF325 *Trop. Mk. IIC bomber.* No. 60 Sqn., Kalewa, Burma; "cab-rank" operations in support of 14th Army, Tiddim-Chindwin Front, **MU-K**, 4-45.

LF331 *Mk. IIC fighter.* No. 309 (Polish) Sqn., Drem; coastal shipping protection, **WC-G**, 6-44.

LF333 *Mk. IIC fighter.* No. 309 (Polish) Sqn., Drem; coastal shipping protection, **WC-H**, 6-44.

LF342 *Mk. IIC bomber (converted to Mk. IIB bomber). Supplied to Portugal*, 1945.

LF360 *Mk. IIC bomber. Supplied to Portugal*, 1945.

LF363 *Mk. IIC fighter.* No. 309 (Polish) Sqn., Drem; coastal shipping protection, Snailwell, **WC-F**, 3-44. No. 41 O.T.U., 1945. Waterbeach Stn. Flt., 1950-54; Biggin Hill, 1959. R.A.F. Battle of Britain Memorial Flight, Coltishall, etc., to date. [*Was the last airworthy Hurricane held on R.A.F. wartime charge.*]

LF366 *Mk. IIC bomber.* No. 41 O.T.U., 11-44. No. 61 O.T.U., 7-45.

LF368 *Mk. IIC bomber.* No. 41 O.T.U., 5-45.

LF374 *Mk. IIC fighter.* Coningsby Stn. Flt., 1944.

LF376 *Mk. IIC fighter.* No. 41 O.T.U., 12-44. No. 61 O.T.U., 7-45.

LF379 *Mk. IIC fighter.* No. 41 O.T.U., 12-44. No. 61 O.T.U., 7-45.

LF380 *Mk. IIC fighter.* No. 1686 (Bomber Defence) Training Flt., Hixon, **FI-D**, 6-44.

LF382 *Mk. IIC fighter.* Coningsby Stn. Flt., 1944.

LF383 *Mk. IIC fighter.* No. 516 (Combined Operations) Sqn., Dundonald, 1944. *Supplied to Portugal*, 1945.

LF386 *Mk. IIC fighter.* No. 41 O.T.U., 12-44. No. 61 O.T.U., 7-45.

LF393 *Mk. IIC fighter.* No 1690 (Bomber Defence) Training Flt., Swinderby, 6-44.

LF395 *Mk. IIC fighter.* Coningsby Stn. Flt., 1944.

LF403 *Mk. IIC fighter.* No. 1689 (Bomber Defence) Training Flt., Holme-on-Spalding Moor, "**A**", 7-44.

LF404 *Mk. IIC fighter.* Waddington Stn. Flt., 8-44.

LF421 *Mk. IIC fighter.* Waddington Stn. Flt., 8-44.

LF422 *Mk. IIC bomber. Supplied to Portugal,* 1945.

LF425 *Mk. IIC bomber. Supplied to Portugal,* 1945.

LF428 *Mk. IIC bomber.* No. 516 (Combined Operations) Sqn., Dundonald, 4-44.

LF430 *Trop. Mk. IV (rocket-armed).* No. 351 (Yugoslav) Sqn., Prkos, Yugoslavia; air strikes in support of the Yugoslav National Army of Liberation, Sarajevo Front, 3-45.

LF458 *Trop. Mk. IV (rocket-armed).* No. 351 (Yugoslav) Sqn., Prkos, Yugoslavia; air strikes in support of the Yugoslav National Army of Liberation, Sarajevo Front, 3-45.

LF464 *Trop. Mk. IV (rocket-armed).* No. 351 (Yugoslav) Sqn., Prkos, Yugoslavia; air strikes in support of the Yugoslav National Army of Liberation, Sarajevo Front, 3-45.

LF469 *Trop. Mk. IV bomber.* No. 34 Sqn., Yazagyo, Burma; air support for the 14th Army, Tiddim Front, "**C**", 1-45.

LF477 *Trop. Mk. IV bomber.* No. 42 Sqn., Ondaw, Burma; long-range offensive strikes, Irrawaddy Front, **AW-C**, 3-45.

LF482 *Trop. Mk. IV (rocket-armed).* No. 6 Sqn., Prkos, Yugoslavia; interdiction operations, 4-45; carried out rocket attack on Risan, 21-11-44.

LF497 *Trop. Mk. IV (rocket-armed).* No. 351 (Yugoslav) Sqn., Prkos, Yugoslavia; air strikes in support of the Yugoslav National Army of Liberation, Sarajevo Front, 3-45.

LF498 *Trop. Mk. IV (rocket-armed).* No. 6 Sqn., Prkos, Yugoslavia; interdiction operations, 4-45; carried out rocket attack on bridge at Spuz, 11-44.

LF507 *Trop. Mk. IV (rocket-armed).* No. 351 (Yugoslav) Sqn., Prkos, Yugoslavia; air strikes in support of the Yugoslav National Army of Liberation, Sarajevo Front, 3-45.

LF514 *Mk. IIC bomber.* No. 516 (Combined Operations) Sqn., Dundonald, 1944. *Supplied to Portugal*, 1945.

LF532 *Mk. IIC fighter.* No. 1696 (Bomber Defence) Training Flt., Gransden Lodge, c.7-44.

LF534 *Mk. IIC fighter.* No. 516 (Combined Operations) Sqn., Dundonald, 3-44; crashed into landing craft at Troon, 18-3-44, during exercise and destroyed.

LF536 *Mk. IIC fighter. Supplied to Irish Air Corps* as "**115**" and delivered, 28-3-45.

LF541 *Mk. IIC fighter. Supplied to Irish Air Corps* as "**116**" and delivered, 7-3-45.

LF564 *Mk. IIC fighter.* No. 1695 (Bomber Defence) Training Flt., Dalton, **3K-Q**, 6-44. *Supplied to Portugal*, 1945; served at Tancos, 1947-50.

LF565 *Mk. IIC fighter. Supplied to Portugal*, 1945; served at Tancos, 1947-50.

LF566 *Mk. IIC fighter. Supplied to Irish Air Corps* as "**117**" and delivered 7-3-45.

LF568 *Mk. IIC fighter. Supplied to Portugal*, 1945.

LF570 *Mk. IIC fighter. Supplied to Portugal*, 1945.

LF577 *Mk. IIC (armament removed).* No. 567 Sqn., Hornchurch; anti-aircraft co-operation, S.E. England (high-speed gun-laying training), **I4-Z**, 11-44.

LF580 *Mk. IIC (armament removed).* No. 289 Sqn., Turnhouse; anti-aircraft co-operation, Scotland (gun-laying training), **YE-W**, 8-44. Became ***5402M.***

LF586 *Mk. IIC fighter. Supplied to Portugal*, 1945; served at Tancos, 1947-50.

LF587 *Mk. IIC fighter.* No. 1687 (Bomber Defence) Training Flt., Scampton, **4E-B**, 3-45.

LF588 *Mk. IIC fighter (armament removed).* No. 1695 (Bomber Defence) Training Flt., Dalton, **3K-S**, 4-45.

LF600 *Mk. IIC (armament removed).* No. 285 Sqn., Woodvale; anti-aircraft co-operation (high-speed gun-laying training), 7-44.

LF620 *Mk. IIC fighter.* No. 309 (Polish) Sqn., Drem; coastal shipping protection, **WC-A**, 7-44. *Supplied to Portugal*, 1945.

LF623 *Mk. IIC fighter (armament removed).* No. 291 Sqn., Hutton Cranswick; anti-aircraft co-operation (high-speed gun-laying training), 8-44.

LF624 *Mk. IIC fighter. Supplied to Irish Air Corps* as "**118**", and delivered 7-3-45.

LF626 *Mk. IIC fighter (armament removed; underwing target winch).* No. 289 Sqn., Turnhouse; anti-aircraft co-operation, **YE-N**, 8-44.

LF628 *Mk. IIC fighter (armament removed; underwing target winch).* No. 289 Sqn., Turnhouse; anti-aircraft co-operation, **YE-S**, 8-44.

LF636 *Mk. IIC fighter (armament removed; underwing target winch).* No. 289 Sqn., Turnhouse; anti-air-

craft co-operation, **YE-Z**, 8-44.
LF643 *Trop. Mk. IIC bomber.* No. 351 (Yugoslav) Sqn., Canne, Italy; anti-shipping attacks in the Adriatic, 1944.
LF644 *Mk. IIC fighter.* No. 309 (Polish) Sqn., Drem; coastal shipping protection, **WC-D**, 7-44.
LF658 *Mk. IIC fighter.* No. 309 (Polish) Sqn., Drem; coastal shipping protection, **WC-E**, 7-44.
LF685 *Mk. IIC fighter.* No. 309 (Polish) Sqn., Drem; coastal shipping protection, **WC-F** (later **WC-D**), 7-44.
LF689 *Mk. IIC fighter.* No. 1684 (Bomber Defence) Training Flt., Little Horwood, 6-44.
LF702 *Mk. IIC fighter.* No. 1682 (Bomber Defence) Training Flt., Enstone, **UH-P**, 7-44.
LF705 *Mk. IIC fighter.* No. 309 (Polish) Sqn., Drem; coastal shipping protection, **WC-K**, 7-44.
LF706 *Mk. IIC fighter. Supplied to Portugal*, 1945.
LF717 *Mk. IIC fighter. Supplied to Portugal*, 1945; served at Tancos, 1947-50.
LF744 *Mk. IIC fighter.* No. 1683 (Bomber Defence) Training Flt., Market Harborough, 7-44.
LF754 *Mk. IIC fighter.* No. 1688 (Bomber Defence) Training Flt., Newmarket, **6H-T**, 9-44.
LF757 *Mk. IIC (armament removed).* No. 289 Sqn., Acklington and Eshott; anti-aircraft co-operation, 1-45. Armament restored. *Supplied to Portugal*, 1945.
LF770 *Mk. IIC (armament removed).* No. 1697 Air Despatch Letter Service Flt., Northolt, **DR-G**, 5-44. Armament restored. *Supplied to Irish Air Corps* as **"119"**, and delivered 7-3-45.
LF772 *Mk. IIC fighter. Supplied to Portugal*, 1945.

MW336 *Mk. IIC (armament removed).* No. 1697 Air Despatch Letter Service Flt., Northolt, **DR-E**, 5-44.
MW339 *Mk. IIC (armament removed).* No. 1697 Air Despatch Letter Service Flt., Northolt, **DR-H**, 5-44.
MW340 *Mk. IIC (armament removed).* No. 1697 Air Despatch Letter Service Flt., Northolt, **DR-N**, 5-44. Became **5463M.**
MW359 *Mk. IIC (armament removed).* No. 1697 Air Despatch Letter Service Flt., Northolt, **DR-A**, 5-44.
MW360 *Mk. IIC (armament removed).* No. 1697 Air Despatch Letter Service Flt., Northolt, **DR-C**, 5-44.
MW361 *Mk. IIC (armament removed).* No. 1697 Air Despatch Letter Service Flt., Northolt, **DR-J**, 5-44.
MW367 *Mk. IIC (armament removed).* No. 1697 Air Despatch Letter Service Flt., Northolt, **DR-B**, 5-44.
MW368 *Mk. IIC fighter.* No. 1685 (Bomber Defence) Training Flt., Ossington, **KA-H**, 6-44.
MW373 *Mk. IIC fighter. Supplied to Portugal*, 1945; served at Tancos, 1946-50.

PG428 *Mk. IIC fighter.* No. 309 (Polish) Sqn., Drem; coastal shipping protection, **WC-W**, 9-44.
PG429 *Mk. IIC fighter.* No. 309 (Polish) Sqn., Drem; coastal shipping protection, **WC-U**, 9-44.
PG440 *Mk. IIC fighter.* No. 601 Sqn., A.A.F., Bellaria, Italy; communications duties, 4-45.
PG469 *Mk. IIC bomber. Converted to Met. Mk. IIC.* No. 518 (Met.) Sqn., Aldergrove, **KI-Y3**, 1946.
PG472 *Mk. IIC (armament removed).* No. 1697 Air Despatch Letter Service Flt., Northolt, **DR-K**, 5-44.
PG488 *Mk. IIC bomber.* No. 286 Sqn., Weston Zoyland; anti-aircraft co-operation, 9-44.
PG512 *Mk. IIC (armament removed).* No. 1697 Air Despatch Letter Service Flt., Northolt, **DR-L**, 5-44.
PG514 *Mk. IIC (armament removed).* No. 1697 Air Despatch Letter Service Flt., Northolt, **DR-M**, 5-44.
PG515 *Mk. IIC (armament removed).* No. 1697 Air Despatch Letter Service Flt., Northolt, **DR-O**, 5-44.
PG521 *Mk. IIC fighter. Supplied to Portugal*, 1945.
PG535 *Mk. IIC fighter. Supplied to Portugal*, 1945.
PG537 *Mk. IIC fighter.* No. 1687 (Bomber Defence) Training Flight, Scampton, 3-45.
PG538 *Mk. IIC fighter. Supplied to Portugal*, 1945.
PG543 *Mk. IIC fighter. Supplied to Portugal*, 1945.
PG546 *Mk. IIC (armament removed).* No. 1697 Air Despatch Letter Service Flt., Northolt, **DR-P**, 5-44.
PG567 *Mk. IIC fighter.* Central Flying School, Hullavington, 1944.
PG568 *Mk. IIC fighter.* Central Flying School, Hullavington, 1944.
PG570 *Mk. IIC fighter.* No. 501 Sqn., A.A.F., Hendon; communications duties, 4-45. Became ***5464M.***
PG571 *Mk. IIC fighter.* Central Flying School, Hullavington, 1944.
PG573 *Mk. IIC fighter.* Central Flying School, Hullavington, 1944.
PG597 *Mk. IIC (armament removed).* No. 1697 Air Despatch Letter Service Flt., Northolt, **DR-Q**, 5-44.
PG599 *Mk. IIC fighter. Supplied to Portugal*, 1945.
PG610 *Mk. IIC fighter. Supplied to Portugal*, 1945.

PZ735 *Mk. IIC fighter.* No. 1321 (Bomber Defence) Training Flt., Bottesford, 9-45. *Supplied to Portugal*, 1945; served at Tancos, 1947.
PZ738 *Mk. IIC fighter. Supplied to Portugal*, 1945.
PZ740 *Mk. IIC fighter.* No. 1690 (Bomber Defence) Training Flt., Scampton, 8-44.
PZ745 *Mk. IIC fighter. Supplied to Portugal*, 1945.
PZ751 *Mk. IIC fighter.* No. 695 Sqn., Bircham Newton; anti-aircraft co-operation duties, East Anglia, **8Q-W**, 11-44.
PZ758 *Mk. IIC (armament removed).* No. 1697 Air Despatch Letter Service Flt., Northolt, **DR-F**, 5-44.
PZ759 *Mk. IIC fighter. Supplied to Portugal*, 1945.
PZ768 *Mk. IIC (armament removed).* No. 1697 Air Despatch Letter Service Flt., Northolt, **DR-U**, 5-44.
PZ769 *Mk. IIC (armament removed).* No. 1697 Air Despatch Letter Service Flt., Northolt, **DR-R**, 5-44.
PZ796 *Mk. IIC fighter. Supplied to Irish Air Corps* as ***"120"***, and delivered 28-3-45.
PZ803 *Met. Mk. IIC (armament omitted).* No. 521 (Met.) Sqn., Langham; weather reconnaissance off East Coast, 11-44.
PZ806 *Met. Mk. IIC (armament omitted).* No. 521 (Met.) Sqn., Langham; weather reconnaissance off East Coast, **T6-B**, 11-44.
PZ809 *Mk. IIC fighter.* No. 8 O.T.U., Mount Farm, "E", 1946.
PZ815 *Met. Mk. IIC (armament omitted).* No. 518 (Met.) Sqn., Tiree, Hebrides, and Aldergrove, Ulster; weather reconnaissance off Scottish coast, 9-45.
PZ818 *Met. Mk. IIC (armament omitted).* No. 521 (Met.) Sqn., Langham; weather reconnaissance off East Coast, 11-44.
PZ819 *Met. Mk. IIC (armament omitted).* No. 521 (Met.) Sqn., Langham; weather reconnaissance off East Coast, **T6-F**, 11-44.
PZ820 *Met. Mk. IIC (armament omitted).* No. 521 (Met.) Sqn., Langham; weather reconnaissance off East Coast, 11-44.
PZ821 *Mk. IIC fighter.* No. 8 O.T.U., Mount Farm, "B", 1946.
PZ823 *Mk. IIC fighter.* No. 8 O.T.U., Mount Farm, "C", 1946.
PZ830 *Trop. Met. Mk. IIC (armament omitted).* No. 520 (Met.) Sqn., Gibraltar; local weather reconnaissance, "**D**", 7-44.
PZ861 *Mk. IIC fighter.* No. 8 O.T.U., Mount Farm, "A", 1946.
PZ863 *Mk. IIC fighter.* No. 8 O.T.U., Mount Farm, "**F**", 1946.
PZ865 *Mk. IIC fighter. Purchased off Contract* by Hawker Aircraft Ltd., and employed for display and demonstration purposes. Named *"Last of the Many"* and entered in numerous sporting events, 1947-52. Registered **G-AMAU** in 1950 (C. of A. issued 23-5-50). Preserved and still in flying condition (1990) and flown by the R.A.F. Battle of Britain Memorial Flight.

HAWKER HURRICANE Mark V. One prototype, *NL255*, undertaken as joint Hawker/Rolls-Royce Ltd. venture, and ultimately covered by Air Ministry/Ministry of Aircraft Production Contract as proposed tropical "low-attack" Hurricane. Joined interim prototypes *KX405* and *KZ193* (converted Mark IVs) in development programme. Original cost of *NL255* offset against loss of Hurricane *LD102* (crashed during manufacturers' flight test, 16-7-43).

LEASE-LEND FINANCING

HAWKER CANADIAN HURRICANE Mark IIB and IIC (originally Mark X and XIB). Fourth production batch of 200 aircraft, *BW835-BX134*, built by Canadian Car & Foundry Corporation, Montreal, Canada, between November 1941 and May 1942. Originally ordered as Mark Xs and XIs with Packard Merlin 28 engines but owing to non-availability of the American engines, aircraft were fitted with Rolls-Royce Merlin XXs to become Mark IIBs and IICs. (*BW835-BW840* and *BW842-BW884* retained in Canada; 107 shipped to Russia, of which 13 were lost in transit at sea.)
BW841 Merchant Ship Fighter Unit. No. 899 Sqn., F.A.A. Became ***4659M.***
BW886 *Converted to Sea Hurricane* and transferred to Admiralty Charge, 4-9-42.
BW906 Shipped to India. No. 2 Sqn., I.A.F.
BW924 No. 247 Sqn. No. 535 (Turbinlite) Sqn. No. 1449 Flt.
BW931 Shipped to India. No. 2 Sqn., I.A.F.; crashed on take-off at Imphal, 8-4-43.
BW939 *Tropicalised* and shipped to the Middle East. No. 335 (Greek) Sqn., Western Desert. S.O.C., 27-10-44.
BW962 *N.F. Mk. IIB.* No. 533 (Turbinlite) Sqn., Charmy Down. *Supplied to Portugal*, 15-8-43.
BW963 *Supplied to Portugal*, 22-6-42.
BW971 *Tropicalised* and shipped to the Middle East. No. 71 O.T.U.; caught fire on the ground at Ismailia, 12-10-44, and S.O.C.
BW973 *N.F. Mk. IIB.* No. 534 (Turbinlite) Sqn., Tangmere. No. 29 O.T.U. S.O.C., 17-7-47.
BX115 *N.F. Mk. IIB.* No. 534 (Turbinlite) Sqn., Tangmere. Shipped to the Far East. S.O.C., 16-11-44.
BX128 No. 247 Sqn. No. 535 (Turbinlite) Sqn. *Supplied to Portugal*, 16-8-43.
BX131 *Tropicalised* and shipped to India. No. 20 Sqn., Chharra, India; shot down by ground fire at Magychaung, Burma, 26-4-43.
BX134 *Tropicalised* and shipped to India. No. 151 O.T.U.; crashed 10 miles N.E. of Peshawar, 18-8-44, following engine failure.

HAWKER CANADIAN HURRICANE Mark XI and XII. Fifth production batch of 248 aircraft built by Canadian Car & Foundry Corporation, Montreal, Canada. Packard Merlin 28 (Mark XI) and Merlin 29 (Mark XII). JS219-JS371, JS374-JS468. 185 aircraft with 122-gun wings (Marks XIB and XIIB), and 63 with four 20-mm cannon wings (Mark XIIC).
JS253 *Sea Hurricane XIIB (Mark IIB wings).* No. 800 Sqn., F.A.A., H.M.S. *Biter*, Oran; Torch landings, 11-42.
JS290 *N.F. Mk. XIIC (Mark IIC wings).* No. 532 (Turbinlite) Sqn., Hibaldstow, *c.*10-42.
JS300 *N.F. Mk. XIIC (Mark IIC wings).* No. 534 (Turbinlite) Sqn., Tangmere, *c.*10-42.
JS310 *Sea Hurricane XIIB (Mark IIB wings).* No. 800 Sqn., F.A.A., H.M.S. *Biter*, Oran; Torch landings, 11-42.
JS327 *Sea Hurricane XIIB (Mark IIB wings).* No. 800 Sqn., F.A.A., H.M.S. *Biter*, Oran; Torch landings, 11-42; shot down by French fighters, St. Leu, 8-11-42.
JS328 *Sea Hurricane XIIB (Mark IIB wings).* No. 800 Sqn., F.A.A., H.M.S. *Biter*, Oran; Torch landings, 11-42.
JS330 *N.F. Mk. XIIC (Mark IIC wings).* No. 245 Sqn., Charmy Down, 10-42.
JS334 *Sea Hurricane XIIB (Mark IIB wings).* No. 800 Sqn., F.A.A., H.M.S. *Biter*, Oran; Torch landings,

11-42.

JS335 *N.F. Mk. XIIC (Mark IIC wings).* No. 245 Sqn., Charmy Down, 10-42.

JS336 *Sea Hurricane XIIB (Mark IIC wings).* No. 800 Sqn., F.A.A., H.M.S. *Biter*, Oran, Torch landings, 11-42.

JS347 *N.F. Mk. XIIC (Mark IIC wings).* No. 537 (Turbinlite) Sqn., Middle Wallop, c.11-42.

JS418 *Trop. Mk. XIIC (Mark IIC wings).* No. 123 Sqn., Mehrabad, Persia; protection of Persian oil installations, 12-42.

JS465 *Trop. Mk. XIIC (Mark IIC wings).* No. 79 Sqn., Chittagong, India; defence of Chittagong, **NV-D**, 12-42.

HAWKER CANADIAN HURRICANE Mark XIIA. Sixtgh production batch of 150 aircraft built by the Canadian Car & Foundry Corporation, Montreal, Canada, during 1942. Packard Merlin 29 engines. *PJ660-PJ695, PJ711-PJ758, PJ779-PJ813, PJ842-PJ872.* Many aircraft shipped to Russia; others either retained in Canada and converted to Sea Hurricane XIIA for service with the Royal Canadian Navy. A small number served with the R.A.F. in the Far East, including:

PJ719 *Trop. Mk. XIIA (Mark IIC wings).* No. 60 Sqn., St. Thomas Mount, India; defence of Madras, 8-43.

PJ745 *Trop. Mk. XIIA (Mark IIC wings).* No. 11 Sqn., Sapam, India, 3-44. No. 42 Sqn., Tulihal, India, 10-44.

PJ847 *Trop. Mk. XIIA (Mark IIC wings).* No. 34 Sqn., Onbauk, Burma, 1-44; "cab-rank" operations in support of the 14th Army, Burma, 1945.

INDEX